CLB 2205
This edition published in 1991 by Gallery Books,
an imprint of W.H. Smith Publishers, Inc.,
112 Madison Avenue, New York 10016
© 1988 Colour Library Books Ltd, Godalming, Surrey, England
All rights reserved
Printed and bound in Italy
ISBN 0 8317 1553 7

Gallery Books are available for bulk purchase for sales promotions
and premium use. For details write or telephone
the Manager of Special Sales, W.H. Smith Publishers, Inc.,
112 Madison Avenue, New York, New York 10016 (212) 532-6600.

The recipes for Chocolate Orange Cake, Loganberry Torte,
Strawberry Box, Chocolate Terrine with Cherry Sauce, Chocolate
Rum Fool, Chocolate Rum Sauce, Mocha Ice Cream, Truffles, Zigzag
Shortbread and Peppermint Sauce are the copyright of Jennie Reekie,
and are reproduced by kind permission of Ward Lock Limited.

Compiled by
Anne D. Ager
Lalita Ahmed
Judith Ferguson
Denise Jarret-Macauley
Maureen McCall
Beverley Piper

Designed by
Philip Clucas and Sara Cooper

THE COMPLETE
COOKBOOK

GALLERY BOOKS
An Imprint of W. H. Smith Publishers Inc.
112 Madison Avenue
New York City 10016

Contents

VEGETARIAN CUISINE

Introduction to Vegetarian Meals

It is amazing how rigid we are when it comes to the subject of food and what we eat. In all other aspects of life virtually anything goes: people walk the streets with pink hair; sail the Atlantic single-handed or jog around the houses for two hours every morning and yet if we prefer beans and lentils to beef and chicken we are considered as being rather odd.

Vegetarians are not cranks, and there is nothing weird and wonderful about a pattern of vegetarian eating; they just prefer to eat dishes which do not contain meat, poultry, game and, quite often, fish. 'Why don't they become ill?' you hear people say; 'Where do they get their energy from if they don't eat meat?'; 'How boring to live on just vegetables and those little dried peas!' As vegetarians will happily tell you, they feel perfectly healthy, have quite sufficient energy to cope with day-to-day activities and, above all, *they really enjoy their food.*

A vegetarian diet can be just as varied and interesting as one based on meat and fish. Meat is much the same the world over, which cannot be said of the wide and wonderful range of fresh fruits and vegetables. And it is variety which is very much the keynote of vegetarian eating: different pastas, rices, cheeses, nuts and pulses are just a selection of the varied ingredients of a vegetarian diet. Most important of all, vegetarian dishes are every bit as nutritious as their meat-rich counterparts. The main difference lies with the types of food which provide us with the necessary nutrients. In a typical vegetarian dish, the protein usually comes from pulses, nuts or cheese, or a combination of these ingredients. Minerals, vitamins, fats and carbohydrates come from all the other basic foods, such as those already mentioned.

Eating 'the vegetarian way' has all sorts of advantages in its favor. A meatless diet is a very healthy one since it is nutritious, low in fat and high in bulk and fiber. Vegetarians rarely need to watch their weight as a diet that is high in natural fiber and low in fat is comparatively low in calories. The traditional pattern of Western eating is relatively expensive to follow, whereas vegetarian dishes are more economical to prepare and cook. In fact, meatless meals can simply make a nice change from the traditional pattern of eating. Vegetarian cooking is fun, and eating vegetarian meals is healthy and good for you.

Vegetarian food really can be exciting and delicious and even if you are not a committed vegetarian many of the ideas in this section are well worth trying. The dishes combine unusual tastes and textures with an imaginative use of spices and fresh herbs for extra flavor. If you served many of the recipes to your family and friends they probably wouldn't even realize that their meal was meatless.

Soups

Cucumber Soup

PREPARATION TIME: 15 minutes

COOKING TIME: 8-10 minutes

SERVES: 4 people

1 large cucumber
1 cup water
2½ cups vegetable stock
1¼ tblsp white wine vinegar
2½ tblsp cornstarch mixed with
2½ tblsp water
2½ tblsp soured cream
2½ tblsp natural yogurt
Salt and ground white pepper to taste
1¼ tblsp chopped chives or scallion
*   tops*
Chili powder

Cut ¼ of the cucumber into wafer thin rounds and keep aside for garnishing. Puree the rest of the cucumber with the water in a liquidizer. Put the vegetable stock and the pureed cucumber into a saucepan and bring to the boil over a medium heat. Add the vinegar and cook for 1 minute. Add the cornstarch mixture gradually. Stir well until the soup starts to thicken. Simmer for 2-3 minutes. Remove from the heat and cool slightly. Blend in the liquidizer and add the soured cream and yogurt. Return to the saucepan and season with salt and pepper. Heat through gently to serve hot or chill to serve cold. Serve garnished with sliced cucumber and chopped chives or scallion tops. Dust with chili powder.

Daal Soup

This is a thick and hearty soup, made from lentils. The lentils most often used for making soup are red lentils, or yellow lentils which are called Toor daal. The recipe below can be made with either variety.

PREPARATION TIME: 15-20
minutes

COOKING TIME: 15 minutes

SERVES: 4-6 people

3 cups red lentils (see above)
3¾ cups water
4 canned tomatoes, drained and
*   crushed*

1 green chili, sliced lengthways and
*   seeded*
2½ tblsp natural yogurt or soured
*   cream*
1 tblsp butter
1 medium onion, peeled and chopped
Salt and freshly ground black pepper
*   to taste*
1-2 sprigs fresh green coriander
*   leaves, chopped*

Wash the lentils in 4-5 changes of water. Drain the lentils and put them into a pan with the water. Cover the pan and bring to the boil; simmer for 10 minutes. Beat until smooth with an egg whisk. Add the crushed tomatoes and green chili and simmer gently for 2 minutes. Stir in the yogurt or soured cream. Melt the butter in a small pan and fry the onion until golden. Season the hot soup with salt and pepper and pour into a serving bowl; sprinkle with the fried onion and chopped coriander. Serve immediately with buttered brown bread, crisp rolls or croutons.

Tomato Saar

This is a thin tomato soup from the South of India. It makes a refreshing and interesting starter.

PREPARATION TIME: 15 minutes

COOKING TIME: 17-18 minutes

SERVES: 4-6 people

2½ tsp butter
1 small onion, peeled and chopped
½lb tomatoes, skinned and chopped
4 cups water
1¼ tblsp tomato paste
4-6 green Cilantro (Chinese Parsley)
*   leaves*
Salt and freshly ground black pepper
*   to taste*
3 cloves of garlic, peeled and crushed

Garnish
1-2 sprigs fresh green coriander or
*   parsley leaves, chopped*
1 green chili, chopped (optional)

Melt half of the butter and fry the onion for 3-4 minutes. Add the skinned and chopped tomatoes and cook for 5 minutes. Blend the

water and tomato paste and add to the onion and tomatoes. Add Cilantro (Chinese Parsley) leaves. Season with salt and pepper. Cover and simmer for 5-7 minutes. Heat the remaining butter and fry the crushed cloves of garlic until dark brown. Pour the mixture over the simmering tomato soup. Remove from the heat. Sprinkle over the chopped coriander and chili. Discard green chili before eating. Serve piping hot either with French bread or with a little plain boiled rice. Alternatively: blend the skinned tomatoes to give a smooth textured soup.

Mixed Vegetable Soup

This Indian recipe can include a wide variety of vegetables. One creates one's own dish by adding or subtracting one or more vegetables.

PREPARATION TIME: 15 minutes

COOKING TIME: about 20 minutes

SERVES: 6 people

2½ tsp butter
1 medium onion, peeled and chopped
6 cloves
1 inch piece cinnamon stick
4 small green cardamoms
1 small bayleaf
1 medium potato, peeled and
*   chopped*
2 carrots, peeled and chopped
1 banana, peeled and chopped
6 flowerets of cauliflower
½ cup shelled fresh or frozen peas
1 leek, washed and chopped
1 stick celery, chopped
½ cup green beans (sliced or
*   chopped)*
4 cups water
Salt and freshly ground black pepper
*   to taste*

Garnish
1-2 sprigs fresh green coriander
1-2 green chilies chopped

Melt the butter in a large saucepan and fry the onion for 3 minutes. Add the cloves, cinnamon, cardamom, bayleaf and fry for 1 minute. Add the potato, carrots, banana and cauliflower. Fry for 3 minutes. Add the remaining vegetables and cook for 2-3 minutes. Add water and salt and

pepper to taste. Cover and simmer gently for 8-13 minutes until vegetables are cooked. Adjust seasoning. Garnish with chopped coriander leaves and green chilies. Discard green chilies before eating. The vegetables should float in the clear soup; do not blend.

Carrot Soup

PREPARATION TIME: 12 minutes

COOKING TIME: 20-25 minutes

SERVES: 4 people

4-6 carrots, peeled and cut into thick
*   slices*
1 medium onion, peeled and
*   quartered*
1 medium turnip, peeled and cut into
*   wedges*
2 cloves garlic, peeled
3 cups water or vegetable stock
¾ tsp dried thyme
Salt and ground white pepper to taste
Hot pepper sauce to taste

Garnish
1 tblsp toasted sunflower seeds,
*   flaked almonds and pistachio nuts*
*   (mixed together)*

Put the carrots, onion, turnip, garlic and water into a large saucepan. Cover and simmer for 15 minutes. Add thyme and salt and pepper to taste and simmer for a further 5 minutes. Cool slightly and blend in a liquidizer. Return to the saucepan and heat the soup through. Ladle the soup into bowls. Add hot pepper sauce to taste. Serve garnished with toasted nuts.

Facing page: Tomato Saar (top right), Daal Soup (center left) and Mixed Vegetable Soup (bottom).

10

Minestrone Soup

This famous vegetable and pasta soup from Italy can be made in many different ways. The recipe below is a simple, but delicious one – served with bread, it is a complete meal in itself.

PREPARATION TIME: 20 minutes
COOKING TIME: 30 minutes
SERVES: 4-6 people

4 tblsp olive oil
1 medium onion, peeled and chopped
2 cloves of garlic, peeled and crushed
2 medium potatoes, peeled and diced
3 carrots, peeled and diced
2 stalks celery, chopped
1½ cups shredded cabbage
4-5 skinned or canned tomatoes, chopped
3¾ cups water or vegetable stock
1 bouquet garni
1½ cups shelled fresh, or frozen peas

Quick Tomato Soup (above right), Minestrone Soup (right) and Onion Soup (far right).

½ cup boiled and cooked red kidney beans
1 cup macaroni or any shaped pasta
Salt and freshly ground black pepper to taste
½ cup grated Parmesan cheese

Heat the olive oil in a saucepan and fry the onion and garlic until the onion is soft, 2-3 minutes. Stir in the potatoes, carrots and celery and fry for 3 minutes; add the cabbage and tomatoes. Cook for 5-6 minutes. Add water or stock and bouquet garni. Add peas, kidney beans, pasta and simmer gently, covered, for 10-15 minutes, or until the pasta is just tender. Season with salt and pepper and ladle into bowls. Sprinkle generously with grated Parmesan cheese before serving. Serve Minestrone soup with crusty bread.

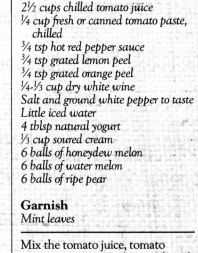

Quick Tomato Soup

This is quite an exotic soup and is made within a few minutes. It is ideal for a hot summer's day.

PREPARATION TIME: 10 minutes plus chilling time

SERVES: 4-6 people

2½ cups chilled tomato juice
¼ cup fresh or canned tomato paste, chilled
¾ tsp hot red pepper sauce
¾ tsp grated lemon peel
¾ tsp grated orange peel
¼-⅓ cup dry white wine
Salt and ground white pepper to taste
Little iced water
4 tblsp natural yogurt
⅓ cup soured cream
6 balls of honeydew melon
6 balls of water melon
6 balls of ripe pear

Garnish
Mint leaves

Mix the tomato juice, tomato paste, pepper sauce, fruit peels and wine together. Season with salt and pepper, cover and refrigerate for 3-4 hours. Thin the soup with a little iced water if necessary. Whisk the yogurt and cream together until smooth and light. Divide the soup amongst 4-6 bowls. Spoon the yogurt and cream mixture into the centre of each portion and float the fruit balls on top. Garnish with mint leaves and serve.

Rice and Mushroom Soup

Ideal for a party or for summer afternoons.

PREPARATION TIME:	10 minutes
COOKING TIME:	40-50 minutes
SERVES:	6-8 people

1 cup wild rice or brown rice
1 cup water
2 tblsp butter
1 medium onion, peeled and finely chopped
1 stalk celery, chopped
1 cup mushrooms, chopped
1 level tsp powdered garam masala (hot aromatic powder)
1 level tsp ground mustard seed
Salt and freshly ground black pepper to taste
4 cups water or stock
2 tblsp cornstarch blended with 2½ tblsp water
⅓ cup light cream

Garnish
1-2 sprigs fresh green coriander or parsley, chopped

Wash the rice in 3-4 changes of water; cook covered in 1 cup water for 25-30 minutes, or until rice is tender. Keep on one side. Melt the butter in a large saucepan; saute the onion until tender for 3-5 minutes. Add the celery and mushrooms. Cook for 1-2 minutes. Stir in the powdered garam masala, mustard and salt and pepper to taste. Add the water or stock. Simmer for 5 minutes. Add the cornstarch mixture and simmer for a further 3 minutes. Add the cooked rice and cream. Gently stir over a low heat for 2 minutes to heat through. Ladle the soup into bowls and garnish with coriander or parsley.

Onion Soup

Onion soup has been made famous by the French. Here is a delicious recipe based on the French style.

PREPARATION TIME:	20 minutes
COOKING TIME:	1 hour
SERVES:	4-6 people

6 tblsp butter
3-4 large onions, peeled and sliced into rings
2½ tblsp flour
3¾ cups vegetable stock

Salt and ground white pepper to taste
6 slices of French bread (¾ inch) thick
2 cloves of garlic, peeled and bruised
6 tblsp grated Parmesan cheese

Melt the butter in a saucepan and fry the onions briskly on a very low heat. Cover and simmer the onions in their own juices for 25-30 minutes, stirring occasionally until golden brown. Remove from the heat. Stir in the flour and add the stock gradually. Season with salt and pepper and return to heat. Bring to the boil quickly; reduce the heat and simmer covered for 15-20 minutes. Rub the bread pieces each side with the bruised garlic. Float the bread rounds in the soup and sprinkle grated Parmesan cheese generously over the top. Put under the broiler and cook for 2-3 minutes or until the top is golden. Serve at once. Alternatively – fry the bread rounds or bread slices in butter prior to rubbing with garlic.

Carrot Soup (top), Rice and Mushroom Soup (center right) and Cucumber Soup (bottom left).

VEGETARIAN CUISINE

Snacks and Appetizers

Flour Pancake

This is a favorite pancake from the southern part of India and it is really worth making; good, wholesome and nutritious.

PREPARATION TIME: 10 minutes

COOKING TIME: 20 minutes

SERVES: 6 people

2½ cups whole-wheat flour
½ tsp salt
⅔ cup natural yogurt
1 egg, beaten
1 small onion, peeled and chopped
1-2 green chilies, chopped
2 sprigs fresh green coriander leaves, chopped
1¼ tblsp grated fresh coconut, or desiccated coconut
2½ tsp sugar
Olive oil

Sieve the flour and salt and add the yogurt and egg. Mix in sufficient water to make a thickish batter of pouring consistency. Beat the mixture well and add the onion, chili, coriander, coconut and sugar. Mix well. Allow to stand for 2-3 minutes. Heat 1¼ tblsp oil in a small frying pan or omelette pan. Spoon in a little of the batter to give a depth of 1¼ inches. Cover with a lid and cook over a low heat for 3-5 minutes. Turn the pancake over and pour a little oil around the edge; cover and cook until the pancake is set and brown on both sides. Repeat with the remaining batter until you have several pancakes. Serve piping hot.

Dosas

Dosas can be eaten plain or with a filling. Eat them as a snack, for breakfast, or as a main meal with a filling and accompanied by chutney and daal (lentil dish).

PREPARATION TIME: overnight, plus 20 minutes

COOKING TIME: 30-45 minutes

SERVES: 6 people

1lb rice
½lb white lentils (urid daal)
½ tsp fenugreek seeds

1¼ tsp dried yeast
1¼ tsp sugar
¾ tsp salt
1¼ tblsp natural yogurt
Olive oil

Wash the rice and white lentils separately in 3-4 changes of water. Soak in fresh water for 1 hour. Grind the rice with a little water to a thick, coarse paste. Grind the white lentils with fenugreek seeds and a little water into a fine paste. (Use a food processor, food liquidizer or food grinder). Mix the dried yeast with 1¼ tblsp tepid water and the sugar. Mix well and leave to stand for 10 minutes until frothy. Mix the ground rice and lentils with the salt, yeast and yogurt and mix well. Cover with a cloth and leave in a dark, warm place overnight. Next day mix well with sufficient water to give a smooth, thickish batter. Heat a medium non-stick frying pan and grease well with 1¼ tsp oil. Pour in 2½-3¾ tblsp of the rice batter,

Bessan Omelette (top right), Flour Pancake (center left) and Dosas (bottom).

spread it around to make a thin pancake. Cover with a lid. Cook for 3-4 minutes; spoon a little oil around the edge of the frying pan and turn the dosa over. Cook for a

14

further 2-3 minutes and serve hot. make the remaining dosa in the same way. Dosas can be made as large as 12-14 inches in diameter.

Vegetable Filling
4 tblsp olive oil
2 large onions, peeled and thinly sliced
1¼ tsp white lentils (urid daal), washed and soaked in water for 5-10 minutes
½ tsp mustard seed
8-10 fresh Chinese parsley leaves
2 green chilies, cut into quarters
1½lb potatoes, boiled in their skins, peeled and cubed
Salt to taste

Heat oil and fry the onions for 4-5 minutes or until light brown. Add the drained lentils and mustard seed. Fry for ½ minute; add the curry leaves and green chilies. Add the potatoes and salt to taste. Cover and cook for 8-10 minutes, stirring occasionally. To serve: make the dosa as above and place 2½ tblsp of the potato filling in the centre; fold the dosa over like an omelette.

Samosa

These crispy triangles with a vegetable filling can be eaten hot or cold.

PREPARATION TIME:	40 minutes
COOKING TIME:	25 minutes
SERVES:	4-6 people

Pastry
2½ cups all purpose flour, sieved
½ tsp salt
½ tsp baking powder
Water

Make the dough by adding water, a little at a time, to the sieved flour, salt and baking powder. Mix to a soft pliable dough. Cover and allow to stand.

Filling
¼ cup oil
1 medium onion, peeled and chopped
4 cups potatoes, peeled and cubed
2 carrots, peeled and grated
½ cup shelled green peas
½ cup green beans, chopped
1¼ tsp chili powder
1¼ tsp salt
1¼ tsp garam masala powder (hot aromatic powder)
¾ tsp ground turmeric
1¼ tblsp dry mango powder, or lemon juice
Oil for deep frying

Heat the oil and fry the onions for 2-3 minutes. Add the potatoes and carrots and cook for 3 minutes. Add peas and beans and cook for 2-3 minutes. Sprinkle chili, salt, garam masala, turmeric and mango powder. Mix well, cover and cook till potatoes are tender. Remove from heat and allow to cool. Divide the dough into 12-14 equal sized balls; roll each one out on a floured surface to a thin circle, 2-3 inches in diameter. Cut each circle in half. Apply the flour paste on the straight edge of each half. bring the edges together, overlapping them so as to make a cone. Fill the cone with the filling. Apply a little flour paste on the open edge and seal by pressing both the edges together. This will make a triangular shape.

Make all the samosas in the same way. Heat the oil for deep frying. When the oil is hot, reduce the heat and fry the samosas, a few at a time, until golden brown on either side (about 4-5 minutes). Drain on kitchen paper and serve with chutney or tomato sauce.

Curry Puffs

Like sausage rolls, curried vegetable puffs make an ideal dish for snacks and cocktails. The size can be varied to suit the occasion.

PREPARATION TIME:	1 hour
COOKING TIME:	20 minutes
SERVES:	4-6

1lb ready-made puff pastry

Filling
¼ cup oil
1 large onion, peeled and chopped
1¼ tsp cumin seeds
4 cups potatoes, peeled and diced
2 carrots, peeled and shredded
1 cup shelled peas
1¼ tsp salt
1¼ tsp freshly ground black pepper
2-3 sprigs fresh green coriander leaves, chopped
1¼ tsp garam masala powder (hot aromatic powder)

Flour paste: mix together 2½ tsp flour with water to make a sticky paste.

Heat the oil and fry the onion for 2 minutes. Add cumin seeds and allow to crackle, then add the diced potatoes. Stir fry over a medium heat for 5-6 minutes. Add the carrots and stir fry for 2 minutes. Add the peas and season with salt, pepper and chopped coriander leaves. Stir well. Cover and cook for 5-6 minutes or until the potatoes are tender. Sprinkle with the garam masala and lemon juice. Mix well. Remove from the heat and allow to cool. Roll out the puff pastry thinly. Cut into 3 inch by 6 inch rectangles. Place 1¼ tblsp filling at one end and roll up the pastry like jelly roll. Secure the ends with the flour and water paste. Preheat the oven to 375°F.

Potato Cutlets (top), Samosa (above left) and Curry Puffs (left).

Arrange the curry puffs on greased cooky sheets and bake for 10-15 minutes or until golden. Serve hot with tomato sauce.

Potato Cutlets

PREPARATION TIME: 30 minutes

COOKING TIME: 30 minutes

SERVES: 6 people

1¼ tblsp oil
1 medium onion, peeled and chopped
1½ cups shelled peas
6 cups potatoes, boiled in their skins, peeled and mashed
1¼ tsp salt
1¼ tsp freshly ground black pepper
2½ tblsp lemon juice
2 eggs, beaten
Breadcrumbs
Oil for shallow frying

Heat 1¼ tblsp oil in a frying pan and fry the onion for 3 minutes; add the peas and fry for 2 minutes. Mix the onion and peas with the mashed potatoes. Add salt and pepper to taste and the lemon juice. Mix well. Divide mixture into 24-30 small even-sized cakes. Dip firstly into beaten egg and then coat evenly with breadcrumbs. Heat sufficient oil in a frying pan for shallow frying. Shallow fry the potato cutlets for 3-4 minutes or until golden. Serve hot or cold with chutney or tomato sauce.

Bessan Omelettes

These vegetarian omelettes are made with chickpea (baisen) flour and can be eaten as a quick snack. Easy to make and quick to prepare, they are ideal for unexpected friends or late night guests.

PREPARATION TIME: 10 minutes

COOKING TIME: 20 minutes

MAKES: 12

2½ cups sieved bessan flour (made from chick-peas)
1 small onion, peeled and finely chopped
1-2 green chilies, chopped (optional)
2 sprigs fresh green coriander, chopped
2 tomatoes, seeded and diced
½ cup shelled peas
¾ tsp salt
Pinch chili powder
Olive oil

Mix the bessan flour with the onion, chilies, coriander, tomatoes and peas. Add sufficient water to made a thick batter, about 1¾ cups. Season with salt and chili powder, Mix well and allow to stand for 5 minutes. Heat a solid based frying pan or griddle pan and brush with oil. Ladle in sufficient batter to cover the base of the pan. Cover and cook over a low heat for 4-5 minutes. Turn the omelette over and cook for 3-4 minutes. Both sides should be browned evenly. Make the rest of the omelettes in the same way. Serve hot with tomato sauce.

Stuffed Summer Squash

Summer Squash can be stuffed with a vegetable or meat filling. Here is a delectable recipe for a vegetable stuffed Summer Squash.

PREPARATION TIME: 15 minutes

COOKING TIME: 45 minutes

SERVES: 4-6 people

2 Summer Squash 6-8 inches in length

Filling
¼ cup oil
1 large onion, peeled and chopped
4 cups potatoes, peeled and diced
1¼ tsp crushed fresh root ginger
1¼ tsp crushed garlic
1¼ tsp chili powder
¾ tsp turmeric powder
1¼ tsp garam masala powder (hot aromatic powder)

1 cup shelled peas
4 tomatoes, chopped
¾ tsp salt
¾ tsp freshly ground black pepper
1 green chili, chopped
2½ tsp melted butter

Heat the oil in a wok or large frying pan and fry the onion for 2 minutes. Add the potatoes and stir-fry for 3-4 minutes. Add the ginger, garlic, chili powder, turmeric and garam masala powder. Mix well and add the peas, tomatoes, salt and pepper and the green chili; cover and cook until the potatoes are tender, about 6-8 minutes. Add the lemon juice. Remove a thin slice from each end of the summer squash. Scoop out the centre pith leaving a ¾ inch shell. Remove the skin in alternate strips to give it firmness. Fill the hollowed summer squash with the prepared potato filling. Place the stuffed summer

squash on a rectangle of foil and brush with melted butter; season with salt and pepper. Wrap the foil around the summer squash; bake at 350°F for 40-45 minutes. Remove the foil from time to time and brush with the juices. Serve hot.

Vegetable Kebabs

This Turkish/Greek recipe makes an ideal side dish for barbecue parties.

PREPARATION TIME: 30 minutes

COOKING TIME: 30 minutes

SERVES: 4-6 people

1 eggplant cut into 1 inch pieces
1 large green pepper, seeded and cut into 1 inch pieces
12-14 small cherry tomatoes (or 6-8 tomatoes, halved)
12-14 small onions, peeled and blanched for 5 minutes
12-14 large mushrooms
2 medium potatoes, boiled in their skins, peeled and cut into 1 inch cubes
Olive oil
2½ tblsp lemon juice
½ tsp salt
¾ tsp freshly ground black pepper

Put all the vegetables into a large bowl and add 60ml (4 tblsp) olive oil, lemon juice and salt and pepper. Mix together and leave to stand for 10-15 minutes, turning the vegetables once or twice. Thread the vegetables alternately onto skewers. Brush with the marinade. Broil for 3-4 minutes, until evenly browned. Brush the vegetables with oil or marinade during grilling. Serve piping hot.

Stuffed Peppers

PREPARATION TIME: 30 minutes

COOKING TIME: 30-40 minutes

SERVES: 6 people

6 even sized peppers (green or red)
¼ cup oil
1 medium onion, peeled and chopped
2 cloves garlic, peeled and chopped
2 tomatoes, chopped
1 green chili, chopped
1 cup plain boiled rice
1 medium potato, peeled and diced
½ tsp salt

¾ tsp freshly ground black pepper
½ cup shelled peas
1¼ tblsp lemon juice
1¼ tblsp chopped parsley or coriander leaves
2½ tblsp vegetable stock

Cut a slice from the top of each pepper; scoop out the centre seeds Heat the oil and fry the onion for 1 2 minutes. Add the garlic, tomatoes and green chili and stir fry for 2-3 minutes. Add the rice, potato, salt and pepper, peas and lemon juice and parsley. Cover and cook for 2-4 minutes. Arrange the peppers in an ovenproof dish and stuff the peppers with the rice mixture. Pour the stock around the peppers. Bake at 375°F for 20-30 minutes, basting occasionally with the juices. Serve hot.

Stuffed Tomatoes

Tomatoes stuffed with a vegetable filling and served with a tangy sauce make a good starter.

PREPARATION TIME: 20 minutes

COOKING TIME: 15-18 minutes

SERVES: 6 people

12 medium size firm tomatoes
2½ tblsp oil
10-12 scallions (only the white part), chopped
2½ tsp chopped parsley or coriander leaves
1 cup cooked rice
2½ tsp pine kernels, or skinned hazelnuts, chopped
2½ tsp roasted sesame seeds
¾ tsp salt
½ tsp freshly ground black pepper
½ tsp ground mixed spice
1 cup vegetable stock
2½ tsp cornstarch
2½ tblsp lemon juice
1 egg, well beaten

Stuffed Summer Squash (top), Vegetable Kebabs (center right) and Stuffed Peppers (bottom).

Slice the tops off the tomatoes and scoop out the center pulp, leaving a ¾ inch "shell". Reserve the tomato pulp. Heat the oil in the frying pan and fry the onions for 2-3 minutes. Add the parsley, cooked rice, nuts, sesame seeds, salt and pepper and allspice. Add the tomato pulp and any juice which may have formed. Cook, uncovered, for 3-4 minutes, until most of the moisture has evaporated. Stuff the hollowed tomatoes with the rice mixture and arrange in a large frying pan. Add the stock and cook for 4 minutes. Remove the tomatoes. Bring the liquid back to the boil and add the blended cornstarch and lemon juice. Remove from the heat. Add the beaten egg a little at a time. Return the mixture to the heat and cook until thickened. Add the stuffed tomatoes and cook over a low heat for 5 minutes, spooning the sauce over the tomatoes from time to time.

Fritters
(TEMPURA)

This is a Japanese dish and is very popular. The batter may be used for meats as well.

PREPARATION TIME: 10 minutes

COOKING TIME: 10-15 minutes

SERVES: 4 people

Batter
225g (8oz) all purpose flour
15ml (1 tblsp) cornstarch
¼ tsp salt
1 cup chilled water
1 egg yolk
2 egg whites, stiffly beaten

Oil for deep frying
1 cup fresh green beans, cut into 2 inch pieces
10-12 fresh asparagus spears, cut in 2 inch lengths
1 eggplant, cut into 1 inch cubes
1 large potato, peeled and sliced ¼ inch thick
10-12 fresh mushrooms, halved
6-8 cauliflower flowerets, halved

Tempura sauce: A
1 cup water
¼ cup sherry
¼ cup soya sauce
1¼ tsp sugar
½ a vegetable stock cube

Mix the ingredients together and bring to the boil. Stir until dissolved.

Tempura sauce: B
1 inch fresh root ginger, peeled and grated
2½ tblsp grated turnip

2½ tblsp grated radish
¼ cup prepared mustard
¼ cup soya sauce

Mix the ingredients together and keep covered.

To make the batter: mix together the flour, cornstarch and salt. Make a well in the center. Mix the chilled water and egg yolk together and pour into the center of the flour. Stir in the flour and blend lightly. Fold in the whisked egg whites.

Heat oil for deep frying. Dip the vegetables into the batter and fry in hot oil for 2-3 minutes until golden. Drain on kitchen paper and serve hot with the Tempura sauces. Use the batter within a few minutes of making. Do not allow it to stand for long.

Cheese and Lentil Balls

PREPARATION TIME: 30 minutes

COOKING TIME: 1 hour

SERVES: 4 people

1½ cups red lentils
1½ cups water
1 cup grated cheese
1 medium onion, peeled and chopped
2 large eggs
½ cup fresh breadcrumbs
1½ tsp mixed dried herbs
1½ tblsp lemon juice
Salt to taste
½ tsp freshly ground black pepper
Oil for shallow frying

Wash the lentils in 3-4 changes of water. Drain the lentils and put them into a pan with the water. Cook until the lentils are tender and the water has been absorbed. Remove from heat and allow to cool. Mix the cooked lentils with the cheese, onion, egg, breadcrumbs, herbs, salt and pepper and the lemon juice. Mix well and shape into balls. Shallow fry the balls for 4-5 minutes on each side until golden brown. Drain on absorbent paper and serve immediately.

Mixed Nut Rissoles

PREPARATION TIME: 15 minutes

COOKING TIME: 20-25 minutes

SERVES: 4 people

2 tblsp hazelnuts, chopped
½ cup shelled peanuts, chopped
½ cup cashew nuts, chopped

2 tblsp pistachio nuts, chopped
1 onion, peeled and chopped
¾ cup fresh breadcrumbs
3 eggs, beaten
Salt and freshly ground black pepper to taste
¾ tsp dried, chopped marjoram
1 carrot, peeled and grated
1¼ tblsp lemon juice
Little milk
Oil for shallow frying

Mix the chopped nuts with the onion, breadcrumbs, eggs, salt and pepper, marjoram, carrot and lemon juice. Add a little milk to bind the mixture, if necessary. Shape into rissoles. Shallow fry the rissoles in oil, for 4-5 minutes on each side, until golden brown. Drain well on absorbent paper and serve immediately. Alternatively, brush the rissoles generously with oil, put them onto a cooky tray and bake in the oven at 425°F for 15 minutes. Turn the rissoles halfway through cooking and brush with extra oil.

Cashew Nut Pie

PREPARATION TIME: 20-25 minutes

COOKING TIME: 30-40 minutes

SERVES: 4 people

Filling
2 medium onions, peeled and chopped
2 tblsp oil
2 cups shredded cabbage
½ cup carrots, peeled and grated

Pie Crust
1 cup crushed cornflakes
½ cup cashew nuts, coarsely ground
1½ cup grated cheese
1 tsp mixed dried herbs
Salt and freshly ground black pepper to taste
2 large eggs
1 cup fresh breadcrumbs
1 tblsp oil
¼ cup butter

To make the filling: fry the onions in the oil for 2 minutes; add the cabbage and carrots and fry for a further 4-5 minutes. Remove from the heat and allow to cool.

To make the pie crust: mix all the ingredients together in a bowl, apart from the oil, butter and ½ cup of the grated cheese. Grease a cake pan with the oil. Press half the pie crust ingredients out to form an even base. Spread the filling mixture on top, and then press over the remaining pie crust ingredients. Sprinkle with the

remaining grated cheese and dot with butter. Bake in oven at 400°F for 25-30 minutes.

Tomato, Onion and Mushroom Flan

PREPARATION TIME: 20 minutes

COOKING TIME: 40-45 minutes

SERVES: 6 people

8oz basic pastry
2 cups grated Cheddar cheese
4 tomatoes, skinnned and chopped
1¼ tblsp chopped chives or parsley
1 cup mushrooms, sliced
2½ tsp corn oil
1 large onion, peeled and chopped
3 eggs, beaten
1⅔ cup milk
¾ tsp salt
½ tsp freshly ground black pepper

Roll out the pastry and use to line a 8-9 inch flan dish. Put ¼ cup of the grated cheese into the pastry case followed by the tomatoes, chives or parsley and the mushrooms. Heat the corn oil and fry the onion for 2-3 minutes. Mix the beaten eggs with the milk, salt and pepper and fried onion. Pour into the flan case and top with the remaining grated cheese. Bake at 400°F for 35-40 minutes, or until set. Serve hot or cold.

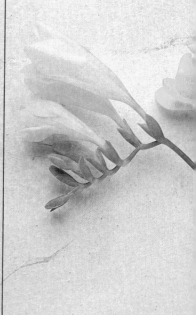

Mixed Nut Rissoles (left),
Cheese and Lentil Rissoles
(below) and Cashew Nut Pie
(bottom).

Pakora

This is the Indian version of vegetable fritters. Fried with or without batter, they make an interesting starter or snack.

PREPARATION TIME: 15 minutes

COOKING TIME: 15-20 minutes

SERVES: 4-6 people

1 large potato, or
2 medium potatoes, peeled and cut
   into ¼ inch thick slices
8-10 cauliflower flowerets, halved
   lengthways
6 carrots, cut into 2 inch lengths and
   halved
1 eggplant, cut into 2 inch cubes
6 zucchini, trimmed and cut into 2
   inch pieces and then quartered
1-2 green peppers, seeded and cut into
   ¼ inch) thick rounds or 1 inch
   pieces
1¼ tsp salt
1¼ tsp red chili powder
¾ tsp turmeric powder
Oil for deep frying
6 lemon wedges

Sprinkle the vegetables with the spices and rub well in. Keep on one side. Heat the oil for deep frying. When it is beginning to smoke, reduce the heat. Fry the vegetables a few at a time, in batches. Fry for 2-3 minutes and drain on kitchen paper. Serve piping hot with wedges of lemon and a sweet and sour chutney or tomato ketchup. (These uncoated fritters are called Bhaja).

Batter

2½ cups bessan flour, sieved (made
   from chick-peas)
1¼ tsp salt
1¼ tsp chili powder
1¼ tsp ground cumin
1 tblsp lemon juice
1¼ cups water

Mix the sieved flour with the salt, chili powder, cumin and lemon juice. Make a well in the centre and add the water; stir in the bessan flour until all the flour has been incorporated. Beat well to give a smooth batter. Adjust seasoning. Allow the batter to stand for a few minutes. Heat the oil as above. Dip the vegetables into the batter and then fry for 2-3 minutes. Drain on kitchen paper and serve piping hot with tomato sauce. Other vegetables which may be used: onions rings, raw banana slices, green tomato slices, spinach leaves.

Stuffed Mushrooms

PREPARATION TIME: 20 minutes

COOKING TIME: 10-15 minutes

SERVES: 4-6 people

Filling

1 small onion, peeled and finely
   chopped
2½ tsp oil
½ inch fresh root ginger, peeled and
   crushed
2 cloves garlic, peeled and crushed
2 cups boiled, peeled and mashed
   potatoes
Salt and freshly ground black pepper
   to taste
1¼ tblsp lemon juice
2½ tsp chopped chives or parsley

20-24 large mushrooms
1½ cup grated Cheddar cheese
Oil for brushing

Fry the onion in the 2½ tsp oil for 2 minutes; add the ginger and garlic. Fry for 1 minute and mix with the mashed potatoes. Season to taste with salt, pepper, lemon juice and chopped parsley. Mix well. Remove the stalks from the mushrooms; stuff the hollows with the potato filling and top with a little Cheddar cheese. Brush the mushrooms with a little oil and arrange them on a baking tray. Bake the mushrooms in a moderately hot oven, 375°F, for 10 minutes until the cheese is brown.

Aloo Bonda

This is an Indian potato fritter recipe made in the shape of spicy balls. Eaten hot or cold, they are ideal for parties, snacks and picnics.

PREPARATION TIME: 25 minutes

COOKING TIME: 30 minutes

SERVES: 4-6 people

Batter

2 cups bessan flour, sieved (made
   from chick-peas)
½ tsp salt
½ tsp baking powder
1¼ cups water

1lb potatoes, boiled in their skins and
   peeled
1 large or 2 medium onions, peeled
   and chopped
1 inch fresh root ginger, peeled and
   finely chopped
2-3 green chilies, chopped
4-5 sprigs fresh green coriander
   leaves, chopped
¾ tsp salt
½ tsp freshly ground black pepper
1¼ tblsp lemon juice
Oil for deep frying

Mix the sieved flour with the salt and baking powder. Make a well in the centre and add the water. Beat well to give a smooth batter. Chop the boiled potatoes into tiny cubes; add the chopped onions, ginger, chilies, coriander leaves, salt and pepper to taste and lemon juice. Mix well and adjust seasoning to taste. Mold into even-sized balls with dampened hands. Heat the oil for deep frying. When hot, dip the vegetable balls into the batter and then fry for 3-4 minutes over a gentle heat until golden brown. Drain on kitchen paper and serve with tomato sauce.

This page: Aloo Bonda (top), Fritters (Tempura) (center right) and Pakora (bottom left).

Facing page: Stuffed Tomatoes (top right), Stuffed Mushrooms (center left) and Tomato, Onion and Mushroom Flan (bottom).

Salads

Onion Salad

This salad is usually served as an accompaniment to kebabs. Onion salad goes very well with a variety of main courses, as a side salad.

PREPARATION TIME: 5-7 minutes
SERVES: 4 people

2 large Spanish onions, peeled and thinly sliced
2-3 sprigs fresh green coriander, chopped
1 green chili, sliced
Juice of 1 lemon
¾ tsp salt
Pinch paprika

Combine the onion rings, coriander leaves and chili in a bowl. Add the lemon juice and salt and mix well. Put the onion salad onto a serving plate and sprinkle with paprika.

Tabbouleh

This is a Lebanese salad and it is very good for parties and picnics.

PREPARATION TIME: 2 hours 30 minutes
SERVES: 6 people

2 cups bulgar or pourgouri (precooked, cracked wheat)
1 cup boiling water
8-10 scallions, chopped
1 green pepper, seeded and chopped
⅔ cup parsley
2½ tblsp chopped mint leaves

Dressing
¼ cup lemon juice
¾ cup olive oil
1¼ tsp grated lemon peel
1¼ tsp ground mixed spice
¾ tsp ground cumin
1¼ tsp salt
¼ tsp freshly ground black pepper
1 small iceberg lettuce, shredded
2 large firm tomatoes, cut into wedges
10-15 pitted black olives, halved
2-3 sprigs mint
1-2 sprigs fresh green coriander

Place the pourgouri or bulgar into a bowl and add boiling water. Cover and stand for 1½-2 hours. Drain the bulgar by squeezing out the excess water. Mix the scallions, green pepper, parsley and mint with the bulgar. Combine all the dressing ingredients in a screw top jar and shake well. Pour the dressing over the bulgar mixture and mix lightly. Line a platter with shredded lettuce. Place the prepared bulgar in the centre. Garnish with tomato, olives, mint and coriander leaves.

Sweet and Sour Coleslaw

A variation on the usual theme, but a definite winner.

PREPARATION TIME: 20 minutes
SERVES: 6 people

½ small red cabbage, shredded
1 small green cabbage, shredded
1 large sweet carrot, peeled and shredded
3 scallions, finely chopped
6½ tblsp cider vinegar
4 tblsp brown sugar
¾ tsp salt
½ tsp freshly ground black pepper
6½ tblsp soured cream
1¼ tsp French mustard

Combine the red and green cabbage, carrots and scallions in a mixing bowl. Mix the vinegar, sugar and salt and pepper in a small saucepan and stir over the heat to dissolve the sugar. Pour the hot vinegar sauce over the cabbage mixture and mix well. Stir the soured cream and mustard together in a separate bowl; stir this mixture into the vegetables. Mix well and serve.

Mixed Bean Salad

This nutritious salad is made from a medley of beans and is very good for health conscious and athletic people. Either cook the dried beans at home or buy ready-cooked ones. Soak the beans separately overnight, and then boil them separately until tender. Drain well.

PREPARATION TIME: 15 minutes
SERVES: 4-6 people

1½ cups cooked red kidney beans
1½ cups cooked black eyed beans (Lobia)
1½ cups cooked chick peas
1½ cups cooked butter beans
1 cup shelled broad beans
2 cups sliced green beans, blanched

Dressing
2½ tblsp brown sugar
½ cup white wine vinegar
¾ tsp salt
½ tsp freshly ground black pepper
½ cup olive oil
¾ tsp dry mustard powder
¾ tsp dried basil leaves
1 large Spanish or red onion, peeled and thinly sliced into rings
2½ tblsp parsley

Mix all the beans together in a large bowl. Mix the sugar and vinegar together with salt and pepper to taste. Stir in the oil, mustard and basil. Pour this vinegar mixture over the beans. Mix thoroughly. Refrigerate until ready to serve. Before serving, mix in the onion rings and parsley.

Nutty Salad

PREPARATION TIME: 20 minutes
SERVES: 4 people

4 cups boiled potatoes, diced
1½ cups shelled green peas
1 cup cooked carrots, diced
1 medium onion, peeled and chopped
1 small green pepper, seeded and chopped
8-10 radishes, chopped
2 stalks celery, chopped
¼ cucumber, chopped
½ cup roasted peanuts, coarsely chopped
½ cup grated fresh coconut
1¼ tblsp sunflower seeds
2-3 sprigs fresh green coriander leaves or parsley, chopped

Dressing
2½ tblsp lemon juice
5¼ tblsp olive oil
1¼ tsp salt
¾ tsp freshly ground black pepper
1 tsp brown sugar

Mix all the vegetables together, except the nuts and sunflower seeds, in a large bowl. Mix the dressing ingredients together in a screw top jar and shake well. Add the dressing to the salad and mix throughly. Sprinkle with the nuts and sunflower seeds before serving.

Rice and Nut Salad

This salad has a very refreshing taste. The main ingredients are nuts, raisins, carrots and rice.

PREPARATION TIME: 15 minutes
SERVES: 4 people

2½ tblsp olive oil
2½ tblsp lemon juice
Salt and freshly ground black pepper to taste
1 cup white raisins
½ cup currants
2½ cups cooked long grain rice, well drained
¾ cup chopped blanched almonds
½ cup cashew nuts, chopped
½ cup shelled walnuts, chopped
15oz can peach slices, drained and chopped
¼ cucumber, cubed
1 cup cooked red kidney beans
1¼ tblsp chopped pitted olives

Mix the olive oil, lemon juice and salt and freshly ground black pepper in a screw top jar; shake vigorously. Soak the raisins and currants in sufficient boiling water to cover, for 10 minutes. Drain the fruits. Mix the rice, nuts and soaked raisins and currants. Add the chopped peaches, cucumber, red kidney beans and olives. Pour the dressing over the salad and toss lightly together. Serve on a bed of chopped lettuce.

Facing page: Onion Salad (top), Nutty Salad (center) and Tabbouleh (bottom).

Cheese Salad

This cheese salad originates from Greece and has many variations; it is popularly known as Horiatiki.

PREPARATION TIME: 10-12 minutes

SERVES: 4 people

½ a head of chicory
½ iceberg lettuce
1 cucumber, peeled and sliced
3-4 large tomatoes, cut into wedges, or
15-20 baby tomatoes, halved

8-10 pitted green or black olives, halved
1 medium Spanish or red onion, peeled and chopped
1 cup Feta cheese, cut into ½ inch pieces

Dressing

⅓ cup olive oil
2½ tblsp red wine vinegar
1½ tsp chopped fresh oregano or
½ tsp dried oregano
¾ tsp salt
½ tsp freshly ground black pepper
¾ tsp brown sugar

Wash and dry the chicory and lettuce leaves; tear into bite size pieces. Place the chicory and lettuce in a large bowl and add the cucumber, tomatoes, olives, onion and cheese. Shake the dressing ingredients together in a screw top jar. Pour the dressing over the salad. Toss lightly and serve.

Cheese Salad (bottom left), Mixed Bean Salad (below) and Rice and Nut Salad (bottom right).

Mixed Fresh Vegetable Salad

This salad can be prepared with any combination of vegetables, in any proportion. Add or subtract according to personal taste.

PREPARATION TIME: 20 minutes
SERVES: 6 people

1 large scallion, peeled and chopped
½ cucumber, diced
3 carrots, peeled and diced
6 large tomatoes, diced, or
8 baby tomatoes, halved
10 mushrooms, diced
3 stalks celery, diced
1 green pepper, seeded and diced
15-20 tiny cauliflower flowerets
15-20 radishes, quartered
1¼ tblsp chopped watercress or
   mustard and cress
2 sprigs fresh green coriander leaves
   or parsley, chopped

Dressing
½ tsp salt
½ tsp freshly ground black pepper
1¼ tsp brown sugar
2½ tsp cider vinegar
1¼ tblsp lemon juice
1¼ tblsp honey
5¼ tblsp olive oil
Pinch mustard powder
8 lettuce leaves

Combine all the vegetables in a large bowl. Mix together all the dressing ingredients. Pour the dressing over the vegetables and serve on a bed of lettuce leaves.

26

Salads

Pasta Salad

This is a popular American salad. It can be eaten as a main dish or as a side salad – it is a wonderful combination of vegetables, pasta and kidney beans.

PREPARATION TIME: 15-20 minutes

SERVES: 6 people

4 cups cooked red kidney beans, drained
3 cups pasta shells or spirals, cooked
1 large green pepper, seeded and sliced into 1 inch long pieces
1 large red pepper, seeded and sliced into 1 inch long pieces
20-30 pitted black olives, sliced in half
1 tblsp capers
4-5 sprigs fresh parsley, chopped

Dressing
1 cup olive oil
¼ cup lemon juice
2½ tsp finely chopped fresh basil leaves
1¼ tsp salt
½ tsp freshly ground black pepper
2 cloves garlic, peeled and minced
1 small head chicory

Combine the beans, pasta, peppers, olives, capers and parsley in a large bowl. Mix all the dressing ingredients together; add to the salad ingredients and toss together. Line the serving platter or bowl with chicory leaves; place the pasta salad in the centre. Alternatively: add ½lb of thinly sliced salami or Italian sausages or can sausages in brine cut into bite size pieces.

This page: Sweet and Sour Coleslaw (top left), Mixed Fresh Vegetable Salad (top right) and Pasta Salad (bottom).

Facing page: Kedgeree (top left), Sweet Savory Rice (center right) and Vegetable Pulao Rice (bottom).

VEGETARIAN CUISINE

Rice and Pulses

Kedgeree

PREPARATION TIME: 15 minutes, plus soaking time

COOKING TIME: 30 minutes

SERVES: 4-6 people

2 cups long grain rice
2 cups red lentils
3 cups tepid water
A stick of butter (or an equivalent
  amount of olive oil)
1 medium onion, peeled and chopped
¾ tsp crushed fresh root ginger
¾ tsp crushed garlic
1 inch piece cinnamon stick
6 cloves
1 bayleaf
1¼ tsp ground coriander
½ tsp ground turmeric
¾ tsp salt
2 green chilies, sliced in half
  lengthwise

Wash the rice and the lentils in 4 to 5 changes of water; soak them in the 3 cups tepid water for 30 minutes. Heat the butter or oil in a large pan; add the onion and fry for 2-3 minutes. Add the ginger, garlic, cinnamon stick, cloves and bayleaf, and fry for 1 minute. Drain the water from the rice and lentils; reserve the water. Add the rice and lentils to the fried onion, together with the coriander, turmeric, salt and green chilies. Stir over the heat for 2-3 minutes, until the rice and lentils are evenly coated with fat. Add the reserved water and bring to the boil; reduce the heat and simmer covered for 8-10 minutes, without stirring, until the water has been absorbed and the rice and lentils are tender. Serve with a vegetable curry.

Vegetable Pulao Rice

PREPARATION TIME: 30 minutes

COOKING TIME: 30 minutes

SERVES: 4-6 people

4 cups long grain rice (Basmati)
3-4 cups water
1 medium onion, peeled and diced
1 inch piece cinnamon stick
1 bayleaf

6 cloves
1¼ tsp black cumin (shah-zeera)
6 small cardamoms
¾ tsp crushed fresh root ginger
¾ tsp crushed garlic
1 medium potato, peeled and diced
1 carrot, peeled and diced
1 cup shelled peas
¾ cup sliced green beans
1¼ tsp garam masala powder (hot aromatic powder)
¾ tsp chili powder
1¼ tsp ground coriander
1¼ tsp ground cumin
1¼ tsp salt
2½ tblsp lemon juice
A stick of butter (or an equivalent amount of olive oil)

Wash the rice in 4-5 changes of water and soak in the 3-4 cups water for 30 minutes. Melt the butter in a pan and fry the onion for 2-3 minutes. Add the cinnamon, bayleaf, cloves, black cumin, cardamoms, ginger and garlic. Fry for 1 minute, stirring, and add the potato, carrot, peas, green beans, garam masala, chili, coriander, cumin and salt. Mix well. Drain the soaked rice, retaining the water and add the rice to the onion and spices. Stir the mixture gently and add the reserved water. Bring to the boil and then reduce the heat; cover and simmer gently for 10-15 minutes, until the rice is tender and the water has been absorbed. Do not stir during cooking. Sprinkle with the lemon juice and serve. To colour pulao: dissolve a pinch of saffron in 1¼ tblsp warm milk; pour over the rice and allow to stand over a very low heat for 5 minutes.

Mixed Daal

This is a mixed lentil stew, using 3 or 4 varieties of daal. Add a few vegetables of your choice to turn it into a substantial meal.

PREPARATION TIME: 15 minutes

COOKING TIME: 30 minutes

SERVES: 4 people

⅔ cup split Bengal grain (Channa)
½ cup yellow lentils (Toor Daal)
1 cup red lentils (Masoor)
½ cup dehusked split mung (Moong), or any other daal
¾ tsp ground turmeric
1¾ tsp ground coriander
4 canned tomatoes, chopped
2 green chilies
3 sprigs fresh green coriander leaves

Salt to taste
A stick of butter
½ inch fresh root ginger, peeled and chopped
1 onion, chopped
1 clove garlic, chopped

As some of these pulses have different cooking times, wash each pulse separately in 3-4 changes of water. Drain. Soak separately in water for 5 minutes. Bring 2½ cups water to the boil; add the drained channa daal. Boil for 15-20 minutes or until the pulses are tender. Add the remaining pulses well drained, and simmer gently with the turmeric and ground coriander for 15-20 minutes, or until all the pulses are soft. Beat with an egg whisk. Add the tomatoes, green chilies and coriander leaves. Simmer for a further 5-6 minutes. Pour into a serving bowl and keep warm. Melt the butter in a frying pan and fry the ginger for 2 minutes. Add the onion and garlic and fry until golden brown. Pour this mixture over the mixed daal and serve immediately.

Sweet Savory Rice

PREPARATION TIME: 20 minutes

COOKING TIME: 30 minutes

SERVES: 4-6 people

4 cups rice (Basmati or long grain)
3-4 cups water
½ cup raisins
¾ cup cashew nuts, chopped
½ cup blanched almonds, split
½ cup pistachio nuts, split
A stick of butter (or an equivalent amount of olive oil)
1 inch piece cinnamon stick
6 cloves
6 small cardamoms
1 bayleaf
¾ tsp black cumin seed (shah-zeera)
1 cup white raisins
1¼ tsp salt
1¼ tsp sugar
Pinch of saffron

Wash the rice in 4-5 changes of water and soak in the 3-4 cups water for 30 minutes. Soak the raisins and nuts in a little water for 10 minutes. Drain the raisins and nuts. Melt the butter in a large pan and fry the cinnamon, cloves, small cardamoms, bayleaf and black cumin for 1-2 minutes. Add the nuts and all raisins. Drain the soaked rice retaining the water; add

the rice to the saucepan. Fry for 1 minute. Add salt, sugar and the reserved water. Bring to the boil. Reduce the heat and add a pinch of saffron. Stir once gently. Cover and simmer gently for 10-15 minutes, without stirring, until the rice is tender and the water has been absorbed. Serve with curries.

Red Kidney Bean Curry

A popular dish from the Punjab province of India. It is similar to Chilli Con-Carne and makes a hearty meal with bread or rice.

PREPARATION TIME: overnight, plus 15 minutes

COOKING TIME: 20-45 minutes

SERVES: 4 people

2 cups dried red kidney beans, washed and soaked overnight in sufficient water to cover
2 medium onions, chopped
4 tblsp oil
1 bayleaf
1 inch piece cinnamon stick
6 cloves
6 small green cardamoms
2 green chilies, quartered
3 cloves garlic, peeled and finely chopped
1 inch fresh root ginger, peeled and finely chopped
¾ tsp chili powder
¼ tsp ground turmeric
2 tsp ground coriander
1¼ tsp ground cumin
1¼ tsp garam masala powder (hot aromatic powder)
15oz can peeled tomatoes, chopped
¾ tsp salt
2-3 sprigs fresh green coriander, chopped

Either pressure cook the red kidney beans for 5-6 minutes, or cook them in their soaking water for 15-20 minutes until soft. Remove from the heat; allow to stand, covered. Fry the onions in the oil in a large saucepan over a moderate heat until tender. Add the bayleaf, cinnamon, cloves and cardamoms and fry for 1 minute. Add the chilies, garlic and ginger and fry until golden. Sprinkle with the chili powder, turmeric, ground coriander, ground cumin and garam masala. Avoid burning the mixture. Stir the mixture to blend the spices. Add the tomatoes and season with salt. Cover and

simmer for 2-3 minutes. Drain the cooked beans and collect the thick red liquid. Add the beans to the spiced tomato mixture. Stir gently and cook for 1 minute. Add the red liquid and chopped coriander; cover and simmer for 3-5 minutes. Serve with bread or boiled rice.

Red Lentil Daal

There is an abundance of natural protein in pulses and there is a great variety of pulses now available.

PREPARATION TIME: 10 minutes

COOKING TIME: 30 minutes

SERVES: 4 people

½lb red lentils
1½ cups water
½ tsp ground turmeric
1¼ tsp ground coriander
1 green chili, cut in half
Salt to taste
4-6 canned tomatoes, chopped
2 sprigs fresh green coriander leaves, chopped
4 tblsp butter
1 small onion, peeled and finely chopped

Wash the lentils in 3-5 changes of water. Put the lentils into a pan with the 1½ cups water; cover and cook over a low heat for 10-15 minutes. Remove any froth with a spoon. Once the lentils are tender and yellow, blend until smooth with an egg whisk. Add the turmeric, ground coriander, chili, salt to taste and chopped tomatoes. Cover and simmer for 10 minutes. Add the coriander leaves and pour into a dish. Keep warm. Melt the butter in a frying pan and saute the onion until golden brown. Pour the onions and butter juices over the daal. Serve with rice or bread.

Facing page: Mixed Daal (top left), Red Kidney Bean Curry (center) and Red Lentil Daal (bottom).

Bread and Pizza

Puri

These deep-fried breads are simple to make once the art has been mastered.

PREPARATION TIME:	10-15 minutes
COOKING TIME:	20 minutes
MAKES:	30-32

4 cups whole-wheat flour
¾ tsp salt
1-1½ cups water
Oil for deep frying

Sieve the flour and salt into a mixing bowl. Mix to a soft dough with water. Knead well and leave to relax for 5 minutes, covered with a damp cloth. Divide the dough into 30-32 small even sized balls; roll out each ball into a small round about 2½-3 inches in diameter. Heat the oil for deep frying and drop in a small piece of dough. If it rises to the top instantly then the correct temperature for frying has been reached. Place one puri at a time into the hot oil, taking care not to splash the oil. Gently stir the puri and it will begin to swell. Turn over and cook on the underside until golden brown – about ½-1 minute. The flip side is always the thick side and it needs extra cooking time. Drain the puris on the side of the frying pan, and place them on kitchen paper to drain,

Puri (above), Roti (right) and Paratha (far right).

before serving. Puris are best when served piping hot. Puris can be served cold and they can also be reheated under the broiler.

Paratha

These shallow-fried breads can either be made plain, or stuffed with a favorite filling, such as cheese, potato etc.

PREPARATION TIME:	15-20 minutes
COOKING TIME:	20-30 minutes
MAKES:	16-18

4 cups whole-wheat flour
¾ tsp salt
1-1½ cups water
Melted butter or oil

Sieve the flour and salt into a mixing bowl. Mix to a soft dough with water. Knead the dough well; leave to relax, covered, for 5 minutes. Divide the dough into 16-18 even-sized balls. Roll each ball into a small round about 2 inches in diameter. Brush each round of dough with oil or melted butter and fold in half. Brush the upper folded surface with oil or butter and fold in half to form a small triangle. On a well floured surface roll out these triangles thinly. Heat a solid based frying pan or a griddle. Put the paratha onto the heated frying pan and cook for ½-1 minute or until small brown specks appear. Cook the other side in the same way. Brush a little oil or butter over the paratha and turn over. Fry for 1 minute and then brush the second side with oil or butter. Fry on both sides until the

paratha is golden and crisp. Make the rest of the paratha in the same way. Keep them soft and warm, well wrapped in a clean tea towel or foil.

Roti

Roti is best made with whole-wheat flour; any variety may be used.

PREPARATION TIME: 20 minutes
COOKING TIME: 20-30 minutes
MAKES: about 24

4 cups whole-wheat flour
¾ tsp salt
1-1½ cups water

Sieve the flour and salt into a mixing bowl. Mix to a soft dough with water. Knead the dough for 2-3 minutes. Cover and allow to relax for 5-6 minutes before shaping the bread. Divide the dough into 1oz balls. Roll each ball into a thin round about 5-6 inches in diameter. Place a solid based frying pan or a griddle over a medium heat; when the pan is hot, place the shaped roti onto it. Cook for ½ minute on each side and then place under a preheated broiler to bloat (little brown specks will appear on the surface). The first 2 rotis do not usually bloat, so do not be alarmed. Make all the rotis and stack them one on top of each other. Keep them covered with a clean tea towel or foil. Serve hot with any curry or spicy savory dish.

Banana and Nut Bread

PREPARATION TIME: 30 minutes
COOKING TIME: 1 hour
MAKES: 1 loaf

A stick of butter
1 cup brown sugar
1 egg, well beaten
2 cups whole-wheat flour
½ tsp salt
¾ tsp baking powder
5 tblsp natural yogurt
2 ripe bananas, peeled and mashed
½ cup raisins
1 cup mixed nuts, chopped

Preheat the oven to 350°F. Cream the butter and sugar until light and fluffy and gradually beat in the egg. Sieve the flour, salt and baking powder together. Add half the yogurt to the butter and sugar mixture and then mix in half the sieved dry ingredients. Beat in the remaining yogurt, flour, mashed banana, raisins and chopped nuts. Mix well. Put the mixture into a greased loaf tin. Bake at 350°F for 1 hour.

Crusty Loaf

PREPARATION TIME: 3 hours 40 minutes
COOKING TIME: 45 minutes-1 hour
MAKES: 2 loaves

1¼ cups tepid water
½oz fresh yeast or 2½ tsp dried yeast
¾ tsp salt
1 tblsp butter
1¼ tblsp sugar
3½ cups sieved all purpose flour
1¼ tblsp melted butter
1½ tblsp caraway, sesame or poppy seeds for topping (optional)

Sprinkle or crumble the yeast into the tepid water; stir to dissolve. Leave for a few minutes until frothy. Mix the salt, butter, sugar and flour together; stir in the yeast liquid and mix to a dough. Knead the dough for 10 minutes on a lightly floured surface. Place the dough in a greased bowl and brush the top lightly with melted butter; cover with a damp cloth and leave it to rise in a warm place (free from draught), until doubled in bulk (about 40-45 minutes). Punch the dough down and let it rise again until almost double its original size about (30 minutes). Punch down once again and turn out onto a floured surface, cut into two equal portions. Roll each one into an oblong about 8-10 inches in length. Beginning with the wide side, roll up each oblong tightly. Seal the edges by pinching together. Holding each end of the roll, roll it gently backwards and forwards to lengthen the loaf and shape the ends. Place the loaves on a greased baking sheet lightly sprinkled with all purpose flour. Brush the loaves either with milk, or with cornstarch glaze, and leave to rise for 1½ hours, uncovered. With a sharp knife, make ¼ inch slashes at regular intervals. Bake in a hot oven, 400°F, for 10 minutes. Brush once again with milk or cornstarch glaze and sprinkle with poppy seeds (or other seeds). Return to the oven and bake for 25-30 minutes

or until golden brown.

To make cornstarch glaze: mix 1½ tsp cornstarch with 1½ tsp cold water. Add ½ cup boiling water and cook for 1-2 minutes until smooth. Cool slightly before use.

Whole-wheat Bread

PREPARATION TIME: 2 hours 30 minutes
COOKING TIME: 50 minutes
MAKES: 1 large loaf

6 cups whole-wheat flour
¾ tsp salt
¼ cup margarine
¼ cup fresh yeast, or
1¼ tblsp dried yeast (see below)
1¼ tblsp granulated or brown sugar
1¼ cups tepid water
⅔ cup tepid milk
1¼ tblsp melted butter

Sieve the flour and salt into a warm bowl and blend the margarine. Cream the fresh yeast with the sugar and stir in the warm water and milk. (If using dried yeast, sprinkle it onto the warm water and milk, with the sugar, and leave to stand for 10 minutes until thick and frothy). Make a well in the centre of the flour and pour in the yeast liquid; gradually mix in the flour to form a dough. Knead the dough well. Cover it with a damp cloth and leave to rise until double in bulk (about 1¼ hours). Grease a loaf tin, 9 inches by 5 inches by 3 inches. Turn the risen dough onto a floured surface and knead well; place in the loaf tin. Leave in a warm place to rise for 40 minutes. Brush the loaf with melted butter and bake at 400°F for about 50 minutes.

Whole-wheat Pizza Dough

PREPARATION TIME: 50-60 minutes

1 cup tepid water
1¾ tsp dried yeast
¾ tsp salt
1¼ tsp sugar

1¼ tsp olive oil
1 cup whole-wheat flour
1¼ cups all purpose flour

Mix the dried yeast with the tepid water. Add the salt, sugar and oil. Mix in the flours a little at a time, to make a dough. Use extra water if needed. Turn the dough onto a lightly floured surface and knead until smooth (about 5-8 minutes). Cover the dough with a clean damp tea towel and leave to stand for 15-20 minutes. Knead once more for 1-2 minutes. You can make either one large pizza base or several smaller ones. Grease one 14 inch pizza pan and roll out the dough to make a round large enough to fit the pizza pan. Shape the pizza dough with the hands to fit the pan. Top with the chosen topping and bake.

Basic Pizza Dough

This is the basic recipe for pizza dough and although there are many variations, the making of the dough is very important. Pizza originated in Italy, around the Naples area, but it is now eaten and enjoyed worldwide. Once the basic dough is perfected, toppings can be adjusted to one's taste. In fact, on one single pizza, each slice can have a different taste (i.e. with a different topping). See Taco Pizza Topping and Mixed Vegetable Pizza Topping recipes.

PREPARATION TIME: about 1 hour 30 minutes

¼ tsp sugar
1¼ tblsp dried yeast
½ cup tepid water
1¼ tsp salt
2 cups all purpose flour, sieved

Mix the dried yeast with 2 tblsp of the tepid water and the sugar. Stir until dissolved. Leave to stand for 10-15 minutes until frothy. Put the flour and salt into a bowl and make

Facing page: Crusty Loaf (top), Banana and Nut Bread (center) and Whole-wheat Bread (bottom).

a well in the centre. Add the yeast liquid and the remaining tepid water; mix to form a dough. Kneed the dough on a floured surface for 8-10 minutes. Cover with a damp cloth and leave to rise in a warm place for 40-45 minutes, until double its original size. Knead once again on a lightly floured surface for 3-5 minutes until soft and elastic. You can make either one large pizza base, or several smaller ones. Grease one 14 inch pizza pan and roll out the dough. Shape the pizza dough with the hands to fit the pan. Top with the chosen topping and bake.

Taco Pizza

This idea is taken from the taco (a Mexican pancake). The pizza base is made with a mixture of cornmeal and flour and some of the topping ingredients are the same as those used in a taco filling.

PREPARATION TIME: 30-40 minutes	
COOKING TIME: 30-35 minutes	
SERVES: 6 people	

Dough

1½ cups all purpose flour
⅔ cup fine yellow cornmeal
2½ tsp baking powder
1¼ tsp salt
½ cup margarine
½ cup milk

Sieve the flour, cornmeal, salt and baking powder into a mixing bowl. Rub in the margarine. Add the milk, gradually, to form a medium soft dough. Knead the dough on a well floured surface for 4-5 minutes, until smooth. Roll into a circle to cover a 13-14 inch pizza pan, with a 1 inch high rim. Grease the pizza pan and cover with the dough. Shape the pizza dough to fit the pan. Pinch the edges to form a deep rim. Keep on one side until the topping is ready.

Topping

2½ tblsp olive oil
1 clove garlic, peeled and crushed
1 small onion, peeled and chopped
½ green pepper, seeded and coarsely chopped
4-6 mushrooms, sliced
½lb cooked red kidney beans (or drained canned ones)
2 scallions, chopped
3 large tomatoes, chopped
6-8 pitted black olives, halved
3-4 pickled Mexican chilies, chopped
½lb Mozzarella, Cheddar or Monterey Jack cheese, cut into slivers
1 carrot, peeled and grated
⅔ cup soured cream
Bottled taco sauce

Heat the oil and fry the garlic, chopped onion, pepper and mushrooms for 2 minutes; add the kidney beans and stir fry for 1-2 minutes. Remove from the heat and stir in the scallions. Spread the above topping mixture over the pizza base. Arrange the tomatoes evenly on top. Add the olives, Mexican chilies and slivers of cheese. Bake at 400°F for 15-20 minutes until the edges turn golden brown and crusty. Serve with grated carrots, whipped soured cream and taco sauce.

Mixed Vegetable Pizza Topping

PREPARATION TIME: 30 minutes	
COOKING TIME: 20 minutes	
SERVES: 4-6 people	

2½ tblsp olive oil
1 small onion, peeled and chopped
2 scallions, chopped
1 medium zucchini, trimmed and thinly sliced
4 mushrooms, sliced
Salt and freshly ground black pepper to taste
6-8 canned tomatoes, chopped
10ml (2 tsp) tomato paste

8 pitted black olives
2 tomatoes, thinly sliced
1 green pepper, seeded and chopped
1 green chili, chopped
1¼ tsp dried oregano
1½ cups Mozzarella cheese, Cheddar cheese or a mixture of the two, cut into thin slivers
2½ tblsp grated Parmesan cheese

Heat the olive oil in a large frying pan; add the onions and sauté for 1-2 minutes. Add the zucchini and sauté for 2 minutes. Add the mushrooms and salt and pepper to taste and stir fry for 1 minute to glaze the vegetables. Remove from the heat and cool. Mix the chopped tomato with the tomato paste and spread evenly over the pizza base. Spoon the vegetable mixture over the pizza and arrange the olives, sliced tomatoes, green pepper and green chili on top. Sprinkle with the oregano, the slivers of cheese and the grated Parmesan cheese. Bake at 450°F for 12-15 minutes, or until the edge of the pizza is golden brown and crusty.

Taco Pizza (top right) and Mixed Vegetable Pizza Topping (bottom right).

VEGETARIAN CUISINE

Main Meals

Okra Curry

A dry vegetable curry made with okra and potato.

PREPARATION TIME: 10-15 minutes
COOKING TIME: 30 minutes
SERVES: 4 people

3¾ tblsp oil
1 onion, peeled and chopped
2 medium sized potatoes, peeled and cut into 1 inch pieces
4 cups okra, topped and tailed, and chopped into ½ inch pieces
Salt to taste
¾ tsp ground turmeric
1¼ tsp chili powder
1¾ tsp ground coriander
2-3 sprigs fresh green coriander leaves, chopped

Heat the oil in a wok or solid based frying pan and fry the onion for 3-4 minutes. Stir in the cubed potatoes; cover and cook for 3-4 minutes. Add the okra, and stir fry for 2 minutes. Sprinkle with salt to taste, turmeric, chili and ground coriander. Mix gently; cover and cook for 8-10 minutes. Stir occasionally and continue cooking until the potatoes are tender. Sprinkle with the chopped coriander leaves. Mix well and serve.

Okra Fry

This is a dry "curry" – no spices are added; the okra supplies the hotness.

PREPARATION TIME: 15 minutes
COOKING TIME: 20-30 minutes
SERVES: 4 people

1-1½ lbs okra
Oil for deep frying
1¼ tblsp oil
1 large onion, peeled and chopped
Salt and freshly ground black pepper to taste

Top and tail the okra; chop them into ¼ inch even-sized pieces. Heat the oil for deep frying; add the chopped okra, a little at a time, and deep fry until brown and crisp. Drain on absorbent paper and keep warm in a dish. Heat the 1¼ tblsp oil and fry the onion until tender about 4-5 minutes. Remove the onion and mix with the fried okra. Sprinkle with salt and pepper to taste. Serve with chapati, or as a side dish.

Eggplant Bake

PREPARATION TIME: 30 minutes
COOKING TIME: 30-40 minutes
SERVES: 6 people

3 large eggplant
2½ tsp salt
Malt vinegar
2½ tblsp oil
2 large onions, peeled and sliced
2 green chilies, chopped
15oz can peeled tomatoes, chopped
¾ tsp chili powder
1¼ tsp crushed garlic
¾ tsp ground turmeric
Oil for deep frying
⅓ cup natural yogurt
1¼ tsp freshly ground black pepper
4 tomatoes, sliced
2 cups Cheddar cheese, grated

Cut the eggplant into ¼ inch thick slices. Lay in a shallow dish. Sprinkle with 1¼ tsp salt and add sufficient malt vinegar to cover. Allow to marinate for 20-30 minutes. Drain well. Heat 2½ tblsp oil in a frying pan and fry the onions until golden brown. Add the chilies, chopped tomatoes, remaining salt, chili powder, garlic and turmeric. Mix well and simmer for 5-7 minutes. Remove from the heat. Cool and blend to a smooth sauce in the liquidizer. Keep the sauce on one side. Heat the oil for deep frying and deep fry the drained, marinated eggplant until brown on both sides (2-3 minutes each side). Drain well on kitchen paper. Grease a large deep baking tray. Arrange half the fried eggplant rounds closely together in the tray. Spoon over half the tomato sauce and beaten yogurt. Season with pepper. Add the remaining eggplant rounds and the rest of the tomato sauce and yogurt. Cover with slices of tomatoes and grated cheese. Bake at 350°F for 10-15 minutes, or until the cheese melts and turns brown. Serve hot as a side dish, or as a main course with brown bread or pitta bread.

Stuffed Zucchini

This is a delightful dish from Southern Italy.

PREPARATION TIME: 30 minutes
COOKING TIME: 30-40 minutes
SERVES: 4 people

½ cup fresh coarse breadcrumbs
5 tblsp milk
8 medium sized zucchini, trimmed
1 onion, peeled and finely chopped
2 tomatoes, chopped
6-8 mushrooms, sliced
1 clove garlic, peeled and chopped
5 tblsp olive oil
2½ tsp dried oregano
Salt and freshly ground black pepper to taste
1 egg, beaten
⅔ cup Mozzarella cheese (or Cheddar), cut into thin slivers
⅔ cup grated Parmesan cheese

Soak the breadcrumbs in the milk for 15-20 minutes. Cook the zucchini in boiling water for 5 minutes. Drain and cool. Slice them in half lengthways and scoop out the flesh, leaving a thick shell at least ¼ inch. Take care not to break or crack the zucchini. Keep the scooped flesh on one side. Squeeze out the excess milk from the breadcrumbs and put them into a bowl. Fry the scooped zucchini flesh, chopped onion, tomatoes,

This page: Eggplant Bake (top left), Okra Curry (center right) and Okra Fry (right).

Overleaf: Zucchini Bake (left), Stuffed Zucchini (center) and Spicy Corn (right).

mushrooms and chopped garlic in half the olive oil for 5 minutes. Mix with the breadcrumbs, oregano, salt and pepper to taste, the beaten egg and half the cheeses. Spoon the mixture evenly into all the zucchini shells. Arrange the stuffed zucchini on a lightly greased baking tray. Sprinkle the remaining cheese over them and brush with the rest of the oil. Bake for 18-20 minutes at 400°F or until the cheese has melted and turned golden brown. Serve at once.

Spicy Corn

This dish originates from East Africa, it makes a tasty hot snack or supper dish.

PREPARATION TIME: 15 minutes

COOKING TIME: 35-40 minutes

SERVES: 6 people

3¾ tblsp oil
1 large onion, peeled and chopped
2 medium potatoes, peeled and cubed
8 fresh Chinese parsley leaves (optional)
¾ tsp cumin seed
¾ tsp mustard seed
1¼ tsp crushed fresh root ginger
1¼ tsp crushed garlic
1½lb frozen sweetcorn kernels
1¼ tsp salt
1¼ tsp chili powder
1¼ tsp ground coriander
¾ tsp ground turmeric
15oz can peeled tomatoes, chopped
1¼ tblsp tomato paste
1-2 green chilies, chopped
2 green peppers, seeded and cut into 1 inch pieces
3 sprigs fresh green coriander, chopped
1¼ tblsp thick tamarind pulp, or
2½ tblsp lemon juice

Heat the oil and fry the onion for 3 minutes; add the potatoes and fry for 5 minutes. Add the Chinese parsley leaves, cumin and mustard seed and stir fry for 1-2 minutes. Add ginger and garlic and stir fry for 1-2 minutes. Add the sweetcorn, salt, chili powder, ground coriander and turmeric. Mix well and cook for 2-3 minutes. Add the chopped tomatoes, tomato paste, chopped chilies, green peppers and coriander leaves.

Stir in the tamarind pulp and mix well adding a little water if the mixture seems too dry. Cover and cook over a low heat until the potatoes are tender about 10-15 minutes. The spicy corn should be thick but moist. Serve hot or cold.

Spiced Peas

PREPARATION TIME: 10 minutes

COOKING TIME: 15 minutes

SERVES: 6 people

2 tblsp oil
1 large onion, peeled and chopped
2 green chilies, sliced in half lengthwise
2lb shelled peas (fresh or frozen)
Salt and freshly ground black pepper to taste
1 tblsp lemon juice
Lemon wedges

Heat the oil in a wok or solid based frying pan and fry the onion until tender. Add the chilies and fry for 1 minute. Add the peas and salt and pepper to taste; stir fry for 5-10 minutes, or until well colored and "dry". Put into a serving dish and sprinkle with lemon juice. Garnish with lemon wedges. Serve as a side dish, or as a snack.

Spinach with Paneer

Paneer is a home-made cheese; it is made by separating milk into curds and whey by means of a souring agent such as lemon juice. It is eaten extensively in northern parts of India and is a good source of protein.

PREPARATION TIME: 15 minutes, plus time for making paneer

COOKING TIME: 20-30 minutes

SERVES: 4 people

To make paneer: (This is an overnight process)
2½ pints milk
2 tblsp lemon juice

Bring the milk to the boil. Reduce the heat and sprinkle with the lemon juice. The milk will separate into pale, watery whey and thick, white paneer (or curds). Remove from the heat and allow the paneer to coagulate (if the milk has not separated properly, add a few more

drops of lemon juice. The whey should be a clear, pale, yellow liquid. Pour the paneer and liquid through a muslin-lined sieve. Discard the liquid whey and tie the muslin over the paneer. Flatten the paneer to ½ inch thick; place it on a tray and rest it in a tilted position. Place more muslin over the top and weight it down. The pressure will drag out the remaining moisture and the tilted position will channel the liquid away from the paneer. Leave to drain overnight. Next day, cut the firm paneer into 1 inch cubes.

6 tblsp butter
1 medium onion, peeled and finely chopped
1 inch piece cinnamon stick
1 bayleaf
1lb frozen spinach paste, or fresh leaf spinach, cooked and pureed
1 tsp chili powder
½ tsp salt
½ cup natural yogurt
3 sprigs fresh green coriander leaves, chopped
1 tsp garam masala powder (hot, aromatic powder)
Oil for deep frying

Heat the butter in a pan and fry the onion until golden brown. Add the cinnamon and bayleaf and fry for 1 minute. Add the spinach and stir to mix. Sprinkle with the chili powder and salt and stir in the yogurt, coriander leaves and garam masala. Cover and cook for 2-3 minutes. Simmer gently. Meanwhile, deep-fry the drained paneer cubes until golden. Add the paneer cubes to the spinach and simmer together for 4-5 minutes. Serve hot with chapati or pulao rice.

New Potato Fry

This Oriental dish is very versatile; it can be served as a side dish, as a snack, or as a main curry. It is also a wonderful way of serving potatoes with traditional roast meats.

PREPARATION TIME: 20 minutes

COOKING TIME: 10-12 minutes

SERVES: 3-4 people

3 tblsp oil
1 tsp mustard seed
1lb small, even sized new potatoes, boiled in their skins and peeled
1 tsp red chili powder

1½ tsp ground coriander
¼ tsp ground turmeric
½ tsp salt
3 sprigs fresh green coriander leaves, chopped (optional)
Lemon juice to taste

Heat the oil in a wok or solid based frying pan and add the mustard seed and the whole, peeled potatoes. Stir fry over a low heat until they are lightly browned. Sprinkle with the spices, salt and chopped coriander leaves. Stir fry over a low heat for 5-6 minutes until golden brown. Remove from heat. Put into a dish and sprinkle with the lemon juice. Serve hot or cold.

Zucchini Bake

Serve this dish as a main course with fried rice, or as a side dish.

PREPARATION TIME: 20-30 minutes

COOKING TIME: 35 minutes

SERVES: 4-6 people

2lbs zucchini trimmed and coarsely grated
1¼ tsp salt
2½ tblsp melted unsalted butter (or oil)
3-4 eggs, well beaten
1½-1¾ cups grated mild cheese (Edam, Samso, etc)
1 medium onion, peeled and finely chopped
2 cloves garlic, peeled and finely chopped
2½ tblsp chopped parsley
1¼ tsp dried basil
¾ tsp freshly ground black pepper
¼-⅓ cup grated Parmesan cheese

Put the grated zucchini into a colander and sprinkle with salt. Leave to drain for 10 minutes. Squeeze the moisture out of the zucchini until quite dry. Lightly grease a baking dish (size approx. 10

Facing page: Spiced Peas (top), Spinach with Paneer (center right) and New Potato Fry (bottom).

x 7 inches). Heat the butter in a non-stick frying pan and fry the zucchini for 3-4 minutes until tender. Mix the beaten eggs, grated cheese, chopped onion, garlic, parsley, basil and pepper. Place the sauteed zucchini in the baking dish and pour egg mixture over the top. Sprinkle with the Parmesan cheese and bake at 350°F for 25-30 minutes until set. Serve cut into squares or diamond shapes. Can be eaten hot or cold.

Vegetable Stir Fry with Tofu (Soybean Curd)

This is a Chinese stir fry dish with soybean curd which makes a filling main course.

PREPARATION TIME: 30 minutes

COOKING TIME: 10 minutes

SERVES: 4 people

2½ tsp soya sauce
2½ tsp Worcestershire sauce
1 inch fresh root ginger, peeled and thinly sliced
3 cloves garlic, peeled and crushed
½lb Soybean Curd, cut into ½inch pieces
2½ tsp cornstarch
1 cup water
3¾ tblsp oil
3 stalks celery, sliced thinly
2 carrots, peeled and cut into thin diagonal slices
2-3 zucchini, trimmed, and cut into thin diagonal slices
1 green pepper, quartered, seeded and sliced thinly
8 mushrooms, thinly sliced
1-2 tomatoes, cut into wedges
½ cup snow peas, or thinly sliced green beans

Mix the soya sauce with the Worcestershire sauce, ginger and garlic. Add the soybean curd cubes and marinate for 8 minutes. Pick out the soybean curd and keep on a plate. Stir the cornstarch into the soya sauce mixture and blend in the water. Heat the oil in a wok over a medium heat. Add the celery and carrots and stir fry for 2 minutes. Add the zucchini and green pepper and stir fry for 2 minutes. Add the tomatoes and snow peas or green beans. Stir fry for 2 minutes. Add the mushrooms and stir fry for 1 minute. Stir in the water and soya sauce mixture. Cook until thickened, stirring for

1-2 minutes. Add the soybean curd. Heat through and serve immediately.

Cheese Bourag

PREPARATION TIME: 30-40 minutes

COOKING TIME: 20-25 minutes

SERVES: 4 people

2 cups flour
Salt
4 tsp baking powder
3 tblsp unsalted butter
½-⅔ cup milk
2 cups strong Cheddar cheese, grated
3 tblsp chopped parsley
Oil for deep frying

Sieve the flour, ¼ tsp salt and baking powder into a bowl; rub in the butter. Add the milk, a little at a time, and mix to a dough with a palette knife. Cover the dough and leave in a cool place to relax. Mix the grated cheese with the chopped parsley and a little salt to taste. Roll the dough out very thinly on a floured board and cut into 2 inch squares. Brush the edges of half the squares with a dampened pastry brush. Place a little filling in the centre of each one and cover with the remaining squares. Seal the edges well by pinching with the fingers or notching with the prongs of a fork. Heat the oil for deep frying. Fry the bourags a few at a time in hot oil until golden and crisp. Drain on kitchen paper and serve hot with sweet and sour sauce.

Avial

This is a mixed vegetable dish made with coconut.

PREPARATION TIME: 30 minutes

COOKING TIME: 20 minutes

SERVES: 4 people

2 medium sized potatoes, peeled and cut into 1 inch cubes
1½ cups lobia beans, trimmed and cut into 2 inch pieces
½ cup green beans, trimmed and sliced
4 drumstick or yard long beans, strung and cut into 1 inch pieces
1½ cups squash, peeled and cut into 1 inch cubes
1 green unripe banana, peeled and cut into 1 inch pieces

1 eggplant, trimmed and cut into 1 inch chunks
1 cup shelled peas
½ fresh coconut, shelled, skin removed and thinly sliced
1½ tsp cumin seeds
2 green chilies, chopped
½ cup water
⅔ cup natural yogurt
3 tblsp coconut oil for cooking

Steam all the vegetables for 10-15 minutes until almost tender, but still slightly crisp. Grind the spices with the water in a liquidizer until smooth. Mix the spice liquid with the coconut. Heat the coconut oil in a saucepan and add the vegetables, spice mixture and yogurt. Bring to the boil and simmer with the lid on for 5 minutes. Serve with rice.

Garlic Hash Brown

This is a favorite American dish eaten with steak and burgers.

PREPARATION TIME: 20 minutes

COOKING TIME: 30 minutes

SERVES: 4 people

5 tblsp oil
4 cloves of garlic, peeled and quartered lengthwise
3 whole red chilies
Salt
1-1½lb potatoes, peeled and coarsely grated

Heat the oil in a wok or a large non-stick frying pan. Fry the garlic until lightly browned. Add the red chilies and fry for 30 seconds. Sprinkle with salt to taste and add the grated potato. Stir fry for 5 minutes. Cover and cook for a further 8-10 minutes. The potatoes should be crisp and golden brown. Cook until the potatoes are tender. Serve as a side dish or for breakfast.

Vegetable Stir Fry with Tofu (top), Avial (center left) and Cheese Bourag (bottom right).

Spiced Chick Peas

This dryish curry is a "must" on any Punjabi menu. It is usually served with milk bread or pitta bread and an onion salad.

PREPARATION TIME: overnight for soaking, plus 15 minutes

COOKING TIME: 40-50 minutes

SERVES: 4-6 people

1lb chick peas
1 tsp baking powder
4 cloves
1 tsp cumin seed
4 large black cardamoms, ground
4 small cardamoms, ground
1 large onion, peeled and chopped
3 tblsp oil
2 bayleaves
1 inch piece cinnamon stick
2 green chilies, sliced in half lengthwise
1 inch fresh root ginger, peeled and finely chopped
4 cloves garlic, peeled and crushed
1½ tsp ground coriander
1-1¼ cups canned tomatoes, chopped
½ tsp freshly ground black pepper
½ tsp salt
5-6 sprigs fresh green coriander leaves, chopped

Wash the chick peas and soak them overnight in 2½ pints water and the baking powder. The following day, cook the chick peas in their soaking liquid in a pressure cooker for 10-15 minutes. If a lot of liquid has been absorbed during soaking, add a little more. Dry roast the cloves and cumin seed in a frying pan. Grind the cloves, cumin, large and small cardamons into a fine powder. Fry the onion in the oil for 2-3 minutes. Add the bayleaves, cinnamon, chilies, ginger and garlic. Fry for 1 minute, add the ground coriander and tomatoes. Fry for 2-3 minutes. Strain the chick peas, retaining any liquid. Add the chick peas to the tomato mixture and add black pepper, salt and the dry roasted spices. Mix well and add 1 cup of the strained chick pea liquid. Sprinkle with chopped coriander; cover and cook for 8-10 minutes. Add a little extra liquid if necessary. Serve with bread or rice.

Vegetable Pancakes (far left) and Spiced Chick Peas (left).

Vegetable Pancakes

A combination of shredded vegetables makes a delicious pancake, when added to the batter before cooking.

PREPARATION TIME: 15 minutes

COOKING TIME: 15 minutes

SERVES: 4-6 people

A stick of butter
2 cups shredded or coarsely grated carrots
2 cups shredded or coarsely grated zucchini
4 cups shredded or coarsely grated potatoes
1 medium onion, thinly sliced
3 eggs, well beaten
1 cup soured cream
5 tblsp cornstarch
¾ tsp salt
¾ tsp freshly ground black pepper
Oil for frying
Wedges of lemon

Melt the butter in a frying pan; add the carrots, zucchini, potatoes and onion. Saute for 3-4 minutes, stirring continuously. Beat the eggs together with the soured cream, cornstarch and salt and pepper. Mix well. Stir in the semi-cooked vegetables. Mix together gently. Heat a large non-stick frying pan and brush with 2½ tsp oil; add 1¼ tblsp batter. Cook until light brown; turn the small pancake over and cook until the other side is also brown. Make 3 or 4 at a time. The size of the pancakes can be increased by using more batter for each pancake. Serve with salads or with tomato sauce as a light meal or snack.

Green Beans with Coconut

PREPARATION TIME: 10 minutes

COOKING TIME: 20 minutes

SERVES: 3-4 people

2½ tblsp oil
2 cloves garlic, peeled and crushed
2 green or red dried chilies
1lb green beans, sliced
½ tsp salt
2½ tblsp desiccated coconut, or grated fresh coconut

Heat the oil in a wok or frying pan. Add the garlic and fry until golden brown. Add the chilies and stir fry for 30 seconds. Add the green beans and sprinkle with salt. Stir fry for 8-10 minutes until the beans are tender but still crisp. Sprinkle with the coconut and stir fry for a further 2-3 minutes. Serve as a side dish.

Mixed Vegetable Raita

Raitas are yogurt-based Indian dishes served as accompaniments to curries etc. Natural yogurt is usually mixed with fruits, vegetables, and herbs such as coriander or mint.

PREPARATION TIME: 10 minutes

SERVES: 4-6 people

1¼ cups natural yogurt
½ cucumber, chopped
1 small onion, peeled and chopped
2 tomatoes, chopped
2 stalks celery, chopped
1 small apple, cored and chopped
2 boiled potatoes, peeled and chopped
¼ tsp salt
¼ tsp freshly ground black pepper
1 sprig fresh green coriander, chopped

Beat the yogurt in a bowl. Add all the remaining ingredients, seasoning well with salt and pepper. Chill before serving.

Cannelloni with Spinach and Ricotta

PREPARATION TIME: 20 minutes

COOKING TIME: 1 hour
               20 minutes

SERVES: 4 people

2½ tblsp olive oil or melted butter
1 large onion, peeled and finely chopped
2 large cloves garlic, peeled and crushed
15oz can peeled tomatoes, chopped
1¼ tblsp tomato paste
Salt and freshly ground black pepper to taste
1¾ tsp dried basil
¾ tsp dried oregano
¾lb cannelloni tubes
5 tblsp thick spinach puree
½lb Ricotta cheese
2½ tblsp grated Parmesan cheese

To make the sauce: heat the oil or butter and fry the onion and garlic for 2-3 minutes. Add the tomatoes and tomato paste and mix well. Simmer for 2 minutes. Add the salt and pepper, basil and oregano. Cover and simmer for 10-15 minutes until thick.

Bring a large pan of salted water to the boil; cook the cannelloni tubes for 10 minutes until just tender. Do not overboil. Lift out the cannelloni tubes and put them into a bowl of cold water to cool quickly. Drain well. Mix together the spinach, ricotta and salt and pepper to taste. Fill the cannelloni tubes with the spinach mixture and arrange them in a greased shallow ovenproof dish. Pour the tomato sauce over the cannelloni; sprinkle with the Parmesan cheese. Bake for 20-30 minutes at 350°F or until the top is brownd and bubbling. Serve at once.

Ginger Cauliflower

This is a very simple and extremely subtle vegetable dish spiced with ginger.

PREPARATION TIME: 15 minutes

COOKING TIME: 15 minutes

SERVES: 4 people

4 tblsp oil
1 medium onion, peeled and chopped
1 inch fresh root ginger, peeled and sliced
1-2 green chilies, cut in half lengthwise
1 medium cauliflower, cut into 1 inch flowerets, along with tender leaves and stalk
Salt to taste
2-3 sprigs fresh green coriander leaves, chopped
Juice of 1 lemon

Heat the oil in a wok or solid based saucepan; fry the onion, ginger and chilies for 2-3 minutes. Add the cauliflower and salt to taste. Stir to mix well. Cover and cook over a low heat for 5-6 minutes. Add the coriander leaves and cook for a further 2-3 minutes, or until the flowerets of cauliflower are tender. Sprinkle with lemon juice, mix well and serve immediately. Serve with pitta bread.

Noodles with Vegetables (top left), Green Beans with Coconut (center right) and Garlic Hash Brown (bottom).

Mung Fritters

These tiny marble-sized fritters are made with mung pulse. They can be eaten as a cocktail snack or made into a curry with a well-flavored sauce.

PREPARATION TIME: 1 hour
30 minutes

COOKING TIME: 30 minutes

SERVES: 4 people

2 cups split mung pulse
1 small onion, peeled and chopped
1 tsp chili powder
1½ tsp garam masala powder (hot
   aromatic powder)
½ tsp cumin seed
4-5 sprigs fresh green coriander
   leaves, chopped
½ tsp salt
Oil for deep frying

Wash and soak the mung pulse for 1 hour in sufficient cold water to cover. Drain and then grind into a thick, coarse paste, adding ½-1 cup water as you go. It should be the consistency of peanut butter. Mix the mung paste with the onion, chili powder, garam masala, cumin seed, coriander leaves and salt. Mix well and adjust seasoning if necessary. Heat the oil for deep frying. Using a teaspoon, shape the paste into small "marbles" and fry in the hot oil until golden brown. Drain on kitchen paper and serve piping hot with chutney, a chili sauce or a dip. To turn into a curry, add the Mung Fritters to the following curry sauce.

Sauce
2 tsp oil
1 small onion, finely chopped
½ tsp chili powder
1 tsp ground coriander
1 tsp ground cumin
4-6 canned tomatoes, chopped
Salt to taste
3-4 sprigs fresh green coriander
   leaves, chopped

Heat the oil in a saucepan and fry the onion for 3 minutes. Stir in all the above ingredients; cover and simmer for 5-8 minutes. Add a little water to make a thickish sauce. Add ready-fried Mung Fritters and simmer for 3-5 minutes.

Noodles with Vegetables

This exotic noodle dish can be served hot or cold, as a main course, as a side dish or as a snack.

PREPARATION TIME: 20 minutes

COOKING TIME: 30 minutes

SERVES: 4 people

Salt to taste
1lb egg noodles, or broken spaghetti
3¾ tblsp oil
1 inch fresh root ginger, peeled and
   thinly sliced
1 large or 2 medium onions, peeled
   and sliced
⅔ cup green beans, sliced
⅔ cup carrots, peeled and cut into
   matchstick strips
1 cup white cabbage, or Chinese
   leaves, shredded
½ cup shelled peas
⅔ cup sprouting mung beans
1 green pepper, seeded and cut into 1
   inch pieces
1-2 stalks celery, chopped
1-2 green chilies, split lengthways
¾ tsp monosodium glutamate
   (optional)
2½ tblsp soya sauce
1¼ tblsp lemon juice
1¼-2½ tsp Chinese red pepper sauce
5 tblsp chicken stock

Bring a large pan of water to the boil and add 1¼ tsp salt. Add the noodles or spaghetti and boil gently for 5-6 minutes. Drain the noodles. Rinse the noodles in cold water and drain once again. Heat the oil in a wok or large frying pan. Fry the ginger for 1-2 minutes. Add the onions and fry for 2-3 minutes. Add the beans and carrots and fry for 2 minutes. Add the remaining vegetables and the chilies and stir fry for 3-4 minutes. Add salt to taste and the noodles. Stir lightly with two forks. Dissolve the monosodium glutamate in the soya sauce and sprinkle over the noodle mixture; stir in the lemon juice, Chinese sauce and stock. Heat through for 2-3 minutes. Serve hot.

This page: Mung Fritters.

Facing page: Ginger Cauliflower (top left), Mixed Vegetable Raita (top right) and Cannelloni with Spinach and Ricotta (bottom).

Sauces, Dips and Chutney

Plum Chutney

Any variety of plum can be used; either singly or in a mixture of one or more varieties.

PREPARATION TIME:	10 minutes
COOKING TIME:	40 minutes
MAKES:	about 6lbs

4½lb plums, pitted
1 inch fresh root ginger, peeled and finely chopped
2 tsp salt
3lb brown sugar
1 tsp cumin seed
1 tsp coriander seed
4 dried red chilies
1 tsp onion seed
2½ tblsp cider vinegar
½ cup chopped blanched almonds
½ cup chopped cashew nuts or hazelnuts
1 cup raisins
1 cup white raisins

Put the plums, ginger, salt and sugar into a saucepan, preferably a non-stick pan. Cover and cook gently until the plums are soft (about 15-20 minutes). Dry roast the cumin seed, coriander seed and red chilies in a frying pan for 1-2 minutes. Remove the red chilies and coarsely grind the cumin and coriander seeds. Add the roasted red chilies, ground spices and onion seed to the cooked plums. Add the cider vinegar, nuts, raisins and white raisins and simmer gently for 5-6 minutes. Allow to cool slightly. Pour into clean, warm glass jars and seal.

Guacamole
(AVOCADO DIP)

This is a popular Mexican dip, usually eaten with crisps, salty biscuits or sticks of raw vegetable, such as cucumber, celery etc.

PREPARATION TIME:	5 minutes
SERVES:	6-8 people

1 avocado, peeled, stoned and mashed
1 large clove garlic, peeled and crushed
1 tsp salt
¼ tsp freshly ground black pepper
1 large tomato, skinned and chopped
1 tsp olive oil
1 tblsp lemon juice
2-3 sprigs fresh green coriander leaves, finely chopped
1 small onion, peeled and grated

Blend the avocado pulp in the liquidizer with the salt, pepper, tomato, olive oil, lemon juice and coriander leaves. Put into a small bowl and mix with the onion. Serve with savory biscuits, crisps or sticks of raw vegetables.

Tamarind Dip

PREPARATION TIME:	20 minutes
MAKES:	about 1½ cups

¾ cup tamarind pods
1 cup boiling water
½ tsp salt
7 tblsp brown sugar
1 green chili, chopped
¼ tsp chili powder

Soak the tamarind pods in boiling water for 5-6 minutes, or until soft. Rub the pods in the water to separate the dried pulp around the seeds. Squeeze out the seeds and skins of the pods. (Do not discard as a second extract can be obtained for future use). Add the salt and sugar to the tamarind pulp. Mix in the chili and chili powder and leave to stand for 5 minutes before using. Salt and sugar can be adjusted according to personal taste.

Savory Coconut Chutney

PREPARATION TIME:	15 minutes
MAKES:	about 1¾ cups

1-2 fresh coconuts, shell removed, outer skin peeled and cut into pieces
½ inch fresh root ginger, peeled and chopped
2 green chilies, chopped
1 tsp cumin seed
1-2 bunches fresh green coriander leaves, chopped
4 tblsp thick tamarind pulp or
5 tblsp lemon juice
1 tsp sugar
½ tsp salt

Put all the ingredients into the liquidizer and blend until smooth and creamy. If the mixture is too thick, add a little water. Serve with hot snacks, such as toasted chicken sandwiches.

Mixed Fruit Chutney

This sweet-sour chutney goes particularly well with pork dishes such as spareribs.

PREPARATION TIME:	30 minutes
COOKING TIME:	40 minutes
MAKES:	about 5¼lb

3 firm pears, cored and sliced
4 apples, cored and chopped
4 peaches, skinned, stoned and sliced or
15oz can peach slices, drained
1lb plums, halved and stoned
6 rings canned pineapple, cut into cubes
1 cup dates, stoned and chopped
2 cups dried prunes, soaked overnight
1 cup dried apricots, soaked overnight
2¼lb brown sugar
2 tsp salt
1 inch fresh root ginger, peeled and thinly sliced
1 cup chopped blanched almonds
1 cup cashew nuts, chopped
5 tblsp cider vinegar
8 cloves, coarsely ground
1 tsp chili powder
2 inch piece cinnamon stick
2 bananas, peeled and sliced

Put all the fruit into a saucepan (apart from the bananas) with the sugar, salt and ginger. Cover and cook for 15-20 minutes. Add the nuts, vinegar, cloves, chili powder and cinnamon stick. Stir well and cook for 6-8 minutes. Simmer gently, stirring occasionally, until most of the liquid has evaporated. The chutney should be thick and sticky. Add the sliced bananas and stir over the heat for 1 minute. Cool slightly. Pour into clean, warm glass jars and seal.

Green Tomato Relish

Use the last crop of tomatoes to make this relish. Serve with any grilled meat, barbecued chicken, etc.

PREPARATION TIME:	4 hours
COOKING TIME:	about 20 minutes
MAKES:	about 3lb

2lb green tomatoes, seeded and chopped
1½ cups shredded white cabbage
2 red peppers, seeded and chopped
1 onion, peeled and chopped
1¼ tblsp salt
1 cup brown sugar
1¼ cups distilled white vinegar
2 tsp mustard seed
2 tsp celery seed
1½ tblsp prepared horseradish sauce

Mix the tomatoes, cabbage, peppers and onion together. Sprinkle with the salt and mix well. Leave to stand for 2-3 hours. Drain well and then rinse under cold running water. Drain and gently squeeze out the excess moisture. Mix the sugar, vinegar, mustard seed, celery seed and horseradish sauce together in a large solid based pan. Bring to the boil over a medium heat. Add the vegetables, cover and simmer gently for another 16-18 minutes until the relish is sticky. Remove from the heat and cool slightly. Pour into clean, warm glass jars and seal. Will keep for up to 2 months.

Facing page: Plum Chutney (top right), Mixed Fruit Chutney (center) and Green Tomato Relish (bottom).

Tamarind Dip (far left),
Savory Coconut Chutney
(center) and Guacamole
(Avocado Dip) (above).

little olive oil or chicken stock.

Chili Sauce

This classic piquant sauce is perfec[t] for those who love hot, spicy food.

PREPARATION TIME:	20 minutes
COOKING TIME:	2 hours 30 minutes
MAKES:	about 600ml (1 pint)

*8 large ripe tomatoes, skinned and
   chopped*
*2-3 small green peppers, seeded and
   chopped*
*2 medium onions, peeled and finely
   chopped*
4 stalks celery, chopped
3 tsp salt
1 cup + 2 tblsp granulated sugar
1½ cups cider vinegar
2-3 bay leaves
1 tsp coriander seeds
1 tsp freshly ground black pepper
¼ tsp ground cloves
½ tsp ground cinnamon
1 tsp ground ginger
1 tsp mustard seed

Mix all the ingredients together in a pan and bring to the boil. Cover and simmer for about 2 hours ove[r] a low heat, until thick. Stir once to mix and simmer again for 10 minutes. Remove from the heat and cool slightly. Pour into clean, warm glass jars and seal.

Mexican Salsa

This is a beautiful fresh sauce which goes well with barbecued meats, curries and, of course, burritos and tacos.

PREPARATION TIME:	10 minutes
MAKES:	about ⅔ cup

5 tomatoes, skinned and chopped
1 small onion, chopped
*1-2 pickled or canned Mexican
   chilies, chopped*
2 cloves garlic, peeled and crushed
2 tsp cider vinegar
½ tsp salt

½ tsp sugar
*2-3 sprigs fresh green coriander,
   chopped*
1 tsp bottled chili sauce

Mix all the ingredients together in a bowl. Chill for 2 to 3 hours before serving.

Salsa Verde

A perfect Italian sauce to serve with any pasta, or with veal.

PREPARATION TIME:	15 minutes
MAKES:	about 1 cup

6 tblsp chopped fresh parsley
2½ tblsp white wine vinegar
3 cloves garlic, peeled and sliced
2 tblsp capers, finely chopped
2 tblsp olive oil
2-3 scallions, chopped
*Salt and freshly ground black pepper
   to taste*

Blend the parsley, garlic and vinegar in the liquidizer. Pour the parsley sauce into a small bowl and mix with the capers, olive oil, scallions and salt and pepper. Mix well. Cover and chill for 10-15 minutes. The sauce can be thinned to the desired consistency with a

This page: Chili Sauce (top left), Salsa Verdi (center) and Mexican Salsa (bottom).

Facing page: Rice Pudding (top), Potato Pudding (center) and Cabbage Pudding (bottom).

Sweets

Carrotella

PREPARATION TIME: 15 minutes
COOKING TIME: 35-40 minutes
SERVES: 4-6 people

2½ pints milk
1lb carrots, peeled and shredded
1 cup canned evaporated milk
½ cup granulated sugar
½ cup raisins
Seeds of 8 small cardamoms, crushed
2 drops rose-water or vanilla essence
½ cup chopped blanched almonds
½ cup pistachio nuts, chopped

Put the milk into a pan and simmer over a low heat until reduced to 2 pints. Add the carrots; cover and cook over a medium heat for 15 minutes. Add the evaporated milk, sugar and raisins. Cover and simmer gently for another 5 minutes. Remove from the heat. Stir in the crushed cardamom seeds and essence and pour into a serving dish. Allow to cool slightly. Sprinkle nuts on the top and serve. On hot summer days, the Carrotella is best chilled.

Carrot Cake

PREPARATION TIME: 30 minutes
COOKING TIME: 45-50 minutes
MAKES: 10 inch loaf

¾ cup butter
¾ cup brown sugar
½ cup granulated sugar
2 eggs, well beaten
2 cups flour
1½ tsp bicarbonate of soda
½ tsp baking powder
¼ tsp ground cinnamon
½ tsp salt
2 cups peeled carrots, shredded
¾ cup raisins
½ cup chopped walnuts
¼ tsp small cardamom seeds, crushed
Confectioner's sugar for dredging

Cream the butter and sugars together. Add the eggs, a little at a time, beating well after each addition. Sieve the flour, bicarbonate of soda, baking powder, cinnamon and salt together. Fold the dry ingredients into the egg mixture. Add the carrots, raisins, nuts and crushed cardamom. Mix well and pour the mixture into a well buttered 10 inch loaf tin. Bake at 350°F for 45-50 minutes, or until a fine metal skewer comes out clean when inserted into the centre of the cake. Cool in the tin for 10-15 minutes, before turning out. Dredge with Confectioner's sugar before serving.

Rice Pudding

There are many ways of making a rice pudding, but this is definitely one of the best. It is suitable for serving on any occasion, from everyday meals to smart dinner parties.

PREPARATION TIME: 10 minutes
COOKING TIME: 1 hour 30 minutes
SERVES: 6 people

¼ cup unsalted butter
1 bayleaf, crumbled
1 inch piece cinnamon stick, crushed
1½ cups pudding rice, washed and drained
2½ pints milk
1½ cups canned evaporated milk
¾ cup granulated sugar
½ cup raisins
½ cup chopped blanched almonds
½ cup pistachio nuts, chopped or cut into slivers
Seeds of 8 small cardamoms, crushed

Melt the butter in a saucepan and fry the bayleaf and cinnamon for 1 minute. Add the rice and stir well. Add the milk and bring to the boil. Reduce the heat and simmer for 40-50 minutes, stirring occasionally to prevent the rice from sticking to the pan. Add the sugar and evaporated milk, and simmer for a further 20-30 minutes, stirring frequently. Thin layers of light brown skin form on the base of the pan, this is what gives the pudding its rich reddish tinge and flavor. Add the raisins and half the chopped almonds. Mix well and simmer for a further 5-10 minutes, or until the pudding is really thick. Mix in the crushed cardamom seeds and pour into a serving dish. Decorate with the remaining chopped almonds and pistachio nuts. Serve hot or cold.

Carrot Halva

A delightful sweet from the mysterious East. Serve it hot or cold, with or without cream.

PREPARATION TIME: 20 minutes
COOKING TIME: 50 minutes
SERVES: 8-10 people

4lb large sweet carrots, peeled and shredded
2 pints canned evaporated milk
3 cups granulated sugar
¾ cup unsalted butter
¾ cup raisins
Seeds of 10 small cardamoms, crushed
1 cup chopped mixed nuts (blanched and chopped almonds, cashews, pistachios etc.)
Light cream

Put the carrots, evaporated milk and sugar into a large, solid based pan and bring to the boil. Reduce the heat and cook the carrots gently for 30-40 minutes, or until the milk has evaporated. Add the butter and raisins and stir over a gentle heat for 8-10 minutes, until the Halva is dark and leaves the sides of the pan clean. Add the cardamom seeds and mix well. Pour into a flat shallow dish about 1 inch deep. Flatten the Halva evenly with a spatula. Sprinkle with the chopped nuts. Serve hot or cold, cut into squares, with light cream.

Potato Pudding

This old-fashioned Oriental pudding has a rich and lovely flavor. It keeps for weeks and can be frozen.

PREPARATION TIME: 15 minutes
COOKING TIME: 1 hour 15 minutes
SERVES: 6 people

2lb potatoes, peeled and shredded
1 cup unsalted butter
1½ pints canned evaporated milk
1½ cups granulated sugar
1 cup ground almonds
¼ tsp saffron
½ cup chopped almonds and pistachios

Wash the potatoes thoroughly and drain them well. Squeeze the potatoes to remove all excess moisture. Put the potatoes, butter and evaporated milk into a large solid based saucepan and cook slowly until mushy. The potatoes will disintegrate into a mashed state as they cook. Add the sugar and stir to dissolve. The mixture will bubble and splatter like bubbling mud from hot springs. Wrap a damp tea towel around your hand and stir the mixture for 20-30 minutes over a gentle heat. Add the ground almonds and saffron. Continue stirring over the heat until the pudding becomes thick, sticky and oily on the surface. Pour the pudding into a shallow dish and decorate with the chopped nuts.

Cabbage Pudding

PREPARATION TIME: 10 minutes
COOKING TIME: 40 minutes
SERVES: 4-6 people

1½ cups finely shredded white cabbage
2 tblsp pudding rice
2½ pints milk
1 cup canned evaporated milk
1 inch piece cinnamon stick
1 bayleaf
½-¾ cups granulated sugar
½ cup raisins

Facing page: Carrot Cake (top), Carrot Halva (center) and Carrotella (bottom).

½ cup chopped blanched almonds
½ cup pistachio nuts, chopped
Seeds of 6 small cardamoms, crushed

Put the cabbage, rice, both milks, cinnamon and bayleaf into a pan. Bring to the boil and simmer gently for 15-20 minutes, stirring occasionally to prevent the mixture from sticking to the pan. Add the sugar and simmer gently until the mixture is thick. Add the raisins and nuts. Remove from the heat when the rice is tender and the milk has been reduced to approx. 1¼ pints. Pour into a serving dish and sprinkle with the crushed cardamom seeds. Mix well and serve.

Frozen Lemon Yogurt Souffle

PREPARATION TIME: 20 minutes

SERVES: 4-6 people

2 pints natural yogurt
1 cup superfine sugar
Juice and finely grated rind of 2
    lemons
1 tsp vanilla essence
2 egg whites
¼ tsp salt
¼ tsp cream of tartar
½ cup heavy cream, whipped
Few thin lemon slices for decoration

Mix the yogurt, sugar, lemon juice, lemon rind and vanilla essence together. Whisk the egg whites, salt and cream of tartar until stiff but not dry. Fold the egg whites gently into the yogurt mixture, and then fold in the whipped cream. Pour the mixture into a souffle dish and freeze overnight. Garnish with lemon slices before serving. Serve either frozen or partially thawed.

Mango Fool

This delicious sweet can be made with fresh or canned mangoes; crushed cardamom seeds give it a characteristic flavor.

PREPARATION TIME: 10 minutes

SERVES: 4-6 people

1lb canned mango slices or the

equivalent amount of fresh mango, stoned and peeled
1 cup canned evaporated milk
Seeds of 6 cardamoms, crushed
Sugar to taste
Whipped cream

Put the mango, evaporated milk and cardamoms into a liquidizer and blend until smooth. Add a little sugar if necessary. Pour into a serving bowl and chill for 20 minutes before serving. Serve with whipped cream.

Tropical Fruit Dessert

An exotic sweet dish to finish any special meal. A delightful dessert from nature's fruit garden.

PREPARATION TIME: 30 minutes

SERVES: 8-10 people

4 bananas, cut into ¼ inch thick
    slices
5 rings pineapple, cut into chunks
    (fresh or canned)
2 semi-ripe pears, peeled, cored and
    cut into chunks
2 medium red-skinned apples, cored
    and cut into chunks
8 peach slices, chopped
2 cups red cherries, pitted
4 tblsp grated fresh coconut
1 honeydew melon, peeled and cut
    into chunks
1lb marshmallows
6-8 slices mango, cut into chunks
    (fresh or canned)
2 kiwi fruit, peeled and cut into
    chunks
20-25 strawberries, halved
Few seedless white and black grapes,
    halved
1½ tblsp confectioners' sugar
1 cup cottage cheese
Few drops vanilla essence

Mix all the ingredients together in a large bowl. Cover and chill for 1 hour.

Tropical Fruit Salad

This medley of fruits is very colorful and it offers a variety of tastes and textures.

PREPARATION TIME: 40 minutes

2 bananas, sliced
4 kiwi fruit, peeled and sliced
10 dates, stoned and sliced in half

2 guavas, halved and then sliced into
    wedges
1 pawpaw, cut into thin crescent
    shapes
1lb canned lychees, drained
8oz canned pineapple chunks,
    drained (or pieces of fresh
    pineapple)
2 fresh mangoes, peeled and sliced
Few seedless grapes, white and black,
    halved
1 small melon, cut into chunks
¼ water-melon, cut into chunks
4 fresh figs, halved

Dressing
2 tblsp lemon juice
Pinch salt
½ cup chopped toasted walnut or
    pine kernels

Prepare the fruits as suggested and arrange in a large glass bowl, in layers. Spoon over the lemon juice and sprinkle with salt. Sprinkle over the chopped nuts.

Semolina and Coconut Slices

PREPARATION TIME: 10 minutes

COOKING TIME: 30 minutes

SERVES: 6 people

¾ cup unsalted butter
1½ cups coarse semolina
2 cups shredded coconut
1½ cups granulated sugar
1 cup canned evaporated milk
1 cup water
1 cup chopped mixed nuts: blanched
    almonds, cashews, walnuts,
    hazelnuts and pistachios
¾ cup raisins
Seeds of 6 cardamoms, crushed

Melt the butter in a frying pan and add the semolina. Dry roast the semolina by stirring it until it turns lightly golden. Spoon onto a plate. Dry roast the coconut in the same pan until lightly golden. Add the

Tropical Fruit Dessert (top right), Frozen Lemon Yogurt Souffle (top left) and Tropical Fruit Salad (bottom).

semolina, sugar, milk and water to the coconut. Stir the mixture over the heat for 5-8 minutes. Add the chopped nuts, raisins and crushed cardamom seeds. Mix well and stir over a gentle heat for 5-6 minutes, until the mixture is thick and the oil begins to separate. Pour into a shallow dish, smooth with a spatula and allow to cool. Cut into diamond shapes or squares.

Mint Barley Sherbet

PREPARATION TIME:	10 minutes
COOKING TIME:	20 minutes
SERVES:	4-6 people

1 cup whole barley
2 pints water
¼ cup mint leaves, minced
Pinch salt

6 tblsp granulated sugar
Juice of 3 lemons
1-2 drops green food coloring
Grated rind of 1 lemon
Few mint leaves and lemon slices to
   decorate

Wash the barley in 2-3 changes of water. Soak the barley in the measured water for a few minutes; add the minced mint leaves and

This page: Yogurt, Almond and Saffron Sherbet (top center), Mango Sherbet (left), Maori Shake (center) and Tropical Blizzard (right).

Facing page: Mint Barley Sherbet (top left), Spiced Tea (top right) and Rich Coffee (bottom).

bring to the boil. Simmer gently for 10-15 minutes. Remove from the heat and strain; discard the barley grains. Dissolve the salt and sugar in the barley liquid; add the lemon juice, colouring and lemon rind. Mix well and make up to 2 pints with water. Pour into glasses and add crushed ice. To make clear sherbet; allow the barley water to stand for 10 minutes, so that the starch settles. Pour off the clear liquid and serve with a twist of lemon and mint leaves floating on the top.

Yogurt Dessert

This yogurt dessert is a light, delicious way of ending a rich meal; it is also simple and easy to make.

PREPARATION TIME: 15 minutes, plus setting time

COOKING TIME: 15 minutes

SERVES: 4-6 people

3 quarts milk
8-10 tblsp granulated sugar or to taste
½ cup finely chopped blanched almonds
½ cup raisins
Seeds of 8 small cardamoms, crushed
2-3 drops rose water or vanilla essence
2½ tblsp natural yogurt
¼ cup pistachio nuts, chopped

Simmer the milk in a large pan until it is reduced by half. Add the sugar to the milk and stir until dissolved. Add half the almonds, the raisins and cardamom seeds. Allow to cool until the milk is just tepid. Add the essence and beaten yogurt to the milk and stir well. Pour into a large, shallow serving dish. Cover and leave in a warm place, such as an airing cupboard, until the yogurt has set (about 5-6 hours). Sprinkle with the chopped pistachio nuts and remaining chopped almonds. Chill for 1 hour before serving. Will keep for up to 15 days in the refrigerator.

Tropical Blizzard

PREPARATION TIME: 3-4 minutes

SERVES: 4 people

1 cup pineapple juice or orange juice
1¼ cups natural yogurt
6 slices mango (canned or fresh)
1 tblsp sugar
Soda water
Ice cubes

Put the fruit juice, yogurt, mango and sugar into the liquidizer; blend for ½ minute. Pour into 4 glasses and dilute with soda water. Serve with ice cubes.

Maori Shake

A new taste experience; kiwi fruit blended with lemon yogurt.

PREPARATION TIME: 5 minutes

SERVES: 4-6 people

1 cup pineapple juice
2 kiwi fruits, peeled and chopped
1¼ cups lemon yogurt
Ice cubes
Lemonade
1 kiwi fruit, peeled and thinly sliced for decoration

Put the pineapple juice, chopped kiwi fruit and lemon yogurt into the liquidizer; blend for 30 seconds-1 minute, until smooth. Pour into 4-6 tall glasses; add ice cubes and top up with lemonade. Stir to mix. Serve with slices of kiwi fruit on top.

Mango Sherbet

This is a pretty green mango sherbet made from unripe mangoes. Windfallen mangoes are usually used for making this refreshing drink in India.

PREPARATION TIME: 20 minutes

COOKING TIME: 5-6 minutes

SERVES: 6 people

2 medium size unripe mangoes
⅓ tsp salt
2¼ pints water
Sugar to taste
Crushed ice

Boil the mangoes in sufficient water to cover for 5-6 minutes. Remove and allow to cool under cold running water. Peel off the skins. Put the water and salt into a punch bowl. Scrape all the mango flesh away from the stones and add to the punch bowl. Discard the stones. Whisk the sherbet until well blended. Pour into tall glasses; add sugar to taste and crushed ice.

Yogurt, Almond and Saffron Sherbet

A good healthy drink, which can be given a sweet or salty flavor.

PREPARATION TIME: 5 minutes

SERVES: 5-6 people

2¼ pints water
1 pint natural yogurt
2 tsp lemon juice
12 blanched almonds
¼ tsp saffron
2 drops vanilla essence or rose water
Salt or sugar to taste

Put 1½ cups water into the liquidizer with the yogurt, lemon juice, almonds, saffron and essence; blend until smooth. Mix in the remaining water. Pour into tall glasses over crushed ice. To make sweet sherbet, stir 2-3 tsp sugar into each glass; and to make a salty sherbet, sprinkle on a pinch of salt.

Rich Coffee

This is an old and traditional method of making coffee from the Orient.

PREPARATION TIME: 8 minutes

SERVES: 6-8 people

2¼ pints water
1 pint milk
2 tblsp freshly ground medium roast coffee
Seeds of 4 small cardamoms, crushed
Sugar to taste

Put the water and milk into a stainless steel pan and bring to the boil. Add the coffee and crushed cardamoms. Cover the pan and remove from the heat. Allow to brew for 2-3 minutes. Stir once. When the coffee grains settle to the bottom, strain off the coffee into cups and add sugar to taste.

Spiced Tea

This is a very different and interesting way of serving tea; it is refreshing served either hot or cold.

PREPARATION TIME: 5 minutes

SERVES: 6 people

2¼ pints water
1 pint milk
½ inch piece cinnamon stick
4 cloves
Seeds of 4 small cardamoms, crushed
6 teabags
or 2 tblsp tea leaves
Sugar to taste

Put the water, milk, cinnamon, cloves and cardamom seeds into a stainless steel pan. Bring to the boil and add the tea. Cover the pan and remove from the heat. Allow to brew for 2 minutes. Stir well. Add sugar to taste. Strain into cups and serve. Alternatively, allow the tea to cool and then chill and serve with ice.

Yogurt Dessert (top left), Mango Fool (left) and Semolina and Coconut Slices (bottom left).

HOME FARE

**Smoked Haddock in
French Mustard Sauce (top),
Chicken Curry (left) and
Poussin in White Sauce (right).**

Meals for Two

Poussin in White Sauce

1 pkt sage and onion stuffing
2 poussins
Fat
1¼ cups milk
¼ cup all-purpose flour
2 tblsp soft margarine
Salt and pepper

Make the stuffing as directed on the packet and use to stuff the poussins. Place the poussins in a roasting pan with melted fat, and cook in the oven for 30-40 minutes at 350°F, until tender. Put the milk, flour, margarine and seasoning into a pan and bring gradually to the boil, beating all the time. Cook gently for 3 minutes, stirring. Serve with baked potatoes and corn with red peppers.
Serves two

Smoked Haddock in French Mustard Sauce

¾lb smoked haddock fillet, skinned and cut into two
A little milk
Salt and pepper
1 tblsp butter
2 tblsp flour
⅔ cup milk
1 tblsp French mustard
Chopped chives (optional)

Place the fish in an ovenproof serving dish. Pour a little milk over the fish and season. Cover and cook in the oven for 15-20 minutes

at 325°F. Heat the butter in a pan, stir in the flour and cook for 2 minutes. Allow to cool, then pour in the milk gradually. Bring to the boil, stirring. Season and stir in the French mustard. Spoon the sauce over the fish and garnish with chopped chives if desired. Serve with potato croquettes and broccoli.
Serves two.

Broiled Meats

2 sausages
Liver
2 pork chops
Tomatoes
Mushrooms, sliced if flat

Broil the sausages, liver, pork chop and tomatoes until tender. Boil mushrooms until soft. Serve with baby new potatoes.
Serves two.

Chicken Curry

2 tblsp butter
1 small chicken, jointed
1 small onion, peeled and chopped
1 small apple, peeled and chopped
1 tsp curry powder
1 tblsp flour
½ tsp curry paste
1¼ cups chicken stock
1 chili (optional)
Pinch of powdered ginger
Pinch of powdered turmeric
1 tsp chutney
Squeeze of lemon juice
Salt and pepper
Shredded coconut
White raisins

Garnish
Thin onion rings, lightly fried
Thin green pepper rings, lightly fried
Lemon rind, lightly fried

Heat the butter and fry the chicken pieces. Remove and drain on paper towels. Fry the onion and apple for 2-3 minutes, then add the curry powder, flour and curry paste. Cook briefly, then carefully blend in most of the stock, reserving ¼ cup. Bring to the boil and cook for a few minutes until it forms a thin sauce. Add the remaining spices, chutney, lemon juice and seasoning. Return the chicken pieces to the pan. Pour the remaining stock over the coconut and allow to stand for a few minutes, then add the strained liquid to the curry. If preferred, fresh coconut or coconut milk can be used instead. Add the white raisins then cover and simmer for 2-3 hours. Garnish with onion, pepper and lemon rind to serve. Serves two

Plaited Lamb

1lb ground lamb
2 onions, peeled and chopped
2 tblsp breadcrumbs
1 tsp dried rosemary
1 tblsp tomato paste
1 tblsp Worcestershire sauce
2 eggs, beaten
Salt and pepper
8oz puff pastry

Mix together the ground lamb, onions, breadcrumbs, rosemary, tomato paste, Worcestershire sauce and one of the eggs. Add salt and pepper. Roll out the pastry into an oblong on a floured surface. Place the lamb mixture in the center and cut diagonal strips from the center to the edges along both sides. Brush all four sides with a little beaten egg. Fold the pastry at each end and then fold the strips over alternately so they meet in the center. Place the plaited lamb on a greased coohy sheet and brush with the remaining beaten egg. Cook in the oven for 15-20 minutes at 425°F. Then reduce the heat to 350°F, and cook for a further 30 minutes. Serve with new potatoes and a green vegetable.
Serves two.

Pasta Fish Pie

3 tblsp macaroni
Salt
8oz white fish

Cheese Sauce
1 tblsp butter or margarine
2 tblsp flour
⅔ cup milk
Salt and pepper
Pinch of dry mustard
3 tblsp Cheddar cheese, grated

Break the macaroni into small pieces (if using long macaroni), and cook in 2 pints of boiling, salted water until tender. Meanwhile, simmer the fish in a little salted water until tender. Lift the fish out and flake with a fork. Heat the butter or margarine in a pan, stir in the flour, and cook the 'roux' for 2-3 minutes over a low heat. Remove the pan from the heat and gradually add the milk, seasoning and mustard. Bring to the boil and cook until thickened, then add the grated cheese. Put the drained macaroni and fish into a hot dish and top with the cheese sauce. Place for 2-3 minutes under a hot broiler until the cheese topping bubbles. Serve with green beans and corn.
Serves two.

Braised Beef

1 tblsp fat
12oz of brisket or chuck roast, cut into pieces
1 carrot, peeled and sliced
1 onion, peeled and sliced
1 turnip, peeled and sliced
1 leek, trimmed and sliced
2 sticks celery, trimmed and sliced
2 tblsp fat bacon, diced
Bouquet garni (mixture of fresh herbs, i.e. parsley, thyme, sage, in muslin bag)
Salt and pepper
⅔ cup beef stock
¼ cup red wine

Heat the fat in a flameproof casserole dish or large saucepan and brown the meat for 3 minutes. Lift the meat onto a plate. Brown the vegetables in the fat together with the diced bacon. Add the bouquet garni, seasoning, stock and wine then return the meat on top of the mixture. Cover tightly and cook very slowly for about 1 hour. Lift the lid from time to time and add more stock if the mixture appears to be running dry. Remove the bouquet garni. Sieve or blend the vegetables and stock to make a sauce and reheat with the meat. Serve with boiled potatoes.
Serves two.

Stuffed Mushrooms

Two large, flt mushrooms
2 tblsp butter
1 rasher of bacon, rinded and chopped
1 tblsp fresh breadcrumbs
1 tsp chopped parsley
Grated rind of ¼ lemon
½ tsp lemon juice
2 tblsp Cheddar cheese, grated
Salt and pepper
Parsley

Remove the stalks from the mushrooms and chop finely. Heat the butter and fry the mushroom stalks and the bacon for a few minutes. Remove from the heat and stir in the breadcrumbs, parsley, lemon rind and juice, and cheese. Season well. Place the mushroom caps on a greased cooky sheet, divide the filling between each cap and cook for 15-20 minutes at 325°F. Sprinkle with chopped parsley. Serve with corn and sauté potatoes.
Serves two.

Veal Cutlets Bonne Femme

2x8oz veal cutlets
Salt and pepper
¼ cup flour
¼ cup clarified butter or butter and oil mixed
½ cup boiled, cold potatoes, thinly sliced
4 tblsp onions
¼ cup sherry
⅔ cup demi-glace sauce
1 tblsp chopped parsley

Sprinkle the veal cutlets with salt and pepper and dredge with flour. Heat the butter, or butter and oil, in a skillet and gently fry the cutlets on both sides for a few minutes. Place the cutlets in an ovenproof dish and cook in the oven for 15-20 minutes at 350°F, until tender. Fry the potatoes in the same pan until golden brown; remove and keep warm. Fry the onions for two minutes. Transfer the onions to a saucepan of water and boil until soft. Drain off the butter and pour the sherry into the pan. Add the demi-glace sauce and bring to the boil, stirring continuously. Arrange the cutlets on a serving dish, surrounded by the fried potatoes and onions. Cover with the demi-glace sauce and decorate with chopped parsley.
Serves two.

Facing page: Plaited Lamb (top left), Pasta Fish Pie (top right) and Veal Cutlets Bonne Femme (bottom).

Bacon and Chestnuts

1lb joint of bacon, boned and rolled
2 tblsp butter
1 small onion, peeled and chopped
¼ cup chestnut pure'e
¼ tsp mixed herbs
¼ tsp mixed spice
1 tsp soft brown sugar
1 beaten egg
1lb puff pastry

Place the bacon in a saucepan, cover with cold water, bring to the boil and simmer for 1 hour. Remove the bacon from the pan and trim off any excess fat; leave until cold. Melt the butter and fry the onion until soft. Mix with the chestnut purée, herbs, spice, and sugar, and half the beaten egg to bind the mixture. Roll out the pastry to a circle large enough to wrap around the bacon joint. Spread the mixture over the top of the bacon. Fold the pastry up over the joint and seal with a little of the beaten egg. Place on a cooky sheet. Brush with beaten egg. Cook in the oven for 30-35 minutes at 425°F. Serve with carrots and broad beans.
Serves two.

Demi-Glace Sauce

2 tblsp dripping or butter
2 tblsp peeled and chopped onion
2 tblsp peeled and chopped carrot
¼ cup flour
1 rasher bacon, rinded and diced
2½ cups brown stock
1 tsp tomato paste
1 tsp mixed herbs
Salt and pepper

Heat the dripping or butter, fry the onion, bacon and carrot until very lightly browned. Do not overcook at this stage as burnt onion gives a bitter taste to the sauce. Add the flour and continue cooking slowly until a rich chestnut color. Draw the pan aside, add the stock and

This page: Braised Beef (top left), Broiled Meats (center) and Stuffed Mushrooms (bottom).

Facing page: Filled Jacket Potatoes (top left), Sausage and Mushroom Pie (top right), Bacon and Chestnuts (bottom right) and Stuffed Eggplant (bottom left).

Pork Fillets and Apricots

8oz pork fillet, cut into small pieces
1 tblsp seasoned flour
2 tblsp butter
7oz can of apricot halves
1 tblsp Worcestershire sauce
1 tblsp soft brown sugar
2 tsp wine vinegar
1 tsp lemon juice
½ tsp powdered cinnamon
4 tblsp water
½ cup long grain rice

Toss the pork pieces in the seasoned flour. Heat the butter in a flameproof casserole dish and fry the pork until lightly browned. Chop all but three of the apricot halves. Mix 4 tablespoons of the apricot syrup with the Worcestershire sauce, sugar, vinegar, lemon juice, cinnamon and water. Pour the apricot sauce and chopped fruit over the pork. Bring to the boil, stirring continuously. Reduce the heat, cover and simmer for 15 minutes. Meanwhile, cook the rice in boiling, salted water. Spoon the pork and sauce onto a serving dish and spoon the drained rice around the meat. Decorate with the reserved apricots. If required serve with a green vegetable.
Serves two.

69

...d has been ... the paste, herbs ...taste. Bring to the ...ghly and simmer, covered, ... minutes. Strain through a fine-meshed strainer, pressing as much as possible of the vegetables through.
Makes 1 pint.

Sausage and Mushroom Pie

8oz pork sausages
2 tblsp butter
1 onion, peeled and sliced
3 tblsp flour
⅔ cup milk
⅔ cup brown stock
Salt and pepper
Pinch of mixed herbs
½ cup sliced mushrooms
8oz puff pastry
1 egg, beaten

Prick the sausages and broil them until golden. Heat the butter in a pan and fry the onion for 5 minutes. Stir in the flour and cook for a further minute. Gradually add the milk and stock and bring to boil. Stir until thickened then add the seasoning, herbs and mushrooms. Place the sausages in a pie dish and pour over the mushroom sauce. Roll out the puff pastry and use to cover the dish. Trim off any excess pastry. Glaze the top of the pie with the beaten egg and cook in the oven for 40 minutes at 390°F. Serve with new or boiled potatoes and a green vegetable.
Serves two.

Stuffed Eggplant

3 medium eggplant, washed and
*   stalks removed*
Salt
1¼ cups butter
1 medium onion, peeled and finely
*   chopped*
1 clove garlic, peeled and crushed
¾ cup ground beef
14oz can of tomatoes
1 tblsp chopped parsley
1 tsp dried marjoram
2 tsp tomato paste
Pepper
2 tsp cornstarch
½ cup Cheddar cheese, grated

Slice the eggplant in half lengthwise. Scoop out the flesh carefully and chop finely. Put the flesh on a large plate, sprinkle with salt and leave for 30 minutes. Blanch the eggplant skins in boiling water for 5 minutes. Remove and place on a serving dish. Heat the butter, add the onion and garlic and cook until soft. Stir in the ground beef and cook until brown. Add the tomatoes, parsley, marjoram and tomato paste. Season with pepper and bring to the boil. Blend the cornstarch with a little cold water and add to the beef and tomato mixture. Return to the boil, then remove from the heat. Drain the eggplant flesh in a sieve and rinse in cold water. Stir half the flesh into the beef and tomato mixture and use to stuff the eggplant halves. Top each one with grated cheese and cook in the oven for about 30 minutes at 350°F. (Use the left-over eggplant flesh in a Bolognese sauce or as a vegetable covered with a cheese sauce.) Serve the stuffed eggplant hot with a tossed green salad.
Serves two.

Hearts and Stuffing

2 lambs' hearts
Seasoned flour
1½ tblsp unsalted butter
1¼ cups brown stock
1 small onion
½ cup carrots
1 celery heart

Stuffing
2 shallots
1 stick celery
1oz belly pork
2 tblsp fresh breadcrumbs
1 rounded tblsp parsley
1 tsp curry powder
Salt and pepper
1½ tblsp melted butter

First make the stuffing. Peel and chop the shallots. Scrub and dice the celery stick. Grind or finely chop the pork. Place these ingredients in a bowl with the breadcrumbs, parsley, curry powder and seasoning. Bind together with the melted butter. Rinse the hearts. Cut out any tubes and discard, and fill the hearts with the stuffing. Sew up the openings and coat the hearts with seasoned flour. Melt the butter in a heavy pan and fry the hearts over a

high heat until brown. Lift the hearts into a casserole dish. Stir in enough seasoned flour to absorb the fat. Cook for 2-3 minutes then add the stock and bring to the boil. Pour over the hearts. Cover the casserole and cook in the oven at 325°F for 2 hours. After 2 hours peel and chop the onion, carrot and celery heart. Add to the casserole and continue to cook for a further 1 hour. Serve with boiled potatoes and green vegetables.
Serves two

Filled Jacket Potatoes

2 medium sized potatoes
2 tblsp butter
Salt and pepper

Cheddar Cheese Filling
¼ cup Cheddar cheese, grated
2 tblsp butter
A little milk
Salt and pepper
1 tblsp Parmesan cheese

Bacon Filling
6 tblsp bacon, rind removed, chopped
*   and fried*
2 tblsp butter
A little milk
Salt and pepper
1 small green pepper, cored, seeded
*   and finely chopped*

Sausage and Onion Filling
2 small pork sausages, chopped and
*   broiled*
2 tblsp butter
A little milk
Salt and pepper
1 small onion, peeled, chopped and
*   fried*

Liver and Zucchini Filling
6 tblsp lambs' liver, chopped and
*   fried*
2 tblsp butter
A little milk
Salt and pepper
2 small zucchini, diced and fried

Scrub the potatoes well. Prick them and dot their skins with butter. Sprinkle lightly with salt and pepper. Cook in the oven for 1-1¼ hours at 400°F. When cooked, cut in half lengthwise and scoop out the centers, keeping the skins intact. Mash the potato in a basin, adding one of the filling mixtures. Return the mixture to the potato skins. Cook for a further 15-20 minutes.
Serves two.

Lasagne

2 tblsp margarine
1 small onion, peeled and sliced
1 cup ground beef
7oz can of tomatoes
1 tsp tomato paste
⅔ cup beef stock
1 tsp dried marjoram
1 tsp mixed herbs
Pinch garlic salt
Salt and pepper
1 tsp cornstarch
6 tblsp lasagne
½ tblsp butter
2 tblsp margarine
¼ cup flour
1 cup milk
6 tblsp Cheddar cheese, grated

Heat the margarine and fry the onion until soft. Stir in the ground beef and cook until browned. Add the tomatoes, tomato paste, stock, herbs and garlic. Season well, cover and simmer for 30 minutes. Meanwhile, mix the cornstarch to a paste with a little cold water, stir into the meat sauce and bring to the boil, stirring continuously. Cook the lasagne in boiling, salted water, adding the ½ tblsp butter, for 10-15 minutes. Drain carefully. Heat the margarine, stir in the flour and cook for a few minutes. Allow to cool and gradually add the milk. Return to the heat and bring to the boil, stirring continuously. Stir in two-thirds of the cheese. Cover the base of a greased ovenproof dish with half the lasagne. Spoon over half the meat and tomato sauce. Cover with the remaining lasagne and spoon over remaining tomato sauce. Pour on the cheese sauce, sprinkle the Cheddar cheese on top and cook in the oven at 375°F for 30-35 minutes.
Serves two

Facing page: Lasagne (top left), Hearts and Stuffing (top right) and Pork Fillets and Apricots (bottom).

HOME FARE
The Family Roast

Lamb

ROASTING TIME: 25 minutes per 1lb + 25 minutes at 325°F.

Place in the center of a preheated oven. If a covered roasting pan is used basting is not necessary, but if the joint is uncovered or pot-roasted, the meat should be basted every 20-30 minutes. The meat should be turned over, using 2 metal spoons, halfway through the cooking. Transfer the meat from the pan to a hot, flat dish large enough to allow for carving. Keep hot. As accompaniments: medium brown, thickened gravy, mint or cranberry sauce. Serve with new potatoes, peas, French or green beans.

Veal

ROASTING TIME: 225 minutes per 1lb + 25 minutes at 325°F.

Place in the center of a preheated oven. If a covered roasting pan is used basting is not necessary, but if the joint is uncovered or pot-roasted, the meat should be basted every 20-30 minutes. The meat should be turned over, using 2 metal spoons, halfway through cooking. Transfer the meat from the tin onto a large, flat carving dish. Keep hot. As accompaniments: medium brown, thickened gravy, veal forcemeat stuffing, squeeze of lemon, bacon rolls. Serve with green vegetables, onions, tomatoes, baked or boiled potatoes.

Turkey

ROASTING TIME: For a 6-8lb turkey cook for 15 minutes at 400°F, then reduce temperature to 350°F and allow 15 minutes per 1lb + 15 minutes.

If the bird is frozen it must be allowed to thaw out completely before cooking. Stuff the bird, sprinkle with salt and place in a roasting pan. Brush the bird with melted dripping, butter or oil. The bird may be wrapped in foil, but the cover should be removed for the last 20-30 minutes to brown the skin. If left unwrapped the bird should be basted frequently. Transfer to a large carving dish when cooked. As accompaniments: sausages, chestnut, sausage meat or veal forcemeat stuffing, bacon rolls, cranberry or celery sauce, thickened gravy. Serve with roast, fried or boiled potatoes, onions, peas or Brussels sprouts.

This page: Turkey (top), Pork (center right) and Lamb (bottom).

Facing page: Mutton (top), Steak (center left), Veal (center right) and Duck (bottom).

Beef

ROASTING TIME: 15 minutes per 1lb + 15 minutes at 350°F.

Place in the center of a preheated oven. If a covered roasting pan is used basting is not necessary, but if the joint is uncovered or pot-roasted, the meat should be basted every 20-30 minutes. The meat should be turned over, using 2 metal spoons, halfway through the cooking. Transfer the meat from the pan to a hot, flat dish large enough to allow for carving. Keep hot. As accompaniments: thin, dark brown gravy, Yorkshire pudding, horseradish sauce, roast parsnips. Serve with baked or boiled potatoes and any vegetable.

Baked Whole Gammon

ROASTING TIME: 30 minutes per 1lb + 30 minutes at 350°F.

Spread gammon with a little melted butter or margarine and wrap in foil. Place in a roasting pan in the center of a preheated oven. Transfer the meat from the pan when cooked, remove the foil and put the gammon onto a large, flat carving dish. Keep hot. As accompaniments: thin, dark brown gravy, sage and onion stuffing, apple sauce. Serve with baked or boiled potatoes, cabbage, celery, Brussels sprouts or cauliflower.

Pork

ROASTING TIME: 30 minutes per 1lb + 30 minutes at 350°F.

Place in the center of a preheated oven. If a covered roasting pan is used basting is not necessary, but if the joint is uncovered or pot-roasted, the meat should be basted every 20-30 minutes. The meat should be turned over, using 2 metal spoons, halfway through the cooking. Transfer the meat from the tin to a hot, flat dish large enough to allow for carving. Keep hot. As accompaniments: thin, dark brown gravy, sage and onion stuffing, apple sauce. Serve with boiled potatoes, cabbage, cauliflower, celery, onion, spinach or Brussels sprouts.

Duck

ROASTING TIME: For a 2-3lb duck, cook for 15 minutes per lb. + 15 minutes at 350-375°F.

If the bird is frozen it must be thawed out completely before cooking. Stuff the bird with sage and onion stuffing, and place in a roasting pan. Brush the bird with melted dripping, butter or oil. Duck must be well pricked all over the breast to allow the fat to run out and leave the breast skin crisp and succulent. Transfer to a large carving dish when cooked. As accompaniments: apple sauce; thin gravy, flavored with orange juice if

liked. Serve with roast potatoes, peas, carrots and any green vegetable.

Steak

Season steak before cooking. Steak can be broiled, fried or roasted until tender and cooked to one's liking. Serve with baked or boiled potatoes and any vegetable.

Mutton

ROASTING TIME: 25 minutes per 1lb + 25 minutes at 325°F.

Place in the center of a preheated oven. If a covered roasting pan is used basting is not necessary, but if the joint is uncovered or pot-roasted, the meat should be basted every 20-30 minutes. The meat should be turned over, using 2 metal spoons, halfway through the cooking. Transfer the meat from the pan onto a large, flat carving dish. Keep hot. As accompaniments: medium brown, thickened gravy, redcurrant, cranberry or mint sauce. Serve with baked or boiled potatoes and any vegetable.

Chicken

ROASTING TIME: 15 minutes per 1lb + 15 minutes at 400°F.

If the bird is frozen it must be allowed to thaw out completely before cooking. Stuff the bird, sprinkle with salt and place in a roasting pan. Brush the bird with melted dripping, butter or oil. The bird may be wrapped in foil, but the cover should be removed for the last 20-30 minutes to brown the skin. If left unwrapped the bird should be basted frequently. Transfer the bird to a large carving dish. As accompaniments: veal forcemeat, bread sauce, bacon rolls and thin gravy. Serve with baked, fried or boiled new potatoes, and green vegetables.

Beef (top), Chicken (far left) and Baked Whole Gammon (left).

HOME FARE
Meals for Special Occasions

to cool completely. Drain the apricots, reserving the juice. Garnish the loaf with apricot halves and the stuffed olives. Mix the cornstarch with a little of the apricot juice, then add the rest of the juice and the wine. Heat, stirring, until thickened. Cool, then brush over the meat loaf and serve the rest separately in a jug. Serve the meat loaf on a bed of lettuce leaves, with potato croquettes and vegetables.
Serves eight-ten.

Boeuf en Croûte

1 tblsp oil
3lb beef round roast
2 tblsp butter
1 onion, peeled and chopped
½ cup mushrooms, chopped
2 tblsp freshly chopped parsley
Salt and pepper
10oz bought or home-made basic puff pastry
A little milk
Few sprigs of watercress to garnish

Heat the oil in a large pan and fry the meat quickly on all sides to seal the juices. Transfer the oil and the meat to a roasting dish. Cook in the oven for 45 minutes at 400°F. Leave to cool. Melt the butter in a pan and fry the onions until soft. Add the mushrooms, parsley and seasoning. Cover and fry for 5 minutes. Roll out the pastry to make a rectangle large enough to cover the meat. Spread ⅓ of the stuffing over the center of the pastry and place the meat on top. Spread the rest of the stuffing over the meat. Dampen the edges of the pastry and fold them over the meat

Turkey and Apricot Loaf

1½lb uncooked turkey meat, ground
¾ cup fresh white breadcrumbs
1 onion, peeled and finely chopped
1 tblsp Worcestershire sauce
1 egg, beaten
Pinch of mixed herbs
Pinch of allspice
Salt and pepper

15oz can apricot halves
½ cup stuffed, green olives, sliced
2 tsp cornstarch
⅔ cup dry white wine

Grease a 1lb loaf pan and set aside. In a large bowl, mix together the turkey, breadcrumbs, onion, Worcestershire sauce, egg, herbs, allspice and seasoning, and combine well. Spoon the mixture

into the loaf pan, making sure the corners are well filled, smooth over the top and bang the pan on a flat surface to release any air bubbles. Cook in the oven for about 90 minutes at 350°F, or until the meat loaf is cooked through. The juices will run clear when a skewer is inserted. Remove from the oven, allow to cool in the pan for 30 minutes, then turn out and leave

This page: Sweet and Spicy Noisettes (top), Veal in Orange (center left) and Peppered Steak (bottom right).

Facing Page: Boeuf en Croûte (top), Turkey and Apricot Loaf (center left) and Stuffed Trout with Almonds (bottom).

like a parcel. Trim as necessary. Place the meat, pastry joins downwards, in a roasting pan. Roll out any pastry trimmings and cut into leaf shapes, to decorate the top. Brush the top with a little milk. Increase the oven temperature to 425°F, and cook the beef for about 40-45 minutes until the pastry is golden. Place the meat on a serving dish and garnish with watercress. Serve with baked potatoes, Brussels sprouts and carrots.
Serves six-eight.

Veal in Orange

1½-2lb veal fillet
1 onion
2½ cups white stock
Salt and pepper
2 oranges
4 small, young carrots
1 cup long grain rice
¼ cup butter
6 tblsp flour
Pinch of powdered saffron
⅔ cup heavy cream
Parsley to garnish

Dice the veal. Peel the onion and keep it whole. Put the veal, onion, stock and seasoning into a pan. Bring to the boil. Lower the heat and simmer for 40 minutes until the meat is tender. Remove the onion. Cut away the peel from 1 orange, remove the white pith, then cut the orange flesh into narrow strips. Soak in ⅔ cup water for 30 minutes. Peel the carrots, cut into neat matchsticks, put with the orange rind and a little seasoning and simmer in a covered pan for 20 minutes. Remove the carrots and orange rind and cook the rice in remaining salted water. Heat the butter in a pan, stir in the flour and cook for several minutes. Add the strained veal stock and bring to the boil. Cook until thickened. Add the orange rind, carrots, cooked rice and any liquid left, together with the pinch of saffron powder and the cream. Stir over a low heat until smooth. Add the cooked veal and mix thoroughly. Arrange a border of rice with the remaining orange cut into slices on a serving dish. Spoon the veal mixture in the center of the dish and sprinkle with parsley. Serve with potatoes and vegetables of your own choice.
Serves six.

Veal with Cucumber

8-12oz fillet veal, cubed
Salt and pepper
1 tblsp cornstarch
¼ cup butter
½ cup mushrooms
2 eating apples, peeled cored and sliced
1 cucumber, peeled and diced
1 green pepper, cored, and deseeded and sliced
1 red pepper, cored and deseeded and sliced
½ cup cooked rice

Sweet and Sour Sauce
1 tblsp cornstarch
2 tblsp sugar
2 tsp soy sauce
3 tblsp vinegar
⅔ cup chicken stock

Toss the veal in seasoned cornstarch and fry in the butter until golden. Remove and keep warm. Fry the mushrooms, apple slices and cucumber. Fry the peppers. Return the meat to the pan. Cover and cook for 10 minutes until the meat is tender. Stir in the cooked rice. Transfer to a serving dish and keep hot. Mix the sweet and sour sauce ingredients together, add to the pan and, stirring gently, boil for 2-3 minutes, until the sauce is transparent. Pour the sauce over the veal and cucumber mixture. This can be served as a meal in its own right, or served with a vegetable if required.
Serves four.

Sweet and Spicy Noisettes

1 tsp honey
1 tsp dry mustard
Salt and pepper
1 garlic clove, peeled and crushed
2 tsp lemon juice
6 noisettes of lamb
3 canned pineapple rings with juice
2 tblsp butter
1½ tblsp chopped mint
1 tomato, quartered
3 glacé cherries

Combine the honey, mustard, seasoning, garlic and lemon juice and spread the noisettes with the mixture. Leave to stand for 20 minutes. Place ¼ cup of the pineapple juice in a pan, add the butter and bring to the boil. Boil until reduced by half and add the mint. Keep warm. Broil the noisettes, basting them occasionally with the pineapple mixture. When the meat is cooked, arrange it on a warmed serving dish and decorate with the tomatoes and the pineapple rings. Garnish with the glacé cherries. Serve with fried mushroom rings and bird's nest potatoes.
Serves three.

Stuffed Trout with Almonds

Salt and pepper
2 medium trout, filleted
8-10 tblsp butter
¼ cup blanched almonds

Stuffing
¾ cup fresh, white breadcrumbs
2 tblsp chopped fresh parsley
1 medium onion, peeled and finely chopped
Salt and pepper
2 tsp mixed dried herbs
1 tart apple, peeled and finely chopped
1 small egg, beaten
A little water

Season the fish lightly and fry for about 10 minutes in the butter, until tender. Transfer to a hot dish. For the stuffing mix together the breadcrumbs, parsley, onion, seasoning, herbs and apple. Stir in the beaten egg, and water if necessary, to give a soft consistency. Stuff the fish with this mixture. Fry the almonds for about 5 minutes, adding extra butter if necessary. Scatter the almonds over the fish. Garnish with parsley, and serve with saute' potatoes and a vegetable.

Three Ring Rice

1 red pepper
A stick of butter
1 cup cooked rice
2 medium onions, peeled and chopped
½ green pepper, cored, deseeded and chopped
1 small garlic clove, peeled and crushed
1 cup ground beef
6oz can of concentrated tomato paste
1 tsp salt
½ tsp chili powder
4oz packet of frozen peas

Core, deseed and cut the red pepper into strips. Arrange at intervals in the bottom of a ring mold. Melt half the butter. Stir in the rice and spoon into the mold over the pepper. Fry the onion and green pepper together with the garlic in the remaining butter until soft. Add the ground beef and cook until brown. Stir in the tomato paste, salt and chili powder. Cook the peas, strain, put on top of the rice, then cover with the beef mixture. Press down each layer firmly. Place the mold in a shallow pan of hot water. Cook in the oven for about 20 minutes at 350°F, or until firm to the touch. Turn out onto a hot dish. Serve with corn or a side salad.

Veal with Cucumber (above right) and Three Ring Rice (below right).

herbs. Pour over the juice from the tomatoes and finish with a layer of potato slices. Pour water in to come halfway up the dish and dot the butter over the top. Cover tightly and cook in oven for 90 minutes at 350°F. Remove the lid and cook for a further 30 minutes to brown the potatoes. Serve with boiled carrots tossed in butter and chopped parsley.
Serves six.

Gammon with Mixed Fruit

4-5lb gammon hock
2 tblsp apricot jam
2 tblsp made mustard
Cloves for decoration
1 small, fresh pineapple, peeled
1 tblsp chutney
5 tblsp unsweetened pineapple juice
2lb canned apricot halves, drained

Cover the gammon with cold water and soak for 4 hours. Drain the gammon and wrap in foil. Place in a roasting pan and cook in the oven for 2 hours at 375°F. Remove the rind from the gammon and score the surface of the meat. Mix half the apricot jam with the mustard and spread the mixture over the gammon. Stud the meat with the cloves in a decorative pattern and return the meat to the oven for about 30 minutes. Cut the pineapple into slices and remove the core from each slice. Heat the remaining apricot jam with the chutney and pineapple juice in a wide pan. Glaze the pineapple slices and the apricot halves in this mixture. Place the finished gammon joint in a serving dish and garnish with the glazed pineapple slices and apricot halves. Serve with an exotic salad.
Serves ten.

Crown Roast of Lamb

2 best ends of lamb, chined
2 tsp butter
1 tart apple, peeled, cored and chopped
8oz pork sausage meat
2 tblsp fresh breadcrumbs
1 tblsp chopped fresh parsley
1 tblsp finely chopped mint
Glacé cherries

Trim the skin and fat from the ends of the rib bones so that 1 inch of the bone protrudes. Place the two joints back-to-back with the bones curving upwards and outwards.

Secure with kitchen thread. Heat the butter and sauté the apple, add the sausage meat, cook for 2-3 minutes and then stir in the rest of the ingredients. Place the stuffing in the cavity of the crown. Cover the tips of the bones with foil and roast in the oven for 30 minutes per 1lb plus 30 minutes at 350°F. Decorate the bone ends with cutlet frills and glacé cherries and serve with roast potatoes and a green vegetable.
Serves six-eight.

Pork Provençal

2lb pork fillets
15oz can tomatoes
1½lb potatoes, peeled and thinly sliced
1½ cups onions, peeled and thinly sliced
Salt and pepper
¼ tsp dried mixed herbs
2 tblsp butter

Slice the meat and trim off any surplus fat. Butter an ovenproof dish then arrange the tomatoes, meat, onions and potatoes in layers. Season each layer and add

This page: Pork Provençal (top) and Turkey Roast with Fruit Sauce (bottom).

Facing page: Crown Roast of Lamb (top), Egg and Melon Salad (bottom left) and Gammon with Mixed Fruit (bottom right).

Egg and Melon Salad

1 small cabbage
1 firm, ripe melon
1 orange
Salt and pepper
2 carrots, peeled and grated
4 hard-boiled eggs
Few sprigs of watercress
Few leaves of Belgian endive
8 radishes

Cooked Salad Dressing

1 tsp flour
1 tblsp sugar
Salt and pepper
½ tsp mustard powder
1 large egg, beaten
2 tblsp water
2 tblsp vinegar
1 tsp butter

To prepare the dressing, combine the flour, sugar, mustard and seasoning in a heavy-based saucepan. Mix in the egg to form a smooth paste. Add the water, vinegar and butter and stir over a low heat until the sauce begins to thicken. Remove from the heat, stir thoroughly and, if necessary, strain to remove any lumps. Cool in the refrigerator. Chop the cabbage very finely. Cube the melon. Peel the orange and cut the segments into pieces. Combine these ingredients with the grated carrots in a mixing bowl. Season as required. Pour over the cooled dressing and spoon the salad mixture onto a large salad dish. Shell and slice the hard-boiled eggs and arrange them with the watercress and Belgian endive leaves round the salad. Cut the radishes into floral shapes and garnish the salad and serve.
Serves four.

Barbados Turkey

¼ cup flour
1 tsp powdered ginger
1 tsp curry powder
4oz turkey escalopes
6 tblsp butter
¼ cup rum
¼ cup shredded coconut
3 tblsp pineapple juice
5 tblsp chicken stock
¼ cup heavy cream
Salt and pepper
Few sprigs of parsley
6-8 slices canned pineapple

Mix together the flour, ginger and curry powder and use to coat the turkey. Heat the butter and fry the escalopes for about 10 minutes each side until cooked and golden. Add the rum and set alight. When the flames subside, remove the

escalopes and keep hot. Add the coconut to the pan and brown quickly. Then stir in the pineapple juice and stock. Boil for 5 minutes, reduce the heat and stir in the cream and seasoning. Arrange the escalopes in a serving dish and cover with the sauce. Garnish with the parsley and pineapple. Serve with boiled rice and green vegetables.
Serves four.

Crown of Chicken

Salt and pepper
¼ cup flour
2lb potatoes
3 tblsp milk
2-4 tblsp butter
6 or 8 chicken legs
4 tblsp olive oil
1 can cherry fruit pie filling
Watercress to garnish

Coat the chicken legs in seasoned flour. Peel the potatoes and cook in boiling, salted water. Drain and mash the potatoes with the milk and butter and keep hot. Meanwhile, fry the chicken in the olive oil until cooked and golden brown. Drain on paper towels and keep hot. Drain excess oil from the frying pan, add the cherry pie filling and heat gently. Place the creamed potatoes in the center of a hot serving dish, stand the chicken legs round the edges. Pour over the hot cherry sauce. Garnish with watercress and serve with a green salad.

Duck and Orange Sauce

1 large duck, e.g. 3lb
1 orange
1¼ cups bought Espagnole sauce
1 tblsp lemon juice
2 tblsp white wine
⅔ cup water
Orange segments to garnish

Place the duck in an open roasting pan. No fat is necessary. Cook in the oven at 300°F. Cook for 25 minutes for every 1lb in weight and 30 minutes over. Prick the breast skin after 30 minutes with a fine skewer. Pare the rind from the orange, cut into wafer-thin strips and simmer in water for about 10 minutes. Strain the Espagnole sauce carefully, reheat with the orange rind, orange juice, lemon juice and wine. Garnish the duck with orange segments and serve with the orange sauce. Serve with

potato croquettes, broccoli and roast turnips.
Serves four.

Peppered Steak

Steak, as required
A little oil or butter
Peppercorns

Brush the steak with oil or melted butter and broil until tender, or as required. When the steak is cooked, place on a serving dish and sprinkle with the peppercorns. Tap with a steak hammer to crush the peppercorns into the steak. Serve with French fries, potato croquettes, onion rings or broccoli, or a mixed side salad.

Turkey Roast with Fruit Sauce

2 tblsp butter
5½lb white turkey roast
1 red pepper
1 small green pepper
1 onion
8oz can mandarin oranges
8oz canned corn

For the Sauce

2 tsp cornstarch
1 tblsp vinegar
1 tsp sugar
1 tsp Worcestershire sauce
1-2 tblsp sherry

Spread the butter over the turkey roast then wrap in foil to make a parcel. Place in a roasting pan and roast in the oven for 90 minutes at 375°F. Core, deseed and chop the peppers. Peel and chop the onion. Drain the mandarins and corn, reserving the juices. Mix the mandarins, corn, peppers and onion together. To make the sauce, mix the cornstarch with a little water to make a smooth paste. Blend the juices from the mandarins and corn with the vinegar, sugar, Worcestershire sauce, sherry and cornstarch and heat until thickened, stirring well. Add the fruit and vegetables. Remove the turkey roast from the oven and unwrap the foil. Pour a little of the sauce all over and

round the turkey and cover again with the foil. Cook the turkey for a further 1-1½ hours or until the turkey is tender and cooked through. Unwrap the turkey and place on a serving dish. Surround with fruit sauce and serve the rest of the sauce separately. Serve with roast potatoes and vegetables of your own choice.
Serves six-eight.

Crown of Chicken (right),
Duck and Orange Sauce
(below) and Barbados
Turkey (bottom).

MICROWAVE COOKING

Introducing the Microwave

The microwave oven is one of the most exciting kitchen appliances available. It may be used to defrost, reheat, and cook foods, and is therefore more versatile than a conventional oven; in fact it can cope with 75% of your normal cooking needs.

The theory behind microwave cooking must be learned and fully understood before a microwave oven can be used to its full extent. It is a very different method of cooking, which is clean, quick, efficient, labor saving and economical.

The Principles of Microwave Cookery

Electricity is converted into microwave energy inside the oven by the magnetron. The 'microwaves' are transferred into the oven cavity where they bounce off the metal interior and penetrate the outer 1"-1½" of the food. They pass through non-metal containers as though they were not there, and simply cause the molecules in the food to vibrate very fast indeed. The heat that is created passes by conduction through to the center of the food and the food is cooked by friction heat. As a rough guide, cooking times by the microwave method are about ⅓ to ¼ of the conventional times.

Different Types of Microwave Ovens

A microwave oven may be either free standing or built-in. If built-in, it is placed in a housing unit, with a conventional oven situated above or below the microwave.

Convected Hot Air and Microwave Combined

These ovens are now widely available. They are more expensive than an ordinary microwave oven as they combine two units in one. The most common criticism of food cooked in a microwave is that it does not appear 'brown'. This is because there is no dry heat available to caramelise or 'brown' the food. Some people prefer to buy the combination ovens, which use traditional cooking methods and microwave cooking combined. In some models both cooking methods may be used simultaneously, whilst in others the

microwave and the hot air ovens are used one after the other.

Broilers
Some microwave ovens offer a browning broiler.

The Output of the Microwave
The cooking time for each dish/recipe is governed by the electrical output of the microwave oven, and the output also controls the running costs of the appliance. The output is measured in watts. A 700w microwave oven consumes about 1.3k per hour and is, therefore, a most economical method of cooking. Microwave ovens are available in a variety of power ratings and the cooking, re-heating and defrosting times vary according to the output. A 3lb chicken takes 21 minutes in a 700w microwave and 28 minutes in a 500w.

There is no pre-heating before use, and no cooling down after cooking.

Versatility
A microwave oven may be used to defrost, cook and reheat food. It is also well suited to the many different methods of cooking – a microwave oven can poach, shallow fat fry, braise, roast, boil and bake. It will even dry herbs for winter use, and may be used to sterilize jars. The oven and cooking containers stay cool, and microwave ovens are, therefore, perfectly safe for elderly people to use, and for households where there are children.

Cleaning
As the oven cabinet does not get very hot, all that is necessary is a

wipe with a clean dish cloth. Should smells cling e.g. curry or fish, simply squeeze a lemon into 1¾ cups of water and bring to the boil. Wipe the oven with the acidulated water. Food does not bake onto the containers so they are easier to wash up.

Turntables

Manufacturers choose different methods of ensuring that the food cooks evenly. Go by personal recommendation wherever possible. Hidden turntables are popular as they do not restrict the shape of dish used. Some ovens offer stirrer fans and turntables.

Standing Times

Standing, or equalizing, time is simply the time that the food takes to finish cooking. The heat is passed from the outside to the center by conduction. The standing time will vary according to the size and density of the food. Standing time may take place either inside or outside the microwave oven; it is an important part of microwave cookery which must be used. It is just as important after defrosting.

Containers for Use in the Microwave Oven

Special containers are available for microwave cookery, but they are not essential. The heat is localized in the food, and not in the container, so the dish itself does not usually become hot. Some plastics, Pyrex, china, glass, and even paper and basketware, may be used. Be guided by the length of time the food will stand in the microwave, and by the temperature that it will reach.

Plastic wrap is a boon to the microwave owner, as it may be used in place of a lid to cover foods and prevent splashing. Do remember to pierce plastic wrap and roasta bags to allow steam to escape.

Metal – including tin foil – may damage the heart of the microwave oven, the magnetron, and should not be used unless specifically directed by the manufacturer.

Browning Dish or Skillet

A browning dish is a special dish which, when preheated in the microwave oven, will become very hot over the base. Several shapes and sizes are available, either with a lid or without. The dish is used to brown such foods as chops, sausages, hamburgers, bacon, eggs etc. The food must be turned to brown on the other side. The deep browning dishes with lids are also used as casserole dishes. *These containers must not be used in conventional ovens.*

Herby Roast Chicken (left), Devilled Pork Chops (below) and Chicken Breasts in Garlic Cream Sauce (right).

Variable Power Chart

MICROWAVE POWER LEVEL	DESCRIPTION AND SUGGESTED USE
10 or Full–High	Microwave energy constant at full wattage. For cooking vegetables, poultry, fish and some sauces, start joints.
8 or Roast	Power on for 13 seconds, auto cut-out for 2 seconds. Repeated continually for time selected, for reheating some joints.
7 and 6 – Medium	Power is on for about 10 seconds, off for 5 seconds, for chops, meat balls, chicken pieces, cakes.
4 and 5 – Simmer	Power is on for 6 seconds, off for 9 seconds, for completing casseroles, defrosting large joints, egg and cheese dishes.
3 – Defrost	Generally for defrosting (allow a standing time afterwards), for melting chocolate, and for delicate sauces.
2 – Very Low	Power is on for 3 seconds, off for 12 seconds. Keep cooked food warm for up to ½ hour. Soften butter and cream cheese from refrigerator.

Please note that this chart is given only as a guide. The variable power dial differs slightly from manufacturer to manufacturer.

Cooked food reheats remarkably quickly without drying out. A chart is provided to give some of the most common foods. Allow a few minutes standing time, after reheating, and before serving.

GENERAL RULES FOR REHEATING.
1. Cover food, allowing steam to escape, unless told specifically not to cover.
2. Stir foods such as casseroles, baked beans, stewed fruits, halfway through reheating.
3. Allow a short standing time – 3-5 minutes before removing covering and serving.
4. Reheat small items, such as sausage rolls or sausages, arranged in ring fashion on outside edge of plate. Reheat on Power 4, or Simmer.

Re-heating Chart

TYPE OF FOOD & WEIGHT	COVER	STIRRING	POWER LEVEL	TIME
1 Plated Meal	Plastic Wrap	–	Full	3-4 minutes
1 Large Macaroni Cheese	Plastic Wrap	Yes, once	Power 7 or Roast	10 minutes
2 Bowls Soup	–	Yes, once	Full	5 minutes
Baked Beans 4ozs	–	–	Power 7 or Roast	2 minutes
Baked Beans 16ozs	Yes	Yes, twice	Power 7 or Roast	7 minutes
Chicken Pieces 8ozs	Yes	–	Full	3-4 minutes
Beef Casserole For 4	Yes	Yes, twice	Full	10-12 minutes
Cooked Vegetables 4ozs	Yes	–	Full	45 seconds
Cooked Vegetables 1lb	Yes	Yes, once	Full	2 minutes
1 Family Meat Pie	No	No	4 or Simmer	7-8 minutes
6 Mince Pies	No	No	4 or Simmer	4 minutes
4 Bread Rolls	Kitchen Roll	No	4 or Simmer	2 minutes
Christmas Pudding 1½lb	Plastic Wrap	No	Power 7 or Roast	3 minutes
Sauce ½ pt	Plastic Wrap	Yes, twice	Full	2 minutes
Fish 12ozs	Plastic Wrap	–	Full	2 minutes

Defrosting Chart

FOOD TO BE DEFROSTED AND WEIGHT	POWER LEVEL	MICROWAVE TIME	STANDING TIME
Ground Meat 1lb	4 or defrost	6 minutes	15 minutes
Chicken 3lb	4 or defrost	30 minutes	30 minutes
Joint of Beef 3lb	4 or defrost	20 minutes	30 minutes
Shepherd's Pie 1lb	4 or defrost	8 minutes	10 minutes
Large Lasagne	6 or simmer	20 minutes	15 minutes
Chops 1lb	4 or defrost	6 minutes	10 minutes
Sausages 1lb	4 or defrost	6 minutes	10 minutes
Cod 8ozs	4 or defrost	6 minutes	10 minutes
Raspberries 8ozs	4 or defrost	4 minutes	15 minutes
1 Victoria Sandwich (2 egg)	4 or defrost	2-3 minutes	15 minutes
Large Sliced Loaf	4 or defrost	7 minutes	10 minutes
Cheese Sauce ½ Pint	4 or defrost	7 minutes	7 minutes
Chicken in Sauce for 4	Simmer	12 minutes	10 minutes
Family Apple Pie	4 or defrost	8 minutes	5 minutes
Family Meat Pie or Quiche Lorraine	4 or defrost	6-7 minutes	10 minutes

The microwave oven makes a perfect partner for your freezer as it enables you to defrost frozen foods in a fraction of the time that it would normally take. Remember to turn or stir the foods, for more even defrosting, and remember that a standing time is very important.

ALTERING TIMINGS

All these recipes can be cooked in any model of variable power microwave oven that is available today. Each of these recipes was tested in a 700W microwave oven. Convert the timings in the following way, if the output of your oven is other than 700W:–

If using an oven of 500W, add 40 seconds for each minute stated in the recipe.

If using an oven of 600W, add 20 seconds for each minute stated in the recipe.

If using an oven of 650W plus, you will only need to allow a slight increase in the overall time.

Stirring and Turning

Stirring and turning are methods used to equalize the heat in the food, i.e. the cooking of the food. The amount of stirring or turning will be governed by the type of food to be cooked, the cooking time and the even distribution of energy in the microwave oven. The recipes in this section give you a guide as to when to stir and turn. Adjust, if necessary, according to your own particular oven. Arrange foods such as baked apples or jacket potatoes in a ring fashion, leaving a space in the center.

Starting Temperature of Food

The starting temperature of food will alter the cooking time. It may be at average room temperature, at cold room temperature or taken from the refrigerator or cold larder. Please note that the timings are calculated for food at average room temperature, unless otherwise stated.

Can You Cook a Complete Meal by Microwave?

The easiest way to use a microwave oven is to employ stage cookery.

The microwave oven cooks according to weight and time, not by temperature, and different types of food require different cooking times. During the standing time of the denser foods, such as joints and jacket potatoes, the less dense items, such as vegetables and sauces, are completely cooked. Foods of similar density may be cooked together, e.g. potatoes and carrots, but remember that the total energy available in the microwave oven must be shared between the foods introduced. If carrots and potatoes are cooked simultaneously, the resulting weight must be checked, and the cooking time calculated accordingly.

Some Things Cannot be Done

Do not try to cook Yorkshire puddings or other batter recipes, boil eggs, deep fat fry, or produce really crisp foods such as roast potatoes, as none of these will be successful. *Pastry* – baking blind, suet crust and some puff pastry recipes work beautifully, but do not try to cook the top of an apple pie.

Soups and Appetizers

Vegetable Soup

PREPARATION TIME: 10 minutes
MICROWAVE TIME: 21-26 minutes
SERVES: 4 people

2 tblsp butter
1lb young leeks, cleaned and sliced
1 medium onion, peeled and sliced
1½ cups potato, peeled and diced
1 carrot, peeled and diced
Salt and freshly ground black pepper
    to taste
1¼ tblsp chopped fresh parsley
1¾ cups homemade chicken stock
1¼ cups milk

Melt the butter in a 3 quart casserole dish. Microwave on Full Power for 1 minute. Stir in all the prepared vegetables, salt and pepper, parsley and 4 tblsp of the stock. Cover the dish, piercing the plastic wrap if used. Microwave on Full Power for 12 minutes. Stir. Set aside, covered, for 5 minutes. Transfer the vegetables into the food processor bowl or blender goblet; add the milk and blend or process until smooth. Return to the casserole dish and stir in the remaining stock. Microwave on Full Power, covered, for 3-5 minutes. Stir well before serving.

Asparagus with Mayonnaise

PREPARATION TIME: 10 minutes
MICROWAVE TIME: 10-12 minutes
SERVES: 4 people

1lb frozen asparagus spears
1 cup corn oil
2 tblsp butter
1 egg
1 egg yolk
²⁄₃ cup olive oil
Salt and freshly ground black pepper
    to taste
2½ tblsp lemon juice
Chopped fresh parsley

Arrange the asparagus in a roasta bag in a suitable dish. Add 4 tblsp water to the bag, with the butter. Seal the bag with a rubber band.

Pierce the bag once at the base. Microwave on Full Power for 10-12 minutes, turning the bag over once halfway through cooking time. Set aside. Put the egg and egg yolk into the goblet of a food processor or blender with the salt and pepper. Blend on maximum. Add the oil, in a steady trickle, blending to a smooth mayonnaise. Add the lemon juice. Carefully drain the asparagus and arrange on a heated serving dish. Sprinkle with the parsley and serve accompanied by the mayonnaise. Serve immediately.

Soured Cream Prawns

PREPARATION TIME: 5 minutes
MICROWAVE TIME: 7-8 minutes
SERVES: 4 people

4 tblsp butter
2 cups peeled shrimps
Freshly ground black pepper to taste
1 egg yolk
²⁄₃ cup soured cream
Paprika

Butter 4 ramekin dishes and divide the shrimps among them. Season well with black pepper. Combine the egg yolk and soured cream and spoon over the shrimps. Dot with the remaining butter. Microwave all 4 ramekins together on Power 4, or Simmer, for 7-8 minutes. (The dishes should be arranged in a ring, leaving a space in the centre.) Serve immediately sprinkled with paprika.

Corn Starter

PREPARATION TIME: 5 minutes
MICROWAVE TIME: 15 minutes
SERVES: 4 people

4 corn cobs
Sprigs of fresh savory
Salt and freshly ground black pepper
    to taste
A stick of butter

Arrange the cobs in a suitable dish. Add 3 tblsp cold water and a few sprigs of savory. Season. Cover with plastic wrap and pierce.

Microwave on Full Power for 6 minutes. Turn each cob over. Re-cover and microwave on Full Power for 6 minutes. Set aside. Put the butter into a 1¼ pint jug and microwave on Power 4 or Simmer for about 3 minutes or until melted. Transfer the cooked cobs to a serving dish. Pour over the butter and sprinkle with extra chopped savory before serving.

Individual Frozen Pizzas

PREPARATION TIME: 2 minutes
MICROWAVE TIME: 6½-8½ minutes
SERVES: 1 person

Preheat a browning dish, without the lid, for 5-7 minutes. Put 1¼ tblsp of oil and 1 individual pizza onto the dish. Microwave uncovered for approximately 1½ minutes on Full Power. Allow to stand for 1 minute before serving. As many pizzas as will fit onto your dish may be microwaved at the same time; increase the microwave time accordingly. Pizzas may be heated directly from the freezer, without the browning dish, on an ordinary non-metallic plate but the base will not be as crisp.

Chestnut Soup

PREPARATION TIME: 15 minutes
MICROWAVE TIME: 34 minutes
SERVES: 4 people

2 tblsp butter
1 stalk celery, chopped
2 large onions, chopped
3¾ cups homemade chicken stock
    (hot)
8oz unsweetened chestnut puree
Salt and freshly ground black pepper
    to taste
4 rashers bacon, de-rinded

Put the butter, celery and onions into a 3 quart casserole dish; cover with a lid and microwave on Full Power for 4 minutes. Stir. Mix 1¼ cups stock with the chestnut puree, in a 2½ pint mixing bowl. Stir into the onion mixture. Season

with salt and black pepper; cover and microwave on Full Power for 7 minutes. Stir in the remaining stock and microwave on Full Power for 20 minutes. Allow to stand whilst preparing the bacon. Arrange the bacon on a microwave roasting rack, or on 2 sheets of absorbent kitchen paper. Microwave, uncovered, on Full Power, for about 3 minutes. Serve the soup sprinkled with the crumbled crispy bacon.

Tomato Baskets

PREPARATION TIME: 5 minutes
MICROWAVE TIME: 5½-6½ minutes
SERVES: 6 people

6 large firm tomatoes
8oz packet frozen mixed vegetables
4 tblsp butter
Salt and freshly ground black pepper
    to taste
Few sprigs of fresh mint

Cut the top off each tomato and reserve. Using a grapefruit knife or a teaspoon, carefully scoop out the centre flesh. (Use in a soup or sauce recipe). Pierce the pouch of frozen vegetables once and place in a dish. Microwave on Full Power for 3½ minutes, turning the bag once halfway through the cooking time. Set aside. Stand the prepared tomatoes upright on a serving dish, in a ring. Dot with half the butter.

Asparagus with Mayonnaise (top), Vegetable Soup (center) and Soured Cream Prawns (bottom).

Microwave on Full Power for about 2-3 minutes until very hot. Mix the drained, cooked vegetables with the remaining butter and salt and pepper and spoon into the tomato shells. Top with the reserved lids, and garnish with sprigs of mint. Serve immediately.

Quick Flat Bun Pizzas

PREPARATION TIME: 10 minutes
MICROWAVE TIME: 6½-7½ minutes
SERVES: 4 as a main meal, 8 as a snack

4 flat buns
1 medium onion, finely chopped
1¼ tsp tomato paste
1¼ tsp dried oregano
8oz can tomatoes, chopped
1¼ tsp French mustard
Salt and freshly ground black pepper to taste
1¼ cups Cheddar cheese, thinly sliced or grated
Stuffed olives, sliced

Tomato Baskets (right), Quick Flat Bun Pizzas (below) and Individual Frozen Pizza (far right).

Cut the flat buns in half and arrange in a ring on a suitable cooky sheet. Place the onion in a 2½ pint mixing bowl; cover and microwave for 1½ minutes on Full Power. Stir in the tomato paste, oregano, chopped tomatoes and the mustard. Season with salt and pepper. Divide among the flat buns, and cover with the cheese. Decorate with the sliced olives. Microwave on Power 4 for 5-6 minutes, until the cheese has melted. Serve immediately.

Garlic Prawn Starter

PREPARATION TIME: 30 minutes
MICROWAVE TIME: 20 minutes
SERVES: 4 people

1½lb zucchini, cleaned, topped and tailed
Salt and freshly ground black pepper to taste
12oz peeled prawns
1¼ tblsp chopped chives
2½ tblsp dry white wine
2 cloves garlic, crushed
1¼ tblsp lemon juice
4 tblsp butter

Garnish
Unpeeled prawns

Slice the zucchini thinly into a colander, sprinkling them generously with salt. Cover with a plate and weigh down; leave to stand for 20 minutes. Rinse well under cold running water. Drain thoroughly. Arrange the zucchini in

a vegetable dish. Season with salt and pepper. Cover and microwave on Full Power for 12 minutes. Stir. Set aside, covered. Put the peeled prawns, chives, wine, garlic, lemon juice and butter into a 2½ pint casserole dish . Cover with a lid. Microwave on Power 4, or Simmer, for 8 minutes. Stir once halfway through cooking time. Drain the excess liquid from the zucchini. Top with the heated prawns and their juices. Garnish with the unpeeled prawns and serve immediately.

Egg and Tuna Starter

PREPARATION TIME: 10 minutes	
MICROWAVE TIME: 10 minutes	
SERVES: 4 people	

7oz can tuna fish in oil, drained
2 hard boiled eggs, cooked
*   conventionally and chopped*
1 cup milk
2 tblsp butter
Salt and freshly ground black pepper
*   to taste*
¼ cup all purpose flour
1¼ tsp made mustard
½ cup grated Cheddar cheese

Garnish
Stuffed olives, sliced

Flake the tuna fish and divide between 4 ramekin dishes. Top with the egg. Melt the butter in a 1 litre jug for 1 minute on Full Power, or until very hot. Stir in the flour and gradually stir in the milk. Microwave on Full Power for 2 minutes. Beat well with a wire whisk. Microwave on Full Power for 2 minutes. Beat well with a wire whisk. Beat in salt and pepper and cheese. Divide the sauce among the ramekins. Garnish with sliced olives. Microwave all 4 ramekins together for 5 minutes on Power 4 or Simmer. Serve immediately.

Mackerel Pate

PREPARATION TIME: 10 minutes, plus chilling	
MICROWAVE TIME: 3 minutes	
SERVES: 6 people	

1 onion, finely chopped
4 tblsp butter
1½ cups cream cheese
2½ tblsp lemon juice
2½ tblsp chopped fresh parsley

¾lb smoked mackerel fillets
1¼ tsp coarse French mustard
Freshly ground black pepper to taste
4 tblsp soured cream
2½ tsp tomato paste

Garnish
Lemon wedges
Fresh parsley and cucumber slices

Put the onion into a soup bowl. Cover with plastic wrap and pierce. Microwave on Full Power for 1 minute. Set aside. Flake the fish into the food processor or blender goblet, discarding skin and bones. Add the onion. Place the butter in the bowl used for the onion and microwave on Power 4, or Simmer, for 2 minutes. Add to the processor or blender with all the remaining ingredients. Process or blend until smooth. Pour into a dampened loaf pan; smooth the surface. Chill until firm. Turn out onto a serving dish and garnish with wedges of lemon, crimped cucumber slices and parsley.

This page: Corn Starter (top), Garlic Prawn Starter (bottom).

Facing Page: Chestnut Soup (top left), Egg and Tuna Starter (top right) and Mackerel Pate (bottom).

95

MICROWAVE COOKING

Vegetables

All types of vegetables, both frozen and fresh, microwave exceptionally well. They keep their color, flavor and shape. Follow a few simple rules and use the charts to help you.

Helpful Hints
1. If you want to add salt, dissolve it in a little water beforehand. Adding salt can cause some vegetables to dry; to be on the safe side season with salt after cooking.
2. Always cover vegetables – roasta or freezer bags are very useful, but remember to pierce them.
3. Stir at least once during the cooking time or, if using a bag, turn it over.
4. Add only the amount of water necessary.
5. Cut the vegetables into even sized pieces.
6. Allow a standing time after cooking and before serving.
7. Cook frozen vegetables from frozen, do not defrost them first.

Fresh Vegetable Chart

VEGETABLE AND WEIGHT	ADDITION	MICROWAVE TIME	STANDING TIME
Sliced Green Beans 1lb	4 tblsp water	8 minutes	5 minutes
Broad Beans 1lb	4 tblsp water	8 minutes	5 minutes
Broccoli Spears 8ozs	4 tblsp water	7 minutes	4 minutes
Sliced Carrots 1lb	2½ tblsp water	7-8 minutes	4 minutes
Cauliflower Flowerets 1lb	4 tblsp water	7-8 minutes	5 minutes
Chopped Celery 8ozs		7 minutes	4 minutes
Zucchini 1lb	2 tblsp butter	10 minutes	3 minutes
Leeks 1lb	2½ tblsp water	7-8 minutes	3 minutes
Mushrooms (Sliced) 8ozs	2 tblsp butter	2 minutes	2 minutes
Sliced Summer Squash 1lb	2 tblsp butter	7 minutes	3 minutes
New Potatoes 1lb	2½ tblsp water	7 minutes	4 minutes
Old Potatoes 1lb	4 tblsp water	9 minutes	5 minutes
Sliced Onions 1lb	2½ tblsp water	8-9 minutes	4 minutes
Brussels Sprouts 1lb	2½ tblsp water	6-7 minutes	4 minutes
Diced Swede 1lb	2½ tblsp water	13 minutes	6 minutes

Baked Stuffed Summer Squash

PREPARATION TIME: 20 minutes
MICROWAVE TIME: 22 minutes
SERVES: 4 people

1 medium size summer squash
2 tblsp butter
1 onion, peeled and finely chopped
1lb raw, lean ground beef
2 tblsp all purpose flour
1½ tsp dried basil or oregano
1 egg, beaten
1 beef stock cube, crumbled
Salt and freshly ground black pepper to taste
1¼ tblsp tomato paste

Wipe the summer squash with a damp cloth. Cut both ends off the summer squash and keep on one side. Scoop out the seeds with a spoon and discard. Melt the butter in a 2 quart mixing bowl for 1 minute on Full Power. Stir in the onion. Microwave on Full Power for 1 minute. Stir in all the remaining ingredients. Mix well. Secure one end of the summer squash with wooden cocktail sticks. Stuff the summer squash with the mixture. Secure the remaining end in place with wooden cocktail sticks. Place the summer squash on a meat roasting rack and cover with plastic wrap. Pierce. Microwave on Full Power for about 20 minutes, turning the summer squash once halfway through cooking time. Allow to stand, covered with foil, for 5 minutes before serving. Cut into rings, and serve piping hot.

Brussels Sprouts with Chestnut and Bacon

PREPARATION TIME: 15 minutes
MICROWAVE TIME: 8 minutes
SERVES: 4 people

1lb fresh Brussels sprouts
1¼ tblsp lemon juice
1½ tsp dried mixed herbs
2½ tblsp cold water
Salt and freshly ground black pepper to taste
6 tblsp butter
8oz canned whole chestnuts, drained
3 rashers bacon, de-rinded, cooked and chopped (see Garlic Mushrooms recipe)

Peel the sprouts and make a cross in the base of each one. Put the sprouts into a 2½ pint casserole dish, or into a roasta bag. Add the lemon juice, herbs, water, and salt and pepper. Cover with a lid, or pierce the bag if used. Microwave on Full Power for 5 minutes. Stir or turn once, halfway through cooking time. Set aside for 5 minutes. Put the butter into a ¾ pint jug and microwave on Power 4 or Simmer until melted (about 3 minutes). If using a roasta bag, tip the sprouts into serving dish. Add the chestnuts to the Brussels sprouts, stirring gently. Cover with a lid. Microwave on Full Power for 1 minute. Coat with melted butter, sprinkle with chopped bacon, and serve.

Brussels Sprouts with Chestnut and Bacon (top), Carrot and Parsnip Puree (center) and Baked Stuffed Summer Squash (bottom).

Frozen Vegetable Chart

VEGETABLE AND WEIGHT	AMOUNT OF WATER	COOKING TIME	STANDING TIME
Asparagus 8ozs	2½ tblsp	7 minutes	5 minutes
Broccoli 8ozs	4 tblsp	10 minutes	5 minutes
Brussels Sprouts 8ozs	2½ tblsp	4 minutes	3 minutes
Carrots 8ozs	2½ tblsp	6 minutes	3 minutes
Cauli Flowerets 8ozs	2½ tblsp	3 minutes	2 minutes
Zucchini 8ozs	Nil	4 minutes	2 minutes
Leeks 8ozs	2½ tblsp	6-7 minutes	2 minutes
Mixed Vegetables 8ozs	2½ tblsp	4 minutes	3 minutes
Mushrooms 8ozs	2 tblsp butter and herbs	4 minutes	2 minutes
Baby Onions 8ozs	2 tblsp butter	5 minutes	4 minutes
Peas 8ozs	Nil	4 minutes	2 minutes
Spinach 8ozs	Nil	5 minutes	3 minutes
Corn 8ozs	Nil	4 minutes	2 minutes

Carrot and Parsnip Puree

PREPARATION TIME: 15 minutes
MICROWAVE TIME: 13 minutes
SERVES: 4 people

8oz carrots, peeled
8oz parsnips, peeled
1 level tsp dried basil
4 tblsp well-flavored stock
2½ tblsp heavy cream
Salt and freshly ground black pepper to taste
Pinch grated nutmeg

Garnish
Carrot curls

Dice the peeled carrots and parsnips and place in a roasta bag in a 2½ pint casserole dish. Add 2½ tblsp water and the basil. Snip the bag once at the base. Microwave on Full Power for 8 minutes, turning the bag over once halfway through cooking time. Set aside for 5 minutes. Empty the contents of the roasta bag into the goblet of a food processor or blender. Add the stock and process until smooth. Add cream, salt and pepper, and nutmeg. Process just to blend. Return to the casserole dish and cover with a lid. Microwave on Power 4, or Simmer, for 5 minutes. Garnish with carrot curls and serve.

Zucchini Choice

PREPARATION TIME: 40-45 minutes
COOKING TIME: 10 minutes
SERVES: 4 people

1lb young zucchini, topped, tailed and washed
Salt and freshly ground black pepper to taste
1lb large firm tomatoes, skinned and sliced
1 tsp dried tarragon
1 clove garlic, crushed
2 tblsp butter

Arrange the sliced zucchini in a colander. Sprinkle generously with salt and leave to stand for 30 minutes. (This draws out the bitter juices.) Rinse well under cold running water. Drain. Layer the zucchini and tomatoes in a 2½ pint casserole dish, starting and finishing with zucchini. Season each layer with salt, pepper, tarragon and garlic. Dot the top with small knobs of butter. Cover tightly with a lid. Microwave on Full Power for 10 minutes. Allow to stand for 3 minutes before serving.

Cauliflower Cheese

PREPARATION TIME: 10 minutes
MICROWAVE TIME: 12 minutes
SERVES: 4 people

1 cauliflower, trimmed and divided into flowerets
1½ tblsp cornstarch
1¼ cups milk
1¼ tsp made mustard
Salt and freshly ground black pepper to taste
¾ cup grated Cheddar cheese
2 tblsp butter
½ red pepper, de-seeded and chopped

Arrange the flowerets of cauliflower in a roasta bag. Add 3 tblsp water. Pierce the bag, and place in a 2½ pint casserole dish. Microwave on Full Power for 7-8 minutes, turning the bag over once halfway through cooking time. Set aside, covered. Cream the cornstarch with a little of the milk to a smooth paste. Stir in the mustard and salt and pepper to taste. Heat the remaining milk in a 2¼ pint jug for 2 minutes on Full Power. Pour the heated milk onto the cornstarch mixture, stirring continuously. Return to the jug and microwave on Full Power for 2 minutes or until boiling. Beat in the cheese and butter, and any liquid from the cauliflower. Transfer cauliflower flowerets to a warmed serving dish. Pour the sauce over evenly. Sprinkle with the red pepper and serve immediately. The red pepper may be heated in a cup in the microwave for 1 minute on Full Power, if liked.

Ratatouille

PREPARATION TIME: 40 minutes
MICROWAVE TIME: 22-24 minutes
SERVES: 4 people

½lb zucchini
1lb eggplant
Salt and freshly ground black pepper to taste
4 tblsp butter
1 medium onion, peeled and sliced
1 large clove garlic, crushed
A little oil
1 red pepper, de-seeded and sliced
15oz can tomatoes, chopped
½ tsp dried oregano
½ cup crumbled Danish Blue cheese

Wash the zucchini and eggplant. Cut off the ends and discard. Slice into ¼ inch slices and layer with a generous sprinkling of salt in a colander. Top with a plate and a weight and set aside to drain for 15 minutes. Rinse well under cold running water and drain. Put the butter in a 1¼ pint measuring jug. Microwave on Full Power for 1-2 minutes until melted. Stir in the onion and garlic. Grease the sides and base of a 2-3 quart casserole or souffle dish with oil. Layer the eggplant, zucchini and red pepper

Ratatouille (top), Zucchini Choice (center left) and Cauliflower Cheese (bottom).

in the dish with the tomatoes, oregano, onion and garlic. Season each layer with salt and pepper. Cover with a lid. Microwave on Full Power for 20-22 minutes, removing the lid for the last 8 minutes. Turn the dish ¼ turn twice during the cooking time, if necessary. Top with the crumbled cheese and serve immediately.

Buttery Mashed Potato

PREPARATION TIME: 10 minutes
MICROWAVE TIME: 17 minutes
SERVES: 4-5 people

2lb old potatoes, peeled
4 tblsp milk
4 tblsp butter
Salt and freshly ground black pepper to taste
2½ tblsp light cream
Chopped fresh parsley

Cut the potatoes into small, even sized pieces and put into a roasta bag with the milk and butter. Season. Secure the bag with an elastic band and stand in a 2 quart mixing bowl. Pierce the bag once at the base. Microwave on Full Power for 17 minutes, turning the bag over once halfway through the cooking time. Allow to stand for 5 minutes. Turn the potatoes and their liquid into the bowl and mash with a fork. Beat with a wooden spoon adding the cream. Turn into a serving dish. Fork up and sprinkle with the parsley. Serve.

Potatoes Gratinee

PREPARATION TIME: 20 minutes
MICROWAVE TIME: 26 minutes
SERVES: 4 people

1½lb old white potatoes, peeled and thinly sliced
1¼ cups pouring white sauce
½ cup grated cheese
4 tblsp milk
Salt and freshly ground black pepper to taste
2 tblsp butter
1 Recipe quantity of Crispy Topping (see recipe)

Soak the potato slices in cold water for a few minutes. Heat the sauce in a large jug for 1 minute on Full Power. Beat in the grated cheese, milk, and salt and pepper to taste. Grease a shallow dish with the butter. Arrange the drained potato slices, overlapping slightly, in the

Spinach Fiesta (top), Buttery Mashed Potato (far left) and Potatoes Gratinee (left).

base of the dish. Pour the sauce evenly over the top. Cover with plastic wrap and pierce. Microwave on Power 7, or Roast, for 25 minutes. Stir once, gently, halfway through cooking time. Serve after 5 minutes standing time, sprinkled with the crispy topping.

Stuffed Baked Peppers

PREPARATION TIME:	10 minutes
MICROWAVE TIME:	14½-15½ minutes
SERVES:	4 people

4 large even-sized peppers, about 8oz each
3 tblsp water
¾lb cooked chicken, pork or turkey
3 tblsp drained, canned corn kernels
5 tblsp soured cream
¾ cup chopped mushrooms
Salt and freshly ground black pepper to taste

Cut the tops off the peppers and reserve. Scoop out the seeds and discard them. Stand the peppers upright in an oblong or round casserole dish. Add the water; cover and microwave on Full Power for 3½ minutes. Set aside. Combine all the remaining ingredients to make the filling and mix well. Drain the water from the peppers and divide the filling among them. Replace the tops. Cover with plastic wrap and pierce. Microwave on Full Power for 11-12 minutes. Stand for 3 minutes before serving.

Garlic Mushrooms

PREPARATION TIME:	20 minutes
MICROWAVE TIME:	12½-14½ minutes
SERVES:	4 people

6 tblsp butter
2 cloves garlic, crushed
¾lb mushrooms, stalks removed
4 rashers bacon, de-rinded
1 cup cream cheese
Salt and freshly ground black pepper to taste
1½ tblsp natural yogurt or soured cream
¾ tsp dried parsley

Garnish
Chopped fresh parsley

Place the butter and garlic into a small bowl and microwave on Power 4, or Simmer, for 3 minutes, or until melted. Using a pastry brush, brush the mushrooms all over, inside and out, with the melted butter. Arrange on a dinner plate, or cooky sheet, in a circular fashion, leaving a space in the centre. Arrange the bacon on 2 sheets of absorbent kitchen paper, on a dinner plate, fat to outside. Cover with 1 piece absorbent kitchen paper. Microwave the bacon on Full Power for 2½-3 minutes. Set aside. Transfer the cream cheese to a 2½ pint mixing bowl. Microwave, uncovered, on Defrost for 2 minutes. Stir in salt and pepper to taste, yogurt, dried parsley and chopped bacon. Soften the chopped onion in a cup for 45 seconds on Full Power. Stir into the cream cheese mixture. Fill the mushrooms with the cheese mixture. Microwave, uncovered on Roast, or Power 7, for 4-6 minutes. Serve immediately garnished with chopped parsley, on croutons of fried bread.

Spinach Fiesta

PREPARATION TIME:	20 minutes
MICROWAVE TIME:	22 minutes
SERVES:	4 people

1¾ cups long grain rice
Salt and freshly ground black pepper to taste
3 frozen cod steaks
½lb frozen spinach
2 tblsp butter
3 tblsp milk
3 tblsp canned tuna fish, drained
½ cup Cheddar cheese, cubed
Chopped fresh parsley

Put the rice into a 2-3 quart mixing bowl. Pour on 1¼ pints boiling water. Add ¾ tsp salt. Cover lightly with plastic wrap and pierce once in the centre. Microwave on Full Power for 12 minutes. Set aside. Snip the fish packets open and microwave all 3 together, arranged on a dinner plate in a ring, for 6 minutes on Defrost. Turn each packet over, halfway through cooking. Set aside. Pierce the packet of spinach and place in a vegetable dish. Microwave on Full Power for 6 minutes. Set aside. Slip the cod steaks out of their packets and arrange on a pie plate in a ring. Dot with butter. Season and spoon over the milk. Cover with plastic wrap and pierce. Microwave on Full Power for 4 minutes. Drain the spinach. Chop and fork into the cooked rice. Add the tuna fish to the rice with the cheese. Drain the cooked cod and flake into the rice. Pile onto a warmed dish and serve, sprinkled with plenty of chopped parsley.

JACKET POTATOES WITH FILLINGS

Plain Jacket Potatoes

PREPARATION TIME:	15-20 minutes
MICROWAVE TIME:	15 minutes
SERVES:	4 people

4 x 7oz potatoes, scrubbed clean

Prick the potatoes with a fork and arrange in a ring on a dinner plate. Microwave uncovered, on Full Power, for 15 minutes. Wrap in a clean tea towel and set aside for 10-15 minutes. (The potatoes will continue to cook). Meanwhile prepare one of the fillings (all fillings serve 4 people).

Cottage Cheese with Prawns and Chives

Instead of pricking the potatoes, make a cross in the top of each one before baking.
2 cups cottage cheese
2 tblsp chopped chives
1 cup peeled prawns
2 tblsp soured cream
1½ tsp tomato paste
Sliced cucumber and whole prawns to garnish

Blend all the ingredients together, apart from the cucumber and prawns. Using a cloth, carefully push up each hot potato from the base, to form a water lily. Divide the filling between the potatoes. Garnish with the cucumber and whole prawns before serving.

Pilchards with Corn

3 tblsp natural yogurt or mayonnaise
Salt and freshly ground black pepper to taste
12oz pilchards in tomato sauce
4 tblsp drained canned corn kernels
4 scallions, chopped

Cut the potatoes in half and carefully scoop out the flesh, leaving the skin intact. Put the potato flesh into a 2 quart mixing bowl. Mash well with a fork, adding the yogurt or mayonnaise and salt and pepper to taste. Open each pilchard and remove the backbone. Flake the pilchards into the potato mix well, adding the corn and chopped scallions. Pile the mixture back into the potato shells. Arrange in a serving dish. Cover with plastic wrap. Microwave on Full Power for 4 minutes.

Baked Beans with Edam Cheese

16oz can baked beans in tomato sauce
2 cups Edam cheese, cubed
Salt and freshly ground black pepper to taste

Garnish
Watercress

Empty the beans into a 2 pint casserole dish. Add the cheese and salt and pepper to taste. Cover with a lid and microwave on Power 7, or Roast, for 2½ minutes. Stir gently. Microwave on Power 7, or Roast, for 2½ minutes. Halve the potatoes after their standing time. Spoon the beans and cheese onto the potatoes. Garnish with watercress and serve.

Stuffed Baked Peppers (top), Jacket Potatoes with Fillings (center) and Garlic Mushroom (bottom).

Supper Dishes

Shish Kebabs

PREPARATION TIME: 10 minutes

MICROWAVE TIME: 8 minutes

SERVES: 3-4 people

12oz raw ground lamb
1 onion, finely chopped
2½ tsp lemon juice
3 tsp hot curry powder
1½ tblsp soured cream
½ egg, beaten
¼ cup all purpose flour
3 tblsp finely chopped fresh parsley
½ tsp salt
2 tblsp tomato sauce

Mix all the ingredients together. Form the mixture into small balls. Arrange the meatballs on a microwave roasting rack in a ring. Microwave, uncovered, on Power 7, or Roast, for 8 minutes. Serve hot with yogurt sauce.

Yogurt Sauce

PREPARATION TIME: 5 minutes

SERVES: 4 people

⅔ cup natural yogurt
1½ tsp granular mustard
3 tsp tomato paste
1½ tsp concentrated mint sauce
1½ tsp lemon juice
1½ tsp superfine sugar
2½ tblsp soured cream

Mix all the ingredients together until well blended. Refrigerate until required. Serve with Shish Kebabs.

Pasta Shells with Cheese and Bacon

PREPARATION TIME: 15 minutes

MICROWAVE TIME: 24 minutes

SERVES: 4 people

6oz dried pasta shapes
½ tsp salt
1¼ tblsp oil
8oz packet frozen mixed vegetables
1¼ tsp cornstarch
1¼ cups milk
1¼ tsp made mustard

Salt and freshly ground black pepper to taste
¾ cup grated mild hard cheese
2 bacon chops
1 Recipe Crispy Topping (see recipe)

Place the pasta in a 3-4 quart mixing bowl. Add the salt and the oil. Pour on 2 quarts boiling water. Cover tightly with plastic wrap and pierce once in the centre. Microwave on Full Power for 8 minutes. Set aside, covered. Microwave the pierced packet of vegetables in a suitable dish, for 4 minutes on Full Power, turning the packet over once halfway through the cooking time. Blend the cornstarch with 1½ tblsp milk until smooth. Put the remaining milk into a 2¼ pint jug and microwave on Full Power for 3 minutes. Beat the blended cornstarch into the hot milk together with the mustard and salt and pepper to taste. Microwave on Full Power for 2 minutes. Beat well adding the cheese. Microwave the bacon chops on 2 sheets of absorbent kitchen paper (with the fat facing outwards). Microwave on Roast for 4 minutes. To assemble the dish: drain the pasta and pile onto a serving dish; drain the vegetables and add to the pasta; chop the bacon and mix into the pasta and vegetables. Pour the cheese sauce evenly over the top and top with crispy crumbs. Microwave on Power 5, or Roast, for 3 minutes. Serve immediately.

Fish Fingers

PREPARATION TIME: 5 minutes

MICROWAVE TIME: 14 minutes

SERVES: 3-4 people

2½ tblsp cooking oil
8 frozen cod fish fingers

Preheat a large browning dish, without a lid, for 7 minutes, on Full Power. Put the oil into the heated dish. Microwave on Full Power for 1 minute. Carefully press the fish fingers into the oil. Microwave, uncovered, on Full Power for 3

minutes. Turn each fish finger over and microwave on Full Power for 3-4 minutes. Drain on absorbent kitchen paper and serve immediately (brown side uppermost).

Crispy Topping

PREPARATION TIME: 10 minutes

MICROWAVE TIME: 8 minutes

5 tblsp butter
1 cup fresh brown breadcrumbs
½ cup oatmeal

Put the butter into a 2 quart mixing bowl and microwave on Full Power for 1½ minutes. Stir in the breadcrumbs and oatmeal. Microwave on Full Power for 2½ minutes. Stir with a fork. Microwave on Full Power for 2 minutes. Stir. Microwave on Full Power for 2 minutes. Allow to stand for 5 minutes before using. Alternatively, the topping may be cooled and stored in an air tight container. Serve as a crispy finish for sweet and savory dishes.

Kidney and Sausage Supper Dish

PREPARATION TIME: 20 minutes

MICROWAVE TIME: 18 minutes

SERVES: 4 people

1lb chipolata sausages
2½ tblsp oil
8oz lambs' kidneys, skinned, halved and cored
3 tblsp tomato sauce
1½ tblsp Worcestershire sauce
Salt and freshly ground black pepper to taste
4 large, ripe tomatoes, skinned and chopped
8oz frozen peas
2½ tsp cornstarch

Preheat the deep browning dish, without the lid, for 4-7 minutes according to size. Prick the sausages and cut into 1 inch pieces. Add the oil and the pieces of sausage to the preheated dish, pressing the sausage against the sides of the browning dish. Microwave on Full

Power for 2 minutes. Stir in the kidneys, tomato sauce and Worcestershire sauce. Cover with the lid and microwave on Power 7, or on Roast, for 5 minutes. Season with salt and pepper and stir in the tomatoes and peas. Mix the cornstarch to a smooth paste with 5 tblsp water and stir in. Microwave on Full Power for 2 minutes. Stir. Microwave on Full Power for a further 2 minutes. Stir and serve immediately.

Cowboy Supper

PREPARATION TIME: 15 minutes

MICROWAVE TIME: 13 minutes

SERVES: 4 people

16oz can baked beans
7oz can corned beef, chilled
Freshly ground black pepper to taste
½ beef stock cube, crumbled
½ cup Cheddar cheese, cubed
1 French loaf

Empty the baked beans into a 2 quart casserole dish. Cover with a lid. Microwave on Power 6 for 5 minutes. Gently stir in the corned beef and season with pepper. Add the stock cube. Cover and microwave on Power 6 for 5 minutes. Add the cheese just before serving.
To warm the bread, cut the bread into pieces and arrange in a bread basket, between absorbent paper napkins. Microwave on Power 4, or Simmer, for 3 minutes. Serve immediately.

Shish Kebabs with Yogurt Sauce (top), Pasta Shells with Cheese and Bacon (center right) and Kidney and Sausage Supper Dish (bottom).

Poached Eggs on Cheese on Toast

PREPARATION TIME: 10 minutes

MICROWAVE TIME: about 10 minutes

SERVES: 4 people

4 eggs
Salt and freshly ground black pepper to taste
Softened butter
4 slices toast
1¼ cups grated cheese
Chopped chives

Put 1½ tblsp cold water into each of the 4 hollows of a microwave muffin pan or into 4 ramekin dishes. If using ramekins, arrange them in a ring on a dinner plate.

Microwave on Full Power until the water boils. Carefully crack 1 egg into each hollow or dish. Prick each yolk once with a cocktail stick. Season with salt and pepper. Microwave on Simmer for about 4 minutes until the whites are just set. Leave aside. Butter the toast and top with the grated cheese. Microwave on Power 5, or Simmer, for about 4 minutes until melted. Slide the toasted cheese onto a serving dish and place an egg on top of each one. Sprinkle with chopped chives and serve immediately.

Cod and Prawn Supper Dish

PREPARATION TIME: 15 minutes

MICROWAVE TIME: 15½ minutes

SERVES: 4 people

4 x 3oz frozen cod steaks, thawed
4 tblsp butter
Salt and freshly ground black pepper to taste
¼ cup flour
1¼ cups milk
¾ cup grated Cheddar cheese
1 cup peeled prawns
1 Recipe Crispy Topping (see recipe)

Garnish
Tomato wedges
Parsley

Arrange the fish steaks in a ring on a dinner plate. Divide half the butter into 4; put a small knob onto each fish steak. Season with salt and pepper and cover with plastic wrap. Microwave on Full Power for 3½ minutes. Set aside. Microwave the remaining butter in a 2¼ pint jug for 1 minute on Full Power. Stir in the flour and then gradually stir in the milk; season to taste. Microwave on Full Power for 2 minutes. Beat well. Microwave on Full Power for a further 2 minutes. Beat in the cheese. Cut the fish into bite-size pieces and arrange in a suitable dish with the prawns. Pour the sauce evenly over the fish. Sprinkle with the crispy crumbs. Microwave on Power 4 for 7 minutes. Serve immediately, garnished with tomato and parsley.

Chicken with Ham

PREPARATION TIME: 15 minutes

MICROWAVE TIME: 13 minutes

SERVES: 4 people

3 cups cooked chicken, roughly chopped
1 cup cooked ham, chopped
5 tblsp drained canned corn kernels with peppers
2 tblsp butter
4 tblsp flour
Salt and freshly ground black pepper to taste
1¼ cups well flavored chicken stock
¾ cup grated cheese
4 tblsp light cream

Garnish
Sliced tomato and parsley

Arrange the chicken, ham and corn in a suitable dish. Melt the butter in a large jug for about 1 minute on Full Power. Stir in the flour and salt and pepper to taste. Stir in a little of the stock, blending it in well. Add the remaining stock. Microwave on Full Power for 2 minutes. Beat well with a wire whisk. Microwave on Full Power for 2 minutes. Beat well. Beat in the cheese and the cream. Pour the sauce evenly over the meat. Microwave on Power 4, or Simmer, for about 8 minutes. Serve immediately, garnished with the tomato and parsley.

Sweet and Sour Pork

PREPARATION TIME: 25 minutes

MICROWAVE TIME: 29 minutes

SERVES: 4 people

1¼ tblsp oil
½ red pepper, de-seeded and chopped
1 carrot, peeled and cut into strips
1 large onion, sliced
4 inch cucumber, seeded and cut into strips
1 stalk celery, chopped
1lb pork fillet, cubed
14oz can pineapple pieces in natural juice
2½ tblsp soya sauce

Fish Fingers (top right), Poached Eggs on Cheese on Toast (far left) and Chicken with Ham (left).

2½ tsp tomato paste
1¼ tblsp wine vinegar
Salt and freshly ground black pepper
   to taste
2½ tsp cornstarch

Preheat the deep browning dish
without the lid for 4-7 minutes

according to size on Full Power. Put
the oil, pepper, carrot, onion,
cucumber and celery into the dish.
Stir well. Cover and Microwave on
Full Power for 4 minutes. Stir in all
remaining ingredients, apart from
the cornstarch. Cover and
microwave on Full Power for 3

minutes and then on Power 4, or
Simmer, for 20 minutes. Cream the
cornstarch with a little water and
stir into the pork mixture.
Microwave on Full Power for 2
minutes. Stir and then serve
immediately on a bed of rice.

**Cowboy Supper (top) and
Sweet and Sour Pork (bottom).**

MICROWAVE COOKING
Fish Dishes

Plaice with Lemon

PREPARATION TIME: 12-15 minutes

MICROWAVE TIME: 9 minutes

SERVES: 4 people

4 plaice fillets (about 3½oz each), skinned
Salt and freshly ground black pepper to taste
Juice of ½ a lemon
3 tblsp milk
1 cup mushrooms, sliced
2 tblsp butter
½ cup soured cream

Lay the plaice fillets out flat; season with salt and pepper and sprinkle with lemon juice. Roll up and secure with wooden cocktail sticks. Arrange the fillets close together in a dish and spoon over the milk; cover and microwave on Full Power for 5 minutes. Set aside. Put the mushrooms and butter into a small dish. Cover and microwave on Full Power for 2 minutes. Add the soured cream and stir in the juices from the fish. Microwave on Full Power for 2 minutes. Arrange the fish on a warmed serving dish. Pour over the sauce and serve immediately.

Curried Prawns with Chicken

PREPARATION TIME: 15 minutes

MICROWAVE TIME: about 22 minutes

SERVES: 4 people

4 tblsp butter
1 medium onion, finely chopped
5 tsp flour
5 tsp mild curry powder
2½ tsp tomato paste
3¾ cups boiling chicken stock
1¼ tblsp apple chutney
1 banana, thinly sliced
¼ cup raisins
Salt and freshly ground black pepper to taste
8oz peeled prawns
8oz cooked chicken, chopped
2½ tblsp lemon juice

Place the butter in a 3 quart

casserole dish. Microwave on Full Power for 1-2 minutes. Stir in the onion. Microwave on Full Power for 1½ minutes. Stir in the flour and curry powder. Microwave on Full Power for 2 minutes. Stir in the tomato paste and gradually add the stock. Add the apple chutney,

banana, raisins and salt and pepper to taste. Cover and microwave on Full Power for 12 minutes. Stir in the peeled prawns, chicken and lemon juice. Microwave on Full Power for 3-4 minutes.

Curried Prawns with Chicken (top left), Scampi Italienne (top right) and Plaice with Lemon (bottom).

Scampi Italienne

PREPARATION TIME: 10 minutes
MICROWAVE TIME: 10 minutes
SERVES: 4 people

½ red pepper, de-seeded and sliced
½ green pepper, de-seeded and sliced
4 tblsp butter
1 small onion, finely chopped
1 clove garlic, crushed
⅔ cup dry white wine
1½ tblsp lemon juice
Salt and freshly ground black pepper
　to taste
1lb frozen shelled scampi, thawed

Garnish
Lemon butterflies
Savory

Put the red and green peppers, butter, onion and the garlic into a 2 quart casserole dish. Cover with the lid. Microwave on Full Power for 3 minutes. Stir in the white wine, lemon juice, salt and pepper to taste and the scampi. Cover and microwave on Full Power for 6-7 minutes, stirring once halfway through. Serve immediately, garnished with lemon butterflies and savory.

Special Fish Pie

PREPARATION TIME: 15 minutes
MICROWAVE TIME: 15 minutes
SERVES: 4 people

1lb young leeks, washed and cut into
　1½ inch lengths
4 large, firm tomatoes, skinned and
　sliced
3 tsp mixed dried herbs
2 tblsp butter
Salt and freshly ground black pepper
　to taste
¾lb cod, skinned and filleted
3 tblsp frozen corn kernels, thawed
½ cup grated Cheddar cheese
1½ tblsp tomato sauce
1lb potatoes, peeled, cooked and
　mashed

Arrange the leeks and tomatoes in the base of a casserole dish; sprinkle with half the herbs. Dot the butter over the surface and season well with salt and pepper. Cover and microwave on Full Power for 5 minutes. Cut the fish into 1 inch pieces. Arrange evenly over the vegetables and season once again. Cover and microwave on Full Power for 7 minutes. Drain

off excess liquid and add the corn. Add the cheese, tomato sauce and remaining herbs to the potato; beat well. Pile or pipe the potato on top of the fish and vegetables. Microwave, uncovered, on Full Power for about 3 minutes. Brown under a pre-heated broiler, if desired, and serve immediately.

Mackerel with Apple Sauce

PREPARATION TIME: 30 minutes
MICROWAVE TIME: 15 minutes
SERVES: 4 people

4 fresh mackerel, heads and fins
　removed, and filleted (approx. 6oz
　per fish)
1 cup fresh brown breadcrumbs
1 eating apple, peeled, cored and
　chopped
½ cup shredded suet
1½ tsp lemon juice
3 tsp finely chopped fresh parsley
1 onion, peeled and finely chopped
Salt and freshly ground black pepper
　to taste
1 egg, beaten
3 tblsp apple juice

Sauce
1½lb cooking and eating apples
　(mixed), peeled, cored and sliced
2½ tsp lemon juice
3 tsp superfine sugar
1 tblsp butter

Put the breadcrumbs, apple, suet, lemon juice, parsley and onion into a mixing bowl. Season to taste with salt and pepper. Mix with the beaten egg to bind. Divide the stuffing among the fish, pressing it well into each cavity. Make an incision with a sharp knife in the thickest side of each fish. Arrange the fish, nose to tail, in a shallow dish. Pour over the apple juice. Cover tightly with plastic wrap and pierce. Microwave on Full Power for 8 minutes. Stand on one side while preparing the sauce. Put the apples into a 2 quart mixing bowl with the lemon juice and sugar. Cover. Microwave on Full Power for 6-7 minutes. Allow to stand for 3 minutes. Beat together with the butter and the juices from the cooked fish. Serve immediately with the fish.

Trout with Almonds

PREPARATION TIME: 10 minutes
MICROWAVE TIME: about
　　　　　　　　　19 minutes
SERVES: 4 people

4 rainbow trout, cleaned and gutted
　(approx 8oz per fish)
5 tblsp butter
1 clove garlic, crushed
Salt and freshly ground black pepper
　to taste
1 cup heavy cream
½ cup flaked almonds

Garnish
Fresh parsley

Use a very small amount of foil to mask the tail of each fish. Make 2 incisions in the thick side of each fish. Put 4 tblsp of the butter into a suitable shallow dish and microwave on Full Power for 1½ minutes. Stir the garlic and salt and pepper into the butter. Arrange the fish, nose to tail, in the flavored butter. Cover with plastic wrap and pierce. Microwave on Full Power for 8 minutes. Turn each fish over once during cooking. Stand aside, covered. Put the almonds and the remaining butter into a soup bowl. Microwave on Full Power for 2 minutes. Stir. Microwave on Full Power for a further 2 minutes. Pour the cream over the fish, and microwave on Power 4 or, Simmer, for 5 minutes. Serve immediately sprinkled with the toasted nuts and garnished with parsley.

Devilled Herrings

PREPARATION TIME: 15-20
　　　　　　　　　minutes
MICROWAVE TIME: 6-7 minutes
SERVES: 4 people

2½ tblsp dry mustard
1¼ tblsp brown sugar
1¼ tblsp malt vinegar
4 fresh herrings, about 8oz each
½ cup white wine
1 medium onion, finely chopped
1½ tblsp finely chopped fresh parsley
Salt and freshly ground black pepper
　to taste
2 tblsp butter

Blend together the mustard, sugar and vinegar. Cut the heads and the tails off the fish and remove the back-bones; flatten each fish. Spread the mustard mixture inside

the herrings and roll up. Secure with cocktail sticks. Arrange the fish in a suitable dish. Add the wine, parsley and salt and pepper to taste. Dot with butter. Cover tightly with plastic wrap or a lid. Pierce if using plastic wrap. Microwave on Full Power for 6-7 minutes. Stand for 3 minutes before serving.

Smoked Haddock with Scrambled Eggs

PREPARATION TIME: 5-10
　　　　　　　　　minutes
MICROWAVE TIME: 11 minutes
SERVES: 3-4 people

1lb smoked haddock fillet
Salt and freshly ground black pepper
　to taste
⅔ cup milk
4 tblsp butter
4 eggs
1½ tblsp finely chopped fresh parsley

Arrange the fish in a shallow container. Season with salt and pepper and add 2½ tblsp of the milk. Dot the fish with half the butter. Cover with plastic wrap and pierce. Microwave on Full Power for 7 minutes. Set aside, covered. Make the scrambled egg: beat the eggs with the remaining milk in a 2 quart mixing bowl; season to taste and add the remaining butter. Microwave on Full Power for 2 minutes; beat well, using a wire whisk. Microwave on Full Power for 2 minutes until light and fluffy. Carefully arrange the fish on a serving dish. Spoon the scrambled eggs either side of the fish. Sprinkle with the chopped parsley and serve immediately.

Special Fish Pie (top), Mackerel with Apple Sauce (center) and Trout with Almonds (bottom).

Prawns Creole

PREPARATION TIME: 15 minutes
MICROWAVE TIME: 18 minutes
SERVES: 4 people

1¾ cups long grain rice
2½ cups boiling chicken stock
2 medium size onions, chopped
½ red pepper, de-seeded and chopped
½ green pepper, de-seeded and chopped

8oz peeled prawns
15oz can pineapple segments in natural juice, drained
¼ cup seedless raisins
Salt and freshly ground black pepper to taste

Put the rice into a 2-3 quart mixing bowl. Pour on the boiling stock. Cover tightly with plastic wrap and pierce once in the centre. Microwave on Full Power for 12 minutes. Set aside, covered with a clean tea towel. Put the onion and red and green pepper into a 2 pint mixing bowl. Cover with plastic wrap and pierce. Microwave on Full Power for 3 minutes. Stir. Fork up the rice after 10 minutes standing time, and add the onions, peppers, prawns, pineapple, raisins and salt and pepper. Cover with plastic wrap and pierce. Microwave on Full Power for 3 minutes to reheat. Serve immediately.

Smoked Haddock with
Scrambled Eggs (below left),
Prawns Creole (below) and
Devilled Herrings (below
right).

MICROWAVE COOKING

Meat Dishes

Sausagemeat Stuffing

PREPARATION TIME: 15 minutes

MICROWAVE TIME: 10 minutes

SERVES: 4 people

1lb pork sausagemeat
¾ cup parsley and thyme mixed
1¼ tblsp tomato sauce
1¼ tsp made mustard
1 small onion, finely chopped
Salt and freshly ground black pepper
*   to taste*
⅔ cup boiling water

Put the sausagemeat into a 2 quart mixing bowl. Add all the remaining ingredients. Leave to stand for 3 minutes. Knead toether until well mixed. Using dampened hands, form the sausagemeat mixture into 20 balls. Arrange on a large roasting rack, or in a ring on a large circular dish, on 2 sheets of absorbent kitchen paper. Microwave on Power 7, or Roast, for 10 minutes.

Savory Ground Meat with Dumplings

PREPARATION TIME: 20 minutes

MICROWAVE TIME: 23 minutes

SERVES: 4 people

2 rashers bacon, de-rinded and
*   chopped*
1 medium onion, chopped
½ green pepper, de-seeded and
*   chopped*
1½lb raw ground beef or pork
1 beef stock cube, crumbled
1 tsp mixed dried herbs
⅔ cup water
1½ tsp chive mustard
Salt and freshly ground black pepper
*   to taste*
16oz can navy beans (or white
*   kidney beans)*

Dumplings
1 cup all purpose flour
1½ tsp baking powder
½ cup suet
½ tsp dried tarragon

Put the bacon, onion and pepper into a soup bowl. Cover with plastic wrap and pierce. Microwave

on Full Power for 2 minutes. Put the ground meat into a 2 quart casserole dish. Microwave on Full Power for 4 minutes. Break down with a fork and stir in the onion mixture, stock cube, herbs, water and mustard. Season well with salt and pepper. Microwave on Power 6, or Roast, for 12 minutes. Stir in the beans. Set aside. To prepare the dumplings: mix together the flour, baking powder, suet and tarragon. Bind with sufficient cold water to make an elastic dough. Divide into 6 dumplings and arrange on top of the ground meat. Cover with a lid and microwave on Power 7 for 4-5 minutes. Stand for 3 minutes before serving.

Mixed Meat Loaf

PREPARATION TIME: 30 minutes

MICROWAVE TIME: 27 minutes

SERVES: 6-8 people

1 clove garlic
6oz lean bacon, de-rinded
1lb raw ground beef
8oz raw ground pork
6oz lambs' liver, finely chopped
6oz Canadian bacon, de-rinded and
*   finely chopped*
½ cup shredded suet
½ cup fresh brown breadcrumbs
½ tsp dried oregano
½ tsp mixed dried herbs
Salt and freshly ground black pepper
*   to taste*
4 tblsp sherry
1 egg, beaten

Glaze
2½ tblsp apricot jam or marmalade,
*   sieved*
1 tsp French mustard
½ tsp meat and vegetable extract

Rub a 2 quart plastic meat loaf pan with the clove of garlic. Lay the bacon in the meat loaf pan to line the base and the sides. In a large mixing bowl, mix the ground beef with the pork, liver, Canadian bacon, suet, breadcrumbs and herbs. Season to taste. Beat together the sherry and the egg; add to the mixture and bind together. Transfer to the prepared loaf pan. Smooth the top. Cover

and microwave on Power 6, or Roast, for 27 minutes. Turn the dish ½ a turn twice during this time. Allow to stand for 10 minutes. Pour off the excess fat and carefully unmold the loaf. Mix all ingredients together for the glaze and brush over the top and sides of the meat loaf. Delicious hot or cold.

Cheesey Beef Cobbler

PREPARATION TIME: 30 minutes

MICROWAVE TIME: 20 minutes

SERVES: 4 people

1lb raw ground beef
1 onion, chopped
8oz can tomatoes, chopped
1 beef stock cube, crumbled
1¼ tblsp bottled brown sauce
Celery salt and freshly ground black
*   pepper to taste*
2½ tblsp frozen peas

Scone Topping
2 cups flour, sieved with 1½ tsp
*   baking powder*
4 tblsp margarine or butter, chilled
½ cup grated Cheddar cheese
1 tsp mixed dried herbs
1 egg, mixed with ½ cup milk
1½ tsp meat and vegetable extract

Put the ground meat and onion into a 7 inch souffle dish. Cover and microwave on Full Power for 4 minutes. Stir well with a fork. Stir in the toatoes, stock cube, brown sauce and celery salt and pepper. Cover and microwave on Power 7, or Roast, for 10 minutes. Stir in the peas and set aside. Put the flour and baking powder into a 2 quart mixing bowl. Blend in the margarine or butter. Mix in the cheese and herbs. Add the beaten egg and milk and mix to a soft dough. Knead lightly. Roll the dough out to a thickness of ½ inch. Using a 2 inch pastry cutter, cut the dough into scones. Arrange the scones on top of the ground meat. Cook, uncovered, on Full Power for 6 minutes. Serve immediately. Note: to improve the color of the scones mix the meat and vegetable

extract with a little water and use to brush the scones prior to cooking.

Lamb Curry

PREPARATION TIME: 20 minutes

MICROWAVE TIME: about 45 minutes

SERVES: 4 people

2 carrots, peeled and chopped
1 medium onion, chopped
2 tblsp butter
¼ cup all purpose flour
4-5 tsp mild curry powder
1lb lamb fillet, cubed
1¾ cups boiling chicken stock
1¼ tblsp shredded coconut
¼ cup white raisins
1 medium sized eating apple, peeled,
*   cored and chopped*
1 peach, peeled, stoned and roughly
*   chopped*
1¼ tomato paste
2½ tblsp lemon juice
Salt and freshly ground black pepper
*   to taste*

Preheat a large browning dish, without the lid, for 3 minutes on Full Power. Put the carrots, onion and butter into the preheated dish. Microwave on Full Power for 2 minutes, covered. Stir in the flour, curry powder and meat. Microwave on Full Power for 4 minutes. Gradually add the stock, stirring all the time. Stir in the coconut, white raisins, apple, peach, tomato paste, lemon juice and seasoning to taste. Cover and

Lamb Curry (top left), Savory Ground Meat with Dumplings (top right) and Mixed Meat Loaf (bottom).

microwave on Full Power for 7 minutes. Stir. Microwave on Power 4, Simmer or Defrost, for 30-35 minutes. Stir twice during this time. Serve immediately.

Pasta with Pork and Liver

PREPARATION TIME: 15 minutes
MICROWAVE TIME: 25 minutes
SERVES: 4 people

2½ tblsp oil
1 medium onion, sliced
12oz raw ground pork
4oz chicken livers, ground
1 cup mushrooms, chopped
8oz can tomatoes, chopped
4 tblsp sherry
Salt and freshly ground black pepper to taste
1 beef stock cube, crumbled

6oz dried pasta shells
Chopped fresh parsley

Heat the browning dish, without the lid, for 4-6 minutes on Full Power, according to size. Put half the oil, the onion and ground meats into the preheated dish. Stir well. Microwave on Full Power for 4 minutes. Stir in all the remaining ingredients, apart from the pasta and the parsley. Cover with the li and microwave on Full Power for minutes. Stir. Microwave, covered on Power 5, or Simmer, for 10 minutes. Allow to stand whilst preparing the pasta. To cook the pasta, place the remaining oil and the pasta into a 3-4 quart bowl. Add 2 quarts water and ½ tsp sal to the pasta. Cover and microwav on Full Power for 8 minutes. Allo to stand for 5 minutes. Drain the pasta and arrange on a serving dis Spoon the meat sauce evenly over the pasta, and garnish with chopped parsley. Serve immediately.

Pasta with Pork and Liver (far left), Cheesey Beef Cobbler (below) and Sausagemeat Stuffing (below right).

117

Chicken Breasts in Garlic Cream Sauce

PREPARATION TIME: 10 minutes

MICROWAVE TIME: 17 minutes

SERVES: 4 people

4 tblsp butter
1 clove garlic, crushed
1 medium onion, sliced
2 rashers bacon, de-rinded and
   chopped
½ cup mushrooms, sliced
½ tsp dried basil
Salt and freshly ground black pepper
   to taste
4 chicken breasts, skinned and boned
   (about 5oz each)
1 cup heavy cream

Garnish
Savory
Toasted flaked almonds

Melt the butter in a 2 quart casserole dish for 1-2 minutes on Full Power. Stir in the garlic, onion, bacon, mushrooms, basil and salt and pepper to taste. Cover and microwave on Full Power for 2 minutes. Arrange the chicken breasts on top of the vegetables. Cover and microwave on Power 7, or Roast, for 10 minutes. Season the cream and pour evenly over the top to coat. Garnish with savory and almonds. Serve immediately.

Chicken Casserole

PREPARATION TIME: 15 minutes

MICROWAVE TIME: about 40 minutes

SERVES: 4 people

4 chicken portions, skinned (about
   8oz each)
2 tblsp butter
1 onion, finely chopped
2 stalks celery, chopped
2 carrots, chopped
2 tblsp drained canned corn kernels
2 tsp cornstarch
1¼ cups chicken stock
Salt and paprika to taste

Put the butter into a 3 quart casserole dish. Microwave on Full Power for 1 minute. Stir in the onion, celery and carrots. Cover with a lid and microwave on Full Power for 3 minutes. Pour the stock into the casserole, and add salt to taste. Arrange the chicken pieces on top of the vegetables, keeping the thickest part to the outside of the dish. Sprinkle each chicken piece with a little paprika. Microwave, covered, on Full Power for 4 minutes. Stir. Microwave on Power 4, Simmer or Defrost, for a further 30 minutes. Using a draining spoon, transfer the chicken to a warmed serving dish. Cover with a piece of foil and set aside. Cream the cornstarch with a little water and stir into the casserole dish. Microwave on Full Power for 2-3 minutes, until boiling and thickened. Stir in the corn. Serve the chicken pieces with the vegetable sauce spooned over the top.

Sausage Suet Pudding

PREPARATION TIME: 30 minutes

MICROWAVE TIME: 21 minutes

SERVES: 4 people

Filling
8oz pork sausages, cut into 1 inch
   pieces
8oz chicken livers, roughly chopped
¼ cup seasoned flour
1 tblsp oil
1 medium onion, chopped
½ green pepper, de-seeded and
   chopped
1¼ cups well flavored boiling stock
Salt and freshly ground black pepper
   to taste

Suet Pastry
2 cups all purpose flour
½ tsp salt
2 tsp baking powder
1 cup finely grated (or shredded) suet
⅔ cup water

Toss the sausages and chicken livers in the seasoned flour. Put the oil into a 2 quart mixing bowl. Microwave on Full Power for 2 minutes. Stir in the onion and green pepper. Microwave on Full Power for 2 minutes. Stir the chicken livers and sausage into the onion. Cover and microwave on Power 8, or Roast, for 5 minutes. Carefully stir in the boiling stock and salt and pepper to taste. Microwave on Full Power for 2-3 minutes, until thickened. Stir and set aside while preparing the pastry. Sieve the flour, salt and baking powder into a bowl. Stir in the suet and mix to a soft dough with the water. Knead lightly. Roll out ⅔ of the pastry and use to line a greased 2 pint boilable plastic pudding basin. Roll the remaining pastry into a circle. Fill the pastry-lined basin with the filling mixture. Dampen the pastry rim with cold water and top with the circle of pastry. Seal edges. Cut a small slit in the top to allow the steam to escape. Cover loosely with absorbent kitchen paper or plastic wrap. Microwave on Power 7, or Roast, for 9 minutes. Stand for 5 minutes before serving.

Herby Roast Chicken

PREPARATION TIME: about 35 minutes

MICROWAVE TIME: about 36 minutes

SERVES: 6 people

¾ cup fresh brown breadcrumbs
½ cup shredded suet
1 tsp finely chopped fresh parsley
1 tsp finely chopped fresh tarragon
1 eating apple, peeled, cored and
   chopped
1 tsp lemon juice
Salt and freshly ground black pepper
   to taste
1 small onion, finely chopped
1 egg, beaten
4lb chicken, giblets removed

Coating
4 tblsp butter
2 tsp chicken seasoning
1 tsp paprika
½ tsp mixed dried herbs

Garnish
Watercress

To make the stuffing, combine the breadcrumbs, suet, parsley, tarragon, apple, lemon juice and seasoning to taste. Put the onion into a small bowl and microwave on Full Power for 1 minute. Add the onion to the other ingredients. Bind together with the beaten egg.

Chicken Casserole (top right), Herby Roast Chicken (top left), Chicken Breasts in Garlic Cream Sauce (bottom right) and Sausage Suet Pudding (bottom left).

Roasting Meats

TYPE OF MEAT	MICROWAVE POWER LEVEL	TIME PER 1lb	INTERNAL TEMPERATURE AFTER MICROWAVING	INTERNAL TEMPERATURE AFTER STANDING
Chops 1. Lamb	Power 7 or Roast (Use pre-heated browning dish)	7-8 minutes	Turn the chops over once during cooking time.	
2. Pork	Power 7 or Roast (Use pre-heated browning dish)	9-10 minutes	Allow to stand for 5-10 minutes before serving.	
Beef (Boned & Rolled)	Power 7 or Roast	5-6 minutes *Rare* 7-8 minutes *Medium* 8-10 minutes *Well done*	130°F 150°F 160°F	140°F 160°F 170°F
Beef on the Bone	Power 7 or Roast	5 minutes *Rare* 6 minutes *Medium* 8 minutes *Well done*	130°F 150°F 160°F	140°F 160°F 170°F
Poultry (Unboned)	Full Power	7 minutes	185°F	190°F
Pork	Power 7 or Roast	10-11 minutes	180°F	185°F
Lamb	Power 7 or Roast	8-9 minutes	170°F	180°F

1. Have joints boned and rolled for best results.
2. Use a <u>microwave</u> meat thermostat to gauge when the meat should be removed from the microwave oven.
3. Any joint which is 3lbs or over will brown in the microwave oven, to increase the colouring, use a browning agent before cooking, or flash the meat under a pre-heated hot broiler after standing time.
4. Turn the joint over once during the cooking time.
5. Use a microwave roasting rack, or an upturned saucer, placed in a suitable dish so as to allow the juices to drain.

Stuff the neck end of the bird with the stuffing. Truss. Weigh the stuffed bird and calculate the cooking time accordingly (7 minutes per 1lb). Use small amounts of foil to mask the wings and the stuffed area, to prevent overcooking. Arrange the chicken in a suitable roasting dish, on two upturned saucers, or on a microwave roasting rack. Melt the butter in the microwave for 1 minute on Full Power. Brush the butter all over the chicken. Combine the chicken seasoning, paprika and herbs together and sprinkle all over the chicken. Cover with a split roasta bag. Microwave on Full Power for the calculated time. Allow the chicken to stand, covered with a tent of foil, before serving. Garnish with watercress.

Devilled Pork Chops

PREPARATION TIME:	10 minutes
MICROWAVE TIME:	16 minutes
SERVES:	4 people

2½ tblsp oil
4 loin pork chops (about 6oz each)
A stick of butter
1¼ tblsp dry mustard
2½ tblsp fresh breadcrumbs
1¼ tblsp soya sauce
2½ tsp Worcestershire sauce
1¼ tblsp tomato chutney
Salt and paprika to taste

Preheat the browning dish (without the lid) for 4-7 minutes, according to size, on Full Power. Put the oil into the heated dish and microwave on Full Power for 1 minute. Put the 4 chops into the dish, pressing them down well. Microwave on Full Power for 2 minutes. Turn the chops over and microwave on Power 7, or Roast, for 10 minutes. Combine all the remaining ingredients in a mixing bowl. Spread over the partly cooked chops. Microwave on Power 7, or Roast, for a further 3 minutes.

Beef or Pork Burgers

PREPARATION TIME:	20 minutes
MICROWAVE TIME:	6-7 minutes
SERVES:	4 people

1lb raw ground beef or pork
1 small onion, finely chopped
½ cup fresh breadcrumbs
1 stock cube, crumbled
½ tsp dried parsley
Salt and freshly ground black pepper to taste
1½ tblsp tomato sauce
1¼ tsp made mustard
2 eggs, beaten
4 buns

Mix the ground beef or pork, onion and breadcrumbs together. Add the stock cube and all the other ingredients, apart from the buns. Mix well. Divide the mixture into 4 and form into burgers. Arrange on a microwave roasting rack, or other suitable dish, in a ring. Microwave on Full Power for 6-7 minutes, turning each burger over once halfway through cooking time. Split the buns and fill with the burgers.

Glazed Leg of Lamb

PREPARATION TIME:	25 minutes
MICROWAVE TIME:	about 50 minutes
SERVES:	6 people

4lb leg of lamb
2-3 cloves peeled garlic, cut into thin strips
Salt and freshly ground black pepper to taste
2½ tblsp tomato sauce
1¼ tsp dry mustard
1¼ tsp brown sugar
1 tsp mixed dried herbs

Devilled Pork Chops (top right), Beef or Pork Burgers (center left) and Glazed Leg of Lamb (bottom).

Make incisions all over the joint with a sharp knife; push a strip of garlic into each one. Season with salt and pepper. Combine the tomato sauce, mustard, brown sugar and herbs, and spread evenly over the joint. Arrange the joint on a roasting rack. Cover with a roasta bag. Microwave for 12 minutes on Full Power. Turn the joint over and microwave on Power 4, or Simmer, for 30-40 minutes or until the meat thermometer registers 160°F. Remove the joint. Cover with a tent of foil and allow to stand for 15 minutes before serving.

Rolled Rib Roast of Beef

PREPARATION TIME: 18 minutes

MICROWAVE TIME: 30 minutes

SERVES: 6-8 people

4lb piece rib roast, boned and rolled
Salt and freshly ground black pepper to taste
1½ tblsp tomato sauce
1½ tsp soft brown sugar

Stand the joint on the microwave roasting rack, in a suitable dish, keeping the fat side of the meat underneath. Season with salt and pepper. Microwave for 7 minutes, on Full Power. Turn the joint over and microwave on Roast, or Power 7, for 21 minutes. Remove from the microwave. Cover loosely with a tent of foil and allow to stand for 15 minutes. Spread the tomato sauce and brown sugar all over the fat. Microwave on Full Power for 2 minutes. (Check temperatures with a microwave thermometer. See chart).

Barbecue Lamb Chops

PREPARATION TIME: 10 minutes, plus marinating time

MICROWAVE TIME: 16 minutes

SERVES: 6 people

Marinade
2½ tblsp wine vinegar
5 tblsp pure orange juice
1¼ tblsp tomato sauce
1¼ tsp soft brown sugar
1¼ tsp French mustard
½ tsp dried tarragon
1¼ tsp mild curry powder
Salt and freshly ground black pepper to taste
1¼ tsp oil
6 loin chops, each about 5oz

Blend all the ingredients together for the marinade, apart from the oil. Lay the chops in a large shallow dish and pour over the marinade. Cover and chill for at least two hours. Turn the chops over in the marinade, once or twice. Preheat a large browning dish for 7 minutes on Full Power. Put the oil and the drained chops into the dish, pressing the chops against the hot dish. Microwave, uncovered, on Full Power for 5 minutes. Turn the chops over. Microwave on Roast, or Power 7, for 3-4 minutes. Serve immediately.

Shepherd's Pie

PREPARATION TIME: 30 minutes

MICROWAVE TIME: 38 minutes

SERVES: 4 people

1 tblsp cooking oil
2 zucchini, thinly sliced
1 small onion, finely chopped
1lb raw lean ground beef
1 tblsp flour
Salt and freshly ground black pepper to taste
1 tblsp tomato paste
4 tblsp water
1 beef stock cube, crumbled
2lb potatoes
½ cup milk
1 egg
1 tblsp butter
2 tblsp mild hard cheese, grated

Preheat a small browning dish on Full Power for 3½ minutes (if using a large browning dish preheat on Full Power for 5 minutes). Add the oil, zucchini and onion, and stir. Cover with a lid and microwave on Full Power for 2 minutes. Add the meat and microwave on Full Power for 3 minutes, stirring once. Add the flour, salt and pepper to taste, tomato paste, water and stock cube. Stir well and cover. Microwave on Power 7, or Roast, for 12 minutes, stirring after the first 4 minutes. Remove from the microwave oven and leave to stand. Meanwhile prepare the potatoes. Peel and dice the potatoes. Put them into a roasta bag with 4 tblsp of the milk. Put the bag into a 2 quart bowl. Secure with a rubber band and pierce once at the base. Microwave on Full Power for 17 minutes (turn the bag over once during this time). Stand, covered, for 5 minutes. Drain the potatoes and mash them together with the egg, remaining milk and the butter. Pile the potato onto the meat mixture and sprinkle with the cheese. Microwave on Full Power for 3-4 minutes, until the cheese

Rolled Rib Roast of Beef (top) and Barbecue Lamb Chops (left).

has melted and the pie is very hot. To speed this recipe up you can use reconstituted powdered potato.

Pork with Leeks and Grapes

PREPARATION TIME: 20 minutes

MICROWAVE TIME: 53 minutes

SERVES: 4-5 people

2½ tblsp oil
1 carrot, peeled and sliced
1 stick celery, chopped
8oz potato, peeled and diced
1lb young leeks, washed and sliced
1½lb boned shoulder of pork, cut into 1 inch cubes
¼ cup all purpose flour
Salt and freshly ground black pepper to taste
1¼ cups well flavored chicken stock
1 cup seedless white grapes

Preheat the browning dish for 4 or 7 minutes, according to size. Add the oil, carrot, celery, potato and leeks to the heated dish. Cover with the lid. Microwave on Full Power for 4 minutes. Using a perforated spoon, transfer the vegetables to a dinner plate. Return the browning dish to the microwave, without the lid, for 1 minute on Full Power. Toss the meat in the flour and seasoning; stir into the dish, turning so that all sides come in contact with the hot skillet. Microwave, uncovered, for 3 minutes on Full Power. Stir in the drained vegetables, stock and extra seasoning to taste. Cover with the lid. Microwave, covered, on Power 5, or Simmer, for 40 minutes. Stir in the grapes and serve after a standing time of 5 minutes.

Turkey Fricassee

PREPARATION TIME: 20 minutes

MICROWAVE TIME: 12 minutes

SERVES: 4 people

2 tblsp butter
¼ cup flour
1¼ cups chicken or turkey stock
Salt and freshly ground black pepper to taste
1 cup mushrooms, sliced
½ red pepper, de-seeded and chopped
4 rashers bacon, de-rinded and chopped

1 medium onion, chopped
12oz cooked turkey, chopped
1 cup stuffed olives, halved
2 tblsp light cream
1 egg yolk

To make the sauce: melt the butter in a 2¼ pint jug for 1 minute on Full Power. Stir in the flour to make a smooth paste. Gradually stir in the stock, mixing well. Season with salt and pepper. Microwave on Full Power for 2 minutes. Beat well with a wire whisk. Microwave on Full Power for 2 minutes. Beat in the sliced mushrooms. Put the red pepper, bacon and onion into a 2½ pint mixing bowl. Cover and microwave on Full Power for 2 minutes. Stir. Arrange the cooked turkey in a serving dish. Add the pepper mixture and most of the halved olives (reserve a few for decoration). Beat the cream and egg yolk into the sauce. Pour the sauce evenly over the vegetables and turkey. Cover with plastic wrap and pierce. Microwave on Power 5 for 5 minutes. Allow to stand for 5 minutes before serving. Garnish with the remaining olives.

Stewed Steak with Garlic

PREPARATION TIME: 25 minutes

MICROWAVE TIME: about 1 hour 40 minutes

SERVES: 4 people

1½lb chuck steak, cubed
1 tblsp seasoned flour
2 leeks, washed and sliced
1 medium onion, sliced
1 carrot, peeled and chopped
2 cloves garlic, crushed
2 tblsp cooking oil
2 rashers bacon, de-rinded and chopped
15oz can tomatoes, chopped
1 tblsp tomato paste
Salt and freshly ground black pepper to taste
1¼ cups well flavored beef stock
½ tsp dried parsley

Toss the meat in the seasoned flour. Put the leeks, onions, carrot and the garlic into a 2½ pint dish. Cover and microwave on Full Power for 3 minutes. Stir and set aside. Preheat the large browning dish, without the lid, for 7 minutes on Full Power. Pour the oil into the

This page: Pork with Leeks and Grapes.

Facing page: Stewed Steak with Garlic (top), Shepherd's Pie (center right) and Turkey Fricassee (bottom).

dish and quickly stir in the bacon and the meat. Press the meat against the sides of the dish. Cover and microwave on Full Power for 4 minutes. Stir, and add all the remaining ingredients. Cover. Microwave on Full Power for 4 minutes, and then on Power 4, or Simmer, for 70 minutes. Stir once after the first 30 minutes. Stir, and allow to stand for 10 minutes before serving.

Sauces and Preserves

Basic Savory White Sauce

PREPARATION TIME: 5 minutes
MICROWAVE TIME: 5 minutes
MAKES: ⅔ pint

2 tblsp butter
¼ cup flour
1¼ cups milk or chicken stock
Salt and freshly ground black pepper
   to taste

Melt the butter in a 2¼ pint jug. Microwave on Full Power for 1 minute until very hot. Stir in the flour to form a roux. Gradually stir in all the milk or stock. Season to taste with salt and pepper. Microwave on Full Power for 2 minutes. Beat well with a wire whisk. Microwave on Full Power for 2 minutes. Beat with a wire whisk and serve.

Variations on Basic White Sauce
Cheese Sauce
Beat ½ cup finely grated cheese and 1 tsp made mustard into the

Mushroom Sauce (above right), Basic Savory White Sauce (far right) and Cheese Sauce (right).

finished sauce. The heat of the sauce will melt the cheese.

Mushroom Sauce
Beat ½ cup finely chopped mushrooms into the prepared

sauce. The heat of the sauce will cook the mushrooms.

Egg Sauce
Chop 1 hard-boiled egg (cooked conventionally). Beat into the prepared sauce.

Parsley Sauce
Beat 1 tblsp chopped fresh parsley into the finished sauce.

Onion Sauce
Finely chop 1 medium sized peeled onion and put it into a bowl. Cover with plastic wrap and pierce. Microwave on Full Power for 1-1½ minutes to soften. Beat the softened onion into the prepared sauce (the onion should be softened before the sauce is made).

Cranberry Sauce

PREPARATION TIME: 10 minutes

MICROWAVE TIME: 4 minutes

MAKES: about ½ pint

1 orange
8oz frozen cranberries, defrosted
½ cup granulated sugar

Finely grate the rind from the orange into a 2½ pint mixing bowl. Squeeze the juice from the orange and make up to ⅔ cup with cold water. Put the cranberries, sugar, orange juice and water into the mixing bowl. Microwave on Full Power for 4 minutes. Stir once, halfway through cooking time. Stir and serve.

Custard Sauce

PREPARATION TIME: 5 minutes

MICROWAVE TIME: 4 minutes

MAKES: 2½ cups

2 cups milk
½ cup granulated sugar
4 egg yolks
1½ tsp vanilla

Put milk into a 2¼ pint jug and microwave on Full Power for 2 minutes. Beat the egg yolks with the sugar in a 2½ pint mixing bowl until the mixture is a pale lemon colour. Very slowly pour the hot milk onto the egg mixture, stirring constantly, until blended. Pour the mixture back into the jug and microwave on Full Power for 2 minutes. Beat well with a wire whisk. Allow to cool slightly and then stir in the vanilla. Serve hot or cold.

Chocolate Sauce

PREPARATION TIME: 5 minutes

MICROWAVE TIME: 5 minutes

MAKES: about ⅔ pint

2 tblsp butter
1 tblsp cocoa powder
1¼ cups milk
1 tblsp corn syrup

Melt the butter in a 2¼ pint jug for 1 minute on Full Power. Stir in the cocoa, mixing well. Gradually add the milk, stirring. Microwave on Full Power for 2 minutes. Beat well with a wire whisk. Microwave on Full Power for 2 minutes. Beat in the corn syrup. Serve immediately.

Beefy Tomato Sauce

PREPARATION TIME: 10 minutes

COOKING TIME: 20 minutes

MAKES: 1¼ pints

¼ cup butter
2 medium sized onions, finely chopped
½ cup flour
3 cups hot beef stock
2 tblsp tomato paste
1 tblsp vinegar
1 tsp French mustard
1 tsp soft brown sugar
1 tsp Worcestershire sauce

1 tblsp tomato sauce
Salt and freshly ground black pepper to taste

Melt the butter in a really large jug or mixing bowl for 1-2 minutes on Full Power. Stir in the onion and microwave, uncovered, for 3 minutes on Full Power. Stir in the flour, mixing well. Gradually add the stock, stirring continuously. Mix the paste with the vinegar and add to the sauce together with the French mustard, sugar, Worcestershire sauce, tomato sauce and salt and pepper to taste. Microwave on Full Power for 10 minutes. Beat well twice during this time. Turn on to Power 4, or Simmer, and microwave for a further 5 minutes. Beat well. Serve with meat balls, meat loaf, etc.

St. Clement's Sauce

PREPARATION TIME: 10 minutes

MICROWAVE TIME: 3½ minutes

MAKES: about ½ pint

3 tblsp fine cut marmalade
Juice of 1 lemon
Juice of 1 orange
1 tsp arrowroot

Put the marmalade and lemon and orange juices into a 2¼ pint jug. Microwave on Full Power for 1½ minutes. Stir well. Microwave on Full Power for 1 minute. Blend the arrowroot to a smooth paste with a little cold water. Stir into the jug. Microwave on Full Power for 30 seconds. Stir. Microwave on Full Power for a further 30 seconds. Stir and serve.

Plum Jam

PREPARATION TIME: 20 minutes

MICOWAVE TIME: 1 hour

MAKES: 2½lb

Juice of 1 orange
2lb plums, halved and stoned
2lb granulated sugar

Put the juice and the plums into a large microwave container. Cover and microwave on Full Power for 10 minutes. Stir in the sugar to dissolve. Cover and microwave on Power 6 for about 40 minutes, or until setting point is reached. Test for setting. Pot and label in the usual way.

Strawberry Jam

PREPARATION TIME: 20 minutes, plus chilling overnight

COOKING TIME: 31 minutes

MAKES: about 2½lb

2lb freshly picked strawberries, hulled
2lb granulated sugar

Place the hulled strawberries in a 6¼ pint microwave dish. Add the sugar and stir. Cover and leave overnight in the refrigerator. Stir well. Cover and microwave on Full Power for 7 minutes, until boiling point is reached. Microwave on Power 5, or Simmer, for 24 minutes, until setting point is reached. Test for setting. Pot and label in the usual way.

Green Tomato Chutney

PREPARATION TIME: 40 minutes

MICROWAVE TIME: 1¾-2 hours

MAKES: about 6lbs

2 medium onions, finely chopped
1½ cups malt vinegar
1 cup wine vinegar
1 small stalk celery, chopped
½ tsp mustard seed
4lb green tomatoes, washed and chopped
2 large tart cooking apples, peeled, cored and chopped
1½ cups seedless raisins
1 clove garlic, crushed
4 peppercorns, 2 cloves and 2 chilies (tied in muslin)
2 cups soft brown sugar
Salt and freshly ground black pepper to taste

Put the onions into a 6 cup pudding basin. Microwave on Full Power for 2 minutes. Put half the vinegar, the celery, mustard seed, tomatoes, apples, raisins, garlic and onions into a very large bowl.

Parsley Sauce (top), Cranberry Sauce (center left), Onion Sauce (center right) and Egg Sauce (bottom).

Crush the muslin bag with a rolling pin and add to the bowl. Stir. Cover and microwave on Full Power for 10 minutes. Stir in the sugar to dissolve. Add the remaining vinegar and season with salt and pepper to taste. Microwave on Full Power for 20-30 minutes. Remove the lid and stir

well. Microwave on Full Power, uncovered, for about 75 minutes until the mixture reduces and thickens. Stir twice during this time. Ladle into clean jam jars. Seal and label when cool. The chutney shld be kept in a cool dark place for 2 months to mature, before using.

This page: Strawberry Jam (top), Plum Jam (center right) and Green Tomato Chutney (bottom).

Facing page: Chocolate Sauce (top), St Clement's Sauce (center left), Beefy Tomato Sauce (center right) and Custard Sauce (bottom).

MICROWAVE COOKING
Sweets

Pear Upside Down Pudding

PREPARATION TIME:	25 minutes
MICROWAVE TIME:	7 minutes
SERVES:	6 people

Oil and superfine sugar
3 tblsp corn syrup
15oz can pear halves, drained
5 glace cherries, halved and rinsed
Recipe quantity Victoria Sandwich
  mixture (see recipe)

Grease a 7 inch souffle dish with oil and sprinkle the base and sides lightly with superfine sugar. Spread the corn syrup over the bottom. Make an attractive pattern over the base with the pears and the glace cherries. Spoon the Victoria Sandwich mixture into the prepared dish. Smooth the top. Microwave on Full Power for 7 minutes. Allow to stand for 7 minutes in the dish before carefully turning out. Serve warm with custard or cream.

Apple and Blackcurrant Flan

PREPARATION TIME:	30 minutes
MICROWAVE TIME:	37 minutes
SERVES:	6 people

Base
1¼ cups white flour
1¼ cups whole-wheat flour
Pinch of salt
¼ cup butter
¼ cup lard
1 egg and 2 tblsp cold water, beaten
  together

Filling
1lb tart cooking apples, peeled, cored
  and sliced
8oz blackcurrants
¼ cup superfine sugar
¾ cup ground almonds
2 tblsp butter
2 egg yolks

Meringue
3 egg whites
¾ cup superfine sugar
Glace cherries and angelica for
  decoration

To make the pastry, sieve the flours and salt into a mixing bowl. Blend the butter and lard until the mixture resembles fine breadcrumbs. Mix to a dough with the egg and cold water. Knead the dough lightly. Roll out and use to line a 10 inch fluted flan dish. Press up pastry to come ¼ inch above the rim of the dish. Prick the sides and base with a fork. Refrigerate for 15 minutes. Using a single strip of foil, about 1 inch wide, line the inside edge of the flan case. Place 2 sheets of absorbent kitchen paper in the base. Weigh down with a few baking beans. Microwave on Full Power for 6 minutes. Remove the foil, beans and absorbent paper. Microwave on Full Power for 2-3

This page: Mille Feuille (top), Apple Mousse (center right) and Pear Upside Down Pudding (bottom).

Facing page: Chocolate Rice Krispie (top), Rhubarb Sunburst (center right) and Creme Caramel (bottom).

minutes. Set aside. Put the fruits into a 2 quart mixing bowl. Cover and microwave on Full Power for about 7-8 minutes, stirring once halfway through. Stir in sugar to dissolve and beat to a puree. Cool. Beat in the ground almonds, butter and egg yolk. Put the egg whites into a large, clean bowl and whisk until stiff and dry. Beat in the sugar, a little at a time, until a thick glossy meringue results. Spread the fruit mixture into the flan case. Pipe or spread the meringue mixture on top to cover completely. Put the flan into a pre-heated moderate oven, 350°F, for 15-20 minutes, until pale golden. Serve sprinkled with tiny pieces of cherry and angelica.

Mille Feuille

PREPARATION TIME: 15-20 minutes, plus cooling time

MICROWAVE TIME: 6 minutes

SERVES: 6 people

8oz puff pastry (you can use a small packet of frozen puff pastry)
8oz fresh strawberries
1¼ cups heavy cream, whipped
2 tblsp superfine sugar
½ cup confectioner's sugar, sieved
Pink food coloring
¼ cup toasted flaked almonds

Roll the pastry out into a circle 8 inches in diameter. Place on a large dinner plate and chill for 10 minutes. Microwave, uncovered, for 5-6 minutes, on Full Power. Turn the plate once halfway through the cooking time. Brown the top under a pre-heated hot broiler for a few seconds, if required. Allow to cool completely. Hull strawberries and roughly chop them. Fold the strawberries into the cream with the superfine sugar. Split the pastry horizontally into 3 layers and place the first layer on a serving dish. Spread thickly with strawberries and cream. Top with the second pastry layer and spread with more strawberries and cream. Add the final layer of pastry, browned side uppermost. Put the confectioner's sugar into a basin. Add a few drops of pink food coloring and just enough boiling water to produce a smooth glacé frosting. Spread the frosting over the Mille Feuille using a teaspoon – see picture. Sprinkle with the cold, toasted almonds and serve immediately.

Creme Caramel

PREPARATION TIME: 15 minutes, plus chilling time

MICROWAVE TIME: 28 minutes

SERVES: 4 people

Caramel
¾ cup granulated sugar
½ cup cold water

Custard
1¾ cups milk
4 eggs, lightly beaten
¼ cup superfine sugar

To make the caramel, place the granulated sugar and water into a large jug. Microwave on Full Power for 9-11 minutes, or until a golden caramel results. Swirl the caramel evenly around the inside of a suitable, lightly-greased 2 pint dish. Leave to set. Put the milk into a large, clean jug and microwave on Full Power for 2 minutes. Add the beaten eggs and superfine sugar. Strain onto the set caramel. Cover with plastic wrap and pierce. Stand the dish in a larger container, which will act as a water bath. Pour in sufficient boiling water to come halfway up the sides of the dish containing the creme caramel. Microwave on Power 5, or Simmer, for about 15 minutes or until the custard has set. Remove from the water bath. Carefully peel away the plastic wrap and allow to cool. Chill until ready to serve. Turn out and serve very cold with whipped cream.

Apple Mousse

PREPARATION TIME: 20 minutes

MICROWAVE TIME: 7 minutes

SERVES: 6 people

1½lb tart cooking apples, peeled, cored and sliced
Juice of 1 lemon
3 cubes of lime jelly (from a packet jelly)
3 tblsp superfine sugar
1 cup heavy cream
2 egg whites
1 red-skinned eating apple

Put the prepared cooking apples into a 2 quart casserole dish with half the lemon juice and the lime jelly. Cover with a lid and microwave on Full Power for about 7 minutes until the apples are pulpy (stir once during this time). Beat with a fork, beating in the sugar until melted. Set aside and allow to cool. Blend the cooled

apple in a food processor or liquidizer until smooth. Add the half-whipped cream and process together for a few seconds. Whisk the egg whites in a clean bowl until they stand in soft peaks. Transfer the apple mixture to a large, clean bowl and fold in the beaten egg whites gently. Turn into a serving dish. Decorate with slices of eating apple, which have been brushed with the remaining lemon juice to prevent discoloration.

Rhubarb Sunburst

PREPARATION TIME: 10 minutes, plus chilling time

MICROWAVE TIME: 6 minutes

SERVES: 4 people

1lb fresh young rhubarb, cut into 1 inch pieces
Finely grated rind and juice of 1 orange
1 tblsp apricot jam
6 canned apricot halves, chopped

Place the rhubarb, orange rind and juice, and the jam into a 2 pint mixing bowl. Cover and microwave on Full Power for 6 minutes. Stir. Set aside to cool, and then chill. Stir in the chopped apricots. Serve with natural yogurt, ice cream or whipped heavy cream.

Chocolate Pudding with Cherries

PREPARATION TIME: 10 minutes

MICROWAVE TIME: 8½ minutes

SERVES: 4-6 people

6 tblsp softened butter
6 tblsp soft brown sugar
¾ cup flour
1 tsp baking powder
¼ cup cocoa powder
2 eggs
2 tblsp milk
15oz can cherry pie filling

Put all ingredients, apart from the cherry pie filling, into a mixing bowl. Beat with a wooden spoon for 1 minute. Spoon into a lightly greased 2 pint plastic pudding basin. Microwave on Full Power for 3½-4 minutes, until well risen and springy to the touch. Set aside. Empty the cherry pie filling into a bowl and microwave on Full Power for 3 minutes, stirring after 1½ minutes. Turn the sponge pudding into a dinner plate. Spoon the hot cherry sauce over the top and serve immediately.

Chocolate Rice Krispie

PREPARATION TIME: 15 minutes, plus chilling time

COOKING TIME: 5 minutes

MAKES: 16-20 wedges

A stick of butter
¼ cup superfine sugar
¼ cup cocoa powder
½ cup corn syrup
1 cup Rice Krispies

Lightly grease 2 x 8 inch sandwich tins with a little of the butter (these are not to be used in the microwave). Put the remaining butter, cut into pieces, into a 2 quart mixing bowl with the superfine sugar, cocoa powder and corn syrup. Microwave on Power 5 or Simmer for 4 minutes. Stir halfway through, and again at the end. Microwave on Full Power for a further 1 minute. Stir in the Rice Krispies, making sure that they are all coated with the chocolate mixture. Divide between the prepared tins and smooth level with a knife. Cool and then chill until set. Cut into finger wedges to serve. As an alternative, ½ cup washed, seedless raisins may be stirred in with the Rice Krispies.

Apple Ginger Crisp

PREPARATION TIME: 15 minutes

MICROWAVE TIME: 9 minutes

SERVES: 4-6 people

1lb tart cooking apples peeled, cored and sliced
¼ cup soft light brown sugar
1 tblsp orange juice
5 tblsp butter
2 cups plain ginger biscuits, crushed
½ cup flaked almonds

Place the apples, sugar and orange juice into a 3¼ pint casserole dish. Cover and microwave on Full Power for 4-5 minutes. Stir and set aside. Put the butter into a 2 quart mixing bowl. Microwave on Power 7, or Roast, for about 2 minutes, until melted. Stir the biscuits and almonds into the melted butter. Mix well. Microwave on Full Power for 2 minutes. Stir well with a fork after 1 minute. Carefully spoon the biscuit crumble over the apples. Serve immediately with whipped cream or ice cream. This pudding can also be served cold.

Chocolate Pudding with Cherries (left), Apple Ginger Crisp (below left) and Apple and Blackcurrant Flan (bottom).

Tea Time Treats

Celebration Gateau

PREPARATION TIME: 40 minutes

MICROWAVE TIME: 14 minutes

MAKES: 1 gateau

Cake
*Superfine sugar and oil for preparing
the dish*
3 eggs
1¼ cups cake flour
¼ cup cocoa powder
1 tsp baking powder
¾ cup softened butter
¾ superfine sugar

Frosting
2 cups confectioner's sugar, sieved
6 tblsp butter
2 tsp boiling water
1 tsp liquid coffee essence
Few drops of vanilla essence

Decoration
1 packet sponge finger biscuits
6oz plain chocolate
*1½ yards brown nylon ribbon, 1 inch
wide*

Lightly grease a deep, 7 inch
diameter souffle dish with oil. Line
the base with a circle of wax paper
and use a little superfine sugar to
dust the sides. Knock out any
surplus. Put all the ingredients for
the cake into a mixing bowl. Beat
for 1 minute. Spoon into the
prepared souffle dish and smooth
the top. Microwave on Power 7, or
Roast, for about 7 minutes, and
then on Full Power for 2-3 minutes
until the sponge has risen to the
top of the souffle dish and is set.
Allow to stand in the container for
10 minutes before turning out onto
a clean tea towel which has been
sprinkled with a little superfine
sugar. Cool completely.
To make the frosting: gradually
beat the sieved confectioner's sugar
into the butter, adding the boiling
water. Take 1 tblsp buttercream out
of the bowl and beat the coffee
essence into it. Beat the vanilla
essence into the remaining
buttercream. Cut the cake in half
horizontally and sandwich together
with some of the vanilla
buttercream. Spread the vanilla
buttercream around the sides and
across the top of the cake. Pipe half
the cake with vanilla buttercream

and the other half with the coffee
buttercream. Arrange the prepared
sponge fingers, like soldiers, around
the edge of the cake – see picture.
Tie brown ribbon around to finish
the gateau.
To prepare the sponge fingers:
measure 1 sponge finger against the
cooked cake. Trim all the sponge
fingers to the same size. Break the
chocolate into a large mixing bowl
and microwave on Power 4 for 3-4
minutes. Stir. Dip the rounded end
of the sponge fingers into the
melted chocolate to coat the top
half of each one. Arrange on a tray
and leave in a cool place for 10-15
minutes to set.

Chocolate Frosting

PREPARATION TIME: 5 minutes

MICROWAVE TIME: 2½ minutes

2 tblsp softened butter
1½ tblsp cocoa powder, sieved
1¼ cups confectioner's sugar, sieved
2 tblsp milk

Put the butter and cocoa into a 2½
pint bowl. Microwave on Power 5,
or Simmer, for 2½ minutes, until
the butter has melted and is very
hot. Stir once, halfway through.
Beat in the confectioner's sugar and
the milk. Beat with a wooden
spoon until thick and glossy. Use to
coat the top and sides of the cake.

Collettes

PREPARATION TIME: 30 minutes

MICROWAVE TIME: 7½ minutes

MAKES: 12

6oz plain chocolate
2oz milk chocolate
4 tblsp heavy cream
1 tblsp butter
2 tsp brandy or coffee essence
*36 paper sweet cases, separated into
twelve groups of three cases*

Break the plain chocolate into
pieces and put into a 2 pint bowl.
Microwave on Power 3, or Defrost,

for 4-5 minutes. Stir. Using a small
paint brush or teaspoon, coat the
base and sides of each group of
paper cases with the melted
chocolate. Leave to set. Put the
milk chocolate and the butter into
a clean bowl. Microwave on Power
3, or Defrost, for 2-2½ minutes.
Beat well for a few minutes. Beat in
the brandy or coffee essence. Half
whip the cream and fold into the
milk chocolate mixture using a
metal spoon. Chill until firm
enough to pipe. Peel the paper
cases away from the set chocolate
and discard. Pipe rosettes of
chocolate filling into the chocolate
case. Serve immediately in new
paper sweet cases.

Fruit and Almond Cake

PREPARATION TIME: 20 minutes

MICROWAVE TIME: 13-16 minutes

MAKES: 1 cake

Use the large spring clip ring mold,
which should be lightly greased and
coated with superfine sugar.
¾ cup softened butter
¾ cup soft brown sugar
½ tsp soy sauce
3 eggs, beaten
1½ cups white flour
1½ tsp baking powder
2-3 drops almond essence
¼ cup ground almonds
½ cup seedless raisins
*½ cup glace cherries, washed and
roughly chopped*

Blend butter and sugar until light
and fluffy. Beat in the soy sauce and
beaten eggs, a little at a time (add 1
tblsp flour with each addition of
egg to prevent curdling). Beat in
the almond essence, ground
almonds and milk. Fold in the
remaining flour, and then the
raisins and cherries. Place in the
prepared ring mold and smooth
the top. Microwave on Power 6, or
Roast, for 12-14 minutes, and then
on Full Power for 1-2 minutes until
just set. Stand for 15 minutes,
before turning out. When quite
cold, the top may be sprinkled with
a little sieved confectioner's sugar.

Cheese and Paprika Scones

PREPARATION TIME: 20 minutes

MICROWAVE TIME: 5-6 minutes

MAKES: about 10

2 cups white flour
2 tsp baking powder
Pinch salt
Pinch paprika
¼ cup firm butter
½ cup mild hard cheese, grated
1 tsp made mustard
1 egg
3 tblsp milk
1 tsp meat extract

Sieve the flour, salt and paprika
into a 2 quart mixing bowl. Blend
the butter and fork-in the cheese.
Beat the mustard and egg together
and mix with the milk. Mix into
the dry ingredients, using a round
bladed knife, to form a soft dough.
Knead on a lightly floured board.
Roll out to a thickness of ½ inch.
Cut into 2½ inch rounds. Arrange
the shaped scones in a ring on a
non-metallic tray, leaving a gap in
the centre. Mix 1 tsp meat extract
with a little boiling water and brush
over the surface of the scones (do
not cover). Microwave
immediately on Power 7, or Roast,
for 5-6 minutes. Transfer to a
cooling rack and allow to stand for
2-3 minutes. Serve hot with butter,
or cold if preferred. As an
alternative to the meat extract
glaze, the cooked scones may be
flashed under a pre-heated hot
broiler to brown and crisp them.

**Celebration Gateau (top),
Collettes (center left) and Fruit
and Almond Cake (bottom).**

Microwave Meringues (right),
Victoria Sandwich (below) and
Porridge (bottom right).

Porridge

PREPARATION TIME: 5 minutes

MICROWAVE TIME: 9 minutes

SERVES: 3 people

2 cups milk and water, mixed
½ tsp salt
1 cup oatmeal
6 tblsp soft brown sugar
6 tblsp butter

Put the milk, water and salt into a 2 quart mixing bowl. Stir in the oatmeal. Microwave on Full Power for 3 minutes. Stir. Microwave on Full Power for 3 minutes. Stir. Microwave on Full Power for 3 minutes. Turn into individual serving dishes. Sprinkle with the brown sugar and top with the butter. Serve immediately.

Microwave Meringues

PREPARATION TIME: 20 minutes

MICROWAVE TIME: about 8 minutes

MAKES: 10 sandwiched meringues

1 egg white
12 tblsp confectioner's sugar, sieved
Pink food coloring
1½ cups chocolate buttercream
Chocolate vermicelli

Put the egg white into a 2 quart mixing bowl and beat until frothy. Gradually work in the confectioner's sugar and mix to give a really stiff frosting. Divide the frosting into two portions. Knead a few drops pink food coloring into one portion of frosting. Roll both the frostings separately into small balls, each about the size of a marble. Arrange 4 balls of frosting in a ring on a large dinner plate. Microwave on Full Power for 1½ minutes. Allow to stand for 2 minutes before removing to a cooling tray. Repeat until all the mixture has been cooked. Fill the cooled meringue halves with the chocolate buttercream. Sprinkle with a little vermicelli and serve in paper cake cases.

Victoria Sandwich

PREPARATION TIME: 15 minutes

MICROWAVE TIME: 7 minutes

MAKES: 1 cake

Oil
Superfine sugar for dusting
3 eggs
1½ cups cake flour
1½ tsp baking powder
¾ softened butter
¾ cup superfine sugar
2 drops soy sauce
2 tblsp milk
3 tblsp strawberry jam

Lightly grease a 7 inch souffle dish with oil; dust the sides with a little superfine sugar. Place a circle of wax paper in the base. Put the eggs, flour, butter, sugar, soy sauce and milk into a mixing bowl. Beat for 1 minute. Spoon into the prepared dish and smooth the top. Microwave on Full Power for about 7 minutes. Test by putting a wooden cocktail stick into the centre of the sponge after a 3 minute standing time. The cocktail stick should come out clean. Stand for 10 minutes. Turn out into a wire cooling rack. When quite cold, split in half horizontally. Sandwich together with the jam. Serve with a little superfine sugar sprinkled over the top.

Cream Slices

PREPARATION TIME: 15-20 minutes, plus cooling time

MICROWAVE TIME: 6-8 minutes

MAKES: about 6 slices

8oz puff pastry (small packet frozen puff pastry can be used)
Black cherry jam
3 tblsp confectioner's sugar, sieved
A few drops of pink food coloring

Roll the pastry into an oblong about 4 inches wide and 12-14 inches long. Cut in half, crossways. Dampen the surface of a suitable container. Lift one half of the pastry onto the prepared tray and microwave on Full Power for 3-4 minutes, until well puffed up (when the door is opened, the pastry should hold its shape). Allow to stand for 2-3 minutes and

and just 'set'. Remove from the microwave oven and allow to stand for 5 minutes before turning out. Allow to become quite cold. To make the buttercream, mix the cocoa with 2 tblsp boiling water to form a smooth paste. Beat with the butter and confectioner's sugar until light and creamy. Split the cooled cake in half horizontally. Sandwich together with a little of the buttercream and arrange on a cake board. Use the remaining buttercream to completely coat the 'hedgehog'. Form a 'snout' for his nose. Fork all over. Cut most of the chocolate chips in half and stud the hedgehog with these to represent the prickles. Use 1 chocolate chip for his nose and 2 raisins for his eyes. Spread some green coconut around the base for grass.

Rich Fruit Cake

PREPARATION TIME: 30 minutes	
MICROWAVE TIME: 40 minutes	
MAKES: 1 cake	

½ cup softened butter
½ cup dark soft brown sugar
2 tblsp dark molasses
1 tsp soy sauce
3 eggs
3 tblsp milk
2 cups flour, sieved with 1 tsp mixed
  spice, a pinch of salt and ½ tsp
  baking soda
1.2lb mixed dried fruit (white raisins,
  raisins, currants and peel)
¼ cup chopped blanched almonds
½ cup glace cherries, washed and
  quartered
3 tblsp sherry or brandy

Lightly grease a deep, 9 inch diameter souffle dish. Line the base with a circle of ungreased wax paper and dust the sides with a little superfine sugar (knocking out any surplus). Beat the butter, sugar,

then remove to a cooling tray. Repeat the process with the remaining half of the pastry. Allow to cool. Using a sharp knife, divide each layer into 3 slices. Sandwich each group of three layers together with the jam. Mix the confectioner's sugar with a little boiling water to make a smooth, glossy frosting. Beat in a few drops pink food coloring. Quickly spread the frosting over the top of each layered slice. Cut each one into 3 slices.

Mr. Hedgehog Cake

PREPARATION TIME: 40 minutes	
MICROWAVE TIME: 3½-7 minutes	
MAKES: 1 cake	

6 tblsp softened butter
6 tblsp superfine sugar
1 cup cake flour
2 eggs
1 tblsp milk
1 tblsp cocoa powder
A stick of butter
2 cups confectioner's sugar, sieved

1 packet large milk chocolate chips
2 raisins
Green colored coconut for grass

To make the sponge, put the butter, the superfine sugar, flour, eggs and milk into a mixing bowl. Beat with a wooden spoon for 1 minute. Lightly grease the base and sides of a 2 pint plastic pudding basin. Fill with the sponge mixture and smooth the top. Microwave on Full Power for 3½ minutes, or on Power 6, or Roast, for 6-7 minutes. The sponge should be well risen

This page: Mr. Hedgehog Cake (top), Cream Slice (center left) and Rich Fruit Cake (bottom).

Facing page: Pineapple Gateau (top right), Chocolate Pear Sponge (center left) and Cheese and Paprika Scones (bottom).

molasses and gravy browning in a large mixing bowl until light and fluffy. Gradually beat in the eggs and the milk. Add 1 tblsp flour with each addition of egg, to prevent it curdling. Fold in the remaining flour using a metal spoon. Fold in the fruits, nuts and glace cherries, together with the sherry or brandy. Spoon the mixture into the prepared container. Microwave on Power 4, Simmer or Defrost, for 40 minutes. Remove from the microwave oven and allow to stand in its dish for 20 minutes before turning out. When quite cold, the cake may be covered with almond paste and frosted, or finished with glace fruits, and glazed. Allow the cake to mature for at least 1 month before using.

Date and Walnut Loaf Cake (below) and Crepes Suzette (bottom).

Crepes Suzette

PREPARATION TIME: 25 minutes

MICROWAVE TIME: about 24 minutes

SERVES: 4-6 people

Pancakes
1 cup flour
Pinch salt
1 egg
⅔ cup milk
⅔ cup water
Cooking oil

Sauce
6 tblsp butter
4 tblsp superfine sugar
Grated rind of 1 orange
Grated rind and juice of ½ a lemon
4-5 tblsp brandy or Cointreau

Sieve the flour and salt into a bowl. Make a well in the centre. Add the egg and half of the milk. Beat well. Gradually beat in the remaining milk and the water. Beat in 1 tsp oil. Allow to stand for 10 minutes. Fry the pancakes in the usual way, making 12 pancakes in all. Fold the 12 cooked pancakes in half and then in half again, to form triangles. Arrange in a shallow dish. To make the sauce, put the butter into a 2¼ pint jug and microwave on Defrost for 5 minutes, or until melted and hot. Stir in the sugar to dissolve. Add the fruit rinds, lemon juice, and the brandy or Cointreau. Microwave on Full Power for 2 minutes. Stir. Pour over the pancakes. Cover with plastic wrap and microwave on Power 5, or Simmer, for 5 minutes. Turn each pancake over in the sauce before serving. Serve piping hot.

Pineapple Gateau

PREPARATION TIME: 30 minutes

MICROWAVE TIME: 7 minutes

MAKES: 1 gateau

Oil and superfine sugar
1 recipe quantity Victoria Sandwich mixture (see recipe)
8oz can pineapple slices, drained
1¼ cups heavy cream, whipped
1 cup chopped blanched almonds, toasted
Angelica for decoration

Lightly grease a 7 inch souffle dish or plastic pan with oil. Put a circle of wax paper into the base of the dish; dust the base and sides with superfine sugar (knock out any surplus). Spoon the prepared Victoria Sandwich mixture into the dish, and smooth the surface. Microwave on Full Power for about

Date and Walnut Loaf Cake

PREPARATION TIME: 15 minutes

COOKING TIME: 6 minutes

MAKES: 1 loaf

2 eggs
4 tblsp milk
1 tblsp corn syrup
1 tsp soy sauce
½ cup softened butter
1½ cups white flour
1½ tsp baking powder
¾ cup soft brown sugar
¾ cup chopped stoned dates
1 small banana, sliced
½ cup walnuts, chopped

Put the eggs, milk, corn syrup, gravy browning, butter, flour and brown sugar into a large mixing bowl. Beat with a wooden spoon. Using a metal spoon, fold in the dates, banana and walnuts. Turn into a lightly greased 2 quart microwave bread baker. Microwave on Full Power for about 6 minutes, turning the dish a half turn, halfway through cooking time. Allow to stand in the bread baker for 10 minutes before turning out. Serve sprinkled with superfine sugar.

7 minutes. Allow to stand for 10 minutes before turning out onto a wire cooling rack. Once the cake is quite cold, remove the wax paper. Split the cake in half horizontally. Chop 1 slice of pineapple and mix with 3 tblsp of the whipped cream; use to sandwich the cake layers together. Spread some of the cream round the sides of the cake and roll it in nuts to coat evenly. Arrange on a serving dish. Spread the top with the remaining cream, piping it if liked. Decorate the top with pineapple and angelica – see picture.

Chocolate Pear Sponge

PREPARATION TIME: 15 minutes

MICROWAVE TIME: 6 minutes

MAKES: 1 sponge cake

14 tblsp cake flour
1 tblsp cocoa powder
1 tsp baking powder
A stick of softened butter
1 tblsp milk
1 tsp mixed spice
4oz ripe pear, peeled, cored and chopped
Oil and superfine sugar for preparing the souffle dish

Put all the ingredients, apart from the pear, into a 2 quart mixing bowl. Mix with a wooden spoon and then beat for 1 minute. Fold in the pear, using a metal spoon. Lightly grease a 7 inch souffle dish; line the base with a circle of wax paper and coat the sides with a little superfine sugar. Turn the mixture into the prepared souffle dish and smooth the top. Microwave on Power 6, or Roast, for 4 minutes, and then on Full Power for 2 minutes. Allow to stand for 10 minutes before turning out onto a cooling rack. The cooling rack should be covered with a clean tea towel, sprinkled with a little superfine sugar. When quite cold, frost the cake with chocolate frosting.

SOME INDIAN SPECIALTIES
Bread and Rice

Ubley Chawal
(BOILED RICE) 1

This method of cooking rice in a large quantity of water is very safe, and is ideal for all grades of rice, especially for starchy short and medium grades. It is also good for cooking large quantities, as the fluffiness can be controlled. Use a few drops of lemon juice to whiten the rice.

COOKING TIME: 10-15 minutes

2 cups Basmati rice
Pinch salt
Few drops lemon juice

Wash rice in 4-5 changes of water until water is clear. Drain rice and put into a large pan. Fill pan with cold or tepid water, to come 2-4 inch above the rice level. Add pinch of salt and bring to boil gradually. When boiling, add drops of lemon juice to bleach the rice and cut the starch formation. Boil for 7-10 minutes, covered, or until the rice is almost cooked and has a hard core in the center. Test by pressing a few grains of rice between thumb and forefinger. Drain well and cover the top of the pan with a clean cloth or foil and put the lid on lightly. Replace on a very low heat. The moisture around the rice is enough to form steam and cook the core of each rice grain in 2-4 minutes. Serve with or without butter/ghee, with daal or curry.

Ubley Chawal
(BOILED RICE) 2

PREPARATION TIME: 5 minutes
COOKING TIME: 15 minutes

This method is only suitable for cooking long grain types of rice such as Basmati, American, Deradun or Pahari. In cooking, the rice absorbs twice its dry measure of liquid; bearing this in mind always measure rice with a cup and then measure twice the amount of water.

2 cups Basmati rice
Pinch salt
Lemon juice

Wash rice in 4-5 changes of water until water is clear. Drain rice and put into a large pan. Fill the pan with measured quantity of water and let the rice soak for 10-15 minutes. The longer it stands the better the result. Add salt and lemon juice and gently bring to boil. Stir once or twice when boiling and simmer, covered, until rice is almost cooked with a hard center, about 7-10 minutes. The water should be totally absorbed. Do not stir rice during cooking. Keep on a low heat for a further 1-2 minutes to evaporate any remaining moisture and complete the cooking of the rice. Serve.

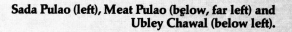

Sada Pulao (left), Meat Pulao (below, far left) and Ubley Chawal (below left).

Sada Pulao
(CUMIN FRIED RICE)

PREPARATION TIME: 5 minutes, plus 15 minutes to soak the rice.

COOKING TIME: 15 minutes

SERVES: 6 people

2 cups Basmati or American long
   grain rice
4 tblsp butter or ghee
1 tsp cumin seed
¼ tsp ground turmeric
1 tsp salt

Wash rice in 4-5 changes of water. Drain well and add 4 cups of water. Cover and set aside for 10-15 minutes. Heat ghee or butter and add cumin seed. Fry for a few seconds; do not allow to burn. Add the strained rice, retaining the water. Add turmeric and salt. Mix well and add the strained water. Bring to the boil, cover, and lower the temperature. Do not stir rice. Cook for 10-12 minutes, until water is absorbed and the rice is tender. Serve with any curry.

Meat Pulao

PREPARATION TIME: 15 minutes

COOKING TIME: 1 hour

SERVES: 6 people

1 small onion, peeled and sliced
4 tblsp ghee or butter
1 inch cinnamon stick
6 green cardamoms
3 large cardamoms
6 cloves
1 bay leaf
1 tsp whole black cumin seeds
1 tsp ginger paste
1 tsp garlic paste
8oz lean pork or lamb, cut into cubes
1 tsp ground coriander
1 tsp ground cumin
⅔ cup natural yogurt
1 tsp salt
2 cups Basmati rice

Fry onion in butter until golden brown. Add cinnamon, cardamoms, cloves, bay leaf and cumin seed. Fry for 1 minute. Add ginger and garlic pastes and fry for ½ minute. Add meat and sprinkle with ground coriander and cumin. Stir and add yogurt and salt. Mix well; cover and cook for 10-12 minutes until yogurt is dry and oil separates. Add 1¼ cups of water and cook until meat is tender (20-25 minutes). Remove from heat.

Strain meat from its liquid. Take a large saucepan and add the measured, washed rice. Add the gravy from the meat, making it up to 4 cups with water. Add the meat and the spices. Adjust seasoning. Bring to the boil and then lower the heat; give a stir, cover, and cook on low heat without stirring for 10-15 minutes, until water is totally absorbed and the rice is tender. Serve with a curry.

Biryani

There are two methods of making biryani: one with uncooked meat and the other with cooked meat. Both styles give equally good results but have slightly different flavors.

Method 1

In this method meat is marinated and cooked with semi-cooked rice.

PREPARATION TIME: 15-20 minutes, and at least 1 hour for meat to marinate.

COOKING TIME: 60-70 minutes

SERVES: 6 people

10oz lean lamb, cut into cubes
2/3 cup natural yogurt
1 tsp salt
1 tsp ground coriander
1 tsp ground cumin
1 tsp chili powder
1/2 tsp ground turmeric
1 tsp ginger paste
1 tsp garlic paste
2 onions, peeled and sliced
Salad or olive oil for frying
3-4 green chilies, chopped
2 sprigs fresh green coriander leaves, chopped
2 cups Basmati rice
1 inch cinnamon stick
6 small cardamoms
6 cloves
2 bay leaves
1 tsp black cumin seed
2 tsp salt
3 tblsp ghee or butter, melted
1-2 tsp saffron dissolved in 6 tblsp milk

In a small bowl, mix the meat, yogurt, salt, coriander, cumin, chili turmeric, ginger and garlic pastes. Cover and set aside to marinate for at least 1 hour. (For best results marinate overnight.)

For boiling rice

Fry onions in plenty of oil, until brown and crisp. Drain on kitchen paper. Put the meat and marinade into a large saucepan. Add half of the fried onions, half of the chopped chilies and the coriander. Mix well. Put the washed rice into a separate saucepan with plenty of water to cover; add the cinnamon, cardamoms, cloves, bay leaf, black cumin and salt. Bring to the boil. Cook for 3-4 minutes until rice is half cooked. Drain well and put the steaming rice over the meat. Sprinkle with the remaining fried onions, chilies and coriander leaves. Make 5-6 holes in the rice

with the handle of a wooden spoon, for the steam to escape, and pour saffron milk all over the rice. Sprinkle with lemon juice and melted butter or ghee. Cover with the lid and place the pan over a moderate heat. As soon as steam is visible, lower the temperature. Cook for 45-50, minutes rotating the pan, so that all areas receive even heat. The rice will cook with the steam formed by the milk and yogurt, and moisture from the meat. Lower heat to minimum and cook for another 10 minutes. Serve biryani from one end of the saucepan, mixing meat with rice with the aid of a spoon. Serve with a mixed vegetable raita.

Method No 2

This method is the layering method. It involves two stages.

Stage 1
Cooking the meat

Stage 2
Layering the meat with rice

1 onion, peeled and chopped
5 tblsp ghee or
5 tblsp salad or olive oil
1 tsp ginger paste
1 tsp garlic paste
10oz lean lamb, cut into cubes
1 tsp ground coriander
1 tsp chili powder
1/4 tsp ground turmeric
1 tsp ground cumin
2/3 cup natural yogurt
1 tsp salt
1/2 tsp saffron
1 tblsp milk
1 onion, peeled and thinly sliced
Salad or olive oil for deep frying
2 cups Basmati rice
1 inch cinnamon stick
6 cloves
1 tsp black cumin seed
1 bay leaf
6 small cardamoms
2 tsp salt
2 sprigs fresh green coriander leaves, chopped
2-3 green chilies, chopped
Juice of 1 lemon

Fry chopped onion in ghee or oil, in a large pan, until light brown. Add ginger and garlic pastes and fry for another 1/2 minute. Add meat and coriander, chili, turmeric and cumin powder. Add yogurt and salt. Mix well and cook with lid on for 10-15 minutes until dry. Add 1 1/2 cups water. Cover and cook for 8-10 minutes, on low heat, until meat is tender and there is about 1/2 cup gravy left.

For rice

Dissolve saffron in milk. Deep fry sliced onion in oil until crisp and brown, and drain on kitchen paper. Wash rice in 4-5 changes of water. Drain and put into a pan. Add plenty of water and the cinnamon, cloves, black cumin, bay leaf and cardamoms. Add salt and bring to boil. Cook until rice is nearly done. (The rice should increase in size but still have a hard center.) Drain well, leaving whole spices in the rice; divide rice in two. Line the saucepan base with half the rice, and top with the drained cooked meat, saving the sauce. Sprinkle with half the fried onion, half the fresh coriander and chili. Cover with the remaining rice. Sprinkle top with the remaining fried onion, chili and coriander. Sprinkle with lemon juice and saffron milk. Pour the meat gravy all round. Make a few holes in the rice with the handle of a spoon for steam to rise. Cover and cook on gentle heat for 4-5 minutes. Mix before serving. Serve with mixed vegetable raita.

Tahiri

PREPARATION TIME: 10 minutes

COOKING TIME: 20 minutes

SERVES: 6 people

1 onion, peeled and sliced
4 tblsp ghee or butter
1 inch cinnamon stick
6 cloves
6 cardamoms
1 tsp black cumin seed
1 tsp whole black pepper
1-2 bay leaves
3/4 cup shelled or frozen peas
2 cups Basmati rice, washed in 4-5 changes of water
3-4 tsp salt

Fry onion in ghee or butter until light brown. Add cinnamon, cloves, cardamom, black cumin, pepper and bay leaf. Fry for 1/2 minute. Add peas and cook for 2 minutes. Add rice and 4 cups water and salt. Bring to boil. Cover and lower heat to simmer. Cook for 10-12 minutes until rice is cooked and water is absorbed. Serve with vegetable or meat curry.

Vegetable Pulao

PREPARATION TIME: 15 minutes

COOKING TIME: 15 minutes

SERVES: 6 people

2 cups Basmati or any long grain rice
4 tblsp ghee or butter
1 onion, peeled and chopped
1 inch cinnamon stick
1-2 bay leaves
6 small cardamoms
4 large cardamoms
6 cloves
1 tsp salt
8oz peeled and sliced mixed vegetables (see below)
1 tsp ground coriander
1 tsp garam masala powder
1 tsp ground turmeric
1 tsp chili powder
Salt to taste

Wash rice in 4-5 changes of water – drain well. Heat butter or ghee and fry onion until light brown. Add cinnamon, bay leaf, cardamoms, and cloves. Fry for 1 minute. Add mixed vegetables and fry for 4-5 minutes. Add drained rice and sprinkle with coriander, garam masala, turmeric and chili powder. Mix well. Add 4 cups of water. Add salt to taste. Bring to boil. Reduce heat; cover and cook gently for 12-15 minutes, without stirring, until water is completely absorbed. Serve by itself, with a raita or with a curry.
Recommended vegetables:- Can be used in any combination. No leafy vegetables or pithy vegetables like marrow, zucchini, gourd etc. are advisable as they will make the pulao soggy.

1-2 eggplant, cut into 1/2 inch chunks
1-2 potatoes, peeled and diced
1-2oz shelled or frozen peas
1-2 carrots, peeled and diced
2oz sliced green beans
1-2oz corn kernels
2-3 cauliflower flowerets, cut into smaller pieces
1-2oz broad beans, frozen or shelled

Facing page: Vegetable Pulao (top), Khichri (left) and Shahi Pulao (bottom).

Khichri
(KEDGEREE)

PREPARATION TIME: 6 minutes	
COOKING TIME: 10-15 minutes	
SERVES: 6 people	

1 cup Basmati rice
1 cup red lentils
¾ tsp salt
½ tsp ground turmeric
1 tsp ground coriander
4 tblsp butter
1 large onion, peeled and chopped
1-2 green chilies, chopped

Mix rice and lentils. Wash in 4-5 changes of water. Drain and add 4 cups of water. Add salt, turmeric and coriander. Bring to boil. Mix well by stirring gently. Lower the temperature; cover and cook over a gentle heat for 10-12 minutes until water is absorbed and rice and lentils are tender. Melt the butter in a skillet and fry onions until golden brown. Add chopped chilies and pour over cooked khichri. Serve with poppadums and chutney.

Shahi Pulao
(NUT AND RAISIN PULAO)

PREPARATION TIME: 5-6 minutes.	
COOKING TIME: 10-15 minutes.	
SERVES: 6 people	

2 cups Basmati or long grain rice
4 tblsp ghee or butter
1 inch cinnamon stick
6 small cardamoms
2 large cardamoms
2 bay leaves
6 cloves
1 tsp salt
4 tblsp raisins
4 tblsp chopped mixed nuts
   (almonds, cashew, pistachio)

Wash rice in 4-5 changes of water, drain. Heat butter or ghee and fry cinnamon, cardamoms, bay leaves and cloves for half minute. Add drained washed rice, salt and 4 cups of water. Bring to boil gently. Stir once or twice. Reduce heat add raisins and nuts, cover and cook for 10-12 minutes or until water is totally absorbed and the rice is tender. Serve with meat or vegetable curry.

Jhinga Pulao
(PRAWN PULAO)

PREPARATION TIME: 6 minutes	
COOKING TIME: 10-15 minutes	
SERVES: 4-6 people	

1 cup long grain or Basmati rice
1 onion, peeled and chopped
4 tblsp ghee or butter
1 inch cinnamon stick
1 bay leaf
6 small cardamoms
6 cloves
1-2 tsp ginger paste
1-2 tsp garlic paste
8 oz large shrimps, peeled and cooked
1 tblsp chopped fresh green coriander
   leaves
1 tsp garam masala powder
1-2 green chilies
¾ tsp salt

Wash rice in 3-4 changes of water. Drain and soak in 2 cups of water. Keep aside. Fry onion in ghee or butter until golden brown. Add cinnamon, bay leaf, cardamoms and cloves; fry for 1 minute. Add ginger and garlic pastes. Cook for ½-1 minute. Add shrimps and sprinkle with coriander and garam masala. Add green chilies and salt. Stir in soaked rice and water. Mix well and bring to boil. Reduce heat, cover and cook until water is absorbed and rice is tender (about 10-15 minutes). Do not stir during cooking. Serve with curry. To color pulao, add a few drops of red or orange food color 2-3 minutes before removing from heat. A pinch of saffron may be added along with the spices.

Pita

PREPARATION TIME: 10 minutes, and 1 hour for dough to rest	
COOKING TIME: 30 minutes	
MAKES: 16	

2 tsp dried yeast
1 tsp fine granulated sugar
3½ cups wholewheat flour
Pinch salt
1½ tblsp butter or margarine

Mix yeast and sugar and add 2 tblsp tepid water. Cover and let it stand in a warm place until frothy. Sift flour and salt; add butter and yeast mixture. Knead with sufficient water to make a pliable dough. Cover and leave for 1 hour. Knead once again and divide into 16 even-sized balls. Roll each one out on a lightly-floured surface to a 6 inch oval or circle. Place on greased baking sheets. Bake at 375°F for 7-10 minutes.

Saag Paratha
(PARATHA MADE WITH A LEAFY VEGETABLE)

PREPARATION TIME: 10 minutes	
COOKING TIME: 20 minutes	
MAKES: 16-18	

3½ cups wholewheat flour (Atta)
Pinch salt
¼ cup drained cooked spinach
Butter or ghee

Sift flour and salt; add spinach and 2 tblsp butter. Knead with sufficient water to make a soft, pliable dough. Knead well and allow to stand for 5 minutes. Heat a non-stick skillet or a Tawa. Make 16-18 even sized balls. Roll each ball out on a lightly-floured surface into a 6-7 inch circle. Place in the skillet or Tawa and cook for 1-3 minutes on low heat. Turn over and cook on the other side. Add a little butter or ghee to each side and shallow fry until light brown. Serve hot or cold.

Kulcha
Kulcha is a deep fried yeast bread.

PREPARATION TIME: 5-6 minutes, and 5-6 hours for yeast to rise.	
COOKING TIME: 30 minutes	
MAKES: 20-25	

1 tsp dried yeast
1 tsp fine granulated sugar
4 cups rice flour
Pinch salt
3 tblsp ghee or butter
2 tblsp natural yogurt
Salad or olive oil

Mix yeast and sugar with 1 tblsp tepid water. Cover and let it stand in a warm place until frothy. Sift flour and salt. Add ghee or butter, and the yogurt. Knead with sufficient water to form a fairly hard dough. Make a well in the center; add yeast mixture and knead. Let it rest for 5-6 hours in a warm place, to rise. Knead once again to a soft, pliable dough. Make 20-25 even-sized balls. Roll each ball into a 2-2½ inch circle. Fry in hot oil for about 2-3 minutes, until lightly golden brown. Serve hot or cold with curry.

Stuffed Paratha

PREPARATION TIME: 10 minutes	
COOKING TIME: 30 minutes	
MAKES: 16-18	

3½ cups wholewheat flour (Atta)
Pinch of salt
2 tblsp ghee or butter
Ghee or oil for frying

Filling
A few flowerets of cauliflower, finely
   chopped
Pinch of salt
1 tsp cumin seed
¼ tsp chili powder
1 tsp ground coriander

Sift flour and salt. Add ghee or butter and knead with sufficient water to make a soft, pliable dough. Make 16-18 even-sized balls. Mix the filling ingredients together. Take a ball of dough and make a slight depression in the center. Fill the center with 1 tsp of cauliflower mixture. Pull the surrounding dough from around the filling to gather at the top. Roll gently into a complete ball. On a lightly floured surface, roll each paratha into a 6-7 inch round. Place the paratha on a preheated non-stick skillet or Tawa. Let it cook for 2 minutes, until little brown specs appear. Flip over on to the other side and cook for 2 minutes. Take a little ghee or oil and shallow fry parathas on both sides. Cook each side on low heat, until golden brown. Serve hot or cold with a curry. Cook all the stuffed parathas in the same way.

Facing page: Biryani (top), Jhinga Pulao (center left) and Tahiri (bottom right).

Nan

The distinctive taste of Nan comes from baking the bread in a clay oven. Nan baked in gas or electric ovens does not have the same charcoal flavor.

PREPARATION TIME: 10-15 minutes and 2-3 hours for dough to rest

COOKING TIME: 30-40 minutes

MAKES: 16-17

2 tsp dried yeast
1 tsp fine granulated sugar
1½ tsp baking soda
1 tblsp sesame or onions seeds
3½ cups all-purpose flour
Pinch salt
4 tblsp melted butter
3 tblsp natural yogurt

Mix yeast and sugar and add 1 tblsp tepid water. Stand in a warm place until frothy. Sift flour and salt, and add baking soda. Make a well and add half the melted butter, yogurt and yeast mixture. Knead with sufficient water to give a smooth dough. Cover and leave to rise for 2-3 hours. Knead again and make 16-17 balls. Roll each ball into either an elongated flat bread – 6 x 10 inches or into a 6-7 inch circle – on a lightly-floured surface. Place on greased baking sheets. Brush with the remaining butter and sprinkle with a few onion or sesame seeds. Bake at 400°F, for 5-6 minutes. When ready the bread will have brown spots on it. Serve hot.

Sheermaal

PREPARATION TIME: 10 minutes

COOKING TIME: 30-40 minutes

MAKES: 10

3½ cups all-purpose flour
Pinch salt
2oz fine granulated sugar
4 tblsp butter or margarine
1 tblsp dried yeast
1 cup tepid water
Milk
Sesame seed

Sift flour and salt, and add all but 1 tsp of the sugar. Add butter or margarine. Mix yeast with the tepid water and remaining sugar mix and stand in a warm place until frothy. Add the yeast liquid to the flour and knead to make a soft dough. Let it rest. When risen to twice its volume, knead once again for 4-5

Below: Saag Paratha (top left), Stuffed Paratha (top right) and Kulcha (bottom).

minutes. Divide into 10 equal portions. Roll each one out into a round or oval shape, ¼ inch thick. Brush with milk and sprinkle with sesame seeds. Place on greased baking sheets. Bake at 375°F for 5 minutes. Turn over and bake for a further 5 minutes until light brown and cooked.

Paratha
Parathas are shallow-fried breads.

PREPARATION TIME: 10 minutes

COOKING TIME: 25 minutes

MAKES: 16-18

3½ cups wholewheat flour (Atta)
Pinch of salt
Ghee or butter for frying

Sift flour and salt. Add sufficient water to knead into a soft dough. Knead well and keep aside to rest for 5 minutes. Make 16-18 even-sized balls. Roll each ball out into a 2 inch circle. Put a ¼ tsp butter in the center. Fold in half; apply a little more butter, and fold in half again to make a triangular shape. On a floured surface, carefully roll each piece of folded dough into a 6

inch triangle. Heat a non-stick skillet or Tawa. Place the paratha on it. Cook for 1-2 minutes. Flip over and cook for 2 minutes. Add a little ghee or butter to the surface and flip over; fry first side again. Repeat for the second side. Both sides should be browned and pressed with a spatula to cook the corners. Cook all parathas in the same way and stack them. Serve hot or cold with curry.

Facing page: Sheermal (top), Nan (center) and Pita (bottom).

Roti/Chapati/Phulka

PREPARATION TIME: 6 minutes
COOKING TIME: 20 minutes
MAKES: 16-20

3½ cups wholewheat flour (Atta)
Pinch of salt
⅔ cup water

Sift flour and salt into a mixing bowl. Knead to a soft pliable dough with water and leave to rest for 5 minutes. Make 16-20 even-sized balls and roll one ball out on a lightly-floured surface to a 7 inch circle. Heat a non-stick skillet or Indian bread griddle known as a "Tawa". Place the rolled circle of dough on it. When little bubbles appear, turn over and cook for ½ minute. Broil on both sides until the roti puffs and swells. Make the rest in the same way and stack them. A little butter can be applied to each roti to keep it soft. Keep them well wrapped in a clean tea cloth or baking foil.

Alternative method:
The roti can be cooked for 1-1½ minutes on each side in the skillet until little brown specs appear. Make them puff up by pressing with a clean tea cloth to rotate the steam.

Puri
These are deep fried little round breads.

PREPARATION TIME: 6 minutes
COOKING TIME: 10 minutes
MAKES: 25-30

3½ cups wholewheat flour (Atta)
Pinch salt
3 tblsp ghee or
3 tblsp salad or olive oil
Salad or olive oil for deep frying

Sift flour and salt and add ghee or oil. Knead with sufficient water to make a soft, pliable dough. Knead well and allow to stand for 5 minutes. Make 25-30 small balls. Roll each ball out into a small circle 2-2½ inches in diameter. Heat oil. The oil is at the correct temperature when a piece of dough dropped into it rises to the surface immediately. If not, then wait for the oil to heat to the right temperature. Slide one puri into the oil. Press gently with a straining spoon. Turn over and the puri will swell. It may need a little pressing. Deep fry for 1-2 minutes until it is light brown. (The side of the puri which goes in first, always has a thin crust, the other side will always have a thick side. When this thick side is light brown the puri is cooked.) Drain. Fry all the puri in the same way and serve, hot or cold, with a curry or chutney, or both.

Roti/Chapati/Phulka (left),
Paratha (top left) and Puri
(above).

153

SOME INDIAN SPECIALTIES

Sherbets and Snacks

Lassi
(YOGURT SHERBET)

PREPARATION TIME: 5-7 minutes
SERVES: 6 people

1¼ cups natural yogurt
¼ cup fine granulated sugar
Pinch of salt
4 cups water
Pinch of saffron
2 tsp lemon juice
Ice cubes

In a mixing bowl beat yogurt well; add sugar and salt, beat again and add water. Dissolve sugar by stirring well. Add saffron and lemon juice and serve with ice cubes.

Tandi Masala Chaaey
(SPICED ICE TEA)

PREPARATION TIME: 10 minutes
SERVES: 4 people

2½ cups water
1 teabag or
2 tsp orange peko tea leaves
Sugar to taste
4 cloves
1 inch cinnamon stick
4 small cardamoms, seeds removed
    and ground
Crushed ice
Fresh lemon juice

Boil ⅔ cup of water. Put tea, sugar, cloves, cinnamon stick and crushed cardamom seeds into a tea pot. Pour on boiling water and allow to stand for 2-4 minutes. Stir well, strain, and mix with remaining cold water. Allow to cool. Mix and serve in tall glasses with crushed ice and lemon juice to taste.

Green Mango Sherbet

PREPARATION TIME: 10-12 minutes
SERVES: 6 people

2 green, unripened mangoes
4 cups water
Pinch of salt
Sugar to taste
Crushed ice

Boil mangoes for 10 minutes. Remove from water and cool. Remove skins gently. Scrape all the pulp from around the stone and skin. Dissolve pulp in water. Add salt and sugar. Stir well to mix. Serve on crushed ice.

Mint Barley

PREPARATION TIME: 15 minutes
SERVES: 4 people

2½-3 cups water
⅓ cup broken barley
6-8 mint leaves, finely chopped
Pinch of salt
Sugar to taste
Fresh lemon juice

Boil 1¼ cups water and add barley; simmer for 5 minutes. Strain and discard barley. Add remaining water and finely chopped mint leaves. Add salt and sugar to taste. Chill and serve on ice with lemon juice.

Lemon Sherbet

PREPARATION TIME: 5 minutes
SERVES: 6 people

Sugar to taste
Pinch salt
5 cups water
Juice of 2 lemons
1 tsp grated lemon rind
Few mint leaves, bruised
Ice cubes

Dissolve sugar and salt in water. Add lemon juice and lemon rind. Add mint leaves and stir well. Serve in tall glasses with ice. ½ cup of gin or vodka may be added.

This page: Lassi (left), Mint Barley (center) and Tandi Masala Chaaey (right).

Facing page: Badam Ka Sherbet (left), Lemon Sherbet (center) and Spiced Grape Sherbet (right).

(Normally served before the meal)

Spiced Grape Sherbet

PREPARATION TIME: 10 minutes

SERVES: 6 people

8oz white seedless grapes
4oz black grapes, seeded
2 cloves
4 cups water
Pinch of salt
6 small cardamoms, seeds removed
　and crushed
Sugar to taste
2 tsp lemon juice
Pinch of freshly ground pepper
Pinch of ground cinnamon
Crushed ice

Wash grapes and liquidize with cloves; strain through a sieve to collect juice. Add 1 cup water to grapes and strain once again to collect the juice. Mix grape juice with remaining water; add salt, crushed cardamom seeds and sugar. Add lemon juice, pepper and cinnamon. Mix well. Serve on crushed ice.

Passion Fruit Sherbet

PREPARATION TIME: 10 minutes

SERVES: 4-6 people

8-10 passion fruit
3 cups water
Sugar
Pinch of salt
1-2 drops of red food coloring
　(optional)
Ice cubes

Cut passion fruits in half. Remove the pulp and blend with the water. Strain and dissolve sugar; add salt. Add red food coloring, if desired, as this will make the sherbet pink. Serve with ice cubes.

Blackcurrant Sherbet

PREPARATION TIME: 10 minutes

SERVES: 1 cup

1 cup fresh or frozen blackcurrants
3 cups water
1/3 cup fine granulated sugar
Pinch of salt
1 tblsp lemon juice
Ice cubes

Mash blackcurrants in a bowl or blend them in a liquidizer. Add water and mix well, then strain. Dissolve sugar and salt in blackcurrant liquid and add lemon juice. Serve with ice cubes.

Badam Ka Sherbet
(ALMOND SHERBET)

PREPARATION TIME: 10 minutes

SERVES: 4 people

1¾ cups milk
2/3 cup water
1/3 cup fine granulated sugar
1½ tblsp blanched almonds, soaked
　in water
1½ tblsp pistachio nuts, soaked and
　skin removed
Pinch of saffron
6 small cardamoms, seeds removed
　and crushed
3-4 drops rosewater
Ice cubes

Mix milk and water and dissolve sugar. Liquidize almonds and pistachio nuts with a little diluted milk. Dissolve saffron, add crushed seeds of cardamom and add rose essence. Serve with ice cubes, or well chilled.

Dahi - Wada
(DAAL DUMPLINGS IN YOGURT)

PREPARATION TIME: 5 minutes
and 1 hour for soaking

COOKING TIME: 30 minutes

SERVES: 4 people

1 cup urid daal, washed and soaked
　for 1 hour
½ cup moong daal, washed and

soaked for 1 hour
½ tsp salt
1 inch root ginger, peeled and finely
　chopped
¼ tsp chili powder or
2 green chilies, finely chopped
4 tblsp mixed sultanas and raisins
Salad or olive oil for deep frying

For Yogurt Sauce:
2 cups natural yogurt
¼ tsp salt
½ tsp cumin seed
2 sprigs fresh green coriander,
　chopped for garnish

Blend drained urid daal and moong daal with sufficient water in a liquidizer to make a very thick purée. Put liquidized urid and moong daal into a mixing bowl; add salt, ginger, chilies and mixed fruits. Mix well. Add small spoonfuls of the mixture to the hot oil to make small dumplings. (To make more uniform wadas, dampen your hands in water, and form a little mixture into a flat, round shape before lowering the mixture gently into the oil.) Fry both sides for 3-4 minutes, or until golden brown. Drain on kitchen paper. Make all the wadas in this way.
To make the sauce, mix yogurt and salt together. Soak fried wadas in water for 2-3 minutes. Gently squeeze out any excess water and arrange on a flat serving dish. Pour the yogurt evenly over them. Dry roast the cumin and coriander

seeds for 1-2 minutes in a skillet. Place the roasted spices in folded kitchen paper and crush with a rolling pin to give a coarse powder. Sprinkle ground spice mixture over the yogurt. Garnish with chopped fresh green coriander. Alternatively, sprinkle with a pinch of paprika powder.

Pakoras or Bhajias
(DEEP FRIED CHICK PEA FLOUR FRITTERS)

PREPARATION TIME: 15 minutes

COOKING TIME: 10 minutes

SERVES: 4 people

1 cup baisen flour
Pinch of salt
½ tsp chili powder
½ tsp baking soda
Salad or olive oil for deep frying

Vegetables and Fruits
1 small potato, peeled and sliced into
　⅛ inch thick wafers
1 small eggplant, cut into thin slices
1 small onion, sliced
1 green pepper, seeded and sliced into
　rings
3-4 flowerets of cauliflower, separated
　into smaller pieces

Mix baisen flour, salt, chili powder and soda; add sufficient water to make a coating batter. Mix well and allow to stand for 3-4 minutes. Dip the prepared vegetables, one by one, into the batter; fry them, a few at a time, for 4-5 minutes in hot oil, until golden brown on both sides. Drain well. Serve hot or cold with chutney.

Other suggestions
Pineapple rings, apples, tomatoes, spinach leaves, green chilies, bread slices cut into quarters, semi-ripe bananas, sweet potatoes, swede, parsnips, chicken and fish pieces.

This page: Blackcurrant Sherbet (center) and Passion Fruit Sherbet (right).

Facing page: Pakoras (top), Ghoogni (center left) and Dahi Wada (bottom).

Crispy Rolls or Curry Patties

PREPARATION TIME: 1 hour	
COOKING TIME: 30 minutes	
MAKES: about 16-20	

2 cups all-purpose flour
Salt
1 tblsp cornstarch
¼ tsp baking soda
1½ tblsp butter or margarine
Chosen filling (see below)
2 tsp flour and a little water to make
    a thick paste.
Salad or olive oil for deep frying

Crispy rolls can be made with either a vegetable or meat filling. The rolls themselves are made in the same way for either filling. Sift flour, salt, cornstarch and soda. Rub in butter. Make dough with water. Knead well and leave to stand for 10 minutes. Knead once again and divide into 4-6 portions. Roll each portion as thinly as possible on a lightly-floured surface, then cut into 4 inch squares. Heat skillet and cook on both sides for ½ minute each. Make the rest similarly. Take a square wrapper and place a little filling slightly above one corner and fold corner over the filling. Bring the two side corners over as if to make the folds of an envelope. Secure with a little flour and water paste and press to seal. Roll over the folded edge to make a neat roll. Seal the flap with flour and water paste. Make all the rolls. Heat oil, and deep fry a few at a time until golden brown. Drain on kitchen paper and serve hot with either chutney or ketchup.

Vegetable Filling
1 onion
2 tblsp salad or olive oil
1lb potatoes, peeled and cubed
⅔ cup shelled or frozen peas
Salt
1 tsp ground black pepper
Salad or olive oil for deep frying

Fry onion in the 2 tblsp salad or olive oil for 3-4 minutes. Add cubed boiled potatoes and peas and sprinkle with salt and pepper. Mix well and cook for 3-4 minutes. Cover and allow to cool.

Meat Filling
1 tblsp salad or olive oil
1 onion, peeled and thinly sliced
⅓ cup grated cabbage
⅓ cup grated carrots
⅓ cup sliced green beans
⅓ cup frozen peas

Salt
½ tsp ground black pepper
⅓ cup sprouted beans
1⅓ cups shredded cooked meat
2-3 tsp lemon juice

Heat oil and fry onions for 2 minutes. Add cabbage and carrots and fry for 3 minutes. Add green beans and peas and sprinkle with salt and black pepper. Cover and cook for 4-5 minutes. Add sprouted beans and stir fry for 2 minutes. Add shredded meat. Mix well, add lemon juice and stir the mixture. Cook for 2-3 minutes. Remove from heat, cool and use for filling.

Aloo-Bonda
(POTATO BALLS IN BATTER)

PREPARATION TIME: 20 minutes	
COOKING TIME: 15 minutes	
SERVES: 6 people	

Batter
1 scant cup baisen flour
Salt
Pinch baking powder
¼ tsp chili powder
⅔ cup water
Oil for deep frying

Filling
1lb potatoes, peeled, boiled and
    cubed
1 onion, peeled and chopped
2 sprigs fresh green coriander,
    chopped
1 inch root ginger, peeled and finely
    chopped
1-2 green chilies, chopped
1 tblsp lemon juice
Freshly ground black pepper to taste
Salt
2 tsp dry mango powder

Sift flour and salt together with baking powder and chili powder. Add water and mix well to make a smooth batter. If the batter is too thick add a little extra water; if too thin, add a little extra sifted baisen flour. Put aside to rest. Put the cubed potatoes into a bowl with the chopped onions, coriander, ginger, chilies and lemon juice; mix well and sprinkle with pepper, salt and mango powder. Shape into small balls about the size of a golf ball. Dip the potato bonda into the baisen batter and slide them into the hot oil. Fry a few at a time until the bonda are golden brown. Drain on kitchen paper and serve hot with chutney. Aloo-bondas can be eaten cold, but they do not freeze well.

Dokhala

PREPARATION TIME: overnight for soaking and 10-12 hours for fermenting	
COOKING TIME: 30-40 minutes	
SERVES: 6 people	

2 cups channa daal (split chick pea),
    washed
1-2 green chilies
1 inch root ginger, peeled and sliced
Salt to taste
Pinch of asafoetida
1 tsp baking soda
4 tblsp salad or olive oil
6-8 curry leaves
½ tsp mustard seed
3 tblsp grated fresh coconut
2 sprigs coriander leaves, chopped

Soak channa daal overnight. Drain and grind with the green chilies, ginger and a little water into a coarse paste. Beat with a circular motion to incorporate air; leave to

ferment for 10-12 hours (use a warm place like an airing cupboard, and cover the pan). After it has fermented, add salt, asafoetida, soda and half the oil. If too thick, add 2 tblsp water. Beat again. Grease a flat, 2-2½-inch-deep pie dish with oil and spread the mixture evenly into it. Steam over

a large saucepan for 15-20 minutes Allow to cool slightly. Heat the remaining oil; add curry leaves and mustard seeds and pour over dokhala evenly. Serve garnished with grated coconut and chopped coriander leaves. Cut dokhala into 1 inch square pieces. Dokhala can be frozen for future use.

Khari Sevian
(SAVOURY MINCE VERMICELLI)

PREPARATION TIME: 10 minutes	
COOKING TIME: 20 minutes for mince and 10 minutes for sevian	
SERVES: 4 people	

1 onion, peeled and finely chopped
1½ tblsp salad or olive oil
½ tsp ginger paste
¼ tsp garlic paste
8 oz ground lean lamb or beef

Salt
1 tsp ground black pepper
¼ cup butter
2 cups broken vermicelli
Juice of 1 lemon

Fry onion in oil for 3-4 minutes. Add ginger, garlic, ground meat and salt. Fry for 6-7 minutes. Add ground black pepper. Mix well. Cover and cook until meat is dry. Remove from heat and put aside. Heat the butter in a non-stick pan and fry vermicelli for 1-2 minutes. Add cooked meat and stir fry for 1 minute. Add 1¼ cups water. Cook until dry. Sprinkle with lemon juice and serve hot.

Khari Sevian (far left), Aloo Bonda (below), Crispy Rolls (center) and Dokhala (bottom).

Ghoogni
(GREEN PEA FRY OR SPICED GREEN PEAS)

PREPARATION TIME: 5 minutes	
COOKING TIME: 10 minutes	
SERVES: 4 people	

1 onion, peeled and chopped
1 tblsp salad or olive oil
2 green chilies, cut in half
1 inch root ginger, peeled and chopped
3 cups shelled or frozen peas
¼ tsp ground black pepper
2 sprigs fresh green coriander, chopped
¼ tsp salt
Juice of 1 lemon

Fry onion in oil until tender (2-3 minutes); add green chilies and ginger. Fry for 1 minute and add green peas. Stir and cook for 5-6 minutes. Add black pepper, chopped coriander and salt. Cook for a further 2 minutes. Pour into a serving dish and sprinkle with lemon juice. Serve hot with tea.

Samosa
(DEEP FRIED STUFFED SAVORY PASTRIES)

PREPARATION TIME: 30 minutes	
COOKING TIME: 15 minutes	
MAKES: 32-40	

1 cup all-purpose flour
Pinch of salt
½ tsp baking powder
1½ tblsp salad or olive oil

Flour paste
1 tblsp all-purpose flour, mixed with a little water to form a thick paste
Oil for deep frying

Samosas may be made with either a vegetable or meat filling (they are made in the same way for either filling). Sift flour and salt and add baking powder. Mix in oil and add the water, a little at a time, to form a dough. Knead well and set aside. When the filling has been made: knead dough again and make 16-20 even-sized balls. On a lightly floured surface roll each ball into a thin circle, 5 inches in diameter. Cut across the center and apply the flour paste along the straight edge and bring the two corners together, overlapping slightly to make a cone. Secure by pressing the pasted edges together. Fill the

cone with the filling, apply paste to te open mouth and seal the edge. Prepare the rest of the samosas in the same way. Fry the samosas, a few at a time, in hot oil until golden brown. Drain on kitchen paper and serve hot or cold with a sweet chutney or ketchup.

For Vegetable Filling
1 tblsp oil
1 onion, peeled and chopped
2 tsp garam masala powder
½ tsp salt
½ tsp chili powder
1lb potatoes, peeled, cubed and boiled for 4 to 5 minutes
4 tblsp frozen or shelled peas
2 tsp dry mango powder

To make the filling: heat the oil and fry onion until just tender. Sprinkle with garam masala, salt and chili powder. Fry for one minute and add drained potatoes and peas. Mix well and fry for 2-3 minutes until potatoes are tender. Sprinkle with mango powder or lemon juice. Allow to cool.

Meat Filling
1 onion, peeled and chopped
2 tblsp salad or olive oil
1lb ground lamb or beef
1 tsp ginger paste
1 tsp garlic paste
2 tsp ground black pepper
½ tsp salt

Fry onion in oil until golden brown. Add the ground meat, ginger and garlic paste, black ground pepper and salt. Fry the mixture for 8-10 minutes until dry. Remove from pan and allow to cool. Samosas made with ground meat can be frozen either half fried, or unfried. Fry straight from the freezer when required. They can also be thawed before frying without any damage or alteration to taste.

Tikias
(POTATO-MINCE PATTIES)

PREPARATION TIME: 20 minutes	
COOKING TIME: 20-30 minutes	
MAKES: 20-25	

1 onion, peeled and chopped
1½ tblsp ghee or
1 tblsp salad or olive oil
8 oz ground lamb or beef
1 cup frozen or shelled peas
2 sprigs fresh green coriander leaves, chopped

2-3 small green chilies, chopped (optional)
1 tsp ground black pepper
1lb boiled potatoes, peeled and mashed
1-2 tsp salt
1-2 eggs, beaten
Salad or olive oil for frying

Fry onion in ghee or oil until just tender (2-3 minutes). Add ground meat, peas, coriander leaves, chilies and black pepper. Fry for 4-5 minutes. Cool and mix with mashed potatoes and salt. Make 20-25 small, flat burger shapes. Heat the oil in a skillet and dip tikias in beaten egg to coat. Shallow fry in hot oil. Fry on each side for 2-3 minutes. Serve hot or cold with chutney.

Khageea
(SPICED SCRAMBLED EGG)

PREPARATION TIME: 6 minutes	
COOKING TIME: 10 minutes	
SERVES: 2-3 people	

1 onion, peeled and chopped
2 tblsp salad or olive oil
½ tsp chili powder
¼ tsp ground turmeric
1 green chili, chopped
2 sprigs fresh coriander leaves, chopped
2 tomatoes, chopped
Salt to taste
1 tblsp water
4 eggs, well beaten

Fry onion in oil for 2 minutes. Add spices, green chili and coriander leaves; stir fry for 1 minute. Add chopped fresh tomatoes. Season with salt and sprinkle in the water. Add beaten eggs. Cover and cook on gentle heat for 6-7 minutes. Stir and mix egg over gentle heat. (Khageea should look like spiced scrambled eggs.) Serve with parathas for any meal, including a hearty breakfast.

Wada
(DAAL FRITTERS)

PREPARATION TIME: 2-3 hours	
COOKING TIME: 20 minutes	
SERVES: 6 people	

½ cup urid daal, washed and soaked for 2-3 hours
½ cup yellow, de-husked moong

daal, washed and soaked for 2-3 hours
1 onion, peeled and finely chopped
1-2 tsp salt
2-3 sprigs fresh green coriander leaves, chopped
1 small green chili finely chopped, or ½ tsp chili powder
1 inch root ginger, peeled and finely chopped
¼ tsp baking soda
Salad or olive oil for deep frying

Grind drained urid and moong daal with a little water to a coarse thick paste. Pour into a mixing bowl and add onion, salt, coriander leaves, chili powder or green chilies, ginger and soda. Mix well and set aside for 4-5 minutes. Fry small spoonfuls of the mixture in hot oil, a few at a time, for 3-4 minutes until golden brown. Drain and serve hot with chutney.

Omelette

PREPARATION TIME: 5 minutes	
COOKING TIME: 5 minutes	
SERVES: 1 person	

2 eggs, separated
1 small onion, finely chopped
1 tomato, thinly sliced
1 green chili, finely chopped
1 sprig coriander leaves, finely chopped
1 tsp water
Salt to taste
1 tblsp salad or olive oil

Beat egg white until stiff. Add egg yolk and beat well. Mix in chopped onion, tomato, chili, coriander and water. Grease a skillet well with oil. Heat the skillet and pour the egg mixture into it. Sprinkle with salt to taste. Cover and cook the omelette for 2-3 minutes until the sides leave the pan. With a flat spoon or spatula, ease up the base of the omelette, and turn it over to cook the other side. Cover and cook for another 2-3 minutes. Serve hot with ketchup or chutney, along with rotis or parathas.

Facing page: Tikias (top left), Samosa (top right) and Wada (bottom).

Ganthia
(BAISEN STICKS)

PREPARATION TIME: 10 minutes

COOKING TIME: 10-15 minutes

MAKES: about 30

Scant 2 cups baisen flour
¼-½ tsp salt
½ tsp baking soda
½ tsp omum (ajowan)
20 whole peppercorns, crushed
Pinch asafoetida
3 tblsp olive oil
Salad oil for frying

Sift flour, salt, soda and omum together. Add crushed peppercorns, asafoetida and 2 tblsp warm olive oil. Rub in well and knead with sufficient water to make a stiff dough. Take 1 tsp olive oil, rub over dough and knead. Repeat twice more until dough is quite smooth. Pass lumps of dough through a sev mould or spaghetti machine with a large hole setting. Fry the shaped baisen sticks in hot oil, over a low heat, until golden brown and crisp. Drain on kitchen paper and store in airtight containers. Serve with tea or drinks.

Egg Curry

PREPARATION TIME: 10 minutes

COOKING TIME: 20 minutes

SERVES: 3 people

1 large onion, peeled and chopped
1½ tblsp ghee or
1 tblsp salad or olive oil
1 inch cinnamon stick
1 bay leaf
4 small cardamoms
6 cloves
1 tsp garlic paste
1 tsp ginger paste
1 tsp ground coriander
1 tsp ground cumin
¼ tsp ground turmeric
1 tsp garam masala powder
1 tsp chili powder
1⅓ cups canned tomatoes, crushed
Salt to taste
¾ cup water
6 eggs, hard boiled and shelled
2 sprigs fresh green coriander leaves, chopped
2 green chilies, chopped

Fry onion in oil for 2-3 minutes. Add cinnamon, bay leaf, cardamoms and cloves. Fry for 1 minute. Add ginger and garlic pastes. Stir the mixture; add coriander, cumin, turmeric, garam masala and chili powder. Add canned tomatoes and salt to taste. Cook the spices for 5 minutes. Add water, cover and bring to the boil. Add eggs and cook for 10-12 minutes. Garnish with green chilies and fresh coriander leaves. The gravy can be increased or reduced as required. Serve with plain boiled rice.

Nimki and Papadi

PREPARATION TIME: 10 minutes

COOKING TIME: 15-20 minutes

MAKES: about 48

Scant 2 cups all-purpose flour
¼ tsp salt
½ tsp baking soda
1 tsp onion seed (kalongi)
½ tsp omum
Pinch of asafoetida
3 tblsp olive oil
Salad oil for deep frying

Sift flour, salt, and soda; add onion seed and omum. Add asafoetida and rub-in olive oil. Knead with sufficient water to make a stiff dough. Knead for 3-4 minutes until smooth. Make 2 equal portions. Roll out each portion as thinly as possible, to about ⅛ inch thick. Then cut the first piece of dough diagonally into strips both ways to make small bite-size diamond shapes and prick with a fork. Roll out the other dough to a similar thickness and cut neat round shapes with a clean, sharp jar lid or a biscuit cutter. Heat the salad oil and fry the shapes until golden brown and crisp. Drain on kitchen paper and allow to cool before storing them in jars or tins. These can be stored for up to 2 months. Serve with tea or drinks. The diamond shapes are called Nimki and the round shapes are called Papadi.

Ganthia (top) and Nimki and Papadi (bottom).

HEALTHY EATING

Introduction

For most of us, eating is one of life's great pleasures, with delectable flavors and aromas, and bright colors and textures, all stimulating our appetites. Unfortunately, these pleasurable aspects of food and eating often lead us to eat more than we need, and to crave for the wrong sorts of food. Wise decisions for healthy eating need to be made with some basic knowledge of nutrition.

What is Healthy Eating?

For optimum health we need a diet that regularly contains carbohydrates, proteins, fat, vitamins and minerals. Some foods are particularly rich in one nutrient, whereas others contain three or more. Each of the following nutrients is essential to the body.

Protein: for body growth and cell replacement.
Carbohydrate: for energy.
Fiber: aids digestion, and helps to prevent digestion-associated complaints.
Fat: concentrated source of energy; also provides vitamins A, D, E and K.
Vitamin A: for healthy eyes and strong bones and teeth.
Vitamin B: necessary for healthy skin, as well as the digestive and nervous systems and blood formation.
Vitamin C: increases resistance to infection; aids healing of wounds.
Vitamin D: helps strengthen teeth and bones.
Calcium: strengthens teeth and bones; essential to the nervous system, muscles, heart and blood.
Iron: maintains haemoglobin in the blood.

Generally speaking, we all eat a diet which is too rich in fat (especially animal fat), too high in refined sugar, too high in salt, and too low in natural fiber.

General Guidelines for a Healthy Eating Pattern.

Eat white fish, chicken, turkey and veal as the main protein meats.
Eat low fat cheeses, such as curd and cottage cheese, rather than the high fat cheeses such as Cheddar.
Use skimmed milk in place of full fat milk, both for drinks and for cooking.
Use the minimum amount of margarine or butter for spreading on bread and toast, and use olive oil for cooking wherever possible.
If dishes need sweetening, use an unrefined sugar or honey – people who are also trying to lose weight can use an artificial sweetener instead (choose a good one).
Choose breads and cereals which are rich in fiber – whole-wheat bread, brown rice, whole-wheat pasta, etc.
Eat plenty of fresh fruits and vegetables, raw whenever possible.
Choose healthy cooking methods – poaching, baking, casseroling, etc. If frying is a necessary stage in a recipe, use the minimum amount of fat.

Recipes

All the recipes in the book have been put together in such a way that they not only offer a good balance of nutrients, but also follow the healthy eating guidelines listed above. They also taste delicious!

Facing page: Noodles with Kidney Beans and Pesto (top) and Cucumber with Yogurt, Dill and Burghul (bottom).

Soups and Appetizers

Houmus with Lime and Pine Kernels

PREPARATION TIME: 15 minutes, plus soaking and chilling time

COOKING TIME: 1 hour

SERVES: 4 people

1 cup dried chickpeas
Salt and freshly ground black pepper to taste
Juice of 2 limes
2 large cloves garlic, peeled and crushed
2½ tblsp natural yogurt
1½ tblsp tahina (sesame seed paste)
1½ tblsp pine kernels, lightly toasted and chopped

Garnish
Wedges of fresh lime

To Serve
Warm whole-wheat pitta bread, or fingers of hot whole-wheat toast

Soak the chickpeas in cold water overnight. Drain the chickpeas and put them into a pan with sufficient fresh cold water to cover; add 1 tsp salt. Bring to the boil and simmer, covered, for 1 hour, until the chickpeas are tender. Drain thoroughly and allow the chickpeas to cool slightly. Put the chickpeas into the blender with the lime juice, garlic, yogurt, tahina, and salt and pepper to taste; blend until smooth. Cover and chill for 2-3 hours. Stir in the toasted pine kernels. Spoon into a bowl, or onto small serving plates, and garnish with wedges of lime. Serve with warm pitta bread, or fingers of hot toast.
Note: this houmus also makes a delicious dip to serve with sticks of raw vegetables.

Avocado and Smoked Salmon Mousses

PREPARATION TIME: 40 minutes, plus chilling time

SERVES: 4 people

1 large ripe avocado
Juice and grated rind of ½ lemon
⅔ cup natural yogurt

Salt and freshly ground black pepper to taste
2 drops Tabasco
4 tblsp dry white wine
2½ tsp powdered gelatin
4oz smoked salmon trimmings, finely chopped
1 tblsp chopped chives

Garnish
Lemon peel leaves
4 small curls smoked salmon

Peel, halve and stone the avocado. Chop the avocado flesh and put it into the blender with the lemon juice and rind, yogurt, salt and

This page: Houmus with Lime and Pine Kernels (top right), Avocado and Smoked Salmon Mousses (top left), Leek and Cashew Nut Soup (bottom). Facing page: Spinach Ramekins (top), Zucchini and Lemon Soup (center left) and Chicken Liver and Tarragon Pie (bottom).

pepper to taste, Tabasco and half the white wine. Blend until smooth. Dissolve the gelatin in the remaining white wine and blend into the avocado mixture. Leave on one side until the mixture starts to thicken. Lightly grease 4 small decorative molds. Mix the smoked salmon and chives into the thickened avocado mixture; spoon into the prepared molds. Chill until set. Unmold the set mousses carefully onto small plates. Garnish with lemon peel leaves and small curls of smoked salmon.

Leek and Cashew Nut Soup

PREPARATION TIME:	15-20 minutes
COOKING TIME:	30-35 minutes
SERVES:	4 people

1 medium onion, thinly sliced.
2 tblsp olive oil
1 clove garlic, peeled and crushed
6 medium size leeks, halved, washed and shredded
1¼ cups skimmed milk
1¾ cups chicken stock
Salt and freshly ground black pepper to taste
3oz shelled cashew nuts, lightly toasted

Garnish
Matchstick strips of leek
A few lightly toasted cashew nuts, finely chopped (optional)

Fry the onion gently in the olive oil for 3 minutes. Add the garlic and shredded leeks and fry together for a further 3 minutes. Add the skimmed milk, chicken stock, and salt and pepper to taste. Bring to the boil and simmer gently for 20-25 minutes. Blend the soup in the blender, together with the toasted cashew nuts, until smooth. Reheat the soup gently in a clean saucepan. Serve each portion garnished with a few strips of leek and a sprinkling of toasted cashews.

Spinach Ramekins

PREPARATION TIME:	25 minutes
COOKING TIME:	35 minutes
OVEN:	350°F
SERVES:	4 people

1lb fresh spinach, cooked and drained thoroughly
Salt and freshly ground black pepper to taste
Pinch ground nutmeg
2 eggs
2 egg yolks
4 tblsp fresh whole-wheat breadcrumbs
2 tblsp natural yogurt
2 tblsp grated Parmesan cheese
8-12 small spinach leaves

Garnish
Sprigs fresh dill
Small twists of lemon

Mix the cooked spinach with the salt and pepper to taste, nutmeg, whole eggs, egg yolks, breadcrumbs, yogurt and Parmesan cheese. Line 4 lightly greased cocotte dishes or ramekins with the spinach leaves, pressing them in well to fit the shape of the dishes. Spoon in the spinach and egg mixture carefully. Stand the dishes in a roasting pan and add sufficient hot water to come halfway up the sides. Bake in the oven for 35 minutes, until just set. The Spinach Ramekins can either be served hot or cold. Unmold each one carefully onto a small serving plate. Garnish with sprigs of fresh dill and twists of lemon, and serve with fingers of lightly buttered brown bread.
Note: the mixture can be baked in a small loaf pan, if preferred, and served cut into slices.

Spicy Rice Stuffed Mushrooms

PREPARATION TIME:	20 minutes
COOKING TIME:	20-25 minutes
OVEN:	375°F
SERVES:	4 people

12 medium size mushrooms
1 small onion, finely chopped
2 tblsp olive oil
1 clove garlic, peeled and crushed
2 tblsp chopped parsley
8 tblsp cooked brown rice
1 egg, beaten
2 tblsp grated Parmesan cheese
Salt and freshly ground black pepper to taste
Generous pinch ground cinnamon

Garnish
A few sprigs of watercress or
Sprigs fresh parsley

Remove the stalks from the mushrooms and chop the stalks finely. Wipe the mushrooms and place them dark side uppermost in a lightly greased ovenproof dish. Fry the onion gently in half the olive oil for 2-3 minutes. Add the garlic and chopped mushroom stalks and fry for a further 3 minutes. Mix with the parsley, cooked brown rice, beaten egg, half the Parmesan cheese, salt and pepper to taste and the cinnamon. Spoon the savory mixture on top of each mushroom and dribble over the remaining olive oil. Bake in the oven for 15-20 minutes. Serve piping hot, garnished with small sprigs of watercress or parsley.

Celery and Hazelnut Soup

PREPARATION TIME:	15 minutes
COOKING TIME:	30-35 minutes
SERVES:	4 people

1 medium onion, thinly sliced
2 tblsp olive oil
6-8 stems celery, finely chopped
1 bayleaf
Salt and freshly ground black pepper to taste
2 tblsp ground hazelnuts
1¼ cups skimmed milk
1¾ cups chicken stock

Garnish
Small celery leaves
A few flaked hazelnuts

Fry the onion gently in the olive oil for 3 minutes. Add the celery and fry for a further 3 minutes. Add the bayleaf, salt and pepper to taste, ground hazelnuts, skimmed milk and chicken stock. Bring to the boil and simmer gently for 20-25 minutes. Blend the soup in the blender until smooth. Reheat the soup gently in a clean saucepan. Serve each portion garnished with a celery leaf and a sprinkling of flaked hazelnuts.

Zucchini and Lemon Soup

PREPARATION TIME:	20 minutes, plus chilling time
COOKING TIME:	about 25 minutes
SERVES:	4 people

1 medium onion, thinly sliced
2 tblsp olive oil
1lb zucchini, topped and tailed, and sliced
Finely grated rind of 1 lemon
1¾ cups chicken stock
Salt and freshly ground black pepper to taste
2 egg yolks
1 cup natural yogurt

Garnish
Thin slices of zucchini
Small sprigs of mint (optional)

Fry the onion gently in the olive oil for 3 minutes. Add the zucchini and fry for a further 2-3 minutes. Add the lemon rind, chicken stock and salt and pepper to taste. Bring to the boil and simmer, covered, for 20 minutes. Blend the soup in the blender until smooth. If you are serving the soup hot, reheat the soup in a clean pan with the beaten egg yolks and yogurt – do not allow to re-boil. To serve the soup cold, cool the blended soup slightly and add the beaten egg yolks and yogurt. Chill thoroughly. Garnish each portion of soup with a thin slice of zucchini and a sprig of mint.

Tomato and Orange Soup

PREPARATION TIME:	15 minutes
COOKING TIME:	about 25 minutes
SERVES:	4 people

2¼lbs ripe tomatoes, skinned, seeded and chopped
1½ tblsp olive oil
1 clove garlic, peeled and crushed
Finely grated rind of ½ an orange
1¾ cups chicken stock
⅔ cup fresh orange juice
Salt and freshly ground black pepper to taste
1½ tsp honey

Garnish
Twists of orange peel
A little natural yogurt

Put the chopped tomatoes, olive oil, garlic and orange rind into a pan; cover the pan and "sweat" gently over a moderate heat for 3-4 minutes. Add the chicken stock, orange juice, salt and pepper to taste, and the honey. Cover and simmer gently for 20 minutes. Blend the soup in the blender until smooth. The prepared soup can either be served hot or chilled. Serve each portion garnished with a twist or two of orange peel and a swirl of natural yogurt.

Spicy Rice Stuffed Mushrooms (right), Tomato and Orange Soup (below) and Celery and Hazelnut Soup (bottom).

Smoked Halibut with Yogurt and Red Caviar

PREPARATION TIME: 10-15 minutes
SERVES: 4 people

8oz smoked halibut, thinly sliced
4 tblsp natural yogurt
2 tblsp red caviar
Salt and freshly ground black pepper to taste
Half a lemon

Garnish
Small sprigs fennel or dill

To Serve
Small triangles lightly buttered brown bread

Arrange the slices of smoked halibut on 4 small plates. Mix the yogurt with half the caviar and salt and pepper to taste. Add a squeeze of lemon juice. Squeeze the remaining lemon juice over the halibut. Spoon a little yogurt sauce into the center of each portion; top with the remaining caviar. Garnish each portion with a few sprigs of fennel. Serve with triangles of buttered brown bread.
Note: if you find smoked halibut difficult to buy, you can use smoked salmon instead.

Eggplant Purée with Crudites

PREPARATION TIME: 25-30 minutes
COOKING TIME: about 10 minutes
SERVES: 4 people

2 medium size eggplants
3 tblsp olive oil
2 cloves garlic, peeled and crushed
Juice of 1 lemon
Salt and freshly ground black pepper to taste
2 tsp chopped fresh mint

Garnish
Sprigs fresh mint

Boil the eggplant under a moderately hot broiler until the skins blister and char – when squeezed with a cloth, the eggplant should feel soft in the center. Rub the skins off the eggplant under a cold running tap. Squeeze the peeled eggplant in a piece of clean muslin to remove as much of the

bitter juices as possible. Put the eggplant flesh into a blender and blend until smooth. Gradually blend in the olive oil, garlic, lemon juice and salt and pepper to taste. Stir in the chopped mint. Cover and chill briefly. Serve with vegetable crudites as dips: sticks of carrot, cucumber, celery, and pepper, small mushrooms, strips of fennel, etc. Garnish with mint.

Chicken Liver and Tarragon Pate

PREPARATION TIME: 10-15 minutes
COOKING TIME: 7-8 minutes
SERVES: 4 people

1 small onion, finely chopped
1 tblsp olive oil
1 clove garlic, peeled and crushed
1 tblsp fresh tarragon, chopped
8oz chicken livers, roughly chopped
1 tblsp brandy
2 tblsp natural yogurt
Salt and freshly ground black pepper to taste

Garnish
Sprigs fresh tarragon or other herbs

To Serve
Hot whole-wheat crusty bread, or toast

Fry the onion gently in the olive oil for 3 minutes. Add the garlic, tarragon and chicken livers and fry gently until sealed on the outside but still pink in the center. Stir in the brandy and allow to bubble for 30 seconds. Put the chicken livers and their liquid into the blender and blend until smooth. Mix in the yogurt and salt and pepper to taste. Spoon into one small terrine, or into several cocotte dishes, and chill. Garnish with fresh tarragon and serve with hot crusty bread or toast.
Note: if you are using small cocotte dishes, the surface of the pate can be smoothed level and a layer of aspic jelly spooned over the top prior to chilling.

Egg and Cheese Mousse with Watercress Sauce

PREPARATION TIME: 25-30 minutes, plus chilling time
COOKING TIME: 2-3 minutes
SERVES: 4 people

1 cup curd cheese, or sieved cottage cheese
2/3 cup natural yogurt
2/3 cup chicken stock
2 tsp powdered gelatin
Salt and freshly ground black pepper to taste
1 tblsp chopped parsley
3 hard boiled eggs, shelled and finely chopped

Sauce
3 tblsp chicken stock
1 bunch watercress
1 clove garlic, peeled and crushed
1 tblsp pine kernels
4 tblsp natural yogurt

Garnish
1 hard boiled egg yolk, sieved
Small sprigs watercress

Lightly grease 4 individual molds or ramekin dishes. Beat the cheese with the yogurt and half the chicken stock until smooth. Dissolve the gelatin in the remaining chicken stock. Stir the gelatin into the cheese mixture, together with salt and pepper to taste, parsley, and the chopped hard boiled eggs. Spoon into the prepared molds. Chill until set – about 3 hours. Meanwhile, make the sauce. Put the chicken stock, trimmed watercress and garlic into a small pan. Cover and simmer for 2-3 minutes. Cool slightly. Blend the watercress and its liquid in the blender, together with the pine kernels, until smooth. Stir in the yogurt and chill. To serve, unmold each set mousse onto a small plate and spoon a pool of watercress sauce around each one. Garnish with a sprinkling of sieved egg yolk and a sprig of watercress.

This page: Eggplant Puree with Crudites (top), Jellied Eggs en Cocotte (bottom).

Facing page: Egg and Cheese Mousse with Watercress Sauce (top) and Smoked Halibut with Yogurt and Red Caviar (bottom).

Stuffed Vine Leaves

PREPARATION TIME: 40 minutes
COOKING TIME: about 1 hour
SERVES: 6 people

½ cup brown or wild rice
Salt and freshly ground black pepper
  to taste
1lb ground chicken
1 small onion, finely chopped
1 clove garlic, peeled and crushed
1 tblsp chopped chives
1 tblsp chopped fresh coriander
2 tblsp chopped parsley
2 tblsp chopped sultanas
1 tblsp chopped pine kernels
Finely grated rind of ½ small orange
Juice of ½ lemon
8oz prepared vine leaves (see below)
2½ cups chicken stock and dry white
  wine, mixed

To Serve
Thinned natural yogurt
Mixed spice (optional)
Feathery sprigs of dill or fennel

Note: vine leaves are preserved in brine, and this needs rinsing off before they can be used. Put the opened vine leaves into a large bowl and cover with boiling water; leave to stand until the vine leaves can be easily separated. Rinse the vine leaves in cold water and then drain on absorbent paper, veined sides uppermost.

Cook the rice in a pan of boiling salted water for 8 minutes. Drain thoroughly. Mix the par-cooked rice with the ground chicken, chopped onion, garlic, chives, coriander, parsley, sultanas, pine kernels, orange rind, lemon juice, and salt and pepper to taste. Line the base of a large, deep frying pan with 4 large leaves. Divide the prepared filling amongst the remaining leaves, placing each portion towards the base of the leaf. Fold the stem of the leaf over the filling and then fold in the sides; roll up to form a sausage shape. Place the prepared stuffed vine leaves close together in the pan; add salt and pepper to taste and the mixed water and wine. Cover the pan and simmer gently for 50 minutes. Allow the stuffed vine leaves to cool in their cooking liquid. Chill the vine leaves for an hour or two before serving. Serve about 5 stuffed vine leaves per person. Place a pool of yogurt onto each serving plate and top with the chilled vine leaves. Sprinkle with mixed spice and garnish with dill. Note: the vine leaves can be marinated in a little oil and vinegar dressing, if preferred, prior to chilling.

My Gazpacho

PREPARATION TIME: 25 minutes, plus chilling time
COOKING TIME: 2-3 minutes
SERVES: 4 people

1¼ cups pure tomato juice
1¼ cups chicken stock
½ small cucumber, seeded and
  chopped
1lb ripe tomatoes, skinned, seeded
  and chopped
6 scallions, chopped
1 green pepper, seeded and chopped
1 red pepper, seeded and chopped
2 cloves garlic, peeled and crushed
2 anchovy fillets, chopped
1 tblsp chopped fresh basil
1 tblsp dry sherry
Salt and freshly ground black pepper
  to taste

Garnish
Thinly sliced cucumber
Small sprigs fresh basil

Put the tomato juice and chicken stock into a pan with the chopped cucumber, tomatoes, scallions, green and red peppers, garlic, anchovies and basil. Bring to the boil, covered, and then remove immediately from the heat. Leave to cool in the covered saucepan (this allows all the flavors to mingle). Once the vegetables and their liquid are quite cool, blend in the blender until smooth, together with the sherry and salt and pepper to taste. Chill the soup thoroughly for at least 4 hours. The soup will be quite thick at this stage, which is characteristic of a "gazpacho"; however, it can be thinned with a little extra chicken stock if preferred. Ladle the soup into bowls (usually glass ones), adding a few ice cubes to each one. Serve each portion garnished with a few slices of cucumber and a sprig of fresh basil.

Jellied Eggs en Cocotte

PREPARATION TIME: 30 minutes, plus chilling time

COOKING TIME: 2 minutes

SERVES: 4 people

4 tomatoes, skinned, seeded and chopped
1 clove garlic, peeled and finely chopped
1 tblsp chopped parsley
Salt and freshly ground black pepper to taste
4 eggs
1½ cups beef consomme

Garnish

Finely chopped tomato, or small tomato "roses"
Sprigs parsley

Mix the chopped tomatoes with the garlic, parsley, and salt and pepper to taste. Divide amongst 4 cocotte dishes. Lower the eggs into a pan of boiling water and cook for 2 minutes – the eggs should be just soft boiled. Cool the eggs under cold, running water. Carefully remove the shells and sit an egg in each cocotte dish. Spoon the consomme into each dish so that it covers the eggs – if the dishes are quite deep, you will need slightly more consomme than the quantity given above. Chill until set. Garnish each dish with a small tomato rose and a sprig of parsley. To make a tomato rose, peel a thin strip of outer flesh from a firm tomato using a small, sharp knife or a potato peeler. Wind the tomato strip round and round, easing it out to form the shape of a rose head.

Stuffed Vine Leaves (far left) and My Gazpacho (left).

HEALTHY EATING
Fish and Seafood

Smoked Haddock and Egg Quiche

PREPARATION TIME: about 25 minutes

COOKING TIME: about 40 minutes

OVEN: 375°F

SERVES: 6 people

½lb whole-wheat pastry
12oz smoked haddock fillet
Chicken stock
2 hard boiled eggs, chopped
1 tblsp chopped chives
6 tblsp grated cheese
1¼ cups skimmed milk
3 eggs
Salt and freshly ground black pepper to taste

Garnish
2 hard boiled eggs
Finely chopped parsley

Roll out the pastry and use to line a 9 inch, deep fluted flan case; press up the edges well. Line with wax paper and baking beans and bake "blind" for 10 minutes. Meanwhile, poach the smoked haddock fillet gently in chicken stock for about 8 minutes, until just tender. Drain the fish and flake it, discarding any skin and bone. Put the flaked smoked haddock into the pastry case with the chopped hard boiled egg, chopped chives and grated cheese. Beat the skimmed milk with the eggs and salt and pepper to taste; pour into the pastry case. Bake for 30 minutes until the filling is just set. Meanwhile, prepare the garnish. Separate the hard boiled egg whites and yolks; chop the whites finely and sieve the yolks. The quiche can either be served hot or cold. Sprinkle the top with chopped egg white, sieved egg yolk and parsley.

Provençal Fish Stew

PREPARATION TIME: about 15 minutes

COOKING TIME: about 35 minutes

SERVES: 4 people

1 medium onion, finely chopped

2 cloves garlic, peeled and crushed
3 tblsp olive oil
1½lb tomatoes, skinned, seeded and chopped
2 tblsp tomato paste
2½ cups dry red wine
Salt and freshly ground black pepper to taste
5 cups mussels in their shells, scrubbed
8 large Mediterranean prawns
½ cup peeled prawns
4 crab claws, partly shelled

To Serve
8 small slices stale French bread, or similar crusty bread
A little olive oil
1 large clove garlic
Bruised chopped parsley

Fry the onion gently in the olive oil for 3 minutes. Add the garlic and chopped tomatoes and fry gently for a further 3 minutes. Add the tomato paste and red wine and bring to the boil; simmer for 15

This page: Zuccini and Lemon Kebabs (top), Smoked Haddock and Egg Quiche (bottom).

Facing page: Provencale Fish Stew (top) and Baked Sea Bass with Fennel and Vegetable Julienne (bottom).

minutes. Add the mussels and simmer, covered, for 5 minutes. Add the whole Mediterranean prawns, peeled prawns and crab claws, and simmer for a further 5 minutes. Meanwhile, prepare the bread croutes. Brush the slices of French bread with a little olive oil and rub with the crushed clove of garlic. Grill until crisp and golden and then sprinkle with chopped parsley. Spoon the fish stew into a deep serving dish and top with the bread croutes. Serve immediately.

Chilled Fish Curry

PREPARATION TIME: 20 minutes, plus chilling time

COOKING TIME: about 6 minutes

SERVES: 4 people

½lb fresh salmon
12oz white fish fillet
Chicken stock
Salt and freshly ground black pepper to taste
⅔ cup mayonnaise
1¼ cups natural yogurt
2 tsp curry powder
Juice and grated rind of ½ lemon
½ cup peeled prawns

Garnish
Sliced, peeled kiwi fruit
Sprigs fresh mint
Flaked coconut

Put the fresh salmon and white fish fillet into a shallow pan and add sufficient chicken stock to just cover. Add salt and pepper to taste; cover and simmer gently until the fish is just tender. Remove the fish carefully from the cooking liquid and allow to cool slightly. Mix the mayonnaise with the yogurt, curry powder, lemon juice and rind, and salt and pepper to taste. Thin the curry sauce down a little with a small amount of the fish cooking liquid. Flake the cooked salmon and white fish and stir lightly into the prepared curry sauce, together with the peeled prawns. Arrange the chilled fish curry on a serving dish and garnish with slices of kiwi fruit, sprigs of fresh mint and a scattering of flaked coconut.

Plaice Tartare

PREPARATION TIME: 25 minutes, plus chilling time

COOKING TIME: 6 minutes

SERVES: 4 people

1lb plaice or sole fillets
Skimmed milk
Salt and freshly ground black pepper

to taste
4 tblsp olive oil
Juice of ½ lemon
½ tsp soft brown sugar
4 anchovy fillets, finely chopped
1 large clove garlic, peeled and crushed
2 tblsp chopped parsley
2 hard boiled eggs

Garnish
Small wedges of lemon
Green olives
Capers

Put the fish fillets into a large, shallow pan with sufficient skimmed milk to just cover; add salt and pepper to taste. Cover the pan and poach the fish gently until just tender – about 6 minutes. Meanwhile, make the dressing. Mix the olive oil with the lemon juice, sugar, anchovy fillets, garlic, and salt and pepper to taste. Stir in the chopped parsley. Separate the egg yolks from the whites; chop the whites finely, and sieve the yolks. Add the chopped egg white to the dressing. Drain the cooked fish and flake it; mix lightly with the prepared dressing. Cover and chill for 1 hour. Spoon the prepared plaice tartare onto serving plates; sprinkle each portion with sieved egg yolk. Garnish with wedges of lemon, green olives and capers.

Baked Sea Bass with Fennel and Vegetable Julienne

PREPARATION TIME: 30 minutes

COOKING TIME: 35-40 minutes

OVEN: 375°F

SERVES: 4-6 people

1 sea bass, about 2½lb in weight, scaled, gutted and cleaned
Salt and freshly ground black pepper to taste
1 tblsp chopped fresh fennel
1 large clove garlic, peeled and finely chopped
Coarsely grated rind of ½ lemon
2 tblsp olive oil
4 tblsp dry white wine

Vegetable Julienne
2 large carrots, peeled and cut into thin strips
3 stalks celery, cut into thin strips
¼lb green beans

Garnish
Feathery sprigs of fennel or dill

Season the sea bass inside and out; put the chopped fennel, garlic and lemon rind into the cavity of the fish. Lay the fish on a rectangle of

greased foil, sitting on a cooky sheet; pinch up the edges of the foil. Brush the sea bass with olive oil and spoon over the dry white wine. Pinch the foil together over the fish to completely enclose it. Bake in the oven for 35-40 minutes (the foil can be folded back for the last 10 minutes cooking time, if liked). For the vegetable julienne, steam all the vegetables over gently simmering water for about 10 minutes – they should still be slightly crunchy. Arrange the cooked sea bass on a large, oval serving platter, and surround with small "bundles" of the steamed vegetables. Garnish with sprigs of fennel.

Cod Steaks with Asparagus Sauce and Chicory

PREPARATION TIME: 25 minutes

COOKING TIME: 25-30 minutes

OVEN: 375°F

SERVES: 4 people

4 even size cod steaks
2 tblsp melted butter
Salt and freshly ground black pepper to taste
1 tsp fennel seed
1lb asparagus
⅔ cup chicken stock
1 egg yolk
3 tblsp natural yogurt

Garnish
Chicory
Feathery pieces of fennel
Thin lemon slices or twists

Put the cod steaks into a lightly greased ovenproof dish. Brush with melted butter; season to taste with salt and pepper and sprinkle over the fennel seed. Cover with a piece of foil and bake for 25-30 minutes, until the fish is just tender. Meanwhile, make the sauce. Trim the asparagus so that you just have nice green tips (use the remaining stems for making soup, etc.). Tie the asparagus tips together and cook upright in a little boiling water until just tender. Drain carefully and reserve 4 tips for garnish. Put the rest of the cooked asparagus tips into the blender with the chicken stock, egg yolk, yogurt and salt and pepper to taste; blend until smooth. Arrange the cooked cod cutlets on a serving dish, and spoon some of the asparagus sauce over the top. Garnish with small pieces of chicory, feathery pieces of fennel, lemon slices and the reserved asparagus tips. Serve the remaining asparagus sauce separately.

Fish, Zucchini and Lemon Kebabs

PREPARATION TIME: 30 minute plus chilling time

COOKING TIME: about 8 minute

SERVES: 4 people

16 small, thin sole fillets, or 8 larger ones, cut in half lengthwise
4 tblsp olive oil
1 clove garlic, peeled and crushed
Juice of ½ lemon
Finely grated rind of ½ lemon
Salt and freshly ground black peppe to taste
3 drops Tabasco
3 medium size zucchini, cut into ¼ inch slices
1 medium green pepper, halved, seeded and cut into 1 inch pieces

Garnish
2 tblsp coarsely chopped parsley

Roll up each sole fillet, jelly-roll fashion, and secure with wooden cocktail sticks. Place them in a shallow dish. Mix the olive oil wit the garlic, lemon juice, lemon rind salt and pepper to taste and the Tabasco. Spoon evenly over the fish. Cover and chill for 2 hours. Remove the wooden cocktail stick and carefully thread the rolled fish fillets onto kebab skewers togethe with the zucchini slices and pieces of green pepper, alternating them for color. Brush each threaded kebab with the lemon and oil marinade. Broil for about 8 minutes, under a moderately hot broiler, carefully turning the kebab once during cooking. Brush the kebabs during cooking with any remaining marinade. Place the kebabs on a serving dish and sprinkle with chopped parsley.

Plaice and Mushroom Turnovers

PREPARATION TIME: 25 minutes plus cooling time

COOKING TIME: about 35 minutes

OVEN: 400°F

SERVES: 4 people

4 large plaice fillets
Salt and freshly ground black peppe to taste
Skimmed milk
Finely grated rind of ½ lemon
½ cup mushrooms, thinly sliced
2 tblsp butter
Juice of 1 lemon
3 tblsp hazelnut stuffing mix

Plaice Tartare (left) and Chilled
Fish Curry (below).

cooked fillets carefully to a shallow serving dish and spoon over the prepared anchovy, caper and mint sauce. The sole fillets can either be served warm or chilled. Garnish with matchstick strips of orange peel and small sprigs of mint.

Taramasalata

PREPARATION TIME: about	20 minutes
SERVES: 4 people	

3 slices whole-wheat bread, crusts removed
5 tblsp water
¼lb smoked cod's roe, skinned
1 large clove garlic, peeled and crushed
Juice of 1 lemon
6 tblsp olive oil
Salt and freshly ground black pepper to taste

To Serve
Whole-wheat pitta bread
Olives (black or green)

Note: for special occasions, serve the taramasalata in a hollowed, cooked globe artichoke. Trim and cook the globe artichoke in the usual way. Drain thoroughly, upside-down, and brush lightly all over with oil and vinegar dressing. Pull out the center leaves and remove the hairy choke. Brush inside with a little more dressing and fill with taramasalata – the outer leaves can then be pulled off and dipped into the taramasalata. Soak the bread in the water for 10 minutes; squeeze the bread lightly between the fingers. Put the bread into the blender with the cod's roe, garlic, lemon juice and 1 tblsp of the olive oil. Blend until smooth, and then gradually blend in the remaining olive oil. Season to taste with salt and pepper. Serve with warm pitta bread and olives, or as suggested above.

12oz puff pastry (preferably the vegetable oil variety)
Beaten egg
Poppy seeds

Season each plaice fillet with salt and pepper to taste. Roll up each one jelly-roll fashion and secure with a wooden cocktail stick. Place in a shallow pan and add sufficient skimmed milk to half cover; cover the pan and poach gently for 5 minutes. Drain the fish and allow to cool. Remove the wooden cocktail sticks. Put the lemon juice, mushrooms and butter into a small pan and cook gently for 5 minutes. Allow to cool and then stir in the hazelnut stuffing mix. Roll out the pastry quite thinly and cut 6 even-sized circles, each about 6 inches in diameter. Brush the pastry edges with beaten egg. Place a fish fillet in the center of each pastry circle and top with the mushroom and

stuffing mixture; pull the pastry edges up and over the fish and pinch together to seal. Place on a lightly greased cooky sheet and glaze with beaten egg. Bake in the oven for about 25 minutes, until well risen, puffed and golden. Serve piping hot.

Sole with Anchovy, Caper and Mint Sauce

PREPARATION TIME: 10-15	minutes
COOKING TIME: 10-12 minutes	
SERVES: 4 people	

2 tblsp chopped fresh mint
4 tblsp dry white wine
4 tblsp olive oil
1 large clove garlic, peeled and finely chopped

Juice of 1 large orange
1 tblsp capers
3 anchovy fillets, finely chopped
Salt and freshly ground black pepper to taste
8 good size sole fillets
Seasoned flour
2 tblsp butter

Garnish
Matchstick strips orange peel
Small sprigs fresh mint

Mix half the chopped mint with the white wine, 3 tblsp of the olive oil, the garlic, orange juice, capers, anchovy fillets and salt and pepper to taste. Dust the sole fillets very lightly in seasoned flour. Heat the remaining oil and the butter in a large, shallow pan with the remaining mint. Fry the sole fillets for 2-3 minutes on either side (you will find this easier if you fry the fillets in two batches). Remove the

This page: Plaice and Mushroom Turnovers (top) and Cod Steaks with Asparagus Sauce and Chicory (bottom).

Facing page: Taramasalata (top) and Sole with Anchovy, Caper and Mint Sauce (bottom).

Meat Dishes

Stir Fried Calves' Liver with Peppers and Carrots

PREPARATION TIME:	15-20 minutes
COOKING TIME:	10-12 minutes
SERVES:	4 people

2 tblsp olive oil
1 onion, thinly sliced
1¼lb calves' liver, cut into thin strips
Seasoned flour
4 tblsp dry sherry
1 green pepper, seeded and cut into thin strips
3 large carrots, peeled and cut into thin strips
Salt and freshly ground black pepper to taste
1 clove garlic, peeled and cut into thin strips
¼lb mung bean sprouts

Garnish
Sprigs fresh sage

Heat the olive oil in a large, shallow pan or wok; add the onion and stir fry for 3 minutes. Dust the strips of calves' liver in seasoned flour and add to the pan; stir fry until sealed on the outside but still pink in the center. Add the sherry and bubble briskly; add ⅔ cup water or stock, green pepper, carrots, salt and pepper to taste and the garlic. Stir over a brisk heat for 3 minutes. Stir in the mung beans and heat through for 1 minute. Spoon into a serving dish and garnish with sprigs of fresh sage.

Chicken Moussaka

PREPARATION TIME:	about 30 minutes
COOKING TIME:	about 1 hour 5 minutes
OVEN:	375°F
SERVES:	6 people

4 tblsp olive oil
1 medium onion, finely chopped
1 clove garlic, peeled and crushed
1lb ground raw chicken
2 tblsp tomato paste
1¼ cups chicken stock
2 tblsp chopped parsley
Salt and freshly ground black pepper to taste
2 medium size eggplants, thinly sliced
⅔ cup natural yogurt
1 egg
¼ cup grated cheese
1 tblsp grated Parmesan cheese

Heat half the olive oil in a pan; add the chopped onion and garlic and fry gently for 3 minutes. Add the ground chicken and fry until lightly browned. Add the tomato paste, chicken stock, parsley and salt and pepper to taste. Cover and simmer gently for 15 minutes. Lay the eggplant slices on lightly greased cooky sheets and brush with the remaining olive oil; bake in the oven for 8 minutes. Arrange a layer of eggplant and then a layer of chicken in a lightly greased ovenproof dish; repeat the layers, finishing with a layer of eggplant. Beat the yogurt with the egg and grated cheese and spoon evenly over the top; sprinkle with the grated Parmesan. Bake in the oven for 35-40 minutes, until the top is bubbling and lightly golden. Serve piping hot.

Veal Casserole with Apricots and Prunes

PREPARATION TIME:	30 minutes
COOKING TIME:	about 1 hour 40 minutes
OVEN:	325°F
SERVES:	4 people

1¼lb boned leg of veal, cubed
Seasoned flour
3 tblsp olive oil
1 large onion, thinly sliced
1lb fresh ripe apricots, skinned, halved and stoned
1¼ cups chicken stock
1¼ cups dry white wine
⅔ cup fresh orange juice
Salt and freshly ground black pepper to taste
6 tblsp dried prunes, soaked overnight
6 tblsp dried apricots, soaked overnight

Garnish
Matchstick strips of orange peel

Dust the cubed veal *lightly* in seasoned flour. Heat the oil in a pan; add the sliced onion and fry gently for 4 minutes. Meanwhile, put the halved and skinned fresh apricots into the blender with the chicken stock and blend until smooth. Add the cubed veal to the onion and fry until evenly colored on all sides. Gradually stir in the apricot puree, white wine and orange juice. Bring to the boil, stirring, and add salt and pepper to taste. Transfer to a casserole and add the drained prunes and apricots. Cover the casserole and cook in the oven for 1½ hours. Serve sprinkled with matchstick strips of orange peel.

Veal Paprika with Noodles

PREPARATION TIME:	10-15 minutes
COOKING TIME:	about 1 hour 15 minutes
SERVES:	4 people

1 medium onion, thinly sliced
2 tblsp olive oil
1¼lb boned leg of veal, cubed
Seasoned flour
1 tblsp paprika
1 tblsp tomato paste
Bayleaf
1¾ cups chicken stock
⅔ cup skimmed milk
Salt and freshly ground black pepper to taste
½ cup mushrooms, sliced

To Serve
Cooked green noodles

Facing page: Veal Casserole with Apricots and Prunes (top) and Chicken Moussaka (bottom).

Fry the onion gently in the olive oil for 3 minutes. Dust the cubed veal *lightly* in seasoned flour and add to the onion; fry until the veal is evenly colored on all sides. Add the paprika, tomato paste and bayleaf, and gradually stir in the stock and skimmed milk. Bring to the boil, stirring, and add salt and pepper to taste. Cover and simmer gently for 55 minutes. Add the sliced mushrooms and simmer for a further 10 minutes. Serve piping hot with cooked green noodles.

Rabbit in Mustard Sauce

PREPARATION TIME: 5 minutes

COOKING TIME: about 1 hour

SERVES: 4 people

4 rabbit joints
Seasoned flour
1 medium onion, thinly sliced
2 tblsp olive oil
1¾ cups chicken stock
⅔ cup skimmed milk

1 tblsp coarse grain mustard
2 tblsp coarsely chopped parsley
Salt and freshly ground black pepper to taste

Garnish
Small puff pastry leaves

Dust the rabbit joints *lightly* in seasoned flour. Fry the sliced onion gently in the oil for 4 minutes; add the rabbit joints and fry until evenly colored on all sides. Add the chicken stock, skimmed milk,

This page: Tarragon Chicken Pancakes (top) and Rabbit in Mustard Sauce (bottom).

Facing page: Stir Fried Calves' Liver with Peppers and Carrots (top) and Veal Paprika with Noodles (bottom).

mustard, parsley and salt and pepper to taste. Bring to the boil; cover and simmer gently for 40 minutes. Arrange on a serving dish or individual plates and garnish with pastry leaves.

Chicken with Blackcurrant Sauce and Snow Peas

PREPARATION TIME: 10-15 minutes

COOKING TIME: 12 minutes

SERVES: 4 people

4 chicken breasts, skinned and boned
Seasoned flour
Oil for shallow frying

Sauce
½lb fresh blackcurrants
Juice of 1 orange
⅔ cup red wine
Artificial sweetener to taste
Chicken stock

Garnish
Julienne strips orange peel
Cooked snow peas
4 lemon slices
Few whole fresh blackcurrants

Dust the chicken breasts lightly in seasoned flour; shallow fry gently in oil, for about 6 minutes on each side, until tender. Meanwhile, make the sauce. Put the blackcurrants into a pan with the orange juice, red wine, and sweetener to taste; cover and simmer gently until the blackcurrants are soft (this will only take a few minutes). Blend the sauce in the blender until smooth. Reheat in a saucepan, adding sufficient stock to give a smooth coating consistency. Arrange the cooked chicken breasts on a serving dish. Spoon over the blackcurrant sauce and garnish with snow peas, strips of orange peel, and lemon slices topped with blackcurrants.

Chicken and Herb Loaf

PREPARATION TIME: 20-25 minutes

COOKING TIME: 50 minutes

OVEN: 375°F

SERVES: 6 people

1lb ground raw chicken
6 tblsp whole-wheat breadcrumbs
1 small onion, grated
1 clove garlic, peeled and crushed
2 tblsp chopped parsley
1 tblsp chopped fresh thyme
1 medium parsnip, peeled and grated
2 eggs, beaten
Salt and freshly ground black pepper to taste

Garnish
A little olive oil
1 tblsp chopped parsley
Sprigs fresh rosemary

Mix the ground chicken with the breadcrumbs, onion, garlic, parsley, thyme, parsnip, beaten eggs and salt and pepper to taste. Spoon the mixture into a greased and lined loaf pin. Cover with a piece of greased foil. Bake in the oven for about 50 minutes, until cooked through – test with a skewer. For a brown top, remove the foil for the last 8-10 minutes. Brush the top of the loaf with the oil, while it is still hot, and sprinkle with the chopped parsley. Carefully take the loaf out of the pan, and serve either hot or cold, garnished with rosemary.

Chicken Andalusia

PREPARATION TIME: 15 minutes

COOKING TIME: 45 minutes

OVEN: 375°F

SERVES: 4 people

4 small Rock Cornish game hens
Salt and freshly ground black pepper to taste
Olive oil
4 small wedges of lime or lemon
4 bayleaves

Sauce
1 small onion, thinly sliced
2 tblsp olive oil
1 clove garlic, peeled and crushed
1lb tomatoes, skinned, seeded and chopped
⅔ cup red wine
⅔ cup chicken stock
1 tblsp tomato paste
2 green chilies, thinly sliced
1 small red pepper, seeded and cut into thin strips
1 small green pepper, seeded and cut into thin strips
2 tblsp chopped blanched almonds
1 tblsp pine kernels
12 small black olives
1 tblsp raisins

Season the Rock Cornish game hens inside and out with salt and pepper. Rub olive oil into the skin and push a wedge of lemon or lime and a bayleaf into the center of each one. Roast the hens in the oven for 45 minutes, until just tender (if they start to get too brown, cover them with foil during cooking). Meanwhile, make the sauce. Fry the sliced onion gently in the oil for 3 minutes; add the remaining sauce ingredients and simmer for 10 minutes. Arrange the hens on a serving dish and spoon over the hot sauce.

Chicken Escalopes

PREPARATION TIME: 20 minutes, plus chilling time

COOKING TIME: 10 minutes

SERVES: 4 people

4 chicken escalopes
Beaten egg
Seasoned flour
4 tblsp whole-wheat breadcrumbs
1 tblsp chopped fresh sage
2 tblsp butter
1 tblsp olive oil

Sauce
⅓ cup low calorie mayonnaise
⅔ cup natural yogurt
1 tsp grated fresh horseradish
2 tblsp chopped walnuts

Garnish
6oz green beans, lightly cooked
4 thin slices lemon
1 tblsp chopped walnuts

Dust the escalopes lightly in seasoned flour; dip into beaten egg and then coat with a mixture of breadcrumbs and sage. Chill for 30 minutes. Heat the butter and oil in a large, shallow pan; add the prepared escalopes and fry gently for 5 minutes on each side until lightly golden and tender. Keep warm. For the sauce: mix all the ingredients together. Arrange the cooked escalopes on a serving dish and garnish with the cooked beans and lemon slices topped with chopped walnuts. Spoon the sauce over the chicken.

Tarragon Chicken Pancakes

PREPARATION TIME: about 10 minutes

COOKING TIME: 5-10 minutes

SERVES: 4 people

8 small whole-wheat pancakes (using whole-wheat flour and skimmed milk in the batter)
A little melted butter
1½ tblsp butter
3 tblsp all-purpose flour
1¼ cups skimmed milk

Chicken with Blackcurrant Sauce and Snow Peas (left) and Chicken Escalopes (below).

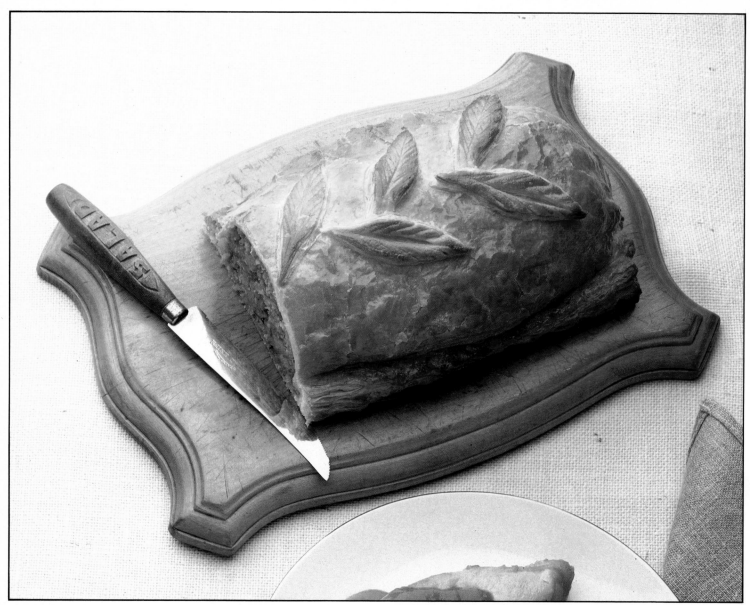

Salt and freshly ground black pepper
　　to taste
½lb cooked chicken, chopped
1 avocado pear (not over-ripe),
　　peeled, halved, stoned and
　　chopped
1 tblsp chopped fresh tarragon

Brush the cooked pancakes lightly
with melted butter and keep them
warm in a parcel of foil in a
moderately hot oven. Melt the
butter and stir in the flour; cook,
stirring, for 1 minute. Gradually stir
in the skimmed milk; bring to the
boil until the sauce has thickened.
Add salt and pepper to taste and
stir in the chopped chicken,
avocado and tarragon. Fold each
pancake in half, and then in half
again, to form a triangle. Fill each
folded pancake with the chicken
and avocado mixture and serve
piping hot. Garnish with sprigs of
fresh tarragon, if liked.

Chicken Breasts with Plum and Cinnamon Sauce

PREPARATION TIME: 15 minutes

COOKING TIME: about 20 minutes

SERVES: 4 people

4 chicken breasts, skinned and boned
Seasoned flour
Olive oil for frying

Sauce
1 small onion, finely chopped
1 tblsp butter
12oz ripe red plums, halved and
　　stoned
Pinch ground cinnamon
Salt and freshly ground black pepper
　　to taste
Artificial sweetener to taste
⅔ cup red wine

Garnish
Whole poached plums
Chopped fresh thyme
Small sprigs fresh thyme

Dust the chicken breasts lightly in
seasoned flour. Shallow fry the
chicken breasts in olive oil for
about 6 minutes on each side, until
tender. Meanwhile, prepare the
sauce. Fry the chopped onion
gently in the butter for 3 minutes;
add the remaining sauce
ingredients and simmer until the
plums are soft and "mushy". The
sauce can either be left as it is, or it
can be blended in the blender or
sieved. Reheat the sauce if
necessary, thinning it to the desired
consistency. Arrange the chicken
breasts on a serving dish and spoon
over the hot plum sauce. Garnish
with a few whole poached plums, a
sprinkling of thyme, and a few
small sprigs of fresh thyme.

This page: Turkey, Chestnut and Sage en Croute.

Facing page: Turkey Meatballs with Sweet and Sour Sauce (top) and Sweetbreads and Zucchini Tarts (bottom).

Turkey, Cauliflower and Almond au Gratin

PREPARATION TIME: 20-25 minutes

COOKING TIME: about 16 minutes

SERVES: 4 people

1 medium size cauliflower
Juice of ½ lemon
Salt and freshly ground black pepper to taste
1½ tblsp butter
3 tblsp flour
1¼ cups skimmed milk
¾ cup cooked turkey, cut into thin strips
½ cup grated cheese
2 tblsp flaked almonds

Divide the cauliflower into good size flowerets; cook in boiling salted water to which you have added the lemon juice and salt to taste, until just tender. Meanwhile, make the sauce. Melt the butter in a pan; stir in the flour and cook for 1 minute. Gradually stir in the skimmed milk and bring to the boil; add salt and pepper to taste and stir until thickened. Add the strips of turkey and half the grated cheese to the sauce. Arrange the flowerets of cooked cauliflower in a greased heatproof dish and spoon over the prepared sauce; sprinkle with the almonds and remaining cheese and brown under a hot broiler.

Turkey Meatballs with Sweet and Sour Sauce

PREPARATION TIME: 20-25 minutes, plus chilling time

COOKING TIME: about 35 minutes

SERVES: 4 people

1 small onion, finely chopped
2 tblsp olive oil
1lb ground raw turkey
1 clove garlic, peeled and crushed
2 tblsp chopped parsley
2 tblsp finely chopped almonds
Salt and freshly ground black pepper to taste
¼ tsp mixed spice
1 tblsp chopped raisins
2 tblsp whole-wheat breadcrumbs
1 egg, beaten

Sauce
1 small onion, thinly sliced
1¼ cups pure tomato juice
2 tblsp tomato paste
Juice of ½ lemon
1 tblsp honey
1 green chili, thinly sliced
2 slices fresh pineapple, finely chopped
1 medium red pepper, seeded and cut into thin strips
2 carrots, peeled and coarsely grated

For the meatballs: fry the onion gently in the olive oil for 4 minutes. Mix with the ground turkey, garlic, parsley, almonds, salt and pepper to taste, mixed spice, raisins, breadcrumbs and beaten egg. Form into small balls, about the size of a table tennis ball. Chill for 30 minutes. For the sauce: put all the ingredients into a shallow pan; bring to the boil and simmer gently for 10 minutes. Add the shaped meatballs and turn them in the sauce. Cover and simmer gently for a further 20 minutes, until the meatballs are tender – if the sauce evaporates too quickly, add a little stock or water. Serve piping hot with cooked brown rice or whole-wheat pasta.
Note: the shaped meatballs can be lightly fried in a little oil, before being added to the sauce, if liked.

Chicken Breasts with Plum and Tarragon Sauce (far right) and Calves' Liver Mousse with Cherry and Marsala (below).

190

Turkey, Chestnut and Sage en Croute

PREPARATION TIME: 35 minutes, plus chilling time
COOKING TIME: about 55 minutes
OVEN: 400°F and then 350°F
SERVES: 6-8 people

1lb ground raw turkey
1 small onion, finely chopped
3 tblsp chestnut puree (unsweetened)
1 tblsp chopped fresh sage
1 clove garlic, peeled and crushed
Salt and freshly ground black pepper to taste
3 tblsp fresh brown breadcrumbs
1 egg, beaten
1lb puff pastry (preferably vegetable oil based)
Beaten egg to glaze

Mix the ground turkey with the onion, chestnut puree, sage, garlic, salt and pepper to taste, and brown breadcrumbs. Bind with the beaten egg. Form into a fat, cylindrical sausage, and chill while you prepare the pastry coating. Divide the pastry into two portions, one slightly larger than the other; roll out thinly on a floured surface into two rectangles, one slightly larger than the other. Trim neatly, reserving the trimmings. Place the smaller rectangle of pastry into a dampened cooky sheet; brush the edges with beaten egg. Place the turkey "sausage" in the center. Lay the larger rectangle of pastry over the top, and pinch the joining pastry edges together to seal (the pastry should fit snugly around the filling). Trim off excess pastry. Glaze the pastry all over with beaten egg and decorate with shapes cut from the pastry trimmings; glaze the pastry decorations. Bake in the oven at the higher temperature for 20 minutes; reduce to the lower temperature and bake for a further 35 minutes, covered with a piece of foil. Serve hot or cold, cut into slices.

Calves' Liver Mousse with Cherry and Marsala

PREPARATION TIME: 25 minutes, plus chilling time
COOKING TIME: 10-12 minutes
SERVES: 6 people

1lb calves' liver
2 tblsp marsala
1¼ cups chicken stock
1 clove garlic, peeled and crushed
Salt and freshly ground black pepper to taste
1¼ cups natural yogurt
4 tsp powdered gelatin
4 tblsp water
4 scallions, chopped

Sauce
½lb fresh cherries, de-stalked and pitted
⅔ cup red wine
3 tblsp marsala
Artificial sweetener to taste
1 tsp cornstarch
Juice of 1 orange

Garnish
Mint leaves
Few fresh cherries

Grease a 3¾ cups mold. Cook the calves' liver in the chicken stock and marsala until just tender – this will only take a few minutes. Put the liver and its liquid into the blender and blend, until smooth, with the garlic and salt and pepper to taste. Stir in the yogurt. Dissolve the gelatin in the water and add to the liver mixture together with the chopped scallions. Spoon into the mold and chill until set. For the sauce: put the cherries into a pan with the red wine, marsala and sweetener to taste; cover and cook until the cherries are just soft. Blend the cornstarch with the orange juice and add to the cherry sauce; stir over the heat until thickened. Unmold the chilled mousse onto a serving dish and garnish with mint leaves and a few fresh cherries. Serve with the *warm* cherry sauce.

Sweetbread and Zucchini Tarts

PREPARATION TIME: 40 minutes, plus chilling time
COOKING TIME: about 35 minutes
OVEN: 375°F
SERVES: 4 people

12oz tart pastry
½lb calves' sweetbreads, soaked for 3 hours
Beaten egg
2 tblsp butter
Finely grated rind of 1 lemon
1 clove garlic, peeled and crushed
4 zucchini, finely shredded
Salt and freshly ground black pepper to taste
Juice of ½ lemon

Divide the pastry into 4 equal portions; roll each one out to a circle and use to line an individual tartlet tin, about 4 inches in diameter. Press up the pastry edges well. Line with wax paper and baking beans, and chill for 30 minutes. Rinse the sweetbreads under cold water. Drain the sweetbreads, put them into a pan and add sufficient cold water to cover; bring to the boil slowly, covered, and simmer for 8 minutes. Drain and rinse; remove any muscly parts and skin, and chop into pieces. Bake the pastry cases for 10 minutes. Remove the paper and beans and brush the rim of each pastry case with beaten egg. Return to the oven for a further 8 minutes. Melt the butter with the lemon rind. Add the garlic and chopped sweetbreads and fry for 4 minutes. Add the shredded zucchini and salt and pepper to taste and fry together for a further 3 minutes. Spoon the hot filling into the pastry cases, squeeze over the lemon juice and serve immediately.

Chicken and Herb Loaf (top right), Chicken Andalusia (center left) and Turkey, Cauliflower and Almond au Gratin (bottom).

HEALTHY EATING
Vegetables and Salads

Stir Fried Peas with Lentil Sprouts and Leeks

PREPARATION TIME:	10 minutes
COOKING TIME:	about 10 minutes
SERVES:	4 people

1 medium onion, thinly sliced
2 cloves garlic, peeled and cut into thin slivers
4 tblsp olive oil
½lb snow peas, topped and tailed
2 large leeks, split, washed, and cut into thin strips
½ cup lentil sprouts
Salt and freshly ground black pepper to taste
1 tblsp chopped coriander

Stir fry the onion and garlic in the olive oil for 3 minutes, either in a wok or in a large, deep frying pan. Add the snow peas and leeks and stir fry for a further 4-5 minutes. Add the lentil sprouts, salt and pepper to taste and the coriander, and stir fry for a further 3 minutes. Serve piping hot with a really good soya sauce, or a peanut sauce. For a quick peanut sauce: put 6 tblsp shelled peanuts into the blender with 1 clove garlic, peeled, 1 small onion, chopped and 1 cup chicken stock; blend until smooth.

Rice and Tuna Stuffed Eggplant

PREPARATION TIME:	40 minutes
COOKING TIME:	about 50 minutes
OVEN:	375°F
SERVES:	4 people

4 small eggplants
3 tblsp olive oil
Salt and freshly ground black pepper to taste
1 small onion, finely chopped
1 clove garlic, peeled and crushed
6 tblsp cooked brown or wild rice
7oz can tuna, drained and coarsely flaked
1 tblsp mayonnaise
1 tsp curry powder
4 tomatoes, skinned, seeded and chopped
1 tblsp coarsely chopped parsley

Cut the eggplants in half lengthwise. Score the cut surfaces lightly with a sharp knife, at regular intervals. Brush lightly with oil and sprinkle with salt. Place on a greased cooky sheet and bake in the oven for 15 minutes. Carefully scoop the center flesh from each half eggplant, making sure that you do not break the skin. Fry the chopped onion gently in 2 tblsp of the olive oil for 3 minutes. Add the garlic, scooped eggplant flesh, and salt and pepper to taste; fry gently for a further 2 minutes. Add the flaked tuna, mayonnaise, curry powder, chopped tomato and parsley, and mix together. Fill the eggplant "shells" with the savory rice mixture and place in a lightly

This page: Okra in Light Curry Sauce (top) and Stir Fried Peas with Lentil Sprouts and Leeks (bottom).

Facing page: Zucchini, Caper and Anchovy Salad (top) and Rice and Tuna Stuffed Eggplant (bottom).

greased ovenproof dish. Sprinkle with the remaining olive oil. Bake in the oven for about 25 minutes. Serve piping hot.

Zucchini, Caper and Anchovy Salad

PREPARATION TIME: 15-20 minutes

SERVES: 4 people

1lb zucchini
1 small onion, thinly sliced
1 tblsp capers
4-6 anchovy fillets, chopped
1 tblsp anchovy oil (drained from the can of anchovy fillets)
2 tblsp olive oil
2 tblsp tarragon vinegar
Juice of ½ lemon
Salt and freshly ground black pepper to taste

Garnish
2 medium size heads of Belgian endive (optional)
2 whole anchovy fillets

The secret of this salad is to slice the raw zucchini really thinly – you can do this with a sharp knife, but it is much easier if you use the slicing blade on a food processor or a mandolin. Top and tail the zucchini, and slice them very thinly. Mix the sliced zucchini with the onion, capers and chopped anchovy fillets. Mix the anchovy oil, olive oil, tarragon vinegar and lemon juice together; add salt and pepper to taste. Stir the dressing into the prepared salad ingredients. Separate the leaves from each head of Belgian endive and use to line a salad bowl. Spoon the prepared salad into the center and garnish with anchovy fillets.

Okra in Light Curry Sauce

PREPARATION TIME: 10 minutes

COOKING TIME: 30-35 minutes

SERVES: 4 people

1 medium onion, roughly chopped
Small piece fresh root ginger, chopped
1 large clove garlic, peeled
¼ cup shelled peanuts
1 tblsp fresh coriander sprigs
1 tblsp chopped parsley
1 tsp ground turmeric
½ tsp ground cumin
2 tblsp olive oil
1 small onion, thinly sliced

1¼ cups chicken stock
Salt and freshly ground black pepper to taste
1lb okra

Garnish
Flaked coconut (optional)
Sprigs fresh coriander

To Serve
Natural yogurt
Wedges of lime

Put the chopped onion, root ginger, garlic, peanuts, coriander, parsley, turmeric and cumin into the blender; blend until smooth. Heat the olive oil in a large, shallow pan; add the sliced onion and fry gently for 3 minutes. Add the blended spice mixture and cook for 1 minute. Add the stock and salt and pepper to taste; bring to the boil and simmer for 5 minutes. Add the okra and cover the pan; simmer gently for 20-25 minutes, until the okra is just tender. Spoon into a serving dish and sprinkle with the flaked coconut. Garnish with fresh coriander. Serve accompanied by a bowl of well-chilled yogurt and lemon wedges for squeezing.

Chicory and Sweetbread Salad

PREPARATION TIME: 40 minutes, plus standing time

COOKING TIME: 18-20 minutes

SERVES: 4

4 calves' sweetbreads
6 tblsp olive oil
1 clove garlic, peeled and crushed
Salt and freshly ground black pepper to taste
2 medium size heads chicory
4 large cooked asparagus tips
¼lb firm white mushrooms, thinly sliced
2 tblsp white wine vinegar
1 tblsp chopped fresh sage (optional)

Garnish
Sprig fresh basil

Soak the sweetbreads in cold water for 3 hours; change the water once or twice during this time. Rinse them under cold water. Drain the sweetbreads; put them into a pan and add sufficient cold water to cover. Bring to the boil slowly; cover and simmer for 8-10 minutes. Drain and rinse under cold water once again. Remove any muscle or fatty parts. Put the prepared sweetbreads between two plates and weight down; leave to stand in a cool place for 1 hour. Slice the

pressed sweetbreads evenly. Heat half the olive oil in a large, shallow pan. Add the sweetbread slices, garlic and salt and pepper to taste and fry gently for 5 minutes; flip the sweetbread slices over and fry for a further 3-4 minutes. Meanwhile, prepare the salad ingredients. Cut the heads of chicory into pieces and arrange on a large, flat plate. Arrange the asparagus tips and mushroom slices between the wedges of chicory. Mix the wine vinegar with the remaining olive oil, salt and pepper to taste and the chopped sage. Spoon the dressing evenly over the salad and top with the fried sweetbread slices and their juices. Garnish with basil. Serve immediately.

Turkey Caesar Salad

PREPARATION TIME: 20 minutes

COOKING TIME: 4-5 minutes

SERVES: 4-6 people

1 Romaine lettuce
Few young spinach leaves
Juice of 1 lemon
1 tsp French mustard
6 tblsp olive oil
2 cloves garlic, peeled and crushed
2 tsp Worcestershire sauce
3 drops Tabasco
4 anchovy fillets, chopped
Salt and freshly ground black pepper to taste
1 egg
2 slices whole-wheat bread, cut into small cubes
6oz cooked turkey, cut into thin strips

Tear the lettuce into pieces and put into a salad bowl with the young spinach leaves. Mix the lemon juice with the French mustard, 3 tblsp of the olive oil, half the garlic, the Worcestershire sauce, Tabasco, anchovy fillets and salt and pepper to taste. Put the egg into a pan of boiling water and cook for *just 45 seconds* – the white and yolk must still be very runny. Carefully crack the egg and scoop all the center egg into the dressing; beat well. Heat the remaining olive oil with the rest of the garlic in a large shallow pan; add the small cubes of whole-wheat bread and fry until crisp and golden. Add the croutons, turkey strips and prepared dressing to the salad greens and toss well together. Serve immediately.

Brown Rice, Pineapple, Peanut and Red Pepper Salad

PREPARATION TIME: 15 minutes, plus cooling time

COOKING TIME: 10-15 minutes

SERVES: 4 people

½ cup brown or wild rice
Salt and freshly ground black pepper to taste
Juice of 1 orange
4 tblsp olive oil
1 tsp clear honey
2 slices fresh pineapple, peeled and chopped
2 tblsp shelled peanuts
1 large red pepper, seeded and cut into thin strips
Peeled segments of 2 large oranges

Cook the rice in boiling salted water until just tender. Meanwhile, prepare the orange dressing. Mix the orange juice, olive oil and

Chicory and Sweetbread Salad (right) and Turkey Caesar Salad (below).

honey together, and season to taste with salt and pepper. Drain the cooked rice thoroughly, and stir in the prepared dressing while the rice is still warm. Allow to cool. Mix in the pineapple, peanuts, and red pepper. Spoon into a shallow salad bowl and garnish with the orange segments.

Fisherman's Whole-wheat Pasta Salad

PREPARATION TIME: 20 minutes, plus cooling time

COOKING TIME: about 10 minutes

SERVES: 4 people

1 cup whole-wheat pasta shapes (shells, wheels, etc.)
Salt and freshly ground black pepper to taste
4 tblsp olive oil
2 tblsp dry white wine
1 tblsp chopped parsley
3 scallions, chopped
½ cup shelled cooked mussels
6 tblsp peeled prawns
½ cup flaked crabmeat
12 black olives

Garnish
Large peeled prawns

Cook the whole-wheat pasta in a large pan of boiling salted water until just tender – about 10 minutes. Meanwhile, prepare the dressing. Mix the olive oil with the white wine, parsley, and salt and pepper to taste. Drain the cooked pasta thoroughly and stir in the prepared dressing. Allow to cool. Mix in the chopped scallions, and then carefully stir in the shellfish; add the black olives. Spoon into one large salad bowl, or four individual ones.

Potato and Hazelnut Nests

PREPARATION TIME: 30 minutes, plus chilling time

COOKING TIME: 35 minutes

OVEN: 375°F

SERVES: 6 people

1½lb potatoes, peeled
Salt and freshly ground black pepper to taste
1½ tblsp butter
2 egg yolks
1 tblsp natural yogurt
2 tblsp finely chopped hazelnuts
1 cup low fat cream cheese
1 tblsp chopped chives (optional)

Garnish
A few flaked or coarsely chopped hazelnuts
Parsley

Cook the potatoes in boiling salted water until just tender. Drain them thoroughly. Mash the potatoes. Return the mashed potato to a clean saucepan and stir over a gentle heat to "dry" them out. Remove from the heat and beat in the butter, egg yolks, salt and pepper to taste, yogurt and chopped hazelnuts. Using a large piping bag fitted with a wide star nozzle, pipe the potato mixture into 6 nest shapes on a lightly greased cooky sheet. Chill for 30 minutes. Bake in the oven until pale golden – about 15 minutes (the potato nests can be glazed with beaten egg before baking, if liked). Beat the cream cheese until

This page: Potato, Lentil and Cheese Pie (top), Potato and Hazelnut Nests (center) and Parsnip, Orange and Ginger Puree (bottom).

Facing page: Fisherman's Whole-wheat Pasta Salad (top) and Brown Rice, Pineapple, Peanut and Red Pepper Salad (bottom).

soft and add the chopped chives and salt and pepper to taste. As soon as the potato and hazelnut nests come out of the oven, put a spoonful of the flavored cream cheese in the center of each one and sprinkle with the flaked hazelnuts. Garnish with parsley. Serve immediately. They make a delicious accompanying vegetable to fish.

Mushrooms Monegasque

PREPARATION TIME: 10 minutes, plus chilling time

COOKING TIME: about 13 minutes

SERVES: 4 people

1lb tomatoes, skinned, seeded and chopped
⅔ cup red wine
2 tblsp tomato paste
Pinch ground ginger
Salt and freshly ground black pepper to taste
1 clove garlic, peeled and finely chopped
2 scallions, finely chopped
2 tblsp raisins
½lb small mushrooms

To Serve
Crusty whole-wheat bread or rolls

Put the chopped tomatoes, red wine, tomato paste, ground ginger, salt and pepper to taste, and the garlic into a shallow pan. Simmer for 6-8 minutes. Add the scallions, raisins and mushrooms; cover the pan and simmer for 5 minutes. Allow to cool and then chill very thoroughly. Serve in small, shallow dishes, accompanied by crusty whole-wheat bread.

Fennel au Gratin

PREPARATION TIME: 15 minutes

COOKING TIME: 25-30 minutes

OVEN: 375°F

SERVES: 4 people

4 medium size heads of fennel
Juice of 1 lemon
Salt and freshly ground black pepper to taste
2 tblsp butter
3 tblsp flour
⅔ cup skimmed milk
⅔ cup dry white wine
4 tblsp natural yogurt
½ tsp chive mustard
6 tblsp grated Gruyère cheese

Garnish
1 tblsp chopped chives

Trim both ends of the fennel – reserve any feathery tops for garnish. Peel off any discolored patches from the fennel. Cut each head in half lengthwise. Put the fennel into a pan of boiling water to which you have added the lemon juice and 1 tsp salt; simmer steadily for 5 minutes. Drain the par-cooked fennel thoroughly. Melt the butter in a pan and stir in the flour; gradually stir in the milk and white wine. Bring to the boil and stir until lightly thickened. Beat in the yogurt, chive mustard, half the grated cheese, and salt and pepper to taste. Arrange the fennel in a lightly greased ovenproof dish and spoon the sauce evenly over the top; sprinkle with the remaining grated cheese. Bake in the oven for 25-30 minutes, until the sauce is golden. Garnish with the chopped chives and any reserved pieces of feathery fennel.

Potato, Lentil and Cheese Pie

PREPARATION TIME: 25 minutes

COOKING TIME: 1 hour
15 minutes

OVEN: 375°F

SERVES: 4 people

½lb lentils, soaked overnight
2½ cups chicken stock
1 small onion, finely chopped
2 tblsp butter
¼ cup flour
4 tblsp natural yogurt
1 egg, beaten
Salt and freshly ground black pepper to taste
1lb medium size potatoes, peeled, par-boiled, and thinly sliced
6 tblsp grated cheese

Garnish
A little crumbled fresh rosemary

Cook the drained, soaked lentils in three-quarters of the stock, with the chopped onion, until tender – about 30 minutes. Drain thoroughly. Melt the butter in a pan and stir in the flour; add the remaining ⅔ cup stock, and stir over the heat until thickened. Season to taste with salt and pepper and stir in half the yogurt. Stir the prepared sauce into the cooked lentils. Put the lentil mixture into a lightly greased ovenproof dish. Beat the remaining yogurt with the egg and salt and pepper to taste. Arrange the potato slices, overlapping, on top of the lentil mixture; brush all the potato slices with the egg and yogurt mixture, and sprinkle with the grated cheese. Bake in the oven for 40-45 minutes, until a rich golden brown. Sprinkle with the rosemary and serve piping hot.

Mushrooms Monegasque (top) and Fennel au Gratin (right).

Broccoli and Almond Risotto

PREPARATION TIME: 5 minutes

COOKING TIME: about 35 minutes

SERVES: 4 people

1 medium onion, finely chopped
2 tblsp olive oil
¾ cup brown or wild rice
3 cups chicken stock
Salt and freshly ground black pepper to taste
2 tblsp chopped, toasted almonds
1lb broccoli, divided into small flowerets
¼ cup grated Parmesan cheese

Garnish
Lightly toasted flaked almonds

Fry the onion gently in the olive oil for 3 minutes. Add the rice and stir over the heat for 1 minute, until the rice is evenly coated with oil. Gradually stir in the chicken stock. Bring to the boil and add salt and pepper to taste and the chopped almonds; cover and simmer for 20 minutes. Add the flowerets of broccoli; cover and simmer for a further 8 minutes, until all the stock has been absorbed. Stir in the Parmesan cheese and spoon into a serving dish; sprinkle with the toasted almonds and serve piping hot.

Parsnip, Orange and Ginger Purée

PREPARATION TIME: 15-20 minutes

COOKING TIME: about 25 minutes

SERVES: 4 people

1½lb parsnips, peeled and roughly chopped
2 thin strips orange peel
Salt and freshly ground black pepper to taste
2 tblsp butter
2 egg yolks
Generous pinch ground ginger
Finely grated rind of ½ orange
1 tblsp chopped preserved stem ginger

Garnish
Finely chopped parsley
Peeled segments of orange

Put the parsnips into a pan with the strips of orange peel, salt and pepper to taste, and sufficient water to just cover. Bring to the boil and simmer, covered, until the parsnips are just tender. Drain very thoroughly, removing the strips of orange peel. Mash the cooked parsnips and return to a clean pan; stir over a gentle heat to "dry" the parsnip puree. Beat in the butter, egg yolks, grated orange rind, salt and pepper to taste and the chopped stem ginger. Heat through and spoon into a serving dish. Garnish with chopped parsley and orange segments, and serve the puree piping hot.

Pasta, Rice and Pulses

Pasta Shells with Agliata Sauce

PREPARATION TIME: 10 minutes
COOKING TIME: about 8 minutes
SERVES: 4 people

10oz whole-wheat or plain pasta shells
Salt and freshly ground black pepper to taste

Sauce
6 tblsp olive oil
3 tblsp coarsely chopped parsley
2 cloves garlic, peeled
1 tblsp pine kernels
1 tblsp blanched almonds

Cook the pasta shells in a large pan of boiling salted water until just tender. Meanwhile, make the sauce. Put all the ingredients into a blender and blend until smooth; add salt and pepper to taste. Drain the hot, cooked pasta shells and toss together with the prepared sauce. Serve immediately.

Chickpea, Mint and Orange Salad

PREPARATION TIME: 15-25 minutes
SERVES: 4 people

¾ cup dried chickpeas, soaked overnight and cooked
2 tblsp chopped fresh mint
1 clove garlic, peeled and crushed
Salt and freshly ground black pepper to taste
Juice of 1 orange
Rind of 1 orange, cut into matchstick strips
3 tblsp olive oil
Segments from 2 large oranges

Garnish
Fresh mint leaves

Mix the chickpeas with half the chopped mint, garlic, and salt and pepper to taste. Mix the orange juice, strips of orange rind and olive oil together; stir into the chickpeas. Lightly mix in the orange segments and garnish with the remaining chopped mint.

Noodle and Ratatouille Bake

PREPARATION TIME: 25-30 minutes
COOKING TIME: 35-40 minutes
OVEN: 375°F
SERVES: 4 people

1 medium onion, thinly sliced
2 tblsp olive oil

2 cloves garlic, peeled and finely chopped
1 large green pepper, seeded and cut into cubes
1 large red pepper, seeded and cut into cubes
1 medium eggplant, cubed
6 tomatoes, skinned, seeded and chopped
1 tblsp tomato paste
3 tblsp red wine
Salt and freshly ground black pepper to taste

This page: Chickpea, Mint and Orange Salad (top) and Spinach and Feta Cheese Lasagne (bottom).

Facing page: Pasta Shells with Agliata Sauce (top) and Noodle and Ratatouille Bake (bottom).

½ cup green noodles, cooked
6 tblsp grated cheese

Fry the onion gently in the olive oil for 4 minutes; add the garlic, red and green peppers, eggplant and chopped tomatoes and cook covered for 5 minutes. Add the tomato paste, wine and salt and pepper to taste; simmer gently for 10-15 minutes, until the vegetables are almost soft. Remove from the heat and stir in the cooked noodles. Spoon into a shallow flameproof dish and sprinkle with the grated cheese. Bake in the oven for 15 minutes (alternatively, the dish can be flashed under a preheated broiler).

Spaghetti with Sweetbread Carbonara

PREPARATION TIME: 10-15 minutes

COOKING TIME: 10 minutes

SERVES: 4 people

1 onion, chopped
3 tblsp olive oil
12oz whole-wheat spaghetti
Salt and freshly ground black pepper to taste
½lb calves' sweetbreads, blanched, skinned and chopped
6 tblsp dry white wine
4 eggs
¼ cup grated Parmesan cheese
2 tblsp chopped fresh basil
1 clove garlic, peeled and crushed

Fry the onion gently in the olive oil for 5 minutes. Meanwhile, cook the spaghetti in a large pan of boiling, salted water for about 10 minutes, until just tender. Add the chopped sweetbreads to the onion and fry gently for 4 minutes. Add the white wine and cook briskly until it has almost evaporated. Beat the eggs with the Parmesan cheese, basil, garlic, and salt and pepper to taste. Drain the hot, cooked spaghetti thoroughly; immediately stir in the beaten egg mixture and the sweetbreads, so that the heat from the spaghetti cooks the egg. Garnish with basil and serve immediately.

Wild Rice and Egg Scramble

PREPARATION TIME: 10 minutes

COOKING TIME: 7-8 minutes

SERVES: 4 people

¾ cup wild or brown rice, cooked
1 tblsp butter
1 small onion, thinly sliced
2 tblsp olive oil
3 eggs
½ tsp mixed herbs
Salt and freshly ground black pepper to taste

Garnish
Chopped parsley

Heat the cooked rice through gently with the butter. Fry the onion gently in the olive oil for 3-4 minutes. Beat the eggs with the herbs, salt and pepper to taste, and 1 tblsp water. Add the beaten egg mixture to the onion and scramble lightly. Combine the hot rice and the scrambled egg and onion and serve immediately.

Pasta Shapes with Green Mayonnaise and Crab

PREPARATION TIME: 25 minutes

COOKING TIME: 8-10 minutes

SERVES: 4 people

Green Mayonnaise
4 tblsp mayonnaise
⅔ cup natural yogurt
3 tblsp cooked spinach
1 clove garlic, peeled
Salt and freshly ground black pepper to taste

12oz pasta shapes – shells, wheels, twists, etc.
Juice of 1 lemon
2 tblsp olive oil
¾ cup flaked crabmeat, or crab flavored sticks, shredded

Garnish
Parsley sprigs

For the green mayonnaise: put all the ingredients into the blender and blend until smooth. Cook the

pasta shapes in boiling salted water until tender. Drain thoroughly and toss in the lemon juice and olive oil, adding salt and pepper to taste. Mix in the flaked crabmeat. Spoon into a serving dish and serve warm, garnished with parsley.

Spinach and Feta Cheese Lasagne

PREPARATION TIME: 20-25 minutes

COOKING TIME: about 35 minutes

OVEN: 375°F

SERVES: 6 people

1lb cooked and drained spinach (or thawed frozen spinach)
Generous pinch grated nutmeg
Salt and freshly ground black pepper to taste
2 tblsp natural yogurt
1 clove garlic, peeled and crushed
1 egg yolk
¾ cup Feta cheese, crumbled
½lb green or whole-wheat lasagne (the non pre-cook variety)

Sauce
⅔ cup natural yogurt
1 egg, beaten
2 tblsp grated Parmesan cheese
3 firm tomatoes, sliced

Mix the cooked spinach with nutmeg and salt and pepper to taste; stir in the yogurt, garlic, egg yolk and crumbled Feta cheese. Layer the lasagne and spinach mixture in a lightly greased ovenproof dish, starting with spinach and finishing with lasagne. For the sauce: mix the yogurt with the beaten egg and half the grated Parmesan cheese; spoon over the lasagne. Top with the sliced tomato and the remaining Parmesan cheese. Bake in the oven for about 35 minutes, until golden. Serve piping hot.

This page: Wild Rice and Egg Scramble (top) and Pasta Shapes with Green Mayonnaise and Crab (bottom).

Facing page: Chicken Liver Risotto with Red Beans (top) and Spaghetti with Sweetbread Carbonara (bottom).

Rice and Vegetable Loaf with Yogurt and Mint Sauce

PREPARATION TIME: 25-30 minutes

COOKING TIME: 53 minutes

OVEN: 375°F

SERVES: 6-8

1 small onion, finely chopped
2 tblsp olive oil
1 clove garlic, peeled and crushed
1 cup wild rice, cooked and drained
   (not rinsed)
3 zucchini, finely shredded
2 medium size carrots, finely
   shredded
2 tblsp chopped parsley
Salt and freshly ground black pepper
   to taste
1 tsp chopped fresh thyme
2-3 eggs, beaten
6 tblsp grated cheese

Garnish
Fresh mint

Fry the onion gently in the olive oil for 3 minutes. Mix together with all the remaining ingredients, adding sufficient beaten egg to give a stiff yet moist consistency. Spoon the mixture into a deep, greased and lined loaf pan, smoothing the surface level. Cover with a piece of lightly greased foil. Bake in the oven for 50 minutes. Allow to cool slightly in the pan before turning out. Serve the rice and vegetable loaf cut into slices, and accompanied by the yogurt and mint sauce. Garnish with mint. For the sauce: mix ⅔ cup natural yogurt with salt and freshly ground black pepper to taste and 1 tblsp chopped mint.

Black-eye Beans with Curry Dressing (far left) and Noodles with Fresh Tomato Sauce (above left).

Noodles with Kidney Beans and Pesto

PREPARATION TIME: 5 minutes

COOKING TIME: about 10 minutes

SERVES: 4 people

½lb whole-wheat or plain noodles
Salt and freshly ground black pepper
  to taste
1 small onion, finely chopped
2 tblsp olive oil
1 clove garlic, peeled and crushed
2 tsp pesto sauce (see recipe)
8oz cooked red kidney beans

Garnish
Sprigs fresh basil

Cook the noodles in a large pan of
boiling salted water until just

tender. Meanwhile, fry the onion
gently in the olive oil for 3 minutes;
mix in the garlic and pesto sauce.
Drain the cooked noodles
thoroughly; add to the onion and
pesto mixture, together with the
red kidney beans. Stir over a gentle
heat for 1-2 minutes and serve
piping hot, garnished with basil.

Black-eye Beans with Curry Dressing

PREPARATION TIME: 10-15
  minutes

COOKING TIME: 35-40 minutes

SERVES: 4 people

½lb black-eye beans, soaked
  overnight

Salt and freshly ground black pepper
  to taste
1 small onion, thinly sliced
1 green pepper, seeded and finely
  chopped
Juice of ½ lemon
2 tblsp cashew nuts, whole or roughly
  chopped

Dressing
⅔ cup natural yogurt
2 tsp curry powder
2 tblsp fresh pineapple juice
1 clove garlic, crushed

Garnish
Curry powder

Simmer the beans in salted water
until tender. Drain. Mix the black-
eye beans with the onion and green
pepper. Stir in the lemon juice, salt
and pepper to taste and the cashew
nuts. For the dressing: mix all the
ingredients together, adding salt
and pepper to taste. Spoon the
bean salad into a bowl, and spoon
the prepared dressing over the top.
Sprinkle with curry powder.

Chicken Liver Risotto with Red Beans

PREPARATION TIME: 15 minutes

COOKING TIME: about 28
  minutes

SERVES: 4 people

1 medium onion, finely chopped
2 tblsp olive oil
1 clove garlic, peeled and crushed
¾ cup brown or wild rice
3 cups chicken stock
Salt and freshly ground black pepper
  to taste
½lb chicken livers, chopped
2 tblsp butter
¾ cup cooked red kidney beans
1 tblsp chopped parsley

Fry the onion gently in the olive oil
for 3 minutes. Add the garlic and
the rice and stir over the heat for 1
minute, until the rice is evenly
coated with oil. Gradually stir in
the chicken stock. Bring to the boil
and add salt and pepper to taste;
cover and simmer for 20 minutes.
Meanwhile, fry the chopped
chicken livers in the butter for
about 4 minutes, until sealed on
the outside but still pink in the
center. Drain the chicken livers
with a slotted spoon and stir into
the cooked rice, together with the
red kidney beans and chopped
parsley. Heat through. Serve hot
with grated Parmesan cheese, if
liked.

Cucumber with Yogurt, Dill and Burghul

PREPARATION TIME: 25 minutes

SERVES: 4 people

6 tblsp burghul
1 clove garlic, peeled and crushed
Juice of 1 lemon
4 tblsp olive oil
1 tblsp fresh dill
Salt and freshly ground black pepper
  to taste
½ a large cucumber, halved, seeded
  and chopped
2 tblsp natural yogurt

Garnish
Coarsely grated lemon rind
Sprigs of fresh dill

Soak the burghul in sufficient
warm water to cover, for 10
minutes. Squeeze the drained
burghul in a clean cloth to remove
excess moisture. Mix the prepared
burghul with the garlic, lemon
juice, oil, dill and salt and pepper to
taste. Stir in the cucumber and the
yogurt. Spoon into a serving dish
and garnish with lemon rind and
dill.
Note: instead of mixing the yogurt
into the burghul, make a well in the
center of the prepared burghul and
spoon the yogurt into the center.

Noodles with Fresh Tomato Sauce

PREPARATION TIME: 10-15
  minutes

COOKING TIME: 6-8 minutes

SERVES: 4 people

1lb tomatoes, skinned and roughly
  chopped
1 small onion, peeled and chopped
1 clove garlic, peeled and chopped
1 tblsp chopped parsley
1 tblsp chopped basil
1 cup olive oil
Salt and freshly ground black pepper
  to taste
12oz noodles (green, yellow, or whole-
  wheat)

Garnish
Sprigs fresh basil

Put the tomatoes, onion, garlic,
herbs, olive oil, and salt and pepper
to taste into the blender and blend
until smooth. Cook the noodles in
boiling salted water until just
tender. Drain thoroughly. Toss the
cooked noodles in the prepared
tomato sauce. Garnish with sprigs
of fresh basil and serve
immediately.

Skillet Rice Cake

PREPARATION TIME: 25 minutes

COOKING TIME: about 15 minutes

SERVES: 4 people

1 medium onion, thinly sliced or
  chopped
1 clove garlic, peeled and chopped
2 tblsp olive oil
1 tblsp chopped fresh thyme
1 red pepper, seeded and thinly sliced
1 green pepper, seeded and thinly
  sliced
4 eggs
Salt and freshly ground black pepper
  to taste
6 tblsp cooked brown or wild rice
3 tblsp natural yogurt
6 tblsp grated cheese

Garnish
Chopped fresh thyme

Fry the chopped onion and garlic
gently in the olive oil in a frying pan
for 3 minutes. Add the thyme and
sliced peppers and fry gently for a
further 4-5 minutes. Beat the eggs
with salt and pepper to taste. Add
the cooked rice to the fried
vegetables and then add the beaten
egg; cook over a moderate heat,
stirring from time to time, until the
egg starts to set underneath. Spoon
the yogurt over the top of the par-
set egg and sprinkle with the
cheese. Place under a moderately
hot broiler until puffed and golden.
Serve immediately, straight from
the pan.

Italian Pasta Pie

PREPARATION TIME: 35 minutes

COOKING TIME: 1 hour 5 minutes

OVEN: 375°F

SERVES: 6-8 people

1¼lbs puff pastry
1lb fresh spinach, cooked and drained
  thoroughly
¾ cup curd cheese
1 clove garlic, peeled and crushed
Salt and freshly ground black pepper
  to taste
Generous pinch ground nutmeg
½ cup pasta shapes, cooked until just
  tender
6 tblsp shelled mussels
1 tblsp chopped fresh basil
1 egg, beaten

To Glaze Pastry
Beaten egg
Grated Parmesan cheese

2 tblsp tomato paste
1 tblsp chopped fresh thyme
Salt and freshly ground black pepper
   to taste
½lb finely chopped cooked chicken
6 tomatoes, skinned, seeded and
   chopped
1 tsp pesto sauce (see recipe)
1 tblsp chopped cashew nuts
1 tblsp chopped walnuts

12oz spaghetti, plain or whole-wheat

Garnish
Chopped walnuts

Fry the onion and garlic in the olive oil for 3 minutes. Add the red wine, tomato paste, thyme and salt and pepper to taste. Bring to the boil and simmer for 10 minutes. Add the chopped chicken, chopped tomatoes, pesto sauce, cashew nuts and walnuts; simmer the sauce for a further few minutes. Meanwhile, cook the spaghetti in boiling, salted water for 8-10 minutes, until just tender. Drain the spaghetti thoroughly. If the sauce is too thick for your liking, thin it down with a little hot stock or water. Pile the cooked spaghetti into a serving dish and spoon the hot sauce over the top. Sprinkle with extra chopped walnuts and serve immediately.

Roll out ⅔ of the puff pastry quite thinly and use to line the sides and base of a loose-bottomed 7 inch round cake tin; press the pastry carefully into the shape of the tin, avoiding any cracks or splits. Roll out the remaining pastry to a circle large enough to cover the top of the cake pan generously. Mix the spinach with the curd cheese, garlic, salt, pepper and nutmeg to taste, cooked pasta, mussels and the beaten egg; spoon the filling into the pastry lined pan. Brush the rim of the pastry with beaten egg; lay the rolled-out portion of pastry over the filling and press the adjoining pastry edges together to seal. Trim off the excess pastry, and pinch the edges decoratively. Cut decorative shapes from the pastry trimmings and fix on top of the pie; glaze with beaten egg and sprinkle with grated Parmesan cheese. Bake in the oven for 45 minutes; cover with a piece of foil and cook for a further 20 minutes. Unmold carefully from the pan and serve the pie hot, cut into wedges. Note: the top of the pie can be sprinkled with a few pine kernels prior to baking, if liked.

Spaghetti with Chicken Bolognaise and Nuts

PREPARATION TIME:	15-20 minutes
COOKING TIME:	15 minutes
SERVES:	4 people

Sauce
1 medium onion, finely chopped
1 clove garlic, peeled and finely
   chopped
2 tblsp olive oil
1 cup red wine

Facing page: Italian Pasta Pie (top) and Spaghetti with Chicken Bolognese and Nuts (bottom).

This page: Rice and Vegetable Loaf with Yogurt and Mint Sauce (top) and Skillet Rice Cake (bottom).

Desserts and Cakes

Ricotta Pancakes with Honey and Raisin Sauce

PREPARATION TIME: 10 minutes

COOKING TIME: 2-3 minutes

SERVES: 4 people

Sauce
4 tblsp clear honey
Juice ½ lemon
1 tblsp raisins
1 tblsp pine kernels

Filling
1 cup curd cheese, or Ricotta
Grated rind of ½ lemon
2 tblsp raisins
1 tblsp chopped pine kernels

8 small, hot pancakes

To Decorate
Twists of lemon

For the sauce: put all the ingredients into a small pan and warm through gently. For the filling: beat the cheese and the lemon rind until soft; mix in the raisins and pine kernels. Divide the filling amongst the hot pancakes and either roll them up, or fold them into triangles. Arrange the pancakes on warm plates, spoon the sauce over the top and decorate with twists of lemon. Serve immediately.

Almond Stuffed Figs

PREPARATION TIME: 25 minutes

SERVES: 4 people

4 large ripe figs
4 tblsp ground almonds
2 tblsp orange juice
2 tblsp finely chopped dried apricots

Sauce
4 tblsp natural yogurt
Finely grated rind of ½ orange

Garnish
Wedges of ripe fig
Wedges of lime
Ground cinnamon

Make a cross cut in each fig, without cutting right down and through the base. Ease the four sections of each fig out, rather like a flower head. Mix the ground almonds with the orange juice and chopped dried apricots; press into the center of each fig. For the sauce: mix the yogurt with the orange rind, and thin down with *a little* water. Spoon a pool of orange flavored yogurt onto each of 4 small plates; sit a stuffed fig in the center of each one. Decorate with wedges of fig and lime and a sprinkling of ground cinnamon.

Honey and Apple Tart

PREPARATION TIME: about 45 minutes

COOKING TIME: 35-40 minutes

OVEN: 375°F

SERVES: 6 people

¾ cup whole-wheat flour
¾ all-purpose flour
6 tblsp butter
1 egg yolk
3 tblsp cold water

Filling
1¼ cups unsweetened apple puree
1 tblsp honey
2 egg yolks
2 tblsp ground almonds
3 large eating apples, quartered, cored and thinly sliced
A little pale soft brown sugar

Glaze
3 tblsp clear honey, warmed

For the pastry: put the flours into a bowl; add the butter in small pieces and blend. Beat the egg yolk with 2 tblsp of the water and add to the dry ingredients; mix to a soft yet firm dough, adding a little extra water as necessary (whole-wheat flour varies from batch to batch as to how much liquid it will absorb). Roll out the dough on a floured surface and use to line a 9 inch loose-bottomed, fluted flan pan; pinch up the edges well. Prick the base. For the filling: mix the apple puree with the brandy, egg yolks, honey and ground almonds. Spread over the base of the pastry case. Arrange the apple slices in overlapping, concentric circles on top of the apple and almond filling. Dust lightly with soft brown sugar. Bake in the oven for 35-40 minutes (if the apples start to brown too much, cover the filling with a circle of foil). As soon as the flan comes out of the oven, brush the apple top with warmed honey. This flan can be served cold, but it is best served warm.

Prune, Apricot and Nut Torten

PREPARATION TIME: 30 minutes, plus "plumping" time

COOKING TIME: 25 minutes

OVEN: 375°F

SERVES: 6-8 people

½ cup dried apricots
½ cup dried prunes
1¼ cups red wine, or dry cider

Nut Shortcake
A stick of butter
¼ cup soft brown sugar
1 cup whole-wheat flour
¼ cup ground hazelnuts
3 tblsp finely chopped walnuts

Glaze
2 tblsp clear honey, warmed

To Decorate
1 tblsp pine kernels
1 tblsp hazelnuts

Put the apricots and prunes into a bowl. Warm the wine or cider and pour it over the dried fruits; leave them to "plump" for 4 hours. For the shortcake: work the butter, brown sugar, flour and ground hazelnuts together. Knead lightly to a smooth dough, working in the chopped walnuts. Press evenly over the base of a 9 inch fluted, loose-bottomed flan pan. Bake in the oven for 15 minutes. Drain the plumped prunes and apricots thoroughly on absorbent paper. Remove the shortcake from the oven and arrange the plumped fruits on top. Cover with a piece of foil and return to the oven for a further 10 minutes. Remove the shortcake carefully from its pan.

Glaze the fruits on top with the warmed honey and sprinkle with the nuts. This is absolutely delicious served warm from the oven, but is equally good served cold.

Ricotta Pancakes with Honey and Raisin Sauce (right) and Almond Stuffed Figs (below).

Passion Fruit Ice Cream

PREPARATION TIME: 20 minutes, plus freezing time

SERVES: 4 people

6 passion fruit
1¼ cups thick natural yogurt
2 egg yolks
2 tsp honey

To Decorate
1-2 passion fruit, halved and scooped

For the ice cream: halve the passion fruit and scoop all the center pulp into a bowl. Add the yogurt, egg yolks and honey, and mix well together. Pour into a shallow container and freeze until firm. Scoop the ice cream into stemmed glasses and trickle a little passion fruit pulp over each portion. Serve immediately. Note: this ice cream goes *very* hard, and needs to be removed from the freezer several minutes before scooping.

Strawberry and Melon Salad

PREPARATION TIME: 25 minutes

SERVES: 4 people

8oz large strawberries, hulled
1 small Charentais or Ogen melon
Juice of 1 orange
1 tblsp brandy

To Decorate
Small sprigs fresh mint

Slice the strawberries quite thinly. Halve and de-seed the melon and then scoop it into small balls (there is a special cutter for doing this, but you can do it with a coffee spoon). Arrange the strawberry slices and melon balls on individual glass plates. Mix the orange juice with the brandy and dribble over the fruit. Decorate with mint.

This page: Prune, Apricot and Nut Torten (top) and Honey and Apple Tart (bottom).

Facing page: Passion Fruit Ice Cream (top) and Strawberry and Melon Salad (bottom).

Jellied Grape Shortcake

PREPARATION TIME: 45 minutes, plus cooling and chilling

COOKING TIME: about 20 minutes

OVEN: 375°F

SERVES: 6 people

¼ cup butter
2 tblsp soft brown sugar
½ cup whole-wheat flour
2 tblsp ground almonds

Jelly Topping

½lb green grapes, halved and de-pipped
2½ cups water
Thinly pared rind of 2 lemons
1 tblsp honey
½oz powdered gelatin
2 tblsp water
Yellow food coloring

Work the butter, brown sugar, flour and ground almonds together. Knead lightly to a smooth dough. Press evenly over the base of a 8 inch loose-bottomed cake pan. Bake in the oven for 12-15 minutes, until the shortcake is pale golden. Remove from the oven and allow to cool completely. Lightly grease the sides of the cake pan above the baked shortcake. Arrange the halved grapes on top of the shortcake. Put the water and lemon rind into a pan; bring to the boil and allow to bubble briskly for 5 minutes. Remove the pan from the heat and allow the liquid to cool. Strain the lemon liquid and measure off 1¾ cups. Stir in the honey. Dissolve the gelatin in the 2 tblsp water and add to the lemon liquid (it can be tinted with a few drops of yellow food coloring at this stage, if liked). Leave in a cool place until it starts to set; pour the setting jelly over the grapes, making sure that the top surface is level. Chill for 2-3 hours until set. Serve cut into wedges.

Hazelnut and Apple Meringue Torten

PREPARATION TIME: 25-30 minutes

COOKING TIME: 45 minutes

OVEN: 375°F then 325°F

SERVES: 6-8 people

A stick of butter
¼ cup soft brown sugar
1 cup whole-wheat flour
¼ cup ground hazelnuts
2 tblsp chopped hazelnuts

Jellied Grape Shortcake (far right) and Chestnut Parfait (right).

2 egg whites
6 tblsp golden granulated sugar
1¼ cups thick, unsweetened apple puree

Work the butter, brown sugar, whole-wheat flour and ground hazelnuts to a soft, smooth dough. Knead lightly and work in the chopped hazelnuts. Press evenly over the base of a 9 inch fluted, loose-bottomed flan tin. Bake in the oven for 10 minutes. Meanwhile, whisk the egg whites until stiff but not "dry"; gradually whisk in the golden granulated sugar. Remove the shortcake from the oven and pipe or swirl the meringue in a border around the edge. Return to the oven, lower the heat, and bake for a further 35 minutes, until golden. Fill immediately with the apple puree and serve while still warm.

Chestnut Parfait

PREPARATION TIME: 15 minutes

SERVES: 4 people

z unsweetened chestnut puree
blsp honey
tblsp brandy
tblsp thick natural yogurt
enerous pinch ground cinnamon

To Decorate
Small cinnamon sticks

Beat the chestnut purée with the honey and brandy; blend in the yogurt and cinnamon. Spoon into glass custard cups or stemmed glasses. Spike each one with a cinnamon stick.
Note: this is very rich, and you may prefer to make the above quantities serve 6 small portions.

Iced Kiwi Fruit and Yogurt Pudding

PREPARATION TIME: 15 minutes, plus chilling time

SERVES: 4 people

1¼ cups thick natural yogurt
Artificial sweetener to taste, or a little honey
4 kiwi fruit, peeled and chopped
2 kiwi fruit, peeled and thinly sliced

Mix the yogurt with sweetener or honey to taste, and stir in the chopped kiwi fruit. Place slices of kiwi fruit so that they stand upright against the sides of 4 stemmed glasses; spoon the yogurt and kiwi fruit mixture into the center. Chill briefly, for about 20-30 minutes, before serving.

Glazed Cherry Rice Pudding

PREPARATION TIME: 20 minutes, plus cooling and chilling time

COOKING TIME: 45 minutes to 1 hour

SERVES: 4-6 people

¼ cup brown rice
2 tblsp soft brown sugar
2½ cups skimmed milk
½ tsp vanilla essence
Generous pinch ground nutmeg
2 tblsp thick natural yogurt

½lb fresh cherries, de-stalked and pitted
⅔ cup pure, red grape juice
⅔ cup water
2 tsp powdered gelatin

Put the rice, sugar, skimmed milk, vanilla essence and nutmeg into a solid based pan; bring to the boil and simmer gently for ¾-1 hour, until the rice mixture is thick and creamy. Allow to cool and then beat in the yogurt. Spoon into a glass bowl and arrange the cherries on the top. Mix the grape juice with half the water; dissolve the gelatin in the remaining water and

then add to the grape juice. Leave in a cool place until syrupy. Spoon the red glaze evenly over the cherries. Chill until set.

This page: Banana, Almond and Orange Truffles (top) and Hazelnut and Apple Meringue Torten (bottom).

Facing page: Iced Kiwi Fruit and Yogurt Pudding (top) and Glazed Cherry Rice Pudding (bottom).

Mango and Orange Mousse

PREPARATION TIME: 35-40 minutes, plus chilling time

SERVES: 4-6 people

1¾ cups fresh mango pulp
Finely grated rind of ½ orange
Artificial sweetener to taste
½oz powdered gelatin
2 tblsp orange juice
2 tblsp natural yogurt
2 egg whites

To Decorate
Twisted strips orange peel

Mix the mango pulp with the orange rind and artificial sweetener to taste. Dissolve the gelatin in the orange juice. Add to the mango pulp, together with the yogurt. Leave until the mixture is on the point of setting. Whisk the egg whites until stiff but not "dry", and fold lightly but thoroughly into the thickened mango mixture. Spoon into stemmed glasses and chill until set. Decorate with twisted strips of orange peel.

No Sugar Fresh Mincemeat Tarts (top right), Lemon Yogurt Cake (above) and Muesli Biscuits (far right).

Banana, Almond and Orange Truffles

PREPARATION TIME: 25 minutes
MAKES: 10

2 bananas, peeled
Juice of ½ orange
Finely grated rind of 1 orange
½ cup ground almonds
2 tblsp finely chopped blanched
    almonds
1 tblsp dark, soft brown sugar
Plain chocolate vermicelli

Mash the bananas with the orange juice and rind; mix in the ground almonds, chopped almonds and brown sugar. Chill the mixture until it is firm enough to shape. Roll into small balls, about the size of a golf ball. Roll each one in chocolate vermicelli so as to give an even coating. Chill once again.

No Sugar Fresh Mincemeat Tarts

PREPARATION TIME: 30 minutes
COOKING TIME: 20-25 minutes
OVEN: 375°F
MAKES: 4

1 eating apple, cored and finely
    chopped
2 tblsp raisins
2 tblsp currants
1 tblsp chopped pitted dates
1 tblsp chopped nuts (any variety)
2 tblsp clear honey

Pastry
1 cup whole-wheat flour
1 cup all-purpose flour
A stick of butter
1 egg yolk
3 tblsp water

Glaze
Beaten egg white
Caster sugar

Mix the chopped apple with the raisins, currants, chopped dates, nuts and honey. Keep covered while you make the pastry. Put the flours into a mixing bowl and blend the butter. Mix the egg yolk with 2 tblsp cold water; add to the sieved flours and mix to a soft, smooth dough, adding a little extra water if necessary. Roll out the dough quite thinly and use to line 4 individual tartlet pans (preferably with loose bottoms). Press up the edges well, trimming off excess pastry. Roll out the pastry trimmings and cut into thin strips. Fill the pastry cases with the fresh mincemeat, and lay a lattice of pastry strips over the top of each one. Press the strips to the side of the pastry case to seal. Glaze the strips and edges of the tarts with beaten egg white and sprinkle lightly with sugar. Bake in the oven for 20-25 minutes, until golden. Serve warm or cold.
Note: these are not little tarts, like jam tarts, and the pastry cases need to be about 4 inches in diameter.

Lemon Yogurt Cake

PREPARATION TIME: 45 minutes
COOKING TIME: about
                    25 minutes
OVEN: 375°F
SERVES: 8-10 people

6 eggs
¾ cup soft brown sugar
1½ cups all-purpose flour
Pinch mixed spice
Finely grated rind of 2 lemons
4 tblsp water
2 tblsp clear honey

Filling
1 cup curd cheese
2 tblsp clear honey
Finely grated rind and juice of ½
    lemon
Few drops vanilla essence
2 tblsp natural yogurt

Langues de chat biscuits
1 cup thick natural yogurt
Matchstick strips lemon peel

Grease 3 large sandwich pans, each 9 inches in diameter; dust each one lightly with flour. Whisk the eggs and brown sugar together until thick, light and creamy (when the whisk is lifted free from the mixture it should leave a trail on the surface). Sieve the flour and spice and fold lightly but thoroughly into the whisked mixture. Divide the mixture amongst the prepared pans, tilting them so that the mixture spreads evenly. Bake the sponge layers for 25 minutes.

Allow them to shrink slightly from their pans before turning the baked sponges onto cooling racks. Put the lemon rind and water into a small pan; boil briskly until reduced by one half. Add the honey to the remaining lemon liquid and heat through together. Trickle the honey and lemon syrup over each sponge layer. For the filling: soften the curd cheese and beat with the honey, lemon rind and juice, vanilla essence and yogurt until smooth. Sandwich the three sponge layers together with the cheese filling, saving a few spoonfuls for fixing the biscuits to the sides of the cake. Fix langues de chat biscuits all around the sides of the assembled cake; attach each one with a little of the cheese filling. Spread the top of the cake with thick yogurt and decorate with matchstick strips of lemon peel.

Lemon and Ginger Cheesecake

PREPARATION TIME: 45 minutes, plus chilling time
SERVES: 6-8 people

3 tblsp butter, melted
2 tblsp soft brown sugar
6 tblsp oatmeal biscuits, crushed

Filling
¾ cup curd cheese
2 eggs, separated
Finely grated rind of 1 lemon
¼ cup light, soft brown sugar
⅔ cup natural yogurt
½oz powdered gelatin
3 tblsp water
Juice of ½ lemon
3 pieces preserved stem ginger, rinsed
    in warm water and chopped

To Decorate
4 tblsp thick natural yogurt
Fine matchstick strips lemon peel, or
    twists of lemon

Lightly grease an 7 inch loose-bottomed cake pan. For the base: mix the melted butter, soft brown sugar and crushed biscuits together; press evenly over the base of the pan. Chill while you make the filling. For the filling: beat the curd cheese with the egg yolks, lemon rind, soft brown sugar and yogurt. Dissolve the gelatin in the water and add to the cheese mixture, together with the lemon juice; leave on one side until the mixture is on the point of setting. Whisk the egg whites until stiff but not "dry", and fold lightly but thoroughly into the cheese mixture, together with the

chopped ginger. Spoon the mixture into the prepared cake pan, smoothing the surface level. Chill for 3-4 hours, until the filling has set. Unmold the cheesecake carefully. Swirl natural yogurt over the top of the cheesecake and decorate with strips of lemon peel or lemon twists.

Muesli Biscuits

PREPARATION TIME: 20 minutes
COOKING TIME: 15 minutes
OVEN: 375°F
MAKES: about 20

½ cup softened butter
½ cup soft brown sugar
1 egg, beaten
1 cup whole-wheat flour
¼ cup muesli
2 tblsp flaked almonds

Beat the butter and sugar together until light and fluffy. Beat in the egg, adding a little flour if the mixture shows signs of curdling. Work in the remaining flour, muesli and flaked almonds. Shape the mixture into small balls, using floured hands. Place on greased cooky sheets, allowing room for spreading. Flatten the balls of biscuit dough slightly. Bake in the oven for 15 minutes until crisp and golden. Allow to cool slightly before removing the baked biscuits to a cooling rack.

Date and Pistachio Shortbreads

PREPARATION TIME: 20 minutes
COOKING TIME: 12-15 minutes
OVEN: 375°F
MAKES: about 12

A stick of butter
¼ cup soft brown sugar
1 cup whole-wheat flour
¼ cup ground almonds
6 tblsp stoned dates, chopped
2 tblsp chopped shelled pistachios

To Decorate
Chopped shelled pistachios

Work the butter, brown sugar, whole-wheat flour and ground almonds to a soft, smooth dough. Knead lightly, working in the chopped dates and pistachios. Press the mixture into small boat-shaped molds. Press a few chopped pistachios into the top of each uncooked shortbread. Bake in the oven for 12-15 minutes.

Apricot and Walnut Teabread

PREPARATION TIME: 20 minutes	
COOKING TIME: 1 hour	
	30 minutes
OVEN: 325°F	
Makes: 1 loaf	

¾ cup softened butter
¾ cup light soft brown sugar
3 eggs, beaten
2 cups whole-wheat flour
1½ tsp baking powder
2 tblsp milk
½ cup dried apricots, chopped
¼ cup chopped walnuts

To Decorate
2 tblsp clear honey, warmed
Extra chopped dried apricots

Lightly grease a 2lb loaf pan, and line the base with a piece of greased greaseproof paper. Cream the butter and sugar until light and fluffy. Gradually beat in the eggs, adding a little flour if the mixture shows signs of curdling. Mix in the flour and baking powder, together with the milk, and finally stir in the chopped apricots and nuts. Put the mixture into the prepared loaf pan, smoothing the top level. Bake in the oven for 1 hour 30 minutes. If the top of the loaf starts to darken too much, cover it with a piece of foil. As soon as the loaf comes out of the oven, brush the top with the warmed honey and sprinkle with the chopped apricots. Leave to cool in the pan for a few minutes before turning out.

Golden Pistachio Meringues

PREPARATION TIME: 15-20	
	minutes
COOKING TIME: 1 hour	
OVEN: 225°F	
MAKES: about 6	

2 egg whites
½ cup golden granulated sugar

Filling
½ cup curd cheese
1 tblsp clear honey
2 tblsp chopped shelled pistachios

To Decorate
Chopped shelled pistachios

Whisk the egg whites until stiff but not dry and then gradually whisk in the golden granulated sugar. Pipe into 6 nest shapes on lightly greased and floured cooky sheets. Bake in the oven for 1 hour. The meringues should be fairly crisp but they should not "color". Allow to cool. For the filling: cream the cheese until soft; beat in the honey and chopped pistachios. Fill the meringue nests with the cheese filling. Sprinkle each one with extra pistachios.

Cinnamon and Peanut Cookies

PREPARATION TIME: 15-20	
	minutes
COOKING TIME: 20 minutes	
OVEN: 350°F	
MAKES: about 20	

A stick of softened butter
½ cup soft brown sugar
1 egg, beaten
4 tblsp clear honey
2¼ cups whole-wheat flour
½ tsp ground cinnamon
1 tsp baking powder
Pinch salt
6 tblsp shelled peanuts

Cream the butter and sugar until well mixed (do not over-beat). Mix in the beaten egg and honey and then mix in the flour, cinnamon, baking powder and salt. Put heaped teaspoons of the mixture onto greased cooky sheets, allowing room for spreading; flatten each one slightly with the rounded side of a dampened spoon. Stud the tops with peanuts. Bake in the oven for 20 minutes.
Note: for really golden, topped biscuits bake them as above for just 15 minutes; brush each one with beaten egg and return to the oven for a further 5 minutes.

This page: (left picture) Cinnamon and Peanut Cookies (top) and Golden Pistachio Meringues (bottom). (Right picture) Mango and Orange Mousse (top) and Lemon and Ginger Cheesecake (bottom).

Facing page: Apricot and Walnut Teabread (top) and Date and Pistachio Shortbreads (bottom).

Drinks, Sauces and Dressings

Tropical Fruit Flummery

PREPARATION TIME: 10 minutes

SERVES: 4 people

3 kiwi fruit, peeled and chopped
2 ripe nectarines, halved, stoned and
  chopped
2 slices fresh pineapple, peeled and
  chopped
Juice of 1 fresh lime
1¼ cups unsweetened pineapple juice

To Decorate
Slices of peeled kiwi fruit, or lime

Put the kiwi fruit, nectarines, pineapple, lime juice and pineapple juice into the blender and blend until smooth. Pour into tall glasses and top up with iced water (either mineral or tap water). Decorate the rim of each glass with a slice of kiwi fruit or lime.

Mulled Apple and Honey

PREPARATION TIME: 5 minutes

COOKING TIME: 4 minutes

SERVES: 4 people

1¾ cups unsweetened apple juice
⅔ cup water
2 tsp honey
2 cinnamon sticks, split in half
6 cloves
3 strips lemon peel

To Serve
4 cinnamon sticks

Put the apple juice into a pan with the water, honey, broken cinnamon sticks, cloves and lemon peel; simmer very gently for 4 minutes. Remove the broken cinnamon sticks and pour liquid into heatproof glasses. Spike each drink with a whole cinnamon stick and serve.

Spicy Fresh Mango Juice

PREPARATION TIME: 15 minutes

SERVES: 4 people

1¼ cups fresh mango pulp
Juice of 1 lemon
1 tblsp clear honey
Generous pinch ground ginger
Generous pinch nutmeg
⅔ cup unsweetened orange juice
⅔ cup water
1 small piece fresh root ginger

To Decorate
4 rings of orange

Put the mango pulp, lemon juice, honey, ground ginger, nutmeg, orange juice and water into the blender and blend until smooth. Pour into 4 glasses, adding two or three ice cubes to each one. Put the piece of root ginger into a garlic crusher and squeeze a few drops into each glass. Slide a ring of orange over the rim of each glass and serve.

This page: Tropical Fruit Flummery (top) and Grapefruit Shrub (bottom).

Facing page: Spicy Fresh Mango Juice (right) and Mulled Apple and Honey (left).

Almond and Tarragon French Dressing

PREPARATION TIME: 5 minutes

MAKES: about 1¼ cups

1 cup good green olive oil
4 tblsp tarragon vinegar
1 tblsp chopped fresh tarragon
1 clove garlic, peeled and crushed
Salt and freshly ground black pepper
    to taste
2 tblsp finely chopped blanched
    almonds

Mix all the ingredients together. Keep in a screw topped bottle or jar, in a cool place (not in the refrigerator).

Pesto Sauce

PREPARATION TIME: 5 minutes

MAKES: about 1¼ cups

1 large bunch fresh basil
4 cloves garlic, peeled
3 tblsp pine kernels
⅔ cup good green olive oil
1 tblsp lemon juice
Salt and freshly ground black pepper
    to taste

Put all the ingredients into the blender and blend until fairly smooth; the sauce should still have a little texture to it. Keep in a screw top jar in the refrigerator, for no more than a week. Serve with cooked pasta, with cold meats such as Italian ham, and with cooked game and poultry.

Fresh Tomato and Basil Sauce

PREPARATION TIME: 10-15
                                minutes

MAKES: 1¾ cups

1 small onion, finely chopped
1lb tomatoes, skinned, seeded and
    chopped
2 tblsp tomato paste
1 tsp honey
1 tsp finely grated orange rind
2 cloves garlic, peeled
Salt and freshly ground black pepper
    to taste
⅔ cup red wine
⅔ cup chicken stock
2 tblsp coarsely chopped fresh basil

Put all the sauce ingredients into

the blender and blend until smooth. If the sauce is too thick for your liking, thin it down a little with extra chicken stock. Can be kept in the refrigerator for up to 3 days. Serve with cooked pasta, with cooked fish, or as the base for a cold soup.

Low Fat Yogurt "Mayonnaise"

PREPARATION TIME: 5-10
                                minutes

MAKES: about 1¼ cups

2 egg yolks
1 tblsp white wine vinegar
1 tsp chive mustard
1 clove garlic, peeled and crushed
Salt and freshly ground black pepper
    to taste
1¼ cups thick natural yogurt

Beat the egg yolks with the vinegar; beat in the remaining ingredients. This is thinner than a standard oil-based mayonnaise, but equally delicious. Serve with salads, cooked fish, over cooked vegetables, etc. Will keep in the refrigerator for up to 4 days.

Grapefruit Shrub

PREPARATION TIME: 10-15
                                minutes

SERVES: 4 people

Peeled segments from 2 grapefruit
1¼ cups unsweetened grapefruit juice
⅔ cup water
2 tblsp clear honey
2 egg whites

To Decorate
Small sprigs fresh mint or grated
    lemon rind

Put the grapefruit segments, grapefruit juice, water and honey into the blender and blend until smooth. Add the egg whites and blend once again until frothy. Pour into glasses, making sure that a good portion of the white "froth" goes into each one. Decorate with mint or lemon rind.

This page: Almond and Tarragon French Dressing (top) and Low Fat Yogurt 'Mayonnaise' (bottom).

Facing page: Pesto Sauce (top) and Fresh Tomato and Basil Sauce (bottom).

CHINESE CUISINE

Introduction to Chinese Cooking

As in any other style of cooking, Chinese food is a symbol of life and good health, forming a central part of family and social activity for many people. Through cooking, one demonstrates personal inventiveness and creativity, as well as one's cultural background, so cooking can always be seen as a pleasurable activity.

In Chinese cooking, the preparation is of great importance. Many dishes require very fine chopping and shredding of the various ingredients, and they are combined in a very orderly manner. Those ingredients which are not easily available in the Western world can be substituted by others in the recipes. It is not necessary to use only Chinese utensils as these dishes can easily be prepared using basic kitchen equipment.

The main cooking technique used to produce good Chinese food is stir-frying. A wok is ideal, but a deep, non-stick pan will serve the purpose just as well. Stir-frying requires good temperature control and this is easily learnt through practice. The wok or pan should be heated, then the temperature reduced before adding oil. If the utensil is too hot the oil will burn, giving a charred, oily taste to the food, which may burn, too! The heat should be progressively raised for the addition of other ingredients. The whole process may take between five and seven minutes. Remember, never overcook, as this will not only destroy the crispness of the food, but also its flavour and goodness.

Chinese food incorporates six basic flavours, just like Indian food. They are: sweet, sour, salty, spicy, pungent and hot. Their employment and respective proportions must be well balanced. Flavouring is always supplemented by ready-prepared sauces, the most essential of which is soya sauce. Others commonly used are oyster and plum sauces.

Finally, garnishing should not be neglected, as presentation is every bit as important as preparation. After all, what appeals to the eye also appeals to the mind and thence to heart and stomach. A slice of cleverly carved carrot, a thin sliver of tomato and carefully arranged parsley or coriander, can add that all-important dash of colour.

Cooking is always a pleasure, especially Chinese cooking. It is a challenge and a way to explore one's creative talents. In any case, who does not want their efforts to be rewarded by the pleasure of an exquisite meal?

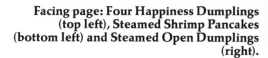

Facing page: Four Happiness Dumplings
(top left), Steamed Shrimp Pancakes
(bottom left) and Steamed Open Dumplings
(right).

Four Happiness Dumplings

PREPARATION TIME: 30-45 minutes for pastry; 20-30 minutes for filling

COOKING TIME: 20 minutes

MAKES: 30-35

Pastry
1¾ cups all-purpose flour
Pinch of salt
1 cup boiling water

Put the flour and salt into a bowl. Add the boiling water and mix quickly to make a dough. Cover and allow to stand for 20-30 minutes. Knead the dough for 2-3 minutes, sprinkling the work surface with a little cornstarch if needed. Divide the dough into 30-35 equal portions and roll each one to a circle 2½ inches in diameter.

Filling
1½ cups ground lean pork
2 black mushrooms, soaked and diced
½ cup finely chopped mixed vegetables (peas, carrots, celery, etc.)
½ tsp brown sugar or maple syrup
2½ tsp light soy sauce
¼ tsp freshly ground black pepper
1 egg
5-6 chives, finely chopped
Salt to taste
1 tblsp salad or olive oil
1½ tsp cornstarch
2 tblsp all-purpose flour mixed with a little cold water to a smooth paste

Mix the pork with the mushrooms, mixed vegetables, sugar, soy sauce, black pepper, egg, chives and salt to taste. Add the oil and cornstarch and mix well with a fork. Divide filling into 30 to 35 equal portions. Fill each dumpling wrapper with a portion of filling and shape into crescent-shaped dumplings. Steam them in an ordinary steamer or a Chinese bamboo steamer for about 20 minutes. Serve with a dip and chili sauce. To make the crescent shape, place a wrapper on a flat surface, put a little filling in the center, spread the edges with a little flour and water paste and pinch the edges of the wrapper together to seal. Pull one corner of the filled wanton around and over the other corner. Press to seal.

Steamed Shrimp Pancakes

PREPARATION TIME: 1 hour

COOKING TIME: 10-15 minutes

MAKES: 25-30

1½ cups all-purpose flour or high gluten flour
1½ tblsp cornstarch
¼ tsp salt
1 tblsp salad or olive oil
3 tblsp beaten egg
2 tblsp water
2 tblsp all-purpose flour mixed with cold water to a smooth paste

Filling
1½ cups peeled shrimps, finely chopped
2 green onions, bulb only, finely chopped
¼ tsp salt, or to taste
1 tsp cornstarch to bind

Sift the flour, cornstarch and salt into a bowl. Add the oil, beaten egg and water and mix to make a stiff dough. Leave for 30 minutes to rest. Knead well for 5-6 minutes and roll into 25-30 6 inch circles on greaseproof paper. To make the filling, mix all the ingredients except the cornstarch together, and then bind with the cornstarch. Place the filling in the center of each pancake and flatten. Spread flour and water paste around the edge of each pancake and fold up from one end to make a roll. Arrange the pancakes in a greased ordinary or Chinese bamboo steamer and cook over boiling water for 10-15 minutes. Serve piping hot with chili or soy sauce dip.

Alternative
To make rice pancakes, soak 4oz rice for 10 minutes. Grind with water to make a very fine paste of batter consistency. Add 1 tblsp oil and mix well. Line a steamer with fine muslin and spoon in a little batter; spread it out into a thin pancake. Steam for 5 minutes. Place a little filling on the pancake and roll up. Steam for 10 minutes and serve piping hot with a dip.

Steamed Open Dumplings

PREPARATION TIME: 1 hour

COOKING TIME: 10-15 minutes

MAKES: 24

Filling
1 cup medium size peeled shrimps, finely chopped
1½ cups ground pork or beef
2 black mushrooms, soaked and finely chopped
Salt to taste
½ tsp brown sugar

Seasoning
½ tsp monosodium glutamate (optional)
1 tblsp cornstarch
1½ tsp dark soy sauce
1 tsp light soy sauce
¼ tsp freshly ground black pepper
1 tblsp sesame oil
24 wonton wrappers

Mix the ground pork, shrimps, mushrooms, salt and sugar together. Add the seasoning ingredients and mix well. Allow to stand for 30 minutes. Take each wonton wrapper and spoon a little filling in the center. Fold up the edges around the filling but do not completely enclose it. (An open ended dumpling is produced with the sides of the wrapper gathered around the filling.) Flatten the base by pressing it slightly so that it will stand upright in a steamer. Grease an ordinary steamer or a bamboo steamer and arrange the dumplings in it. Steam for 15-20 minutes. Serve hot with a dip.

Wontons with Pork and Shrimp Filling

PREPARATION TIME: 30 minutes

COOKING TIME: 10-15 minutes

MAKES: 40-50

1½ cups lean ground pork
Salad or olive oil
1½ cups peeled small shrimps, finely chopped
3 green onions, finely chopped
½ tsp ground white pepper
1¼ tblsp soy sauce
1½ tsp rice wine or dry sherry
½ tsp salt, or to taste
1½ tsp cornstarch blended with 2 tblsp water
40-50 wonton wrappers
2 tblsp all-purpose flour, mixed with a little cold water to a smooth paste

Fry pork in 2 tblsp oil until it loses its pink color. Add shrimps and onions and fry for 3-4 minutes. Add pepper, soy sauce and wine. Season with salt and stir fry for 1-2 minutes. Add the blended cornstarch and stir over a moderate heat until thickened. Allow to cool before filling the wontons. Divide filling into 40-50 equal portions. Take a wonton wrapper, moisten the edges with the flour and water paste. Place a portion of filling in the center of the wonton and gather up the edges to make a neat round, or shape in such a way as to make a triangle or any other shape that you prefer. Once you have shaped all the wontons, deep-fry them in hot oil until crisp and golden. You will need to fry them in 3 or more batches. Drain well on absorbent paper before serving.

Fried Meat Dumplings

PREPARATION TIME: 10 minutes

COOKING TIME: about 15 minutes

MAKES: 48 dumplings

2 tblsp salad or olive oil
2 cups lean ground beef or lamb
2 green onions, chopped
2½ tblsp light soy sauce
½ tsp salt
1¾ tblsp rice wine or dry sherry
2 tsp cornstarch mixed with 2 tblsp water
Dumpling wrappers (see recipe)

2 tblsp all-purpose flour mixed to a paste with cold water
Oil for deep frying

Heat the 2 tblsp oil in a pan and fry the ground meat and onion for 2-3 minutes. Add the soy sauce, salt and wine. Cook gently for 2 minutes and then stir in the cornstarch and water mixture. Stir over the heat until the mixture thickens. Put the meat mixture into a dish and leave to cool. Divide into equal portions – about 48. Take a round dumpling wrapper and place a portion of filling in the center. Moisten the edges of the wrapper with a little flour and water paste, gather the edges up and over the filling and pinch together to seal. Shape neatly. Continue to make the remaining dumplings in the same way. Deep-fry the dumplings in moderately hot oil, cooking a few dumplings at a time, until they are golden brown. Drain thoroughly on absorbent paper. Serve with chili sauce dip.

Dumpling Wrappers (Chiao Tze P'i)

PREPARATION TIME: 50-60 minutes

MAKES: 40-50 wrappers

2¼ cups all-purpose flour
¾ cup cold water

Sift the flour into a bowl and add the cold water, a little at a time, and mix to a firm dough. Knead the dough on a flat surface for 4-5 minutes. Cover with a damp cloth or wrap in plastic wrap. Leave to stand at room temperature for 30-40 minutes. Roll out on a well-floured surface as thinly as possible, until almost transparent. Cut into round or square pieces to suit your requirements. Use within a few hours of making otherwise they will dry out.

Wonton Wrappers

PREPARATION TIME: 5-6 hours (including standing time)

MAKES: 40-50 wrappers

1 cup all-purpose flour
2 tblsp beaten egg
2 tblsp cold water
Cornstarch

Sift flour and gradually add the beaten egg and water mixed together. Mix to a stiff dough. Knead firmly for 5-6 minutes and wrap in plastic wrap. Leave to stand at room temperature for 4-5 hours. Roll out into a very large square on a work surface dusted with cornstarch. The pastry should be almost transparent. Cut into 40-50 3 inch round or square wrappers. Dust each wrapper with cornstarch before stacking. Store the wrappers, wrapped securely in plastic wrap, in the refrigerator, for up to 24 hours. If they are allowed to dry out they will split during cooking.

Spring Roll Wrappers

PREPARATION TIME: 20 minutes, plus chilling time

MAKES: 12 wrappers

1 scant cup all-purpose flour
1 egg, beaten
A little cold water

Sift the flour into a bowl. Make a well in the center and add the beaten egg and a little cold water. Mix to a soft yet firm dough, adding a little extra water if necessary. Knead the dough until it is really pliable (this helps to make the gluten work). Chill, covered, for 4 hours or overnight. Allow to come back to room temperature. Roll out the dough on a well-floured surface to about ¼ inch thick. Cut into 12 equal pieces, and then roll each piece to a square about 6x6 inches – each square should be very thin.

Spring Rolls

PREPARATION TIME: 20-30 minutes

COOKING TIME: about 20 minutes

MAKES: 12

2 cups lean, raw pork or beef, finely shredded
1 cup small to medium, shelled shrimps (either uncooked or boiled)
4 green onions, finely chopped
Salad or olive oil
2 tsp fresh root ginger, peeled and shredded
1⅓ cups white cabbage, shredded
1-1¼ cups bean sprouts
1¼ tblsp soy sauce
Salt to taste
12 spring roll wrappers, each 6 inches square (see recipe)
2 tblsp all-purpose flour, mixed with a little cold water to a smooth paste

Fry the shredded pork and the shrimps with the spring onions in 1 tblsp of oil for 2-3 minutes. Add the ginger, cabbage and bean sprouts, and stir fry for 2-3 minutes. Add soy sauce, and season with a little salt if desired. Remove from the heat and allow to cool. Lay out the spring roll wrappers on a clean working surface, with one point of each wrapper facing you. Divide the

filling mixture into 12 equal portions and place one portion of filling just above the front point of each wrapper. Fold in the opposite side points, so that they overlap slightly like an envelope – secure the side points with a little flour and water paste. Starting with the point facing you, roll each wrapper up around the filling, securing the remaining point with a little flour

and water paste. Repeat in exactly the same way with the remaining spring roll wrappers. They will keep a better shape if you chill them for 1 hour before cooking. Deep fry over a medium heat until golden brown and crisp. Drain thoroughly on absorbent paper and serve hot with a selection of dips or chili sauce. The spring rolls can be frozen, uncooked.

This page: **Fried Meat Dumplings (top right), Spring Rolls (center left) and Wontons with Pork and Shrimp Filling (bottom). Facing page: Spiced Beef (top), Steamed Beef Szechuan Style (bottom left) and Beef with Green Pepper and Chili (bottom right).**

CHINESE CUISINE
Meat Dishes

Spiced Beef

PREPARATION TIME: 30 minutes

COOKING TIME: 5-6 minutes

SERVES: 4 people

Marinade
1 tsp fine granulated sugar
2-3 star anise, ground
½ tsp ground fennel
1¼ tblsp dark soy sauce
¼ tsp monosodium glutamate
    (optional)

1lb fillet of beef, cut into 1 inch strips
1 inch fresh root ginger, peeled and
    crushed
½ tsp salt
2 tblsp salad or olive oil
4 green onions, sliced
½ tsp freshly ground black pepper
1¼ tblsp light soy sauce

Mix the marinade ingredients
together. Add the beef strips,
ginger and salt, and marinate for 20
minutes. Heat the oil in a wok and
stir fry the onions for 1 minute.
Add beef, ground pepper and soy
sauce and stir fry for 4-5 minutes.
Serve with a dip.

Steamed Beef Szechuan Style

PREPARATION TIME: 40 minutes

COOKING TIME: 15 minutes

SERVES: 4 people

3 slices fresh root ginger, minced
1 tsp salt
1 tsp fine granulated sugar
Freshly ground black pepper
1 tblsp salad or olive oil
2 tblsp rice wine or dry sherry
1½ tblsp chili bean paste
2½ tblsp dark soy sauce
3-4 green onions, finely chopped
1lb fillet of beef, cut into 2 inch long
    strips
⅔ cup ground rice
1 large lotus leaf or several cabbage
    leaves

For the marinade, mix the ginger,
salt, sugar, pepper, oil, wine, bean
paste, soy sauce and half of the
onions. Add beef strips and mix

well. Leave to marinate for 15-20
minutes. Heat the wok and dry
roast the ground rice for 2-4
minutes till rice changes color from
white to light brown. Roll the
marinated beef in the roasted
ground rice to give a thin, even
coating. Line the bamboo steamer
with a well-oiled lotus leaf or a few
old and tough cabbage leaves.
Arrange the coated beef strips in a

neat pile on top. Steam fairly
quickly for 10-15 minutes over
boiling water. Garnish with the
remaining chopped onions before
serving. Serve hot with chili sauce.

Beef with Green Pepper and Chili

PREPARATION TIME: 30 minutes

COOKING TIME: 10-12 minutes

SERVES: 4 people

1lb fillet of beef, cut into 1 inch strips

Seasoning
2 tblsp dark soy sauce
1 tsp sesame oil
Pinch baking soda
¼ tsp ground black pepper

½ tsp salt

Oil for frying
2 green peppers, seeded and thinly
   sliced
1 onion, peeled and sliced
2 green onions, chopped
1 inch fresh root ginger, peeled and
   sliced
2 garlic cloves, peeled and chopped
3 green chilis, sliced

Sauce
2½ tblsp chicken broth
½ tsp monosodium glutamate
   (optional)
1½ tsp dark soy sauce
Salt to taste
Few drops sesame oil

Marinate beef with the seasoning
ingredients for 15 minutes. Heat 2
tblsp oil in a wok and stir fry green
peppers and onions for 2 minutes.
Remove to a plate. Reheat wok,
add 2-3 tblsp oil and fry ginger,
garlic, and green chilis for 1 minute.
Add beef and stir fry for 4-5
minutes. Add sauce ingredients,
mixed together, and the fried
peppers and onions. Stir fry for a
further 2 minutes and serve.

Diced Pork with Sweet Corn

PREPARATION TIME: 25 minutes
COOKING TIME: 15-20 minutes
SERVES: 2 people

Marinade
Pinch salt
2½ tsp dark soy sauce
¼ tsp fine granulated sugar
1 tsp rice wine
1 tblsp water

1½ cups pork loin, diced
Oil for deep frying
2 slices fresh root ginger, peeled and
   diced
1 clove garlic, peeled and chopped
1 cup chicken broth

Seasoning
¼ tsp salt
¼ tsp freshly ground black pepper
¼ tsp fine granulated sugar
1 tsp rice wine or dry sherry
Few drops sesame oil

1 tsp cornstarch mixed with 1 tblsp
   water
1 cup canned creamed sweet corn
1 egg, well beaten
4 green onions, chopped

Mix the marinade ingredients
together. Add the pork and leave
to marinate for 15 minutes. Drain
the pork and discard the liquid.
Heat the wok and pour in the oil
for deep frying. Fry the pork until
light brown. Remove the pork and
drain. Reserve the oil for future
use. Heat 1 tblsp oil in the wok and
add the ginger and pork. Stir fry for
3 minutes. Add the broth and
simmer for 3 minutes. Add the
seasoning ingredients and simmer
for 2-3 minutes. Add the blended
cornstarch and water and simmer
until the sauce thickens. Add the
sweet corn and beaten egg and
cook for 2-3 minutes. Serve
sprinkled with chopped onions.
Serve this dish with plain boiled
rice or noodles.

Pork Stuffed Mushrooms

PREPARATION TIME: 15-20
                             minutes
COOKING TIME: 12 minutes
SERVES: 4 people

Filling
1 egg
2 tsp cornstarch
2 tsp rice wine or dry sherry
¼ tsp minced fresh root ginger
6 water chestnuts, finely chopped
½ cup peeled medium shrimps,
   chopped
1½ cups ground lean pork
¼ tsp salt
¼ tsp freshly ground black pepper
½ tsp fine granulated sugar
2 tsp chili sauce

16 large, open mushrooms
2½ cups chicken broth
Oil

Mix all the filling ingredients
together. Remove the mushroom
stalks. Divide the filling into 16
portions. Bring the chicken broth
to the boil. Add the mushrooms
and leave to stand off the heat for 5
minutes, covered. Drain the
mushrooms and discard the broth.
Top each mushroom with a portion
of filling. Put the stuffed
mushrooms into a well oiled
steamer. Steam for 10-12 minutes
over boiling water. Serve as a snack,
as a starter or as a side dish.
Alternatively, serve with a simple
sauce made from thickened
chicken broth. Pour the sauce over
the steamed mushrooms.

Sliced Pork in Wine Sauce

PREPARATION TIME: 30 minutes

COOKING TIME: about 16 minutes

SERVES: 4 people

Seasoning

1¼ tblsp wine-flavored vinegar
1¼ tblsp light soy sauce
1 tblsp rice wine or dry sherry
2 tsp soy paste
1 tsp freshly ground black pepper
1 tsp salt
1 tsp Shao Hsing wine
1lb pork fillet, cut into 2 inch long, thin slices
1 tblsp cornstarch
4 tblsp salad or olive oil
½ inch fresh root ginger, finely chopped
3 green onions, chopped
1 green pepper, seeded and diced

Sauce

2 tsp cornstarch
4 tblsp dry white wine
½ cup chicken broth
2 tsp dark soy sauce
1 tsp fine granulated sugar
½ tsp salt

Mix the seasoning ingredients together. Add the pork slices and leave to marinate for 10-15 minutes. Drain the pork and roll in the cornstarch. Leave on one side. Discard the marinade. Heat half the oil in the wok until smoking. Add the pork, reduce the heat, and stir fry for 4-6 minutes until lightly browned. Remove the pork and keep on one side. Discard any oil

Diced Pork with Sweet Corn (far left), Sliced Pork in Wine Sauce (top left) and Pork Stuffed Mushrooms (left).

the meat balls and serve with chopped green onions and green pepper rings sprinkled on top. Serve as a snack, as a starter or as a side dish.

Pork Chop Suey

PREPARATION TIME: 35 minutes
COOKING TIME: 10 minutes
SERVES: 3-4 people

Marinade
1 tblsp water
½ tsp baking soda
2½ tsp dark soy sauce

½lb pork fillet, sliced into 2 inch pieces
3 tblsp cooked oil or cooking oil
1 onion, peeled and cut into pieces
1 clove of garlic, peeled and sliced
⅓ cup bamboo shoots, sliced
2 cups bean sprouts

Seasoning
Pinch salt
Pinch freshly ground black pepper
Pinch monosodium glutamate (optional)
3 tblsp light soy sauce
1 tsp fine granulated sugar
1 tsp cornstarch

Sauce
1 tsp cornstarch
1 tblsp water

Mix the marinade ingredients together. Add the pork and leave for 15 minutes to marinate. Drain the pork and discard the marinade. Heat the oil in the wok and stir fry pork for 2-3 minutes. Remove the pork. Add the onion, garlic and bamboo shoots to the wok and stir fry for 1-2 minutes. Add the bean sprouts and stir fry for 2 minutes. Remove onto a dish and add the mixed seasoning ingredients. Leave for 10 minutes. Return the pork and the vegetables to the wok. Add the blended sauce ingredients. Bring to the boil gently, stirring until the sauce thickens. Serve immediately.

This page: Steamed Pork with Salted Cabbage (top), Pork with Green Pepper (center right) and Pork Chop Suey (bottom). Facing page: Fried Pork with Vegetables (top left), Bean Sprouts with Chopped Pork (center right) and Deep Fried Pork Meat Balls (bottom).

left in the wok. Add the remaining oil to the wok and stir fry the onions, ginger and green pepper for 3-5 minutes. Return the fried pork to the wok and cook for a further 2-3 minutes with the vegetables. Remove onto a serving dish. Mix the cornstarch from the sauce ingredients with 2 tblsp water. Add the remaining sauce ingredients to the wok and bring to the boil. Add the blended cornstarch. Stir and simmer until the sauce thickens, simmer for 1-2 minutes. Pour over the pork and serve.

Deep Fried Pork Meat Balls

PREPARATION TIME: 25 minutes
COOKING TIME: about 12 minutes
MAKES: 16 meat balls

1lb coarsely ground lean pork
1 small onion, finely chopped
1 green chili, chopped
Salt and freshly ground black pepper to taste
½ inch fresh root ginger, peeled and finely chopped
1 egg, beaten
1 tblsp cornstarch
2 tsp dark soy sauce
2 sprigs Chinese parsley, finely

chopped
1 tsp cooked oil
Oil for deep frying
2 green onions, chopped (for garnishing)
1 green pepper, seeded and cut into rings (for garnishing) (optional)

Mix the ground pork with the chopped onion, chili, salt and pepper to taste, chopped ginger, beaten egg, cornstarch, soy sauce, parsley and cooked oil. Leave to stand for 10 minutes. Mould into 16 even-sized balls. Heat the oil in the wok for deep frying and slide a few pork balls into the oil. Fry over a gentle heat for 5-6 minutes until golden brown and tender. Remove and drain on kitchen paper. Fry all

Braised Hong Kong Beef

PREPARATION TIME: 30 minutes

COOKING TIME: about 15-17 minutes

SERVES: 4 people

2 tblsp salad or olive oil
1lb fillet of beef, sliced into matchstick size strips
1 onion, peeled and sliced
1 inch fresh root ginger, peeled and cut into thin strips
3-4 fresh tomatoes, cut into thin wedges
½lb carrots, scraped and cut into 2 inch sticks
2½ tsp brown sugar
½ tsp five spice powder
2¼ tblsp light soy sauce
1 tblsp rice wine or dry sherry
2 tblsp water
Salt to taste

Heat the oil in a wok and fry the beef for 3-4 minutes. Add the onion, ginger, tomatoes and carrots. Stir fry for 2-3 minutes. Add the sugar, five spice powder, soy sauce, wine and water. Season with salt to taste and cook gently for 8-10 minutes. Serve as a side dish.

Pork with Green Pepper

PREPARATION TIME: 20 minutes

COOKING TIME: 1 hour 15 minutes

SERVES: 4 people

1lb pork fillet, cut into 2 inch strips

Seasoning
¼ tsp fine granulated sugar
¼ tsp monosodium glutamate (optional)
1¼ tsp light soy sauce
2 tsp sweet bean paste
2 tsp Shao Hsing wine or dry sherry
4 tblsp chicken broth

Oil for deep frying
2 cloves garlic, peeled and cut into thin strips
1 green pepper, seeded and sliced into strips
1 green chili, sliced into strips
1 red chili, cut in half then sliced into strips

Sauce
1 tsp cornstarch
1 tblsp water

Boil the pork in water for ¾ hour until cooked. Drain the pork and discard the water. Mix the seasoning ingredients together and stir in the pork. Leave to stand for 10 minutes. Heat the wok and add

the oil for deep frying. When oil is very hot fry the drained pork for a few minutes until golden brown. Remove and drain the pork and keep the oil for future use. Reheat the wok and add 1 tsp oil and stir fry the garlic for 1 minute. Add the pepper and chilies and stir fry for 1 minute. Add the remaining seasoning mixture and the pork. Stir fry over a gentle heat for 1-2 minutes and then add the blended sauce ingredients. Cook until the sauce thickens. Remove from the heat and serve immediately. Serve with mixed fried rice or rice noodles.

Steamed Pork with Salted Cabbage

PREPARATION TIME: 25 minutes

COOKING TIME: 2 hours

SERVES: 4 people

1lb pork fillet cut into ½ inch thick slices
Salt
2 cups cabbage, shredded (Chinese white or plain green cabbage)

Seasoning
1 tblsp fine granulated sugar
2 tblsp cooked oil
1 tsp monosodium glutamate (optional)
4 tblsp broth or water
Salt and freshly ground black pepper

1¼ tblsp dark soy sauce
Oil for deep frying

Sauce
1 tsp cornstarch
1 tblsp water

Boil the pork in 2 cups water for ¾ hour until tender. Drain the pork and discard the water. Boil 2 cups fresh water with 1 tsp salt and add the cabbage. Cook for 2 minutes. Drain, rinse in cold water and then drain again. Season the cabbage with 1 tsp of the sugar and 1 tblsp of the cooked oil. Mix well and keep on one side. Place the pork in a dish and mix with the dark soy sauce. Leave for 10 minutes. Drain. Mix all the seasoning ingredients together. Heat the oil for deep frying and fry the pork until it turns lightly golden. Drain and add to the seasoning mixture. Keep the oil for future use. Place the pork and the seasoning mixture into a deep dish and put the boiled cabbage on top. Cover and steam over boiling water for 1 hour. Drain off any excess liquid and retain. Heat the wok and add the cabbage liquid.

Add the blended sauce thickening of cornstarch and water. Stir over the heat until the sauce thickens. Pour over the cabbage and pork and serve.

Bean Sprouts with Chopped Pork

PREPARATION TIME: 15 minutes

COOKING TIME: 10 minutes

SERVES: 4 people

2 cups ground lean pork

Marinade
½ tsp salt
1¼ tblsp light soy sauce
1 egg white, beaten
1 tsp cornstarch

3 cups bean sprouts
Salad or olive oil for cooking

Seasoning
½ tsp salt
½ tsp fine granulated sugar
½ tsp monosodium glutamate (optional)
2 tsp soy sauce
1 tsp rice wine or dry sherry
1 tblsp oyster sauce

½ inch fresh root ginger, peeled and thinly sliced
2-3 green onions, chopped
½ cup chicken broth

Sauce
½ tsp cornstarch
1 tblsp water or broth
Few drops of sesame oil

Mix the pork with the marinade ingredients and keep on one side for 10 minutes. Trim the bean sprouts and chop them coarsely. Heat 2 tblsp oil in the wok. Stir fry the bean sprouts for 1 minute to evaporate excess water and moisture. Remove the bean sprouts and keep on a plate. Mix the seasoning ingredients together. Heat 3 tblsp oil in the wok until it smokes. Stir fry the pork for 2 minutes and then add the ginger, onions and bean sprouts. Stir fry for 2-3 minutes. Add the seasoning ingredients and stir fry for 1 minute. Add the chicken broth and the blended sauce ingredients. Cook until the sauce thickens. Serve immediately.

Spiced Liver (top), Sliced Beef in Oyster Sauce (center right) and Braised Hong Kong Beef (right).

Oil for frying
1 small onion, peeled and thickly
   sliced
3 green onions, chopped lengthwise
2 leeks, white part only, cut into 1½
   inch slices
1 tsp sesame oil

Mix the marinade ingredients with
the beef strips. Leave to marinate
for 20 minutes. Mix all the
seasoning ingredients together in a
small bowl. Heat 2 tblsp oil in a
wok and when it is smoking, add
the beef. Reduce the heat and stir
fry for 4-5 minutes. Remove the
meat and keep the oil for future
use. Heat the wok, add 2 tblsp
fresh oil and stir fry the onion and
leeks for 2 minutes. Add seasoning
mixture and beef and stir fry for 1-2
minutes. Sprinkle sesame oil over
the top and mix well. Serve
immediately. Use as a main dish or
a side dish.

Shredded Beef with Vegetables

PREPARATION TIME:	15 minutes
COOKING TIME:	10 minutes
SERVES:	2-3 people

8oz lean beef, cut into thin strips
Pinch salt
4 tblsp salad or olive oil
2 red and green chilies, cut in half
   then sliced into strips
1 tsp black vinegar
1 stem of celery, cut into 2 inch thin
   strips
2 carrots, cut into 2 inch thin strips
1 leek, white part only, sliced into 2
   inch thin strips
2 cloves, garlic, peeled and finely
   chopped

Seasoning
1 tsp light soy sauce
1 tsp dark soy sauce
2 tsp Shao Hsing wine
1 tsp fine granulated sugar
Pinch monosodium glutamate
   (optional)
½ tsp freshly ground black pepper

**This page: Stir Fried Beef with
Onions (top), Shredded Beef
with Vegetables (center left)
and Sesame Beef with Dates
(bottom). Facing page: Beef
with Green Beans (top), Beef
Steak with Ginger (center
right) and Sweet and Sour Beef
(bottom).**

Spiced Liver

PREPARATION TIME:	10 minutes
COOKING TIME:	20 minutes
SERVES:	4 people

1lb lamb's liver, cut into 1 inch cubes
½ cup soy sauce
3-4 green onions, chopped
2¼ tblsp rice wine or dry sherry
2 tsp fine granulated sugar
1 inch fresh root ginger, peeled and
   finely chopped
½ tsp freshly ground black pepper
Pinch anise powder

Boil the liver in sufficient water to
just cover, for 3-4 minutes. Drain
well. Add soy sauce, green onions,
wine, sugar, ginger, pepper and
anise powder. Simmer gently for
10-15 minutes, covered, until the
liver is tender. Serve as a side dish.

Stir Fried Beef with Onions

PREPARATION TIME:	30 minutes
COOKING TIME:	10 minutes
SERVES:	4 people

Marinade
1 tblsp cornstarch
1 egg white
1 tblsp salad or olive oil
1 tsp baking soda

1lb beef fillet, cut into 1 inch strips

Seasoning
1 tsp Shao Hsing wine
1¼ tblsp light soy sauce
1 tsp dark soy sauce
½ tsp salt
½ tsp freshly ground black pepper
1 tsp monosodium glutamate
   (optional)

Put the beef into a bowl and sprinkle with salt; rub salt into meat. Heat 1½ tsp oil in a wok until it begins to smoke. Reduce heat and add beef and chilies and stir fry for 4-5 minutes. Add remaining oil and stir fry beef until it turns crispy. Add vinegar and mix until it evaporates, then add celery, carrots, leeks and garlic. Stir fry for 2 minutes. Mix the seasoning ingredients and pour over the beef and cook for 2 minutes. Serve immediately.

Steamed Lamb with Mushroom Sauce

PREPARATION TIME: 20-25 minutes

COOKING TIME: 2 hours 10 minutes

SERVES: 6 people

2¼lb boned leg of lamb, cut into 1 inch cubes
2 onions, thinly sliced
Salt and freshly ground black pepper
2 tsp salad or olive oil

2 cloves of garlic, peeled and sliced
1 tsp cornstarch
Pinch monosodium glutamate (optional)
6 tblsp light soy sauce
3½ tblsp rice wine or dry sherry
1 tsp crushed black pepper
1 inch fresh root ginger, peeled and thinly sliced
Few drops sesame oil

Put the lamb into a saucepan and add sufficient water to cover. Boil for 5 minutes. Drain the lamb and retain the water. Arrange the lamb cubes in a deep dish and sprinkle the onions on top. Season with pepper and salt. Heat the oil in a wok and fry the garlic until brown. Remove the garlic and discard. Mix together the cornstarch, monosodium glutamate, soy sauce, wine, crushed pepper, ginger and 4 tblsp reserved lamb broth. Stir the cornstarch mixture into the oil in the wok and cook for 1-2 minutes. Pour over the lamb. Cover the lamb with overlapping foil and tie around the rim. Put the dish in a steamer and steam over boiling water for 2 hours. Serve with the sesame oil sprinkled over the lamb.

Lamb with Tomatoes

PREPARATION TIME: 20 minutes

COOKING TIME: about 10 minutes

SERVES: 2 people

2 tsp cornstarch
½ tsp salt
1½ tblsp light soy sauce
4½ tblsp water
3 tblsp salad or olive oil
½ inch fresh root ginger, sliced
8oz lamb fillet, cut across the grain in thin strips of ½x2 inch
2 green onions, chopped
1 onion, peeled and cut into 1 inch pieces
1 green pepper, seeded and cut into strips
1 tsp curry powder
3-4 small, firm tomatoes, cut into ½ inch pieces

Mix the cornstarch, salt, soy sauce, water and 1 tsp of the oil together. Keep on one side. Heat the remaining oil in a wok and fry the ginger and lamb for 2-3 minutes. Add the onions, green pepper and curry powder and stir fry for 3-4 minutes. Stir in the cornstarch

mixture and cook for 1 minute. Add the tomatoes and cook until the sauce thickens. Serve as a side dish.

Mongolian Lamb with Onions

PREPARATION TIME: 20 minutes

COOKING TIME: 8-10 minutes

SERVES: 4 people

1lb lean, boned lamb, cut into ¼x2 inch strips
1 egg white
2 cloves of garlic, sliced
½ tsp five spice powder
½ inch fresh root ginger, peeled and thinly sliced
1 tblsp cornstarch
1¼ tblsp light soy sauce
3½ tblsp rice wine or dry sherry
2 tblsp water
3 tblsp cooked oil
6 green onions, chopped

Mix the lamb with the egg white, garlic, five spice powder, ginger root and 1 tsp cornstarch and 1 tsp soy sauce. Keep on one side. Mix the

Lamb with Tomatoes (below left), Steamed Lamb with Mushroom Sauce (right) and Mongolian Lamb with Onions (below right).

remaining cornstarch, soy sauce, wine and water together. Heat the wok and add the oil. When it begins to smoke, add the beef mixture. Reduce the heat and stir fry for 3-4 minutes until the meat browns slightly. Remove and keep on one side. Add the onions and the cornstarch, soy sauce and wine mixture to the wok. Stir until it thickens. Return the meat to the wok and simmer gently for 3-4 minutes, or until the meat is tender. Serve as a main dish.

Sweet and Sour Beef

PREPARATION TIME: 15 minutes
COOKING TIME: 15 minutes
SERVES: 4 people

Batter
A generous ½ cup all-purpose flour
1½ tsp baking powder
4 tblsp cornstarch
1 tblsp salad or olive oil

3 tblsp salad or olive oil

8oz fillet of beef, cut into 1 inch cubes
1 onion, peeled and cut into wedges
1 inch fresh root ginger, peeled and thinly sliced
1 clove garlic, peeled and thinly sliced
1 green pepper, seeded and chopped

Sweet and Sour Sauce
4 tblsp brown sugar
¼ tsp salt
4 tblsp wine-flavored vinegar
1 tsp fresh root ginger, peeled and minced

⅓ cup water
1 tblsp cornstarch
2 tsp cooked oil
Few drops food coloring
Oil for deep frying

For the batter: sift the flour, baking powder and cornstarch. Beat in the oil and add sufficient water to make a thick, smooth batter. Heat the 3 tblsp oil in a wok and stir fry the beef for 2 minutes. Remove the beef. Fry the onion, ginger, garlic and green pepper for 2-3 minutes in the same oil. Remove the wok from the heat. Mix the sauce ingredients together and add to the wok. Return the wok to the heat and bring to the boil gently. Lower the heat and simmmer gently for 2-3 minutes until thick and clear. Meanwhile, dip the beef cubes into the batter and deep fry in hot oil until golden brown and crisp. Drain on absorbent paper. Arrange in a deep dish and pour the hot sauce over the beef. Serve with a chow mein dish or fried rice. Thinly sliced carrots, cucumber and zucchini may also be added along with the onion, ginger and green pepper.

Barbecued Pork
(Kan Hsiang Ch'a Shao or Char Siu)

PREPARATION TIME: 3 hours

COOKING TIME: 1 hour to 1 hour 30 minutes

SERVES: 6-8 people

4½lb loin of pork

Seasoning
1 tblsp ginger juice
Few drops red food coloring
5 tblsp brown sugar
1 cup light soy sauce
1 tsp salt
1 tblsp Mue Kwe Lo wine (or a mixture of 2 tsp dry sherry and 1 tsp apricot brandy)

8oz honey, melted

Remove the bones from the loin of pork. Cut pork into 1½ inch wide strips. With the aid of a fork scrape the surface of the pork lightly to form grooves in which the seasoning can lodge. Mix the seasoning ingredients together and rub well into the pork strips. Leave to marinate for at least 1½ hours. Thread the pork strips onto a long metal skewer and hang to dry for 1 hour. Put the pork onto a wire rack in a roasting tin. Brush with melted honey and roast in the oven at 350°F, for 1-1½ hours, basting with honey frequently. When cooked, brush the pork with any remaining honey and leave to 'dry' slightly. Serve hot or cold, sliced thinly on a serving plate.

Pork Spare Ribs

PREPARATION TIME: 25 minutes

COOKING TIME: 40-45 minutes

SERVES: 4 people

16-20 pork spare ribs
1 tsp salt
Salad or olive oil
1 tsp ginger paste

Pork Meat Balls in Sauce (left), Pork Spare Ribs (above) and Barbecued Pork (right).

1 tsp garlic paste
1 tsp onion paste
Pinch monosodium glutamate
 (optional)
1 tsp light soy sauce
1 tsp cornstarch
1 egg
½ tsp Shao Hsing wine
½ tsp chili oil

Sauce
3 tblsp brown sugar
3 tblsp black vinegar
1 tblsp ketchup
1 tsp cornstarch
1 tsp water
1 tblsp dark soy sauce
½ tsp salt
½ tsp freshly ground black pepper

Trim excess fat from spare ribs and rub with salt. Add 4 tblsp oil to the wok and fry the ginger, garlic and onion for 1-2 minutes. Add the spare ribs and stir fry for 6 minutes. Remove to a dish and add the monosodium glutamate, light soy sauce, cornstarch, egg, wine and chili oil. Marinate for 10 minutes. Prepare the sauce by mixing all the ingredients together in the wok and bringing them gently to the boil. Simmer for 2-3 minutes and add the spare ribs along with their marinade. Stir fry until the liquid is reduced to half its original quantity.

Put all the ingredients onto a baking tray and spread out evenly. Bake at 375° for 25 minutes. Baste occasionally with the liquid from the tray and oil. The spare ribs should have browned well and be well coated with seasoning. Serve hot or cold.

Pork Meat Balls in Sauce
(Sha Kwo Shih-tzu-Tou)

PREPARATION TIME:	25 minutes
COOKING TIME:	45 minutes
SERVES:	4 people

Seasoning
Pinch monosodium glutamate
 (optional)
1 tblsp Shao Hsing wine
1 inch fresh root ginger, peeled and
 ground
2 green onions, white part only,
 minced
½ tsp salt
2 tsp cornstarch

2 cups ground lean pork
¼ cup bamboo shoots, chopped
⅓ cup dried Chinese mushrooms,
 soaked, drained and sliced
1 egg, beaten

Cornstarch to roll the meat balls in
6oz Chinese white cabbage, cut into
 3 inch pieces or 8oz ordinary green
 leafy cabbage, cut into 3 inch
 pieces
1 tblsp cooked oil
Oil for deep frying
1 tblsp cornstarch
3 tblsp water
1 small onion, peeled and finely
 chopped
1 inch fresh root ginger, peeled and
 finely chopped
1¼ chicken broth

Sauce
Salt to taste
½ tsp monosodium glutamate
 (optional)
1¼ tblsp light soy sauce
1 tsp dark soy sauce
1 tblsp cooked oil
1 tsp sesame oil

Mix seasoning ingredients together. Add the pork, bamboo shoots, mushrooms and egg and mix well. Shape into 15-16 even-sized balls and roll them in cornstarch. Keep aside on a dish. Blanch cabbage for 1 minute in boiling water and the cooked oil. Drain the cabbage and discard the water. Heat the wok and add the oil for deep frying. When quite hot deep-fry the meat balls, a few at a time, for 4-5

minutes. Remove and drain. Keep warm in a large casserole dish. Keep oil for future use. Mix the 1 tblsp cornstarch with the 3 tblsp water and keep aside. Reheat the wok and add 1 tsp deep frying oil. Stir fry the onion and ginger for 2 minutes. Add the chicken broth and stir in the blended sauce ingredients. Bring to the boil and add the meat balls. Simmer gently for 30 minutes. Add the cabbage, sesame oil and the blended cornstarch mixture. Stir over the heat until the sauce thickens.

Sesame Beef with Dates

PREPARATION TIME: 20 minutes, plus 30 minutes to marinate

COOKING TIME: 12-15 minutes

SERVES: 4 people

Seasoning A
½ tsp baking soda
1¼ tblsp light soy sauce
1 tblsp salad or olive oil
1¾ tsp cornstarch

1lb beef fillet, thinly sliced into 2 inch pieces
20 dried dates (red or dark), soaked and stoned

Seasoning B
1 tsp monosodium glutamate (optional)
1½ tsp brown sugar
2 tsp bean paste
A generous ¾ cup beef broth
Salt to taste

4 tblsp cooked oil, or plain oil
1 inch fresh root ginger, peeled and thinly sliced
2 green onions, sliced

Sauce
1¼ tblsp cornstarch
2½ tblsp water or broth
2 tblsp sesame seeds

Mix the ingredients for seasoning A. Mix with the beef and marinate for 30 minutes. Drain meat and discard marinade. Drain soaked dates; slice most of them into 4 long pieces, leaving a few whole. Mix the dates with seasoning B. Heat oil in a wok and stir fry beef for 4-5 minutes. Add ginger, green onions, dates and seasoning B and gently bring to the boil. Add the blended sauce ingredients. Cover and simmer for 3-4 minutes over a gentle heat until the sauce thickens and becomes clear. Remove from the heat, place on a serving dish and keep warm. Heat a wok or

skillet and add the sesame seeds. Dry roast for 2 minutes until they begin to crackle and turn golden brown. Sprinkle over the beef and serve immediately.

Shredded Pork with Preserved Vegetables

PREPARATION TIME: 30 minutes

COOKING TIME: 6-8 minutes

SERVES: 3 people

Pinch monosodium glutamate (optional)
2 tsp cornstarch
Salt and freshly ground black pepper to taste
½lb lean pork, shredded
Oil for deep frying
1 inch fresh root ginger, peeled and shredded
½ cup shelled green peas, lightly cooked
½ tsp fine granulated sugar
2 tsp Shao Hsing wine or dry sherry
8oz mixed Shanghai preserved vegetables, in brine
1 tsp sesame oil

Mix the monosodium glutamate, cornstarch and a pinch of salt. Add the pork and let it stand for 15 minutes. Heat the oil in a wok and deep fry the pork for 3 minutes. Remove the pork and drain. Reserve oil for future use. Reheat wok and add 2 tsp deep fried oil. Stir fry the ginger and green peas for 1 minute. Add the pork and sprinkle with the sugar, wine and salt and pepper to taste. Stir fry for another minute and add the well-drained preserved vegetables. Allow to heat through and then stir gently. Sprinkle on the sesame oil and serve. Serve as a side dish or on a bed of plain fried noodles.

Beef Steak with Ginger

PREPARATION TIME: 20-25 minutes

COOKING TIME: 10-12 minutes

SERVES: 2-3 people

Seasoning
½ tsp baking soda
3 tblsp light soy sauce
2 tblsp rice wine or dry sherry
½ tsp salt
½ tsp ground black pepper

½ tsp fresh root ginger, peeled and minced
½lb beef fillet, sliced into 1 inch pieces

Sauce
1 tsp fine granulated sugar
¼ tsp monosodium glutamate (optional)
1¼ tblsp) dark soy sauce
3½ tblsp broth
Few drops sesame oil
1 tsp Shao Hsing wine

4 tblsp salad or olive oil
1 inch fresh root ginger, peeled and thinly sliced
4 green onions, chopped
½ cup bamboo shoots, thinly sliced
2 green chilies, sliced

Mix the seasoning ingredients with the minced ginger. Add the beef and marinate for 20 minutes. Drain the beef and discard the marinade. Mix the sauce ingredients together. Heat 3 tblsp oil in the wok and fry the sliced ginger and onions for 2 minutes. Add the bamboo shoots and chilies and stir fry for 1-2 minutes. Remove to a plate. Add the remaining oil to the wok and fry the beef for 2-3 minutes. Add the fried vegetables and stir fry for 2 minutes. Add the well-stirred sauce ingredients and simmer gently until the mixture thickens. Simmer for another 1-2 minutes. Remove from heat and serve.

Beef with Green Beans

PREPARATION TIME: 30 minutes

COOKING TIME: 12 minutes

SERVES: 4 people

Seasoning
½ tsp baking soda
1 tsp cornstarch
1¼ tblsp light soy sauce
2 tblsp water
1 tsp cooked oil

1lb lean beef, thinly sliced into 1 inch pieces

Sauce
¼ tsp salt
1 tsp monosodium glutamate (optional)
1½ tsp light soy sauce
1½ tsp dark soy sauce
1 tsp Shao Hsing wine (optional)
½ cup broth
2 tsp cornstarch

3 tblsp salad or olive oil
2 cloves of garlic, peeled and sliced
1 onion, peeled and cut into wedges
1 inch fresh root ginger, peeled and thinly sliced
6oz Chinese long beans, cut into 3 inch pieces (or whole tender green

beans)
Salt and freshly ground black pepper to taste

Mix seasoning ingredients together. Add the beef and marinate for 20 minutes. Drain the meat and discard the marinade. Mix the sauce ingredients together. Heat 2 tblsp oil in the wok until it smokes. Reduce the heat and add the garlic and the beef and stir fry for 3-4 minutes. Remove the meat and keep on one side. Add the remaining oil to the wok and add the onion, ginger and long beans and stir fry for 2-3 minutes. Add the fried beef. Cover and fry for a further 1 minute. Stir in the sauce ingredients and bring to the boil. Simmer gently for 2-3 minutes. Season with salt and pepper. Remove from heat and serve.

Sweet and Sour Pork

PREPARATION TIME: 20 minutes plus 20 minutes to marinate

COOKING TIME: 15-20 minutes

SERVES: 4 people

Batter
3 tblsp all-purpose flour
1 tblsp cornstarch
1½ tsp baking soda
2 tblsp salad or olive oil

12oz lean pork, cut into 1 inch cubes

Seasoning
1 tsp fine granulated sugar
1 tsp salt
2½ tblsp light soy sauce
1½ tsp dark soy sauce
1 tblsp cooked oil
1 tblsp water

Cornstarch
Oil for deep frying
2 cloves garlic, cut into thin strips
1 large onion, peeled and cut into ½ inch pieces
1 carrot, sliced into ⅛x1x2 inch thin pieces
Pinch salt

Sweet and Sour Sauce
3 tblsp brown sugar
1 tblsp ketchup
1 cup chicken broth or water
4 tblsp wine-flavored vinegar
1½ tsp light soy sauce
Few slices fresh root ginger, peeled
1 tblsp cornstarch
Few drops of red food coloring
2 tsp cooked oil

Mix the batter ingredients together, adding sufficient water to make a

Diced Pork with Walnuts

PREPARATION TIME: 30 minutes
COOKING TIME: 16-18 minutes
SERVES: 3 people

¾ cup shelled walnuts
Oil for deep frying

Seasoning
1¾ tsp light soy sauce
Few drops sesame oil
Salt and freshly ground black pepper
    to taste
1 tblsp salad or olive oil
1 tblsp water
1 tblsp cornstarch
Pinch monosodium glutamate
    (optional)

½lb pork fillet, cut into cubes
1 carrot, thinly sliced
1 onion, peeled and cut into pieces
3 green onions, chopped
1 inch fresh root ginger, peeled and
    thinly sliced

Sauce
⅓ cup broth
1 tsp cornstarch

Cook the walnuts in boiling water
for 3-4 minutes. Drain the nuts
thoroughly. Deep fry the walnuts
until lightly browned. Remove and
drain. Use oil for cooking. Mix the
seasoning ingredients together and
add the pork. Leave to marinate for
15 minutes. Discard marinade.
Heat 2 tblsp oil in the wok and stir
fry the carrots for 2 minutes. Add
the onions and root ginger and stir
fry for 1 minute. Add 2 tsp of the
sauce broth and remove to a plate.
Add the drained pork cubes and 1
tblsp oil to the wok and stir fry for
4-5 minutes. Mix the remaining
broth and the cornstarch together
for the sauce. Return the walnuts
and carrots to the wok, together
with the blended sauce ingredients.
Mix well and simmer until the
sauce thickens. Remove and serve
immediately. Serve with rice
noodle or fried rice.

hick coating batter. Wash and
drain the pork. Mix with the
easoning ingredients and marinate
or 15-20 minutes. Drain the pork
nd discard the marinade. Roll the
ork cubes in cornstarch. Heat the
il for deep frying. Dip the pork
ubes in batter and fry in the hot
il until golden brown. Fry a few at
time until all the pork has been
fried. Drain well and keep warm in
a low oven. Heat wok and add 2
tsp deep fried oil. Stir fry the garlic,
onions and carrots for 3-4 minutes.
Season with salt and fry for a
further minute. Mix the sweet and
sour sauce ingredients together and
add to the wok. Stir the mixture
until it thickens. Pour over the fried
pork cubes and serve immediately.

Note: sliced green peppers can also
be added along with the carrots
and onions.

**Sweet and Sour Pork (top
right), Diced Pork with
Walnuts (center) and Shredded
Pork with Preserved Vegetables
(bottom left).**

CHINESE CUISINE
Poultry Dishes

Roast Crispy Duck

PREPARATION TIME: 15-20 minutes plus 6-8 hours to dry

COOKING TIME: 1 hour 30 minutes

SERVES: 4-6 people

4½lb duck, prepared for cooking
1 cup water
6 large green onions cut into 2 inch lengths
5 tblsp maple syrup
½ tsp red food coloring
2½ tblsp ketchup

Wash the duck and pat it dry on a clean cloth. Ease the fingers between the skin and flesh of the duck, starting at the neck end and working the length of the bird. Put a stick or large skewer through the neck and the cavity of the duck to wedge it securely. This will make the duck easier to handle. Hold the duck over the sink and pour boiling water all over it. Pat the duck dry. Melt half the maple syrup and dissolve in the water. Stand the duck on a rack over a deep tray. Slowly pour the dissolved syrup over the duck. Pour the syrup liquid over the duck 3 or 4 times. Leave the duck in a cool place for 6-8 hours, or overnight, until the skin is dry. Remove the stick. Stand the duck on a rack in a roasting tin. Preheat the oven to 400°F, and cook for 30 minutes. Turn over and cook the underside for a further 30 minutes. Melt the remaining maple syrup with the ketchup and add the food coloring. Spread over the duck and cook for a further 30 minutes. (The duck should have a crisp, red skin.) Remove the duck skin in squares. Slice the duck flesh and serve with the skin on the top. Serve the following dip as an accompaniment.

Duck Dip
4oz brown sugar
5 tblsp sweet bean paste
2½ tblsp sesame oil
½ cup water

Heat the wok and add the mixed ingredients. Cook for 3-4 minutes until the sugar has dissolved and the dip is smooth. Serve in individual cups.

Sliced Duck with Bamboo Shoots

PREPARATION TIME: 30 minutes

COOKING TIME: 10 minutes

SERVES: 2-3 people

2¼lb small duck
1 tsp monosodium glutamate (optional)
3 tsp cornstarch
2½ tblsp water
4oz broccoli, chopped
3 tblsp salad or olive oil
2-3 green onions, chopped
1 inch fresh root ginger, peeled and thinly sliced
1 clove garlic, peeled and finely chopped
⅔ cup bamboo shoots sliced
½ tsp fine granulated sugar
Salt and freshly ground black pepper to taste
5 tblsp chicken broth
2 tsp rice wine or sweet sherry
Few drops sesame oil

Cut the duck flesh into bite-size

pieces, removing all the bones. Mix the MSG, with ⅔ of the cornstarch and 1 tblsp water. Stir into the duck. Marinate for 20 minutes. Cook the broccoli in boiling water for 1 minute. Drain thoroughly. Heat the wok and add the oil. Stir fry the onions, ginger, garlic and bamboo shoots for 1-2 minutes. Add the duck pieces and stir fry for 2-3 minutes. Add the sugar, salt and pepper to taste, broth rice wine and sesame oil. Stir fry for 3 minutes. Add the remaining cornstarch and water blended together. Stir over the heat until the sauce thickens. Serve immediately, as a side dish.

Duck with Ginger and Pineapple

PREPARATION TIME: 20 minutes

COOKING TIME: 2 hours to 2 hours 45 minutes

SERVES: 4-6 people

½ inch fresh root ginger, peeled and crushed
1½ tblsp soy sauce
4½lb duck, prepared for cooking
Salt and freshly ground black pepper to taste
3 tblsp salad or olive oil
4 inches fresh root ginger, peeled and thinly sliced
¾ cup bean sprouts
3 green onions, chopped
2 carrots, peeled sliced and blanched in boiling water for 2 minutes
2 tsp brown sugar
1½ tblsp wine-flavored vinegar
1½ cups canned pineapple chunks in syrup
1¼ tblsp cornstarch mixed with 2½ tblsp water

Mix together the crushed ginger, half of the soy sauce and salt and pepper to taste. Wash the duck and pat it dry. Rub the outside of the duck with salt and put on a wire rack in a roasting tin. Roast at 350°F, for 30 minutes. Brush the ginger and soy sauce mixture over the duck. Baste frequently with the sauces from the pan and roast for 2 hours, turning the bird occasionally to brown all sides. Remove and slice the duck in small pieces. Heat the oil in a wok and stir fry the sliced ginger, bean sprouts, onions and carrots for 1-2 minutes. Add the duck slices and cook for 1 minute. Then add the brown sugar vinegar and pineapple chunks in their syrup. Bring to the boil and cook for 2-3 minutes. Add the blended cornstarch and remaining soy sauce and cook until the sauce thickens. Serve as a main dish along with noodles or rice.

This page: Stewed Chicken and Pineapple (top right), Fried Shredded Chicken on Cabbage (center left) and Chicken and Cashew Nuts (bottom right). Facing page: Sliced Duck with Bamboo Shoots (top), Duck with Ginger and Pineapple (bottom left) and Roast Crispy Duck (bottom right).

Chicken Green Chili

PREPARATION TIME: 10 minutes, plus 10 minutes to marinate

COOKING TIME: 10 minutes

SERVES: 4 people

Sauce
1 tsp light soy sauce
1 tsp dark soy sauce
Salt to taste
2 tsp cornstarch
1 tsp sesame oil
1 tsp vinegar
1 cup chicken broth

Seasoning
Salt to taste
Freshly ground black pepper to taste
Pinch monosodium glutamate (optional)
2½ tblsp) dark soy sauce
1¼ tblsp light soy sauce
1 tsp cornstarch
2 tsp rice wine or dry sherry

1lb boned chicken, cut into bite-size pieces
3 tblsp salad or olive oil
3 green onions, chopped
1 inch fresh root ginger, peeled and sliced
2 cloves of garlic, peeled and sliced
1 green pepper, seeded and chopped
2-3 green chilies, sliced lengthwise

Mix the sauce ingredients together. Mix the seasoning ingredients together and add the chicken. Marinate for 10 minutes. Drain the chicken and discard the liquid. Heat 1 tblsp oil and stir fry the onions, ginger and garlic for 2 minutes. Remove to a dish. Add the remaining oil and stir fry the chicken for 3 minutes. Add the blended green peppers and chilies and stir fry for 2 minutes. Add the onion mixture and the well blended sauce ingredients and cook for 3-4 minutes until the sauce thickens. Serve immediately.

Chicken Fry with Sauce (below right), Chicken Green Chili (below center) and Chicken and Mushrooms (far right).

Chicken and Mushrooms

PREPARATION TIME: 15 minutes, plus 10 minutes to marinate

COOKING TIME: 10-12 minutes

SERVES: 3-4 people

Seasoning
½ tsp salt
2½ tblsp light soy sauce
2 tsp cornstarch
1 tsp rice wine or dry sherry
Pinch monosodium glutamate (optional)

½lb chicken breast, cut into bite-size pieces

Sauce
Salt to taste
Freshly ground black pepper to taste
1¼ tblsp light soy sauce
1 cup chicken broth
2 tsp cornstarch

1 tsp oyster sauce

2 tblsp salad or olive oil
1 onion, peeled and chopped
1 clove of garlic, sliced
½ inch fresh root ginger, peeled and thinly sliced
3 dried black mushrooms, soaked and sliced
½ cup open mushrooms, sliced
½ cup buttom mushrooms, sliced

Mix the seasoning ingredients together. Marinate the chicken in the seasoning mixture for 10 minutes. Mix the sauce ingredients together. Heat the oil in a wok and fry the onion, garlic and ginger for 2-3 minutes. Remove and keep on one side. Fry the drained chicken in the remaining oil for 4 minutes. Add the mushrooms and stir fry for 1 minute. Add a little extra oil if necessary. Return the fried onion mixture to the wok and stir fry until well mixed. Pour the blended sauce ingredients into the wok and cook gently until the sauce thickens. Serve piping hot.

Chicken Fry with Sauce

PREPARATION TIME: 20 minutes

COOKING TIME: about 24 minutes

SERVES: 4 people

1 tblsp cooked oil
1 tsp sesame oil
2 tblsp sesame seeds

Sauce
2 cloves garlic, minced
2 green onions, finely chopped or minced
1 tsp Chinese black vinegar, or brown vinegar
3½ tblsp dark soy sauce
1 tsp light soy sauce
½ tsp monosodium glutamate (optional)
½ tsp salt
1½ tsp fine granulated sugar

8 chicken thighs, or 1lb chicken, cut into small joints

Heat the wok and add the oils. Stir fry the sesame seeds till they change color to golden brown. Remove to a dish. Mix sauce ingredients together and add the sesame seeds. Wipe the wok and add the chicken. Add sufficient water to cover, and cook for 20 minutes until the chicken is tender. De-bone the chicken and quickly cut into bite-size pieces. Arrange the chicken on a plate and spoon the sauce over the top. Serve immediately.

Stewed Chicken and Pineapple

PREPARATION TIME: 30 minutes

COOKING TIME: 15 minutes

SERVES: 4 people

Seasoning
2½ tblsp light soy sauce
1 tblsp salad or olive oil
1 tblsp cornstarch
1 tsp salt
½ tsp sesame oil
2 tblsp water

1½lb boned chicken breast, cut into cubes

Sauce
1½ tsp cornstarch
1 cup water or chicken broth
2½ tsp dark soy sauce
Salt to taste

2 tblsp salad or olive oil
1 onion, peeled and cut into chunks
2 green onions, finely chopped
1 inch fresh root ginger, peeled and thinly sliced
4-5 pineapple rings, cut into chunks

Mix the seasoning ingredients together. Add the cubed chicken and marinate for 10-12 minutes. Mix the sauce ingredients together

in a bowl. Heat the oil in a wok and fry the onions for 2 minutes until just tender. Add the drained chicken and fry for 3-4 minutes. Add the root ginger and fry for 1 minute. Add any remaining marinade and the sauce ingredients and bring to the boil. Cook, stirring, until the sauce thickens then add the pineapple chunks. Heat through. Remove from the heat and serve with fried rice.

Chicken Chop Suey

PREPARATION TIME: 30 minutes

COOKING TIME: 15 minutes

SERVES: 4 people

2½ tblsp light soy sauce
1 tsp brown sugar
Salt to taste
1lb boned chicken, cut into 1 inch pieces
2 tblsp salad or olive oil
1 onion, cut into chunks
2½ cups bean sprouts
2 tsp sesame oil
¼ tsp monosodium glutamate (optional)
1 tblsp cornstarch
1 cup chicken broth

Mix the soy sauce with the sugar and salt and add the chicken pieces. Allow to marinate for 5 minutes. Drain the chicken and reserve the marinade. Heat the wok and add the oil. Fry the chicken for 2-3 minutes. Remove the chicken. Fry the onions for 2-3 minutes and add the bean sprouts. Stir fry for 4-5 minutes. Return the chicken to the pan and add the sesame oil. Dissolve the monosodium glutamate and the cornstarch in the broth and pour over the chicken mixture. Cook for 2-3 minutes, stirring, until the sauce thickens. Serve as a side-dish.

Deep Fried Crispy Chicken

PREPARATION TIME: 3 hours

COOKING TIME: 13-14 minutes

SERVES: 4 people

3-3½lb chicken, prepared for cooking

Seasoning
1 tsp salt
½ tsp five spice powder
2 tblsp maple syrup
2 tblsp brown vinegar
⅔ cup wine-flavored vinegar

Oil for deep frying

Wash the chicken and hang it up by a hook to drain and dry. The skin will dry quickly. Pour boiling water over the chicken 4-5 times to partially cook the skin. This will make the skin crisp during frying. Rub salt and five spice powder well inside the chicken cavity. Dissolve the maple syrup and vinegars in a pan over a gentle heat. Pour over the chicken. Repeat several times, catching the syrup solution in a drip tray. Leave the chicken to hang and dry for 1½-2 hours, until the skin is smooth and shiny. Heat the oil for deep frying. Deep fry the chicken for 10 minutes. Ladle hot oil carefully over the chicken continually, until the chicken is deep brown in color. (The skin puffs out slightly.) Cook for a further 3-4 minutes and remove from the oil. Drain on absorbent paper. Cut into small pieces and serve with a dip.

Chicken and Cashew Nuts

PREPARATION TIME: 15 minutes

COOKING TIME: 15 minutes

SERVES: 4 people

12oz chicken breast, sliced into 1 inch pieces
1 tblsp cornstarch

Seasoning
1 tsp salt
1 tsp sesame oil
1¼ tblsp light soy sauce
½ tsp brown sugar

Oil for deep frying and stir frying
¾ cup cashew nuts
2 green onions, chopped
1 small onion, peeled and cubed
1 inch fresh root ginger, peeled and sliced
2 cloves of garlic, sliced
1 cup snow peas (mange tout)
½ cup thinly sliced bamboo shoots

Sauce
2 tsp cornstarch
1 tblsp Hoi Sin sauce
1 cup chicken broth
Pinch monosodium glutamate (optional)

Roll the chicken pieces in cornstarch. Discard the remaining cornstarch. Mix the seasoning ingredients together and pour over chicken. Leave to stand for 10 minutes. Heat oil for deep frying in a wok and fry cashew nuts until golden brown. Remove the nuts and all but 2 tblsp of the oil; drain the nuts on kitchen paper. Heat the oil remaining in the wok and stir fry the onions, ginger and garlic for 2-3 minutes. Add snow peas and bamboo shoots and stir fry for 3 minutes. Remove the fried ingredients. Add 1 tblsp oil to the wok and fry the chicken for 3-4 minutes. Remove the chicken. Clean the wok and add a further 2 tblsp oil and return chicken, cashew nuts and fried onions etc. to the wok. Prepare the sauce by mixing the cornstarch, Hoi Sin sauce, chicken broth and monosodium glutamate together. Pour over the chicken. Mix well and cook until the sauce thickens and becomes transparent. Serve hot with a chow mein dish. Alternatively, a few chunks of pineapple will add extra zest to the dish.

Fried Shredded Chicken on Cabbage

PREPARATION TIME: 20 minutes

COOKING TIME: 12 minutes

SERVES: 4 people

1lb Chinese white cabbage, cut into 1 inch pieces
Pinch baking soda

Seasoning
1¼ tblsp light soy sauce
1 tblsp cornstarch
¼ tsp sesame oil
¼ tsp freshly ground black pepper
½ tsp fine granulated sugar
½ tsp salt
1¼ tblsp water
1 tblsp salad or olive oil
Pinch monosodium glutamate (optional)

2 tblsp salad or olive oil
1 onion, peeled and roughly chopped
1 inch fresh root ginger, peeled and thinly sliced
1lb boned chicken breasts, shredded
4-6 mushrooms, sliced

Sauce
3 tblsp chicken broth
¼ tsp sesame oil
1 tsp light soy sauce
1 tsp cornstarch
1 tsp monosodium glutamate (optional)

Wash cabbage and blanch in boiling water with a pinch of

baking soda for 2 minutes. Drain well. Mix the seasoning ingredients together. Heat the wok and add the oil. Fry the onions, ginger and chicken for 2-3 minutes. Add the mushrooms and fry for further 2 minutes. Add the broth and cook for 4-5 minutes. Mix the sauce ingredients together and pour over the chicken. Cook for 2 minutes. Serve immediately.

Steamed Chicken

PREPARATION TIME: 20-30 minutes

COOKING TIME: 15-20 minutes

SERVES: 4 people

1½lb boned chicken

Seasoning
1¼ tblsp light soy sauce
1 tsp brown sugar
1 tsp salt
1 tblsp cornstarch
2 tblsp oil or cooked oil
½ tsp monosodium glutamate (optional)

4oz dried mushrooms, soaked in boiling water for 5 minutes and sliced, (or ordinary mushrooms)
½ inch fresh root ginger, peeled and sliced
4 green onions, finely chopped
2 tblsp broth or water, if needed

Cut the chicken into 1 inch pieces. Mix the seasoning ingredients together and mix with the chicken. Leave to marinate for 15 minutes. Place a plate in a steamer and put the chicken, mushrooms, ginger, half the onion and the broth on top. Steam over boiling water for 15-20 minutes. Serve with the remaining onions sprinkled over the chicken. The steaming can also be done on a greased lotus leaf or a banana leaf. The flavor is quite stunning.

Tangerine Peel Chicken

PREPARATION TIME: 30 minutes

COOKING TIME: 12-15 minutes

SERVES: 4 people

1lb boned chicken breast, cut into 1 inch pieces

Facing page: Chicken Chop Suey (top left), Steamed Chicken (center right) and Deep Fried Crispy Chicken (bottom left).

Seasoning

½ tsp salt
1½ tsp brown sugar
½ tsp monosodium glutamate
    (optional)
1 tsp dark soy sauce
2½ tsp light soy sauce
1 tsp rice wine or dry sherry
2½ tsp brown vinegar
1 tsp sesame oil
2 tsp cornstarch

Oil for deep frying
1-2 red or green chilies, chopped
½ inch fresh root ginger, peeled and
    finely chopped
2 inches dried tangerine peel, coarsely
    ground or crumbled
2 green onions, finely chopped

Sauce

½ tsp cornstarch
1-2 tblsp water or broth

Mix the chicken pieces with the seasoning ingredients and stir well. Leave to marinate for 10-15 minutes. Remove the chicken pieces and reserve the marinade. Heat wok and add the oil for deep frying. Once it starts to smoke add the chicken pieces and fry for 4-5 minutes until golden. Drain chicken on kitchen paper. Tip off the oil, leaving 1 tblsp oil in the wok, and stir fry the chilies, ginger, tangerine peel and onions for 2-3 minutes. When they begin to color add the chicken and stir fry for 1 minute. Mix the reserved marinade with the sauce ingredients and pour over the chicken. Stir and cook for 2-3 minutes until the sauce thickens and the chicken is tender. Serve immediately.

Roast Spiced Duck

PREPARATION TIME: 3-4 hours to
dry, and 1 hour to glaze

COOKING TIME: 1 hour

SERVES: 4-6 people

4½lb duck, prepared for cooking
1 tsp five spice powder
1½ tsp salt
5 tblsp maple syrup
1½ tblsp wine-flavored vinegar
Salad or olive oil

Wash and dry the duck. Rub in the five spice powder and salt. Close the cavities of the duck by securing both ends with small skewers. Mix the maple syrup and vinegar together with a little water and bring to the boil. Spoon this liquid over the duck several times, collecting the liquid in a tray. Hang the duck by its neck for 3-4 hours to dry. Preheat the oven to 450°F.

Place the duck in a roasting tin. Rub oil into the skin. Roast in the oven for 1 hour, basting with any remaining maple syrup and vinegar liquid. If the duck is not quite tender, cook for a little longer. Slice the duck onto a warmed serving dish and serve immediately.

Roast Peking Duck

PREPARATION TIME: 15 minutes
plus 2-3 hours to dry out the skin

COOKING TIME: 1 hour
                  20 minutes

SERVES: 4-6 people

4½lb duck, prepared for cooking
4½ cups boiling water
2½ tblsp maple syrup
1 cup water
2-3 seedless oranges, peeled and cut
    into rings
2 tblsp salad or olive oil
Salt and freshly ground black pepper

Sauce

2½ tsp cornstarch
5 tblsp water or broth
Pinch monosodiumm glutamate
    (optional)
2½ tsp light soy sauce
1 tsp rice wine or dry sherry

To Garnish

4 green onions, cut into 2 inch lengths

Wash and dry the duck. Put a stick or skewer through the neck and the cavity of the duck so that it is easier to handle. Hold the bird over the sink and pour the boiling water over it. Hang the duck up to dry. Melt the syrup and water together and spoon over the duck several times, catching the liquid on a drip tray each time. Leave the duck to dry for 2-3 hours in a cool place. Save any liquid that drops off. Preheat the oven to 400°F. Place the duck, breast side down, in a roasting tin and roast for 30 minutes. Lift out the duck. Put the orange rings into the tin and sit the duck on top, breast side uppermost. Baste with the oil and season with salt and pepper. Roast for a further 45-50 minutes until tender. Cut off the duck joints and slice the breast meat. Arrange with the orange slices on a serving dish and keep warm.

To Make the Sauce

Mix the sauce ingredients together and add any reserved maltose liquid. Bring to the boil gently, stirring, until the sauce thickens. Pour over the cooked duck and sprinkle with the onions.

Steamed Duck in Wine Sauce

PREPARATION TIME: 20 minutes

COOKING TIME: 30 hours
                  30 minutes

SERVES: 4-6 people

4½lb duck, prepared for cooking
Generous ½ cup Kao Liang wine, or
    mild red wine
½ tsp monosodium glutamate
    (optional)
1 inch fresh root ginger, peeled and
    thinly sliced
3 green onions, chopped
1 tsp salt

**Roast Spiced Duck (top), Roast
Peking Duck (above) and
Steamed Duck in Wine Sauce
(right).**

1 tsp fine granulated sugar
1¼ tsp) cornstarch

Place the duck in a large pot. Add water to cover and boil for 5-7 minutes. Remove the duck and drain well. Mix all the remaining ingredients together apart from the cornstarch. Place the duck in a deep dish and stand over a steamer. Pour the wine mixture over the duck. Cover and steam for 2-3 hours until the duck is quite tender. Remove the duck and strain the cooking liquid. Place the duck on a serving dish, either whole or cut into slices. Blend the cooking liquid with the cornstarch.

Bring to the boil and stir until thickened. Pour over the duck. Serve immediately

Chicken Chow Mein

PREPARATION TIME: 30 minutes

COOKING TIME: 20 minutes

SERVES: 4 people

1lb egg noodles or spaghetti, broken into small pieces
1 onion, peeled and thinly sliced
½ cup mushrooms, sliced
3 green onions, chopped
2 cloves of garlic, peeled and chopped
Salt to taste
Pinch monosodium glutamate
4 tblsp salad or olive oil
1½ cups chicken meat, finely shredded
2½ tblsp light soy sauce
1 tsp fine granulated sugar
1 tblsp rice wine or dry sherry
⅓ cup chicken broth

Cook the noodles in boiling, salted water for 4-5 minutes until tender. Drain and rinse under cold water. Drain once again and add 2 tblsp oil; mix well to prevent the noodles from sticking together. Heat 2 tblsp oil in a wok and fry the onions and garlic for 2 minutes. Add chicken and stir fry for 3-4 minutes. Add mushrooms. Sprinkle over the wine, sugar, soy sauce, monosodium glutamate and salt to

taste. Cook until the mixture is fairly dry. Add noodles and stir well to mix. Sprinkle over the broth and cook once again until dry. Serve with chili sauce and dark soy sauce. ½ cup sliced green beans, ⅓ cup lightly cooked peas or ⅓ cup shredded carrot may also be added, along with the chicken pieces.

Peking Duck with Pancakes

PREPARATION TIME: for duck 2-3 hours; for pancakes 6 minutes

COOKING TIME: for duck 1 hour 20 minutes; for pancakes 15 minutes

SERVES: 6-8 people

4½lb Peking duck, roasted
16-20 green onions, sliced into 3 inch pieces

Pancakes (Po Ping)
1lb all-purpose flour
Pinch salt
1¼ tblsp salad or olive oil
1 tsp sesame oil
Tepid water for kneading
Flour for rolling

To Make Pancakes
Sift the flour and salt into a mixing bowl. Make a well in the center and add the oils and water, a little at a time, and work in the flour. Make a pliable dough. Remove from the bowl and knead well for 2-3 minutes. Cover with a damp, clean

cloth and allow to rest for 10 minutes. Knead again for 1 minute and divide the dough into 16-20 even-sized balls. Roll each ball in flour and roll out into a 4-6 inch circle. Place a skillet on the heat and when moderately hot place the rolled circle of dough on it; cook for ½-1 minute. Little bubbles will appear; flip over and allow to cook for 1-1½ minutes. Pick the pancake up and check whether little brown specs have appeared on the undersides; if not, then cook for few seconds more. Use a clean tea towel to press the pancakes gently, this will circulate the steam and cook the pancakes. Prepare the rest of the pancakes in the same way and keep them stacked, wrapped in foil to keep them warm.

To Make Dip
5 tblsp brown sugar
4 tblsp bean paste (sweet)
1 tblsp sesame oil
1 tblsp olive oil or peanut oil
1 cup water

Other Dips, Ready Prepared
4 tblsp Hoi Sin sauce
4 tblsp Chinese barbecue sauce

Mix sugar, bean paste and water

together. Warm the wok, add the oil and then the sugar mixture. Bring to boil and, when the sugar has melted, remove and put in a bowl. Place the duck on a cutting board and cut thin slices from the breast area and thighs. Place a pancake on an individual plate, cover with a slice of duck and a few strips of onion, spread on a dip of your choice, roll up like a pancake and eat. To make very crisp duck, cut duck into large joints and deep fry them till crispy.

Sweet and Sour Chicken

PREPARATION TIME: 30 minutes
COOKING TIME: 20 minutes
SERVES: 3-4 people

½ tsp salt
3 tsp cornstarch
2 chicken breasts, cut into ½ inch cubes
1 onion, peeled and roughly chopped into ½ inch pieces
¼ cup sliced bamboo shoots
1 green pepper, seeded and thinly

sliced
1 inch fresh root ginger, peeled and thinly sliced
2 carrots, scraped and thinly sliced into 1 inch long pieces
1 garlic clove, peeled and chopped
2 tblsp salad or olive oil

Batter
1 cup all-purpose flour
1 tblsp cornstarch
1 small egg

Oil for deep frying

Sauce
1 tblsp brown sugar
1¼ tblsp wine-flavored vinegar
1¼ tblsp soy sauce
1 tblsp ketchup
2 cups chicken broth
Pinch monosodium glutamate (optional)
2½ tsp cornstarch

Mix salt and cornstarch and roll chicken pieces in it. Make the batter by mixing the sieved flour and cornstarch with the egg and sufficient water to make a thick batter. Beat well. Heat oil for deep frying. Dip the chicken pieces into the batter and deep-fry until golden brown and crisp. Drain on

absorbent paper and keep warm. Heat the 2 tblsp oil in a wok and stir fry the onion, ginger and garlic for 2-3 minutes. Add the carrots and fry for 2 minutes. Add the green pepper and fry for 2 minutes. Add bamboo shoots, season with salt and stir well. Mix all the sauce ingredients together. Pour over the cooked vegetables. Cook 2-3 minutes until the sauce thickens. The sauce should become transparent. Arrange fried chicken pieces on a serving dish and pour the sweet and sour sauce over them. Serve as a side dish.

This page: Peking Duck with Pancakes.

Facing page: Tangerine Peel Chicken (top), Sweet and Sour Chicken (center left) and Chicken Chow Mein (bottom).

Fish and Seafood

Prawns with Broccoli

PREPARATION TIME: 10 minutes

COOKING TIME: 8-10 minutes

SERVES: 4 people

1lb peeled medium size shrimp
Oil for deep frying

Sauce
½ cup chicken broth
2 tsp cornstarch
Freshly ground black pepper and salt to taste
Pinch monosodium glutamate (optional)
1 tsp fine granulated sugar

Seasoning
2 tblsp cooked oil, or oil from deep frying the shrimps
Pinch salt
½ tsp fine granulated sugar
Pinch monosodium glutamate (optional)
2 tsp cornstarch

8oz Chinese broccoli, or Continental broccoli, cut into 3 inch pieces
1 carrot, peeled and sliced
2 cloves garlic, peeled and chopped
½ inch fresh root ginger, peeled and chopped

Deep fry the shrimps in hot oil for 1-2 minutes. Drain the shrimp and keep on one side. Keep the oil. Mix the sauce ingredients together. Mix seasoning ingredients together in a separate bowl. Cook the broccoli in boiling water for 1 minute. Drain and add cold water to cover. Drain once again and mix the broccoli with the seasoning ingredients. Heat the wok and add 2 tblsp cooked oil. Add the carrot, garlic and ginger and stir fry for 1 minute. Add the broccoli and stir fry for 1 minute more. Add the shrimps and stir fry for ½ minute then add the blended sauce ingredients. Cook gently until the sauce thickens. Serve immediately.

Shrimps with Bean Curd

PREPARATION TIME: 10 minutes

COOKING TIME: 8 minutes

SERVES: 4 people

1lb peeled medium size shrimp

Seasoning
1 tsp light soy sauce
Pinch salt
1 tsp fine granulated sugar
1 tsp cornstarch

1 inch fresh root ginger, peeled and finely choppped
2 tblsp salad or olive oil
1 clove of garlic, peeled and chopped
1 red chili, chopped

2-3 beancurd cakes, cubed
4 tblsp chicken broth
1 tsp cornstarch
2 tblsp water

Mix the shrimps with the seasoning ingredients and half of the ginger. Heat the oil and stir fry the ginger and shrimps for 2 minutes. Add the garlic and fry for 1 minute. Add the chili, cubed beancurd and broth. Simmer for 2-3 minutes. Mix the cornstarch with the water and remaining crushed ginger and pour over the shrimp mixture. Simmer gently until the sauce thickens. Serve immediately.

Shrimp in Hot Sauce

PREPARATION TIME: 10 minutes

COOKING TIME: 6 minutes

SERVES: 4 people

12oz cooked unshelled shrimp

Seasoning
1 tsp brown vinegar
1 tsp Shao Hsing wine
Pinch salt

Sauce
1 tsp cornstarch mixed with 1 tblsp water
2 tsp ketchup
Salt and freshly ground black pepper to taste

2 tsp fine granulated sugar
½ tsp monosodium glutamate (optional)
1 tsp hot chili sauce
1 cup chicken broth
2 tblsp cooked oil

Wash shrimps and drain well. Mix the seasoning ingredients together. Mix the sauce ingredients together in a separate bowl. Heat the oil in a wok and deep fry the shrimps for 1 minute. Remove the shrimps and drain. Keep the oil. Reheat the wok and add 2 tsp oil and stir fry the onion, celery and garlic for 1 minute. Add shrimps and the blended sauce ingredients. Bring to the boil and simmer gently for 3-4 minutes. Stir in the seasoning mixture.

Fish in Wine Sauce

PREPARATION TIME: 20 minutes

COOKING TIME: 15 minutes

SERVES: 3-4 people

Marinade
¼ tsp salt
1 egg white
2 tsp cornstarch
1 tsp wine-flavored vinegar

10-12oz mullet or carp fillet, cut into 2 inch slices
Oil for deep frying

Shrimp in Hot Sauce (top right), Shrimps with Bean Curd (center right) and Prawns with Broccoli (bottom right).

1 cup chicken broth

Seasoning
Pinch monosodium glutamate
  (optional)
Pinch salt
Pinch freshly ground black pepper
1 tsp fine granulated sugar
2½ tsp cornstarch
1½ tblsp water
1 cloud ear fungus, soaked and boiled
  for 2 minutes, and then chopped
2 dried Chinese mushrooms, soaked
  and sliced

Mix the marinade ingredients
together. Marinate the fish in the
marinade for 10 minutes. Heat a

generous quantity of oil in the wok
and deep fry the drained fish
pieces, a few at a time, until the
flesh is white. Remove and drain
the fish. Keep the oil for future use.
Clean the wok. Add the chicken
stock to the wok and bring to the
boil. Simmer gently and stir in the
seasoning ingredients. Simmer for
few seconds and then add the
cornstarch blended with the water.
Add the fish and simmer until the
sauce thickens. Add the fungus
and mushrooms. Simmer for 1
minute. Serve immediately.

Fish with Chicken and Vegetables

PREPARATION TIME: 25 minutes

COOKING TIME: 15 minutes

SERVES: 4 people

1lb plaice or lemon sole fillets, cut into 2 inch pieces
8oz boned chicken, cut into 2 inch slices
6 dried Chinese mushrooms, soaked and sliced
½ cup button mushrooms, sliced
½ cup bamboo shoots, sliced
½ cup shredded mustard green, kale, or broccoli or 4 asparagus tips, chopped
1 cup mixed diced vegetables (peas, carrots, bean sprouts, etc)
1 small onion, peeled and sliced
1 tsp salt
Cooked oil

Marinade
¼ tsp salt
1 tsp white pepper
½ tsp monosodium glutamate (optional)
2 tsp cornstarch
1 tblsp cooked oil
¼ tsp sesame oil

Sauce
1 cup chicken broth
Salt to taste
Freshly ground black pepper to taste
½ tsp monosodium glutamate (optional)
2 tsp cooked oil
1 tsp lemon juice

Wash the fish and drain. Mix the marinade ingredients together and marinate fish for 10-15 minutes. Blanch the mustard green, kale or broccoli in boiling, salted water for 1 minute. Drain and keep on one side. Heat the wok with 1 tblsp cooked oil and stir fry the mixed vegetables and the onions for 2 minutes. Add the mustard green and stir fry for 1 minute. Drain and remove onto a plate. Brush a deep plate with cooked oil and arrange the drained fish, mushrooms, chicken and bamboo shoots in alternate rows. Place the dish over a steamer. Cover and steam over boiling water for 7 minutes until cooked. Remove the steamer from heat and keep on one side. Heat the wok and add the sauce ingredients and fish marinade. Bring to the boil and simmer for 1 minute, until thickened. Put the steamed fish, mushrooms etc. onto a serving plate and pour the hot sauce over the top. Serve immediately.

Fish with Vegetables and Bean Curd

PREPARATION TIME: 20 minutes

COOKING TIME: 15 minutes

SERVES: 4 people

4 squares bean curd, cut into 1 inch squares

Sauce B
1 tblsp Shao Hsing wine
1¼ tblsp dark soy sauce
1¼ tblsp light soy sauce
2½ tsp brown sugar
Pinch salt
Pinch white pepper
3¾ cups chicken broth

8oz cod fillet, cut into 2 inch slices

Seasoning for Fish A
½ tsp salt
½ tsp Shao Hsing wine
1¾ tblsp cornstarch

3 tblsp salad or olive oil
1½ cups shredded Chinese cabbage, or Chinese leaves

Seasoning for Cabbage C
½ tsp brown sugar
Pinch salt

1 tsp cornstarch
1 inch fresh root ginger, peeled and shredded
2 green onions, chopped
1½ tblsp cornstarch mixed with 2 tblsp water
½ cup bean sprouts
Few slices of green pepper, diced
1 small carrot, chopped
2 tblsp frozen peas (or lightly cooked fresh ones)

Soak the bean curd in cold water for 2 minutes. Drain well. Mix the sauce B ingredients and keep on one side. Wash the fish and drain well. Mix seasoning A ingredients and marinate fish for 10-12 minutes. Heat the wok and add half the oil. When very hot, add the cabbage and seasoning C ingredients and stir fry for about 2 minutes. Drain the cabbage well. Discard any liquid. Heat wok and add the remaining oil. Add the ginger and onions and stir fry for 1 minute. Add sauce B ingredients and bring to the boil. Add fish and boil for 1 minute. Add the bean curd and simmer over a low heat for 5-6 minutes. (The bean curd should become spongy to the touch). Add the blended

cornstarch and water. Stir and simmer until the sauce thickens. Add the cabbage and other vegetables and simmer for a further 2 minutes. Serve immediately.

Boiled Shrimp

PREPARATION TIME: 5 minutes, plus 10 minutes for the sauce

COOKING TIME: 10-15 minutes

SERVES: 6 people

Sauce
2½ tblsp dark soy sauce
3½ tblsp light soy sauce
½ inch fresh root ginger, peeled and shredded
2 green onions, finely chopped
1 red chili, seeded and shredded
4 tblsp cooked oil
2 tsp ketchup

2lbs medium or large uncooked shrimps in their shells
Salt

Mix the sauce ingredients together. Wash the shrimps and drain. Place the shrimps into a wire basket and lower into a large pan of boiling, salted water. Boil for 10-12 minutes. Drain. Serve the drained hot shrimps with small bowls of sauce for dipping.

Cantonese Prawns

PREPARATION TIME: 10 minutes

COOKING TIME: 15 minutes

SERVES: 4 people

3 tblsp salad or olive oil
2 cloves garlic, finely crushed
1lb peeled medium shrimps
2 inches root ginger, peeled and finely chopped
1 cup uncooked pork or bacon, finely chopped

Sauce
1¼ tblsp rice wine or dry sherry
1¼ tblsp light soy sauce
1 tsp fine granulated sugar
1 cup broth or water
1 tblsp cornstarch mixed with 2 tblsp broth or water

2-3 green onions, chopped
2 eggs, lightly beaten

Heat 1 tblsp oil in a wok. Add the garlic and fry for 1 minute. Add the shrimp and stir fry for 4-5 minutes. Remove to a dish. Keep warm. Add the remaining oil to the wok and fry the ginger and pork for 3-4 minutes until it loses its color. Add

the mixed sauce ingredients to the wok and cook for 1 minute. Add the onions and cook for 1 minute. Add the beaten eggs and cook for 1-2 minutes, without stirring, until it sets. Spoon the egg mixture over the shrimps. Alternatively, add the shrimps along with the beaten eggs. Allow the eggs to set and then mix gently. Serve at once.

Shrimp and Ginger

PREPARATION TIME:	10 minutes
COOKING TIME:	10 minutes
SERVES:	4-6 people

2 tblsp salad or olive oil
1½lb peeled medium shrimp
1 inch fresh root ginger, peeled and finely chopped
2 cloves garlic, peeled and finely chopped
2-3 green onions, chopped lengthwise into 1 inch pieces
1 leek, white part only, cut into strips.
1 cup shelled peas, lightly cooked
2 cups bean sprouts

Seasoning
2½ tblsp dark soy sauce
1 tsp fine granulated sugar
Pinch monosodium glutamate (optional)
Pinch of salt

Heat the oil in a wok and stir fry the shrimps for 2-3 minutes. Remove the shrimps to a dish. Reheat the oil and add the ginger and garlic and fry for 1 minute. Add the onions and stir fry for 1 minute. Add the leek, peas and beansprouts. Stir fry for 2-3 minutes. Sprinkle over the seasoning ingredients and return the shrimps to the wok. Cover and cook for 2 minutes. Serve immediately.

Shrimp and Cauliflower

PREPARATION TIME:	15 minutes
COOKING TIME:	14-15 minutes
SERVES:	4-6 people

3 tblsp salad or olive oil

Facing page: Fish with Vegetables and Bean Curd (top), Fish in Wine Sauce (center right), Fish with Chicken and Vegetables (bottom). This page: Shrimp and Ginger (top), Boiled Shrimp (center) and Cantonese Prawns (bottom right).

1 clove garlic, peeled and finely
    chopped
1lb medium size shrimps, peeled
10oz cauliflower florets, cut into
    smaller pieces
1 cup water or broth
Salt to taste
1½ cups shelled peas, lightly cooked

Sauce
2 tsp cornstarch
2 tblsp broth or water
Freshly ground black pepper to taste

Heat the oil in a wok and fry the
garlic for 2 minutes. Add the
shrimps and cook for 3 minutes.
Remove the shrimps. Add the
cauliflower and fry for 2-3 minutes,
stirring constantly. Add broth,
cover and simmer for five minutes.
Add salt to taste and the peas and
cook for a further 2-3 minutes.
Return the shrimps to the wok and
stir well. Add the blended sauce
ingredients and gently simmer until
it thickens. Serve immediately.

Snow Peas with Shrimp

PREPARATION TIME:	10 minutes
COOKING TIME:	6-8 minutes
SERVES:	4-6 people

1 tsp cornstarch
1 tsp fine granulated sugar
1 tsp dark soy sauce
1 tblsp water
3 tblsp salad or olive oil
1lb peeled medium size shrimps
1 cup chicken broth
½ tsp salt
1⅓ cups snow peas (mange tout)
¾ cup water chestnuts, sliced
1 small onion, peeled and cut into
    small pieces
1 stem celery, cut into ¼ inch pieces
Pinch monosodium glutamate
    (optional)

Mix together the cornstarch, sugar,
soy sauce and water. Heat the oil in
a wok. Add the shrimps and stir fry
for 2 minutes. Add the broth, salt,
snow peas, water chestnuts, onions
and celery. Cover and cook for 2
minutes. Stir in the monosodium
glutamate. Stir in the cornstarch
mixture and simmer gently until
the sauce thickens. Serve as a side
dish.

Prawns with Cashew Nuts

PREPARATION TIME:	10 minutes
COOKING TIME:	7-8 minutes
SERVES:	4 people

3 tblsp salad or olive oil
¾ cup cashew nuts
2 tsp cornstarch
1 cup chicken broth or water
1 onion, peeled and cut into small
    pieces
⅓ cup sliced green beans
⅔ cup Chinese cabbage, or white
    cabbage, shredded
½ cup bamboo shoots, sliced
1lb peeled medium shrimp
Salt and freshly ground black pepper
    to taste
4 rings pineapple, cut into chunks

Pinch monosodium glutamate
    (optional)

Heat 1 tblsp oil in a wok and stir fry
the cashew nuts until light brown.
Remove the nuts and keep on one
side. Mix the cornstarch with 2
tblsp water or broth and keep on
one side. Reheat the wok with the
remaining oil and fry the onion for
1 minute. Add the beans, cabbage
and bamboo shoots and stir fry for
2-3 minutes. Add the cashew nuts
and shrimps and then add the

remaining broth, salt and pepper,
and the pineapple. Simmer for 1
minute and then add the MSG
and cornstarch mixture and cook
until the sauce thickens. Serve
immediately.

**Shrimp and Cauliflower (top
right), Prawns with Cashew
Nuts (center left) and Snow
Peas with Shrimps (bottom).**

CHINESE CUISINE
Vegetables

Braised Cauliflower with Chili

PREPARATION TIME: 5 minutes
COOKING TIME: 10 minutes
SERVES: 4 people

4 tblsp salad or olive oil
1 inch fresh root ginger, peeled and
    thinly sliced
1 small cauliflower, cut into 1 inch
    florets
2-3 green or red chilies, sliced into
    quarters and seeded
3 green onions
Salt to taste
1 tsp fine granulated sugar
1¼ cups chicken broth
1½ tsp cornstarch
1½ tblsp water

Heat the wok and add the oil. Stir
fry the ginger for 1 minute. Reduce
the heat and add the cauliflower
and chilies. Stir fry for 3-4 minutes.
Add the green onions, season with
salt and sprinkle with sugar. Mix
for 1 minute and then add the
broth. Cover and cook for 2
minutes. Add the blended
cornstarch and water and stir over
the heat until the sauce has
thickened.

Fried Bean Curd with Mushrooms

PREPARATION TIME: 15 minutes
COOKING TIME: 12-15 minutes
SERVES: 4 people

8oz large cap mushrooms, sliced

Seasoning
1 tblsp rice wine or dry sherry
2 tsp fine granulated sugar

4 dried Chinese mushrooms, soaked
    and sliced
Pinch baking soda
8oz mustard green or spinach, cut
    into 3 inch pieces
4 squares beancurd (tofu), cubed
Salad or olive oil
1 inch fresh root ginger, peeled and
    shredded
2 green onions, chopped
½ cup cooked ham, shredded

Sauce

1½ tblsp oyster sauce
1½ tsp dark soy sauce
1½ tblsp cornstarch
6 tblsp broth or water
Freshly ground black pepper

Blanch the fresh mushrooms in
water for 1 minute. Drain the
mushrooms and discard the water.
Mix the seasoning ingredients
together and marinate all the
mushrooms for 5-6 minutes.
Discard marinade. Bring 5 cups of
water to the boil and add the
baking soda and salt. Blanch the
greens for 2 minutes. Drain the
greens. Discard water. Sprinkle ½
tsp salt over the beancurd. Deep
fry in hot oil until golden brown.
Drain and remove. Heat 2 tblsp oil
in the wok and stir fry the ginger,
onions and ham for 2-3 minutes.
Return the mushrooms to the wok
and mix with the ginger and
onions. Add the blended sauce
ingredients and bring to boil. Add
the bean curd and simmer until the
sauce thickens. Arrange the greens
on a dish and pour the sauce over
them. Sprinkle with freshly ground
black pepper.

Fried Vegetables with Ginger

PREPARATION TIME: 10 minutes
COOKING TIME: 13-15 minutes
SERVES: 6 people

2¼lb mixed Chinese green vegetables
    (cabbage, spinach, kale, broccoli,
    Chinese leaf etc.)
½ cup snow peas (mange tout)
1 tsp baking soda
2 tsp fine granulated sugar
1 tsp salt
1 tblsp cooked oil
4 tblsp salad or olive oil
1 inch fresh root ginger, peeled and
    shredded
1 green pepper, seeded and diced
1 green or red chili, sliced into strips

Sauce
2 tsp dark soy sauce
1 tsp fine granulated sugar
1 cup chicken broth
2 tsp cornstarch
1 tsp five spice powder

To Serve

½ tsp sesame oil
Freshly ground black pepper to taste

Cut the green vegetables into 3
inch pieces. Bring a large pan of
water to the boil and add the
seasoning ingredients. Add the
snow peas and greens and cook for
4-5 minutes. Drain green
vegetables and discard water. Add 1
tblsp oil to the vegetables and keep
covered. Heat the remaining oil in
the wok and stir fry the ginger for 1
minute. Add the green pepper and
chilies and stir fry for 1-2 minutes.
Add the blended sauce ingredients
and stir well. Simmer gently for 3-4
minutes. Add the green vegetables
and cook for 1 minute. Serve
immediately, sprinkled with sesame
oil and pepper.

Bamboo Shoots with Green Vegetables

PREPARATION TIME: 10 minutes
COOKING TIME: 10-12 minutes
SERVES: 4 people

Salad or olive oil for cooking
8oz spinach, or chopped broccoli

Seasoning
½ cup chicken broth or water
¼ tsp monosodium glutamate
    (optional)
¼ tsp salt
¼ tsp fine granulated sugar

1 cup bamboo shoots, sliced

Sauce
1½ tsp light soy sauce
Pinch monosodium glutamate
1½ tsp cornstarch
3 tsp water
1 tblsp cooked oil

Heat 2 tblsp oil in the wok. Fry the
spinach for 2 minutes and add the
mixed seasoning ingredients.

**Fried Vegetables with Ginger
(top right), Mustard Green
with Crab Sauce (center left)
and Fried Bean Curd with
Mushrooms (bottom).**

2 cups chicken, shredded (cooked or uncooked)

Seasoning
2 tblsp light soy sauce
½ tsp fine granulated sugar
1½ tblsp cornstarch
3 tblsp broth or water

Heat 4 tblsp oil in the wok and stir fry the garlic for 2 minutes. Add the eggplant, which will soak up all the oil. Stir fry for 3-4 minutes, stirring constantly to avoid burning. Add the bean paste, chili powder, and salt to taste and mix well. Add the chicken broth. Cover and cook for 4-6 minutes, simmering gently. Remove the eggplant and arrange on a dish. Save the sauce. Clean the wok and heat the remaining oil. Stir fry the ginger for 1 minute. Add the onions and chicken and stir fry for 2 minutes. Add the blended seasoning ingredients and the reserved eggplant sauce and simmer gently until it thickens. Pour over the eggplant and serve immediately.

Szechuan Eggplant

PREPARATION TIME: 15 minutes
COOKING TIME: 18-20 minutes
SERVES: 3-4 people

Salad or olive oil
1 large eggplant, cut into strips 2 inches long and ½ inch thick
3 cloves garlic, peeled and finely sliced
1 inch fresh root ginger, peeled and shredded
1 onion, peeled and finely chopped
2 green onions, chopped
1 cup cooked and shredded chicken
1 red or green chili, cut into strips

Seasoning
1 cup chicken broth
1 tsp fine granulated sugar
1½ tsp wine-flavored vinegar
½ tsp salt
½ tsp freshly ground black pepper

Sauce
1½ tsp cornstarch
1½ tblsp water
1 tsp sesame oil

Heat the wok and add 3 tblsp oil. Add the eggplant and stir fry for 4-5 minutes. The eggplant absorbs a lot of oil; keep stirring or else it will burn. Remove from wok and keep on one side. Heat the wok and add

Simmer for 1 minute and remove from the wok onto a dish. Heat the wok and add 1 tblsp oil. Add the bamboo shoots and fry for 1-2 minutes. Return the spinach mixture to the wok. Cook for 3 minutes. Mix together the ingredients for thickening the sauce. Add to the wok and cook for 1-2 minutes. Serve with roast Peking duck, or as a side dish.

Braised Eggplant and Chicken with Chili

PREPARATION TIME: 10 minutes
COOKING TIME: about 15 minutes
SERVES: 4 people

⅓ cup salad or olive oil
2 cloves of garlic, peeled and sliced

1lb eggplant, cut into 2x2½ inch pieces
1 tblsp soy bean paste (or canned red kidney beans, made into paste)
½ tsp ground dry chili or chili powder
Salt
1¾ cups chicken broth
1 inch fresh root ginger, peeled and sliced
2-3 green onions, chopped

2 tblsp oil. Add the garlic and ginger and fry for 1 minute. Add the onions and fry for 2 minutes. Add the chicken and chili. Cook for 1 minute. Return the eggplant to the wok. Add the blended seasoning ingredients and simmer for 6-7 minutes. Stir in the blended sauce ingredients and simmer until the sauce thickens. Serve with extra sesame oil if desired. This dish goes well with Yung Chow fried rice or rice supreme.

Lettuce and Bean Sprouts with Soy Sauce

PREPARATION TIME: 15 minutes

COOKING TIME: 5 minutes

SERVES: 4 people

1½ cups bean sprouts (moong or soya)
8oz lettuce
1 tblsp salad or olive oil
1 inch fresh root ginger, peeled and shredded

1 green or red chili, seeded and split in half
Salt and freshly ground black pepper

Sauce

3 tblsp light soy sauce
2 tsp dark soy sauce
1½ tblsp medium white wine or rice wine
½ tsp fine granulated sugar
Salt and freshly ground black pepper to taste
½ tsp sesame oil

Trim the bean sprouts by pinching off the grey and brown ends, as they impart a bitter taste to the dish. Pick off bean seed skin if using soya beans. Cut soya bean sprouts in 2-3 pieces. Rinse in cold water and drain. Wash and drain lettuce before shredding into 2 inch pieces. Heat the oil in the wok and stir fry the ginger and chili for 1 minute. Add the lettuce and toss for 1 minute. Drain and remove on to a plate. Place the bean sprouts in a colander and pour boiling water over them. Drain throughly and add to the lettuce. Sprinkle with salt and pepper and keep covered.

Mix the sauce ingredients together in the wok. Stir over the heat until blended. Pour this sauce over the vegetables and serve immediately.

Sweet and Sour Cabbage

PREPARATION TIME: 10 minutes

COOKING TIME: 10 minutes

SERVES: 4 people

1lb white cabbage, shredded
½ tsp baking soda
1 tsp salt
2 tsp fine granulated sugar
1 tblsp salad or olive oil

Sauce

2½ tblsp fine granulated sugar
2½ tblsp wine-flavored vinegar
1 cup chicken broth or water
Pinch salt
1¼ tblsp) cornstarch
Few drops red food coloring
1 tsp ketchup

Boil the cabbage in a large pan of

water with the baking soda, salt, and sugar for 2-3 minutes. Drain the cabbage and discard the boiling water. Keep the cabbage in cold water for 5 minutes. Drain and keep on one side. Heat the wok and add the oil. Fry the cabbage until it is heated through. Remove onto a serving dish. Add the well-stirred sauce ingredients to the wok and gently bring to the boil, stirring. Stir over the heat until the sauce thickens. Pour over the cabbage and serve immediately.

Facing page: Bamboo Shoots with Green Vegetables (top right), Sweet and Sour Cabbage (center left), Szechuan Eggplant (bottom).

This page: Lettuce and Bean Sprouts with Soy Sauce (left), Braised Eggplant and Chicken with Chili (center) and Braised Cauliflower with Chili (right).

Egg Dishes and Curry

Lamb Curry

PREPARATION TIME: 15 minutes

COOKING TIME: 50 minutes

SERVES: 4 people

2 tblsp salad or olive oil
1 onion, peeled and chopped
1 inch fresh root ginger, peeled and chopped
2 cloves of garlic, chopped
1lb lean, boned lamb, cut into cubes
1-2 carrots, scraped and sliced
1 tsp five spice mixture
Salt to taste
2 chilies, chopped
2 tblsp ketchup
2½ tblsp cornstarch
1 green pepper, seeded and chopped

Heat the oil and fry the onion for 2 minutes. Add the ginger and garlic and fry for 1 minute. Add the lamb and carrots and stir fry for 3-4 minutes. Sprinkle over the five spice powder and add the salt, chilies and ketchup. Stir in 1¼ cups water. Cover and simmer for 30-35 minutes. Mix 2 tblsp water with the cornstarch and add to the curry. Add the green pepper and simmer for 5 minutes. Serve with rice.

Prawn Curry

PREPARATION TIME: 10 minutes

COOKING TIME: 8 minutes

SERVES: 4 people

2 tblsp salad or olive oil
1 onion, peeled and chopped
1 carrot, cut into strips
1 cup snow peas (mange-tout)
1 inch fresh root ginger, peeled and chopped
2 cloves garlic, chopped
1lb large shrimps, peeled and de-veined
2 tsp curry powder
Salt to taste
2 green chilies, sliced
2 tblsp cornstarch

Heat the oil and fry the onion for 2 minutes. Add the carrot and snow peas and fry for 2 minutes. Add the ginger, garlic and shrimp and stir fry for 1-2 minutes. Sprinkle over the curry powder and add the salt, green chilies, and 1¼ cups water. Mix the cornstarch with 1 tblsp water and add to the curry. Cook gently until the curry thickens. Serve with rice.

Chicken Curry

PREPARATION TIME: 15 minutes

COOKING TIME: 40 minutes

SERVES: 4-6 people

2 tblsp salad or olive oil
1 onion, peeled and chopped
2 cloves of garlic, peeled and chopped
1 inch fresh root ginger, peeled and finely chopped
3lb chicken, boned and cut into small pieces
3 tsp curry powder
1½ tsp chili powder
½ tsp salt
⅔ cup mixed frozen vegetables
1 green pepper, seeded and chopped
3 tsp cornstarch

Heat the oil and fry the onion for 2 minutes. Add the garlic, ginger and chicken and fry gently for 5 minutes. Add the curry powder, chili powder, salt and 1¾-2 cups of water. Cover and cook gently until the chicken is tender. Add the mixed vegetables and green pepper and cook for 3-4 minutes. Add the cornstarch, dissolved in 2 tblsp water, and simmer until the sauce thickens. Serve with plain boiled rice.

Shrimp Fu Yung

PREPARATION TIME: 10 minutes

COOKING TIME: 4 minutes for filling; 3-4 minutes for each pancake

SERVES: 6 people

Salad or olive oil
1-2 cloves of garlic, chopped
1 cup small shrimps, peeled
1 cup green beans, sliced
1 carrot, shredded
6 eggs
Sauce
Salt and freshly ground black pepper to taste
1 cup chicken broth
¼ tsp salt
3 tsp soy sauce
1 tsp fine granulated sugar
1 tsp vinegar
1½ tsp cornstarch

Heat 2 tblsp oil in a wok. Add the garlic and stir fry for 1 minute. Add the shrimps and stir fry for 1 minute. Add the beans and carrot and stir fry for 2 minutes. Remove

and keep on one side. Beat the eggs with salt and pepper to taste, and add the cooled shrimp mixture. Clean the wok and heat 1 tsp oil. Pour in 5 tblsp of the egg mixture and cook like a pancake. When the egg is set, turn the pancake over and cook on the other side until lightly golden. Place on a warm platter and keep warm.

To Make the Sauce
Beat the broth with the other sauce ingredients and stir over a gentle heat until the sauce thickens. Serve the pancakes with this sauce.

Egg Fu Yung

PREPARATION TIME: 5 minutes

COOKING TIME: 8-10 minutes

SERVES: 3-4 people

6 eggs
1½ tblsp soy sauce
3-4 green onions, chopped
Salt and freshly ground black pepper to taste
3 tblsp oil
1½ cups bean sprouts

Beat the eggs and soy sauce together and add the green onions and salt and pepper to taste. Heat the oil in a skillet or wok and stir fry the bean sprouts for 2-3 minutes. Pour in the beaten egg mixture. Leave over a moderate heat to set. Broil to set and brown the top. Cut into wedges and serve immediately. Alternatively, stir the mixture while it is cooking so that it turns out like scrambled egg.

Prawns in Egg Custard

PREPARATION TIME: 5 minutes

COOKING TIME: 20 minutes

SERVES: 6 people

8 eggs
Salt and freshly ground black pepper to taste
Pinch monosodium glutamate (optional)
1 tsp Shao Hsing wine
1¼ cups chicken broth
1¼ cups water
1lb large shrimps, peeled and de-veined
2 tsp cooked oil

Beat the eggs in a bowl, add the

seasoning, MSG and wine. Bring the broth and water to the boil and add to the eggs. Add shrimps and set the bowl over a steamer. Cover and steam over simmering water for about 15-20 minutes, until the custard has set. Serve with the cooked oil spooned over the top.

Stir Fried Eggs with Shredded Meats and Vegetables

PREPARATION TIME: 15-20 minutes

COOKING TIME: 15 minutes

SERVES: 4 people

½ cup cooked chicken, shredded
¾ cup cooked pork or beef, shredded
Salt to taste
¼ tsp soy sauce
4 tblsp salad or olive oil
4 eggs, beaten
2 green onions, chopped
⅓ cup dried mushrooms, soaked and sliced
⅓ button mushrooms, sliced
2 cloud ear fungus, boiled in water for 3 minutes and thinly sliced
2 cups Chinese white cabbage, broccoli or green leafy cabbage, shredded
1-2 green or red chilies, chopped
2 sprigs Chinese parsley, chopped
Pinch monosodium glutamate (optional)

Put the chicken and pork into a bowl with ¼ tsp salt and the soy sauce. Leave for 10 minutes. Heat the wok and add 2 tblsp oil. Add the beaten eggs and stir fry for 2-3 minutes until they resemble scrambled egg. Keep on one side. Reheat the wok and add the remaining oil. Fry the onions and meats for 2 minutes. Remove from the wok and keep on one side. Stir fry the cabbage and chilies in the wok for 1-2 minutes. Cover and gently cook in its own juice until tender – approx 3-4 minutes. Return the meats, mushrooms and egg to the cabbage and add the parsley and MSG. Stir fry for 1-2 minutes. Serve with extra soy sauce and Shao Hsing wine sprinkled over it, if desired.

Lamb Curry (right), Prawn Curry (below) and Chicken Curry (bottom).

Marbled Eggs

PREPARATION TIME: 10 minutes

COOKING TIME: 1 hour 10 minutes to 1 hour 15 minutes

MAKES: 6-8

These are eaten cold, dipped in a sauce, as a starter or a snack. Allow 1 egg per person.

6-8 eggs
4 tblsp tea leaves
1 inch cinnamon stick
2-3 star anise
3 tblsp dark soy sauce
2 tblsp light soy sauce

Boil the eggs for 8-10 minutes until hard boiled. Drain and cool quickly by placing in iced water. Tap each egg shell with the back of a spoon until cracks appear all over. Bring enough water to the boil to cover the eggs. Add tea leaves, cinnamon, star anise, soy sauces and stir. Add the eggs and simmer gently for at least 1 hour. Allow to cool and then shell before serving.

Egg Pancakes with Filling

| **PREPARATION TIME:** 10 minutes |
| **COOKING TIME:** 6-7 minutes for each pancake |
| **SERVES:** 4-6 people |

6 eggs
Salt and freshly ground black pepper to taste
1 cup lean pork, finely chopped or ground
½ cup small cap mushrooms, chopped
1 tsp rice wine or dry sherry
1 tsp light soy sauce
½ tsp fine granulated sugar
1 tsp fresh root ginger, minced
Oil

Beat the eggs and season with salt and pepper. Mix the pork with the mushrooms, wine, soy sauce, sugar and ginger. Add salt and pepper to taste and mix well. Heat the wok and add 1 tsp oil. Spoon in 3 tblsp of the beaten egg and spread into a 3 inch circle. Place 3 tsp filling into the center of the egg. When the underside of the egg sets but the top is still moist, fold the egg circle over to make a crescent shape; press gently to seal the edges. Cook for 4 minutes on a low heat to cook the filling. Make the remaining pancakes in the same way. Serve with a chili sauce or dip, or with stir fried vegetables as a main dish.

Noodles with Pork Fu Yung

| **PREPARATION TIME:** 20 minutes |
| **COOKING TIME:** about 20 minutes |
| **SERVES:** 4 people |

½ tsp baking soda
1 tblsp water
8oz lean pork, thinly sliced
8oz cake noodles
2 tsp cornstarch
Few drops sesame oil
Salt and freshly ground black pepper to taste
½ tsp fine granulated sugar
Salad or olive oil
2 cloves of garlic, finely chopped
1 inch fresh root ginger, peeled and sliced
2-3 green onions, chopped
6 eggs, well beaten

Mix the baking soda and the water together. Mix in the pork and marinate for 10-12 minutes. Drain. Cook the noodles in boiling, salted water for 3-4 minutes. Drain, rinse in cold water and drain once again. Toss in 1 tblsp oil. Heat 2 tblsp oil in the wok and brown the garlic. Add 1 tsp salt and the noodles and stir fry for 3-4 minutes, until they turn light brown. Remove and keep on one side. Heat sufficient oil for deep frying in the wok and deep fry the pork for 3-4 minutes, drain and remove. Tip off the oil. Heat 1 tblsp oil in the wok. Add the ginger and onions and stir fry for 1-2 minutes. Add the pork and then pour in the beaten eggs, mixing well. Add the cornstarch, sesame oil and sugar and cook until the mixture thickens. Pour over the noodles and serve immediately.

This page: Marbled Eggs (top), Noodles with Pork Fu Yung (center right) and Stir Fried Eggs with Shredded Meats and Vegetables (bottom left).

Facing page: Prawns in Egg Custard (top left), Egg Pancakes with Filling (top right), Shrimp Fu Yung (center left) and Egg Fu Yung (bottom right).

Rice and Noodles

Rice with Ground Beef

PREPARATION TIME: 10 minutes
COOKING TIME: 25 minutes
SERVES: 6 people

2 tblsp salad or olive oil
8oz ground beef
3 green onions, chopped
½ inch fresh root ginger, peeled and sliced
2 cloves garlic, peeled and sliced
1½ tblsp soy sauce
1 green pepper, seeded and chopped
1lb rice, thoroughly washed
½ tsp salt
1 tsp freshly ground black pepper, or to taste

Heat the oil and fry the ground beef, onions, ginger and garlic for 5 minutes. Add the soy sauce and green pepper and fry for 5-6 minutes. Cook the rice with sufficient water to come 1 inch above the rice level, and the salt, for 5-6 minutes or until the rice is semi-cooked, and the water is almost absorbed. Spread the beef evenly over the rice. Cover and cook for 6-8 minutes over a very gentle heat. Remove and serve well mixed. Season with salt and pepper to taste.

Assorted Meat Congee

PREPARATION TIME: 20 minutes
COOKING TIME: 1 hour 45 minutes
SERVES: 6 people

1lb rice
9½ cups chicken broth
4oz tripe, well washed and chopped (optional)
4oz pig's or lamb's liver, sliced
1 cup cooked beef, ham, lamb, chicken or pork, chopped
4oz white fish fillets, thinly sliced
1 tsp sesame oil
3 green onions, chopped
1½ tsp salt, or to taste
1½ tsp freshly ground black pepper
½ inch fresh root ginger, peeled and sliced

Wash the rice well and put it into a large saucepan. Add the chicken

broth and the tripe (if used). Cook gently for 1-1½ hours, or until the tripe is well cooked and the rice has become a soft pulp. In a separate saucepan, boil the sliced liver for 5 minutes in water. Drain and add to the rice. Add the cooked meat, fish, sesame oil, half the onions, salt and pepper and the slices of ginger. Cook for further 10-15 minutes covered. Pour into large bowls and serve topped with the remaining chopped onions.

Rice Supreme

PREPARATION TIME: 10 minutes
COOKING TIME: 15 minutes
SERVES: 6 people

3 tblsp salad or olive oil
1½ tblsp) light soy sauce
2 eggs, beaten
1 small onion, peeled and finely sliced
½ cup small shrimps, peeled
½ cup large shrimps, peeled

½ cup white fish, cubed
2 green onions, finely chopped
½ a small green pepper, seeded and cut into strips
1lb rice, cooked and cooled
Salt to taste
1 tsp freshly ground black pepper
3 tblsp ketchup
½ cup frozen peas

Heat 1 tblsp oil in the wok and pour in the beaten eggs. Cook to make a thin omelette. Cut into thin strips. Heat 1 tblsp oil in the wok and stir fry the onion for 2 minutes. Add the shrimps and fish and stir fry for 3-4 minutes. Remove the fish mixture to a plate. Heat the remaining oil in the wok. Add half the green onions and the green pepper and stir fry for 2 minutes. Add the rice and season with salt and pepper. Add the ketchup, peas, fried fish and shrimps. Add the soy sauce and stir fry for 3 minutes. Serve with the egg strips arranged on top of the rice. Sprinkle with the remaining chopped green onions.

Vegetable Rice

PREPARATION TIME: 10 minutes
COOKING TIME: 5-8 minutes
SERVES: 6-8 people

1lb rice, cooked
2 cups Chinese cabbage, or Chinese leaves, shredded
1 cup sliced green beans
¾ cup frozen peas
3 green onions, chopped
1½ tblsp light soy sauce
Salt to taste

Rinse the cooked rice in cold water and drain. Put the moist rice into a pan. Arrange the Chinese cabbage, sliced beans, peas and onions on top. Cover and cook over a gentle heat for 4-6 minutes. Sprinkle with soy sauce and add salt to taste. Stir the vegetables evenly into the rice and raise the heat for a few seconds. Serve immediately.

Plain Fried Rice

PREPARATION TIME: 5 minutes, plus cooling time
COOKING TIME: 10-11 minutes
SERVES: 4-6 people

1lb Patna or long grain rice
¼ tsp monosodium glutamate
2 tblsp salad or olive oil
Salt

Wash the rice in 4-5 changes of cold water. Drain the rice and put into a large pan or wok. Add sufficient cold water to come 1 inch above the level of the rice. Bring to the boil. Stir once and reduce the heat to simmer. Cover and cook gently for 5-7 minutes until the water has been totally absorbed and the rice is separate and fluffy,

This page: Vegetable Rice (top), Assorted Meat Congee (center right) and Rice Supreme (bottom).

Facing page: Yang Chow Fried Rice (top), Plain Fried Rice (center left) and Rice with Ground Beef (bottom).

with the necessary amount of stickiness to be handled by chopsticks. (If necessary cook for a little longer.) Spread the rice out on a tray and cool. Sprinkle with the monosodium glutamate. Heat the oil in a wok or large skillet and add the rice. Stir fry for 1-2 minutes. Add salt to taste and stir fry for a further 1-2 minutes.

Yang Chow Fried Rice

PREPARATION TIME: 10 minutes

COOKING TIME: 6-8 minutes

SERVES: 6 people

3 tblsp salad or olive oil
1 egg, beaten
1 cup cooked meat, chopped (pork, lamb, beef)
1 cup medium shrimps, shelled and chopped
½ cup shelled green peas, lightly cooked
2 green onions, chopped
1lb dry, cooked rice
Salt to taste
1 tsp monosodium glutamate (optional)

Heat 1 tblsp oil in a wok. Fry the beaten egg until set, and break into small lumps. Remove the egg. Add the remaining oil and fry the meat, shrimps, peas and onions for 1-2 minutes. Add the cooked rice and sprinkle with salt and monosodium glutamate. Fry for 3 minutes. Mix in the cooked egg and serve immediately.

Sizzling Rice or Singing Rice

PREPARATION TIME: 50 minutes

COOKING TIME: 2 hours, plus time for deep frying sizzling rice

4oz short grain rice

When rice is cooked, the crust that forms on the bottom of the pot can be dried and then deep fried. When it is immersed in gravy or soup it makes a sizzling noise, hence the name. Once made or collected, the rice crusts can be kept for months.

To Make a Rice Crust

Wash rice in 4-5 changes of water until the water runs clear. Drain the rice and put it into a pan with 1¼ cups of water; bring to the boil. Reduce heat to low and cook for 20 minutes, simmering gently. Turn off the heat and let the rice stand, covered, for 25-30 minutes. Take a non-stick skillet and transfer the rice to it. Spread evenly to a thickness of ½ inch. Cook on a very gentle heat for 40-50 minutes. Turn over and cook gently for another hour. The rice should be very dry. Break into 2 inch squares and store in a glass jar with a lid.

To Cook Sizzling Rice

Pour oil into a pan to a depth of 2 inches and bring to a moderately high temperature (375°F). Add the rice squares and fry until golden

brown. Remove and drain on kitchen paper. Serve with soup or any stir fried dish.

Shrimp Egg Rice

PREPARATION TIME: 20 minutes

COOKING TIME: 17-18 minutes

SERVES: 4-6 people

1lb long or medium grain rice
2 eggs
½ tsp salt
4 tblsp oil
2 green onions, chopped
1 large onion, peeled and chopped
2 cloves garlic, peeled and chopped
1 cup small peeled shrimps
½ cup shelled peas, lightly cooked
2 tblsp dark soy sauce

To Cook the Rice

Wash rice in 4-5 changes of water. Add cold water to come 1 inch above the rice level and bring to the boil. Stir once and reduce the heat to simmer. Cover the pan and gently cook the rice for 5-7 minutes until the rice is dry and the liquid has been totally absorbed. Remove from the heat, add cold water to cover and drain throughly. Spread the rice on a large tray and separate the grains with a fork.

Beat the eggs in a bowl and season with a pinch of salt. Heat the wok and add 1 tblsp oil. Add the onions and stir fry for 2 minutes. Add the beaten eggs. Allow to set slightly and then stir the mixture until it scrambles. Remove onto a plate. Heat the wok and add 1 tblsp oil. Fry the garlic for 1 minute then add the shrimps and cook for 2 minutes. Add the peas, and stir fry for 1 minute. Remove onto a plate.

Heat the wok and add the remaining oil, a little salt to taste and the cooked rice. Stir fry to heat the rice through. Stir in the soy sauce, shrimp mixture and the cooked eggs, gently stirring the mixture to blend. Serve immediately.

Shrimp Egg Rice (below), Sizzling Rice or Singing Rice (bottom left) and Plain Rice (bottom right).

Plain Rice

PREPARATION TIME: 5 minutes
COOKING TIME: 5-7 minutes
SERVES: 4-6 people

1lb rice
Pinch salt
2 tsp salad or olive oil

To make a bowl of plain rice, take any grade of long or medium grain rice. Wash the rice in 4-5 changes of water and then add enough cold water to come 1 inch above the rice level. Add the salt and oil and bring to the boil. Stir once. Cover and simmer gently for 5-7 minutes until the water has been totally absorbed. Remove from the heat and serve. Plain boiled rice should be fluffy, yet have enough moisture around the rice so that the grains can be picked up easily by chopsticks.

Noodles in Soup

PREPARATION TIME: 10 minutes
COOKING TIME: 6-8 minutes
SERVES: 4-6 people

1lb small rounds of cake noodles
Salt
5½ cups chicken or beef broth
1 cup cooked shredded chicken
2 eggs, hard boiled and sliced
1⅓ cups Chinese napa cabbage, or iceberg lettuce, finely shredded
2 green onions, thinly sliced

½ cup bamboo shoots, sliced
2 sticks celery, chopped
1 leek, chopped
2 green onions, shredded
4 tblsp broth
3 tblsp soy sauce

Soak the rice noodles in warm water for 10-15 minutes. Drain thoroughly. Heat half the oil in a wok. Add the chicken, shrimps, bamboo shoots, celery, leeks and green onions and stir fry for 2-3 minutes. Add the broth and salt and pepper to taste. Simmer for 2 minutes and then drain the chicken and vegetables. Heat the remaining oil, add the rice noodles and stir over the heat for 1 minute. Add the soy sauce and stir into the chicken and vegetable mixture. Cook together for 2-3 minutes. Serve immediately.

Meat and Prawn Chow Mein

PREPARATION TIME: 20 minutes

COOKING TIME: 12-15 minutes

SERVES: 4-6 people

1lb dried Chinese noodles, or broken
    spaghetti
Salt to taste
4 tblsp salad or olive oil
2-3 green onions, chopped
1 cup cooked ham, shredded
1 cup large shrimps, peeled and de-
    veined
1 cup shredded carrots
1 cup green beans, sliced
1 tsp fine granulated sugar
1½ tblsp rice wine or dry sherry
1 cup cooked chicken, shredded
1½ cups bean sprouts
3½ tblsp soy sauce

Cook the noodles in boiling, salted water for 4-5 minutes. Rinse under cold water and drain thoroughly. Toss in 1 tblsp oil. Heat the remaining oil in a wok. Add the onions, ham, prawns, carrots and green beans and stir fry for 2-3 minutes. Add the salt, sugar, wine, chicken and bean sprouts. Cook for 2 minutes. Add the cooked noodles and soy sauce. Cook for 1-2 minutes. Serve immediately.

Cook the noodles in boiling, salted water for 5 minutes. Drain thoroughly. Heat the broth and add salt to taste. Serve the cooked noodles in bowls, and pour over the hot broth. Garnish with chicken, sliced eggs, cabbage and green onions.

Stir Fried Shanghai Noodles

PREPARATION TIME: 10 minutes

COOKING TIME: 5-6 minutes

SERVES: 4 people

1½ cups white cabbage, shredded
½ tsp sesame oil
3 tblsp cooked oil
1 cup cooked chicken or pork,
    shredded
1lb thick Shanghai noodles, cooked
    until just tender
2½ tblsp) soy sauce
½ tsp monosodium glutamate
    (optional)
Freshly ground black pepper to taste

Cook the cabbage in boiling water for 1 minute. Drain thoroughly. Heat the oils in a wok. Add the meat and stir fry for 2-3 minutes. Add the cooked noodles, soy sauce, monosodium glutamate and salt and pepper to taste. Add the cabbage, heat through and serve immediately.

Deep Fried Noodles

Boil noodles for 5 minutes. Drain thoroughly on absorbent paper. Deep fry in hot oil until crisp and golden.

Fried Rice Noodles

PREPARATION TIME: 25 minutes

COOKING TIME: 10 minutes

SERVES: 4-6 people

1lb rice noodles
3 tblsp salad or olive oil
1 cup cooked chicken, shredded
½ cup small shrimps, peeled and de-
    veined

This page: Deep Fried Noodles (top), Stir Fried Shanghai Noodles (center), Fried Rice Noodles (bottom). Facing page: Meat and Prawn Chow Mein (top), Noodles in Soup (center), Rice Noodles Singapore Style (bottom).

Rice Noodles Singapore Style

PREPARATION TIME: 15 minutes, plus soaking time for noodles

COOKING TIME: about 15 minutes

SERVES: 4-6 people

8oz rice noodles
Salad or olive oil
2 eggs, beaten
½ inch fresh root ginger, peeled and shredded
1½ cups bean sprouts
1 cup cooked ham, pork or chicken, shredded
3 tblsp chives, finely chopped
2 cloves garlic, finely chopped
Salt to taste
2 tblsp chicken broth
3 tblsp soy sauce
3 green onions, chopped

Soak the rice noodles in warm water for 10 minutes and then drain well. Heat 1 tblsp oil in a skillet or wok and fry the beaten eggs to make a thin pancake. Slide onto a plate and cut into thin strips. Heat the wok or skillet and add 1 tblsp oil. Fry the ginger and bean sprouts for 2 minutes. Slide onto a plate. Heat the wok or skillet with a further 1 tblsp oil and fry the pork or chicken and the chives for 1-2 minutes. Slide onto a plate. Heat 2 tblsp oil in the wok or skillet and brown the garlic. Add the rice noodles and stir fry for 2-3 minutes. Add salt to taste, chicken broth, bean sprouts and pork or chicken. Mix well, sprinkle with soy sauce and stir over the heat for 1 minute. Top with the strips of egg pancake and spring onions and serve immediately.

Noodles with Beef and Almonds

PREPARATION TIME: 15 minutes

COOKING TIME: 10 minutes

SERVES: 4 people

3 tblsp salad or olive oil
1 onion, chopped
4 cloves of garlic, chopped
1 inch fresh root ginger, peeled and sliced
8oz lean beef, thinly sliced
½ cup carrots, diced
½ cup sliced green beans
½ cup water chestnuts, sliced
½ cup mushrooms, sliced
2 green chilies, sliced in half

Salt
1 tsp fine granulated sugar
1 tsp monosodium glutamate (optional)
1 cup chicken broth
⅔ cup blanched almonds
1lb noodles, cooked until just tender

Heat 2 tblsp oil in a wok. Fry the onion, garlic, ginger and beef for 3 minutes. Add the carrots and green beans and fry for 2 minutes. Add the water chestnuts, mushrooms and green chilies and fry for 1 minute. Add salt, sugar, MSG and broth. Simmer for 1 minute. Remove to a dish and keep warm. Clean the wok and add the remaining oil. Fry the almonds and noodles for 1-2 minutes. Mix with the cooked vegetables and season with soy sauce. Serve immediately.

Egg Noodles with Meat Sauce

PREPARATION TIME: 15 minutes

COOKING TIME: 20-22 minutes

SERVES: 4-6 people

3 tblsp salad or olive oil
3 cloves garlic, chopped
1 inch fresh root ginger, peeled and shredded
1 onion, chopped
1 green pepper, seeded and sliced
1lb ground beef
½ tsp salt
1 tblsp ketchup
1 tblsp soy sauce
½ tsp freshly ground black pepper
½ cup chicken broth
1 tsp cornstarch
1lb egg noodles
2 green onions, chopped

Heat 2 tblsp oil in a wok. Fry the garlic and ginger for 1-2 minutes. Add the onion and fry for 2-3 minutes. Add the green pepper and the ground beef and fry for 1 minute. Add half the salt, ketchup, soy sauce and ground pepper. Fry for a further 3 minutes. Blend the broth and cornstarch and add to the wok. Cook until thickened and the meat is tender. Meanwhile, cook noodles in boiling, salted water for 3-4 minutes, and drain. Rinse in cold water and drain once again. Heat the remaining oil in a

pan. Add the noodles and toss over the heat until heated through. Arrange on a plate and top with the meat sauce. Garnish with chopped green onions.

Fried Noodles with Shredded Chicken

PREPARATION TIME: 15 minutes

COOKING TIME: about 10 minutes

SERVES: 4 people

Salad or olive oil
2 cups cooked chicken, shredded
1 clove of garlic, chopped
2-3 green onions, chopped
4oz whole green beans (or long Chinese beans, cut into 3 inch pieces)
1lb noodles, cooked until just tender
1½ tblsp cornstarch
1 cup chicken broth
2 tblsp soy sauce
2 tblsp oyster sauce
½ tsp wine
½ tsp fine granulated sugar
¼ tsp salt

Heat 2 tblsp oil in a wok and cook the chicken for 2 minutes. Remove the chicken. Add the garlic, green onions and beans and fry for 2 minutes. Remove the vegetables. Heat 2 tblsp oil in the wok and toss the pre-boiled noodles over the heat for 2 minutes. Arrange on a plate and keep warm. Return the fried chicken, onion and green beans to the wok and stir fry for 1 minute. Dissolve the cornstarch in the chicken broth and add to the wok. Add the soy sauce, oyster sauce, wine, sugar and salt and pepper to taste. Simmer until the sauce is thick. Pour over the bed of noodles and serve immediately.

This page: Noodles with Beef and Almonds (top), Egg Noodles with Meat Sauce (center) and Fried Noodles with Shredded Chicken (bottom).

Facing page: Chinese Bean Buns (top), Red Bean Filled Dim Sums (center right) and Candied Apples (bottom).

CHINESE CUISINE
Sweets

again for 2 minutes and then divide the dough into 12-14 portions. Flatten into thick, circular shapes 4 inches in diameter. Place a chopstick on each circle of dough to mark it in half, and then in half again. Cut along the marks to within ⅓ of the center. Place one portion of filling in the center of the dough circle and fold the cut ends in to meet in the center, to form a rosette. Secure by pinching ends of dough together. Place a piece of greased foil over the pinched ends and place the buns on a greased baking tray. Brush with a little milk. Bake at 375°F for 20-25 minutes.

Red Bean Filled Dim Sums

PREPARATION TIME: 45-50 minutes

COOKING TIME: 10-12 minutes

MAKES: about 24

¼ cup fine granulated sugar
1¼ cups warm water
1¼ tblsp dry yeast
3¾ cups all-purpose flour
2 tblsp melted shortening
1 egg white, beaten

Filling
¾-1 cup sweet bean paste
Red food coloring

Dissolve the sugar in the warm water and add the yeast. Stir until dissolved. Leave in a warm place until frothy. Sift the flour into a mixing bowl and add the melted shortening and the yeast mixture. Mix together. Turn the mixture onto a floured surface and knead to a smooth and elastic dough. Roll into a long sausage and divide into 24 equal portions. Roll each portion into a 2 inch flat circle. Brush edges of dough with beaten egg white. Place 1 tblsp of filling into the center of each circle and pull the dough around it to enclose the filling. Pleat the open edges in a circular fashion, so that a small opening is left in the middle of the pleating. Place a small piece of greased foil over the pleats on each dim sum. Leave for 10-12 minutes until the dough becomes springy to

Chinese Bean Buns

PREPARATION TIME: about 2 hours, including proving time

COOKING TIME: about 30 minutes

MAKES: about 14

¼ cup milk
⅓ cup fine granulated sugar
½ tsp salt
1½ tblsp shortening
¼ cup warm water
2 tsp dry yeast
1 egg, beaten

2¼ cups all-purpose flour

Bring the milk almost to the boil. Stir in the sugar, salt and shortening. Cool slightly. Put the warm water and yeast into a bowl and stir to mix. Add the lukewarm milk mixture. Add the beaten egg and 1 cup of the flour and beat until smooth. Add the remaining flour and mix to a dough. Turn dough out on to a well-floured board and knead until smooth and elastic. Place in a greased bowl. Brush the dough with oil and

cover. Leave to rise in a warm place until doubled in size (about 1 hour).

Filling
⅓ cup sweet bean paste
2 tblsp fine granulated sugar
2 tblsp chopped walnuts
1 tblsp shortening

Heat the filling ingredients together in a wok for 5-6 minutes until smooth and shiny. Remove and cool. Divide the filling into 12-14 portions. Knead the risen dough

the touch. Put a dab of red food coloring on each dim sum. Arrange the dim sums in a bamboo steaming basket and steam over boiling water for 10-12 minutes. The dim sums are ready when they are dry and smooth. Alternatively they can be baked at 350°F for about 20 minutes.

Agar-Agar Pudding

PREPARATION TIME: 5 minutes

COOKING TIME: 4-5 minutes

SERVES: 4 people

2½ cups milk
½ cup fine granulated sugar
2 tblsp ground almonds
4 tblsp agar-agar (also called Chinese grass)
2 tblsp blanched and chopped almonds

Mix the milk, sugar and ground almonds together in a pan and stir over the heat for 4 minutes. Add the agar-agar and stir until dissolved. Stir in the chopped almonds. Pour into a shallow dish 1 inch deep. Cool and keep in refrigerator until set. Serve chilled, cut into diamond or square shapes.

Almond Cookies

PREPARATION TIME: 20 minutes

COOKING TIME: 12-15 minutes

MAKES: 60 cookies

1 generous cup shortening
½ cup fine granulated sugar
⅓ cup brown sugar
1 egg, beaten
Few drops almond essence
2¼ cups all-purpose flour
Pinch salt
1½ tsp baking powder
½ cup blanched almonds
1 egg yolk
2 tblsp water

Cream the shortening with the sugars until light and fluffy. Add the egg and almond essence and beat until smooth. Sift the flour, salt and baking powder. Mix the dry ingredients into the creamed mixture. Shape into small balls on a lightly floured surface. Flatten slightly and press an almond into the center of each one. Place onto a greased cooky sheet. Mix the egg yolk with the water. Brush the cookies with the egg glaze. Bake at 350°F for 12-15 minutes.

Sweet Almond Pudding

PREPARATION TIME: 4-5 minutes

COOKING TIME: 6 minutes

SERVES: 4-6 people

1 cup blanched almonds
1¾ cups water
¾ cup fine granulated sugar
4 tblsp rice powder, or ground rice

⅔ cup milk

Blend the blanched almonds and water in the blender. Put into a pan and bring to the boil. Add the sugar and stir over the heat until the sugar has dissolved. Add the rice slowly to the milk and stir gradually into the simmering sugar and almond mixture. Cook gently until the mixture thickens. Remove from the heat and pour into a serving dish. Serve hot or cold.

Sweet Dumplings

PREPARATION TIME: 10 minutes

COOKING TIME: 15-20 minutes

MAKES: 10-12

Salad or olive oil
½ cup fine granulated sugar
⅓ cup plain red bean paste
⅓ cup desiccated coconut
4 egg whites
1½ tblsp all-purpose flour
4 tblsp cornstarch
Confectioner's sugar

Heat 1 tblsp oil in a wok and add the sugar, bean paste and coconut. Stir fry for 4-5 minutes until the sugar melts and the paste is smooth and shiny. Fry for a few minutes more and then allow to cool on a dish. Whip the egg whites until stiff and mix with the flour and cornstarch to a smooth batter. Beat well. Clean the wok and heat sufficient oil for deep

frying. Make 10-12 even-sized balls from the bean paste mixture. Dip each ball into the batter and then deep fry for 3-4 minutes until golden and crisp. Fry a few at a time and drain on kitchen paper. Dust with sifted confectioner's sugar before serving.

Stuffed Lychees

PREPARATION TIME: 20 minutes

SERVES: 6 people

3 cups canned lychees, stones removed
4-5 rings canned pineapple
Few drops vanilla essence or almond essence

Drain the lychees into a bowl, reserving the juice. Slice each pineapple ring into ½ inch long strips. Press one or two strips of pineapple into each lychee. Arrange the pineapple-filled lychees in a deep serving dish. Mix the pineapple and lychee liquid with a few drops of essence. Spoon over the stuffed fruits. Serve well chilled. Alternatively, stuff the lychees with maraschino cherries, mango, canned pears, oranges etc.

Facing page: Sweet Dumplings (top), Almond Cookies (center left) and Date Cake (bottom right).

Chocolate Roulade (above),
Devil's Food Cake (right) and
Family Chocolate Cake (far
right).

COOKING WITH CHOCOLATE

Introduction

Rich, dark and luxuriously smooth and enticing, chocolate remains one of the most popular ingredients for both everyday and exotic desserts, cakes and confectionery. This section combines a wealth of mouth-watering creations that have been specially selected for their variety as well as their relative ease of preparation: recipes which are bound to delight all those with a passion for chocolate cuisine.

Hints For Cooking With Chocolate
The amount of cocoa butter added to chocolate determines how the chocolate can be used.

Cooking Chocolate
This is not to be confused with cake covering. Cooking chocolate has some cocoa butter replaced with palm kernel oil or coconut oil. Flavorings are used to make the chocolate less expensive and easy to use; it can be used for any chocolate cooking or decoration.

Milk Chocolate
This is rarely used in cooking as it does not give a strong enough flavor, but it can be used for making Easter Eggs and in other recipes that require a delicate flavor.

Couverture
This is a chocolate containing a high proportion of cocoa butter, which gives it a smooth, glossy appearance. Couverture chocolate requires repeated heating and cooling, or tempering; a professional method of working with chocolate.

White Chocolate
This variety has a relatively high sugar content. It is used in some recipes but great care should be taken when using this as it is difficult to melt and has a tendency to go grainy if overheated.

Semi-Sweet Chocolate
This chocolate has a rich, dark flavor and is used in most recipes where chocolate is called for. Semi-sweet eating chocolate can always be used but there are also some varieties available which are specially recommended for cooking.

Bitter Chocolate
This is not easy to buy but it can be made as required. To make plain chocolate bitter add 1 tsp instant coffee powder or granules (or 1 tsp cocoa powder) for every 2oz of chocolate.

Chipped and Grated Chocolate
Chocolate can be chipped and grated either manually or in a food

processor. When grating chocolate, refrigerate for 30 minutes, then hold the chocolate with kitchen paper to prevent it from melting.

Cocoa Powder and Drinking Chocolate

Often used in baking but make sure the lumps are removed. It is best used blended with hot (not boiling) water, so that it forms a smooth paste. Add the paste to the recipe as required.

Melting Chocolate

This should be done carefully as it is particularly important. Break the chocolate into pieces and put in a bowl over a pan of simmering water, or into the top of a double boiler if you have one. When using an electric cooker turn off the heat once the water has boiled. Make sure the bowl fits well into the saucepan so that no steam or water goes into the chocolate. Note: if the chocolate goes solid add a little vegetable oil and beat well.

Microwave Melting

This is a clean and easy way to work with chocolate. Break the chocolate into pieces and put into a suitable bowl. Cover with plastic wrap and melt following the manufacturers instructions. The timing will depend on the quantity of chocolate and the size of the bowl.

Decorating with Chocolate

Chocolate for Dipping

This chocolate has a high proportion of vegetable fat and is less expensive than couverture. Melt the chocolate, which you may find easier to use if you add 1 tblsp of vegetable oil to every 6oz of chocolate.

Chocolate Leaves

These are made by using rose leaves, although any leaves with good strong veins can be used. *Make sure that the leaves you select are not poisonous.* Wash and dry the leaves thoroughly, melt the chocolate and, using a small paintbrush, brush the underside of the leaves with the chocolate. Alternatively you can dip the undersides of the leaves in the chocolate, then place them on non-stick silicone paper or wax paper, chocolate side up. When the chocolate is hard peel off the leaves.

Chocolate Curls

Make sure the chocolate is neither too warm, as it will be too soft to hold a cult, nor too cold, since it will become brittle and may crumble. Using a small knife or even a vegetable peeler make curls by gently shaving the chocolate with the blade.

Craque

To produce these glamorous, long curls, melt the chocolate and spread it with a palette knife onto an ungreased, laminated or marble surface. The chocolate should be ¼ inch thick. Leave it to set, then scrape it up in curls by holding a knife at an angle of 45° and pushing it away from you.

Shapes

To make shapes, melt and pour the chocolate onto an ungreased, laminated or marble surface then, when set, cut into shapes with a sharp knife.

COOKING WITH CHOCOLATE
Cakes and Gateaux

Chocolate Fudge Cake

PREPARATION TIME:	15 minutes
COOKING TIME:	45-50 minutes
OVEN TEMPERATURE:	325°F
MAKES:	1 cake, 9 inches in diameter

1¾ cups regular flour
1 tsp bicarbonate of soda
1 tsp baking powder
2½ tblsp cocoa powder
10 tblsp brown sugar
2½ tblsp corn syrup
2 eggs
⅔ cup oil
1¼ cups milk

Chocolate Frosting
6oz semi-sweet chocolate, grated
2½ tblsp light cream

To Decorate
Chocolate shavings

Grease and line a 9 inch cake pan.
Sieve the dry ingredients together
in a bowl and add the sugar. Make
a well in the center and add the
syrup, eggs, oil and the milk. Beat
them all together until smooth.
Pour the cake mixture into the cake
pan. Bake in the oven for 45
minutes. When cooked, leave the
cake in the pan for a few minutes
before turning it out onto a wire
rack. To make the frosting: heat the
chocolate and cream in a small,
heavy saucepan until melted. Cool
the mixture slightly and pour over
the cake; drag the surface with a
fork when it is nearly dry, and
decorate with the chocolate
shavings.

Chocolate Spice Cake

PREPARATION TIME:	30 minutes
COOKING TIME:	40-50 minutes
OVEN TEMPERATURE:	350°F
MAKES:	1 cake, 8 inches in diameter

5 eggs, separated
¾ cup sugar
3oz semi-sweet chocolate, melted
¾ cup flour
½ tsp ground nutmeg
½ tsp ground cinnamon
½ tsp ground cloves

Cinnamon Topping
Ground cinnamon
Confectioner's sugar

Butter and line a 8 inch spring form
cake pan with wax paper (use a pan
that has a central funnel). Brush
the paper with melted butter and
dust with flour. Put the egg yolks
and sugar into a mixing bowl and
beat them well until the mixture
will fall from the whisk in a thick
ribbon. Stir in the melted
chocolate. Sieve together the flour,
nutmeg, cinnamon and cloves, and
fold into the cake mixture. Beat the
egg whites until stiff but not dry.
Gently fold in the beaten egg
whites, a little at a time. Pour the
mixture into the pan. Bake in a pre-
heated oven for 40-50 minutes, or
until a skewer inserted into the
middle comes out clean. Remove
the cake from the oven and let it
cool in the pan on a wire rack, for
10 minutes. Turn the cake out to

**This page: Chocolate Fudge
Cake (top) and Chocolate
Almond Cake (bottom).**

**Facing page: Chocolate Spice
Cake (top) and Chocolate
Potato Cake (bottom).**

282

Chocolate Roulade (above) and
Chocolate Orange Cake (right).

cool completely. Dust the top of the cake with a little ground cinnamon and/or confectioner's sugar.

Chocolate Roulade

PREPARATION TIME: 35 minutes
COOKING TIME: 15-20 minutes
OVEN TEMPERATURE: 350°F
MAKES: 1 roulade, 9 inches long

1¼ tblsp instant coffee
1¼ tblsp hot water
4oz semi-sweet chocolate, chopped or grated
4 eggs, separated
½ cup fine sugar

To Decorate
1¼ cups heavy cream
Confectioner's sugar

Grease and line a 13x9 inch jelly roll pan. Mix the coffee with the hot water and add the chocolate; stand in a bowl over a saucepan of hot water and stir until the chocolate has melted. Allow the mixture to cool. Beat together the egg yolks and sugar until thick, then fold into the chocolate mixture. Beat the egg whites until stiff but not dry, and fold lightly into the mixture. Pour the mixture into the prepared pan. Bake in the oven for 15-20 minutes. Immediately after taking the cake out of the oven, cover the cake in its pan with a damp tea towel, and leave it to stand overnight. To decorate: carefully turn the cake out onto a sheet of wax paper which has been sprinkled with confectioner's sugar; remove the lining paper. Whip the cream until it holds its shape and spread over the cake (reserve a little for decorating). Roll up the cake like a jelly roll, and dust it with icing sugar. Decorate the remaining cream down the center or around the roulade.

Chocolate Orange Cake

PREPARATION TIME: 30 minutes
COOKING TIME: 40 minutes
OVEN TEMPERATURE: 350°F
MAKES: 1 cake, 8 inches in diameter

2 cups regular flour
9 tblsp cocoa powder
1 cup butter
1¼ cups fine sugar
2 eggs, beaten
1 cup buttermilk

Frosting
1 cup butter
Grated rind of 1 orange
½ cups confectioner's sugar, sieved
Juice of ½ an orange

To Decorate
Fresh orange segments or slices

Grease and line two 8 inch cake pans. Sieve together the cocoa and the flour. Cream the butter and sugar together until light and fluffy; gradually add the beaten eggs. Stir the buttermilk into the mixture, and then fold in the cocoa and flour. Turn the mixture into the prepared pans. Bake for 40 minutes. Remove the cakes from the oven; turn out of the pans and allow to cool on a wire rack. When the cakes are cold, split each cake into two layers. To make the frosting: cream the butter with the orange rind until soft; beat in the confectioner's sugar, alternately with the orange juice. Sandwich the cakes together with some of the butter frosting and spread the remaining frosting on the top and the sides of the cake. "Rough" with a fork and decorate with the orange slices or segments.

Austrian Sachertorte

PREPARATION TIME:	40 minutes, plus cooling time
COOKING TIME:	1 hour 15 minutes
OVEN TEMPERATURE:	350°F
MAKES:	1 cake, 8 inches in diameter

Torte

5oz dark semi-sweet chocolate, grated
1 tblsp warm water
10 tblsp butter
10 tblsp confectioner's sugar
5 eggs, separated
1¼ cups regular flour
1½ tsp baking powder
1oz cornstarch
1 tblsp rum, or strong black coffee
5 tblsp sieved apricot jam

Frosting

½ cup heavy cream
2 tsp brandy
4oz dark semi-sweet chocolate, grated
2oz sweet chocolate, grated
Confectioner's sugar to dust

Grease and flour an 8 inch round cake pan. Melt the chocolate in a basin with the warm water. Cream the butter and confectioner's sugar together until light and fluffy. Beat in the chocolate gradually. Beat in the egg yolks one at a time. Sieve together the flour and the cornstarch and fold it into the chocolate mixture. Beat the egg whites until stiff but not dry. Beat a third of the egg whites into the mixture then fold in the remainder. Spoon the mixture into the prepared cake pan. Bake for 50 minutes to 1 hour, until firm to the touch. Turn out and cool on a wire rack. Split the cake in half horizontally, sprinkle with rum or coffee, and sandwich together with 2 tblsp apricot jam. Place the cake on a wire rack. Brush all over with the remaining jam. To make the frosting: place the cream in a

Chocolate and Almond Cake

PREPARATION TIME:	45 minutes
COOKING TIME:	40-45 minutes
OVEN TEMPERATURE:	325°F
MAKES:	1 cake, 8 inches in diameter

¾ cup butter or margarine
¾ cup fine sugar
4oz semi-sweet chocolate, melted
¼ cup ground almonds
4 eggs, separated
½ cup regular flour
1 tsp baking powder
3 tblsp cornstarch

Frosting

2½ tblsp cocoa powder
2½ tblsp hot water
6 tblsp butter or margarine
1½ cups icing sugar

To Decorate

½ cup chopped toasted almonds
16 whole almonds, half dipped in melted chocolate

Grease and line two 8 inch cake pans. Cream the butter and sugar together until light and fluffy. Beat together the melted chocolate, ground almonds, and egg yolks, and add to the butter and sugar mixture. Fold the flour and cornflour into the mixture. Beat the egg whites until stiff but not dry; fold into the cake mixture. Divide the mixture between the two pans. Bake in the oven for 40-45 minutes. Turn out and cool on a wire rack. To make the frosting: blend the cocoa powder with the hot water. Beat together the butter and confectioner's sugar until well mixed. Mix in the cocoa mixture. Use two-thirds of the frosting to sandwich the cakes together and cover the sides. Put the toasted nuts on a sheet of wax paper and roll the sides of the sandwiched cakes over the nuts. Smooth the remaining frosting over the top of the cake. Decorate with the whole almonds, half dipped in melted chocolate.

This page: Humpty Dumpty (top) and Moon Cake (bottom).

Facing page: Raspberry Torte (top) and Austrian Sachertorte (bottom).

saucepan with the brandy and bring just to the boil. Add the grated dark semi-sweet chocolate and stir until thick and smooth. Pour the chocolate mixture evenly over the cake and leave it to set. Melt the milk chocolate and place in a wax pastry bag fitted with a plain "writing" tip. Write "Sachertorte" across the top. Dust with confectioner's sugar if liked.

Chocolate Raspberry Torte

PREPARATION TIME: 45 minutes
COOKING TIME: 35-40 minutes
OVEN TEMPERATURE: 325°F
MAKES: 1 cake, 12 inches in diameter

1 recipe Family Chocolate Cake mixture (see recipe)
⅓ cup rum or Framboise
6 tblsp raspberry jam
1lb fresh raspberries
Bittersweet Butter Cream (see recipe)
20 chocolate leaves (see recipe)

Chocolate Frosting
2 tsp oil
2 tblsp butter
6oz semi-sweet chocolate, grated
1¼ tblsp Framboise or rum

Grease and flour a 12 inch deep pizza pan. Fill with the cake mixture. Bake until it springs up when pressed on top. Leave to cool in the pan for 5 minutes. Remove from the pan and let the cake cool on a wire rack for at least 2 hours. Slice the cake into two layers, horizontally, using a long knife. Sprinkle the cut surfaces with either the Framboise or rum. Spread one layer of the cake with raspberry jam and then with bittersweet butter cream; sandwich the cake back together again. Turn the cake upside down and chill. To make the frosting, put the oil and butter into a saucepan and stir constantly over a medium heat. Let the mixture simmer for a minute. Remove from the heat and add the chocolate and the Framboise or rum. Beat until the chocolate has

melted and the frosting is smooth. Let the frosting cool and spread the frosting over the top and sides of the cake. Put the raspberries on the top of the cake, in the middle, and put the chocolate leaves round the circle of raspberries. Refrigerate the cake for 1 hour. Note: this cake is best consumed on the day it is made.

Raspberry Torte

PREPARATION TIME: 25 minutes
COOKING TIME: 45 minutes
OVEN TEMPERATURE: 350°F
MAKES: 1 cake, 8 inches in diameter

4 eggs, separated
½ cup fine sugar
3 tblsp cocoa powder
¼ cup fresh white breadcrumbs
½ cup ground almonds

Filling
4 tblsp Raspberry jam
⅔ cup heavy cream, whipped

To Decorate
Fresh raspberries
Cocoa powder to dust

Grease and line an 8 inch round cake pan. Beat the egg yolks and sugar until thick and fluffy. Sieve the cocoa powder into the breadcrumbs. Fold into the egg yolks. Beat the egg whites in a large, dry bowl until they are fluffy and stiff. Fold half the egg whites into the cake mixture taking care not to deflate the meringue; fold in the almonds followed by the remaining egg whites. Put the mixture into the prepared cake pan. Bake in the oven for 45 minutes. Cool in the pan for a few minutes, and then turn onto a wire rack to cool. Split the cake in half horizontally. Spread one layer of the cake with the jam, and then with half the whipped cream. Decorate with the remaining cream on the top of the cake and garnish with raspberries. Dust the cake with cocoa powder.

Devil's Food Cake

PREPARATION TIME: 35 minutes
COOKING TIME: 1 hour
45 minutes-2 hours
OVEN TEMPERATURE: 300°F
MAKES: 1 cake, 8 inches in diameter

¾ cup butter or margarine
¾ cup soft brown sugar
2 eggs, beaten
¾ cup corn syrup
¼ cup ground almonds
1½ cups regular flour
6 tblsp cocoa powder
⅔ cup milk
¼ tsp bicarbonate of soda

American Frosting
1 egg white
1⅛ cups confectioner's sugar
1¼ tblsp corn syrup
3½ tblsp water
Pinch of salt
1 tsp lemon juice

To Decorate
Chocolate curls

Grease and line an 8 inch cake pan with wax paper. Cream the butter and sugar together until light and fluffy. Add the eggs gradually, beating well after each addition. Sieve together all the dry ingredients. Add the corn syrup and the milk to the creamed mixture. Fold in the dry ingredients and beat well with a wooden spoon. Pour the mixture into the prepared cake pan. Bake until a skewer inserted in the center comes out clean. Turn out and cool on a wire rack. To make the frosting: place all the frosting ingredients into a basin over a saucepan of hot water; beat until the frosting stands in peaks. Remove from the heat and continue beating until the mixture has cooled. Spread over the cake using a palette knife. (The frosting must be used as soon as it is made.) Decorate with the chocolate curls.

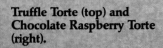

Truffle Torte (top) and Chocolate Raspberry Torte (right).

Humpty Dumpty

PREPARATION TIME: 50 minutes
COOKING TIME: 40-50 minutes
OVEN TEMPERATURE: 325°F
MAKES: 1 cake

1 cup butter or margarine
1 cup fine sugar
4 eggs, lightly beaten
1½ cups regular flour
1½ tsp baking powder
2½ tblsp cocoa powder
12oz Butter Frosting (see recipe)
Colored chocolate buttons
Liquorice strips
8oz marzipan

Grease a 1¼ pint pudding basin, and grease and line a 7 inch square shallow pan. Cream the butter and sugar together until light and fluffy. Beat in the eggs and then sieve the flour and baking powder into the mixture. Mix the cocoa powder with a little water to make a paste. Mix this into the cake mixture. Put two-thirds of the cake mixture into the pudding basin and the rest into the pan. Bake the pudding cake for 40-50 minutes, and the square cake for 30 minutes. Cool on a wire rack. To frost the cake: cut the square cake in half and then cut each half into 4 rectangles. Using the rectangles of cake as bricks, make a wall 2 bricks high and 4 across, sandwiching them together with butter frosting. Spread some of the remaining frosting on the top of the wall. Cover the pudding basin cake completely with butter frosting and put Humpty's eyes and nose on, using chocolate buttons. Use the liquorice to make a mouth.

Roll out the marzipan and shape legs and arms. Fix in position with cocktail sticks. You can even make a little hat by making a marzipan cup and pulling out a brim.

Chocolate Potato Cake

PREPARATION TIME:	55 minutes, plus cooling time
COOKING TIME:	30 minutes
OVEN TEMPERATURE:	375°F
MAKES:	1 two layer cake, 7 inches in diameter

½ cup hot mashed potato
2½ tblsp heavy cream
¾ cup + 2 tblsp sugar
2oz semi-sweet chocolate, melted
5 tblsp unsalted butter, softened
4 tsp bicarbonate of soda
2½ tblsp water
3 eggs, separated
1 cup flour
1 tsp baking powder
½ tsp rum
¼ cup milk
¼ tsp salt

Cocoa and Rum Frosting

3 tblsp unsalted butter
1¾ cups confectioner's sugar
2½ tblsp cocoa powder
¼ tsp salt
2 tsp rum
1½ tblsp strong black coffee

Butter and line two 7 inch round cake pans with wax paper. Brush the paper with a little melted butter and dust with flour. Mix the mashed potato and cream together in a bowl over a saucepan of hot water. Beat the softened butter and sugar together until soft and creamy. Add the potato and cream mixture to the butter and sugar and stir in the melted chocolate. Dissolve the bicarbonate of soda in the water and add to the mixture. Beat the egg yolks into the mixture one at a time. Sieve together the flour, baking powder and salt. Fold the flour into the mixture, adding the milk and rum alternately. Beat the egg whites until stiff but not dry. Gently fold in a third of the egg whites, and then fold in the remainder. Divide the mixture between the pans. Bake in a pre-heated oven for 30 minutes, or until a skewer inserted into the center comes out clean. Leave the cakes in the pans for 5 minutes before turning them out onto a wire rack to cool. For the frosting:

beat the butter until soft and creamy. Sieve together the confectioner's sugar, cocoa powder and salt; beat into the butter. Stir in the rum and coffee. Spread a layer of frosting on top of one cake and sandwich the cakes together; frost the top and sides of the cake with the remaining frosting.

Black Forest Gateau

PREPARATION TIME:	35 minutes
COOKING TIME:	55 minutes
OVEN TEMPERATURE:	325°F
MAKES:	1 cake, 7 inches in diameter

4oz semi-sweet chocolate, grated
1 cup regular flour
1¼ tsp baking powder
3 tblsp cornstarch
Generous pinch salt
10 tblsp butter, softened
½ cup fine sugar
4 eggs, separated
1¼ cups heavy cream, whipped
4 tblsp black cherry jam

To Decorate

4oz semi-sweet chocolate, grated

Grease and line a 7 inch round cake pan. Melt the chocolate in a basin over hot water. Sieve the flours and salt together. Cream the butter and sugar together until light and fluffy. Add the melted chocolate and egg yolks and beat well. Beat the egg whites until they are stiff and form peaks. Fold the egg whites lightly but thoroughly into the cake mixture. Spoon the mixture into the prepared cake

This page: Chocolate Mushroom Cake (top) and Chocolate Valentine Basket (bottom).

Facing page: Black Forest Gateau (top) and Devil's Food Cake (bottom).

pan. Bake in the oven for 55 minutes. Cool the cake in the pan and then turn it out onto a wire rack. Split the cake into two, horizontally. Spread one half with the jam and then with a third of

the cream; sandwich together with the remaining cake layer. Spread one half of the remaining cream over the top of the cake. Fit a large star tip to a pastry bag and fill with the remaining cream. Shape 8 rosettes on the top of the cake. Sprinkle the grated chocolate on the top of the cake. (You can top each rosette of cream with a black cherry, if liked.)

Chocolate Lemon Cake

PREPARATION TIME:	30 minutes
COOKING TIME:	40-45 minutes
OVEN TEMPERATURE:	350°F
MAKES:	1 2lb cake

¾ cup butter or margarine
¾ cup soft brown sugar
3 eggs
Grated rind of 1 lemon
2 cups regular flour
2 tsp baking powder
4oz semi-sweet chocolate, melted

Frosting
¾ cup butter
1lb confectioner's sugar, sieved
2½ tblsp lemon juice

To Decorate
Crystallized orange and lemon slices

Grease and line a 2lb rectangular pan or loaf pan. Cream the butter and sugar together until light and fluffy. Beat in the eggs, one at a time, adding a little sieved flour with each egg. Beat in the lemon rind and remaining flour, and then the chocolate. Pour into the prepared pan. Bake in the oven for 40-45 minutes. Turn onto a wire rack to cool. To make the frosting: put all the ingredients into a mixing bowl and beat together with a wooden spoon until well mixed. Cut the cake in half and use half the butter cream to sandwich the cake together. Spread the remaining frosting on the top of the cake and decorate with crystallized orange and lemon slices.

Chocolate Valentine Basket

PREPARATION TIME:	25 minutes
COOKING TIME:	40-45 minutes
OVEN TEMPERATURE:	325°F
MAKES:	1 heart-shaped cake

1 recipe Family Chocolate Cake mixture (see recipe)

Frosting
10 tblsp butter
1¼ cups confectioner's sugar
1¼ tblsp milk
2½ tblsp hot water
1¼ tblsp cocoa powder
Sweets for filling

Bake the Family Chocolate Cake mixture in two 8 inch heart-shaped cake pans for 40-45 minutes. Leave to cool on a wire rack. Cream the butter and the confectioner's sugar together with the milk. Mix the hot water and cocoa powder into a paste. Add this to the butter mixture and cream well. Fit two pastry bags with tips; one a ribbon tip, and the other a plain writing tip. Fill the bags with the butter cream. Hold the ribbon tip sideways and draw three evenly-spaced lines, one above the other, on one of the cakes. The three lines should all be the same length. Draw a vertical line, using the writing tube, along the edge of the basket weaving. Continue this process until the cake is covered. Cover the outermost edge and the sides of the remaining cake in the same way. This will now be the base, and the completely covered cake the lid. Arrange the lid at an angle on top of the lower cake and fill the inside with sweets.

Moon Cake

PREPARATION TIME:	20 minutes
COOKING TIME:	35 minutes
OVEN TEMPERATURE:	350°F
MAKES:	1 cake, 9 inches in diameter

This cake is fun to make and to eat. The mixture bubbles during baking and leaves a cake with a rocky, moon-like surface.

1¾ cups regular flour
½ cup granulated sugar
½ cup brown sugar
1 tsp salt
5 tblsp cocoa powder
6 tblsp melted butter
1 tsp vanilla essence
2½ tsp baking powder
1¼ tblsp white wine vinegar
⅔ cup milk
4oz marshmallows
Confectioner's sugar

Put the flour, sugar, salt and cocoa directly into a 9 inch cake pan and stir well until you have a light brown moon sand texture. Make a big crater in the middle of the sand so you can see the base of the pan, then a medium sized crater somewhere else in the sand, and a smaller crater on the other side (make sure that they are well apart). Spoon the baking powder into the medium sized crater. Spoon the melted butter into the large crater and the vanilla into the smallest crater. Now pour the vinegar into the medium sized crater and it will bubble and foam and become "volcanic". When this stops, pour the milk over the moon sand and stir well. The sand will now look like mud. Scatter the marshmallows over the surface. Bake for 35 minutes. (Test with a cocktail stick or skewer to see that the cake is done.) Dust with confectioner's sugar and serve from the pan.

Chocolate Mushroom Cake

PREPARATION TIME:	1 hour
COOKING TIME:	3 hours
OVEN TEMPERATURE:	225°F
MAKES:	1 cake, 9 inches in diameter

1 recipe Family Chocolate Cake mixture (see recipe)
Frosting recipe for Family Chocolate Cake
2oz white chocolate, melted
3 chocolate flakey bars
Confectioner's sugar

Meringue Mushrooms
2 egg whites
½ cup fine sugar
Oil for greasing
Cocoa powder
3oz dark semi-sweet chocolate, melted

Make the Family Chocolate Cake as instructed. Bake as directed and coat with frosting. Fill a pastry bag fitted with a small writing tip with the melted white chocolate. Make a spiral of melted white chocolate on top of the cake, working from the middle outwards. Cut the chocolate flakey bars in half, dust them with confectioner's sugar, and stick them around the sides of the cake to represent bark. To make the meringues: beat the egg whites in a bowl until they are stiff but not dry. Add the sugar slowly, beating well after each addition. Lightly oil a cooky sheet and cover with wax paper. Fit a pastry bag with a ½-¾ inch plain tip. Fill the bag with the meringue mixture. Pipe 12 mushroom stems on half the cooky sheet. Lift the bag vertically until the stems are 1½-2 inches high. Cut the meringue away from the tip. Then pipe 12 even rounds of meringue 1½-2 inches in diameter and 3-4 inches thick. (These make the mushroom tops; make sure that they are flat.) Sieve the cocoa powder over the meringues and then bake in a pre-heated oven until they are dried out (about 3 hours). Leave to cool. When the meringues are cool, spread melted chocolate on the underside of each mushroom top and fix the stem onto the chocolate. Leave to cool until the chocolate has set. Remove the mushrooms and stick a few of them on the cake, using a little more melted chocolate. Lay the others around the cake, to be eaten separately.

Chocolate Rolled Wafer Gateau

PREPARATION TIME:	40 minutes
COOKING TIME:	25-30 minutes
OVEN TEMPERATURE:	350°F
MAKES:	1 gateau, 8 inches in diameter

3 eggs
6 tblsp fine sugar
1½ tblsp cocoa powder
½ tsp baking powder
10 tblsp regular flour

Filling and Decoration
1¼ cups heavy cream
4oz packet English rolled wafers
1 oz semi-sweet chocolate, melted

Grease and line two 8 inch cake pans. Place the eggs and sugar in a basin and beat over a saucepan of hot water until thick and pale. Remove from the heat and beat until cool. Sieve together the cocoa powder, baking powder and flour, and gently fold into the mixture. Divide the mixture between the two prepared pans. Bake for 25-30 minutes. Turn out carefully onto a wire rack and cool. Whip the cream until thick and use a little to sandwich the cakes together. Spread a little cream around the sides and secure the English rolled wafers round the edge of the cake. Spread the remaining cream on the

top of the cake. Put the melted chocolate into a wax pastry bag with a small hole, and drizzle over the cream; swirl it with a skewer.

Chocolate Rolled Wafer Gateau (right) and Chocolate Lemon Cake (below).

291

Truffle Torte

PREPARATION TIME: 1 hour

COOKING TIME: 1 hour
              15 minutes

OVEN TEMPERATURE: 350°F

MAKES: 1 cake, 7 inches in
              diameter

½ cup unsalted butter, softened
½ cup fine sugar
3 eggs, separated
4oz semi-sweet chocolate, melted
¼ cup regular flour
10 tblsp finely ground hazelnuts

Chocolate Frosting

⅔ cup heavy cream
5oz semi-sweet chocolate, broken into
    pieces

Butter and line a 7 inch springform cake pan with wax paper. Brush the paper with a little melted butter and dust with flour. Beat the butter until soft and creamy. Add the sugar and continue to beat until light and fluffy. Add the egg yolks, one at a time, and beat well. Stir in the melted chocolate. Sieve together the flour and the ground hazelnuts and fold them into the cake mixture. Beat the egg whites until stiff but not dry. Gently fold in the beaten egg whites. Pour the mixture into the prepared pan. Bake in the pre-heated oven for about 1 hour. (When cooked the cake should be springy to the touch.) Remove from the oven and leave the cake in its pan for 5 minutes. Turn onto a wire rack and cool completely. To make the chocolate frosting: put the cream into a saucepan and bring to the boil. Add the chocolate, stirring until the chocolate has melted, and the mixture is thick and smooth. Pour the frosting evenly over the cake before it has a chance to set. Decorate with shaped chocolate whirls (see Cookies and Confections recipe).

Family Chocolate Cake

PREPARATION TIME: 25 minutes

COOKING TIME: 45-50 minutes

OVEN TEMPERATURE: 325°F

MAKES: 1 cake, 9 inches in
              diameter

1¾ cups regular flour
1 tsp bicarbonate of soda
1¼ tsp baking powder

2½ tblsp cocoa powder
10 tblsp soft brown sugar
2½ tblsp corn syrup
2 eggs
⅔ cup oil
⅔ cup milk

Frosting

6oz semi-sweet chocolate, chopped or
    grated
2½ tblsp light cream

To Decorate

Walnut halves

Grease and line a 9 inch cake pan. Sieve all the dry ingredients together in a large bowl. Put the sugar, syrup, eggs, oil and milk into a well in the center of the dry ingredients. Beat thoroughly until the mixture is smooth. Pour the mixture into the prepared cake pan. Bake for 45-50 minutes until a skewer inserted in the center of the cake comes out clean. Leave the baked cake in its pan for a few minutes and turn onto a wire rack to cool. To make the frosting: place the chocolate and cream into a small, heavy-based pan and heat gently until melted. Cool slightly and pour evenly over the cake. Decorate with walnuts.

Chocolate Cup Cakes

PREPARATION TIME: 20 minutes

COOKING TIME: 15 minutes

OVEN TEMPERATURE: 350°F

MAKES: 18

½ cup soft margarine
½ cup fine sugar
2 eggs
¾ cup regular flour
1 tsp baking powder
3 tblsp cocoa powder

Fudge Frosting

1 tblsp corn syrup
1lb granulated sugar
¼ cup unsalted butter
6 tblsp cocoa powder

Line 2 bun trays with 18 paper cake cases. Put all the cake ingredients into a bowl and beat together with a wooden spoon, until smooth and glossy. Put one small spoonful of the mixture into each of the cake cases. Bake in the center of the oven for 15 minutes or until they are firm to touch. To make the frosting: put the syrup into a saucepan with 1 cup cold water, the sugar, butter and cocoa powder; stir over a low heat until the sugar dissolves. Boil the mixture until a

little will form a soft ball when dropped into cold water. (Do not stir the mixture, just cut it with a wooden spoon occasionally.) Remove the mixture from the heat and allow it to cool for 10 minutes. Beat it with a wooden spoon until the mixture begins to thicken to a coating consistency. Pour the mixture over the cup cakes and allow it to set. (If the frosting sets before it has covered all the cakes, melt it gently.)

Spider's Web

PREPARATION TIME: 50 minutes

COOKING TIME: 35 minutes

OVEN TEMPERATURE: 375°F

MAKES: 1 cake, 7½ inches in
              diameter

1¼ cups regular flour
6 tblsp cocoa powder
½ tsp bicarbonate of soda
½ cup soft margarine
1 cup dark soft brown sugar
2 eggs
2 tsp peppermint essence
2 tblsp ground almonds
⅔ cup soured cream

To Decorate

4oz unsweetened chocolate, grated
1⅛ cups confectioner's sugar
1 dark chocolate button
Green food coloring
Peppermint essence
1 cup Butter Frosting (see recipe)
1 liquorice shoe-lace
1 chocolate-covered marshmallow
1 packet white chocolate buttons

Grease and line two 7½ inch cake pans. Sieve the flour, cocoa powder and bicarbonate of soda into a bowl and then add all the other ingredients. Mix well until they are blended. Divide the mixture between the two pans. Slightly hollow out the centers so that the

This page: Chocolate Cup Cakes (top) and Family Chocolate Cake – shown with candy covered chocolate sweets – (bottom).

Facing page: Nouvelle – Truffle Cake (top) and Sherry Cream Pie (bottom).

tops will be flat when baked. Bake in the oven for 35 minutes, until a wooden skewer inserted through the center comes out clean. Cool the cakes slightly in their pans and then turn onto a wire rack. Melt half the chocolate in a bowl over a pan of simmering water. Mix the sieved confectioner's sugar with a few drops of water to give a coating consistency. Put the melted chocolate into a pastry bag fitted with a small, plain tip. Cover the top of one of the cakes with the white frosting. Immediately shape a spiral of chocolate onto the white frosted cake, working outwards from the center. To make the web, mark out 12 lines by drawing a skewer across the frosting, from the center outwards. Put the dark chocolate drop in the center and leave to set. Add a little green coloring and peppermint essence to the butter frosting. Spread some of the green peppermint butter frosting over the un-frosted cake and place the frosted cake on top. Spread some of the remaining green frosting around the sides of the cake. Sprinkle the remaining grated chocolate around the sides of the cake. To make the spider: cut the liquorice into 8 equal lengths. Stick each length into the side of the chocolate marshmallow and trim the two front legs, making them a little shorter than the others. Using a little frosting, stick two white buttons on the front of the marshmallow for eyes. Put small liquorice trimmings onto the white chocolate drops, fixing them in place with a little more frosting. Place the spider on the cake.

Birthday Salute
Tanks

PREPARATION TIME:	45 minutes
COOKING TIME:	25 minutes
OVEN TEMPERATURE:	375°F

1 recipe Family Chocolate Cake mixture (see recipe)
12oz Chocolate Butter Frosting (see recipe)
1 packet chocolate chips
6 chocolate flakey bars

Grease and line a 7 inch square cake pan. Fill the pan with the family chocolate cake mixture and spread evenly in the pan. Bake as instructed, then leave to cool on a wire rack. Cut the cake in half. Cut off a piece from each half, measuring 2x2 inches. Cover the larger cake pieces with butter icing.

Spider's Web (above) and Birthday Salute (right).

Put the smaller pieces of cake on top of the larger pieces of cake, slightly towards the back. Stick 5 chocolate chips along both of the longer sides of each lower cake. Then put one chip on top for the hatch lid. Reserve two chocolate flakey bars, then cut the rest into short lengths. Lay the short lengths as tracks around the outer edges of the cakes. Push the whole flakey bars into the front of the smaller cakes to make the gun barrels.

Cannon

PREPARATION TIME: 10 minutes
COOKING TIME: 12 minutes
OVEN TEMPERATURE: 400°F

3 eggs
6 tblsp fine sugar
Vanilla essence
¾ cup regular flour
3 tblsp cocoa powder
1½ tblsp warm water

1 recipe Chocolate Butter Frosting

To Decorate
Confectioner's sugar
4 large chocolate flakey bars
Chocolate balls

Grease and line a 9 inch jelly roll pan. Beat the eggs, sugar, and a few drops of vanilla essence in a bowl over a pan of hot water until pale and thick (use an electric beater if possible). Sieve together the flour and cocoa powder, and then fold into the egg mixture with the water. Turn the mixture into the prepared pan and spread evenly. Bake for 12 minutes until the cake has risen. Sprinkle some confectioner's sugar onto a sheet of wax paper and turn the cake out onto the paper. Peel off the lining paper which may be stuck to the cake, and trim off any crisp edges that may be around the cake. Lay a piece of wax paper over the top of the cake and roll up the cake with the wax paper inside. Leave to cool on a wire rack. Unroll the cake and remove the paper. Spread with some of the butter frosting and re-roll. Dust the cake with confectioner's sugar. To decorate: fit a star tip onto a pastry bag and fill with some of the butter cream. Cut the jelly roll into 12 pieces,

then cut 4 of the slices in half. Place two halves side by side, standing them on their flat edges. With a dab of butter cream, attach two whole slices on each of the sides. Make stripes of butter frosting down the middle of each cannon and lay the flakey bar on it, angled up at one end. Next to the cannon place a pile of chocolate balls, to represent cannon balls.

Chocolate Nut Gateau

PREPARATION TIME: 30 minutes, plus chilling

MAKES: 1 gateau, 7 inches in diameter

2 tblsp butter
1 tblsp corn syrup
1½ cups crunchy breakfast cereal

Filling
4½ tblsp cornstarch
1¼ tblsp cocoa powder
1¾ cups milk
⅔ cup chocolate flavored yogurt
1½ tblsp hazelnuts, skinned and roughly chopped

Topping
⅔ cup hazelnut-flavored yogurt
6 tblsp heavy cream, whipped

To Decorate
Grated chocolate
8 whole hazelnuts

Melt the butter and syrup in a saucepan. Add the crunchy cereal and mix well until they are coated with the butter syrup. Press the mixture into the base of a 7 inch fluted flan ring placed on a serving plate. Leave to cool. For the filling: mix the cornstarch and cocoa powder with a little of the milk. Heat the remaining milk until boiling and pour onto the cornstarch mixture, stirring constantly. Return the mixture to the pan and return to the heat; simmer for a few minutes, until thickened. Remove the saucepan from the heat and stir in the chocolate yogurt and chopped hazelnuts. Pour the mixture over the crisp base. For the topping: mix the nut yogurt with the whipped cream and spread it over the chocolate mixture. Put the flan in the refrigerator and chill until set. Carefully remove the flan ring and decorate with grated chocolate and whole hazelnuts. Serve with chocolate sauce if desired.

Chocolate Pistachio Loaf

PREPARATION TIME: 20 minutes

COOKING TIME: 1 hour 15 minutes-1 hour 30 minutes

OVEN TEMPERATURE: 350°F

MAKES: One 1lb loaf

1 cup regular flour
1¼ tsp baking powder
½ cup butter or margarine, softened
¼ cup fine sugar
2oz semi-sweet chocolate, chopped
½ cup pistachio nuts, chopped
2 tblsp ground almonds
2 eggs
2½ tblsp milk

Frosting
6oz semi-sweet chocolate, chopped or grated
A knob of butter

To Decorate
A few pistachio nuts, chopped

Grease and line a 1lb loaf pan. Put all the cake ingredients into a mixing bowl and beat until they are well mixed. Pour the mixture into the prepared pan. Bake in a pre-heated oven for 1 hour 15 minutes, or until cooked. Turn the cake out of the pan and leave to cool on a wire rack. For the frosting: melt the chocolate in a basin over a pan of hot water; beat the knob of butter

(the size of a walnut) into the chocolate and pour evenly over the cake. Sprinkle with chopped pistachio nuts.

Chocolate Knitting

PREPARATION TIME: 45 minutes

COOKING TIME: 40-45 minutes

OVEN TEMPERATURE: 325°F

MAKES: 1 cake, 9 inches square

1 recipe Family Chocolate Cake mixture (see recipe)
Butter frosting (see recipe)
2 tsp cocoa powder
1 packet of sugar strand cake decorations
2 large wooden knitting needles
10 chocolate flakey bars
10 inch square cake board

Bake the family chocolate cake mixture in a 9 inch square cake pan as directed. Cut the cake in half and sandwich the two halves together using some of the butter frosting. Put on the cake board. Mix the cocoa powder with 2 tsp boiling water and add this to the remaining butter frosting. Mix until smooth. Then add an extra 1¼ tblsp confectioner's sugar to the frosting so it will work better. Spread some of this frosting over the top of the cake. With a

warmed knife, cut 4 flakey bars in half and arrange them along the edge of the cake. Cut 4 flakey bars into quarters and place them with two pieces alternately, vertically and horizontally. Then cut two flakes into eight and repeat this process. Put the knitting needles into the cake; one goes on top, and the other goes through the center filling, so that the handles cross. Use the remaining frosting to fill a pastry bag fitted with a star tip. Make sticks of frosting over the top needle. Sprinkle the sugar strands over the top of the cake in a flaked pattern.

Dart Board

PREPARATION TIME: 45 minutes

COOKING TIME: 35 minutes

OVEN TEMPERATURE: 325°F

MAKES: 1 cake, 10 inches in diameter

1 cup butter
¾ cup soft light brown sugar
4 eggs
¾ cup corn syrup
3 tblsp cocoa powder
2 cups regular flour
2 tsp baking powder
1 tsp mixed ground spice
½ tsp ground ginger

To Decorate
12 inch cake board
4 tblsp apricot jam
12oz Butter Frosting (see recipe)
Generous pinch ground ginger
Grated chocolate
1 liquorice wheel
Small darts

Grease and line two 10 inch round cake pans. Cream the butter and sugar together; beat in the eggs slowly, followed by the corn syrup. Mix the cocoa powder with a few drops of water and make into a paste. Fold the flour into the cake mixture and then divide the mixture into two. Add the cocoa paste to one portion; sieve the mixed spice and ground ginger into the other portion, and add a little milk if necessary. Spread the two mixtures into their separate pans and hollow out the centers so the cakes will have a flat top when cooked. Bake in a pre-heated oven for 35 minutes. Leave to cool upside down on a wire rack, removing the paper. Put a 7 inch

round plate on each cake and, using it as a guide, cut out a circle from the middle of each cake. Remove the circles and cut them into 20 even wedges. Put the ginger outer circle on the cake board and put the wedge slices – alternating between chocolate and ginger – in a circular pattern in the center. Spread the top of the cake with jam and lay the chocolate ring on top of the ginger ring. Then repeat the process with the remaining

wedges, reversing the colors to get a chequered effect. Beat the butter frosting with the ginger and spread some of it around the sides of the cake. Cover the sides of the cake with grated chocolate. Fill a pastry bag fitted with a plain writing tip with butter frosting. Write the numbers on the cake in the correct order. Fit a star tip to the pastry bag, refill with the remaining butter icing, and shape shells for the scoring circles. Make a line around

the top and bottom of the outer edges and stick the liquorice wheel in the center for the bullseye. Put on the darts for decoration.

Facing page: Chocolate Knitting (top) and Dart Board (bottom).

This page: Chocolate Pistachio Loaf (top) and Chocolate Nut Gateau (bottom).

COOKING WITH CHOCOLATE

Desserts and Pastries

Chocolate Pear Pie

PREPARATION TIME: 25 minutes, plus chilling

SERVES: 4-6 people

6 tblsp butter
8oz semi-sweet chocolate graham
    crackers, crushed
14½oz can of pear halves
2½ tsp arrowroot

To Decorate
Grated chocolate

Melt the butter in a saucepan and mix with the crushed biscuits. Press the crumb mixture into the base and up the sides of an 7 inch loose-bottomed, fluted quiche pan. Place in the refrigerator to set. Carefully remove the crumb case from the quiche pan; leave it on the base as this will make serving easier. Drain the juice from the pears and reserve. Arrange the pear halves in the pie case. Mix the arrowroot with half of the pear juice in a small saucepan and bring to the boil. Stir gently until the mixture thickens and clears. Cool slightly and then spoon over the pears. Chill briefly. Sprinkle with grated chocolate and serve with cream.

Chocolate Orange Pudding

PREPARATION TIME: 25 minutes

COOKING TIME: about 1¾ hours

SERVES: 4-6 people

1 recipe Steamed Chocolate Pudding
    mixture (see recipe)
2 oranges

Make the chocolate pudding mixture as directed. Finely grate the rind of 1 orange and add this to the mixture. Thinly slice the second orange and press the orange circles around the inside of a greased 2½ pint pudding basin; put one orange slice in the base. Fill with the pudding mixture. Cover and steam the pudding for about 1¾ hours. Serve with orange or chocolate sauce.

Chocolate Mousse

PREPARATION TIME: 20 minutes, plus chilling time

SERVES: 4-6 people

4oz semi-sweet chocolate, grated
2½ tblsp water
1¼ tblsp instant coffee

4 egg whites
½ cup sugar

To Decorate
A little reserved chocolate

Put most of the chocolate, and the water and coffee into a bowl; stand it over a pan of hot water. Stir the mixture occasionally until the

This page: Chocolate Brandy Cheesecake (top left), Chocolate Orange Pudding (top right) and Chocolate Pear Pie (bottom)

Facing page: Chocolate Eclairs (top) and Chocolate Strudel (bottom).

chocolate has melted and the mixture is smooth. Beat the egg whites until stiff but not dry, gradually beating in half the sugar. Mix the remaining sugar into the chocolate mixture and fold in the meringue. Divide the mixture among 4-6 glasses and sprinkle with remaining grated chocolate. Chill briefly.

Strawberry Box

PREPARATION TIME: 50 minutes, plus chilling

SERVES: 6 people

Chocolate Case
8oz semi-sweet chocolate, chopped or grated
1 tblsp vegetable oil

Filling
6oz semi-sweet chocolate, chopped or grated
1¼ tblsp kirsch
2 egg yolks
⅔ cup heavy cream
⅔ cup light cream

Topping
8oz strawberries, hulled and halved
4 tblsp strawberry jam, sieved
1¼ tblsp kirsch
1oz unsweetened chocolate, chopped or grated
⅔ cup heavy cream

Line either a 6 inch square cake pan or an 7 inch round cake pan with a double thickness of foil. (Make sure that the foil comes above the top of the pan to make removal of the set chocolate case easy.) For the chocolate case: melt the chocolate with the vegetable oil; pour two-thirds into the prepared pan and turn and tilt the pan so that the sides and base are coated evenly. Allow the chocolate to set slightly and then repeat the process with the remaining melted chocolate. Leave it in a cool place until the chocolate has set completely. Remove the chocolate case from the pan by pulling the foil lining gently; peel the foil away carefully from the chocolate case. To make the filling: melt the chocolate. Remove from the heat and beat the kirsch and the egg yolks into the chocolate. Whip the heavy and light creams together until thick and then fold into the chocolate. Pour the chocolate cream into the prepared chocolate case. Chill until set. Arrange the strawberries on the top of the filled case. Bring the jam and the kirsch to the boil together and remove from the heat; allow to cool slightly. Spoon the topping glaze over the strawberries, but do not allow the

hot jam to run to the edge of the chocolate case or it will melt. The glaze will set in about 5 minutes. Melt the chocolate and allow it to cool. Whip the heavy cream until thick and beat in the chocolate. Shape the chocolate mixture decoratively around the case using a pastry bag.

Chocolate Eclairs

PREPARATION TIME: 20 minutes

COOKING TIME: 20-25 minutes

OVEN TEMPERATURE: 425°F

MAKES: 10-12

¼ cup butter or margarine
⅔ cup water
10 tblsp regular flour, sieved
2 eggs, beaten
⅔ cup heavy cream, whipped

Frosting
4oz semi-sweet chocolate, chopped or grated
1 tblsp butter

Melt the butter (or margarine) in a saucepan over a gentle heat. Add the water and bring it just to the boil. Remove the pan from the heat and add the flour. Beat the mixture well until it leaves the sides of the pan clean. Cool the mixture slightly, and beat in the eggs gradually, beating between each addition. Spoon the mixture into a pastry bag fitted with a ½ inch plain tip. Make 3 inch lengths onto a lightly dampened cooky sheet. Bake in a preheated oven for 20-25 minutes until crisp and golden brown. Make a slit in the side of each eclair to allow the steam to escape, and cool on a wire rack. Fit a pastry bag with a ½ inch plain tip and spoon the whipped cream into the bag. Push the cream into each of the eclairs. Melt the chocolate and butter on a plate over a pan of hot water, stirring until smooth. Dip each eclair into the chocolate to give an even top coating and place on a wire rack to set.

Chocolate Strudel

PREPARATION TIME: 1 hour 30 minutes

COOKING TIME: 40 minutes

OVEN TEMPERATURE: 375°F

MAKES: a 14 inch strudel

1 cup regular flour
½ a beaten egg
½ tsp salt
⅓ cup water

A few drops of vinegar
6 tblsp butter, melted and cooled

Filling
3 tblsp butter
¼ cup vanilla sugar
2 eggs, separated
⅓ cup raisins
⅓ cup heavy cream
A pinch of ground cinnamon
2 tblsp fine sugar
2oz semi-sweet chocolate, grated
2½oz chopped walnuts
Confectioner's sugar

Sieve the flour into a large mixing bowl and make a well in the center. Beat together the egg, salt, water, vinegar and 1¼ tblsp of the melted butter. Pour this mixture into the well. Mix all the ingredients together to a dough. Knead the dough on a well-floured board until smooth and elastic (this will take about 15 minutes). Put the dough into a floured bowl and cover with a cloth. Leave for 15 minutes. While the dough is resting make the filling. Beat together the butter and vanilla sugar until light and fluffy. Add the egg yolks one at a time, beating after each addition. Add the walnuts, cream, cinnamon, chocolate and raisins and mix well. Beat the egg whites until stiff but not dry, and then gradually beat in the fine sugar. Fold this mixture gently into the

chocolate mixture. Cover the work surface with a large, clean cloth and dust the cloth with flour. Put the dough into the middle of the cloth and brush the tp with melted butter. Working around the dough, roll it out to a thickness of ⅛ inch. Brush it with more butter and, using four hands (you'll need to enlist help!), stretch the dough outwards as thinly as possible. Try to work around the dough so it does not tear. Cut the dough into a rectangle measuring 14x18 inches. Butter a large cooky sheet. Spoon the filling onto the strudel pastry, leaving a margin of 2 inches around three of the edges. Fold the margins over the filling and brush the remaining pastry with the melted butter. Gently lift the cloth so that the dough rolls itself up. Roll the dough onto the prepared cooky sheet. Bake for 40 minutes, basting with melted butter once or twice, until golden and crisp. Remove the strudel from the oven and dust with confectioner's sugar. Serve warm or cold. (Do not be put off by the thought of handling strudel pastry. Although a professionally thin pastry is needed for good results, it is not as difficult to achieve as its reputation would suggest.)

Strawberry Box (top right) and Chocolate Mousse (right).

Chiffon Pie

PREPARATION TIME:	40 minutes, plus chilling
COOKING TIME:	1 hour
OVEN TEMPERATURE:	375°F
MAKES:	1 pie, 9 inches in diameter

Shortcrust Pastry
2 cups regular flour
2 tblsp fine sugar
1 tsp salt
¼ cup ground almonds
10 tblsp unsalted butter, cut into pieces
1 egg yolk

Filling
1 cup milk
9 tblsp fine sugar
7oz unsweetened chocolate, broken into pieces
2 eggs, separated
1¼ tblsp powdered gelatin
4 tblsp strong black coffee
1½ cups heavy cream, whipped

Topping
1 cup heavy cream, whipped
Grated chocolate

To make the pastry: sieve the flour, sugar and salt and add the almonds. Make a well in the center of the dry ingredients and add the butter and egg yolk. Working quickly, use the fingertips to mix all the ingredients together. Shape the dough into a ball and wrap in foil or plastic wrap. Leave to chill for 1 hour. Roll out the pastry on a floured work surface to a thickness of ⅛-¼ inch and use to line a 9 inch fluted deep pie pan. Cover the pastry with a sheet of wax paper and weight it down with rice or beans. Bake blind in a pre-heated oven for 15 minutes, or until the edges begin to color. Remove the paper and beans and bake for a further 15 minutes. Leave to cool on a wire rack before removing from the pan. To make the filling: mix the milk, 6 tblsp of the sugar and the chocolate pieces in a saucepan; cook over a moderate heat. Stir constantly until the chocolate melts. The chocolate mixture should be thick and smooth when removed from the heat. Leave to cool. Beat the egg yolks into the chocolate mixture. Dissolve the gelatin in the coffee, over a low heat, and stir into the warm chocolate mixture. Chill until it begins to set. Beat the egg whites until stiff but not dry. Beat the remaining sugar into the beaten egg whites until stiff and glossy.

Gently fold the egg whites into the chocolate mixture, followed by the whipped cream. Pour the mixture into the pie shell. Decorate with whipped cream and grated chocolate.

Chocolate Terrine with Cherry Sauce

PREPARATION TIME:	40 minutes, plus freezing
COOKING TIME:	about 8 minutes
MAKES:	1 3lb terrine

8oz unsweetened chocolate, chopped or grated
1 cup unsalted butter
½ cup fine white sugar
⅓ cup confectioner's sugar
⅓ cup cocoa powder
½ cup granulated sugar
⅔ cup water
4 egg yolks, beaten
1⅓ cups heavy cream
4oz pitted black cherries

Sauce
2½ tblsp cornstarch
1¼ cups water
1lb pitted black cherries
½ cup granulated sugar
5 tblsp kirsch

Grease a 3lb loaf pan, and line with greased wax paper. Melt the chocolate in a bowl over a pan of hot water; remove from the heat and cool. Cream the butter and fine sugar until light and fluffy. Sieve the confectioner's sugar and cocoa together and beat into the butter mixture; beat in the cooled melted chocolate. Put the granulated sugar and water into a small, heavy-based pan and stir over a gentle heat until the sugar has dissolved. Boil quickly to 225°F on a sugar thermometer. Beat the egg yolks in a basin and add the sugar syrup; beat into a mousse-like consistency. Beat into the butter and chocolate mixture. Whip the cream and lightly fold it into the mixture. Fold in the pitted cherries and turn the mixture into the prepared pan. Freeze for 6 hours or until firm.

Cherry Sauce
Blend the cornstarch with 3 tblsp water in a small bowl. Put the cherries into a pan with the remaining water and sugar and bring to the boil. Remove the pan from the heat and stir in the cornstarch mixture. Bring back to the boil, stirring continuously. Remove from the heat and add the kirsch. Serve the Chocolate Terrine in slices, accompanied by the hot cherry sauce.

Banana and Chocolate Trifle

PREPARATION TIME:	30 minutes
SERVES:	6 people

1 packet pineapple jelly
3 bananas
1 chocolate jelly roll
1¼ tblsp cornstarch
2½ tblsp fine sugar
2½ cups milk
2½ tblsp cocoa powder
⅔ cup heavy cream

To Decorate
4 glace cherries

Make up the jelly following the instructions on the packet. As the jelly is about to set, slice two bananas and stir them into the jelly. Pour into a pretty glass dish. When the jelly has cooled (but not set), cut the jelly roll into eight pieces and arrange the slices around the sides of the dish, standing up in the jelly. Mix the cornstarch and the sugar with a little of the milk; add the cocoa powder and mix well. Add the remaining milk. Put the chocolate mixture into a small saucepan and boil for a few minutes, stirring until it thickens. Leave to cool. Lightly whip the cream and fold into the cold custard. Pour the mixture into the dish on top of the jelly. Before serving, decorate the top of the trifle with slices of the remaining banana and the glace cherries.

This page: Chocolate Terrine with Cherry Sauce (top) and Tarte au Chocolat (bottom).

Facing page: Banana and Chocolate Trifle (top) and Chiffon Pie (bottom).

Chocolate Rum Fool

PREPARATION TIME: 20 minutes, plus chilling

SERVES: 4-6 people

⅔ cup raisins
5 tblsp dark rum
1 cup cold cooked potato
¼ cup sugar
7oz semi-sweet chocolate cake
  covering
1 cup butter
⅔ cup heavy cream

Soak the raisins in the rum for one hour. Sieve the potato and beat in the rum-soaked raisins and the sugar. Melt the chocolate and the butter together. Remove from the heat and beat into the potato mixture. Whip the cream until thick, and gently fold two-thirds of it into the mixture. Turn the mixture into a serving dish and chill in the refrigerator for at least one hour. Decorate with the remaining cream when ready to serve.

Chocolate and Cherry Mousse

PREPARATION TIME: 35-40 minutes, plus chilling

SERVES: 6 people

Cherry Mousse
12oz pitted cherries, fresh or canned
1½ tsp gelatin powder
2½ tblsp cold water
¼ cup sugar
2 eggs, separated
⅔ cup heavy cream

Chocolate Mousse
6oz semi-sweet chocolate, chopped or
  grated
2 tsp instant coffee
1 tblsp water
4 eggs, separated
⅔ cup heavy cream

To Decorate
⅔ cup whipped cream
A few whole cherries

Rub the cherries through a sieve, or puree them in a blender or food processor. Sprinkle the gelatin over the cold water and leave in a basin to soften for a few minutes; dissolve the gelatin over a pan of simmering water. Remove from the heat and cool. Beat the sugar and egg yolks together until thick and creamy and then beat in the gelatin; stir in the cherry puree and mix well. Beat the egg whites in a dry bowl until stiff but not dry. Whip the cream lightly until it

holds its shape and then fold the cream gently into the cherry mixture. Fold the egg whites into the cherry mixture lightly but thoroughly. Pour into 6 individual serving dishes and chill for 30 minutes. For the chocolate mousse: melt the chocolate with the coffee and the water. Remove from the heat and beat in the egg yolks. Whip the cream lightly until it holds its shape, then beat the egg whites in a separate bowl until stiff but not dry. Fold the cream into the chocolate mixture and then the egg whites. Pour the chocolate mousse over the chilled cherry mousse and chill for at least an hour. Decorate with whipped cream and cherries before serving.

Chocolate Quiche

PREPARATION TIME: 30 minutes, plus chilling time

COOKING TIME: about 1 hour

OVEN TEMPERATURE: 375°F and then 350°F

SERVES: 10 people

1 cup regular flour
1¼ tsp baking powder
Pinch of salt
½ cup ground almonds
10 tblsp butter
1 egg yolk
Cold water

Filling
1lb 2oz cooking chocolate, grated
3 cups heavy cream
7 egg yolks

Mix the flour, salt and almonds in a bowl. Add the butter in small pieces and rub into a crumb-like texture. Beat the egg yolk with 2½ tblsp of water. Add to the crumble mixture and mix to a firm dough, adding a little extra water if required. Shape the dough into a ball; wrap and chill in the refrigerator. Flour a pastry slab or work surface and roll out the dough; use to line a large loose-bottomed quiche pan, 12 inches in diameter. Line the pastry with wax paper and beans and bake "blind" at the higher temperature for 10 minutes. Remove the paper and beans and bake for a further 3 minutes. Leave to cool. Melt the chocolate and cool slightly. Beat the cream and the egg yolks until they are well blended, and add the melted chocolate. Pour into the pastry case. Bake for 45 minutes at the lower temperature, until the top is firm to the touch. Allow the quiche to cool a little, and then serve in small portions with whipped cream and/or fruit.

Nouvelle – Truffle Cakes

PREPARATION TIME: 40 minutes

COOKING TIME: 18-20 minutes

OVEN TEMPERATURE: 375°F

MAKES 6

This is a very rich, sophisticated dessert, ideal for special occasions.

5 eggs, separated
3 tblsp granulated sugar
6 tblsp regular flour
3 tblsp cocoa powder
1 tsp baking powder
Pinch salt
2 tblsp melted unsalted butter
3oz semi-sweet chocolate, melted
Cocoa powder
Rum, Grand Marnier or Amaretto
  liqueur
⅔ cup heavy cream, well chilled
Frosting or vanilla sugar
1 recipe Nouvelle Chocolate Sauce
  (see recipe)
1 cup split almonds, lightly toasted
  and broken into pieces

To make the cake mixture: butter and flour six 4 inch individual souffle dishes. Line the base of each dish with buttered wax paper. Put the egg yolks and half the sugar into a bowl and beat well, preferably with an electric mixer, until the eggs are thick and pale. Sieve the flour, cocoa, baking powder and salt together. Beat the egg whites until stiff but not dry, gradually adding the remaining sugar. Fold the flour and melted butter alternately into the egg yolk mixture. Fold in the beaten egg whites lightly but thoroughly. Divide the mixture among the prepared dishes. Stand them on a cooky sheet and bake for 18-20 minutes, or until a skewer inserted in the center comes out clean. Take the cakes out of the oven and let them cool in their dishes. Remove them from their dishes, right way up, and cool on a wire rack. Trim the cakes a little so that they are rounded. Brush the tops and sides of the cakes with the melted chocolate and let it harden slightly before rolling them in the cocoa powder. Dig a little hole in the top of each cake. Sprinkle the inside of each cake with some of the liqueur you have chosen. About 30 minutes before serving, whip the cream until thick and flavor it with frosting or vanilla sugar and more of the chosen liqueur. Fit a pastry bag with a small rosette tip and fill with the cream. Fill the little hole in each cake with the cream and place the truffle cake hole-side down on

a small plate. Shape a small rosette of cream to decorate each cake. Mix the Nouvelle Sauce with the almonds: spoon it around the bottom of each cake, and a little over the top.

Chocolate and Cherry Mousse (right) and **Chocolate Quiche (below).**

Tarte au Chocolat

PREPARATION TIME: 25 minutes, plus chilling

COOKING TIME: 45 minutes

OVEN TEMPERATURE: 375°F

MAKES: 1 tart, 10 inches in diameter

2 cups regular flour
1 tsp salt
¼ cup ground almonds
2½ tblsp fine sugar
10 tblsp unsalted butter
1 egg yolk

Filling
1 cup heavy cream
2 tblsp brandy
7oz semi-sweet chocolate, chopped or grated
2 egg whites, beaten
¼ cup fine sugar

Topping
1¼ cups heavy cream
2 tblsp fine white sugar
Praline (see recipe) or grated chocolate

Grease and line a 10 inch quiche pan with wax paper. Sieve together the flour and salt and add the almonds and sugar; make a well in the center. Add the butter and egg yolk. Mix all the ingredients together, using the fingertips, to form a dough. Shape the dough into a ball and wrap in foil or plastic wrap. Chill for 1 hour. Roll the dough out on a floured work surface to about ⅛-¼ inch thick. Use the dough to line the prepared quiche pan. Cover with wax paper and weight it down with rice or beans. Bake "blind" for 10-15 minutes until it begins to turn pale golden. Remove the paper and beans and bake for a further 15 minutes. Leave the pastry case to cool in its pan. To make the filling: put the cream and brandy into a saucepan and bring just to the boil. Add the chocolate and stir until the mixture is thick and smooth. Leave to cool for at least 1 hour. Beat until fluffy. Beat the egg whites until stiff but not dry, adding the sugar slowly. Fold the meringue into the chocolate mixture. Remove the pastry case from its pan and fill it with the chocolate mixture. For the topping: beat the cream with the sugar until it is light and fluffy, and then spread it over the chocolate filling. Decorate with crushed praline or chocolate.

Chocolate Honeycomb

PREPARATION TIME: 20 minutes, plus chilling

SERVES: 4-6 people

½oz gelatin
3 eggs, separated
¼ cup sugar
1¾ cups milk
3oz semi-sweet chocolate, grated
Vanilla essence

Put the gelatin, sugar and egg yolks into a basin and beat until creamy. Heat the milk in a small saucepan; add the grated chocolate and stir until dissolved. Pour the chocolate milk over the beaten egg yolk and gelatin mixture; put the bowl over a pan of gently simmering water and stir continuously until the mixture is thick. Leave the mixture to cool. Add a few drops of vanilla essence to the thickened chocolate mixture. Beat the egg whites until stiff but not dry and fold in. Turn the mixture into a dampened mold and chill until set. Unmold carefully before serving.

Marbled Rum Cream Pie

PREPARATION TIME: 35 minutes, plus chilling

COOKING TIME: 10 minutes

SERVES: 6-8 people

1 cup sugar
A pinch of salt
5 tblsp water
1¼ tblsp gelatin
2 eggs, separated
¾ cup milk
5 tblsp dark rum
12oz semi-sweet chocolate, finely chopped
1 cup heavy cream
1 tsp vanilla essence
1 baked sweet shortcrust pastry pie case, 9 inches in diameter

Mix ¼ cup of the sugar with the salt, water and gelatin in a small, heatproof bowl; stand over a pan of simmering water and stir until the gelatin has dissolved. Remove the bowl from the heat and beat in the egg yolks, milk and rum. Return to the heat, and continue to beat until the mixture has thickened slightly. Remove from the heat and stir in

the chocolate until it has melted. Chill until thickened but not set. Beat the egg whites until stiff but not dry and gradually beat in ½ cup of the remaining sugar. Fold the meringue mixture into the chilled chocolate mixture. Whip the cream with the remaining sugar and vanilla essence until thick. Pile alternate spoons of cream and chocolate mixture into the cold cooked pastry pie case. Cut through the layers with a knife, to give a marbled effect. Chill well until firm.

Sherry Cream Pie

PREPARATION TIME: 30 minutes, plus chilling time

COOKING TIME: 35 minutes

OVEN TEMPERATURE: 375°F

MAKES: 1 pie, 8 inches in diameter

1¼ cups flour
¼ cup sugar
⅓ cup butter
1 egg yolk

Filling
8oz semi-sweet dark chocolate, chopped or grated
4 tblsp medium sherry
1 tsp gelatin
4 eggs, separated

To Decorate
2oz semi-sweet chocolate, melted
⅔ cup heavy cream
1 tblsp sherry

Put the flour and the sugar into a bowl; add the butter, cut into small pieces, and the egg yolk. Knead to a smooth dough. Wrap the dough and chill for 30 minutes. Lightly flour the work surface and roll out the dough; use to line a 8 inch loose-bottomed pie pan. Prick the base of the pan with a fork. Line with wax paper and baking beans. Bake for 15 minutes; remove the paper and beans and bake for a further 15 minutes. Remove the pastry case from the pan and cool on a serving plate or platter. Put the chocolate into a small, heavy-based saucepan with the sherry and 2½ tblsp cold water. Sprinkle the gelatin over the top and stir over a low heat until the gelatin has dissolved. Beat the egg yolks into the sauce, one at a time, and cool the mixture. Whisk the egg whites until stiff but not dry and then fold it into the sauce. Pour the mixture into the prepared pastry case and

chill until set. Melt the chocolate. Lightly whip the heavy cream. Divide the cream in half; stir the sherry into one half, and the chocolate into the other. Fit two pastry bags with star tips and fill each bag with a different cream. Decorate the top of the pie with alternate stars of the different creams.

Steamed Chocolate Pud

PREPARATION TIME: 25 minutes

COOKING TIME: 1¾-2 hours

SERVES: 6 people

1 cup sugar
1 cup butter
4 eggs, beaten
1½ cups regular flour
6 tblsp cocoa powder
2½ tblsp rum

Butter a 2½ pint pudding basin. Beat the sugar and butter together until light and fluffy. Add the eggs gradually, beating well after each addition. Fold in the sieved flour, cocoa and the rum and mix well. Turn the mixture into the greased pudding basin. Cover the top with a double thickness of wax paper or foil, making a pleat in the top to give room for the pudding to rise. Tie round with string. Steam for 1¾-2 hours until well risen and spongy to the touch. Unmold the

pudding and serve hot with a sauce of your choice.

Facing page: Marbled Rum Cream Pie (top) and Chocolate Honeycomb (bottom).

This page: Steamed Chocolate Pud (top) and Chocolate Rum Fool (bottom).

COOKING WITH CHOCOLATE

Fruits and Fantasies

Chocolate Dipped Pineapple with Melba Sauce

PREPARATION TIME: 40 minutes, plus chilling

SERVES: 6-8 people

1 good sized fresh pineapple
Rum
½ cup granulated sugar
1lb raspberries
6oz unsweetened chocolate, chopped or grated

Peel and slice the pineapple into rings, ½ inch thick. Sprinkle the slices first with the rum, and then with a little sugar. Cover and chill for at least one hour. Puree the raspberries and sieve them to remove the seeds. Sweeten with a little sugar to taste and add a little rum. Chill until needed. Melt the chocolate in a bowl over a saucepan of hot water. Remove the pineapple from the refrigerator and pat dry with absorbent paper. Cover a cooky sheet with waxed paper and partially dip each ring of pineapple into the melted chocolate. Leave on the waxed paper to harden (you can put them in the refrigerator). Put each pineapple ring onto an individual plate and pour a pool of melba sauce over just before serving.

Chocolate Souffle with Sour Cherries

PREPARATION TIME: 40 minutes

COOKING TIME: 10-12 minutes

OVEN TEMPERATURE: 400°F

SERVES: 6 people

½ cup sugar
3 eggs, separated
Vanilla essence
Grated rind of half a lemon
5 egg whites
1¼ tsp instant mashed potato powder
Melted butter for greasing
Sugar to dust
1¼ tsp arrowroot
13oz can sour cherries

Beat 2 tblsp of the sugar with the egg yolks, vanilla essence and

lemon rind. Beat the egg whites with the remaining sugar until stiff but not dry; beat in the potato powder. Fold the snowy egg whites into the egg yolk mixture. Brush the surface of a metal serving dish with melted butter and sprinkle with a little sugar. Put ¾ of the souffle mixture into the dish with a spatula and smooth it out into a

boat shape, hollowing out the middle. Fit a pastry bag with a star tip and fill with the remaining souffle mixture. Shape a border around the top and bottom of the boat. Bake in the oven for 10-12 minutes. Drain the canned cherries and keep the juice. Mix the juice with the arrowroot and stir over a low heat until it thickens. Add

This page: Locksmiths Lads (top) and Banana Fritters with Chocolate Rum Sauce (bottom).

Facing page: Chocolate Souffle with Sour Cherries (top) and Chocolate Dipped Pineapple with Melba Sauce (bottom).

most of the cherries. Fill the top of the souffle with the reserved cherries. Serve the cherry sauce separately. Note: the metal of the dish will conduct the heat evenly through the souffle.

Chocolate Waffles and Fruit Kebabs

PREPARATION TIME: 15 minutes

COOKING TIME: 15 minutes

SERVES: 4 people

2oz semi-sweet chocolate, chopped or grated
¼ cup water
⅓ cup unsalted butter
2 eggs
6-7 tblsp sugar
1½ cups regular flour
2½ tsp baking powder
½ cup milk
¾ cup chopped walnuts
Whipped cream or ice cream to serve

Stir the chocolate and water together in a small, heavy-based saucepan until the chocolate melts. Remove the pan from the heat when the chocolate forms a paste. Beat the butter into the melted chocolate, and then add the eggs and the sugar. Sieve the flour and baking powder onto a sheet of wax paper. Add the sieved flour and milk alternately to the chocolate mixture. Stir in the walnuts. Pour the batter into a hot, oiled waffle iron. Bring the cover down and cook for 2-3 minutes on either side. Serve with whipped cream, ice cream, and cocktail sticks threaded with pieces of fresh fruit.

Banana Fritters with Chocolate Rum Sauce

PREPARATION TIME: 20 minutes, plus standing time

COOKING TIME: 14-15 minutes

SERVES: 6 people

Almost any kind of fruit can be battered, and the accompanying sauces that can be used range from fruit purees to liqueured sauces, like the rum sauce in this recipe.

1¼ cups flour
⅔ cup white wine
2 eggs, separated
½oz drinking chocolate
1 tblsp sugar
6 bananas
Oil for deep frying
Confectioner's sugar for dusting

Sauce

A stick of butter
½ cup sugar
A pinch of salt
2½ tblsp dark rum
6 tblsp cocoa powder
⅔ cup heavy cream
1¼ tsp vanilla essence

Sieve the flour into a bowl and beat in the wine, egg yolks and drinking chocolate. Beat until smooth and let the batter stand for 15 minutes. Beat the egg whites and sugar until fluffy. Fold the fluffy egg whites into the batter. Slice the bananas into bite-sized pieces. Put each piece onto a fork and dip into the batter. Lower immediately into the hot oil, frying until the batter is golden brown. Lift out of the oil with a slotted spoon and leave to drain on a piece of absorbent paper. Dust with confectioner's sugar and serve with the sauce. To make the sauce: melt the butter in a small saucepan. Stir in the sugar, salt, rum and cocoa powder. Mix well over a low heat. Add the cream and bring to the boil. Simmer very gently for 5 minutes. Remove from the heat and add the vanilla essence. Note: you can use fresh butter to fry the fritters and this will give a very rich flavor, unlike lard or vegetable oil, which are usually well refined, and will not alter the natural flavor of the ingredients. The crisper the better, but be careful not to burn the fritters. You may have a tempura set which can be used when entertaining informally, or a thermostatically controlled deep fat fryer which will give you perfect results.

Locksmiths Lads
Beignets De Prunes Au Chocolat

PREPARATION TIME: 35 minutes

COOKING TIME: about 4 minutes

SERVES: 4 people

1¼ cups regular flour
2 eggs, separated
⅔ cup white wine
A pinch of salt
2½ tblsp cooking oil
2 tblsp sugar
16 large tenderized prunes
16 blanched almonds
Oil for deep frying
2oz grated chocolate
Confectioner's sugar to dust

Zabaione Sauce
3 egg yolks
1 whole egg
9 tblsp sugar
7½ tblsp marsala

Sieve the flour into a mixing bowl; make a well in the center and pour in the egg yolks, white wine, salt and the oil. Mix using a wire whisk, and leave the batter to stand for 20 minutes. Beat the egg whites until stiff and fold in the sugar. Fold the egg whites into the batter. Carefully remove the stone from each prune and replace it with an almond. Spike the prunes with a fork and dip them into the batter. Fry the coated prunes in hot oil until they are golden brown; remove and drain them on absorbent paper. Scatter the grated chocolate over the prunes when they are nearly cold. Dust with confectioner's sugar. To make the sauce: cream the egg yolks, whole egg and sugar together in a heatproof bowl over a saucepan of simmering water. Add the marsala to the mixture and beat it with a wire whisk until it doubles in volume, and is foamy. Serve immediately with the Locksmiths Lads.

Strawberry Shortcake

PREPARATION TIME: 15 minutes

COOKING TIME: 7-10 minutes

OVEN TEMPERATURE: 450°F

SERVES: 6 people

A wonderful dessert for the summer, with a luxurious topping.

2 cups regular flour
2½ tsp baking powder
¼ cup butter
2 tblsp sugar
1 egg, lightly beaten
Milk
12oz strawberries, hulled
1¼ cups heavy cream
1 recipe Chocolate Fudge Sauce (see recipe)

Chocolate Waffles and Fruit Kebabs (top right) and Strawberry Shortcake (right).

Sieve the flour and baking powder into a mixing bowl. Cut the butter into the mixture until it resembles breadcrumbs. Stir in the sugar. Add the beaten egg, and enough milk to bind the mixture into a stiff scone dough. Roll out the dough to a thickness of approximately ½ inch and cut out two circles. Put the circles of dough onto greased cooky sheets. Bake for 10 minutes (the shortcakes should be pale golden). Cool on a wire rack. Slice 8oz of the strawberries and whip the cream. Place one circle of the shortcake on a plate. Spoon half of the cream onto it and top with the sliced strawberries. Add a little more cream and place the second shortcake on top. Top the shortcake with spoonfuls of the remaining cream and the remaining strawberries. Drizzle over a little chocolate fudge sauce. Serve the remaining sauce separately.

Strawberry Fondue

PREPARATION TIME:	50 minutes
COOKING TIME:	20 minutes
SERVES:	6 people

Stand
*Oasis cone (from a florist) 12-15
   inches high
Kitchen foil
Dress net
Ribbon bows*

*2lb large strawberries, washed and
   hulled
Cocktail sticks*

Vanilla Fondue
*12oz white chocolate, grated
⅓ cup evaporated milk
¼ tsp vanilla essence*

Grand Marnier Fondue
*6oz semi-sweet chocolate, grated
6oz sweet chocolate, grated
¾ + 2 tblsp cup heavy cream
2½ tblsp Grand Marnier*

To make the stand: cover the oasis with kitchen foil and then cover it with the dress net (use a color that will go with the strawberries and with your table decoration). Place ribbon bows at random, fixing them into the oasis. Stick the strawberries into the stand, using cocktail sticks, so that they almost cover the cone completely. To make the vanilla fondue: melt the white chocolate with ⅔ of the evaporated milk in a pan over a low heat. Add the vanilla essence and then add the remaining evaporated milk as required. (The fondue should coat the back of a spoon.) To make the Grand Marnier fondue: melt together the chocolates and then add the cream. Stir well and remove from the heat. Finally add the liqueur. Pour the two fondues into separate warmed bowls. Keep these on a warming tray, or on a fondue tray, or on stands with night light candles beneath. Your guests can then pick strawberries and dip them into the fondues.

Chocolate Apricot Horns

PREPARATION TIME:	15 minutes
COOKING TIME:	15-20 minutes
OVEN TEMPERATURE:	425°F
MAKES:	10

*8oz puff pastry
Beaten egg to glaze
4oz semi-sweet chocolate
1 tblsp butter
2½ tblsp brandy
¾ cup apricot puree
¾ cup heavy cream, whipped*

To Decorate
Chocolate curls

Roll out the pastry into a rectangle about 10x13 inches and trim the edges. Cut into strips 1 inch wide. Dampen one long edge of each strip with water and wind round a metal cornet mold (start at the point and overlap the dampened edge as you go). Put the horns on a lightly dampened cooky sheet and chill for 15 minutes. Brush the horns with beaten egg and bake for 15-20 minutes until golden brown. Leave for 5 minutes, before carefully removing the molds; cool the pastry horns on a wire rack. Melt the chocolate with the butter on a plate, over a pan of hot water; dip each of the horns into the chocolate. Mix the brandy with the apricot puree and spoon a little into each of the horns. Fit a star tip to a pastry bag and fill the pastry bag with the whipped cream. Push the cream into the horns. Decorate with chocolate curls.

Profiteroles Vine

PREPARATION TIME:	30 minutes, plus cooling
COOKING TIME:	25-30 minutes
OVEN TEMPERATURE:	400°F
SERVES:	4-6 people

Choux Pastry
*⅔ cup water
¼ cup butter
10 tblsp flour, sieved
2 eggs, beaten*

Filling
*1¼ cups cold chocolate vanilla sauce
   (English chocolate custard)
⅔ cup heavy cream, whipped
6oz semi-sweet chocolate, melted
Chocolate Butter Sauce (see recipe)*

For the pastry: heat the water and butter in a small saucepan until the butter melts. Bring to the boil; remove the pan from the heat and beat in the flour. Beat with a wooden spoon until it leaves the sides of the pan clean. Cool the mixture slightly, and gradually beat in the eggs, beating between each addition. (The mixture should be smooth and glossy.) Fill a pastry bag, fitted with a large, plain tip, with the choux pastry. Shape 20 even-sized balls onto two dampened cooky sheets. Bake in a pre-heated oven for 20-25 minutes, until well risen. Split each of the choux balls and let the steam escape; return to the oven for a further 2 minutes. To make the filling: follow a recipe for English custard and add 1¼ tblsp of cocoa. Stir the cream into the sauce, making sure that there are no lumps (beat if necessary). Fill a large pastry bag, fitted with a plain tip, with the cream sauce and fill the choux buns. To decorate and serve: coat a large leaf with melted chocolate; pipe a few curls and a stem onto a sheet of silicone paper. Leave them to set; gently peel off the paper and the leaf. Arrange the profiteroles to look like a bunch of grapes on a large serving tray or dish; add the chocolate leaf, stem and curls. Finally pour over the chocolate sauce.

This page: Strawberry Fondue (with Grand Marnier Fondue).

Facing page: Profiteroles Vine (top) and Chocolate Apricot Horns (bottom).

COOKING WITH CHOCOLATE
Frozen Desserts

Mocha Ice Cream

PREPARATION TIME: 25 minutes,
plus freezing

SERVES: 6 people

2½ tblsp instant coffee granules
¼ cup butter
½ cup soft brown sugar
5 tblsp cocoa powder
6 tblsp water
1¾ cups canned evaporated milk,
  chilled

Put the coffee, butter, sugar, cocoa
and water into a saucepan, and
heat gently. Stir the mixture until
melted, and bring it to the boil.
Cool. Beat the chilled evaporated
milk in a bowl, until it is thick and
frothy. Mix it into the cooled
mixture, beating until it is well
blended. Turn the mixture into a
freezer container and freeze
uncovered until slushy. Beat the ice
cream well and re-freeze until firm.

Rum Ice Cream Gateau

PREPARATION TIME: 30 minutes,
plus freezing

COOKING TIME: 1 hour

OVEN TEMPERATURE: 300°F

SERVES: 6-8 people

Oil for greasing
1 cup sugar
3 egg whites
1¼ tblsp instant coffee
2½ tblsp boiling water
1¾ cups heavy cream
2½ tblsp dark rum
⅔ cup chocolate ice cream

Lightly oil a baking sheet and line
the base of a 7 inch round, loose-
bottomed cake pan with greased
wax paper. Beat ¼ cup of the sugar
into the egg whites and continue to
beat until stiff. Add the remaining
sugar and beat until it peaks. Fill a
pastry bag, fitted with a star tip,
with the meringue mixture. Shape
small rosettes onto the cooky
sheet, keeping them well apart.
Bake them in a pre-heated oven for
1 hour; leave in the oven for a
further 20 minutes, with the oven
turned off. Remove the meringues

from the oven and allow them to
cool. Mix the coffee with the water
in a small bowl. Beat the cream
until thick; fold in all but 4 of the
meringues. Add the coffee and the
rum, taking care not to crush the
meringues. Use the mixture to fill
the prepared cake pan. Cover and
freeze until firm. Soften the ice
cream. When the gateau is hard
enough, remove it from the pan.

Beat the ice cream and use it to fill
a pastry bag fitted with a ½ inch
star tip. Quickly shape rosettes on
top of the gateau. Return the
gateau to the freezer and leave until
firm. Put the reserved meringues in
the center of the gateau.
Refrigerate for 10 minutes before
serving.

**This page: Mocha Ice Cream
(top) and Rum Ice Cream
Gateau (bottom).**

**Facing page: Chocolate Chip Ice
Cream (top) and Chocolate Ice
Box Cake (bottom).**

Chocolate Ice Cream

PREPARATION TIME: 1 hour
40 minutes, plus freezing time

COOKING TIME: 15-20 minutes

SERVES: 8 people

4oz semi-sweet chocolate, chopped or
    grated
2½ cups milk
7 egg yolks
½ cup sugar

Put the chopped chocolate into a saucepan with a little milk. Stir over a low heat until the chocolate melts and forms a smooth paste. Add the remaining milk. Beat the egg yolks and sugar together until thick and light. Beat into the chocolate milk. Beat continuously over a low heat until thick. Pour the mixture into a bowl and stand over ice. (If you do not have a lot of ice, chill in the refrigerator.) Either pour into an ice cream churn, and follow the manufacturer's instructions, or pour into ice trays and freeze for 30 minutes. Tip the par-frozen ice cream into a bowl and beat until smooth. Return to the freezer. Repeat this process every 30 minutes, until the ice cream is really thick. Freeze until ready to serve.

Nougat Ice Cream Cake

PREPARATION TIME: 40 minutes,
plus freezing

SERVES: 6-8 people

¼ cup ground hazelnuts
16 small wafer biscuits
15½oz can pineapple chunks, or
8oz crystallised pineapple
1¾ cups vanilla ice cream
1¾ cups chocolate ice cream
4oz semi-sweet chocolate, finely
    chopped
4oz nougat
1¾ cups heavy cream, whipped

Grease a 1lb loaf pan and sprinkle the inside with ground hazelnuts. Put 12 of the wafer biscuits around the sides and base of the pan. Drain the pineapple chunks (or chop the crystallised pineapple). Soften the ice creams by placing them in the refrigerator. Spoon the vanilla ice cream into the pan and smooth it down. Add the chopped chocolate to the chocolate ice cream, and ¾ of the chopped pineapple. Spoon this mixture on top of the vanilla ice cream. Chop the nougat into small pieces and sprinkle it on top of the chocolate ice cream. Cover the chocolate ice cream with the remaining 4 wafer biscuits. Freeze for 3-4 hours, until firm. Spoon or decorate the whipped cream over the unmolded ice cream cake. Decorate with the reserved pineapple. Serve cut into slices.

Chocolate Ice Box Cake

PREPARATION TIME: 1 hour,
plus freezing

COOKING TIME: 25-30 minutes

OVEN TEMPERATURE: 375°F

SERVES: 8 people

Melted butter for greasing
7 eggs, separated
6 tblsp vanilla sugar
6 tblsp regular flour
Pinch of salt
Superfine sugar

Filling
12oz semi-sweet chocolate, chopped
    or grated
2½ tblsp strong black coffee
¼ cup brandy
2 egg yolks
5 egg whites, stiffly beaten
½ cup heavy cream, lightly whipped

Frosting
⅔ cup heavy cream
5oz semi-sweet chocolate, chopped or
    grated

Grease and line two 9x12 inch jelly roll pans with wax paper. Brush the paper with melted butter and dust with flour. Beat the egg yolks and vanilla sugar together until thick and light; fold in the flour and salt. Beat the egg whites until stiff but not dry. Gently fold the beaten egg whites into the mixture. Divide the mixture between the two pans. Bake in a pre-heated oven for 15-20 minutes, or until golden. When the sponges are baked, spread two tea towels on a work surface and cover each one with a sheet of wax paper. Sprinkle with superfine sugar and turn the sponges out onto the sugared paper. Peel off the lining paper and leave the sponges to cool. Line the bottom of an 8 inch spring form cake pan with greased wax paper. Cut a circle of sponge from each rectangular sponge to fit the pan. Put one on top of the paper lining. Reserve the other. Cut three strips of sponge, 2 inches wide, to line the sides of the pan. Place in position. To make the filling: put the chocolate, coffee and brandy into a saucepan and stir over a low heat until the chocolate has melted. Leave to cool. Beat in the egg yolks, and then gently fold in the beaten egg whites, taking care not to over-mix. Finally, fold in the whipped heavy cream. Pour the mixture into the sponge-lined cake pan and put the remaining sponge circle on top as a lid. Cover the top of the pan with a plate 8 inches in diameter, weighted down lightly. Put the cake pan into the freezer for 2-3 hours, or chill in the refrigerator for at least 5 hours. To make the frosting: pour the cream into a pan and bring to the boil. Stir in the chocolate until it melts, and the mixture thickens. Carefully take the set cake out of its pan and pour frosting over it. Open freeze, or refrigerate, until the frosting has set.

Chocolate Chip Ice Cream

PREPARATION TIME: 30 minutes,
plus freezing time

COOKING TIME: 6-8 minutes

SERVES: 8 people

3½oz semi-sweet chocolate, chopped
    or grated

1¼ cups milk
3 egg yolks
3oz sugar
1¼ cups heavy cream, lightly
    whipped
2½oz finely chopped chocolate

Stir the chopped or grated chocolate into the milk in a small, heavy-based saucepan; stir over a gentle heat until the chocolate melts. Put the egg yolks into a bowl with the sugar and beat until thick and creamy. Add the chocolate milk and beat. Return the chocolate mixture to the saucepan and stir continuously over a moderate heat until the mixture is thick and will coat the back of a spoon. Strain the chocolate custard into a bowl and cool in the refrigerator. When quite cold, fold in the whipped cream. (If you are using a churn, pour in the mixture and follow the manufacturer's instructions, adding the chopped chocolate at the appropriate stage.) Pour into ice trays and freeze until the mixture begins to set around the edges. Pour into a bowl and beat. Stir in the chopped chocolate. Return the ice cream to the ice trays and freeze for 30 minutes. Repeat the beating and

Chocolate Ice Cream (above right) and Nougat Ice Cream Cake (right).

freezing method every 30 minutes,
until the ice cream is really thick.
Freeze until firm.

Luxury Lace Ice Cream

PREPARATION TIME: 50 minutes,
plus freezing

COOKING TIME: 6-8 minutes

SERVES: 6-8 people

1¼ cups light cream
5oz semi-sweet chocolate, chopped or
    grated
1¼ tsp instant coffee powder
4 egg yolks
½ cup sugar
1¼ cups heavy cream

To Decorate

4oz semi-sweet chocolate, chopped or grated

Put the light cream into a saucepan and heat gently. Add the chocolate and coffee powder and stir until the mixture is smooth, and the chocolate has melted. Beat the egg yolks and sugar until thick, pale and creamy. Continue beating, and slowly pour in the chocolate cream mixture. Return the mixture to the saucepan and stir it over a gentle heat until it reaches coating consistency. Remove from the heat and cool. Whip the cream lightly and fold it into the chocolate mixture. Pour the mixture into a shallow container and freeze it until firm. To make the chocolate lace decoration: put a large cake pan upside down. Smooth a piece of plastic wrap over alternate domed shapes. Melt the plain chocolate and use it to fill a wax pastry bag fitted with a writing tip. Decorate around the edge of each dome and then decorate parallel lines in every direction over the dome, joining up all the lines with circles. Repeat the pattern so that it is "double" in thickness. Chill the chocolate domes until set. Carefully lift them off the cake pan. Keep them chilled until you are ready to serve the ice cream. To serve: put a generous scoop of ice cream into each chocolate lace cup and top it with another cup.

Frozen Chocolate Soufflé

PREPARATION TIME: 30 minutes, plus freezing time

COOKING TIME: 15 minutes

SERVES: 6-8 people

This delicate and light chocolate dessert makes an unusual end to a meal.

¼ cup sugar
3 eggs, separated
3½ oz semi-sweet chocolate, melted and cooled
1½ cups heavy cream, lightly whipped

To Decorate

Chocolate scrolls
Confectioner's sugar

Tie a collar of greased wax paper around a 1¼ pint soufflé dish,

making sure that it extends at least 2 inches above the rim of the dish. Beat the sugar and egg yolks in a bowl over a pan of simmering water, until thick and light. The mixture should fall off the whisk in ribbons). Remove from the heat and beat in the melted chocolate. Beat until the mixture has cooled. Fold the lightly whipped cream into the chocolate mixture. Beat the egg whites until stiff but not dry; fold lightly into the mixture. Pour the mixture into the prepared soufflé dish. Freeze for at least 4 hours. Just before serving, remove the paper collar by gently easing it off. Decorate the top with chocolate scrolls and dust lightly with confectioner's sugar.

Minted Chocolate Chip Gateau

PREPARATION TIME: 25 minutes, plus freezing

COOKING TIME: 20 minutes

OVEN TEMPERATURE: 400°F

SERVES: 6 people

3 large eggs
⅓ cup sugar
¾ cup regular flour, sieved
1 tsp baking powder
Filling
6 scoops chocolate chip ice cream
To decorate
1 box chocolate mint sticks

To make the sponge: beat the eggs and sugar together until they are thick and light in color. Fold the sieved flour lightly but thoroughly into the mixture. Put into a greased and lined shallow loaf pan. Bake in the oven for 20 minutes. Turn out and cool. Slice the cake through into layers; sandwich together with 4 scoops of the ice cream. Spread the remaining ice cream over the sides of the cake, omitting the top; stick on the chocolate mint sticks (you may have to use a piece of string or ribbon to hold them in position). Freeze the cake until firm. Cut the cake into slices to serve.

Iced Lake

PREPARATION TIME: 35 minutes, plus freezing

COOKING TIME: 10-15 minutes

OVEN TEMPERATURE: 350°F

SERVES: 6 people

Lemon Ice Cream

Grated rind of 2 lemons
Juice of 3 lemons
¾ cup sugar
1¼ cups heavy cream
1¼ cups milk

Chocolate Cookies

¼ cup butter
¼ cup sugar
1 egg yolk
½ cup regular flour
¼ cup rice flour
1¼ tsp cocoa powder

To Serve

Nouvelle Chocolate Sauce (see recipe)

To make the ice cream: put the lemon rind, juice and sugar into a bowl and stir well. Add the cream and beat until thick. Beat in the milk slowly. Pour the mixture into a large freezer container and freeze it until slushy. Tip the ice cream into a bowl and beat it until smooth. Re-freeze in its container until firm. To make the cookies: lightly grease a cooky sheet. Cream the butter and sugar together. Add the egg yolk, beat the mixture well. Add the regular flour, rice flour and cocoa and work them well into the mixture. Lightly flour the work surface and roll out the dough. Cut out shapes with animal cutters. Place on a cooky sheet. Bake for 10-15 minutes. Cool on a wire rack. To serve: place scoops of ice cream onto small serving plates and top each one with an animal biscuit. Spoon Nouvelle Chocolate Sauce around each portion.

This page: Iced Lake (top) and Minted Chocolate Chip Gateau (bottom).

Facing page: Frozen Chocolate Soufflé (top) and Luxury Lace Ice Cream (bottom).

COOKING WITH CHOCOLATE
Cookies and Confections

Chocolate Ravioli

PREPARATION TIME: 30 minutes, plus chilling

MAKES: 25 pieces

1 cup roasted hazelnuts
1¼ tblsp granulated sugar
2½ tblsp melted butter
2oz semi-sweet chocolate melted
1¼ tblsp brandy
9oz white chocolate, melted

Line a square cooky sheet with a rim of tinfoil, making sure that it is smooth and even, with neat corners. Crush the hazelnuts and mix them with the sugar and butter. Stir in the melted dark chocolate and brandy to form a paste. Form into 25 small balls and arrange them in rows over the bottom of the cooky sheet, pressing the balls flat. Pour the melted white chocolate evenly over the small balls so as to cover them completely. Place the tray in the refrigerator until firm. Cut the ravioli into rows with a knife or ravioli cutter and then separate each one.

Chocolate Meringues

PREPARATION TIME: 35 minutes

COOKING TIME: 15-20 minutes

OVEN TEMPERATURE: 350°F

MAKES: about 8

2 egg whites
¾ cup confectioner's sugar, sieved
½ cup nuts

Filling
4oz semi-sweet chocolate, chopped or grated
5 tblsp water
1¼ tblsp strong black coffee
¼ cup butter
2 egg yolks
1¼ tblsp dark rum

Beat the egg whites until stiff and dry. Add the confectioner's sugar a spoonful at a time and continue to beat until very thick. Carefully fold in the chopped nuts; spoon or shape small mounds onto a cooky sheet lined with silicone paper.

Bake for 15-20 minutes. Leave to cool slightly and then transfer onto a wire rack. Gently spoon out a little meringue from the underside of each of the meringues. For the filling: melt the chocolate and stir in the coffee and water; boil the mixture, stirring continuously for 2 minutes. Remove the pan from the heat and allow the mixture to cool; beat the butter into the cooled mixture and blend in the egg yolks and the rum. Refrigerate until the mixture thickens. When cool, spoon it into a pastry bag fitted with a plain tip, and push the filling into the meringues. Sandwich them together in pairs.

This page: Toffee Bars (top left), Chocolate Fudge (top right) and Chocolate Ravioli (bottom).

Facing page: Florentines (top) and Chocolate Meringue Biscuits (bottom).

Chocolate Eggs

PREPARATION TIME: 50 minutes
COOKING TIME: 12-15 minutes
MAKES: 6

6 small eggs
Food coloring
¾ cup heavy cream
10 oz semi-sweet or sweet chocolate, melted
5 tblsp white rum
Sticking plaster or tape

Using a needle, make a small hole in one end of each egg; carefully make a larger hole in the other end. Blow the egg contents out into a bowl. Pour running water into the egg shells and shake them well until clean. Put a little food coloring of your choice into a saucepan of water and boil the egg shells until they take on the color. Dry the shells in a low oven for 5 minutes. Boil the cream and stir it into the melted chocolate. Stir in the rum. Put a small piece of plaster over the smallest hole in each egg shell; fill a pastry bag fitted with a plain tip with the chocolate cream. Fit the tip gently into the egg shell and push in the chocolate cream until full. Clean off any chocolate on the shell and chill. Remove the plasters. These eggs are fun to give as gifts, or use uncolored, as a joke for a chocolate breakfast. Note: stand the eggs in their box to make filling and chilling easier.

Artichoke

PREPARATION TIME: 1 hour 30 minutes, plus setting overnight
MAKES: 1 artichoke, serving 8-10 people

After dinner mints with a difference.

1lb semi-sweet chocolate, chopped or grated
2½ tblsp oil
Few drops of peppermint oil
1 globe artichoke

To Make the Artichoke

2 tblsp sugar
2 tblsp butter
2½ tblsp water
⅓ cup confectioner's sugar, sieved
3 tblsp cocoa powder
A piece of cake the size of the artichoke

Artichoke (above), Chocolate Eggs (right) and Truffles (far right).

Melt the semi-sweet chocolate with the oil and stir occasionally until melted. Cool this mixture slightly and stir in the peppermint oil. Take the leaves off the artichoke; dip the front of each leaf into the melted chocolate and lay them on silicone paper. Leave overnight to set before peeling off the artichoke leaves. To make the frosting: dissolve the sugar in the butter and water over a low heat; remove from the heat and stir in the frosting sugar and the cocoa powder. Cut the cake into a pyramid shape and cover it with some of the cooled frosting. Stick the chocolate artichoke leaves around the cake, in the same order as the real artichoke was assembled. You will need to use some of the frosting to help them to stick. Serve with the peppermint creams at the end of the meal.

Chocolate Fudge

PREPARATION TIME: 35 minutes
COOKING TIME: 10-15 minutes
MAKES: about 1½lbs

This fudge is much easier to make if you have a sugar thermometer, but do not worry if one is not available; the temperature of the fudge can be tested without one.

2 tblsp butter
8oz semi-sweet chocolate, melted
1 cup granulated sugar
1¾ cups canned evaporated milk

To Decorate
3 tblsp cocoa powder or drinking chocolate

If you have a sugar thermometer put it in your saucepan before you start the fudge. Heat the butter, sugar and evaporated milk in the saucepan, stirring continuously, until the sugar has dissolved. Boil the mixture until the thermometer reads 240°F (if you do not have a thermometer, take out a little of the fudge with a small spoon and drop it into a jug of cold water; if it stays in a ball it is ready). Remove the saucepan from the heat and plunge the bottom of the pan into cold water to stop mixture from cooking. After a few minutes beat the fudge until it is thick and grainy. Beat in the melted chocolate. Butter a shallow 12x7 inch cake pan and pour in the fudge. Cool until set. Cut the fudge into squares. Dust the fudge in either cocoa powder or drinking chocolate.

Truffles

PREPARATION TIME: 15 minutes
MAKES: about 10

4oz semi-sweet chocolate, chopped or grated
1¼ tblsp dark rum
2 tblsp unsalted butter
1 egg yolk
½ cup ground almonds
½ cup cake crumbs
2oz chocolate vermicelli

Melt the chocolate with the rum in a small bowl over a saucepan of hot water. Beat in the butter and egg yolk and remove the mixture from

the heat. Stir in the ground almonds and cake crumbs to make a smooth paste. Divide into balls and roll them in the vermicelli until evenly coated.

Dipped Fruit

PREPARATION TIME:	10 minutes, plus drying
MAKES:	1½lb dipped fruit

1½lb prepared fruit (grapes, strawberries, etc.)
Melted plain chocolate

Wash the fruits, but leave the stems on them if possible. Holding each piece of fruit by the stem, dip into the melted chocolate, leaving the top section uncovered. Allow any excess to run off and leave to set on a tray lined with silicone paper.

Chocolate Meringue Cookies

PREPARATION TIME:	20 minutes
COOKING TIME:	15-20 minutes
OVEN TEMPERATURE:	350°F
MAKES:	about 10

½ cup butter or margarine
¼ cup sugar
1 egg yolk
¼ cup ground almonds
1½ cups regular flour

Filling
4oz semi-sweet chocolate
1 tblsp butter

Meringue Topping
For meringue ingredients see
Chocolate Meringues recipe

Grease a cooky sheet and line with silicone paper. Cream the butter or margarine and sugar together; add the egg yolk and beat well. Add the ground almonds and flour and mix well. Knead the mixture and roll it out thinly. Cut into rounds using a 2½ inch cutter. Place the rounds on the prepared cooky sheet and bake for 15-20 minutes. Make up the meringue mixture. Shape into 1 inch swirls on a cooky sheet lined with silicone paper. Follow the baking instructions for chocolate meringues. When cool, gently ease them off the cooky sheet. To make up the filling: melt the chocolate with the butter over a gentle heat.

Mix well and spread over the top of each of the almond cookies. Top each one with a meringue and leave until set.

Florentines

PREPARATION TIME:	15 minutes
COOKING TIME:	8-10 minutes
OVEN TEMPERATURE:	350°F
MAKES:	12

⅓ cup butter
⅓ cup corn syrup
⅔ cup flaked almonds, chopped
¼ cup regular flour
2 tblsp chopped mixed peel
4 tblsp candied cherries, chopped
1¼ tsp lemon juice
4oz semi-sweet chocolate, chopped or grated

Line a cooky sheet with silicone paper. Melt the butter and syrup together in a small saucepan. Stir in the almonds, flour, mixed peel, cherries and lemon juice. Put small spoonfuls of the mixture onto the prepared cooky sheet. Keep them well apart and flatten with a fork. Bake in a pre-heated oven for 8-10 minutes. Remove the Florentines carefully to a wire rack to cool. Melt the chocolate in a bowl over a pan of hot water. Spread over the flat side of each Florentine. Place the cookies chocolate sides uppermost, and mark the liquid chocolate with wavy lines, using a fork. Leave until set.

Toffee Bars

PREPARATION TIME:	40 minutes
COOKING TIME:	25-30 minutes
OVEN TEMPERATURE:	350°F
MAKES:	15 bars

Cooky Base
½ cup butter
¼ cup sugar
1½ cups regular flour, sieved

Toffee Caramel
½ cup butter or margarine
¼ cup sugar
2½ tblsp golden syrup
⅔ cup condensed milk

Chocolate Topping
4oz semi-sweet chocolate
1 tblsp butter

For the cooky base: cream the butter and sugar together until light and fluffy. Add the flour and knead until smooth. Press the dough into a greased, 8 inch square shallow cake pan, and prick with a fork. Bake in a pre-heated oven for 25-30 minutes. Cool. Put the ingredients for the toffee caramel into a small saucepan and stir until dissolved; bring slowly to the boil, and cook stirring for 5-7 minutes. Cool slightly and then spread over the cooky base. Leave to set. For the topping: melt the chocolate with the butter over a low heat; spread it carefully over the toffee. Leave it to set and cut into fingers.

Chocolate Muesli

PREPARATION TIME:	25 minutes
COOKING TIME:	10-12 minutes
OVEN TEMPERATURE:	375°F
MAKES:	about 12

½ cup margarine or butter
½ cup sugar
1 egg, beaten
Few drops vanilla essence
1 cup regular flour, sieved
½ tsp bicarbonate of soda
¼ cup rolled oats
⅓ cup cocoa powder

Chocolate Coating
4oz semi-sweet chocolate, chopped or grated
1 tblsp butter

Beat the margarine or butter with the sugar until light and fluffy. Beat in the egg, adding the essence, flour and bicarbonate of soda. Stir in the oats and the cocoa powder. Spread the mixture onto a lightly greased cooky sheet, and mark out into bars with a knife. Bake for 10-12 minutes until lightly browned. Re-mark with a sharp knife and cool on a wire rack. To make the chocolate coating: melt the chocolate and butter together and pour evenly over the bars. Separate the bars when set.

This page: **Chocolate Meringues (top)** and **Dipped Fruit (bottom)**.

Facing page: **Praline Orange Log (top), Chocolate Muesli (center right)** and **Mint Creams (bottom left)**.

Chocolate Chip Cookies

PREPARATION TIME: 15 minutes, plus chilling

COOKING TIME: 10-12 minutes

OVEN TEMPERATURE: 350°F

MAKES: about 30

2 cups regular flour
Pinch of salt
10 tblsp butter
½ cup sugar
1 egg, lightly beaten
2oz semi-sweet chocolate, grated

Sieve the flour and salt into a mixing bowl. Cut the butter into the flour and cut in until the mixture looks like breadcrumbs. Stir the sugar into the mixture. Add the egg and mix to a stiff dough. Knead the grated chocolate into the dough. Chill the dough for 30 minutes. Roll out the dough and cut into 2 inch rounds with a plain cutter. Grease a cooky sheet and put the rounds on it, placing them well apart. Prick the rounds with a fork. Bake in a pre-heated oven for 10-12 minutes until golden. Cool on a wire rack.

Chocolate Crunch

PREPARATION TIME: 20 minutes, plus chilling

MAKES: 1 1lb loaf

4oz chocolate shortbread finger cookies
¼ cup whole hazelnuts
½ cup firm margarine
⅓ cup sugar
2½ tblsp cocoa powder
1 egg, beaten
7 tblsp white raisins

To Decorate
Confectioner's sugar

Line a 1lb loaf pan with plastic wrap. Chop up the shortbread fingers. Brown the hazelnuts and rub off the skins. Put the margarine and sugar into a small saucepan and stir over a low heat until the sugar dissolves. Stir the cocoa into the mixture, and remove from the heat. Stir in the egg, hazelnuts, white raisins and chopped cookies. Pour the mixture into the lined pan and smooth it level. Chill until set. Dust with confectioner's sugar and serve cut in slices.

Chocolate Palmiers

PREPARATION TIME: 30 minutes

COOKING TIME: 12-15 minutes

OVEN TEMPERATURE: 425°F

MAKES: 6

8oz puff pastry
Superfine sugar
3oz semi-sweet chocolate, coarsely grated

To decorate
¾ cup heavy cream, whipped
2oz strawberries, halved
Confectioners sugar for dusting

Roll out the pastry on a well-sugared surface to a rectangle measuring approximately 12x10 inches. Sprinkle with the chocolate and press down with a rolling pin. Take the shorter edge of the pastry and roll it up to the center. Roll the opposite side to meet it at the center. Moisten with water and press together the adjoining rolls. Cut into ½ inch slices and place them cut side down on a dampened cooky sheet. Keep them well apart and flatten them a little. Bake in a pre-heated oven for 12-15 minutes, until puffed and golden. (Turn the palmiers over once they begin to brown.) Cool them on a wire rack. Whip the cream and use it to fill a pastry bag fitted with a ½ inch fluted tip. Shape swirls of cream on half of the palmiers and arrange the fruit on top of the cream. Use the other palmiers to sandwich the fruit. Sprinkle with confectioner's sugar.

Praline Orange Log

PREPARATION TIME: 20-25 minutes, plus chilling

COOKING TIME: 30-35 minutes

OVEN TEMPERATURE: 350°F

MAKES: 30 slices

6oz semi-sweet chocolate, chopped or grated
1¼ tblsp strong black coffee
2 tblsp sugar
1¼ tblsp orange liqueur
⅓ cup butter
2 egg yolks

Praline
1½ cups shelled nuts (see below)
1 cup granulated sugar
⅓ cup water
1 egg white, beaten

Use either almonds, hazelnuts, walnuts or pistachio nuts. Use the nuts chopped or whole, with or without the skins, toasted or plain. For praline powder, the nuts must be peeled.

Melt the chocolate in a bowl with the coffee, sugar, orange liqueur and butter, over a low heat. Remove from the heat and allow to cool thoroughly. Stir in the egg yolks. Chill for 3½-4 hours. To make the praline: put the nuts on a cooky sheet and warm them in the oven for 10 minutes. Butter a marble slab or large cooky sheet. Put the sugar and water into a small, heavy saucepan, stirring until the sugar has dissolved. Bring to the boil and boil until the sugar caramelizes; remove from the heat and plunge the base of the pan into cold water to halt the cooking process. Stir in the nuts. Pour onto the marble or onto a cooky sheet. Spread out and leave until set and hard. Put the praline into a strong plastic bag and crush with a rolling pin. To make praline powder, grind it in a coffee grinder. Shape the chilled chocolate mixture into a log, 2 inches in diameter. Brush the log with the beaten egg white and roll gently in the crushed praline, pressing firmly with the hands to help the praline stick. Chill the log until very firm. Cut into slices about ¼ inch thick.

Chocolate Crunch (top right), Chocolate Palmiers (center left) and Chocolate Chip Cookies (bottom).

Mint Creams

PREPARATION TIME: 20 minutes, plus setting overnight

MAKES: about 16

The white of 1 egg
¼ tsp peppermint essence
2¼ cups confectioner's sugar
4oz semi-sweet chocolate, chopped or grated

Beat the egg white and essence together in a bowl and gradually add the confectioner's sugar. Lightly dust the work surface with extra confectioner's sugar and knead the peppermint frosting until smooth. Using plenty of extra icing sugar, roll out the frosting to a thickness of about ¼ inch and cut out shapes with a 1½ inch cutter, either fluted or plain. Place the shaped mints on a cooky sheet lined with wax paper, and leave them in a warm place to dry out, preferably overnight. Melt the chocolate; dip the mints in so that half is coated in chocolate. Shake off any excess chocolate and place the mints on a sheet of buttered wax paper or foil until set.

Dominoes

PREPARATION TIME: 25 minutes

COOKING TIME: 10-15 minutes

OVEN TEMPERATURE: 350°F

MAKES: about 14

½ cup butter or margarine
½ cup sugar
1 egg, beaten
2¼ cups regular flour
3 tblsp cocoa powder
Salt

Butter Frosting
⅓ cup butter
1 cup + 2 tblsp confectioner's sugar, sieved
Few drops of vanilla essence

Cream the butter and sugar together and add the egg. Sieve the flour, cocoa powder and salt together and work into the butter mixture. Knead the dough and roll it out between two sheets of wax paper. Cut out rectangles, about 1¼x2¾ inches. Mark a line across the center of the biscuits using a skewer. Bake the cookies on a

greased cooky sheet for 10-15 minutes. Cool them on a wire rack. To make the frosting: soften the butter and beat in the frosting sugar. You may need to add a few drops of hot water if the frosting is too firm. Add vanilla essence to taste. If you want to sandwich the cookies together, do so with a little of the butter frosting. Decorate the top of the dominoes with dots, using a pastry bag fitted with a plain tip and filled with the remaining butter frosting.

Zigzag Shortbread

PREPARATION TIME: 20 minutes

COOKING TIME: 30-35 minutes

OVEN TEMPERATURE: 325°F

MAKES: about 14 fingers

1¼ cups regular flour
¼ cup sugar
½ cup butter
1¼ tblsp cocoa powder
1¼ tblsp drinking chocolate

Grease a 7 inch square cake pan. Sieve the flour into a bowl, reserving ½oz. Add the sugar. Cut in the butter until it forms a crumble texture. Divide the

mixture in half; add the cocoa and the drinking chocolate to one half. Add the remaining flour to the other half. Knead both mixtures to doughs. Turn the chocolate dough onto a lightly floured surface. Roll out and cut into strips 1½ inches wide. Do the same with the plain dough. Lay the strips alternately in the pan, in a diagonal pattern, easing them in so that they fit. Bake until lightly crisp but not brown, for 30-35 minutes. Mark out into fingers and leave to cool in the pan. Note: the shortbread trimmings can be cut into small shapes and baked separately for 5 minutes.

Chocolate Whirls

PREPARATION TIME: 10 minutes

COOKING TIME: 15 minutes

OVEN TEMPERATURE: 350°F

MAKES: 10

¼ cup butter or margarine
2 tblsp brown sugar
1¼ tblsp molasses
1 tsp cocoa powder
Pinch of salt
1 cup regular flour

1¼ tsp baking powder
10 hazelnuts

Grease a cooky sheet. Put the butter and sugar into a mixing bowl and beat until soft and creamy. Add the molasses and stir well. Sieve the cocoa powder, flour and salt together and knead into the molasses mixture. Spoon the mixture into small balls on a floured work surface. Roll the balls into long sausage shapes; curve round one end and continue winding the rest of the sausage round so you have a Catherine wheel shape. Place the "wheels" on the cooky sheet; push a hazelnut into the center of each one. Bake for 15 minutes. Cool on a wire rack.

This page: Chocolate Whirls (left), Zigzag Shortbread (center) and Dominoes (right).

Facing page: Iced Chocolate (left) and Chocolate Egg Cream Soda (right).

COOKING WITH CHOCOLATE

Drinks and Sauces

Iced Chocolate

PREPARATION TIME: 5 minutes, plus chilling

COOKING TIME: 15 minutes

MAKES: 8-10 drinks

¾ cup granulated sugar
1 cup water
4½ tblsp cocoa powder
Chilled milk

Put the sugar and water into a heavy-based saucepan and stir over a moderate heat until the sugar dissolves. Brush off any sugar crystals that may form on the inside of the pan with a pastry brush dipped in cold water. Raise the heat and boil the syrup until it spins fine threads from a spoon or fork. Remove from the heat. Add the cocoa powder and stir until well mixed over a low heat. Cool the chocolate syrup and chill in the refrigerator until required. To make the drink: put 1 tblsp chilled syrup into a jug or blender with 1¼ cups chilled milk and stir or blend until blended. Pour the chocolate drink over ice cubes in chilled glasses.

Bittersweet Butter Cream

PREPARATION TIME: 15 minutes

MAKES: 1¾ cups

10oz unsweetened chocolate
1½ cups butter softened
1½ cups sugar
2 tsp vanilla essence
3 eggs
3 tblsp cocoa powder
1 tsp instant coffee powder
2 tsp dark rum
Pinch of salt

Melt the chocolate. Beat the butter until creamy and add the sugar and vanilla. Add the eggs, one at a time, beating well after each addition. Stir cocoa and coffee powder into the melted chocolate and add it to the buttercream. Stir in the rum and salt, making sure that all the ingredients are well incorporated. Use to fill Chocolate Raspberry Torte, or other chocolate recipe.

Banana Shake

PREPARATION TIME: 10 minutes

MAKES: 1 drink

3 tblsp chocolate ice cream
2 tblsp drinking chocolate powder
²/₃ cup milk
1 banana
Ice cubes

Blend together all the ingredients in a blender or food processor, or beat with a hand whisk (if using a hand whisk, mash the banana first). Serve in a tall glass with ice cubes.

Chocolate Butter Sauce

PREPARATION TIME: 5 minutes

COOKING TIME: 10 minutes

MAKES: 1³/₄ cups

1 cup water
8oz semi-sweet chocolate, chopped or grated
1 tblsp brandy
7 tblsp butter, cut into small pieces

Put the water, chocolate and brandy into a saucepan. Stir over a low heat until the chocolate has melted. The mixture should be smooth. Remove from the heat and slowly stir in the butter until it melts. The sauce should then become thick and glossy. This sauce can be served hot or cold.

Praline Sauce

PREPARATION TIME: 40 minutes, including making of praline

MAKES: about 1¼ cups

1 tblsp cocoa powder
6oz canned evaporated milk
3oz semi-sweet chocolate, chopped or grated
5 tblsp crushed praline (see recipe)

Beat together the cocoa and evaporated milk in a small saucepan. Heat the mixture and bring it to the boil. Remove the pan from the heat and stir in the chocolate. Return to the heat and continue stirring over a gentle heat until the chocolate has melted. Add the praline.

Chocolate Toffee Sauce

PREPARATION TIME: 10 minutes

COOKING TIME: 15 minutes

MAKES: about 1¼ cups

4oz semi-sweet chocolate, chopped or grated
⅓ cup water
¼ cup granulated sugar
4 tblsp chilled unsalted butter
1 tsp vanilla essence
8oz nut brittle, broken into small chunks

Using a small, heavy-based saucepan, gently heat the chocolate and water until the chocolate has melted. Stir continuously. Stir in the sugar and continue to heat

gently for 2 minutes, until the sugar has dissolved and the mixture has thickened. Remove the sauce from the heat and beat in the butter. Stir in the vanilla and the broken nut brittle. Serve hot. This sauce can be kept in the refrigerator for a few days. To serve warm, heat it gently to a pouring consistency.

Peppermint Sauce

PREPARATION TIME: 15 minutes

MAKES: about 1 cup

3oz chocolate covered peppermint creams
²/₃ cup light cream

Break up the peppermint creams and melt over a pan of hot water. Remove from the heat and slowly stir in the cream. Serve the sauce hot or cold with ice cream.

This page: Praline Sauce – shown with Nougat Slice – (top), Bitter Chocolate Sauce – shown with Cherries – (center right) and Chocolate Butter Sauce (bottom left).

Facing page: Hot Fudge Sauce (left) and Chocolate Toffee Sauce (right).

Chocolate Custard

PREPARATION TIME: 10 minutes

COOKING TIME: 3 minutes

MAKES: about 2½ cups

4 egg yolks
¼ cup sugar
2 cups milk
4oz semi-sweet chocolate, chopped or
   grated

Heat the milk until very hot. Add the chocolate and stir until melted. Beat the egg yolks and sugar together until pale and creamy. Slowly pour the milk onto the egg mixture and blend. Return mixture to pan and heat over medium heat, stirring constantly, until sauce thickens. Serve hot.

Bitter Chocolate Sauce

PREPARATION TIME: 5 minutes

COOKING TIME: 15 minutes

MAKES: 1 cup

4 tblsp strong black coffee
4oz semi-sweet chocolate, chopped or
   grated
½ cup heavy cream
⅓ cup apricot jam

Put all the ingredients into a small, heavy-based pan. Stir continuously over a low heat until smooth.

Honey Nut Spread (above), Chocolate Custard – shown with Steamed Pudding – (center right) and Bittersweet Butter Cream (far right).

Nouvelle Sauce

PREPARATION TIME: 10 minutes

COOKING TIME: 5 minutes

MAKES: 1¾ cups

This is a thin chocolate sauce which is served slightly cooled.

8oz semi-sweet chocolate, chopped or grated
½ cup granulated sugar
2 cups water
2½ tsp brandy

Melt the chocolate with the sugar and water; simmer for 4-5 minutes, stirring continuously. Remove the pan from the heat and let the chocolate mixture cool. Stir in the brandy. Strain the sauce and serve.

Honey Nut Spread

PREPARATION TIME: 10 minutes

MAKES: about 6oz

¼ cup butter, softened
1¼ tblsp cocoa powder
2 tsp orange liqueur
2½ tblsp honey
3 tblsp confectioner's sugar
½ cup nuts, chopped

Cream the butter with the cocoa powder and the orange liqueur; beat in the honey and the confectioner's sugar, and then fold in the nuts. This spread is now ready to serve on hot toasted crumpets, or muffins, and is delicious with pancakes.

Chocolate Cream Sauce

PREPARATION TIME: 5 minutes

COOKING TIME: 10-15 minutes

MAKES: 1¾ cups

1¼ cups heavy cream
1 tblsp brandy
1 tblsp strong black coffee
8oz semi-sweet chocolate, chopped or grated

Pour the cream, brandy and coffee into a small, heavy-based saucepan and bring to the boil. Remove from the heat and add the chopped chocolate. Stir the chocolate until it melts and the sauce is smooth. Serve this sauce hot or cold.

Cocoa Rum

PREPARATION TIME: 5 minutes

MAKES: 1 drink

½oz semi-sweet chocolate, chopped or grated
⅔ cup milk
1 tblsp rum
1 tblsp whipped cream
Grated nutmeg

Put the chocolate and milk into a saucepan and bring it to the boil. Stir the chocolate milk a few times, and then remove it from the heat. Beat in the rum and pour into a heatproof glass. Put a spoonful of cream on the top and sprinkle with grated nutmeg.

Malted Chocolate Shake

PREPARATION TIME: 10 minutes, plus chilling

COOKING TIME: 5 minutes

MAKES: 2 drinks

¼ cup soft brown sugar
4½ tblsp cocoa powder
1¼ cups milk
2 tblsp vanilla ice cream
1 tblsp whiskey

Put all the ingredients except the whiskey and ice cream into a saucepan and mix well. Bring gently to the boil. Cook gently for 5 minutes, stirring frequently. Remove from the heat and leave to cool. Beat in the ice cream. Cover and chill in the refrigerator until required. Pour into two glasses and add the whiskey.

Chocolate Egg Cream Soda

PREPARATION TIME: 8 minutes

MAKES: 2 drinks

2oz semi-sweet chocolate, melted
1 egg
1¼ cups full cream milk
2 scoops chocolate ice cream
Chilled soda water
2 scoops vanilla ice cream

Put two tall glasses in the freezer until they are frosted. Put the melted chocolate, egg, milk and chocolate ice cream into the blender; blend for 1 minute. Divide this mixture between two glasses; add a scoop of vanilla ice cream to each one and top up with chilled soda water. Serve while it is still frothing.

Hot Fudge Sauce

PREPARATION TIME: 10 minutes

COOKING TIME: 10 minutes

MAKES: about 1¾ cups

10 tblsp unsalted butter
6 tblsp cocoa powder
2oz semi-sweet chocolate, chopped or grated
⅓ cup granulated sugar
½ cup evaporated milk
Pinch of salt
A few drops of vanilla essence

Melt the butter in a small, heavy-based saucepan. Remove from heat and add the cocoa powder. Beat until smooth. Stir in the chopped chocolate, sugar and evaporated milk; bring to the boil over a moderate heat, stirring continuously. Remove the sauce from the heat and stir in the salt and vanilla essence. This sauce will keep in the refrigerator for 2-3 days.

Coffolate

PREPARATION TIME: 10 minutes, plus chilling time

COOKING TIME: about 15 minutes

MAKES: 4 drinks

1 tblsp cornstarch
1¾ cups boiling coffee
1¾ cups hot milk
2oz semi-sweet chocolate, chopped or grated
½ tsp ground cinnamon
½ cup sugar

To Decorate
Whipped cream

Mix the cornstarch to a paste with a little of the coffee. Place the hot milk in a bowl over a pan of simmering water (or into a double boiler). Mix in the cornstarch paste and stir well. Add the chocolate, cinnamon, sugar and remaining coffee. Simmer the mixture for 15 minutes, beating with a whisk; cool and chill. Serve in tall glasses with the cream to decorate.

This page, top picture: Cocoa Rum (left) and Coffolate (right). Bottom picture: Nouvelle Sauce (top left), Chocolate Cream Sauce (top right) and Peppermint Sauce – shown with Pear Pie – (bottom).

Facing page: Malted Chocolate Shake (left) and Banana Shake (right).

SWEET SURPRISE

Chocolate Lime Tart

PREPARATION TIME: 20 minutes

8oz graham crackers
5oz semi-sweet chocolate
2 tablespoons butter
2oz white marshmallows
⅓ cup milk
2 limes
⅓ cup heavy cream
2oz semi-sweet chocolate, grated
The grated rind of 1 lemon
⅓ cup heavy cream, whipped
  for decoration

Crush the cookies. Melt the chocolate and butter together and mix in the cookies. Lightly grease the sides and base of a 9 inch tart pan. Press the cooky mixture onto the base and sides of the dish. Melt the marshmallows in a basin over hot water and add the milk. Stir in the juice from one lime and grate the rind. Mix in the lemon rind, whip the heavy cream and fold into the marshmallow mixture. Pour into the crumb base and leave to set. Decorate the tart with the remaining cream, grated chocolate and slices of the second lime.

Cointreau and Mandarin Mousse

PREPARATION TIME: 10 minutes

10½oz can of mandarin oranges
1 tablespoon gelatin
4 tablespoons Cointreau or orange
  liqueur
3 egg yolks
2 tablespoons sugar

Strain the mandarins, reserving the juice. Sprinkle the gelatin over the juice. Pour two tablespoons of Cointreau over the mandarins and leave them to soak. Add the remaining Cointreau, egg yolks and sugar to the gelatin. Beat the egg mixture over a bowl of hot water until thick and frothy (with an electric beater this should take 4 minutes). Pour into individual glass dishes and chill until set. Spoon the soaked mandarins on top. Serve.

Cheese Mousse with Strawberries

PREPARATION TIME: 45 minutes

1 cup cottage cheese
5oz strawberries
3 tablespoons confectioners' sugar
2 tablespoons Cointreau or orange
  liqueur
2 tablespoons lemon juice
2 tablespoons orange juice
1 tablespoon gelatin
⅔ cup heavy cream
6 meringue rosettes

Chocolate Sauce
8oz chocolate
2 tablespoons milk
2 tablespoons butter

Put the cottage cheese into a bowl and add the strawberries, reserving a few strawberries for decoration. Sift the confectioners' sugar over the cheese and sprinkle over the Cointreau. Cover and leave to stand in the fridge for about half an hour. Heat the orange and lemon juice and dissolve the gelatin in it. Whilst the gelatin is still warm, stir in the cheese mixture. Stiffly whip the cream and fold it in. Serve the mousse on the plate and decorate with the reserved strawberries. Serve with some chocolate sauce and meringue rosettes.

Chocolate Sauce
Melt the chololate, milk and butter in a bowl over hot water. Stir rapidly. Serve.

This page: Chocolate Lime Tart.

Facing page: Cointreau and Mandarin Mousse (top) and Cheese Mousse with Strawberries (bottom).

Special Desserts

Ginger Rum Trifle

PREPARATION TIME: 20 minutes

1½ cups ginger cake, sliced
1½ cups canned pear quarters
9 tablespoons rum
1¾ cups cold thick vanilla sauce
1¼ cups heavy cream
2-3 teaspoons confectioners' sugar
Toasted flaked almonds
Stem ginger cut into strips

Line the bottom of a glass dish with half the ginger cake. Drain the canned pears and mix the rum with the juice. Sprinkle half over the cake. Place the pears on the top of the cake and cover with the remaining slices. Pour over a little more rum mixture. Spoon the sauce over the cake. Whip the cream and gradually add confectioners' sugar until it peaks. Spoon the cream over the sauce and decorate with lightly toasted almond flakes and stem ginger strips.

Lemon Brandy Cream

PREPARATION TIME: 15 minutes

1¼ cups light cream
1¼ cups heavy cream
6 tablespoons soft brown sugar
2 large lemons
6 tablespoons sponge cake
2 tablespoons brandy
2 tablespoons toasted flaked almonds

Mix the light and heavy cream in a small saucepan and add the sugar. Stir over a low heat until the cream begins to bubble. Grate the rind of the lemons and gently stir into the cream. Leave the mixture to cool and crumble the cake crumbs into glasses or serving dish. Stir the brandy into the cream mixture with the juice from both lemons. Pour the mixture into the glasses or dish over the cake crumbs and refrigerate for 30 minutes. Decorate with toasted almond flakes.

Exotic Fruit Salad Basket

PREPARATION TIME: 15 minutes

1 large melon
1 persimmon
3 kiwi fruit, washed
4oz blackberries, washed
6oz raspberries, washed
6oz redcurrants, washed
6oz strawberries, washed
6oz blackcurrants, washed
6oz grapes, red and green

1 mango, peeled and sliced
Strawberry leaves
Use as many fruits in season as are available
Sugar syrup (see Sauces)

Hollow out a melon and reserve the pulp. Slice the persimmon and kiwi fruit, and make melon balls using the reserved melon. Arrange the fruit in the melon basket and spoon over with sugar syrup (see Sauces).

Inset illustration: Lemon Brandy Cream (right), Berry Whip (left).

These pages: Exotic Fruit Salad (top left), Cranberry Fool (top right) and Ginger Rum Trifle (bottom).

Cranberry Fool, Chilled

PREPARATION TIME: 30 minutes

1lb cranberries
10 tablespoons sugar
2 tablespoons lemon juice
⅔ cup carton soured cream

Bring the cranberries to the boil in 1¾ cups water in a saucepan, then simmer for about 15 minutes. Cool and stir in the sugar until dissolved. Purée the mixture until most of it is smooth by rubbing it through a sieve to remove the cranberry skins. Make sure the mixture is cool, stir in the lemon juice, cover and chill. Spoon into serving dish and serve with sour cream.

Berry Whip

PREPARATION TIME: 15 minutes

3 egg whites
A few grains of salt
¾ cup confectioners' sugar
½lb blackberries
Sponge fingers

In a deep bowl beat the egg whites. Add the sugar and salt and beat until very stiff. Fold in the berries. Spoon into glasses and chill. Serve with sponge fingers.

Cremets

PREPARATION TIME: 10 minutes

1½ cups curd cheese
2 tablespoons vanilla sugar or
     superfine sugar with a few drops of
     vanilla essence
1¼ cups heavy cream

Beat the curd cheese until smooth. Add the sugar and gradually beat in the cream. Pile into a bowl and chill.

Almond Galette

PREPARATION TIME: 1 hour

COOKING TIME: 10 minutes for each batch of rounds

OVEN: 375°F

1½ cups butter
2 cups superfine sugar
2 eggs
2¾ cups all-purpose flour
2 tablespoons ground almonds
3¾ cups heavy cream, whipped
Confectioners' sugar
Heavy cream
Whole almonds

Cut out 9 inch circles of non-stick baking paper. Cream the sugar and butter together and beat in the eggs. Fold in the sifted flour and ground almonds. Divide the mixture into 12 and using a large palette knife coat the individual paper rounds with the mixture. Work from the center outwards with smooth strokes. Wet a cooky sheet and bake the rounds. Leave until cool and carefully peel off the paper. When all the rounds are cooked use them to form layers, spreading each one with whipped cream. Reserve ⅔ cup of cream for

decoration. Dust the top with confectioners' sugar and decorate with almonds and cream.

Blackberry, Raisin and Walnut Jelly

PREPARATION TIME: 10 minutes
Note: In order that the fruit should be plump, soak overnight.

½ cup seedless raisins
2 tablespoons rum
1 packet blackberry jelly
1¼ cups port
1lb frozen blackberries (keep
     frozen)
6 walnuts halved
Cream
Flowers

Soak the raisins in the rum for a few hours, preferably overnight. Dissolve the jelly in 1¼ cups of boiling water. Add the port and cool, making sure the jelly does not set. Put the fruit and nuts in individual glasses or a mold, making sure they are quite full. Spoon over the jelly and leave to set. Decorate with flowers and/or cream.

French Plum Pudding

PREPARATION TIME: 20 minutes

COOKING TIME: 40 minutes

OVEN: 400°F

¾ cup all-purpose flour
¾ cup butter
6 tablespoons superfine sugar
¼ cup ground almonds
1 egg yolk
1 tablespoon cold water
1½lb plums, halved and stoned

Sift the flour into a mixing bowl. Cut in two-thirds of the butter and 2 tablespoons of the sugar. Add the ground almonds and mix into a firm dough with the egg yolk and water. Chill. Melt the reserved butter in a 9 inch round ovenproof dish. Add the remaining sugar until caramelized. Remove from heat. Arrange the plums, skin side down, in the ovenproof dish. On a lightly floured surface roll out the dough into a round slightly bigger than the dish. Place the dough on top of the plums and gently press down, tucking in the edges as you go. Bake in the oven until golden. To serve, turn out onto a serving dish. Serve instantly.

Chocolate Meringues

PREPARATION TIME: 40 minutes

COOKING TIME: 2 hours
(leave the meringues to cool for as long as necessary)

OVEN: 250°F

4 egg whites
1 cup superfine sugar
¼ cup hazelnuts, finely ground
1¼ cups heavy cream
1 tablespoon cocoa powder
Chocolate curls

Beat the egg whites until stiff. Gently whisk in the sugar a little at a time and fold in the hazelnuts with a metal spoon. Spoon out rounds of meringue onto a cooky sheet lined with non-stick wax paper. Bake until well dried out. Cool on wire racks. Whip the cream until stiff and fold in the cocoa powder. Use the cream to sandwich the meringues and decorate with chocolate shavings or curls.

Coconut Cup

PREPARATION TIME: 35 minutes

3 coconuts sawed in half
3 scoops soft-scoop vanilla ice cream
     per half coconut
3 tablespoons dark rum
1lb dried mixed fruit

Soak fruit in rum overnight. Saw coconuts in half and remove the flesh. Grate half the flesh, and incorporate in the ice cream along with the fruit, reserving some of the fruit for decoration. Fill coconut halves with mixture and place in freezer until firm. To serve, top with remaining fruit and grated coconut.

This page: Cremet (left), Almond Galette (right).

Facing page: Blackberry, Raisin and Walnut Jelly (top right), French Plum Pudding (center left) and Chocolate Meringues (bottom).

Blackberry Ice Cream Dessert

PREPARATION TIME: 20 minutes plus freezing time

6 tablespoons sugar
1½ tablespoons Curaçao
1⅓ cups blackberry purée
¾ cup low-fat plain yogurt
Generous pinch of cinnamon
⅔ cup heavy cream, whipped
⅔ cup water

Boil the sugar with the water for a minute and add the Curaçao. Stir in the blackberry purée (rub the fruit through a nylon sieve). Stir in the yogurt and cinnamon, and lastly fold in the whipped cream. Freeze until creamy and serve.

Kiwi Cheesecake

PREPARATION TIME: 45 minutes
COOKING TIME: 20 minutes
OVEN: 350°F

Base
¼ cup soft butter
¼ cup superfine sugar
1 egg
10 tablespoons all-purpose flour
½ teaspoon baking powder
Finely grated rind of ½ medium
    orange

Filling
¾ cup cream cheese
¼ cup superfine sugar
3 eggs, separated
Juice of 1 medium orange
Finely grated rind of ½ medium
    orange
½oz gelatin
4 tablespoons cold water
⅔ cup natural yogurt
⅔ cup heavy cream

To decorate
⅔ cup heavy cream
3 kiwi fruit, peeled and sliced
Nuts

Base
Grease and line the base and sides of an 8 inch loose bottom cake pan with wax paper. Note: The paper should come over the top of the pan. In a mixing bowl add the butter, egg and superfine sugar and cream the mixture until fluffy. Sieve the flour and baking powder into the bowl and beat. Add the

orange rind. Use either a wooden spoon or electric beater for two or one minute respectively. Spoon the mixture into the cake pan and cook for 20 minutes, 350°F. Leave in pan when cooked and allow to cool.

Filling
While the base is cooking, beat the sugar with cream cheese and add the egg yolks, orange juice and rind. Beat until very smooth. In a heatproof basin put the cold water and sprinkle in the gelatin, leaving it to stand for 10 minutes until soft. Stand the basin in a pan of simmering water until gelatin dissolves. Stir constantly. Leave to cool but not set. Pour the gelatin in a constant stream into the cheese mixture and stir. Beat in the yogurt. Whip the cream and fold carefully into the mixture using a metal spoon. Beat the egg whites in a clean bowl until stiff and fold into cheese mixture. Pour the cheese mixture over the base and smooth

the top. Leave to set in the fridge for several hours.

To decorate
Remove from the pan and carefully peel off the paper, serve decorated with cream, kiwi fruit and nuts (an alternative could be orange segments). Serve chilled.

Poached Minty Pears

PREPARATION TIME: 40 minutes plus chilling

6 large pears, peeled
6 tablespoons sugar
Fresh mint leaves
6 tablespoons clear honey
3 tablespoons Creme de Menthe
    liqueur

Put the pears in a saucepan. Stand upright and pour water over.

Cover all the pears. Boil and then simmer for 30 minutes. Pour off half the water and sprinkle over with sugar. Add the fresh mint and simmer for 10 minutes. Transfer the pears to a bowl. Reserve ⅔ cup water from the pan and stir in the honey and liqueur. Pour this mixture over the pears and allow it to cool. Cover the pears and chill for 2 hours. Stand each pear on an individual serving dish and spoon over the mint sauce.

This page: Blackberry Ice-Cream Dessert (top), Coconut Cups (bottom).

Facing page: Kiwi Cheesecake (top), Poached Minty Pear (bottom).

Coffee Truffles

PREPARATION TIME: 10 minutes

1 cup cake crumbs
2 tablespoons ground almonds
¼ teaspoon coffee powder
Heaped tablespoon apricot jam, melted
2-3 tablespoons coffee liqueur
2oz chocolate vermicelli

Put the crumbs and ground almonds into a bowl. Mix in the jam and coffee liqueur and mix together to form a stiff paste. Shape into small balls and roll in chocolate vermicelli.

Crystal Fruits

1 egg white
8oz bunch of grapes
2 large red apples
2 large pears
½ cup plums
Any other soft fruit in season

Beat the egg white well and brush onto the fruit. Leave for a few minutes but not until dry. Dip the fruit into superfine sugar and place on wax paper until dry. Arrange in fruit bowl or stand.

Apricot Mountain

PREPARATION TIME: 20 minutes

COOKING TIME: 4 minutes or until meringue is brown

OVEN: 450°F

About ¾lb canned apricot halves
4-6 tablespoons Marsala or sweet sherry
3 egg whites
½ cup superfine sugar
8 inch sponge tart case
1¾ cups vanilla ice cream

Strain the apricots and sprinkle them with the sherry. Beat the egg whites until stiff and fold in the sugar. Beat again until the meringue peaks. Stand the tart case on a heatproof dish and sprinkle with a little more sherry. Pile the apricots into the tart case. Cover the apricots with a mountain shape of ice cream. Using the meringue mixture, quickly cover the ice cream and the sponge base. Bake immediately until the meringue is light brown. Serve from the oven.

For a very special effect bury half an egg shell at the top of the mountain before baking the meringue. As you serve fill it with warmed brandy, ignite and serve flaming.

Petits Fours

PREPARATION TIME: 40 minutes
OVEN: 400°F

Sponge
3 eggs
½ cup superfine sugar
¾ cup all-purpose flour
1 tablespoon hot water

Topping
Fruits in season
Apricot jam to glaze

Sponge
Beat eggs and sugar until thick and creamy. Sift in flour and fold in with the hot water. Place mixture in a greased and floured jelly roll pan. Bake for 8 to 10 minutes until cake springs back when pressed. Turn out and cool. Cut shapes out of the sponge using pastry cutters.

Topping
Place sponge shapes on a wire rack and top with attractively arranged fruit. Melt apricot jam on low heat and spoon over shapes to glaze. When surplus has dripped off and jam has set remove and place on serving plate.

Chocolate Leaf, Filled with Orange Mousse

PREPARATION TIME: 1 hour
plus chilling

For the Leaf
6oz semi-sweet chocolate
1 cabbage leaf (with veins)

Mousse
3 whole eggs plus 2 yolks
¼ cup superfine sugar
Juice of ½ lemon
1½ tablespoons powdered gelatin
⅔ cup heavy cream
⅔ cup freshly squeezed orange juice
Finely grated rind of 2 oranges

Leaf
Put the chocolate in a basin over simmering water and stir until smooth. With a pastry brush, paint the chocolate over a well-veined cabbage leaf and leave to cool and harden. Repeat the process until there is a thick build up of chocolate on the leaf. When hard the cabbage leaf can be easily removed.

Mousse
Put the eggs and yolks in a basin with the sugar. Beat until pale and frothy. This can be done over a saucepan of simmering water, but make sure that the basin doesn't touch the water. Beat until thick. Remove from the heat and beat until cold. Put the lemon juice and a little water into a small saucepan and sprinkle in the gelatin and leave it to soak for a few minutes. Whip the cream and stir it into the egg mixture, gradually adding the orange juice and grated rind. Gently heat the gelatin until clear and stir it quickly into the mixture. Fill the serving dish and refrigerate until set. This mousse can either be served with one leaf or several small leaves to go with each portion of mousse.

Crystal Fruits (left), Coffee Truffles (bottom left) and Petits Fours (bottom right).

Fruit Salad with Mango Purée

PREPARATION TIME: 20 minutes plus 1 hour chilling in the refrigerator

3 peaches
3 tamarillos (tree tomatoes)
3 kiwi fruit
1½ tablespoons lemon juice
3 tablespoons sugar syrup

Mango Purée
2 well-ripened mangoes weighing
   about 12oz
Juice of ½ a lime, or lemon
3 teaspoons honey
5oz redcurrants
Strawberry leaves for decoration

Blanch the peaches briefly and peel. Halve and remove stones and cut into delicate wedges. Peel and slice the tamarillos, nectarines and kiwi fruit, arrange in serving dish and scatter over with redcurrants. Pour over the lemon juice mixed with sugar syrup. Leave the fruits to stand in syrup for 1 hour in a cool place.

Mango Purée
Either liquidize or rub through a wire sieve the flesh of the mangoes and mix with the lime juice. Mix in the honey and pour the mixture over the fruit. Decorate with strawberry leaves.

Pineapple Malibu

PREPARATION TIME: 30 minutes

1 medium ripe pineapple
2 cups heavy cream
6 tablespoons macaroons, roughly
   crushed
3 tablespoons coconut liqueur

Cut the pineapple a few inches below the top. Scoop out as much of the fruit as possible, discarding the core if hard. Chop the fruit into bite-size pieces. Whip two-thirds of the cream until it begins to stiffen and fold in the macaroons, having first soaked them in the coconut liqueur. In another bowl whip up the remaining cream and fold into the coconut cream. Spoon alternate spoonfuls of diced pineapple and cream mixture into the hollowed pineapple and chill. Serve straight from the fridge.

Chocolate Ginger Tart

PREPARATION TIME: 30 minutes

4oz semi-sweet chocolate
1¼ cups milk
½ cup superfine sugar
3 tablespoons flour
½ cup butter
2 egg yolks
6oz ginger nut cookies
Whipped cream
4oz stem ginger cut into thin slices

Melt the chocolate in the milk in a saucepan, stirring constantly. Remove pan from heat. Mix the superfine sugar, flour and ¼ cup butter into the chocolate milk and stir in the egg yolks. Put on a low heat and slowly bring to the boil. Simmer for 5 minutes until the mixture begins to thicken, stir until smooth. Remove from heat and cool. While the filling is cooling, melt the remaining ¼ cup of butter and crush the ginger nut cookies. Mix the cookies with the melted butter and press in a greased pie pan. When the filling is cool, pour onto the ginger nut base. Chill and decorate with whipped cream and sprinkle with stemmed ginger cut into thin slices (an alternative decoration is chocolate vermicelli).

Coffee Charlotte

PREPARATION TIME: 1½ hours
COOKING TIME: 12 minutes
OVEN: 475°F

Sponge
4 egg yolks
¼ cup sugar
Generous pinch of salt
3 egg whites
5 tablespoons flour mixed with 2
   teaspoons coffee powder
¾ cup apricot jam
3 tablespoons brandy
2 tablespoons cornstarch

set, caref...
fill the spong...
the marinated...
the top of the m...
from the sponge ro...
charlotte set for three...
refrigerator and turn on...
dish. Brush with the apric...

Orange Campari Mousse

PREPARATION TIME: 45 minutes
plus chilling

1 teaspoon powdered gelatin
2 medium oranges, washed and dried
7 tablespoons superfine sugar
2 eggs, separated
3 tablespoons Campari
²⁄₃ cup heavy cream
1 tablespoon cold milk
Red grapes

Add gelatin to two tablespoons of water in a saucepan. Leave to one side. Grate peel of 1 orange. Squeeze oranges and if necessary make up juice to ¾ cup with water. Melt gelatin and water over a low heat. Stir in orange juice. Pour mixture into a bowl, beat in sugar, egg yolks, Campari and orange peel. Place in fridge until the mixture begins to thicken and set. In one bowl beat egg whites until stiff. In another beat milk and cream together until thick. Gradually mix egg whites and cream alternately into the orange mixture until totally incorporated. Pour into a bowl and place in refrigerator until firm and set. Serve in glasses decorated with sliced red grapes.

Charlotte

6 apricot halves
1 tablespoon vanilla sugar
1 tablespoon brandy
4 egg yolks
½ cup sugar
Plus 1 tablespoon sugar
1 cup milk
½ vanilla pod
½oz powdered gelatin
1 cup heavy cream
⅓ cup apricot glaze (warmed apricot jam)

Sponge
Beat the egg yolks with a spoonful of sugar and the salt. Beat the egg whites and fold the egg yolk mixture into the meringue. Sift together the cornstarch and flour and stir them in. Line a jelly roll pan with non-stick wax paper. Spread the sponge mixture evenly in the jelly roll pan using a spatula. Bake until golden. Turn it out at once onto a clean, damp cloth and peel off the paper. Blend the jam with the brandy and spread the sponge cake with it. Roll it up. Let it cool and cut into thin slices ¼ inch thick. Line the mold with the slices as close together as possible.

Charlotte
Place the apricot halves in a dish and sprinkle them with vanilla sugar. Pour over the brandy. Leave them to marinate in the refrigerator for half an hour. Cream the egg yolks and sugar together in a mixing bowl and put the milk in a small saucepan with the vanilla pod. Heat the milk and bring to the boil and pour into the egg yolks. Return the sauce mixture to the saucepan and stir until it is thick enough to coat the spoon. Remove from heat. Dissolve the gelatin in warm water and stir in the tablespoon of brandy. Add to the sauce mixture and stir well. Cool the sauce. Meanwhile stiffly whip the cream, adding the remaining sugar. When the sauce begins to

Facing page: Apricot Mountain (left), Orange Campari Mousse (right).

This page: Chocolate Leaf, Filled with Orange Mousse (top), Chocolate Ginger Tart (center left) and Fruit Salad with Mango Purée (bottom right).

lly fold in the cream and
re-lined mold. Stir in
apricot and cover
ld with slices
l. Let the
hours in the
o a serving
t glaze.

347

Chestnut Parfait

PREPARATION TIME: 40 minutes
plus freezing

4 egg yolks
10 tablespoons sugar
2/3 cup milk, warmed and flavored
  with a vanilla pod
14 tablespoons unsweetened chestnut
  purée
2 tablespoons dark rum
2 egg whites
1/4 cup sugar
2 cups heavy cream
Chocolate leaves
A few cranberries
Whipped cream

Beat the egg yolks with the sugar
and add the warmed milk flavored
with the vanilla pod and cook until
thickened, stirring gently. The
mixture should coat the spoon.
Transfer to a mixing bowl. Add the
chestnut purée and rum while the
mixture is still lukewarm. Chill
well. Whip the egg whites with the
sugar until very stiff. Beat the
cream until it peaks. Fold the egg
white into the chestnut cream and
carefully fold in the whipped
cream. Pour into a 6 cup mold and
freeze for 4 hours. Decorate with
small rounds of sweetened
chestnut purée dusted with
chocolate powder or melted
chocolate sauce.

Strawberry Shortcake

PREPARATION TIME: 1 hour
COOKING TIME: 25 minutes
OVEN: 425°F

Shortcake
2 cups all-purpose flour
Pinch of salt
4 teaspoons baking powder
6 tablespoons butter
1 large egg
3 tablespoons superfine sugar
3 tablespoons milk
1 tablespoon melted butter

Filling
2 egg yolks
2 drops vanilla essence
1 1/4 cups milk
2 tablespoons sugar
2/3 cup heavy cream
1lb fresh or thawed, frozen
  strawberries
8 toasted almonds

Shortcake
Sift the flour, salt and baking
powder into a bowl. With a knife,
mix in the butter. Beat in the egg,
sugar and milk and pour into the
center of the dry ingredients. Mix
into a dough. On a lightly floured
surface knead gently and divide
into two. Brush an 8 inch cake pan
with melted butter and shape half
the dough into a circle to fit. Place
the second circle on top and bake
until risen and golden brown. Cool
and separate the two halves.

Filling
Make up the vanilla sauce. Heat
the milk in a saucepan with the
sugar and vanilla essence. Beat the
yolks in a bowl and pour on the
hot milk. Blend and return to the
pan. Stir over a gentle heat until
the sauce thickens enough to coat
the back of a wooden spoon.
Cover and leave to cool. Whisk

the cream until just stiff. Fold the
cream into the cooled sauce,
reserving two tablespoons for
decoration. Reserving 8 whole
strawberries and one-third of the
sauce mixture, halve the remaining
strawberries and mix into the
sauce. Spread the strawberry sauce
on the bottom layer of the
shortbread and sandwich with the
top layer. Spread the top with the
reserved sauce mixture and
decorate with whole strawberries
and almonds.

Green Devils

PREPARATION TIME: 20 minutes
plus chilling

1 1/2 lb dessert gooseberries
3/4 cup superfine sugar
2 1/2 cups water
3 tablespoons grenadine
Juice 1/2 lemon
1 level tablespoon cornstarch
Cream

Rinse and top and tail the
gooseberries. Put the superfine
sugar in a small saucepan and
dissolve it in the water. Simmer
and bring to the boil. Take off heat
and stir in the grenadine, lemon
juice and gooseberries and bring
back to simmer. Cook very gently
for five minutes until the fruit is
tender. Remove from heat. Lift out
the fruit and put into the serving
dish. Mix the cornstarch with a
little water to make a thin paste.
Stir into the fruit juice till it begins
to thicken. Stir all the time. When
the syrup is clear, pour over the
fruit. Chill, preferably overnight,
and serve with thick pouring
cream.

Facing page: Pineapple Malibu (top), Coffee Charlotte (center right) and Chestnut Parfait (bottom).

This page: Green Devils (top), Strawberry Shortcake (bottom).

CAKES
AND
CAKE DECORATION

Introduction

Cake decorating is both rewarding and interesting. It is hoped that this book will show how simple it can be and encourage those who use it to improve on their basic skills.

Starting with the simplest frostings, such as butter frosting, which is easy to use and can create elaborate novelty cakes, the book gradually introduces the more complex techniques required to master the frosting and decoration of wedding and other celebration cakes.

Always try to avoid last-minute rushes; many of the decorations can be made in advance and stored. Try to plan ahead when you know that you will be making a special cake and remember that frosting and decorating can take time and patience. If you have not had much

practice, start with the simpler designs before trying to tackle a royal-frosted celebration cake. You will be anxious that the result should be stunning, so practice first!

Never push the frosting design straight onto the cake, as you may ruin the surface you have created. If you are using a complex design, apply it first in white frosting then go over it in color. This way, if you make a mistake, you will not have not stained the surface of the cake. The cakes in this book will certainly give you some new ideas and may encourage you to design versions of your own.

Cakes and their decoration is an absorbing hobby. By following and practising some of the designs suggested, it is hoped you will be able to produce a highly professional result – cakes for every occasion.

Note:
All eggs are size 2.
All spoon measures are level.
Cooking times may vary as they depend upon the efficiency of your oven. Dishes should always be placed in the center of the oven unless otherwise stated.
Fan-assisted ovens may cook slightly quicker, so follow the manufacturer's instructions.
Always preheat the oven to the specified temperature.

CAKES AND CAKE DECORATION
Basic Cakes and Frosting

Lining Cake Pans
All pans must be greased and lined unless you are using a non-stick cake pans, in which case follow the manufacturer's instructions.
If using a shallow pan, only the base needs to be lined for beaten sponges and the quick cake mixture.
If you are making a fruit cake, which will take longer to bake, then the sides as well as the base need lining using a double thickness of wax paper.

To Grease the Pan
Brush with melted lard, margarine or oil. Grease the wax paper with melted fat or oil; if you are using non-stick silicone paper do not grease it. In the preparation of pans, it is necessary to grease and dust them with flour if you are not lining them.

Round Pans
To line a deep, round pan, draw with a pencil round the edge of the cake pan on double thickness wax paper and cut the resulting shape out.
Using a piece of string, measure round the pan. Use another piece of string to measure the height plus 1 inch. Cut out one long strip or two shorter lengths of wax paper to the equivalent of these measurements. If making two lengths, add on a little extra for them to overlap. Make a fold ¼ inch deep along one edge and cut into the fold at regular intervals at a slight angle. Place one of the circles of paper in

the bottom of the pan, followed by the side pieces and, finally, the second paper circle which will cover the slashed edges.

Square Pans
To line a deep, square pan follow the instructions above as for a round pan, but fold the long strips so they fit into the corners of the pan.

Rich Fruit Cake

CAKE SIZES	5in round 4in square	6in round 5in square	7in round 6in square	8in round 7in square	9in round 8in square	10in round 9in square
APPROX COOKING TIME:	2½ hours	2¾ hours	3¼ hours	3¼ hours	4 hours	4¼-4½ hours
OVEN:	275°F	275°F	275°F	275°F	275°F	275°F
	Note for all recipes: First ⅔ of cooking time at 300°F.					
Butter	¼ cup + 1 tblsp	6 tblsp	½ cup	½ cup + 2 tblsp	¾ cup + 2 tblsp	1 cup + 2 tblsp
Eggs	2	2	3	4	5	6
Flour	¾ cup	1 cup	1½ cups	1¾ cups	2¼ cups	2¾ cups
Dark soft brown sugar	⅓ cup	⅓ cup + 1 tblsp	10 tblsp	¾ cup	1 cup	1¼ cups
Molasses	½ tblsp	½ tblsp	1 tblsp	1 tblsp	1 tblsp	1 tblsp
Ground almonds	2 tblsp	2 tblsp	3 tblsp	¼ cup	5 tblsp	⅓ cup
Ground mixed spice	¾ tsp	¾ tsp	1 tsp	1¼ tsp	1½ tsp	1¾ tsp
Grated lemon rind	½ lemon	½ lemon	1 lemon	1 lemon	1 lemon	2 lemons
Grated orange rind	½ orange	½ orange	1 orange	1 orange	1 orange	2 oranges
Grated nutmeg	¼ tsp	¼ tsp	¼ tsp	½ tsp	½ tsp	¾ tsp
Chopped almonds	¼ cup	⅓ cup	½ cup	¾ cup	1 cup	1¼ cups
Currants	1 cup	1¼ cups	1⅔ cups	2 cups	2⅔ cups	3¼ cups
Raisins	¼ cup	½ cup	¾ cup	1 cup	1¼ cups	1½ cups
White raisins	⅔ cup	1 cup	1¼ cups	1¾ cups	2 cups	2⅓ cups
Chopped mixed candied fruits	1oz	1½oz	2oz	2½oz	3½oz	4oz
Candied cherries	1oz	1½oz	2oz	2½oz	3½oz	4oz
Orange juice	1¼ tblsp	1¼ tblsp	1¼ tblsp	1¼ tblsp	2¼ tblsp	2¼ tblsp
Brandy	1¼ tblsp	1¼ tblsp	1¼ tblsp	1¼ tblsp	2¼ tblsp	3¼ tblsp

Jelly Roll Pans (Long, Shallow Pans)

Grease and line a shallow pan so that the cake may be easily removed. Line the sides of the pan with paper at least 1½ inches longer than the pan, cutting into each corner.

Loaf Pans

When lining a loaf pan the method is again the same, but the paper should be 6 inches higher than the top of the pan.

1in round 0in square	12in round 11in square
¾ hours	6 hours
75°F	275°F
⅓ cups	1½ cups + 2 tblsp
7	8
½ cups	4 cups
½ cups	1¾ cups
½ tblsp	2 tblsp
7 tblsp	½ cup
¾ tsp	2½ tsp
lemons	2 lemons
oranges	2 oranges
¼ tsp	1 tsp
½ cups	1¾ cups
3⅓ cups	3½ cups
¾ cups	2 cups
2¾ cups	3 cups
5oz	6oz
5oz	6oz
2¼ tblsp	3¼ tblsp
3¼ tblsp	4¼ tblsp

Rich Fruit Cake

This is a traditional recipe which cuts well and is rich, dark and moist. Traditional fruit cake improves with keeping and is used for celebration cakes – weddings, birthdays and Christmas – with almond paste and royal frosting. Prepacked dried fruit is ready washed, but if you are buying your fruit loose rinse it through with cold water and dry it well with kitchen paper or clean cloths. Then spread it out on a tea towel placed on a cooky sheet in a warm (not hot) place for 24 hours. Do not use wet fruit in a cake as the fruit will sink.

Mix the white raisins, currants and raisins together. Cut the glacé cherries into quarters, rinse in warm water and dry with kitchen paper. Add the cherries to the fruit together with mixed peel, almonds, and grated orange and lemon rind.

Oiling and lining cake pans.

Sift the flour with a pinch of salt, ground cinnamon and mixed spice. Cream the butter until soft, then add the sugar, and cream until light and fluffy (do not overbeat). Add the eggs one at a time, beat well and after each egg add a spoonful of flour. Add the dark molasses, orange juice and brandy, if desired. Spread the mixture evenly into a greased and double-lined pan. Use the back of a spoon to make a slight hollow in the center of the cake so it will be flat when cooked. Tie two thicknesses of brown paper round the pan then bake in the center of the oven at 300°F, (see chart for the suggested time).

With large cakes turn the oven down to 275°F, after two-thirds of the cooking time. To test the cake, push a toothpick into the center. It should come out clean if the cake is cooked. When the cake is cooked, remove the pan from the oven and leave the cake in the pan to cool. Turn the cake onto a wire rack and remove the lining paper. Spike the top of the cake with a skewer and spoon a few tablespoons of brandy or other spirit over the top. To store the cake, wrap it in cheesecloth and foil. If possible, repeat the spooning over of brandy or spirit every few weeks. The cake can be allowed to mature for 2-3 months.

Quick Mix Cake

This is a quick cake, which is ideal for novelty cakes, and the mixture is firm enough to cut into any shape; it is moist and crumbly and can be filled with cream, butter or jam.

Put the margarine, sugar, eggs, sifted flour and baking powder in a bowl. Mix together all the ingredients with either a wooden spoon or electric mixer. Beat for 1-2 minutes until the mixture is smooth and glossy. In a food processor this will take 30 seconds-1 minute. Put the mixture in a prepared pan. Level the top with the back of a spoon and bake in the center of the oven at 325°F (see chart for the suggested time). When baked, the cake will be firm to the touch and shrink away from the sides of the pan. Loosen the sides of the cake from the pan and leave it to cool on a wire rack. Turn the cake right way up onto another wire rack.

Beaten Sponge Cake

This cake mixture is ideal for afternoon tea and the cake may be filled with cream, butter frosting or fruit. It does not keep well and is best eaten the same day it is made, although it can be kept in the freezer for up to 2 months.

Put the eggs and sugar in a

heatproof bowl over a saucepan of hot, not boiling, water. The bowl must not touch the water. Beat the mixture until it becomes thick enough to leave a trail when lifted. Sift the flour and baking powder together and fold into the egg mixture with a metal spoon, taking care not to knock the air out. Pour the mixture into a prepared pan and gently shake the mixture level. Bake in the center of the oven (see chart for oven temperature and suggested time). Remove from the pan and cool on a wire rack. When making a jelly roll, turn out the cake onto a sheet of wax paper sprinkled with confectioners' sugar. Quickly peel off the lining paper and trim the cake edges. Fold and roll the cake up without cracking it. Let it cool a little, then unroll and remove the wax paper. Fill and re-roll the cake.

Madeira Cake

Madeira cake is a moist cake that can be covered with almond paste and then frosted with royal frosting or any other frostings.

PREPARATION TIME: 15 minutes

COOKING TIME: 1 hour 15 minutes to 1 hour 30 minutes

OVEN TEMPERATURE: 325°F

¾ cup butter
¾ cup sugar
Grated rind of 1 lemon
3 eggs
2 cups flour
2 tsp baking powder
2 tblsp warm water

Cream the butter and sugar until they are light and fluffy. Beat the eggs in one at a time, adding a spoonful of flour after each egg. Sift in the remaining flour and fold it into the mixture with lemon rind and juice. Turn into a prepared cake pan and bake in the oven for 1¼-1½ hours. When cooked, the cake should be firm to the touch. Leave it in the pan to cool for 5-10 minutes, then turn onto a wire rack and remove the lining paper.

Beaten Sponge Cake

CAKE SIZES	2 x 7in cake pans	8in cake pan 7in square cake pan	11 x 7in jelly-roll pan	18 sponge drops	8in round cake pan	2 x 8in cake pans
APPROX COOKING TIME:	20-25 minutes	25-30 minutes	10-12 minutes	5-10 minutes	35-40 minutes	20-25 minutes
OVEN:	350°F	350°F	375°F	375°F	350°F	350°F
Eggs	2	2	2	2	3	3
Fine white sugar	⅓ cup	⅓ cup	⅓ cup	⅓ cup	½ cup	½ cup
Cake flour	½ cup	½ cup	½ cup	½ cup	¾ cup	¾ cup
Baking powder	¾ tsp	¾ tsp	¾ tsp	¾ tsp	¾ tsp	¾ tsp

Quick Mix Cake

CAKE SIZES	2 x 7in cake pans	18 paper cake cases or small tart tins	8in cake pan / 8in ring mold / 7in deep square cake pan	*1¾ pint pudding mold / *add 3 tblsp cornstarch sifted with the flour	About 26 paper cases of small tart tins	2 x 8in cake pans
APPROX COOKING TIME:	25-30 minutes	15-20 minutes	35-40 minutes	about 50 minutes	15-20 minutes	30-35 minute
OVEN:	325°F	325°F	325°F	325°F	325°F	325°F
Shortening	½ cup	½ cup	½ cup	½ cup	¾ cup	¾ cup
Fine white sugar	⅔ cup	⅔ cup	⅔ cup	⅔ cup	1 cup	1 cup
Eggs	2	2	2	2	3	3
Flour	1 cup	1 cup	1 cup	1 cup	1½ cups	1½ cups
Baking powder	1¼ tsp	1¼ tsp	1¼ tsp	1¼ tsp	1½ tsp	1½ tsp
Vanilla essence	4 drops	4 drops	4 drops	4 drops	6 drops	6 drops

For Victoria Sponge see "Tea Time Treats."

Variations

Chocolate Victoria Sponge
Replace 1oz flour with 1oz sifted cocoa powder. Add this to the other flour.

Coffee Victoria Sponge
Replace the water with coffee essence, or dissolve 2 tsp instant coffee powder in 1 tblsp boiling water.

Lemon Victoria Sponge
Add the very finely grated rind of 1 lemon.

Basic Frosting Recipes and Their Uses

Quick Frosting

This is an easy white frosting which is a quick version of the traditional American frosting. A sugar thermometer is not required for this recipe, but the frosting must be used very quickly before it sets.

PREPARATION TIME: 7-10 minutes

1 egg white
¾ cup confectioners' sugar
Pinch of salt
2 tblsp water
Pinch of cream of tartar

Put all the ingredients into a heatproof bowl and mix. Put the bowl over a pan of simmering water and beat the mixture. If possible, use an electric mixer until the frosting peaks. Remove the frosting from the heat and pour it over the cake, spreading it quickly. This will cover a 7 inch cake.

Chocolate Fudge Frosting

PREPARATION TIME: 10 minutes

This is a delicious chocolate frosting which is quick and easy to make.

¼ cup butter
3 tblsp milk
1 cup confectioners' sugar, well sifted
2 tblsp cocoa powder, sifted

Melt the butter in a small saucepan with the milk. Add the confectioners' sugar and cocoa and beat well until smooth and very glossy. Cool until lukewarm and pour over cake. This is enough to fill and frost the top of a 8 inch cake.
NB: if the frosting is too thick to pour, reheat gently to thin. This frosting can also be made in a small bowl over a pan of gently simmering water.

Sponges: Beaten Sponge, Madeira Cake.

Tables

11 x 7 x 1½in cake square	12 x 9in jelly-roll pan
30-35 minutes	12-15 minutes
350°F	400°F
3	3
½ cup	½ cup
¾ cup	¾ cup
¾ tsp	¾ tsp

9in cake pan	11 x 7 x 1½in cake square / 8in round cake pan / 8in square cake pan	2½ pint pudding mold	11½ x 8½ x 1½in cake square	9in round cake pan / 9in square cake pan	12 x 10 x 2in cake square
about 25 minutes	35-40 minutes	about 1 hour	about 40 minutes	about 1 hour	50-60 minutes
325°F	325°F	325°F	325°F	325°F	325°F
¾ cup	¾ cup	¾ cup	1 cup	1 cup	1¼ cups
1 cup	1 cup	1 cup	1⅓ cups	1⅓ cups	1⅔ cups
3	3	3	4	4	5
1½ cups	1½ cups	1½ cups	2 cups	2 cups	2½ cups
1½ tsp	1½ tsp	1½ tsp	2 tsp	2 tsp	2¼ tsp
6 drops	6 drops	6 drops	8 drops	8 drops	10 drops

Marzipan or Almond Paste

This is a paste which is made firm and rollable, and is traditionally used as a base cover for fruit cakes before coating with royal frosting or any other decorative frosting. Prepare the cake by levelling the top, if necessary. Dust a work surface with confectioners' sugar and roll out half the almond paste 1 inch larger than the top of the cake. Brush the top of the cake with the apricot glaze, or the egg white and brandy. Invert the cake onto the almond paste and, using a palette knife, draw up the top of the almond paste around the cake. Put the top of the cake down on a board and brush the sides of the cake with apricot glaze. Cut two pieces of string or thread, one the height of the cake and the other equal in length to the circumference. Roll out the remaining almond paste into a strip, equal in width and length to the circumference of the cake, using the strings as a guide, or cut two short strips of paste instead. Carefully wrap the almond paste round the cake, pressing firmly round the sides and joins. For a square cake, cut the string into four lengths, equal to the sides of the cake and cut the paste to match. Press lightly on the paste when it is placed round the cake in order to produce sharp corners. When covered, leave the cake for 24 hours to dry. Wedding cakes should be left for up to 1 week before frosting, otherwise almond oil will stain the frosting if the cake is kept after the wedding.

Marzipan or Almond Paste

PREPARATION TIME: 15 minutes

½ cup sugar
½ cup confectioners' sugar
1 cup ground almonds
1 tsp lemon juice
A few drops almond essence
1 or 2 egg yolks, beaten

Mix the sugars and the ground almonds in a bowl. Make a well in the center and add the lemon juice, almond essence and egg yolk or yolks to the mixture and form into a pliable dough. Lightly dust the work surface with confectioners'

Guide to Almond Paste Quantities Required for Cakes

Square	Round	Almond Paste/ Marzipan
5 inch	6 inch	12oz
6 inch	7 inch	1lb 4oz
7 inch	8 inch	1½lb
8 inch	9 inch	1½lb
9 inch	10 inch	2lb
10 inch	11 inch	2¼lb
11 inch	12 inch	2½lb
12 inch		3lb

sugar and turn out the dough. Knead until smooth. The almond paste can be stored in a polythene bag or wrapped in foil for 2-3 days before use. Makes 1lb.

Apricot Glaze

PREPARATION TIME: 10 minutes

This glaze can be stored in an airtight container for up to 1 week, if kept in the refrigerator. Re-boil the glaze and cool before applying to the cake.

6-8oz apricot jam
2 tblsp water

Put the jam and water in a saucepan and heat until the jam has melted, stirring occasionally. Pour the jam through a sieve and return it to a clean saucepan. Re-boil and simmer until you have a slightly thickened consistency. Cool before applying to the cake.

How to Royal Frost

It does not matter whether you frost the top or the sides first, the important point to remember is that the frosting should be applied in several thin coats. Try frosting a section first, rather than doing all of it in one go. Your aim is to achieve a smooth surface and you must let each coat dry before applying another. Most cakes require 2 coats on the top and sides, with maybe 3 on the top for a very smooth finish. Wedding cakes require three coats all over and the bottom tiers need 4 coats. For a 2 or 3-tier cake apply 4 coats to the bottom tier; for a 4-tier cake apply 4 coats to the bottom 2 tiers.

Method for Frosting a Cake – Frosting the Sides of a Round Cake

A flat-sided scraper is essential for

producing smooth sides. Put plenty of frosting on the side of the cake and, using a small palette knife, move it back and forth to get a relatively smooth surface and to remove little air pockets. For round cakes, put your arm round the back of the cake and move the scraper forwards on the cake as this will help you to get a smooth, sweeping movement without stopping. The scraper should be upright against the side of the cake. Move the scraper off the cake at an angle so the join is not noticeable. If you use a turntable, it will make frosting larger cakes easier. Hold the scraper to the side of the cake and use the other hand round the cake so the turntable moves round quickly and smoothly in one revolution. Scrape off any extra frosting with a small palette knife. Wipe the cake board and allow each coat to dry for 2-3 hours or overnight before frosting the top.

Frosting the Top

When frosting the base tier of a wedding cake, remember not to add glycerine. Spread the frosting on the cake and, using a metal, or firm plastic, ruler held at a 30° angle, draw it gently across the cake with a positive movement. Try not to press down too hard or the frosting will be too thin. Remove any surplus frosting from the sides of the cake with a clean palette knife. Leave the frosting to dry for at least a day. Remove any rough edges round the joins with clean, fine-graded sandpaper. If the coating is not enough, repeat this 2-3 times. Wait 24 hours before applying frosting decoration onto the cake.

Frosting a Square Cake

Ice 2 opposite sides first, then the other 2 sides to produce sharp corners. Hold the palette knife parallel with the side of the cake when frosting.

Royal Frosting

The consistency of royal frosting depends upon its use. For rosettes and flat frosting it should be quite firm, whereas for applying latticework and writing it should be a little thinner. When frosting is required for any flooding and runouts, it should be thin and smooth. Royal frosting can be made in any quantity in the proportion of 1 egg per cup of sieved confectioners' sugar. Keep the frosting bowl covered with a damp cloth to keep it moist. As an egg substitute, egg albumen (white) can be bought in specialist cake decoration shops and the instructions for use are given on the packet. The addition of glycerine will aid the softening of the frosting when it is dry. This makes it easier to cut.

Wedding Cakes

When frosting wedding cakes, do not add glycerine to the two top layers of frosting on the bottom tier, so the cake can support the other tiers. Made frosting can be stored in an airtight container in a cool atmosphere for 2 days. Before use the stored frosting should be stirred well.

Beat the egg whites with a wire whisk until frothy, making sure that the bowl is clean and dry first. Gradually beat in half the confectioners' sugar using a wooden spoon. Beat in the remaining half of the confectioners' sugar with the glycerine and, if using lemon juice, add it now. Beat the mixture thoroughly until smooth and white. Beat in enough icing sugar to give the mixture a consistency which is stiff and stands in peaks. Add the color, if required. Cover the bowl with a damp cloth and leave the frosting to stand for several hours. This allows any air bubbles to rise to the surface of the frosting and burst. Before using, stir well with a wooden spoon. Do not overbeat. Note: if you are using an electric mixer, use the slowest speed and leave the frosting for 24 hours as this will incorporate more air and will need longer to stand.

Facing page: covering with almond paste, and using apricot glaze.

Guide to Royal Frosting Quantities Required to Flat Frost in Two Thin Coats

Square	Round	Icing Sugar
5 inch	6 inch	1½lb
6 inch	7 inch	2lb
7 inch	8 inch	2½lb
8 inch	9 inch	3lb
9 inch	10 inch	3½lb
10 inch	11 inch	3½lb
11 inch	12 inch	4½lb
12 inch		4½lb

Molding Frosting

PREPARATION TIME: 20 minutes

This is also known as kneaded fondant. It is very easy to use and can be rolled out like pastry. It is ideal for covering novelty cakes and even rich fruit cake. The frosting sets and becomes firm. Molding frosting can be used to cover a cake directly or over almond paste. If using almond paste first, allow the paste to dry before covering with the frosting, which can also be used to make flowers and other decorations.

2 cups confectioners' sugar
1 egg white
¼ cup liquid glucose
Food coloring or flavoring, if desired

Sift the confectioners' sugar into a mixing bowl and add the egg white and the liquid glucose to the center of the sugar. Beat the ingredients with a wooden spoon, gradually incorporating the confectioners' sugar to result in a stiff mixture. Knead the frosting until you have a pliable paste. This icing can be stored by placing it into a bag, wrapping it in plastic wrap or sealing it in a plastic container and storing it in a cool place for up to 3 days. If adding a color, sprinkle with a little more sifted confectioners' sugar to keep the frosting the same consistency.

To Apply Molding or Gelatin Frosting
Brush either the cake with apricot glaze or the almond paste with egg white. Roll out the frosting on a surface dusted with confectioners' sugar or cornstarch, or between two sheets of dusted polythene. Roll out the frosting at least 3 inches larger than the top of the

cake. Support the frosting on a rolling pin and drape it over the cake. Dust your hands with cornstarch or confectioners' sugar and rub the surface of the cake, working in circular movements with the palms of your hands to make the frosting thinner and ease it down the sides of the cake. Smooth out any folds in the frosting and cut off the excess. If frosting a square cake, mold the corners so that the square keeps its shape. Leave to dry.

Gelatin Frosting

PREPARATION TIME: 20 minutes

This frosting can be used in the same way as molding frosting, but when it dries it becomes quite brittle. The frosting can be used to make decorations such as flowers and leaves.

2 tsp gelatin powder
2 tblsp water to dissolve the gelatin
2 cups confectioners' sugar
1 egg white

Put the gelatin powder into the water, which is contained in a small, heatproof basin held over a saucepan of hot water. Stir until the gelatin has dissolved. Sift the confectioners' sugar into another bowl and add the dissolved gelatin and egg white. Stir well until firm, then knead with the fingers until smooth. Dust with extra confectioners' sugar, if necessary. If adding food coloring, sprinkle with more confectioners' sugar to keep the frosting to the same consistency. This frosting can be stored for 2 to 3 days before use. To do so, wrap it in plastic wrap or

a polythene bag and keep it in a sealed container. If it begins to dry, place the frosting in its sealed polythene bag and dip briefly in hot water. Leave for 1 hour and knead well before use.

Glacé Frosting

PREPARATION TIME: 10 minutes

Probably the quickest frosting to make, it is used on sponges, small cakes and cookies. To keep the frosting liquid, place the bowl over a pan of hot water.

1 cup confectioners' sugar
2 tblsp warm water
Various flavorings and colorings

Sift the confectioners' sugar into a mixing bowl and gradually add the water. The frosting should be thick enough to coat the back of a spoon when it is withdrawn from the mixture. Add the flavoring and the coloring, if desired. This quantity will frost 18 small cakes and half the amount will frost the top of a 8 inch cake.

Variations

Coffee
Replace 1 tblsp warm water with 1 tblsp coffee essence.

Orange or Lemon
Replace 1 tblsp warm water with 1 tblsp orange or lemon juice. Add the grated rind of one orange or lemon and a few drops of food coloring.

Chocolate
Sift 3 tblsp cocoa powder with the confectioners' sugar.
NB: you must be careful not to keep the frosting in too hot a bowl of water, otherwise it will lose its gloss. Also, if a newly-frosted cake is moved around without being given a chance to set, the glacé frosting could crack and spoil the smooth surface.

Buttercream Frosting

This frosting is good for covering sponge and quick cake mixture cakes. Butter frosting is ideal for covering novelty cakes, as it can be flavored and colored easily and is no problem to use.

PREPARATION TIME: 10 minutes

½ cup butter
1 cup sifted confectioners' sugar
2 tblsp milk
Flavorings (see 'Variations')

Beat the butter and some of the confectioners' sugar until smooth. Add the remaining confectioners' sugar with the milk and flavoring. Beat until creamy. This frosting will cover and fill a 8 inch 2-layer cake. Store in an airtight container in the refrigerator, for several weeks if necessary.

Variations

Lemon or Orange
Add the grated rind of 1 lemon or orange to the butter. Replace the milk with lemon or orange juice. Add a few drops of orange or lemon coloring.

Molding frosting, Royal frosting, Butter frosting, American frosting and Buttercream frosting.

Chocolate
Blend 2 tblsp cocoa powder with 2 tblsp boiling water. Cool, then add to the mixture with 1 tblsp milk.

Coffee
Replace 1 tblsp milk with 1 tblsp coffee essence.

Crème au Beurre

PREPARATION TIME: 15 minutes

2 egg whites
½ cup confectioners' sugar, sifted
½ cup unsalted butter
Flavorings (see 'Variations')

Place the egg whites and confectioners' sugar in a bowl over a pan of simmering water. Beat until the mixture holds its shape. Cool. Cream the butter until soft

then beat into the egg white mixture, a little at a time. Flavor or color as required.

Variations

Chocolate
Melt 2oz plain chocolate in a bowl over a pan of hot water. Cool and beat into the egg white mixture.

Coffee
Add 1 tblsp coffee essence to the egg white mixture.

Praline
Gently heat ¼ cup of both sugar and blanched almonds in a small pan until the sugar turns brown round the nuts. Turn the mixture onto an oiled cooky sheet, cool and crush with a rolling pin. Add the 3 tblsp of this crushed praline to the egg white mixture.
NB: this frosting can be stored in an airtight container in the

refrigerator for several weeks.

Confectioners' Custard

PREPARATION TIME: 10-15 minutes

3 egg yolks
¼ cup sugar
¼ cup all-purpose flour
1¼ cups milk
2 tblsp butter
1 tblsp sherry

Put the egg yolks and sugar in a bowl and beat until smooth and creamy. Stir in flour and mix well. Heat the milk until hot, but not boiling, and stir into the egg mixture. Return the mixture to the pan and stir, bringing it gently to the boil. Remove from the heat

and beat in the butter and the sherry. Pour into a bowl, stirring occasionally to prevent a skin forming. Makes 1¾ cups of custard. NB: the custard can be stored in the refrigerator for up to 48 hours.

Basic Equipment and Practising Skills
You will probably have most of the basic pieces of equipment needed for decorating simple cakes: various-sized bowls and basins, measuring cups, measuring spoons, wooden spoons, spatula, pastry brush, rolling pin, kitchen scales, airtight containers, cocktail sticks, artist's brush and a wooden skewer, to name but a few. However, special frosting equipment is often required, so it is wise to invest in a good, basic selection. You can extend your range as the need

arises. Palette knives are ideal for smoothing and spreading frosting. They come in various sizes and one would prove most useful. A frosting ruler is essential for flat icing the tops of cakes. Choose a firm, not flexible, ruler – at least 12 inches long, but preferably 14 inches. A frosting rule is even better. A frosting turntable is invaluable for frosting and decorating large cakes. There are several types of frosting scraper and these are used for pulling round the sides of the cake until it is smooth. Frosting cones come into the same category and have serrated teeth of various sizes.

Decorating Tips
Decorating tips come in various forms, the metal types giving the best definition. Try to start with a few basic tips. The range available starts from size 00. A basic frosting tip kit should consist of a fine, a medium and a thick writing tip; a shell tip; a leaf and a scroll tip; a ribbon tip (which is also used for basketwork); a forget-me-not and an 8-point and 10-point star tip. Tips are available in two styles: plain or screw-on types. Screw-on tips are used in conjunction with nylon pastry bags and a screw connector. Plain tips can be used with paper or nylon pastry bags. With this type of tip remember that the frosting has to be removed in order to change a tip. You can either make your own, or use a nylon pastry bag or frosting pump. To make a paper pastry bag, cut a piece of good quality wax paper or non-stick silicone paper into a 10 inch square. Fold in half to form a triangle. Fold the triangle in half to make a yet smaller triangle. Open out the smaller triangle and re-shape into a cone. Turn over the points of the cone so that it stays conical. Secure the join with a little sticky tape. Cut about ½ inch off the tip of the bag and push in a tip.

Nylon Pastry Bags
Nylon bags are sold in various sizes and can be easily filled. These bags are used with a screw connector. The connector is pushed into the bag and protrudes through the hole at the tip of the bag. This allows the tip to be placed at the end and secured with a screw-on attachment, allowing the tip to be changed without emptying the pastry bag.
Nylon pastry bags are most useful for gâteaux as they can be filled with cream, and a meringue tip (a

large decorative tip) can be attached to make rosettes.

Frosting Pumps
These are bought as part of a frosting set; some are made of metal and others of plastic. They consist of a tube with a screw attachment for the screw-on type of tip. The frosting is controlled with a plunger which is unscrewed to refill the tube. Unfortunately, pumps are difficult to use for delicate work as you cannot feel the movement of the frosting to help control it.

Decorations

Frosting Decorations

Stars
Stars can be made with various-shaped tips ranging from 5 to 8, or more, points. With the 5-point star, use a tip number 13 or 8. These are the most useful sizes. Place the star nozzle in the bag and fill with frosting. Hold the bag upright and push out enough frosting to form a star. Remove the tip from the surface of the star swiftly. Stars should be fairly flat without a point in the center.

Rosettes
These are made with a star tip, but using a circular movement. Start at one side of the circle and finish slightly higher than the surface of the frosting in the middle of the circle.

Shell
Use either a star tip or a special shell tip No. 12. Shell tips give fatter shells. Hold the pastry bag at an angle to the surface on which the shell is required and start pushing out frosting towards the center of where the shell will rest. First move the tip away from you and then towards you. Push out more frosting for the thicker parts of the shell. Link the shells together by starting the second shell over the tail of the first.

Leaves
Use a leaf tip, which is No. 10 and has a pointed tip, or sometimes an indentation in the center of the point. Leaves can be decorated straight onto the cake or on non-stick silicone paper, left to dry and then placed onto the cake for decoration. Two or three overlapping movements can be used to give the leaf some form.

Basket Weaving
See 'Tracy Rose Wedding Cake'.

Templates
These are patterns made of paper or card which are used to transfer the pattern onto the top of a cake. It is easy to create your own or, for simple decorations, i.e. circles and squares, draw round a saucepan lid or plastic storage container. On the 21st birthday cake we use a round template. Draw a circle of the required size onto a piece of wax paper and cut it out with a pair of scissors.
Fold the circle in half, into quarters and into eighths, ending with a flattened cone shape. Draw a line in a concave shape from one point to another and cut it out. When the circle is opened, the edge of it will be scallop shaped.

Frosted Flowers
Use a large, medium or fine petal tip, depending on the size of flower required, and a frosting nail, or a piece of waxed paper cut into squares and attached to a cork. Once made, leave the flowers to dry for at least 1 day before transferring them to a cake.

Rose
Hold the pastry bag with the thin part of the tip upright. Push out a cone of frosting, twisting the nail quickly through the fingers and thumb. Push out frosting to make three, four or five petals round the center of the rose by curving them outwards.

Forget-me-nots
Push out the frosting straight onto the cake, using a No. 2 writing tip for the petals, by joining five or six dots together round the edge of the frosting nail and frosting a curved petal in the center. Alternatively use a forget-me-not tip.

Holly Leaves
Color some almond paste green, roll out onto waxed paper and cut into rectangles. Using a frosting tip, cut each holly leaf into shape by cutting first two corners of the rectangle and working your way down the sides until you have a holly leaf shape. Mark the 'veins' with a knife point. Roll out a little more almond paste and color it red for the holly berries.

Christmas Roses
Cover the top of an essence bottle with a little foil and take a piece of

molding frosting the size of a pea and dip it into cornstarch and roll it into a ball. Shape another piece into a petal (see 'Molded Roses'). Repeat until you have five petals. Place the small ball in the foil and surround it with the petals, overlapping them. Leave to dry. Remove from the foil and paint the center yellow with a little food coloring.

Mistletoe
Roll out a little molding frosting or almond paste colored green. Cut into tongue shapes and round the ends. Mark a definite vein down the middle of the leaf with a knife and leave it to dry. Make small, pea-sized balls out of either natural almond paste or white molding frosting.

Molded Roses
Make a cone with a little colored molding frosting and press it out at the base so that it stands. Place a piece of frosting the size of a pea in a little cornstarch and roll it into a ball. Using a hard-boiled egg, flatten the frosting in your hand with quick strokes into a petal shape. Use more cornstarch if it gets too sticky. Gently try to get the frosting very thin. Carefully wrap the petals round the cone and turn the edges outwards. Repeat the process until a fully shaped rose is achieved. Leave the rose to dry and cut off the base. It may be necessary to use a cocktail stick to curl the petals.

Chocolate Leaves
Break the chocolate into small pieces and place in a bowl over a pan of hot water. Gently heat until the chocolate melts. Do not overheat the chocolate or let any water dilute it. With an artist's small paintbrush, paint the underside of the freshly-picked, undamaged and washed rose leaf, making sure that the chocolate spreads evenly over the surface of the leaf. Allow the chocolate to set and, when hard, carefully peel the leaf away from the chocolate, starting from the tip.

Facing page: a variety of cake decorations.

CAKES AND CAKE DECORATION
Novelty Cakes

These are fun cakes enjoyed by all ages, but particularly by children. There follows a variety of designs which can be used for every occasion. It is suggested that you use the quick cake mixture or maderia cake for these. Hopefully, this will inspire you to design your own novelty cakes which might be more appropriate for a specific occasion. If you find it difficult to find a cake board for an unusual cake, make your own by covering a sheet of thick card with silver foil.

Birthday Box

12x10x2 inch quick mix cake
Recipe apricot glaze
8oz almond paste (optional) – this makes the cake a little smoother
Recipe molding frosting
Thin 12x10 inch cake board or piece of thick card
Food coloring – yellow
8oz candies
8oz royal frosting
Egg white, beaten, for attaching molding frosting

Put the cake on a larger cake board. Brush with apricot glaze and cover, if desired, with a thin layer of almond paste. Color the molding frosting and save 4oz in a plastic bag. Brush the cake with egg white, roll out the molding frosting and use it to cover the almond pasted cake. With a knife or ruler press lines diagonally into the frosting. Roll out the reserved 4oz of molding frosting and cover the white side of a thin, rectangular, silver cake board (the same size as

the top of the cake). Fit a pastry bag with a small star tip and fill with royal frosting. Pipe shells round the bottom edge of the cake. Put the lid on a basin and apply frosted shells round the edge of the lid. Decorate the lid with either fresh or piped flowers and a bow secured with royal frosting. Place the candies on top of the cake and put the lid on, leaving them partially revealed.

Clown

1lb molding frosting
    6 tblsp colored pale orange
    ¾ cup colored yellow
    ⅔ cup colored red
    ¼ cup colored green
1 large jelly roll
4 small jelly rolls
2 Lady fingers (sponge fingers)
1 marshmallow
1 recipe apricot glaze
1 recipe royal frosting, colored red

Using the orange molding frosting, break off 2 small rounds and gently flatten them. Make 4 cuts halfway into the balls to make fingers. Roll out the remaining orange frosting into a strip which is 8x3 inches. Brush the ends of the jelly roll with the apricot glaze and use the orange strip to cover the ends of the jelly roll. Brush the rest of the jelly roll with the glaze and with a third of the yellow frosting rolled out into a strip 8x5 inches, cover the glazed area of jelly roll. Squeeze the join of the yellow and orange frosting so that it forms a head and body. Stand the jelly roll upright on a cake board with something for support. Put the small jelly rolls lengthways for the legs and brush with glaze. Take a small ball of yellow molding frosting and roll it out into a 4x1 inch width. Divide it into 2 and cut slashes in each

This page: Birthday Box.

Facing page: Clown.

halfway up. These will be used for the hair (reserve). Brush the sponge fingers with glaze and cover them with yellow fondant. Stick them with jam onto the sides of the body. Roll out the remaining yellow frosting into a strip 8x5 inches and cut it down the middle. Use each strip to cover the legs. Roll out a small piece of red frosting and mold it over the marshmallow and leave to dry. Roll out 2 pea-sized balls of red frosting and use them as buttons. Roll out another small piece of red frosting and cut with a pastry cutter. Divide the green frosting into two balls, rolling out one and cutting with the same round pastry cutter. Using a cocktail stick, create folds in the circles which radiate from the center. Work your way round. Cut one of the circles in two and the other into four. Roll out the red frosting into an oblong 7x3 inches and attach it to the legs in thin strips. Using the reserved green frosting, flatten it a little and cut it into two, shaping each half into an oval. Stick them upright on to the end of the legs as boots. Put half red and half green frills round the neck of the clown, securing them with a little apricot glaze. Put quarter frills round his wrists and ankles, with a little glaze to attach them to the hands. Secure the hair

to his head with glaze. Do the same with the hat. Fill a pastry bag fitted with a writing tip with the red frosting and pipe features onto the clown's face. Surround him with sweets or put balloons in his hand.

Giant Sandwich Cake

12x10x2 inch quick mix cake
Food colorings – brown, green, yellow, pink, red
Recipe molding frosting
Egg white to brush almond paste
½ x recipe butter cream frosting
8oz almond paste, if required

Cut the cake diagonally so you have 2 triangles. Color half of the frosting pale brown. Divide a further quarter into four and color the pieces green, yellow, salmon pink and red. Remember to keep frosting in a plastic bag when you are not using it, to prevent it from drying out. For the lettuce, roll out an irregular shape with the green frosting and crinkle it up using a cocktail stick so it looks like ruched material. Reserve on a sheet of non-stick silicone paper. To make the ham, roll out the pink frosting with a pinch of white frosting, making sure the colors stay separate. Roll out into an oval shape and reserve. For the cheese, roll the yellow frosting into a 4 inch square and reserve. For the tomato slices, roll the red frosting into a 4 inch square and with a small, plain round pastry cutter cut rounds. Roll out the pale brown frosting into 6 strips all 2 inches wide: two

12 inches long, two 10 inches long, two 16 inches long. Use the egg white to brush the sides of the triangles. Stick the brown strips onto the appropriate length sides. Roll out the remaining white frosting into a triangle large enough to cover the top of one triangular cake piece. Brush the top of the cake triangle and fix on the molding frosting triangle. Spread the top of the other cake, the one without white molding frosting, with a little butter frosting to make the bottom half of the sandwich and make sure it is on either a presentation plate or a cake board. Around the edges of the bottom triangle lay the lettuce, ham, tomato and cheese so they spill out of the cake. Stick together with the frosted triangle. Fit a pastry bag with a star tip and fill with the remaining butter frosting. Frost irregular swirls in between the lettuce, tomato, cheese and ham. Dust the top of the triangular cake with a little confectioners' sugar.

Birthday Breakfast

Rich fruit cake (measure the size of your skillet and bake a cake that will fit)
Recipe apricot glaze
4oz white molding frosting
Food colorings – brown, pink
15oz can apricot halves

Transfer the fruit cake to the frying pan. Brush the top with apricot glaze. Roll out the white molding frosting and cut into several irregular shapes, rounding off any sharp corners. Roll the remaining frosting into sausage shapes and brush them with a little brown and pink food coloring. Drain the can of apricot halves. Place the irregular white molding frosting shapes on top of the cake, putting an inverted apricot half on each one. Put the sausages in the pan. Brush the sausages and the apricot halves with a little apricot glaze.

Camelot Castle

2 8 inch square 6-egg Victoria sponges
Recipe butter cream frosting
Recipe apricot glaze
4 ice cream cones
4 miniature jelly rolls
1 rectangular plain cooky
1 water cooky
½ cup granulated sugar
4oz molding frosting
Recipe royal frosting
Sugar flowers
Silver balls
3 or 4 small paper flags
Food colorings – pink, green, red

Toffee Water (To Fill Moat)
1 cup granulated sugar
⅔ cup water
Blue food coloring
Sugar thermometer, if available

Cut a 2 inch wide slice from one cake. Put the other cake towards the back of the cake board. Stick the large section of cake to the cake on the board with some butter frosting. Make sure it sits towards the back of the base cake. With apricot glaze, secure the 2 inch slice on the front edge of the cake board. Using apricot glaze, brush the ends of the small jelly rolls and place them in the four corners of the cake, placing the ice cream cones on top. Cover the small jelly rolls, ice cream cones and the top and sides of the cake with butter frosting. Also frost the 2 inch slice. Put the water cooky on the front side of the cake between the 2 jelly roll towers. Put the granulated sugar, with a few drops of pink food coloring, in a bowl and stir well until the sugar takes up the color. Sprinkle the colored sugar over the ice-cream cones, the top of the castle and the grounds. Fit a star tip to a pastry bag and fill with royal frosting. Pipe round the top of the castle walls and over the front surface of the water cooky. When the stars are just drying, go round the top of the walls and frost another row of stars on top of each alternate star. Put a silver ball in the center of each of the stars round the edge of the door and 2 for doorknobs. Color a little of the royal frosting green, and a little red, and frost the green vine with red stars for flowers. You can also use sugar flowers.

To Make the Water to Fill the Moat
Color the molding frosting green and roll it out to form a long sausage which will go round the edge of the board. Use the frosting

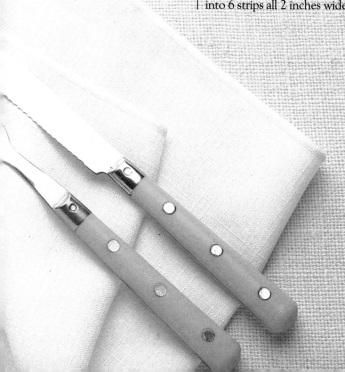

Giant Sandwich Cake (top left) and Birthday Breakfast (bottom left).

with a pastry wheel. With a little water, attach the ribbons of fondant to the inside of the shoes approximately halfway between the toe and heel. With a cocktail stick, gently mark round the top of the shoe, then the sole. Cut two 6 inch long, string-width strips of fondant and make a little bow out of each and put them in place. As an alternative, pink satin ribbon can be used in place of fondant. Fill the shoes with the candies.

Football Boot

10x8 inch quick mix cake
Jam for filling
Recipe apricot glaze
Recipe molding frosting
Recipe butter frosting
¼ cup shredded coconut
¼ cup chocolate chips
Food coloring – red, yellow, black and
*   green*
Medium star tip and pastry bag
2 liquorice laces
12 inch square cake board
1 cocktail stick

Cut the cake horizontally and stick together with jam for filling. Put the cakes on the board. With a cocktail stick mark out the outline of the boot. When you are happy with the outline, cut it out with a sharp knife and brush with apricot glaze. Divide the molding frosting into two, remembering to keep the frosting in a plastic bag when not in use. Roll out half the frosting into an oblong and cover the boot shape (top and sides). Do not frost the leg. Cut the frosting at the ankle to indicate the top of the boot. Divide the remaining frosting into two, coloring half red and the rest yellow. Draw out the shapes for the patches, tongue of the boot and the flash on some wax paper. Draw a large 'E' with a double line and cut it out. This should be used as a template to guide you when you roll out the red frosting to cover the ankle and the flash for the side of the boot. Roll out the yellow molding frosting and cut the

---

to form a wall and stick it down by smoothing it onto the board, then leave it to dry for one hour. Heat the sugar and water so the sugar dissolves and boils. Continue to boil the mixture until it reaches 'soft crack' point, that is, just before it starts to color. If a sugar thermometer is available, the reading should be 270-290°F. Pour the sugar mixture into the moat. Put the sugar flowers on the green banks of the moat and lay the cooky across from the castle to the land to form a drawbridge. Use the flags to decorate.

Ballet Shoes

2 jelly rolls
12 inch square cake board
2lb fondant frosting
Food coloring – pink
Recipe apricot glaze
Cornstarch to dust
4 tblsp jam
1 yard pink satin ribbon (as an
*   alternative to fondant ribbons)*

To Make Shoes
Cut the edge of one end of the cake into a point. Then cut the tip of the point. This will be the toe end of the shoe. Repeat for the other shoe and place them both on

---

the cake board. Cut the other end of the cake, rounding it slightly. Cut out a long oval towards the heel end of the cake. Press the cake in firmly, but gently, to create an instep. Color all the fondant pale pink. Brush the cake with the glaze. Roll out the fondant on the cornstarch-dusted work surface. Press the fondant down and smooth out any cracks. Mold it gently round the toe and take special care to squeeze and tuck it into the inside of the shoe. Cut off any excess and re-mold it into a ball. Roll out. Cut 4 long strips 1 inch wide and cut the shortest ends with pinking shears or cut

---

This page: Camelot Castle.

Facing page: Ballet Shoes (top) and Football Boot (bottom).

same shapes, but smaller, to go on top of the red. Cut the liquorice laces and tie into a bow. With a little frosting place it at the ankle. Mix half of the butter frosting yellow and half red. Fill a pastry bag with the red butter frosting and pipe a band about 6 stripes wide, then repeat with the yellow frosting. Work your way up the leg until you have 3 red bands and 2 yellow. Put rows of chocolate chips on the side of the boot to represent studs. Put the shredded coconut in a bowl and add a few drops of green food color. Stir in and use to sprinkle on the board to represent grass.

Shirt and Tie

15x3½x¾ inch quick mix cake
2 x recipe butter cream frosting
4oz colored fondant, if using design with tie
1 small packet round candies, e.g. jellies
Food coloring – red

In a clean bowl reserve ¼ of the butter cream frosting and with the food coloring make up a darker shade of the color previously used. Wash the pan used for baking the cake and, if the pan is old or marked, line with foil so that it is totally covered both inside and out. Alternatively, you could make or use a cardboard shirt box. Put the cake into the cake pan or box, and spread with the lighter frosting. If the cake fits snugly into its box or pan, only frost the top; if not, frost all the visible cake. Make the neck and collar shaping by first marking it out. Draw a line in the frosting with a cocktail stick 3 inches from one end of the cake. (The 9 inch sides are top and bottom.) This marks the shoulder line, so use this line to guide you when building up the collar with more frosting. Half the collar (front and back) should be on either side of the faint line. Fill the pastry bag with the darker frosting and with a writing tip outline the collar and shoulder seam. Roll out a thin strip of fondant 1½ inches wide and 14 inches long, pinch it in to form the tie knot and place on the cake. If you are using the design with center placket (shirt front) pocket and sleeves use the darker frosting in the pastry bag and frost the shirt front, pocket and sleeves. Put the candies in position as buttons.

Artist's Palette

9 inch square quick mix cake
Recipe apricot glaze
¾lb molding frosting
½ cup granulated sugar
Food colorings – red, blue, green, yellow, orange, violet and brown

Cut a kidney shape out of the cake and carefully cut a circle slightly off center. Place the cake on the cake board and brush with apricot glaze. Color all except 2oz of the molding frosting pale brown. Roll out and use to cover the palette, pushing in gently at the hole so that the frosting coats the inner wall of the circle. Push down to reveal the cake board. Using a dry brush, dip gently into the brown food coloring and drag hesitantly across the palette. Wipe the brush with kitchen paper to absorb some of the food coloring and continue to cover the palette with the wood grain. Leave to dry. Color 1 tblsp of granulated sugar with each of the food colorings. This is done by adding a few drops and stirring until the sugar absorbs the color. Roll out the remaining molding frosting into a long sausage shape and cut in half. Make a point at the end of one sausage and leave to dry and gently flatten the end of the other.

To Make the Pencil and Paintbrush

When the molding frosting shapes are dry, copying a pencil, color the one with the pointed end by painting in the lead and the outside. Copy the brush you are using and place them next to the palette. When the palette is dry, put little mounds of the colored sugar on the top.

Artist's Palette (left) and Shirt and Tie (below).

CAKES AND CAKE DECORATION

Celebration Cakes

round the bottom of the cake. With a medium, plain tip make bulbs between each of the stars on the inner edge of the cake. Make another row of bulbs on the side of the cake above the stars. Colour a little of the frosting pink and fit a pastry bag with a writing tip. Make a row of dropped loops from each of the bulbs on the top of the cake. From the point of alternate stars on the top edge of the cake make a row of dropped loops. Go round the cake again making loops on the stars omitted on the first round. Make a bulb on the point of each of the stars. With the pink frosting, make a scallop on the cake board round the stars. Write the message with swirls round it in the shape of 'S's and 'C's on the top of the cake and place the flowers, a little fern and the ribbon in position.

Boy's Birthday Cake

8 inch square, rich fruit cake
Recipe apricot glaze
1¾lb almond paste
Royal frosting, made with 3lb
*   confectioners' sugar*
Food coloring – blue
8 silver leaves for the top
16 silver leaves for the side panels

Brush the top of the cake with the apricot glaze. Cover the cake with the almond paste and leave it to dry. Attach the cake to the board with a little frosting. Flat frost the sides and top of the cake and let it dry. Fit a pastry bag with a large tip and make a continuous 'S' pattern on the top edge and the base of the cake. Make 4 bars horizontally across and down the corners of the cake. At each of the 4 corners, and

Mother's Day Cake

7 or 8 inch square or round cake
Recipe apricot glaze
1½lb almond paste
Royal frosting, made with 2lb
*   confectioners' sugar*
Food colorings – green, yellow
Green ribbon
Frosted flowers

Brush the top and sides of the cake with apricot glaze and cover with almond paste; leave to dry. With a little frosting, attach the cake to the cake board and flat frost the top and sides; leave to dry. Using a pastry bag fitted with a leaf tip, make a row of leaves in white frosting facing outwards around the

bottom of the cake. Then make an overlapping circle of white leaves around the top edge of the cake. Fill another pastry bag with green-colored frosting and make a row of leaves facing outwards on top. Finally, make an overlapping circle of green leaves on the top. Fill a pastry bag with a little yellow-colored frosting and fit a medium writing tip and write 'Mother' on the top surface of the cake. Attach the frosted flowers on the top surface with a dab of frosting and, using the pastry bag with green frosting and the leaf tip again, make a few leaves around the flowers to finish. Decorate with the green ribbon.

Girl's Birthday Cake

8 inch round, rich fruit cake
Recipe apricot glaze
1¾lb almond paste
Royal frosting, made with 3lb
*   confectioners' sugar*
3 frosted flowers
Food coloring – pink
Pink ribbon
Frond of asparagus fern

Brush the top and sides of the cake with apricot glaze. Cover the cake with the almond paste. Attach the cake to the board with a little frosting. Flat frost the top and the sides of the cake. Fit a pastry bag with a large star tip and make a circle of stars round the top edge of the cake. Make a row of stars

This page: Girl's Birthday Cake and Boy's Birthday Cake.

Facing page: Mother's Day Cake.

on the top of the cake, make a single line from the flat surface of the cake crossing the continuous 'S' and ending in the corner. Fit a small star tip and frost vertically down the corners of the cake, covering the ends of the bars. Frost the decorative lines on the top of the cake, starting with a long line with a dot at each end and working out and down with shorter lines towards the outer edge. Write the name in the center of the cake. Color a little of the frosting blue and fit a writing tip onto the pastry bag. Make 2 rows of scallops on the top edge of the cake, a row on each side of the continuous 'S', ending at the corner where the corner bars start. Go over the name in blue. Make a dropped loop round the base of the cake, with the point of the loops at each of the corners. Attach 2 silver leaves at the base corners of each of the 4 side panels, and 2 silver leaves on the top of the cake at each of the 4 corners attached to the flat surface of the cake.

Silver Wedding Anniversary Cake

8 or 9 inch square, rich fruit cake
Recipe apricot glaze
1¾-2lb almond paste
Royal frosting, made with 2½lb
  confectioners' sugar
8 silver leaves
Silver non-toxic coloring

Brush the top and the sides of the cake with apricot glaze and cover with almond paste. Leave the cake to dry. Attach the cake to the board with a little frosting. Flat frost the top and sides of the cake, giving 2 or 3 coats. Fit your pastry bag with a medium writing tip. Using a saucepan lid or a round template, draw a circle in the center of the top of the cake. Using a medium-sized five-star tip, pipe a continuous swirl round the bottom edge of the cake and finish off each corner with a shell. With a smaller star tip, pipe a small dot on the top edge of the cake in the center of the top edge of each of the side panels and divide the space between the original dot and the corner of the cake with a further

dot. You should have 3 dots on each of the top sides of the cake. Using these as a guide, join them together by making a scallop, with the dots marking the points of the scallop. Using a writing tip, pipe with a scribbling line between the scallop on the sides of the cake and the template circle drawn on the top of the cake. The scribbling should be done with a continuous line that never crosses itself. Using the same tip, overfrost the template-drawn circle with a continuously twisting line. On the side panels and on the corners of the cake, create three beads in descending size below each of the points of the scallop. Overfrost the continuous swirls round the bottom of the cake with a plain, continuous swirl beginning and ending with an 'S' shape. Make the '25' in the circle on top of the cake, then – when dry – overfrost this again with white. Fit your pastry bag with a medium star tip and, having positioned the silver leaves, secure them with a frosted rosette. Using a fine paintbrush, gently paint the continuous swirl overfrost on the circle on the top surface of the cake and also the top of the '25' with a single silver line.

It is most important that a celebration cake should feed the desired number of guests, so here is a guide:

Round	Square	Portions
6 inch	5 inch	20-30
7½-8 inch	7 inch	40-45
10 inch	9 inch	70-80
11 inch	10 inch	100-110
12 inch	12 inch	130-140

NB: for decorating simple cakes, candies can be utilised and are easily applied to butter frosting. These are much used in novelty cake designs.

Silver Wedding Anniversary Cake.

Golden Wedding Cake

10 inch)round, rich fruit cake
Recipe apricot glaze
2¼lb almond paste
Royal frosting, made from 3lb
 confectioners' sugar
Food coloring – yellow
6 gold leaves
Yellow ribbon

Brush the sides and top of the cake with the apricot glaze. Cover the cake with the almond paste and leave to dry. Attach the cake to the board with a little frosting. Flat frost the top and sides of the cake. Fit a pastry bag with a large star tip and make a row of shells round the top of the cake. Create a row of shells round the bottom of the cake. Fit the pastry bag with a smaller star tip and create continuous 'C's on the shells on the top of the cake. Fit the pastry bag with a medium-sized plain tip and make a scallop on the top of the cake round the shells. Round the bottom of the cake, on the board, make a scallop round the shells. Repeat the scallop on the side of the cake under the shells on the top edge of the cake. Colour a little of the frosting yellow and, using a writing tip, repeat the pattern of continuous 'C's on the top edge of the cake. Make a dropped loop on top of the shell at the base of the cake. Fit the same pastry bag with a leaf tip and make inverted leaves between the shells at the base of the cake, with the point of the leaves creeping up the sides of the cake. With a writing tip, write the words and surround them with 'S's and 'C's. Decorate with a real rose or any other flower, or frosted flowers and/or gold leaves.

Diana Wedding Cake

Two-Tier Round Cake
10 inch round, rich fruit cake
6 or 7 inch round, rich fruit cake
2 x recipe apricot glaze
3lb almond paste
Royal frosting, made from 3½lb
 confectioners' sugar
Silver cake boards: 13 inch and 8 or
 9 inch
32 silver leaves
8 frosted flowers
4 round pillars

Brush the top and sides of the cake with apricot glaze and cover with almond paste. Leave the cake to dry. Attach the cake to the board

with a little frosting. Flat frost the top and sides of the cake, giving three coats and an extra coat on the base cake. Fit a pastry bag with a large star tip and make shells round the bottom of each of the cakes. Using the same tip, mark the cake surface lightly at the edge as though it were square – treat it as though it had four corners, putting a dab of frosting in each of the four corners and a smaller dab at the center of each of the four sides. From each of the dabs which mark the center of the sides make an inverted 'S', finishing at the corner

mark. Repeat this from where you started and mirror the original shape towards the other corner point. Repeat this round the cake. Make a 'C' facing the center of the cake, with its back marking the center point of the side. Overpipe all the decorative swirls, the 'S's and 'C's twice. Fit a pastry bag with a medium-sized plain tip and make a continuously twisting scallop on the upper edge of the sides of the cakes. Repeat this pattern on the cake board around the shells. With the same tip, frost over the decorative swirls, 'S's and 'C's on

the tops of the cakes. Make a scallop on the top surface of the cake, encompassing the 'C's in the curves; three curves to each imaginary side. Make dropped loops under the continuously twisting scallop on the sides of

This page: Golden Wedding Cake. Facing page: Diana Wedding Cake.

Lindsey Jane
Wedding Cake.

cakes. On the sides of the cake below the loops, attach the flowers and leaves with a little frosting, four flowers per cake below each 'C' and a frosting rosette to attach the other leaves between each of the flowers. Assemble the cake using the pillars and decorate the top with flowers.

Lindsey Jane Wedding Cake

Two-Tier Square Cake
6 inch square, rich fruit cake
10 inch square, rich fruit cake
2 x recipe apricot glaze
3¼lb almond paste
Royal frosting made with 4lb
*   confectioners' sugar*
28 pink frosted roses, to decorate
Asparagus fern, to decorate
Silver cake boards, 8 inch and 12
*   inch*
4 square pillars
2 narrow ribbon bows

This design is suitable for a 1, 2 or 3-tier cake. The roses are chosen to match the bridal attire.
Brush the sides and tops of the cakes with apricot glaze and cover with almond paste. Leave to dry. Attach the cakes to the cake boards with a dab of frosting. Flat frost the cakes, giving two or three coats all over. Fit a pastry bag with a medium-sized shell tip and decorate shells on the top edge of the cakes, the bottom edge and up each of the corners. Apply with frosting on the top of the cakes in each corner 2 shells facing each other. Fit the pastry bag with a medium-sized plain tip and create a shallow scallop round the top side of the cake. Create an 'S'-shaped swirl, filling each of the small scallops. On the bottom tier, put a cluster of roses in the middle of the cake, surrounded by fern, two roses in each of the corners and one rose

at the base of each of the corners. On the top tier, repeat but with a single rose at the top of each corner and the ribbon bows on top of the cake. Assemble the cake using the pillars.

Christening Cake

8 inch round, rich fruit cake
Recipe apricot glaze
1¾lb almond paste
Royal frosting, made with 3lb
*   confectioners' sugar*
Food coloring – blue
½oz almond paste
1 narrow, white ribbon bow

Brush the top and sides of the cake with the apricot glaze. Cover the cake with the almond paste and leave it to dry. Attach the cake to the board with a little frosting. Flat frost the top and sides of the cake with the royal frosting. Fit a pastry bag with a large star tip. With a frosting comb, comb the sides of the cake with a swirling line and make a row of shells round the top of the cake. Fit a pastry bag with a small star tip and make a scallop round the top of the shells. Make a graduated rope round the bottom of the cake with a large, dropped loop round the rope. Fit the pastry bag with a small plain tip and make a scallop on the top of the cake next to the shells. Write the name of the baby on the top of the cake. Color a little royal frosting blue. Using a writing tip, make beads at the points of each of the tips. Make another scallop onto the silver board. Go over the name with the blue, making small 'C's and scrolls. To make the bootees, color a little molding frosting pale blue and shape two. Press a small hole towards the end of each of the oval shapes. With a writing tip, pipe round the holes, making a little bow at the front. Decorate with a silver ball and put the small bow between the bootees.

Tracy Rose Wedding Cake

Three-Tier Square
5 inch square, rich fruit cake
8 inch square, rich fruit cake
11 inch square, rich fruit cake
3 x recipe apricot glaze
5lb almond paste
Royal frosting, made with 8lb
confectioners' sugar
2 x recipe molding frosting, peach
color (to make 60 molded roses)
3 cake boards: 7 inch, 10 inch and 14
inch
Food colorings – green, peach (brown)
8 square cake pillars
2 rectangular silver boards

Brush the top and sides of the cakes with apricot glaze and cover with almond paste; leave to dry. Attach the cakes to the silver cake boards with a dab of frosting. Flat frost the tops of the cakes with the peach colored royal frosting. Cut the thin, rectangular cake boards lengthways down the middle and then cut each widthways with a sharp knife. Cut the corners off each piece diagonally so that they will go together to form a square with a square hole in the center. Place each on a sheet of wax paper and flat frost onto the white side with a palette knife; leave to dry. Fit a pastry bag with a medium writing tip and the other with a basket weave tip. Hold the basket weave tip sideways and on the side of the first cake pipe 3 lines, evenly spaced, one above the other and all of the same length. Pipe a vertical line using the writing tip along the edge of the basket weaving. Continue this process until the cake is covered. Repeat the basket weave method on each of the cardboard lids. To make the molded flowers see chapter on decorations. Color a little of the royal frosting green and fit a pastry bag with a leaf tip. Color a little more royal frosting a dark peach and use it to fill a bag fitted with a star tip. Continue to use the writing tip filled with the tinted peach royal frosting as used in the basket weave. Position the molded frosting roses facing outward round the top edges of the 2 bottom tiers and in a radiating pattern on the small top tier. Make frosted dark peach stars between each of the roses and dot the center of each star using the tinted peach royal frosting. Make frosted leaves at random round the flowers. Place the pillars on a tray and frost small stars dotted with tinted peach for the center of the flower. Again, frost leaves at random and leave to dry.

To Assemble the Cake

Place the basket lids round the outer edge of each of the cake's bottom two tiers and, with a little frosting, secure them to the top of the cake. Make sure that there is enough room in the square at the center of each cake for the four pillars.

Note: the cake board can be frosted with a palette knife to surround each of the cakes, if required.

This page: Christening Cake.

Facing page: Tracy Rose Wedding Cake.

BARBECUES & SALADS

Before gas and electricity were harnessed for our cooking convenience, our ancestors employed barbecue cooking, although they didn't know it by that name. Flaming food, however, seemed to go out of fashion for a time in northern Europe, except in chafing dishes in expensive restaurants. Countries with sunnier climates kept up the art and the United States, where informality is the spirit of entertaining, adopted barbecue cooking as its own.

A barbecue grill can be a very primitive arrangement of a firebowl – a place to hold charcoal or wood – and a rack, or some support to hold the food. Modern design has added several different interpretations:

Portable barbecue grills – These are small and are often called picnic barbecues. They have folding or telescopic legs. Table-top models with short legs and hibachis in various sizes are popular styles.

Semi-portable grills – These are slightly larger and have fixed legs, sometimes with wheels for easy movement. They are often round with rotating racks, good for moving food quickly off hot-spots, or adjustable shelves. Rotisseries can be fixed to these grills and most have windshields along the back.

Hooded grills – These keep the food at an even temperature and the smoke out of the cook's eyes! With practice, whole meals can be cooked, and food can be smoked over aromatic wood chips for extra flavor.

Home-made grills – Barbecues can be built of brick or stone with oven shelves for racks.

Electric and gas grills – These use special rocks that radiate heat from electric coils or gas flames. They give the taste and appearance of charcoal-grilled food along with control over the intensity of heat. A dial with a number of settings allows more delicate foods to be cooked through without charring on the outside. These grills are cleaner and heat much faster than charcoal or wood-fired grills, which must be lit at least an hour before cooking. They are also practically self-cleaning. The recipes in this book were cooked on an electric grill from Redring Electric Company.

When choosing a fuel for barbecueing, you should bear in mind that charcoal compressed into briquettes will burn for twice as long, with more uniform heat than lumpwood charcoal – irregular-sized pieces of kiln-charred hardwood. However, lumpwood charcoal is easier to light than briquettes. Vine wood cuttings are an alternative to charcoal, but do not burn as long. Hardwood, such as birch or cherry, can be used, but takes a long time to light and is expensive.

Firelighters, either liquid or solid, get the fire going faster. Use them to start a fire, but never, for safety reasons, on coals that are already hot. With any grill that uses charcoal or wood, be sure the firebowl has perforations in the bottom and sides, or that the coals can sit on a perforated rack inside. This allows air to circulate underneath and makes the fire easier to light and keep going.

Special equipment is not necessary, but long-handled cooking utensils are easiest and safest to use. When grilling fish, a hinged wire rack, specially shaped for both small or large fish, is a great help. So too are square, hinged racks for turning a number of hamburgers, sausages or steaks at the same time.

Cooking times for barbecued food cannot be very exact. There is room for variation depending on the type of grill and source of heat. For grills without adjustable shelves, results are better if the food is cooked in the oven for about half to three-quarters of the cooking time and the remaining time on the barbecue grill for color and flavor. Similarly, larger cuts of meat, such as Butterflied Lamb, will cook faster and be juicer if pre-cooked in the oven. In fact, employ this method with any food cooked for a large group and you will avoid the problem of eating in shifts.

Salads are a natural accompaniment to barbecued food. On a warm summer's day or evening they can also be a light and refreshing meal in themselves. So when summer arrives, abandon your oven occasionally and try barbecues and salads and discover why food tastes so much better when cooked and eaten outdoors.

Appetizers and Side Salads

Satay

PREPARATION TIME: 25 minutes	
COOKING TIME: 10-15 minutes	
SERVES: 4 people	

*1lb chicken, skinned, boned and cut into
    1 inch cubes*

MARINADE
2 tbsps soy sauce
2 tbsps oil
2 tbsps lime juice
1 tsp ground cumin
1 tsp turmeric
2 tsps ground coriander

SAUCE
2 tbsps oil
1 small onion, finely chopped
1 tsp chili powder
1 cup peanut butter
1 tsp brown sugar
Remaining marinade

GARNISH
Lime wedges
Coriander leaves

Combine the marinade ingredients in a deep bowl. Put in the meat and stir to coat. Leave covered in the refrigerator for 1 hour. Drain and thread the meat on 4 large or 8 small skewers. Grill about 10-15 minutes, turning frequently to cook all sides. Baste often. Meanwhile heat the oil in a small saucepan. Add the onion and the chili powder. Cook until the onion is slightly softened. Remove from the heat and set aside. When the meat is nearly cooked combine the marinade with the oil and onion and chili powder. Stir in the remaining sauce ingredients, thinning with water if necessary. Brush the Satay with the sauce 1-2 minutes before the end of cooking time. Spoon over a bit more sauce and serve the rest separately. Garnish each serving with lime wedges and

This page: Rumaki (left) and Satay (right). Facing page: Grilled Garlic Shrimp (left) and Smoked Fish Kebabs with Horseradish Sauce (right).

coriander leaves.

PREPARATION TIME: 15 minutes
COOKING TIME: 10-15 minutes
SERVES: 4 people

¾ cup soy sauce
1lb chicken livers, trimmed and cut into 2
    inch pieces
1 7oz can water chestnuts, drained
8 slices smoked streaky bacon
1 red pepper, cut in 1 inch pieces
Brown sugar

Combine half the soy sauce and all the chicken livers in a deep bowl. Leave to marinate in the refrigerator for 1 hour. Place the bacon slices on a wooden board. Stretch the bacon by running the back of a knife backwards and forwards over each slice. Cut the slices in half across. Drain the chicken livers and discard the soy sauce. Put a piece of liver and a water chestnut on each slice of bacon and roll up. Thread onto skewers, alternating with a piece of red pepper. Grill on an oiled rack above hot coals for 10-15 minutes, basting with the remaining half of the soy sauce and turning frequently. One minute before the end of cooking, sprinkle lightly with brown sugar and allow to glaze. Garnish serving dishes with parsley if desired.

Greek Salad

PREPARATION TIME: 15 minutes
SERVES: 4 people

1 head romaine lettuce
16 black olives, stoned
1 cup crumbled feta cheese
1 small can anchovies, drained
8 mild pickled peppers
2oz cherry tomatoes, halved
½ cucumber, cut in small dice
2 tbsps chopped fresh oregano or 1 tbsp
    dried oregano

DRESSING
½ cup olive oil
3 tbsps red wine vinegar
1 clove garlic, finely minced
Salt and pepper

Wash and dry the romaine lettuce and tear the leaves into bite-size pieces. Place the leaves in a large salad bowl and arrange or scatter all the other ingredients on top of the lettuce. If the anchovies are large, cut them into thinner strips or chop into small pieces. Sprinkle the fresh or dried oregano over all the ingredients in the salad bowl. Mix the dressing together well and pour over the salad just before serving.

Caesar Salad

PREPARATION TIME: 20 minutes
COOKING TIME: 3 minutes
SERVES: 4-6 people

1 large or two small heads romaine lettuce
8 slices white bread, crusts removed
½ cup oil
1 clove garlic, peeled
1 small can anchovies
3oz fresh Parmesan cheese

DRESSING
1 egg
½ cup olive oil
Juice of 1 lemon
1 clove garlic, finely minced
Salt and pepper

Wash the lettuce and dry well. Tear the lettuce into bite-size pieces and place in a large salad bowl, or four individual bowls. Cut the slices of bread into ½ inch dice. Heat the vegetable oil in a small frying pan. When the oil is hot put in the clove of garlic and the cubes of bread. Lower the heat slightly and, using a metal spoon, keep stirring the cubes of bread to brown them evenly. When they are golden brown and crisp, remove them to paper towels to drain. Add the anchovies to the lettuce in the salad bowl and sprinkle on the fried bread croûtons. To prepare the dressing, place the egg in boiling water for 1 minute. Break into a small bowl and combine with remaining dressing ingredients, whisking very well. Pour the dressing over the salad and toss. Using a cheese slicer, shave off thin slices of Parmesan cheese and add to the salad. Alternatively, grate the cheese and add to the salad with the dressing.

Smoked Fish Kebabs with Horseradish Sauce

PREPARATION TIME: 15 minutes
COOKING TIME: 6 minutes
SERVES: 4 people

1 smoked kipper fillet, skinned and cut
    into 1 inch pieces
1 smoked haddock fillet, skinned and cut
    into 1 inch pieces
8 bay leaves
1 small red onion, quartered
Oil

SAUCE
2 tbsps grated fresh or bottled horseradish
1 cup sour cream
2 tsps fresh dill, chopped
Salt and pepper
Squeeze of lemon juice
Pinch sugar

Thread the fish, bay leaves and slices of onion on skewers, alternating ingredients and types of fish. Brush with oil and place on an oiled grill rack above hot coals. Mix the sauce ingredients together and divide onto side plates. Grill the kebabs for about 6 minutes, turning and basting with oil frequently. When the onion is cooked, remove to serving dishes. Place kebabs on lettuce leaves, if desired, for serving.

Grilled Garlic Shrimp

PREPARATION TIME: 15 minutes
COOKING TIME: 8-10 minutes
SERVES: 4 people

2lbs uncooked jumbo shrimp
4 tbsps melted butter

Facing page: Greek Salad (top) and Caesar Salad (bottom).

MARINADE
3 cloves garlic, finely chopped
4 tbsps oil
½ cup lemon juice
4 tbsps chopped basil
Salt
Coarsely ground black pepper

Shell and de-vein the shrimp. Leave the shell on the ends of the tails. Combine the marinade ingredients in a plastic bag. Put in the shrimp and seal the bag. Refrigerate for 1 hour, turning frequently. Place the bag in a bowl to catch possible drips. Drain the shrimp and thread onto 4 skewers. Mix the marinade with the melted butter and brush the shrimp with the mixture. Grill for 8-10 minutes about 4-6 inches above the coals. Brush frequently with the

marinade while the shrimp cook. Pour over remaining marinade before serving.

Carrot Salad with Creamy Sesame Dressing

PREPARATION TIME: 1 hour

SERVES: 4 people

4 large carrots, peeled
1 cup raisins
1 cup chopped walnuts
2 tbsps sesame seeds
2 tbsps oil
1 tbsp lemon juice
6 tbsps sesame paste (tahini)
6 tbsps warm water

2 tbsps heavy cream
Salt and pepper
1 tbsp sugar

Place the carrots in iced water for 1 hour. Dry them and grate coarsely into a bowl. Add the raisins, nuts and sesame seeds. Mix the dressing ingredients together, adding more cream if the dressing appears too thick. If dressing separates, whisk vigorously until it comes together before adding additional cream. Toss with the carrot salad and serve.

Curried Rice Salad

PREPARATION TIME: 20 minutes

COOKING TIME: 12 minutes

SERVES: 6 people

¾ cup long grain rice
1 tbsp curry powder, hot or mild as desired
4 green onions, sliced
2 sticks celery, sliced
1 small green pepper, diced
10 black olives, halved and stoned
¼ cup golden raisins
¼ cup toasted sliced almonds
4 tbsps flaked coconut
2 hard-boiled eggs, chopped

DRESSING
½ cup mayonnaise
1 tbsp mango chutney
Juice and grated rind of ½ a lime
4 tbsps natural yogurt
Salt

GARNISH
2 avocados, peeled and cut in cubes
Juice of ½ lemon or lime

Cook the rice in boiling salted water for about 12 minutes or until tender. During the last 3 minutes of cooking time drain away half the water and stir in the curry powder. Leave to continue cooking over a gentle heat until the rice is cooked and the water is evaporated. Leave covered to stand for about 5 minutes. Toss the

This page: Carrot Salad with Creamy Sesame Dressing. Facing page: Curried Rice Salad.

rice with a fork, drain away any excess water and leave to cool. Combine with the remaining salad ingredients, stirring carefully so that the hard-boiled eggs do not break up. Mix the dressing ingredients together thoroughly. Chop any large pieces of mango in the chutney finely. Stir the dressing into the salad and toss gently to coat. Arrange the rice salad in a mound on a serving dish. Sprinkle the cubed avocado with the lemon juice to keep it green and place around the rice salad before serving.

Cheese and Vine Leaves

PREPARATION TIME: 20 minutes

COOKING TIME: 6 minutes

SERVES: 4 people

4 pieces goat's, feta or haloumi cheese
1 cup olive oil
4 tbsps chopped fresh herbs such as basil,
   tarragon, oregano, marjoram, parsley
2 cloves garlic, peeled and crushed
   (optional)
1 bay leaf
Squeeze lemon juice

TO SERVE
4 fresh vine leaves, washed, or 4 brine-
   packed vine leaves, soaked 30 minutes
1 head radicchio
8 leaves curly endive, washed and torn in
   bite-size pieces

If using goat's cheese, make sure it is not too ripe. Lightly score the surface of whichever cheese is used. Mix together the oil, herbs, garlic and lemon juice. Place the cheese in a small, deep bowl or jar and pour over the oil mixture. If cheese is not completely covered, pour on more oil. Leave, covered, overnight in the refrigerator. Drain the cheese and place in a hinged wire rack. Grill the cheese over hot coals until light golden brown and just beginning to melt. Drain and dry the vine leaves. Wash the radicchio and break apart the leaves. Arrange radicchio and endive leaves on 4 small plates and place a vine leaf on top. Place the

cooked cheese on top of the vine leaf and spoon some of the oil mixture over each serving.

Gorgonzola and Bean Salad with Pine Nuts

PREPARATION TIME: 20 minutes

COOKING TIME: 4-5 minutes

SERVES: 4 people

12oz green beans, ends trimmed
½ cup pine nuts, toasted if desired
1 cup crumbled gorgonzola or other blue
   cheese
2 tbsps red wine vinegar
6 tbsps olive oil
½ clove garlic, finely minced
Salt and pepper
2 heads radicchio

This page: **Cheese and Vine Leaves.** Facing page: **Gorgonzola and Bean Salad with Pine Nuts (top), and Spinach Salad with Bacon, Hazelnuts and Mushrooms (bottom).**

If the beans are large, cut across in half or thirds. Place in boiling salted water and cook for 4-5 minutes or until tender-crisp. Rinse under cold water and leave to drain. Toast pine nuts, if desired, at 350°F (180°C), for 10 minutes. Allow to cool. Mix the vinegar, oil, garlic, salt and pepper until well emulsified. Toss the beans in the dressing and add the cheese and nuts. Separate the leaves of radicchio, wash and dry. Arrange on salad plates and spoon the bean salad on top. Alternatively, tear radicchio into bite-size pieces and toss all the ingredients together.

Beet and Celeriac Salad

PREPARATION TIME: 25 minutes

COOKING TIME: 20 minutes

SERVES: 4 people

1 large celeriac root, peeled
4-6 cooked beets
4 green onions chopped
Juice of ½ a lemon

DRESSING
1½ cups sour cream
2 tsps white wine vinegar
Pinch sugar
2 tsps celery seed
1½ tbsps parsley

Cut the celeriac into ½ inch dice. Cook in boiling salted water with the juice of half a lemon for about 20 minutes or until tender. Drain and set aside to cool. Dice the beets the same size as the celeriac. Mix the beets with the green onions and carefully combine with the celeriac. Mix the dressing ingredients together, reserving half of the parsley. Combine the dressing with the celeriac and the beets, taking care not to over mix. Sprinkle the remaining parsley over the salad before serving.

Parsley Salad Vinaigrette

PREPARATION TIME: 20 minutes

COOKING TIME: 2 minutes

SERVES: 4 people

2 large bunches parsley (preferably flat Italian variety)
8oz tomatoes, quartered and seeded
1 cup stoned black olives, sliced
½ cup vegetable oil
1 clove garlic, finely minced
3 tbsps white wine vinegar
1 tsp dry mustard
Pinch sugar
Salt and pepper
½ cup grated fresh Parmesan cheese

Pick over the parsley and discard any yellow and thick stems. Break parsley into individual leaves. Cut the

This page: Red Cabbage, Celery and Carrot Salad. Facing page: Parsley Salad Vinaigrette (top), and Beet and Celeriac Salad (bottom).

tomatoes into ½ inch dice. Use 2 tbsps of measured oil and heat in a small frying pan. Add the finely chopped garlic and cook slowly to brown lightly. Combine with the remaining oil, vinegar, mustard, sugar, salt and pepper and beat well. Toss the dressing with the parsley, tomatoes and olives before serving. Sprinkle over the Parmesan cheese.

Red Cabbage, Celery and Carrot Salad

PREPARATION TIME: 15 minutes

SERVES: 6-8 people

1 small head red cabbage
4-6 carrots, peeled
4-6 sticks celery

DRESSING
½ cup oil
1 tbsp white wine vinegar
2 tbsps lemon juice
1 tbsp honey
1 tbsp celery seed
2 tsps chopped parsley
Salt and pepper

Cut the cabbage in quarters and remove the core. Grate coarsely or

slice finely. Grate the carrots coarsely. Cut the celery into very fine strips. Combine all the vegetables in a large salad bowl or in individual bowls. Mix the salad dressing ingredients very well. This can be done by hand with wire whisk or in a blender. Once the dressing is well emulsified, add the celery seeds and whisk again. Pour over the salad and toss before serving.

Three Bean Salad

PREPARATION TIME: 15 minutes plus marinating time

SERVES: 6-8 people

1 8oz can chickpeas
1 8oz can red kidney beans
1 8oz can green flageolet beans
6-8 tomatoes, quartered

DRESSING
½ cup olive oil and vegetable oil mixed
4 tbsps white wine vinegar
2 tbsps chopped parsley
1 tbsp chopped basil
1 shallot, finely chopped
1 clove garlic, finely minced
Salt and pepper

Drain and rinse all the beans. Mix the dressing ingredients together thoroughly and combine with the beans. Allow to marinate for 2 hours. Mound the beans into a serving dish and surround with the quartered tomatoes to serve.

Pea, Cheese and Bacon Salad

PREPARATION TIME: 20 minutes

COOKING TIME: 15-20 minutes

SERVES: 6 people

6 strips bacon, rind and bones removed
1lb fresh or frozen shelled peas
4oz Colby cheese
4 sticks celery, diced
4 green onions, sliced thinly or 1 small red onion, diced
1 red pepper, cored, seeded and diced

1 head Buttercrunch lettuce
¾ cup sour cream or natural yogurt
1 tbsp chopped fresh mixed herbs
1 tsp white wine vinegar
1 tsp sugar
Salt and pepper

Dice the bacon and cook gently in a small frying pan until the fat runs. Turn up the heat and fry the bacon until brown and crisp. Remove to paper towels to drain. Meanwhile cook the peas in boiling salted water for 15-20 minutes for fresh peas and 5 minutes for frozen peas. When the peas are cooked, drain and refresh under cold water and leave to drain dry. Cut the cheese into dice slightly larger than the peas. Dice the celery and red pepper to the same size as the cheese. Combine the peas,

This page: Tomato and Mozzarella Salad with Fresh Basil. Facing page: Three Bean Salad (left), and Pea, Cheese and Bacon Salad (right).

cheese, celery, green onions, red pepper and bacon in a bowl. Mix the dressing ingredients together, reserving half of the chopped mixed herbs. Combine the vegetables and bacon with half of the dressing. Separate the leaves of the lettuce and wash well. Pat dry and arrange on serving dishes. Spoon on the salad mixture and top with the remaining dressing. Sprinkle the reserved chopped herbs on top of the dressing.

Tomato and Mozzarella Salad with Fresh Basil

PREPARATION TIME: 15 minutes

SERVES: 4 people

3 large beefsteak tomatoes, sliced ¼ inch thick
6oz mozzarella cheese, drained, dried and sliced ¼ inch thick
4 tbsps coarsely chopped fresh basil leaves

DRESSING
6 tbsps olive oil and vegetable oil mixed
2 tbsps balsamic vinegar or white wine vinegar
¼ tsp Dijon mustard
Salt and pepper

GARNISH
Fresh basil leaves

Arrange the tomato slices and mozzarella cheese slices in overlapping circles on four individual salad plates. Sprinkle the fresh chopped basil leaves on top and garnish in the center with the whole basil leaves. Mix all the dressing ingredients together very well and spoon some over the salads before serving. Serve the rest of the dressing separately.

Cracked Wheat Salad

PREPARATION TIME: 20 minutes

SERVES: 4-6 people

2 cups bulgur wheat, washed and drained
4 green onions, chopped
1 cucumber, cut in small cubes
Juice and rind of 1 lemon
4 tomatoes, cubed
4 sticks celery, diced
½ cup toasted sunflower seeds
1 cup crumbled feta cheese
½ cup olive oil
1 clove garlic, minced
Salt and pepper
4 tbsps chopped mixed herbs

Place the washed bulgur wheat in clean water and leave to soak for 5 minutes. Drain and squeeze as much moisture out as possible. Spread the wheat out onto a clean towel to drain and dry. When the wheat is dry put into a large bowl with all the remaining ingredients and toss together carefully so that the cheese does not break up. Allow the salad to chill for up to 1 hour before serving. If desired, garnish the salad with whole sprigs of herbs.

Spinach Salad with Bacon, Hazelnuts and Mushrooms

PREPARATION TIME: 20 minutes

COOKING TIME: 2-3 minutes

SERVES: 4 people

1½ lbs spinach, stalks removed, washed and dried
6 strips bacon, bones and rind removed
8oz mushrooms, sliced
1 cup hazelnuts, roasted, skinned and roughly chopped

DRESSING
½ cup oil
3 tbsps white wine vinegar
1 tsp Dijon mustard
1 shallot, finely chopped
Salt and pepper
Pinch sugar (optional)

Tear the spinach leaves into bite-size pieces and put into a serving bowl. Fry or broil the bacon until brown and crisp. Crumble the bacon and sprinkle over the spinach. Add the hazelnuts and mushrooms to the spinach salad and toss. Mix all the dressing ingredients very well and pour over the salad just before serving.

Cucumber and Mint Salad

PREPARATION TIME: 30 minutes

SERVES: 4 people

1 large or 2 small cucumbers, peeled for a striped effect or scratched with the prongs of a fork lengthwise along the skin
Salt

DRESSING
1 cup sour cream or natural yogurt
2 tbsps chopped fresh mint
1 tbsp chopped parsley
Pinch sugar
Squeeze lemon juice
Salt and pepper

GARNISH
Whole sprigs of mint

Slice the cucumber thinly in rounds. Place the cucumber in a colander and sprinkle lightly with salt. Leave for 30 minutes to drain. Rinse the cucumber under cold water to remove the salt and pat dry. Mix the sour cream or yogurt with the sugar, lemon juice, salt, pepper, mint and parsley. Pour over the drained cucumber and toss. Leave refrigerated for 30 minutes before serving, and garnish with whole sprigs of mint.

Potato Salad with Mustard-Chive Dressing

PREPARATION TIME: 25 minutes

COOKING TIME: 20 minutes

SERVES: 6 people

3lbs potatoes, new or red variety
6 sticks celery, thinly sliced
1 red pepper, seeded, cored and diced
3 hard-boiled eggs

DRESSING
1 cup prepared mayonnaise
1 cup natural yogurt
4 tbsps Dijon mustard and mild mustard mixed half and half
1 bunch chives, snipped
Salt and pepper

Facing page: Cucumber and Mint Salad (top), and Cracked Wheat Salad (bottom).

Cook the potatoes in their skins for about 20 minutes in salted water. When the potatoes are tender, drain and peel while still warm. Cut the potatoes into cubes and mix with the celery and red pepper. Set the potato salad aside to cool while mixing the dressing. Combine the mayonnaise, yogurt, mustard, half the chives, salt and pepper and mix well. Toss carefully with the potato salad so that the potatoes do not break up. Spoon the salad into a serving dish and slice the hard-boiled eggs into rounds, or chop roughly. Arrange the hard-boiled eggs in circles on top of the potato salad or scatter over, if chopped. Sprinkle over reserved chives and refrigerate for about 1 hour before serving.

Red, Green and Yellow Pepper Salad

PREPARATION TIME: 20 minutes

SERVES: 6 people

3 sweet red peppers
3 green peppers
3 yellow peppers
Oil
½ cup small black olives, stoned
2 tbsps finely chopped coriander leaves
3 hard-boiled eggs

DRESSING
6 tbsps oil
2 tsps lemon juice
2 tbsps white wine vinegar
1 small clove garlic, finely minced
Pinch salt
Pinch cayenne pepper
Pinch sugar (optional)

Cut all the peppers in half and remove the seeds and cores. Press lightly with palm to flatten. Brush the skin side of each pepper with oil and place under a preheated broiler about 6 inches from the heat. Cook until the skin chars. Remove and wrap the peppers in a clean towel. Leave them to cool 10-15 minutes. Mix the dressing ingredients and quarter the eggs. Unwrap the peppers and peel off the skin. Cut the peppers into strips about 1 inch wide and arrange

in a circle, alternating colors. Arrange the olives and quartered egg in the center. Sprinkle the coriander leaves over the peppers and spoon over the dressing. Leave the salad, covered, in the refrigerator for 1 hour before serving. Peeled peppers will keep covered in oil up to 5 days in the refrigerator.

Coleslaw

PREPARATION TIME: 25 minutes

SERVES: 6 people

DRESSING
1 cup prepared mayonnaise
4 green onions finely chopped
1 cup sour cream
2oz Roquefort or blue cheese

This page: Zanzibar Shrimp. Facing page: Coleslaw (top), and Potato Salad with Mustard-Chive Dressing (bottom).

¼ tsp Worcestershire sauce
1 tsp vinegar
2 tbsps chopped parsley
Pinch sugar
Salt and pepper

SALAD
1 medium size head white cabbage, shredded
6 carrots, peeled and coarsely grated
1 green pepper, cut into thin short strips
1 cup roasted peanuts or raisins

Combine all the dressing ingredients,

reserving half the parsley, and refrigerate in a covered bowl for about 1 hour to allow the flavors to blend. Combine the dressing with the salad ingredients and toss to serve. Sprinkle on reserved chopped parsley.

Zanzibar Shrimp

PREPARATION TIME: 25 minutes

COOKING TIME: 18-23 minutes

SERVES: 4 people

1lb jumbo shrimp, shelled and de-veined
1 large fresh pineapple, peeled, cored and cut into chunks
Oil

SAUCE
½ cup orange juice
1 tbsp vinegar
1 tbsp lime juice
1 tsp dry mustard
1 tbsp brown sugar
Remaining pineapple

GARNISH
Flaked coconut
Curly endive

Thread the shrimp and pineapple pieces on skewers, alternating each ingredient. Use about 4 pineapple pieces per skewer. Place the remaining pineapple and the sauce ingredients into a food processor and purée. Pour into a small pan and cook over low heat for about 10-15 minutes to reduce slightly. Place the kebabs on a lightly oiled rack above the coals and cook about 6 minutes, basting frequently with the sauce. Sprinkle cooked kebabs with coconut and serve on endive leaves. Serve remaining sauce separately.

Egg Mayonnaise with Asparagus and Caviar

PREPARATION TIME: 25 minutes

COOKING TIME: 10 minutes

SERVES: 4-6 people

12 asparagus spears, trimmed and peeled
6 hard-boiled eggs
1½ cups prepared mayonnaise
1 tbsp lemon juice
Hot water
Red caviar

Tie asparagus in a bundle and cook in a deep saucepan of boiling salted water, keeping the asparagus tips out of the water. The tips will cook in the steam and the thick stalks will cook in the water, thus helping the asparagus to cook evenly. Cook about 5-8 minutes or until just tender. Rinse under cold water and drain. Meanwhile, place eggs in

This page: Red, Green and Yellow Pepper Salad. Facing page: Egg Mayonnaise with Asparagus and Caviar.

boiling water. Bring water back to the boil and cook eggs for 10 minutes. Cool completely under cold running water and peel. Combine mayonnaise and lemon juice. If very thick, add enough hot water until of coating consistency. Arrange eggs cut side down on a plate and coat with the mayonnaise. Surround with asparagus and garnish the eggs with caviar.

Meat and Poultry

Kashmiri Lamb Kebabs

PREPARATION TIME: 20 minutes

COOKING TIME: 10 minutes

SERVES: 4 people

1½ lbs lamb shoulder or leg
2 tbsps oil
1 clove garlic, finely minced
1 tbsp ground cumin
1 tsp turmeric
1 tsp grated fresh ginger
Chopped fresh coriander or parsley leaves
Salt and pepper
1 red pepper, cut in 1 inch pieces
1 small onion, cut in rings

Cut the lamb in 1 inch cubes. Heat the oil and cook the garlic, cumin, turmeric and ginger for 1 minute. Add the coriander, salt and pepper. Allow to cool and then rub the spice mixture over the meat. Leave covered in the refrigerator for several hours. Thread the meat on skewers, alternating with the pepper slices. Cook about 10 minutes, turning frequently. During the last 5 minutes of cooking, thread sliced onion rings around the meat and continue cooking until the onion is cooked and slightly browned and meat has reached desired doneness.

Ground Lamb Kebabs with Olives and Tomatoes

PREPARATION TIME: 20 minutes

COOKING TIME: 10 minutes

SERVES: 4 people

4 tbsps bulgur wheat, soaked and drained

1¼ lbs ground lamb
1 clove garlic, finely minced
2 tsps ground cumin
Pinch cinnamon
Salt and pepper
1 egg, beaten
Oil
16 large green olives, stoned
16 cherry tomatoes

This page: Mustard Grilled Pork with Poppy Seeds. Facing page: Kashmiri Lamb Kebabs (left) and Ground Lamb Kebabs with Olives and Tomatoes (right).

SAUCE

1 cup yogurt
2 tbsps chopped fresh mint
Salt and pepper

Soak the bulgur wheat until soft. Wring out and spread on paper towels to drain and dry. Mix with the remaining ingredients and enough of the beaten egg to bind together. The mixture should not be too wet. Form into small balls about 1½ inches in diameter. Thread onto skewers with the olives and tomatoes. Brush with oil and grill about 10 minutes, turning frequently. Mix the yogurt, mint, salt and pepper and serve with the kebabs.

Mustard Grilled Pork with Poppy Seeds

PREPARATION TIME: 20 minutes plus marinating time	
COOKING TIME: 45 minutes to 1 hour	
SERVES: 4-6 people	

4 6-7oz pieces whole pork tenderloin
2 tbsps black poppy seeds

MARINADE

1 tbsp mild mustard
4 tbsps oil
4 tbsps unsweetened apple juice
1 clove garlic, finely minced
Salt and pepper

SWEET MUSTARD SAUCE

1 cup mild mustard
¼ cup brown sugar
¼ cup dry cider or unsweetened apple juice
2 tsps chopped fresh or crumbled dried tarragon
Pinch cayenne pepper
Salt

Mix the marinade and rub into the pork. Place the pork in a dish or pan and cover. Refrigerate for 4 hours or overnight. Using a grill with an adjustable rack, place the pork over the coals on the highest level or set an electric or gas grill to a medium temperature. Cook the pork for

45 minutes-1 hour, basting with the marinade and turning frequently. Lower the shelf or raise the temperature. Baste frequently with the sauce during the last 10 minutes of cooking time. During the last 5 minutes, sprinkle the pork with the poppy seeds. Serve the pork sliced thinly with the remaining sauce.

Turkey and Pancetta Rolls

PREPARATION TIME: 30 minutes	
COOKING TIME: 20-30 minutes	
SERVES: 4-6 people	

2 turkey breasts, 1lb each, skinned
⅓ cup butter softened
1 clove garlic, minced
1 tbsp oregano leaves
16 slices pancetta or prosciutto ham
Salt and pepper
Oil

Cut the turkey breasts in half, lengthwise. Place each piece between two sheets of plastic wrap and bat out each piece with a rolling pin or meat mallet to flatten. Mix the butter, garlic, oregano, salt and pepper together. Spread half of the mixture over each slice of turkey. Lay 4 slices of pancetta on top of each piece of turkey. Roll up, tucking in the sides and tie with fine string in 3 places. Spread the remaining butter on the outside of each roll. Cook the rolls over medium-hot coals until tender. Insert a meat thermometer into each roll to check doneness. The temperature should read 190°F (90°C). Cooking should take approximately 20-30 minutes. Slice each roll into ½ inch rounds to serve.

Niçoise Chicken

PREPARATION TIME: 30 minutes	
COOKING TIME: 20 minutes	
SERVES: 4 people	

4 boned chicken breasts, unskinned
4 tbsps oil
2 tbsps lemon juice

TAPENADE FILLING

1lb large black olives, stoned
2 tbsps capers
1 clove garlic, peeled and roughly chopped
4 anchovy fillets
2 tbsps olive oil
Raw tomato sauce

1lb ripe tomatoes, peeled, seeded and chopped
1 shallot, very finely chopped
2 tbsps chopped parsley
2 tbsps chopped basil
2 tbsps white wine vinegar
2 tbsps olive oil
1 tbsp sugar
Salt and pepper
1 tbsp tomato paste (optional)

Cut a pocket in the thickest side of the chicken breasts. Combine half the olives, half the capers and the remaining ingredients for the tapenade in a blender or food processor. Work to a purée. Add the remaining olives and capers and process a few times to chop them roughly. Fill the chicken breasts with the tapenade. Chill to help filling to firm. Baste the skin side with oil and lemon juice mixed together. Cook skin side down first for 10 minutes over medium hot coals. Turn over, baste again and grill for another 10 minutes on the other side. Meanwhile, combine the sauce ingredients and mix very well. Serve with the chicken.

Orange Grilled Duck with Sesame and Spice

PREPARATION TIME: 20 minutes plus marinating time	
COOKING TIME: 40 minutes	
SERVES: 4 people	

4 boned duck breasts
4 tbsps sesame seeds

Facing page: Turkey and Pancetta Rolls (top) and Niçoise Chicken (bottom).

minutes before the duck is cooked, sprinkle the orange slices with brown sugar and grill on both sides to glaze. Serve with the duck.

Herb and Onion Grilled Lamb Chops

PREPARATION TIME: 10 minutes

COOKING TIME: 15 minutes

SERVES: 4 people

4 leg chops, cut ¾ inch thick

MARINADE
1 large onion, finely chopped
1 tbsp parsley, finely chopped
1 tbsp fresh thyme or mint leaves, roughly chopped
2 fresh bay leaves, cut in thin shreds with scissors
1 clove garlic, finely minced
3 tbsps oil
Juice of ½ lemon
Salt and pepper

Combine all the marinade ingredients and pour over the chops in a dish. Leave, covered, 2 hours in the refrigerator. Place on a rack over hot coals and cook the chops 15 minutes, turning often and basting frequently with the remaining marinade.

Barbecued Flank Steak

PREPARATION TIME: 25 minutes

COOKING TIME: 45-55 minutes

SERVES: 6 people

3½ lbs flank steak, in one piece

BARBECUE SEASONING
4 tbsps salt
1½ tsps freshly ground pepper
1½ tsps cayenne pepper (or paprika for a milder tasting mixture)

This page: Orange Grilled Duck with Sesame and Spice. Facing page: Herb and Onion Grilled Lamb Chops (top), and Barbecued Flank Steak (bottom).

MARINADE
4 tbsps soy sauce
½ cup dry white wine
3 tbsps oil
Pinch ground nutmeg
Pinch ground ginger
Pinch ground mustard
Salt and pepper

SAUCE
Reserved marinade
¾ cup orange juice
1 shallot, finely chopped
2 tsps cornstarch

GARNISH
1 orange, peeled and thinly sliced in rounds
Brown sugar

Score the fat side of each duck breast with a sharp knife. Mix the marinade ingredients together and pour over the duck in a shallow dish. Cover and refrigerate for 2 hours. Turn the duck frequently. Place the duck breasts fat side down on grill. Cook for 20 minutes per side, basting frequently. If the duck appears to be cooking too quickly, turn more often. Combine the sauce ingredients and add any remaining marinade. Cook 1-2 minutes over moderate heat until boiling and, just before the duck is finished cooking, brush the fat side lightly with the sauce and sprinkle on the sesame seeds. Turn fat side down onto the grill for 1 minute. Serve remaining sauce with the duck. Five

Barbecued Ribs

PREPARATION TIME: 15 minutes

COOKING TIME: 2 hours

SERVES: 4-6 people

2-3 racks pork spare ribs (about 5lbs)
Barbecue sauce (see recipe for Barbecued
*   Flank Steak)*
or
Sweet mustard sauce (see recipe for
*   Mustard Grilled Pork with Poppy*
*   Seeds)*

Leave the ribs in whole racks. Combine the ingredients for either sauce and pour over the meat in a roasting pan. Cover with foil and bake, turning and basting frequently, for 1 hour in a 325°F (150°C) oven. Uncover and bake 30 minutes more in the oven. Finish on a barbecue grill over moderately hot coals for about 30 minutes, basting frequently with the sauce. Cut between the bones into pieces. Serve with the remaining sauce.

Javanese Pork

PREPARATION TIME: 20 minutes

COOKING TIME: 30-45 minutes

SERVES: 4 people

4 pork rib or loin chops cut 1 inch thick
4 tbsps dark soy sauce
Large pinch cayenne pepper
3 tbsps lime or lemon juice
1 tbsp ground coriander
2 tbsps oil
2 tbsps brown sugar
4 medium-sized sweet red peppers
Oil
1 bunch fresh coriander

Snip the fat around the edges of the chops at ½ inch intervals to prevent curling. Mix soy sauce, cayenne pepper, lemon juice, coriander and oil together in a dish or pan. Place the pork chops in the marinade and leave, covered, in the refrigerator for

This page: Javanese Pork. Facing page: Chinese Pork and Eggplant Kebabs (left), and Barbecued Ribs (right).

BARBECUE SAUCE
4 tbsps oil
1¼ cups tomato ketchup
3 tbsps Worcestershire sauce
6 tbsps cider vinegar
4 tbsps soft brown sugar
4 tbsps chopped onion
1 clove garlic, crushed (optional)
1 bay leaf
4 tbsps water
2 tsps dry mustard
Dash tabasco
Salt and pepper

First prepare the barbecue sauce. Combine all the ingredients, reserving salt and pepper to add later. Cook in a heavy saucepan over low heat for 30 minutes, stirring frequently and adding more water if the sauce reduces too quickly.

Remove the bay leaf and add salt and pepper to taste before using. The sauce should be thick. Use the sauce for basting while cooking, or serve hot to accompany cooked meat and poultry. Score the meat across both sides with a large knife. Mix together the barbecue seasoning and rub 2 tbsps over the meat, reserving the rest of the seasoning for other use. Sear the meat on both sides over hot coals. Raise the grill rack or lower the temperature on a gas or electric grill. Baste with the sauce and grill the meat slowly. During last 5 minutes, lower the rack or raise the temperature and grill the meat quickly on both sides, basting with the sauce. Slice the meat thinly across the grain and serve with any remaining sauce.

**This page: Stuffed Hamburgers.
Facing page: Butterflied Lamb.**

1 hour. Turn over after 30 minutes. Place on grill over medium hot coals or on a middle rack. Mix sugar into remaining marinade. Cook chops for 15-20 minutes on each side until well done. Baste with the marinade frequently during the last 10-15 minutes of cooking. Meanwhile, wash and dry the peppers and brush with oil on all sides. Place alongside pork for half of its cooking time. Turn the peppers often. They will soften and char on the outside. Serve the pork chops with peppers, and garnish with coriander leaves.

Butterflied Lamb

PREPARATION TIME: 30 minutes plus marinating time	
COOKING TIME: 40-50 minutes	
SERVES: 6-8 people	

4lbs leg of lamb
5 tbsps oil
Juice and rind of one lemon
Small bunch mint, roughly chopped
Salt and coarsely ground black pepper
1 clove garlic, crushed

To butterfly the lamb, cut through the skin along the line of the main bone down to the bone. Cut the meat away from the bone, opening out the leg while scraping against the bone with a small, sharp knife. Take out the bone and remove excess fat. Flatten thick places by batting with a rolling pin or meat mallet.

Alternatively, make shallow cuts halfway through the thickest parts and press open. Thread two or three long skewers through the meat – this will make the meat easier to handle and turn on the grill. Place in a plastic bag or large, shallow dish. Mix the other ingredients together and pour over the lamb, rubbing it in well. Cover the dish or seal the bag and leave at room temperature for 6 hours or overnight in the refrigerator. Turn the lamb frequently. Remove from the dish or the bag and reserve the marinade. Grill on the skin side first, at least 6 inches away from the coals. Grill 20 minutes per side for pink lamb and 30-40 minutes per side for more well done lamb. Baste frequently during grilling. Remove the skewers and cut the slices across the grain. If fresh mint is unavailable, use rosemary, fresh or dried. Alternatively, roast lamb in a 350°F (180°C) oven for half of the cooking time and grill for the last half of cooking.

Stuffed Hamburgers

PREPARATION TIME: 30 minutes	
COOKING TIME: 20 minutes	
SERVES: 4-8 people	

2lbs ground beef
1 onion, finely chopped
4 tbsps Worcestershire sauce
Salt and pepper
8 hamburger buns

GUACAMOLE BURGERS

FILLING
4oz Monterey Jack cheese, cubed
1 mild chili pepper, thinly sliced and seeds removed

TOPPING
1 avocado, peeled and mashed
1 small clove garlic, crushed
2 tsps lemon or lime juice
1 tomato, peeled, seeded and finely chopped
Salt and pepper

BLUE CHEESE BURGERS
FILLING
4oz blue cheese, crumbled
¼ cup chopped walnuts

TOPPING

1 tbsp steak sauce
5 tbsps prepared mayonnaise
6 tbsps sour cream or yogurt
Salt and pepper

GRUYÈRE AND MUSHROOM BURGERS

FILLING

2oz mushrooms, roughly chopped
4oz Gruyère or Swiss cheese, cubed

TOPPING

1lb tomatoes
1 clove garlic, finely minced
2 tbsps tarragon, chopped
1 tbsp tarragon vinegar
Pinch sugar
2 tbsps oil
Salt and pepper

Mix the hamburger ingredients well, mold the meat around the chosen fillings and press carefully into patties. Mix the guacamole topping ingredients together and set aside while grilling the hamburgers. Mix the topping for the blue cheese burgers and refrigerate until needed. For the Gruyère burger topping, roughly chop tomatoes and then finely chop in a blender or food processor. Sieve to remove the seeds and skin, combine with the remaining tomato sauce ingredients and mix well. Grill hamburgers over hot coals 10 minutes per side. Quickly grill cut sides of the hamburger buns to heat through and place the hamburgers inside. Spoon on the appropriate toppings for each filling.

Chicken Tikka

PREPARATION TIME: 20 minutes	
COOKING TIME: 10-15 minutes	
SERVES: 4 people	

3lb chicken, skinned and boned

MARINADE

½ cup natural yogurt
1 small piece ginger, grated
1 clove garlic, finely minced
1 tsp chili powder, hot or mild

½ tsp ground coriander
½ tsp ground cumin
¼ tsp turmeric
¼ tsp red food coloring (optional)
Juice of one lime
Salt and pepper

Half head Iceberg lettuce, shredded
4 lemon wedges
4 small tomatoes, quartered

Cut chicken into 1 inch pieces. Mix all the marinade ingredients together. Pour over the chicken and stir well. Cover and leave for several hours in the refrigerator. Thread chicken on skewers and grill 10-15 minutes, turning frequently. Baste with any remaining marinade. Serve on a bed of shredded lettuce with tomatoes and lemon wedges.

Indian Chicken

PREPARATION TIME: 15 minutes plus marinating time	
COOKING TIME: 45 minutes to 1 hour	
SERVES: 4-6 people	

3lbs chicken, cut into 8 pieces
2 cups natural yogurt
2 tsps ground coriander
2 tsps paprika
1 tsp ground turmeric
Juice of 1 lime
1 tbsp honey
½ clove garlic, finely minced
1 small piece ginger, peeled and grated

Pierce the chicken all over with a fork or skewer. Combine all the remaining ingredients and spread half the mixture over the chicken, rubbing in well. Place the chicken in a shallow dish or a plastic bag and cover or tie and leave for at last 4 hours or overnight in the refrigerator. If your barbecue has adjustable shelves, place on the level furthest from the coals. Arrange the chicken skin side down and grill until lightly browned, turn over and cook again until lightly browned. Baste frequently with remaining marinade. Lower the grill for the last 15 minutes and cook, turning and basting frequently, until the chicken is brown and the skin is crisp. Alternatively, cook the chicken in a covered pan in the oven at 325°F (150°C) for 45 minutes to 1 hour and grill for the last 15 minutes for flavor and color. Serve any remaining yogurt mixture separately as a sauce.

Chinese Pork and Eggplant Kebabs

PREPARATION TIME: 20 minutes	
COOKING TIME: 15-20 minutes	
SERVES: 4 people	

1lb pork tenderloin, cut in 1 inch cubes
2 medium onions, cut in 1 inch pieces
1 large eggplant, cut in 1½ inch cubes
2 tbsps hoisin sauce
3 tbsps soy sauce
4 tbsps rice wine or dry sherry
1 clove garlic, finely minced
Sesame seeds
Salt

Sprinkle the eggplant cubes with salt and leave in a colander to drain for 30 minutes. Rinse well and pat dry. Pre-cook in 2 tbsps oil to soften slightly. Thread the pork, onion and eggplant on skewers, alternating the ingredients. Mix the hoisin sauce, soy sauce, rice wine or sherry and garlic together. Brush the kebabs with the mixture and place them on a lightly-oiled grill. Cook about 15-20 minutes, turning and basting frequently. During the last 2 minutes sprinkle all sides with sesame seeds and continue grilling to brown the seeds. Pour over any remaining sauce before serving.

Facing page: Indian Chicken (top), and Chicken Tikka (bottom).

Burgundy Beef Kebabs

PREPARATION TIME: 20 minutes
plus marinating time

COOKING TIME: 10 minutes

SERVES: 4 people

*4oz shallots or button onions, parboiled 3
  minutes and peeled*
*1½ lbs sirloin or butt steak, cut in 1 inch
  thick cubes*

MARINADE
1 cup burgundy or other dry red wine
3 tbsps oil
1 bay leaf
1 clove garlic, peeled
1 sliced onion
6 black peppercorns
1 sprig fresh thyme
Pinch salt

SAUCE
1 cup sour cream
*2 tbsps chopped fresh mixed herbs (such
  as parsley, thyme, marjoram and
  chervil)*
1 tbsp red wine vinegar
Pinch sugar
2 tsps Dijon mustard
Salt and pepper

Bring the marinade ingredients to the
boil in a small saucepan. Remove
from the heat and allow to cool
completely. When cold, pour over
the meat in a plastic bag. Seal the bag
well, but place it in a bowl to catch
any drips. Marinate overnight in the
refrigerator, turning the bag
occasionally. Thread the meat onto
skewers with the onions and grill
10 minutes, turning and basting
frequently. Mix the sauce ingredients
together and serve with the kebabs.

Smoked Sausage and Apple Kebabs

PREPARATION TIME: 20 minutes

COOKING TIME: 6 minutes

SERVES: 4 people

*Two rings smoked pork or beef sausage,
  cut in 1 inch thick slices*

4 small apples, quartered and cored
8 sage leaves
Lemon juice
*Quarter quantity sweet mustard sauce
  (see recipe for Mustard Grilled Pork
  with Poppy Seeds)*

Brush the apples with lemon juice.
Thread onto skewers, alternating
with sausage pieces and bay leaves.

Brush with the mustard sauce and
grill 10 minutes, turning frequently
and basting with the sauce. Serve any
remaining sauce with the kebabs if
desired.

Ham and Apricot Kebabs

PREPARATION TIME: 15 minutes

COOKING TIME: 12 minutes

SERVES: 4 people

1½ lbs cooked ham cut in 2 inch cubes
8oz canned or fresh apricots, halved and
    stoned
1 green pepper, cut in 2 inch pieces

APRICOT BASTE
¾ cup light brown sugar
4 tbsps apricot jam, sieved
6 tbsps wine or cider vinegar
1 tsp dry mustard
3 tbsps light soy sauce
Salt and pepper

Thread ham, apricots and pepper
pieces onto skewers, alternating the
ingredients. Mix the apricot baste
ingredients together and cook over
gentle heat to dissolve the sugar.
Brush over kebabs as they cook. Turn
and baste several times, grilling for
about 12 minutes over hot coals. If
using canned apricots, reserve the
juice and add to any baste that
remains after the kebabs are cooked.
Bring this mixture to the boil to
reduce slightly and serve as a sauce
with the kebabs.

Spicy Madeira Steaks

PREPARATION TIME: 20 minutes

COOKING TIME: 15 minutes

SERVES: 4 people

4 butt steaks about 6oz each

MARINADE
4 tbsps oil
½ cup ketchup
¾ cup red wine vinegar
1 clove garlic, crushed
1 tsp pepper
1 tsp ground cloves
½ tsp cinnamon
½ tsp thyme leaves

SAUCE
½ cup reserved marinade
2 tbsps flour
½ cup beef stock
½ cup Madeira
Salt

Combine marinade ingredients and

pour over steaks in a dish. Cover and
refrigerate at least 4 hours. Remove
from marinade and place over hot
coals. Grill, basting frequently, until
of desired doneness. Combine flour
with reserved marinade, beating well
to mix to a smooth paste. Gradually
beat in stock. Bring to the boil in a
small saucepan, stirring constantly.
Cook until thickened, about

1 minute. Reduce heat and simmer
5 minutes. Stir in Madeira and add
salt to taste. Serve with the steak.

**Facing page: Spicy Madeira Steaks
(left), and Burgundy Beef Kebabs
(right). This page: Ham and
Apricot Kebabs (left), and Smoked
Sausage and Apple Kebabs (right).**

BARBECUES & SALADS

Fish and Seafood

Marsala Fish

PREPARATION TIME: 25 minutes	
COOKING TIME: 10-15 minutes	
SERVES: 4 people	

4 medium sized mackerel, trout or similar
   fish
Juice of 1 lemon
2 tsps turmeric
2 green chili peppers, finely chopped
1 small piece ginger, grated
1 clove garlic, finely minced
Pinch ground cinnamon
Pinch ground cloves
4 tbsps oil
Salt and pepper
Fresh coriander leaves

ACCOMPANIMENT
½ cucumber, finely diced
½ cup thick natural yogurt
1 green onion, finely chopped
Salt and pepper

Clean and gut the fish. Cut three slits on each side of the fish. Combine spices, lemon juice, oil, garlic and chili peppers and spread over the fish and inside the cuts. Place whole sprigs of coriander inside the fish. Brush the grill rack lightly with oil or use a wire fish rack. Cook the fish 10-15 minutes, turning often and basting with any remaining mixture. Combine the accompaniment ingredients and serve with the fish.

Scallops, Bacon and Shrimp Kebabs

PREPARATION TIME: 25 minutes	
COOKING TIME: 20-25 minutes	
SERVES: 4 people	

12 large, raw scallops
12 raw jumbo shrimp, peeled and de-
   veined
12 slices smoked bacon
Juice of 1 lemon
2 tbsps oil
Coarsely ground black pepper

This page: Scallops, Bacon and Shrimp Kebabs. Facing page: Marsala Fish.

RED CHILI YOGURT SAUCE
2 cloves garlic, finely chopped
1 red pepper, grilled and peeled
1 red chili pepper, chopped
3 slices bread, crusts removed, soaked in water
3 tbsps olive oil
½ cup natural yogurt

Wrap each scallop in a slice of bacon and thread onto skewers, alternating with shrimp. Mix the lemon juice, oil and pepper and brush over the shellfish as they cook. Turn frequently and cook until the bacon is lightly crisped and the scallops are just firm. Meanwhile, prepare the sauce. Squeeze the bread to remove the water and place the bread in a blender. Add the finely chopped garlic, the chopped red chili pepper and peeled red pepper and blend well. With the machine running, pour in the oil through the funnel in a thin, steady stream. Keep the machine running until the mixture is a smooth, shiny paste. Combine with the yogurt and mix well. Serve with kebabs.

Grilled Sardines with Lemon and Oregano

PREPARATION TIME: 15 minutes
COOKING TIME: 6-8 minutes
SERVES: 4-6 people

8-12 fresh sardines, gutted, scaled, washed and dried
8-12 sprigs fresh oregano
⅓ cup olive oil
Juice and rind of 2 lemons
Salt and pepper
1 tbsp dried oregano

Place one sprig of oregano inside each fish. Mix oil, lemon juice and rind, salt and pepper together. Make two slits on each side of the fish. Brush the fish with the lemon mixture and grill over hot coals for 3-4 minutes per side, basting frequently. When the fish are nearly done, sprinkle the dried oregano on the coals. The smoke will give the fish extra flavor. May be served as a appetizer or main course.

Gray Mullet with Fennel

PREPARATION TIME: 15 minutes
COOKING TIME: 18-22 minutes
SERVES: 4 people

2-4 gray mullet, depending upon size, gutted and cleaned

MARINADE
⅓ cup oil
1 tbsp fennel seeds, slightly crushed
1 clove garlic, finely minced
Juice and rind of one lemon
2 tbsps chopped fennel tops
Salt and pepper

Heat oil and add the fennel seeds. Cook for one minute. Add the garlic and remaining ingredients except the fennel tops. Leave the mixture to cool completely. Pour over the fish in a shallow dish. Cover and refrigerate for 1 hour. Grill over hot coals 10-12 minutes per side. Sprinkle over fennel tops halfway through cooking. Tops may also be placed directly on the coals for aromatic smoke.

Swordfish Steaks with Green Peppercorns and Garlic Oregano Sauce

PREPARATION TIME: 25 minutes
COOKING TIME: 15 minutes
SERVES: 4 people

2 tbsps fresh green peppercorns (substitute well-rinsed canned green peppercorns)
6 tbsps lemon juice
4 tbsps olive oil
Salt
4 swordfish steaks (tuna steaks may also be used)

SAUCE
1 egg
1 clove garlic, roughly chopped
½ cup oil
1 tbsp lemon juice
2 sprigs fresh oregano
Salt and pepper

Crush the green peppercorns slightly

and mix with lemon juice, oil and salt. Place the swordfish steaks in a shallow dish and pour over the lemon oil mixture. Cover and refrigerate several hours, turning frequently. Process the egg and garlic in a blender or food processor. With the machine running, pour oil through the funnel in a thin, steady stream. When the sauce is thick, strip the leaves off the oregano and process to chop them finely. Add lemon juice, salt and pepper. Grill the swordfish over hot coals for 15 minutes, basting frequently and turning once. Serve with the sauce. (Peppercorns will pop when exposed to the heat of the grill.)

Grilled Red Mullet with Tarragon

PREPARATION TIME: 15 minutes
COOKING TIME: 10-16 minutes
SERVES: 4 people

4 large or 8 small red mullet, gutted, scaled, washed and dried
4 or 8 sprigs fresh tarragon

MARINADE
4 tbsps oil
2 tbsps tarragon vinegar
Salt and pepper

SAUCE
1 egg
½ cup oil
1 tsp Dijon mustard
1 tbsp chopped tarragon
1 tbsp chopped parsley
1 tbsp tarragon vinegar
2 tbsps heavy cream
1 tsp brandy
Salt and pepper

Place a sprig of tarragon inside each fish. Cut two slits on the side of each fish. Mix the marinade ingredients together, pour over the fish in a shallow dish and refrigerate for 30

Facing page: Swordfish Steaks with Green Peppercorns and Garlic Oregano Sauce (top), and Grilled Sardines with Lemon and Oregano (bottom).

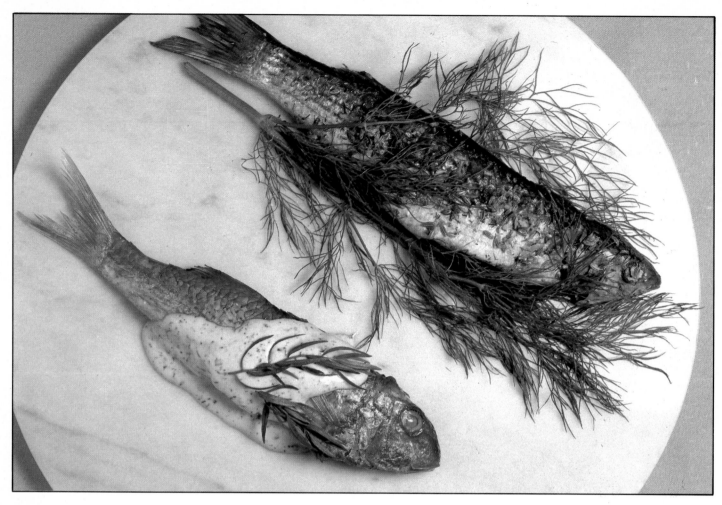

minutes, covered. Put the egg in a blender or food processor. Add the mustard, salt and pepper and process to mix. Add the oil through the funnel, with the machine running, in a thin, steady stream. When all the oil has been added, add the herbs, vinegar and brandy and process to mix well. Fold in the heavy cream and pour into a serving dish. Keep in the refrigerator until ready to use. Cook the fish for 5-8 minutes per side, depending upon size of fish. Baste frequently with the marinade while cooking. Serve with the sauce.

This page: Gray Mullet with Fennel (top), and Grilled Red Mullet with Tarragon (bottom). Facing page: Monkfish and Pepper Kebabs with Bernaise Butter Sauce.

Monkfish and Pepper Kebabs with Bernaise Butter Sauce

PREPARATION TIME: 30 minutes
COOKING TIME: 25 minutes
SERVES: 4 people

1lb monkfish, cut into 2 inch pieces
8 strips bacon, rind and bone removed
2 pieces lemon grass
1 green pepper, cut in 2 inch pieces
1 red pepper, cut in 2 inch pieces
12 mushroom caps
8 bay leaves
Oil
BERNAISE BUTTER SAUCE
½ cup dry white wine
4 tbsps tarragon vinegar
2 shallots, finely chopped
1 tbsp chopped fresh tarragon
1 tbsp chopped fresh chervil or parsley
1 cup butter, softened

Salt and pepper

Cut the bacon in half lengthwise and again in half across. Peel the lemon grass and use only the core. Cut into small pieces. Place a piece of fish on each strip of bacon and top with a piece of lemon grass. Roll up. Thread the rolls of fish on skewers, alternating with peppers, mushrooms and bay leaves. Brush with oil and grill 15 minutes, turning and basting often. While the fish cooks, heat the white wine, vinegar and shallots in a small saucepan until boiling. Cook rapidly to reduce by half. Add the herbs and lower the heat. Beat in the softened butter a bit at a time until the sauce is the thickness of hollandaise sauce. Season with salt and pepper to taste and serve with the fish kebabs.

Barbecued Vegetables

Grilled Fennel

PREPARATION TIME: 15 minutes
COOKING TIME: 20 minutes
SERVES: 4 people

4 small bulbs fennel
Juice and rind of 1 lemon
4 tbsps oil
1 shallot, finely chopped
Salt and pepper

Remove the fennel tops and reserve them. Cut the fennel bulbs in half and remove the cores. Parboil the fennel for 5 minutes. Combine the juice and rind of the lemon, salt, pepper, oil and shallot. Pour over the fennel and set aside for 15 minutes. Place the fennel bulbs on hot coals and cook 15 minutes, turning often and brushing with the lemon mixture. Chop the fennel tops finely and sprinkle over the grilled fennel. Pour over any remaining lemon juice mixture to serve.

Grilled Tomatoes

PREPARATION TIME: 15 minutes
COOKING TIME: 6 minutes
SERVES: 4 people

4 beefsteak tomatoes cut in half
1 tbsp oregano, fresh or dried
2 tbsps olive oil
1 tbsp lemon juice
Salt and pepper
4oz feta cheese, crumbled

Mix the oil, lemon juice, salt, pepper and oregano together. Brush over the cut side of the tomatoes and grill that side first for 3 minutes over hot coals. Brush the skin side of the tomatoes and turn them over. Grill 3 minutes more on skin side and remove the tomatoes to a serving dish. Sprinkle over the crumbled feta cheese and pour over the remaining basting mixture to serve.

Grilled Corn-on-the-Cob

PREPARATION TIME: 20 minutes
COOKING TIME: 15 minutes
SERVES: 4 people

4 large ears of corn, husks and silk removed, parboiled 5 minutes
½ cup butter, melted
Salt and pepper
Chili powder or paprika (optional)

Brush the drained corn liberally with melted butter. Sprinkle with salt and pepper. Chili powder or paprika can be substituted for the pepper, if desired. Grill over medium hot coals for 15 minutes, turning often and basting frequently with butter. To serve, pour over any remaining butter.

Grilled Eggplant

PREPARATION TIME: 30 minutes
COOKING TIME: 20-24 minutes
SERVES: 4 people

2 eggplants
¾ cup olive oil
6 tbsps lemon juice
1 tbsp cumin seed
1 clove garlic, finely chopped
2 tbsps parsley, chopped
Salt and pepper

Cut the eggplant into rounds about 1 inch thick. Score the surface of each round lightly with a sharp knife, sprinkle with salt and leave to stand for 30 minutes. Heat oil for 1 minute and add the cumin seed and cook for the 30 seconds. Add the garlic and cook for a further 30 seconds. Add the lemon juice. Rinse the salt from the eggplant slices and pat dry. Brush one side of the slices with the basting mixture. Grill on a lightly oiled rack or place in a hinged wire rack. Cook for 10-12 minutes per side until soft, basting frequently. Place the slices in a serving dish and pour over the remaining basting mixture. Sprinkle with parsley just before serving.

Grilled Mushrooms

PREPARATION TIME: 10 minutes
COOKING TIME: 15-20 minutes
SERVES: 4 people

1lb large mushrooms, cleaned

MARINADE
1 tbsp chopped tarragon, fresh or dried
Grated rind and juice of 1 orange
1 tbsp tarragon vinegar
2 tbsps oil
Salt and pepper

Mix together the marinade

Facing page: Grilled Tomatoes (top), and Grilled Fennel (bottom).

ingredients. Cut the stalks from the mushrooms and place the mushroom caps in a shallow dish. Pour over the marinade and leave the mushrooms for 15-20 minutes. Place the mushrooms in a wire rack and cook 15-20 minutes over hot coals. Brush the mushrooms frequently with the marinade and turn them once or twice. Remove to a serving dish and pour over the remaining marinade to serve.

Zucchini, Pepper and Onion Kebabs

PREPARATION TIME: 20 minutes

COOKING TIME: 10-12 minutes

SERVES: 4 people

4-6 zucchini, ends trimmed
1 large onion
1 large green pepper
1 large red pepper
Oil
4 tbsps dry white wine
1 tsp thyme
2 tsps chopped parsley
1 tsp chopped chives
½ cup melted butter

Peel the zucchini with swivel peeler for a striped effect. Parboil 4 minutes. Refresh under cold water. Cut in 2 inch pieces. Quarter the onion and cut in large pieces, separating the layers. Cut the peppers in half and remove the core and seeds. Cut into pieces the same size as the onion. Thread the vegetables onto skewers. Melt the butter and add the wine and cook 1 minute. Add the herbs, salt and pepper. Brush the kebabs lightly with oil and grill 5-6 minutes per side. Brush frequently with the butter mixture. When the zucchini are tender, remove to a serving dish. Pour over the remaining butter.

Barbecued Baked Potatoes

PREPARATION TIME: 15 minutes

COOKING TIME: 25 minutes

SERVES: 4-6 people

4 large potatoes, scrubbed but not peeled
Salt and pepper
Paprika
½ cup melted butter

SAUCE
1 cup sour cream
2 tsps red wine vinegar

This page: Zucchini, Pepper and Onion Kebabs. Facing page: Grilled Eggplant and Grilled Mushrooms.

1 tsp sugar
1 tsp mustard powder
1 tsp celery salt
1 tsp chopped fresh herbs

Parboil the potatoes for 10 minutes in their skins. Cut the potatoes in quarters lengthwise. Brush the potatoes with a mixture of butter, paprika, salt and pepper on all surfaces. Grill the potatoes for 15 minutes, basting frequently with the remaining butter. Meanwhile, combine all the sauce ingredients and set aside in the refrigerator until ready to serve with the potatoes.

This page: Grilled Corn-on-the-Cob (top), and Barbecued Baked Potatoes (bottom). Facing page: Hungarian Sausage Salad.

Main Dishes and Pasta Salads

Hungarian Sausage Salad

PREPARATION TIME: 25 minutes

COOKING TIME: 20-25 minutes

SERVES: 4-6 people

4 small potatoes
½ cup oil
3 tbsps wine vinegar
1 tsp Dijon mustard
1 tsp dill seeds, slightly crushed
1 tbsp chopped parsley
1 tsp chopped dill
Pinch hot paprika
Salt
1lb sausage such as kielbasa, smoked pork
    sausage, knockwurst or bratwurst
1 large red onion, thinly sliced
2 green peppers, cored and sliced
4 tomatoes, quartered

Scrub and peel potatoes and cook in salted water in a covered saucepan for 20 minutes or until soft. Mix all the dressing ingredients together in a medium-sized bowl. Dice the potatoes while still warm and coat with the dressing. Leave the potatoes to cool in the dressing. If using knockwurst boil for 5 minutes. Broil the bratwurst until evenly browned on all sides. Slice the sausage in ½ inch slices and combine with the onion, pepper and tomatoes. Carefully combine with the potatoes in the dressing, taking care not to over mix and break up the potatoes. Pile into a large serving dish and allow to stand for 1 hour before serving.

Salade Niçoise

PREPARATION TIME: 20 minutes

COOKING TIME: 15-20 minutes

SERVES: 4 people

2 large potatoes, or 6 small new potatoes
6oz green beans
4 hard-boiled eggs
1 can tuna
4oz shrimp

1 can anchovies
4 ripe tomatoes
¾ cup black olives, stoned
1 small cucumber, diced

DRESSING
6 tbsps olive oil
2 tbsps white wine vinegar

1 head radicchio, leaves separated and
  washed
1 head romaine lettuce, washed
4 chicken breasts, cooked, skinned and
  thinly sliced
4oz Bresse Bleu or other blue cheese, cut
  in small pieces
16 cornichons (small pickled gherkins)
  thinly sliced
4oz cherry tomatoes, halved and cored
½ cup walnut halves

DRESSING
2 tbsps vegetable and walnut oil mixed
2 tsps white wine vinegar
¾ cup crème frâiche
2 tsps chopped fresh tarragon
Salt and pepper

Tear the radicchio and romaine
lettuce into bite-size pieces. Leave
the lamb's lettuce in whole leaves.
If using watercress, remove the thick
stems and yellow leaves. Toss the
lettuces together and pile onto a
salad plate. Place the chicken, cheese,
cornichons, tomatoes and walnuts on
top of the lettuce. Mix the oils and
vinegar together and whisk well to
emulsify. Fold in the crème frâiche
and add the tarragon, salt and
pepper. Drizzle some of the dressing
over the salad to serve and hand the
rest of the dressing separately.

Pasta and Vegetables in Parmesan Dressing

PREPARATION TIME:	25 minutes
COOKING TIME:	13-15 minutes
SERVES:	6 people

1lb pasta spirals or other shapes
8oz assorted vegetables such as:
Zucchini, cut in rounds or matchsticks
Broccoli, trimmed into very small
  flowerets
Pea pods, ends trimmed
Carrots, cut in rounds or matchsticks

**This page: Salade Niçoise (top),
and Salade Bresse (bottom). Facing
page: Pasta and Vegetables in
Parmesan Dressing.**

3 tbsps chopped mixed fresh herbs
2 tsps French mustard
Salt and pepper

Peel and cook the potatoes (skins
may be left on new potatoes if
desired) until tender. If using old
potatoes, cut into ½ inch dice (new
potatoes may be sliced into ¼ inch
rounds). Trim the ends of the beans,
put into boiling salted water for
about 3-4 minutes or until just barely
cooked. Drain and rinse under cold
water, then leave to drain dry.
Quarter the tomatoes, or, if large, cut
into eighths. Quarter the hard-boiled
eggs. Cut the anchovies into short
strips. Mix the dressing ingredients

together and blend well. Drain oil
from the tuna and mix the tuna and
all the salad ingredients together.
Pour over the dressing and toss
carefully so that the potatoes do not
break up. Serve the salad on top of
lettuce leaves if desired.

Salade Bresse

PREPARATION TIME:	20 minutes
SERVES:	4-6 people

1 bunch lamb's lettuce or watercress,
  washed

Celery, cut in matchsticks
Cucumber, cut in matchsticks
Green onions, thinly shredded or sliced
Asparagus tips
Green beans, sliced
Red or yellow peppers, thinly sliced

DRESSING
½ cup olive oil
3 tbsps lemon juice
1 tbsp sherry pepper sauce
1 tbsp chopped parsley
1 tbsp chopped basil
¼ cup freshly grated Parmesan cheese
2 tbsps mild mustard
Salt and pepper
Pinch sugar

Cook pasta in a large saucepan of boiling salted water with 1 tbsp oil for 10-12 minutes or until just tender. Rinse under hot water to remove starch. Leave in cold water. Place all the vegetables except the cucumber into boiling salted water for 3 minutes until just tender. Rinse in cold water and leave to drain. Mix the dressing ingredients together very well. Drain the pasta thoroughly and toss with the dressing. Add the vegetables and toss to coat. Refrigerate for up to 1 hour before serving.

Cob Salad

PREPARATION TIME: 25 minutes

SERVES: 4-6 people

1 large head romaine lettuce, washed
2 avocados, peeled and chopped
3 tomatoes, cut in small dice
1 cucumber, cut in small dice
1 cup blue cheese, crumbled
4 green onions, chopped or 1 small red onion, chopped
4oz cooked chicken breasts, cut in small pieces
2 hard-boiled eggs, chopped

GREEN GODDESS DRESSING
½ can anchovies
4 tbsps chopped parsley
2 tbsps chopped basil or tarragon

2 tbsps chopped chives
Small bunch watercress, leaves only
1½ cups mayonnaise
1 tbsp white wine vinegar

Dry the lettuce and cut it into strips. Tear the strips into small pieces and put into a salad bowl. Arrange all the ingredients on top. To prepare the dressing, combine all the ingredients in the blender or food processor and purée until smooth and very green. Serve the dressing separately with the salad.

Crab Louis

PREPARATION TIME: 20 minutes

SERVES: 4 people

DRESSING
1 cup mayonnaise
½ cup yogurt
4 tbsps tomato chutney/chili sauce
2 green onions, finely chopped
½ green pepper, finely diced
1 tsp lemon juice
Salt and pepper

1lb crabmeat, flaked
1 head Buttercrunch or ½ head Iceberg lettuce
4 hard-boiled eggs, quartered
1 cup black olives, stoned

Combine all the dressing ingredients and mix half with the flaked crabmeat. Arrange a bed of lettuce on a serving dish and mound on the crabmeat. Coat the crabmeat with the remaining dressing. Arrange the quartered egg and black olives around the salad.

Julienne Salad

PREPARATION TIME: 25 minutes

SERVES: 4-6 people

1 small head Iceberg lettuce
1 small Buttercrunch lettuce
4 tomatoes, quartered
1 small red onion, chopped
½ cucumber, sliced
6 radishes, sliced
2oz cooked ham
2oz cooked tongue

4oz cooked chicken
2oz Gruyère or Swiss cheese
2oz Colby cheese

CREAMY HERB DRESSING
1 cup natural yogurt
½ cup heavy cream
3 tbsps fresh mixed herbs, chopped (use chervil, tarragon, basil, dill or parsley)
2 tbsps prepared mayonnaise
Salt and pepper

Tear the lettuce into bite-sized pieces and mix with the remaining vegetables. Divide into four salad bowls. Slice the meats and the cheeses into thin strips. Arrange on top of the salad ingredients. Mix the dressing thoroughly and serve separately.

Lobster and Cauliflower Salad

PREPARATION TIME: 30 minutes

SERVES: 4-6 people

1 large cauliflower, washed
½ cup vegetable oil
3 tbsps lemon juice
1 tsp dry mustard
Salt and pepper
1 large cooked lobster
1 cup prepared mayonnaise
2 tsps Dijon mustard
4 hard-boiled eggs
16 black olives, halved and stoned
2 bunches watercress, washed
Red caviar

Break the cauliflower into small flowerets and mix with the vegetable oil, lemon juice, mustard and salt and pepper. Leave for at least 2 hours in a cool place. Crack the lobster and remove all the meat from the shell and set aside in a small bowl. Mix the mayonnaise and Dijon mustard. Thin if necessary with a spoonful of hot water. Add half the dressing to the lobster and mix carefully. Combine

Facing page: Julienne Salad (top), and Cob Salad (bottom).

the cauliflower with the eggs and olives. Stir to coat the eggs with dressing but do not over-mix or break up the eggs. Remove the thick stems from the watercress and any yellow leaves. Arrange beds of watercress on four small plates. Spoon in equal portions of the cauliflower salad onto the watercress and top with an equal portion of the lobster. Coat the lobster salads with

the remaining mustard mayonnaise and spoon some red caviar over the dressing.

Tuna and Pasta with Red Kidney Beans

PREPARATION TIME: 20 minutes

This page: Tuna and Pasta with Red Kidney Beans. Facing page: Crab Louis (top), and Lobster and Cauliflower Salad (bottom).

COOKING TIME: 10 minutes

SERVES: 4-6 people

1½ cups small pasta shells
1 8oz can red kidney beans, drained and rinsed

4oz small mushrooms, quartered
1 can tuna, drained and flaked
4 green onions, sliced
2 tbsps chopped mixed herbs

DRESSING
½ cup olive oil
3 tbsps white wine vinegar
Squeeze lemon juice
1 tbsp Dijon mustard
Salt and pepper

Cook the pasta shells in boiling salted water with 1 tbsp oil for 10 minutes or until just tender. Rinse under hot water and then place in cold water until ready to use. Mix the dressing ingredients together thoroughly and drain the pasta shells. Mix the pasta with the beans, mushrooms, tuna, green onions and chopped mixed herbs. Pour over the dressing and toss to coat. Chill up to 1 hour in the refrigerator before serving.

Mariner's Salad

PREPARATION TIME: 25 minutes

COOKING TIME: 15 minutes

SERVES: 6 people

1lb pasta shells, plain and spinach
4 large scallops, cleaned
1 cup frozen mussels, defrosted
½ cup lemon juice and water mixed
4oz shelled and de-veined shrimp
½ cup cockles or small clams, cooked
4 crab sticks, cut in small pieces
4 green onions, chopped
1 tbsp chopped parsley

DRESSING
Grated rind and juice of ½ lemon
1 cup mayonnaise
2 tsps paprika
⅓ cup sour cream or natural yogurt
Salt and pepper

Cook the pasta for 10 minutes in a large pan of boiling salted water with 1 tbsp oil. Drain and rinse under hot water. Leave in cold water until ready to use. Cook the scallops and mussels in the lemon juice and water mixture for about 5 minutes or until fairly firm. Cut the scallops into 2 or 3 pieces, depending upon size. Mix

the dressing and drain the pasta thoroughly. Mix all ingredients together to coat completely with dressing. Stir carefully so that the shellfish do not break-up. Chill for up to 1 hour before serving.

Italian Pasta Salad

PREPARATION TIME: 25 minutes

COOKING TIME: 10 minutes

SERVES: 4-6 people

1lb pasta shapes
8oz assorted Italian meats, cut in strips: salami, mortadella, prosciutto, coppa, bresaola
4oz provolone or fontina cheese, cut in strips
15 black olives, halved and stoned
4 tbsp small capers
4oz peas
1 small red onion or 2 shallots, chopped
6oz oyster mushrooms, stems trimmed and sliced

DRESSING
3 tbsps white wine vinegar
½ cup olive oil
½ clove garlic, minced
1 tsp fennel seed, crushed
1 tbsp chopped parsley
1 tbsp chopped basil
1 tbsp mustard
Salt and pepper

Cook the pasta in a large saucepan of boiling water with a pinch of salt and 1 tbsp oil. Cook for about 10 minutes or until just tender. Add the frozen peas during the last 3 minutes of cooking time. Drain the pasta and peas and rinse under hot water. Leave in cold water until ready to use. Mix the dressing ingredients together well and drain the pasta and peas thoroughly. Mix the pasta and peas with the Italian meats and cheeses, olives, capers, chopped onion or shallot and sliced mushrooms. Pour the dressing over the salad and toss all the ingredients together to coat. Do not over-mix. Leave the salad to chill for up to 1 hour before serving.

Shrimp and Cashews in Pineapples with Tarragon Dressing

PREPARATION TIME: 30 minutes

COOKING TIME: 10 minutes

SERVES: 4 people

2 small fresh pineapples
8oz small cooked shrimp
1 cup roasted unsalted cashew nuts
2 sticks celery, thinly sliced
4 tbsps lemon juice

DRESSING
1 egg
2 tbsps sugar
1 tbsp tarragon vinegar
¼ pint whipping cream
2 tsps chopped fresh tarragon or 1 tsp dried tarragon, crumbled

Cut the pineapples carefully in half lengthwise, leaving the green tops attached. Carefully cut out the flesh and remove the cores. Cut the flesh into bite-size pieces. Combine the shrimp, cashews and celery and toss with the lemon juice. Spoon the mixture into the pineapple shells and refrigerate to chill. To prepare the dressing, beat the egg and sugar together until light in a heat-proof bowl. Add the vinegar and tarragon, place the bowl over hot water. Whip with a wire whisk until thick. Take off the heat and allow to cool, whipping occasionally. When cold, lightly whip the cream and fold into the dressing. Spoon over the salad and serve in the pineapple shells.

Facing page: Italian Pasta Salad (top), and Mariner's Salad (bottom).

Oriental Salad

PREPARATION TIME: 25 minutes

COOKING TIME: 2 minutes

SERVES: 4-6 people

1 cake tofu, cut in small cubes
½ cup vegetable oil
4oz pea pods, ends trimmed
2oz mushrooms, sliced
2oz broccoli flowerets
2 carrots, peeled and thinly sliced
4 green onions thinly sliced
2 sticks celery, thinly sliced
½ cup unsalted roasted peanuts
4oz bean sprouts

½ head Chinese cabbage, shredded

DRESSING
3 tbsps lemon juice
2 tsps honey
1 tsp grated ginger
3 tbsps soy sauce
Dash sesame oil

Drain tofu well and press gently to remove excess moisture. Cut into ½ inch cubes. Heat 2 tbsps from the ½ cup oil in the wok or frying pan. Save the remaining oil for the dressing. Cook the pea pods, mushrooms, broccoli, carrots and celery for 2 minutes. Remove the

This page: Oriental Salad. Facing page: Shrimp and Cashews in Pineapple with Tarragon Dressing.

vegetables and set them aside to cool. When cool mix them together with the onions, peanuts and bean sprouts. Mix the dressing and pour over the vegetables. Add the tofu and toss carefully. Arrange a bed of Chinese cabbage on a serving dish and pile the salad ingredients on top to serve.

Salads with Fruit

Waldorf Salad

PREPARATION TIME: 20 minutes

SERVES: 6 people

4 sticks celery, diced
4 apples, mixture of red-skinned and
    green-skinned, diced
6oz grapes, black and white, halved and
    seeded
1 cup walnuts or pecans, roughly chopped
1 cup prepared mayonnaise
4 tbsps heavy cream
Juice of half a lemon

Mix the celery, apples, grapes and
nuts together and toss with the
lemon juice. Lightly whip the cream
and fold into the mayonnaise. Fold
the dressing into the salad and serve
chilled. If desired, substitute raisins
for the grapes and garnish with
2 tbsps chopped parsley.

Fruit Salad with Coconut Cream Dressing

PREPARATION TIME: 30 minutes

SERVES: 6-8 people

2lb fresh assorted fruit, such as:
Pineapple, peeled, cored and cut in
    wedges
Melon, skinned and sliced
Bananas, peeled, cut in thick rounds and
    sprinkled with lemon juice
Apricots, halved and stoned and sprinkled
    with lemon juice
Peaches, peeled and sliced and sprinkled
    with lemon juice
Strawberries, hulled and washed
Raspberries or blackberries, washed
Papaya, peeled and sliced

Currants, stems removed
Blueberries, washed
Kiwi, peeled and sliced
Kumquats, thinly sliced, seeds removed
Fresh figs, quartered
Pears, peeled, cored and sliced

DRESSING
1 cup natural yogurt
½ cup coconut cream
2-3 tbsps lime juice
Seeds of 1 fresh pomegranate

Arrange assortment of fruit on
plates. Mix together the ingredients
for the dressing and drizzle over the
fruit. Sprinkle on the pomegranate
seeds.

Green and Gold Sunflower Salad

PREPARATION TIME: 15 minutes

SERVES: 4 people

2 large ripe avocados
8 ripe apricots

DRESSING
3 tbsps sunflower oil
1 tbsp lemon juice
Salt and pepper

YOGURT DRESSING
½ cup natural yogurt
2 tsps honey
Grated rind of 1 lemon
2 tsps chopped parsley
4 tbsps toasted sunflower seeds
1 small Buttercrunch lettuce, washed and
    separated into leaves

Prepare the oil and lemon juice
dressing. Cut avocados in half and
remove the stones. Peel and cut into

slices. Cut apricots in half and
remove the stones. If the apricots are
large, cut in half again. Add the
apricots to the avocados, spooning
over the dressing. Mix all the
ingredients for the yogurt dressing
together except the sunflower seeds.
Place the lettuce leaves on salad
plates and arrange the avocado and
apricots on top. Spoon over some of
the yogurt dressing and sprinkle the
sunflower seeds onto the dressing.
Serve immediately and hand extra
dressing separately.

Watercress and Orange Salad

PREPARATION TIME: 20 minutes

SERVES: 4-6 people

3 large bunches watercress, well washed
    and thick stalks removed
4 oranges, peeled and segmented

DRESSING
6 tbsps vegetable oil
Juice and rind of 1 orange
Pinch sugar
Squeeze lemon juice
Salt and pepper

Break watercress into small sprigs
and discard any yellow leaves.
Arrange the watercress with the
orange segments on plates or toss in
one large salad bowl. Mix the
dressing ingredients together very
well and pour over the salad just
before serving.

**Facing page: Watercress and
Orange Salad (top), and Waldorf
Salad (bottom).**

Fennel, Orange and Tomato Salad

PREPARATION TIME: 25 minutes

COOKING TIME: 3-4 minutes

SERVES: 4 people

*2 bulbs fennel, green top trimmed and
 reserved*
2 large, ripe tomatoes
2 oranges

DRESSING
2 tbsps orange juice
1½ tbsps lemon juice
Zest of 1 orange
*⅓ cup olive oil and vegetable oil mixed
 half and half*
1 tsp chopped fresh oregano or basil

Pinch sugar
Salt and pepper

Choose fennel with a lot of feathery green top. Reserve the tops. Cut the cores out of the bottom of the fennel bulbs and discard. Bring water to the boil in a large saucepan. Slice the fennel thinly, lengthwise, and place the slices in the boiling water. Cook until translucent and slightly softened, about 3-4 minutes. Carefully remove the slices to a colander and rinse under cold water. Leave to drain. Place the tomatoes into the boiling water for 5-10 seconds. Put immediately into cold water. Peel and slice into ¼ inch rounds. Grate or use a zester to remove the peel from 1 orange. Peel

This page: Fruit Salad with Coconut Cream Dressing. Facing page: Green and Gold Sunflower Salad (top), and Fennel, Orange and Tomato Salad (bottom).

off the pith with knife and peel the remaining orange. Slice both oranges into ¼ inch rounds. Prepare the dressing by whisking all the ingredients very well and reserving the orange zest. Arrange the fennel, tomato and orange slices in circles on a round serving dish. Pour over the dressing and sprinkle on the orange zest. Chop the fennel tops and sprinkle over or use whole to garnish the salad.

JAPANESE COOKING

The words simplicity and elegance define Japanese cooking best. With no complicated sauces to distract from the main ingredients, Japanese cooking calls for a few perfect ingredients, exquisitely prepared. Garnishes are kept to a minimum, but they are like miniature sculptures. The Japanese love of pure ingredients stems from the people's love and reverence for nature and all that comes from it. Often, food is garnished with leaves, pine needles or sea plants to remind each person of its origins. Study the artistic arrangement of a Japanese dish and you will see the roots of nouvelle cuisine.

The chapters in this book follow the order of courses at a formal Japanese banquet. Each of the following courses illustrates an important technique in Japanese cooking:

1 Zensai – hors d'oeuvres
2 Sumashi-jiru – clear soups (we have combined this course with miso soups, which normally appear later in the meal)
3 Sashimi – raw fish and garnishes
4 Yakimono – broiled and pan-fried food
5 Mushimono – steamed and baked food
6 Nimono – simmered food
7 Agemono – deep-fried food (Nabemono, one pot dishes such as Sukiyaki, are included in the chapter on simmered food, and sometimes take the place of courses 4-7)

8 Sunomo or Aemono – vinegared food and salads
9 Gohan – rice
10 Miso-shiru – miso soups
11 Tsukemono – pickles
12 Green tea
13 Fresh fruit or desserts

If the number of courses seems daunting, remember that each course is a small serving by Western standards, and that two or three courses can make an excellent meal on their own. Also, don't imagine that you need a vast kitchen filled with specialized equipment – average kitchens in Japan are small, with very basic appliances – everyday kitchen utensils are quite adequate, and sharp knives are an absolute must. Woks are not traditional Japanese cookware, but they adapt well for steaming or frying. Ingredients do not have to be unusual, merely as fresh and good looking as possible, to maintain the Japanese standard. It is, however, useful to have a basic understanding of the following Japanese ingredients:

Adzuki beans – Small dried red beans. Used in rice dishes and sweets.
Agar-agar – Vegetable gelatin sold in blocks or powder. Needs soaking in liquid before use. Use normal gelatin.
Bamboo shoots – First shoots of the bamboo plant. Fresh shoots are best, but the canned variety is more readily

available. Rinse canned shoots before use.

Bonito flakes, dried – Used to make dashi, the basic stock for soups and simmering. Also sprinkled on food to garnish. Sold pre-packaged, the flakes are made from fillets of a mackerel-like fish.

Daikon – A large, white radish, used cooked or raw. Often used grated as a garnish or ingredient in a dipping sauce. Do not substitute pink or red radishes.

Ginger – Knobbly root with a spicy, hot taste. Peel and grate for use. Pickled ginger is often used as a garnish, grated or sliced, for broiled meats. Red or pink in its pickled form.

Glutinous rice – A round-grain variety which cooks to a sticky consistency essential for sushi or vinegared-rice dishes and for picking up with chopsticks. Short-grain rice can be substituted. Rice is so important in Japanese cooking that it is used as a course in itself. For plain boiled rice use long-grain or Patna rice.

Kamaboko – Fish paste sold in a rectangular cake, tinted pink or light green with a white center.

Konbu – A greenish-brown kelp and an important flavoring in dashi. Sold dried, it should be stored tightly covered.

Konnyaku – Gelatinous vegetable paste formed into a cake. It absorbs tastes and colors of foods it is cooked with. Stored in water, it will keep for up to two weeks if the water is changed every day.

Lotus root – Root of the waterlily. Cross-section slice looks like a flower. Available fresh or canned from Japanese groceries.

Mirin – Fermented soy bean paste. Used as a soup base, condiment, sauce ingredient or salad dressing. It comes in a light or white variety, or dark, reddish color. A yellow variety is the most common.

Noodles – Harusame are transparent noodles made from rice. Shirataki noodles are made from devil's tongue root. Both are often called cellophane noodles. Soba are buckwheat noodles. Udon are white noodles made from wheat flour and vary in length and thickness. Somen noodles are the thinnest. Both buckwheat and udon noodles are available dried or fresh in vacuum-sealed packs.

Nori – Laver (seaweed) used to wrap sushi, or shredded to use as a garnish. Sold in thin sheets.

Sesame seeds – Both black and white varieties are used.

Seven-taste (or spice) pepper – A combination of red pepper, sanso pepper, ground orange peel, sesame seed, hemp seed, poppy seed and ground nori seaweed. Usually used to season food at the table.

Shiitake mushroom – Available fresh or dried, the latter being the more common form. Dried mushrooms must be soaked in water for 30 minutes before use, and the stems are removed before cooking.

Shiso leaves – Bright green leaves from a small herb plant. Used as a garnish and available fresh from Japanese groceries. They have a mint-like flavor.

Soy sauce – Japanese type is lighter and sweeter than Chinese. Light variety is saltier than the dark.

Tofu – White cake made from soy bean curd, and custard-like in texture. Usually sold in water-packed cartons, it needs to be thoroughly drained before use. Can be stored in the refrigerator if kept in water that is changed daily.

Trefoil – A herb related to parsley. Use salad cress as a substitute.

Vinegar – Made from rice and pale yellow in color.

Wasabi horseradish – Pale green powdered root with a very hot, pungent taste. Mix with water to a smooth paste and shape into mounds or small leaf shapes. Use as an accompaniment to sashimi or an addition to dipping sauce.

Japanese garnishes are beautiful and, with practice, not difficult to make. The following are the easiest and the ones used in these recipes:

Carrot spurs – Cut a carrot into 3 inch sections and peel. Place in boiling water for about 4 minutes. Carve lengthwise with a sharp knife or dannelle knife. Cut triangular grooves down the length of each carrot. Cut crosswise into slices.

Carrot twists – Cut carrot into 3 inch sections and peel. Slice thinly, lengthwise. Make a 1 inch slit in the center of each slice. Soak the pieces in salt water for at least 10 minutes. Rinse. When pieces are pliable, slip one end of each piece through the slit in the middle and pull back.

Carrot blossoms – Cut carrot in 3 inch sections. Slice five sides to form a pentagon. with a knife or cannelle knife make five lengthwise triangular cuts on all five sides. Trim the top of the carrot so that one end is higher than the other. Slice the flowers thinly, turning as you slice. Go around twice to make double flowers.

Cucumber twigs – Cut 2 inch sections from an unpeeled cucmber. Slice one side lengthwise off this section, about ¼ inch thick. Cut a center section from this piece about 2 inches wide. In this section, make two lengthwise cuts from either end. Do not cut all the way through. Each cut should end ¼ inch from the opposite end. Twist the two outer strips so that they cross over. The same thing can be done with a thick piece of lemon rind.

Zucchini fan or comet – cut the ends off. Slice in half, lengthwise. Make a series of cuts, close together down the length of one half, leaving a spine along the side to hold the slices together. Soak in salt water for at least 10 minutes. Rinse. Spread out on a serving plate. Add a carrot spur.

Radish flowers – Cut stems and tips from radishes. Make two cuts in each of the four sides. Tip should be uppermost. Cut a cross in the top. Soak in ice water until the slice opens.

Radish fans – Choose radishes with leaves. Cut the tip off the radish and cut lengthwise, but not quite through to the leaf end. Soak in salt water and spread out on a plate.

Radish jacks – Slice a radish into thin rounds, Cut a notch in each slice. Slide one slice into the notch of the other.

Lemon and cucumber whirls – Thinly slice lemons and cucumbers. Notch each slice and twist.

Scored mushrooms – Soak dried shiitake mushrooms in hot water for 30 minutes. Cut off the stems and make a cross in the middle of the top of each cap.

JAPANESE COOKING

Hors d'Oeuvres

Lemon-Ikura

PREPARATION TIME: 5 minutes
SERVES: 4 people

4 rounded tsps salmon roe (large grain)
4 thin slices lemon
2 chives, very finely shredded

Arrange the lemon slices on a serving dish. Mound a spoonful of roe on top of each slice. Garnish each with a few shreds of chive. Serve cold as part of a selection of hors d'oeuvres.

Fresh Vegetables with Sauces

PREPARATION TIME: 30 minutes
COOKING TIME: 2 minutes
SERVES: 4 people

Selection of the following:
Pea pods (2 per person, stems trimmed)
Zucchini (if small, 1 per person, sliced in half. If large, cut 1 into thin strips)
Carrots (as for zucchini)
Green beans (2 per person, stems trimmed)
Shiitake mushrooms, dried (1 per person, cut in quarters if large)
Daikon radish (as for carrots)
Turnips (1 large or 2 small, peeled, quartered and sliced)
Leeks (1 small thin one cut into 1 inch pieces)

SOY AND LEMON SAUCE
6 tbsps soy sauce
4 tbsps fresh lemon juice

SESAME SAUCE
3 tbsps white sesame seeds

2 tbsps mirin
6 tbsps soy sauce
4 tbsps dashi

Fresh Vegetables with Sauces.

Place the vegetables in a steamer or on a rack above boiling water. Cover well and cook 2 minutes. Mix the ingredients for each sauce and divide the mixture among 8 small bowls. Arrange the vegetables attractively on 4 serving plates and serve with the dipping sauces.

Shrimp in Nori Packages

PREPARATION TIME: 20 minutes

COOKING TIME: 2 minutes

SERVES: 4 people

4 jumbo shrimp

This page: Lemon-Ikura. Facing page: Pink, White and Green Rolls (top) and Shrimp in Nori Packages (bottom).

1 square nori
4 chives

BROILING SAUCE
2 tbsps soy sauce
1 tbsp mirin
1 tbsp grated ginger squeezed for juice

GARNISH
Zucchini fan (see introduction)

Shell and de-vein the shrimp, but leave on the tail ends. Pass the sheet of nori over a gas flame on both sides to freshen it. Cut it into 4 strips. Mix all the sauce ingredients together and brush the shrimp. Brush the nori strips and wrap one around each shrimp, but do not completely cover. Place under a pre-heated broiler and cook for 1 minute on each side, brushing with the remaining sauce. Tie each with 1 chive. If desired, prepare double quantity sauce and use some for dipping. Garnish with prepared zucchini fan.

Tofu-Dengaku

| PREPARATION TIME: 20 minutes |
| COOKING TIME: 5-6 minutes |
| SERVES: 4 people |

3oz tofu, well drained, pressed for 15 minutes and sliced into rectangles 2 inches long and ½ inch thick
1½ tbsps miso
1½ tbsps mirin
1½ tbsps dashi
½ oz spinach, cooked and puréed or defrosted and well drained
1 tbsp white sesame seeds

GARNISH
Radish flower (see introduction)

Prepare the garnish. Place the tofu in a steamer or on a rack above boiling water. Cover and cook for 5-6 minutes. Combine the remaining ingredients, except spinach and sesame seeds, in a small pan and cook slowly until very thick. Add the spinach and mix well. Place tofu on serving dishes and insert small

bamboo skewers lengthwise. Spread the spinach mixture evenly over each piece of tofu and sprinkle with sesame seeds. Garnish with radish flower.

Chicken Livers with Cucumber

| PREPARATION TIME: 25 minutes |
| COOKING TIME: 5-6 minutes |
| SERVES: 4-6 people |

1 tbsp oil
6oz chicken livers, picked over and trimmed
2 tsps grated ginger, squeezed for juice
2 tsps mirin
2 tsps soy sauce
½ cucumber, peeled in stripes
1 tbsp white sesame seeds

Heat the oil in a frying pan. Cut the chicken livers into even-sized pieces, but not too small. Put into the hot oil and cook over high heat, turning frequently to brown on the outside. Pour in the soy sauce, mirin and ginger juice and continue to cook 1-2 minutes over medium heat. Livers may be served slightly pink inside. Toss half the livers with sesame seeds to coat. Cut the cucumber half in quarters, lengthwise, and then into pieces the size of the livers. Thread one sesame-seed-coated liver, one piece of cucumber and one plain liver onto small bamboo skewers to serve.

Pink, White and Green Rolls

| PREPARATION TIME: 30 minutes, plus chilling time |
| COOKING TIME: 2 minutes |
| SERVES: 8 people |

3 inch piece of daikon (white) radish, peeled
8 large or 16 small spinach leaves
4oz smoked salmon, thinly sliced
Pinch salt

3 tbsps rice vinegar
3 tbsps sugar

Trim the piece of daikon radish into a large cube. Cut the cube into 16 very thin slices. Soak in 2 cups water with 2 tsps salt for about 20 minutes to soften. Wash spinach leaves well and remove thick stalks. Cook 2 minutes in a covered saucepan with a pinch of salt until just wilted. Rinse in cold water and pat dry. Place the salmon slices in 4 rows. Place the spinach leaves, evenly divided, on top of the salmon. Divide the radish slices evenly among the four rows and place on top of the spinach. Roll up and secure with wooden picks. Mix the vinegar and sugar and pour over the rolls. Refrigerate for 2-3 hours, turning once or twice. When ready to serve, remove the picks and slice each roll in half, crosswise. Serve cut side up so that a spiral of pink, white and green shows.

Beef and Scallion Rolls

| PREPARATION TIME: 25 minutes |
| COOKING TIME: 12-15 minutes |
| SERVES: 4 people |

4-6 green onions, trimmed and cut into 2 inch lengths
4oz sirloin, fat trimmed, sliced very thin and cut into 5 x 2 inch pieces
1 tbsp oil
2 tbsps soy sauce
1 tbsp sugar
1 tbsp saké
1 tbsp dashi
1 tbsp mirin

GARNISH
Carrot blossoms (see introduction)
Cucumber twigs (see introduction)

Prepare the garnishes. Divide onions equally into 4-6 groups. Roll 1 slice of beef around 1 group of onions. Tie

Facing page: Tofu-Dengaku (top) and Chicken Livers with Cucumber (bottom).

rolls with string. Repeat with remaining onions and beef. Heat oil in a large heavy-based frying pan. Add the beef rolls, seam side down, and cook about 1 minute over moderate heat. Turn the rolls several times to brown evenly. Reduce the heat and add all remaining ingredients except the mirin. Cook a further 3 minutes and remove the meat with a slotted spoon. Turn up the heat and cook the pan juices to reduce by half. Add the mirin. Remove the string from the rolls and return them to the pan. Cook the rolls, turning them often, until well

This page: Beef and Scallion Rolls.

glazed. Cut each roll into ½ inch thick rounds. Thread the rounds on skewers and garnish.

JAPANESE COOKING

Soups

Summer Chilled Miso Soup

PREPARATION TIME: 25 minutes plus chilling time	
COOKING TIME: 25 minutes – 1 hour	
SERVES: 4 people	

4 cups chicken stock or dashi
3oz miso
½ small cucumber, thinly sliced
1-2 tomatoes, skinned and sliced
½ oz salad cress

Make the stock as for Sumashi Jiru or dashi as for Butaniku no Dango. Chill thoroughly. Cream the miso with about 1 cup of the stock and add to the remaining stock with all the remaining ingredients.

Butaniku no Dango

PREPARATION TIME: 20 minutes	
COOKING TIME: 15 minutes	
SERVES: 4 people	

DASHI
6 cups water
½ oz konbu seaweed
½ oz shaved, dried bonito fillet

8oz ground pork
½ tsp ground ginger
2 tbsps soy sauce
½ oz somen noodles
4 green onions shredded

This page: Sumashi Jiru (Basic Clear Soup) (top) and Butaniku no Dango (bottom).

Bring the water to the boil in a heavy-based pan, add the seaweed and simmer gently 1-2 minutes. Remove the seaweed and add the bonito flakes. Bring back to the boil and then remove from the heat. Allow the bonito flakes to sink to the bottom of the pan and then strain the stock through cheesecloth, or a fine-meshed strainer. Combine the pork and ginger and form into small balls. Return the stock to the rinsed-out pan. Add the soy sauce and bring the stock back to the boil. Add the pork balls, cover and simmer gently for 5 minutes. Add the noodles and continue simmering for 5 minutes, until the meat balls and noodles are cooked. Add the green onions and serve.

This page: Summer Chilled Miso Soup. Facing page: Soup with Fish Dumplings (top) and Shrimp Noodle Soup (bottom).

Shrimp Noodle Soup

PREPARATION TIME: 20 minutes

COOKING TIME: 25-35 minutes

SERVES: 4 people

STOCK
8oz fish trimmings (head, bones and skin)
1 small onion, studded with 6 cloves
1 small piece ginger root
5 cups water

SOUP
Strained stock
1oz soba noodles
8oz cooked, peeled shrimp

GARNISH
Parsley sprigs

Place all the stock ingredients into a heavy-based pan. Bring to the boil and simmer gently for 20-25 minutes. Do not over-boil or stock will taste bitter. Remove scum from the surface and strain through cheesecloth, or a fine-meshed strainer. Return the stock to the rinsed-out pan. Add the noodles and simmer for 5-10 minutes until they are cooked. Add the shrimp to the hot soup and pour into individual dishes to serve. Garnish with small sprigs of parsley.

Vegetable Miso Soup

PREPARATION TIME: 30 minutes

COOKING TIME: 25 minutes – 1 hour

SERVES: 4 people

4 cups dashi or chicken stock
2 tbsps oil
4oz daikon radish, cut into matchsticks
2 carrots, peeled and cut into matchsticks
1 small onion, diced
4 whole okra, stems removed and cut into rounds
4 dried mushrooms, soaked 30 minutes, stalks removed
4oz miso

Make stock as for Sumashi Jiru or dashi as for Butaniku no Dango. Heat oil in a heavy-based pan and sauté radish, carrot and onion. When soft, add the okra, mushrooms (with caps scored if desired), and stock or dashi. Bring almost to the boil and mix about 1 cup of the hot stock with the miso. Add this slowly back to the soup. Remove from heat and serve.

Sumashi Jiru (Basic Clear Soup)

PREPARATION TIME: 20 minutes

COOKING TIME: 55 minutes – 1 hour 10 minutes

SERVES: 4 people

STOCK
1 chicken carcass or about 1lb chicken trimmings (bones, giblets, skin etc.)
1 carrot, peeled and roughly chopped
1 small onion, peeled and roughly chopped
2 sticks celery
4 cups water

SOUP
Stock (as above), strained
1 tbsp sherry
2 tbsps soy sauce
4oz diced, cooked chicken
1 medium carrot
4 sprigs watercress

Break the chicken bones into small pieces and add with the remaining stock ingredients to a heavy-based pan. Bring to the boil and then simmer gently for 45 minutes to 1 hour, occasionally skimming off fat if necessary. Strain through cheesecloth, or a fine-meshed strainer. Return to the rinsed out pan. Peel the carrot for the soup and pare off small strips with a cannelle knife, or small paring knife, down the length of the carrot. Cut the carrot into slices to form "flowers". Bring the stock to the boil and add the sherry and soy sauce. Season with salt and pepper, if necessary. Add the carrot flowers and chicken and cook gently for 5-10 minutes until the chicken is hot and the carrot is just tender. Pour into individual bowls and garnish with watercress.

Miso Soup with Shrimp and Fried Tofu

PREPARATION TIME: 25 minutes

COOKING TIME: 25 minutes – 1 hour

SERVES: 4 people

4 cups chicken stock or dashi
2 tbsps oil
4oz tofu, drained and cubed
4 tbsps miso
4oz shrimp
2 green onions, sliced diagonally

GARNISH
4 unshelled shrimp

Make stock as for Sumashi Jiru or dashi as for Butaniku no Dango. Heat the oil in a frying pan and fry the tofu 2 minutes. Remove from the pan and pour over boiling water to remove excess oil. Drain. Heat most of the stock or dashi in a heavy-based pan until just boiling. Remove from the heat. Mix the remaining stock or dashi with miso and add gradually to the pan. Add the tofu and shrimp and garnish with sliced green onion and whole shrimp.

Soup with Fish Dumplings

PREPARATION TIME: 25 minutes

COOKING TIME: 25-35 minutes

SERVES: 4 people

STOCK
12oz-1lb whole whitefish (to give 4oz fillets)
1 small onion, studded with 6 cloves
1 small piece ginger root
5 cups water

¼ tsp ground ginger
2 green onions

Facing page: Miso Soup with Shrimp and Fried Tofu (top) and Vegetable Miso Soup (bottom).

1 egg white
4-5 tbsps (approx) all-purpose flour
2 tbsps oil
4 spears asparagus cut diagonally into
    1 inch pieces
Salt and pepper
Rind and juice of 1 lemon
1 tbsp soy sauce

Fillet and skin the fish, using the
trimmings to make stock as for
Shrimp Noodle Soup. Mince the fish
fillets in a food processor with the
ground ginger, green onions, egg
white, salt and pepper. Gradually
blend in flour until mixture is stiff
enough to shape into small balls. The
mixture will be sticky. Heat the oil in
a heavy-based pan and sauté the
asparagus until just tender. Add the

stock and return to the boil gently.
Carefully add the fish dumplings,
lemon rind and juice and soy sauce,
and simmer for 5-10 minutes until
cooked. Serve immediately.

Clear Tofu Soup

PREPARATION TIME: 20 minutes
COOKING TIME: 55 minutes – 1 hour
SERVES: 4 people

4 cups chicken stock or dashi
3 tbsps soy sauce
4oz tofu, drained and cubed

**This page: Clear Tofu Soup. Facing
page: Salmon or Tuna Sashimi.**

2 small leeks, washed, trimmed and sliced
2oz bean sprouts

Make up stock as for Sumashi Jiru
(Basic Clear Soup) or dashi as for
Butaniku no Dango. Bring to the boil
in a heavy-based pan and add soy
sauce and leek slices. Simmer until
leeks are tender. Divide between
individual dishes and add the tofu
and bean sprouts to the hot soup.
Serve immediately.

JAPANESE COOKING

Raw Fish

Tuna Sashimi

PREPARATION TIME: 50 minutes

SERVES: 4 people

8oz tuna fillet
½ cup light soy sauce

GARNISH
Carrot twists (see introduction)
Cellophane noodles

Prepare the carrot twists. Skin the fillets and treat as in Salmon Sashimi. Slice the tuna across the grain. Place in shallow serving bowls. Cover cellophane noodles with hot water and soak for 5 minutes. Drain and leave to cool. Arrange carrot twists and a portion of cellophane noodles next to the tuna on each plate.

Salmon or Tuna Sashimi

PREPARATION TIME: 50 minutes

SERVES: 4 people

8oz raw salmon or tuna fillet
½ daikon radish, finely grated

SAUCE
6 tbsps soy sauce
3 tbsps lemon juice

GARNISH
4 zucchini fans (see introduction)
4 carrot spurs (see introduction)

Skin the fish fillet, place in a colander and pour over boiling water. This will not cook the fish. Place immediately into ice-cold water. Pat the fish dry and slice across the grain into ⅜ inch-thick strips. Arrange daikon radish in mounds in 4 serving bowls. Place the slices of fish against the daikon radish mounds. Mix the soy sauce and lemon juice and divide into 4 small bowls. Garnish with prepared zucchini fans and carrot spurs arranged to look like a comet.

Scallop Sashimi

PREPARATION TIME: 50 minutes

SERVES: 4 people

4 large or 8 small, fresh scallops with roe, if possible
4 shiso leaves
4 lemon twigs (see introduction)
2 tbsps wasabi horseradish powder mixed with water to a thick paste

SAUCE
6 tbsps light soy sauce
2 tbsps lemon juice

Wash the scallops in cold, salted water. Pat dry and slice into very thin rounds, leaving the roe in one piece. Overlap slices of scallops in serving dish or place roe on one side. Decorate with shiso leaves and lemon twigs. Mix the soy sauce and

lemon juice together and serve one bowl of the sauce with each serving of sashimi.

Squid Sashimi

PREPARATION TIME: 50 minutes

SERVES: 4 people

1 squid (prepared squid are available from fishmongers and Japanese markets)
1 carrot, finely grated

SAUCE
½ cup soy sauce
Pinch wasabi powder

GARNISH
Fennel or dill fronds
4 radish fans (see introduction)

Prepare the radish fans. Wash the squid in cold, salted water and pat dry. Lightly score one side of the squid and then cut into ⅜ inch-thick strips, crosswise. Place a mound of

carrot on each serving dish. Place the squid against the mound of carrot. Mix the soy sauce and the wasabi and pour into 4 small bowls. Garnish with fennel or dill and prepared radish fans.

This page: Tuna Sashimi. Facing page: Scallop Sashimi (top) and Squid Sashimi (bottom).

JAPANESE COOKING

Broiling and Pan Frying

Beef and Leek Skewers

PREPARATION TIME:	25 minutes
COOKING TIME:	8-10 minutes
SERVES:	4 people

1lb butt steak, cut in 1½ inch cubes
4 leeks, cut in 1½ inch pieces, white and
    pale green part only
3 tbsps oil
4 tbsps sugar
2 tbsps mirin
1 tbsp grated ginger
½ cup soy sauce
Pinch black pepper

GARNISH
Lemon slices

Thread the leeks and beef alternately
onto bamboo skewers. This should
fill 2-3 skewers per person. Pour oil
into a large frying pan. When hot,
add 2 skewers at a time and brown all
sides well, about 1-2 minutes. Drain
off any excess oil and mix the
remaining ingredients. Pour over the
meat and cook a further 2-3 minutes.
Remove the meat and simmer until
the sauce is thick and syrupy, about
5 minutes. Pour over the meat and
garnish with lemon slices.

Chicken Yakitori

PREPARATION TIME:	30 minutes
COOKING TIME:	5-6 minutes
SERVES:	4 people

4 tbsps mirin
4 tbsps sake
½ cup soy sauce

Pinch cayenne pepper
1 clove garlic
1 small piece ginger
1 tsp sugar

**This page: Chicken Yakitori. Facing
page: Pork Kebabs with Vegetables
(top) and Beef and Leek Skewers
(bottom).**

1 chicken, skinned, boned and cut in
1 inch pieces
2 large green peppers, cored, seeded and
cut in 1 inch pieces
2-4 leeks, depending on size (substitute
green onions when leeks are out of
season)

GARNISH
Radish jacks (see introduction)

Combine the first 7 ingredients in a small pan and bring to the boil. Remove from the heat and set aside to cool. Pour over the chicken and marinate for 30 minutes. Wash the leeks well and cut off the dark green tops. Cut the white and pale green parts into 1 inch pieces. If the leeks are very thick, cut in half. Thread 2 pieces of chicken onto bamboo or metal skewers, followed by a piece of pepper and leek, until all the ingredients are used. This will make 2-3 skewers per person. Reserve the marinade. Pre-heat a broiler and cook the chicken skewers 5-6 minutes per side, basting frequently with the marinade. May be cooked on a charcoal grill as well. Garnish with radish jacks.

Pork Kebabs with Vegetables

PREPARATION TIME: 30 minutes

COOKING TIME: 5-6 minutes

SERVES: 4 people

1 small eggplant
2 green peppers
1 onion, cut in 1 inch pieces
12oz pork tenderloin

SAUCE
2 tbsps oil
2 tbsps soy sauce
3 tbsps Worcestershire sauce
3 tbsps ketchup
1 tbsp grated ginger, squeezed for juice
1 clove garlic, finely minced

GARNISH
Lemon and cucumber twists (see
introduction)

Slice the eggplant in half and score lightly. Sprinkle with salt and leave to stand 30 minutes. Cut the peppers in half and remove seeds. Cut into 1 inch pieces. Cut the pork into 1 inch pieces. Squeeze the juices from the eggplant and rinse well. Pat dry and cut into pieces the size of the pork. Thread the ingredients onto bamboo or metal skewers, beginning with pork and alternating between pork and vegetables, ending with pork. This should make 2-3 kebabs per person. Mix the sauce ingredients thoroughly. Brush the kebabs and place under a pre-heated broiler. Cook 5-6 minutes, turning every 2 minutes, until the pork is cooked. Brush frequently with the sauce. Serve remaining sauce in separate bowls. Garnish with lemon and cucumber twists.

Beef Teriyaki

PREPARATION TIME: 30 minutes

COOKING TIME: 12-14 minutes

SERVES: 4 people

Light cooking oil, such as soya or peanut
oil
1 large onion, sliced
4 very small zucchini, ends trimmed
8 small or 4 large mushrooms, halved and
scored
4 butt steaks about 4oz in weight

SAUCE
4 tbsps dark soy sauce
4 tbsps sake
3 tbsps mirin
1 clove garlic, finely chopped
1 small piece ginger, finely chopped

Pour about 2 tbsps oil into a large frying pan. When hot, place in the onion slices in one layer. Fry until golden brown on both sides, about 1-2 minutes. Remove and keep warm. Cut the zucchini into thin rounds. Add 2 tbsps more oil to the pan and cook the zucchini quickly over high heat. Set aside and add the mushrooms to the pan. Cook 1 minute and set aside. Keep all the

vegetables warm while cooking the steaks. Add more oil to the pan and keep the heat high. Cook 1 steak at a time until both sides are brown, about 1 minute per side. Put all the steaks into the pan, pour over the sauce and cover. Cook over moderate heat 1-2 minutes. Divide all the vegetables evenly among 4 plates. Place steaks on the plates and cut in half, lengthwise, then into about 8 short strips. Pour the sauce over the steaks to serve.

Tuna Teriyaki

PREPARATION TIME: 20 minutes

COOKING TIME: 17 minutes

SERVES: 4 people

4 tuna fish steaks
2 tbsps oil
4 tbsps soy sauce
1 tbsp mirin
1 tbsp sugar
1 tbsp miso

GARNISH
Radish flowers and leaves (see
introduction)

Heat the oil in a large frying pan. Add the tuna and cook until slightly browned, about 2 minutes. Drain away excess oil and add the soy sauce, mirin and sugar. Cook over very low heat to cook the fish, about 5 minutes. Remove the fish from the pan and keep warm. Cook liquid over high heat to reduce by half. Stir in the miso. Skin tuna steaks and separate carefully in half. Discard bones and skin. Pour sauce over the fish and garnish with radish flowers and leaves.

Facing page: Beef Teriyaki (top) and Tuna Teriyaki (bottom).

Broiled Green Peppers

PREPARATION TIME: 15 minutes

COOKING TIME: 4-5 minutes

SERVES: 4 people

4 medium-sized green peppers
2 tbsps oil
Sesame seeds
Pickled ginger

Quarter the peppers and remove the seeds and cores. Heat a broiler and brush the peppers on all sides with oil. Cook for 4-5 minutes, turning the peppers every minute. During the last minute of cooking, turn the peppers skin side up and sprinkle over the sesame seeds. Allow the seeds to brown slightly and then remove the peppers to a serving dish. Serve with grated pickled ginger, if desired.

Flying Fish

PREPARATION TIME: 40 minutes

COOKING TIME: 4-10 minutes

SERVES: 4 people

4 fresh small sea bream, trout or red
* mullet*
Salt
Soy sauce

GARNISH
4 shiso leaves
4 lemon twigs

Scale the fish and gut them through the gills (a fishmonger will prepare the fish in this way). Rinse the fish very well and pat dry. Place the fish with the heads all pointing to the right and the stomach in front of you. Starting just behind the eye area, thread one or two metal skewers 3 times through 1 side of the fish. Do not allow the skewers to penetrate both sides of the fish. Bend the fish slightly every time the skewers are threaded through. Rub salt into the fins to make them stand up. Coat the tail with salt as well. Make sure the salt coating is quite heavy. Pre-heat a broiler and place the fish on a rack, the side not penetrated by skewers

uppermost. Broil 2-5 minutes per side. Twist the skewers occasionally to make them easier to remove. Place the fish on individual serving plates with the side broiled first uppermost. Remove the skewers and garnish with the shiso leaves and lemon twigs. Serve the soy sauce in individual bowls for dipping.

Egg Roll

PREPARATION TIME: 20 minutes

COOKING TIME: 1-2 minutes

SERVES: 3 people

4 eggs, beaten
⅓ cup dashi
Pinch salt
¼ tsp light soy sauce
2 green onions, roughly chopped
1 shiitake mushroom, roughly chopped
1 sheet nori, finely shredded

GARNISH
½ daikon radish, finely grated

This is best made in a special oblong Japanese omelet pan. A large frying pan may be substituted. Mix the eggs with the dashi, salt and soy sauce. Brush the pan with a light film of oil. Heat until slightly smoking. Pour in enough of the egg to coat the bottom of the pan. Cook for a few seconds, until the egg is just set. Sprinkle over the onions and mushroom. Roll up the omelet and push to one side of the pan. Brush the pan again with oil and pour in more of the egg. Cook again until just set. Roll up the first omelet inside the second and repeat until all the egg is used. Lift out of the pan and cut into nine rolls. Pass the nori over a gas flame on both sides to freshen. Shred finely. Arrange nori strips on plates and place 3 rolls on top. Garnish with a little grated daikon radish.

This page: Flying Fish. Facing page: Egg Roll (top) and Broiled Green Peppers (bottom).

Steaming and Baking

Shrimp Egg Custard

PREPARATION TIME: 20 minutes	
COOKING TIME: 20-25 minutes	
SERVES: 4 people	

STOCK
2 cups dashi
1 tsp soy sauce
1 tsp mirin
Pinch salt

4 dried shiitake mushrooms, soaked
*   30 minutes, drained and scored*
4 jumbo shrimp
4 pea pods, blanched and cut in half
1oz bean sprouts
5 eggs, beaten

GARNISH
1 piece pickled ginger, grated

Bring stock ingredients to the boil. Take off the heat and leave to cool. Strain the stock and when cool mix with the beaten eggs. Divide the mixture evenly among 4 heat-resistant cups or small bowls. Add the bean sprouts and position the shrimp so the tail shows. Add the pea pods and float a mushroom on top of the custard. Pour water into a steamer or a large, deep saucepan and bring to the boil. Place the cups on a steamer or a rack above the boiling water. Cover the pan or steamer and cook over high heat for about 2 minutes. Reduce the heat and steam until just set, about 15 minutes. A toothpick inserted into the middle of

This page: Shrimp Egg Custard. Facing page: Steamed Abalone (top) and Baked Stuffed Trout (bottom).

the custard should come out clean when the custard is cooked. Garnish with the pickled ginger.

Baked Stuffed Trout

PREPARATION TIME: 20 minutes	
COOKING TIME: 16-19 minutes	
OVEN TEMPERATURE: 400°F (200°C)	
SERVES: 4 people	

4 small trout, cleaned and boned

STUFFING
4 tbsps red miso
2 green onions, chopped
2 tbsps sugar
1 tbsp mirin
1 tbsp dashi
1 tbsp grated ginger

GARNISH
Lime slices

Make sure the heads and tails of the fish are left on. Cut 4 pieces of foil large enough to enclose each fish. Brush lightly with oil. Combine stuffing ingredients in a saucepan. Cook over moderate heat 4 minutes to thicken. Place each fish on a piece of foil and spread the stuffing in the cavity. Fold the foil over the fish tightly and twist the ends. Bake 12-14 minutes. Partially open the foil to serve. Garnish with a slice of lime.

Beef Roasted with Vegetables

PREPARATION TIME: 25 minutes	
COOKING TIME: 15 minutes	
OVEN TEMPERATURE: 400°F (200°C)	
SERVES: 4 people	

1lb sirloin or rib roast, sliced in very thin strips

8 shiitake mushrooms, quartered lengthwise
1 green pepper, cored, seeded and cut in 8 pieces, lengthwise
1 carrot, quartered
4 tbsps mirin
4 tbsps soy sauce
Seven spices pepper

DIPPING SAUCE
4 tbsps lemon juice
4 tbsps orange juice
½ cup soy sauce
½ cup dashi

GARNISH
1 small piece daikon radish
1 small red chili pepper
4 shiso leaves
4 orange slices

Cut 4 pieces of foil about 10 inches square. Brush with oil. Place an equal portion of beef, bamboo shoots, peppers, mushroom and carrot on the foil. Mix mirin, soy sauce and seven spice pepper together and pour over each portion. Wrap well and cook 15 minutes. Combine sauce ingredients and pour into 4 small bowls. Remove core from the radish with a vegetable peeler. Insert chili pepper and grate together, finely. Arrange a leaf on each serving plate. Add grated daikon radish and chili pepper and an orange slice. Open the foil packets and place one on each dish. Serve each person with a sauce bowl for dipping.

Steamed Abalone

PREPARATION TIME: 30 minutes	
COOKING TIME: 20 minutes	
SERVES: 4 people	

4 fresh abalone in the shell, if possible
Salt
4 tbsps sake

MISO SAUCE
⅓ cup red miso
4 tbsps dashi
2 tbsps sugar
2 tbsps mirin

GARNISH
4 large pieces konbu seaweed
2oz pickled ginger, sliced

Use a strong spatula to remove the abalone if in the shell. Scrub the shells well and reserve. Sprinkle the abalone liberally with salt and scrub to remove black portion. Peel off green edges with a knife. Lightly score the surface of the abalone and line the shells or serving dishes with the seaweed. Replace the abalone in the shell on top of the seaweed and put into a steamer or on a rack above boiling water. Spoon the sake over each abalone, cover and steam for 20 minutes on moderate heat. Brush with miso sauce after about 12 minutes steaming. Remove the abalone, cut in half horizontally and then into ½ inch strips. Replace in the shells. Garnish with cucumber and ginger. Use any remaining miso sauce as a dipping sauce.

Steamed Chicken

PREPARATION TIME: 25 minutes	
COOKING TIME: 15 minutes	
SERVES: 4 people	

1lb chicken breasts, boned
2 tsps salt
2 tbsps sake
1 tbsp light soy sauce
1 tbsp dark soy sauce

4 leaves of Chinese cabbage
1 piece daikon radish
1 small red pepper

Prick the skin of the chicken and salt lightly. Mix the sake and soy sauce and pour over the chicken. Rub in well. Place chicken in a steamer or in a dish on a rack over boiling water. Cover and cook 15 minutes on moderate heat. Cut into ½ inch strips. Meanwhile, insert a vegetable peeler lengthwise into the daikon radish and remove a core. Push in the

Facing page: Beef Roasted with Vegetables.

pepper. Grate the two together, finely. Place the Chinese cabbage on a plate and arrange the chicken. Garnish with small mounds of grated daikon radish. Reduce the cooking liquid from the chicken by boiling rapidly in a small saucepan. Use as a sauce.

Steamed Fish Rolls

PREPARATION TIME:	25 minutes
COOKING TIME:	10-15 minutes
SERVES:	4 people

2 large sole or flounder to give 4 whole
   fillets
4 green onions, blanched 2 minutes
6oz shrimp
2 tsps cornstarch
1 tsp sake
2 eggs, beaten
Salt

GLAZE
1 tbsp white miso
1 tbsp mirin

GARNISH
1 small piece pickled daikon radish,
   fanned
4 whole shrimp

Skin the fish fillets and lay them skin side up on a flat surface. Chop the shrimp finely and mix with cornstarch and sake. Divide the shrimp filling between the 2 fillets and spoon into a mound across the middle of the fillet. Trim off the white part of the onions and use only the green. Place the onions next to the shrimp filling. Cook the eggs with a pinch of salt until softly scrambled. Place in a mound next to the onions. Roll up the fish fillets, folding the thicker end over the filling first. Secure with wooden picks. Place in the top part of a steamer. Boil water in the bottom part. Alternatively, use a large pan and place the fish on a rack over boiling water. Steam for 10-15 minutes, until the fish is cooked. Five minutes before the end of cooking, brush with combined glaze ingredients. Cut in slices and serve garnished with pickled daikon

radish cut in a fan shape and whole shrimp.

Hakata-Mushi (Steamed Ground Pork)

PREPARATION TIME:	30 minutes
COOKING TIME:	50 minutes
SERVES:	4 people

1lb Chinese cabbage, parboiled 2 minutes
3 eggs, beaten
1lb ground pork
2 tbsps all-purpose flour
1 tbsp soy sauce
Pinch salt

SAUCE
2 cups dashi
3 tbsps soy sauce
½ clove garlic, finely minced
1 tbsp cornstarch

Line the bottom of a greased 1lb loaf pan with ⅓ of the cabbage leaves. Mix ⅓ of the beaten egg with the meat, flour, soy sauce and salt. Pour half of the remaining egg into the pan over the cabbage leaves. Press half of the meat mixture on top of the egg. Cover with another ⅓ of the cabbage leaves and add another layer of meat. Pour remaining egg over the meat and cover with remaining cabbage leaves. Press the mixture down and

cover the pan with foil. Bring water to the boil in a steamer or large, deep pan with a tight-fitting lid. Place the pan in the steamer or on a rack above the water and cook 50 minutes, covered. Mix the cornstarch with 2 tbsps of dashi. Bring the remaining dashi to the boil and add the soy sauce and garlic. Gradually stir in the cornstarch and cook, stirring constantly, until the mixture thickens. Cover the surface of the

Facing page: Steamed Chicken (top) and Hakata-Mushi (Steamed Ground Pork) (bottom). This page: Steamed Fish Rolls.

sauce with wax paper to prevent a skin forming. Allow the sauce to cool. Cool the hakata-mushi to room temperature and cut into squares or slices. Serve with the cooled sauce for dipping.

Simmering and One Pot Cooking

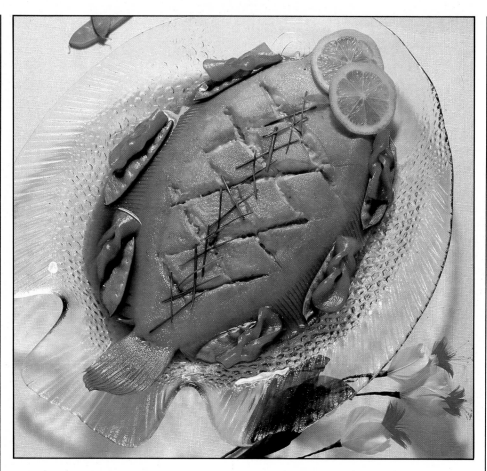

dashi, mirin and soy sauce. Gut the fish or buy already prepared. Leave on the heads and tails. Score the white side of the fish with a sharp knife. Put the fish cut sides down into a large, shallow pan. Pour over the stock and cook gently on top of the heat for 15-20 minutes. Remove the fish to serving dishes and turn cut side up. Keep warm. Cut the konnyaku cake into rectangles about ¼ inch thick. Cut a slit in the middle and pull the end of the konnyaku through the slit, twisting as you pull. Place in the fish cooking liquid and cook 5 minutes on gentle heat. Arrange the blanched pea pods and konnyaku against the fish and spoon some of the cooking liquid over each.

Simmered Vegetables

PREPARATION TIME: 30 minutes

COOKING TIME: 7 minutes

SERVES: 4 people

2lbs of a selection of the following:
Shiitake mushrooms, soaked 30 minutes, stalks removed
Turnips, peeled and pared into thick barrel shapes
Carrots, peeled

Simmered Flounder

PREPARATION TIME: 35 minutes

COOKING TIME: 27 minutes

SERVES: 4 people

½ cup sake
1½ cups dashi
½ cup mirin
½ cup soy sauce
4 small flounder or sole

4oz pea pods, steamed 2 minutes
1 cake konnyaku

GARNISH
Lemon Slices
Shredded chives

Pour sake into a small saucepan and warm gently. Ignite the fumes and allow to burn until the flames die off naturally. Keep a pan lid handy in case the flames shoot up. Add the

**This page: Simmered Flounder.
Facing page: Simmered Vegetables (top) and Simmered Coltsfoot and Carrots (bottom).**

Konnyaku cake, cut in ¼ inch slices
Zucchini cut in ¼ inch diagonal slices
Pea pods, strings removed if necessary,
   ends trimmed on the diagonal
Green onions, cut in 1 inch diagonal
   pieces

BROTH
1½ cups dashi
2 tsps sake
4 tbsps soy sauce
3 tbsps mirin

Score the mushroom caps if desired. Use a sharp, small knife to cut the turnips into thick hexagonal shapes. Take strips off the carrots, lengthwise, with a cannelle knife or paring knife. Cut crosswise into "flower" shapes. Cut a lengthwise slit in the konnyaku cake slices. Pull one end through the slit, twisting as you pull. Bring the dashi and sake to the boil in a saucepan and add the turnip and konnyaku. Blanch 1 minute. Remove the vegetables and set aside. Put in the pea pods and zucchini. Blanch 30 seconds. Return the turnips and konnyaku to the pan and add the mushrooms and carrots. Add the sugar, soy sauce and bring to the boil. Allow to simmer 5 minutes. Add the green onions during the last minute of cooking. Remove all the vegetables with a draining spoon and arrange in serving dishes. Allow the sauce to boil rapidly to reduce it. Add the mirin and cook 30 seconds. Allow to cool slightly and pour over the vegetables.

Chicken One Pot

PREPARATION TIME: 35 minutes
COOKING TIME: 30 minutes
SERVES: 6 people

2 tbsps oil
1lb boned chicken, thinly sliced
1 cup chicken stock
4 tbsp soy sauce
2 tbsps sugar
1 carrot, sliced diagonally
1 medium green pepper, cut in thin strips
8oz fresh spinach leaves, well washed
8 shiitake mushrooms, soaked 30 minutes

1 piece tofu, sliced
1 small bunch coriander leaves
8oz buckwheat noodles, cooked

SAUCE AND GARNISH
6 tbsps soy sauce
6 tbsps lemon juice
1 piece daikon radish, peeled and stuck
   with 1 small red chili pepper

Heat oil in an electric frying pan or chafing dish at the table. Start frying the chicken a few slices at a time. Mix stock, soy sauce and sugar. When chicken pieces are cooked, push to the side of the pan and add some of each vegetable and a small portion of noodles. Moisten all with stock mixture. Make a hole in the center of the daikon radish with a vegetable peeler and push in the chili pepper. Grate the two together finely and serve in small mounds next to mounds of onion. Serve the soy sauce and lemon juice in individual bowls. As the ingredients are cooked, each person takes food from the pan. A bit of the radish and onion may be mixed into the dipping sauce. Dip food into the sauce and continue to cook ingredients as the meal goes on.

Simmered Chicken with Okra

PREPARATION TIME: 20 minutes
COOKING TIME: 12 minutes
SERVES: 4 people

1½ cups dashi or chicken stock
3 tbsps mirin
5 tbsps soy sauce
2 chicken breasts, boned and cut in slivers
½ cup dashi or chicken stock
6 okra pods, stems trimmed and cut in
   rounds
1 piece tofu, cut in slices
Bamboo shoots cut in thin matchsticks

GARNISH
Carrot flowers (see introduction)

Prepare the garnish. Mix the first 3 ingredients and bring to the boil in

a shallow pan. Add the chicken and cook 10 minutes on moderate heat. Take off the heat and set aside. Add remaining dashi to a small saucepan with the okra, tofu and bamboo shoots. Cook 2 minutes. Arrange the chicken and vegetables in shallow serving bowls. Pour over a small amount of chicken cooking liquid. Garnish with carrot flowers.

Simmered Coltsfoot and Carrots

PREPARATION TIME: 25 minutes
COOKING TIME: 14 minutes
SERVES: 4 people

2 coltsfoot stems (4 sticks celery may be
   substituted)
2 cups dashi
1 tbsp sugar
2 tbsps mirin
2 tbsps soy sauce
1 small carrot, cut in thin ribbons
Bonito flakes

Cook the coltsfoot stems or celery sticks whole in 4 cups salted water. Cook 4 minutes. Rinse under cold water. Peel the stems from the bottom of the coltsfoot and drain. Cut coltsfoot or celery into 2 inch sticks. Combine dashi, sugar, mirin and soy sauce in a saucepan and bring to the boil. Add the coltsfoot and simmer 10 minutes. Simmer only 5 minutes for celery. Add the carrot ribbons 2 minutes before the end of cooking. Remove the vegetables and arrange in dishes. Allow the vegetables and cooking liquid to cool. Pour some of the liquid over each serving of vegetables and serve cold, garnished with bonito flakes.

Facing page: Simmered Chicken with Okra (top) and Chicken One Pot (bottom).

1½ cups dashi
1 tbsp mirin
1 small piece ginger, peeled and left whole

Cut strips from the carrot lengthwise with a cannelle knife or paring knife. Cut the carrot crosswise into ¼ inch "flower" slices. Trim the ends of the beans on the diagonal. Slice the daikon pieces into thin rectangles. Cut the kamaboku paste into slices and cut a lengthwise slit in the middle of each. Pull one end of the paste through the slit, twisting gently. Place the paste and all the vegetables, except the mushrooms, in a shallow pan and cover with water. Add a pinch of salt and cover the pan tightly. Cook about 2 minutes on high heat, until the carrots are almost tender. Add the bamboo shoots halfway through cooking time. Meanwhile, bring the dashi, mirin and ginger to the boil in a shallow pan. Leave the shells on the very ends of the tails of the shrimp. Place them in the hot dashi and cook 2 minutes or until just pink. Do not allow them to boil. Arrange all the ingredients attractively in 4 shallow bowls. Spoon over some of the dashi mixture and serve immediately.

Sukiyaki

PREPARATION TIME: 40 minutes

COOKING TIME: 30 minutes

SERVES: 6 people

6 eggs, beaten
3 tbsps oil
1 ½ lbs sirloin, sliced paper thin
1 bunch green onions, cut in ½ inch
    diagonal pieces
8 shiitake mushrooms, soaked 30 minutes
    and scored
5oz shiratake noodles, soaked 5 minutes
    and cut in 5 inch lengths
5oz udon noodles, cooked
8oz Chinese cabbage
8oz fresh spinach, leaves washed and
    stems removed
2 bamboo shoots, cut in triangular pieces
1 5oz cake konnyaku, sliced
1 5oz cake tofu, sliced
Salad cress or watercress

Simmered Shrimp with Vegetables

PREPARATION TIME: 30 minutes

COOKING TIME: 2 minutes

SERVES: 4 people

8oz shrimp or 1lb jumbo shrimp
2 medium carrots, peeled
16 green beans

This page: Sukiyaki. Facing page: Cod and Cabbage One Pot (top) and Simmered Shrimp with Vegetables (bottom).

1 small piece daikon radish, cut into
    matchsticks
1 piece kamaboku fish paste or konnyaku
2oz bamboo shoots, cut into matchsticks

483

BROTH
1 cup dashi
½ cup soy sauce
3 tbsps mirin
1 tbsp sugar

Break one egg into each of 6 bowls and beat lightly. Arrange all the ingredients on a large tray. Heat oil in an electric frying pan or chafing dish at the table. Brown the meat a few pieces at a time. Add onions. Move meat to one side of the dish and add equal portions of the other ingredients. Mix broth ingredients together and add some to the pan. Each person takes some of the cooked food and dips it into the egg, which quickly glazes the hot food. Keep adding ingredients and simmering liquid as the meal progresses.

Eternity Patties

PREPARATION TIME: 20 minutes
COOKING TIME: 13-15 minutes
SERVES: 4-5 people

12oz ground chicken
½ egg, beaten
2 tbsps all-purpose flour
½ tsp ground ginger
½ cup all-purpose flour
2½ cups dashi
3 tbsps soy sauce
2 tbsps sugar
1 tbsp sake

GARNISH
Radish flowers and leaves

Combine the chicken, egg, 2 tbsps flour, ginger and salt in a large bowl and mix well. Divide the mixture into 10 (mixture will be soft). Lightly flour hands and form mixture into patties. Coat the patties with the remaining flour mixed with a pinch of salt. Score a lattice on the top of each patty using the blunt side of a knife. Combine remaining ingredients in a large frying pan and bring to the boil. Add the patties to the pan, scored side up, and swirl liquid over the tops. Reduce heat and simmer 3-4 minutes. Gently turn the patties over

and cook 5-6 minutes. Turn again and increase the heat to bring the liquid up to a rapid boil. Quickly swirl the liquid over the patties for about 2 minutes. Transfer the patties to a serving dish and spoon over some of the cooking liquid. Garnish with radish flowers and leaves.

Cod and Cabbage One Pot

PREPARATION TIME: 40 minutes
COOKING TIME: 30 minutes
SERVES: 4 people

10 dried shiitake mushrooms, soaked 30 minutes
1lb cod fillet, skinned and cut in 1 inch pieces
3 small leeks, washed and cut in 2½ inch lengths
8oz Chinese cabbage
8oz tofu, drained
1½ oz cellophane noodles, soaked 5 minutes
5 cups dashi

SAUCE
2 tbsps rice vinegar
2 tbsps soy sauce
4 tbsps mirin
2 tbsps lemon juice
4 tbsps sake
1 small piece konbu seaweed

GARNISH
2 green onions, finely chopped
3oz piece daikon radish, stuck with 1 red pepper, finely grated

Drain mushrooms and cut off stalks. Trim down spines of the cabbage leaves and cut the leaves into 3 irregular-shaped pieces. Cut the tofu into 10 pieces. Drain the noodles and arrange all the ingredients on a large tray. Bring the stock to the boil. Mix the sauce ingredients and pour into 4 small bowls. Arrange a mound of onion and one of grated daikon radish on each of 4 separate plates or trays. Put the pot of stock on an electric ring on the table. Add the fish, then the mushrooms and then

the cabbage leaves. Add the leeks, noodles and tofu. Each person mixes small amounts of onion and radish into the sauce and takes food from the main pot to dip into the sauce. A fondue pot may also be used for cooking.

Simmered Pork and Vegetable Casserole

PREPARATION TIME: 25 minutes
COOKING TIME: 1 hour
SERVES: 4 people

2 tbsps oil
1lb pork spare ribs, cut in 1 inch pieces
1oz piece ginger, sliced thinly
3 tbsps sake
4 tbsps soy sauce
2 tbsps sugar
2oz green beans, cut in 2 inch lengths
2 sticks celery, cut in 2 inch lengths
2oz bamboo shoots, cut into strips

Heat the oil in a large sauté pan. Cook the sliced ginger briefly and remove. Add the pork to the pan, turn up the heat and brown on all sides. Pour in water to just barely cover. Return the ginger to the pan. Add the sake, cover and cook for 1 hour. Check the level of liquid and add more water if the meat begins to dry out. When the pork is tender, add the soy sauce, and sugar and cook, uncovered, to reduce the sauce to syrupy consistency. Meanwhile, put beans and celery into a small pan and barely cover with water. Add a pinch of salt and bring to the boil. Cook 2-3 minutes until tender-crisp. Add the bamboo shoots after about 2 minutes. Place the pork in individual serving dishes and scatter over the vegetables. Pour over any remaining sauce.

Facing page: Simmered Pork and Vegetable Casserole (top) and Eternity Patties (bottom).

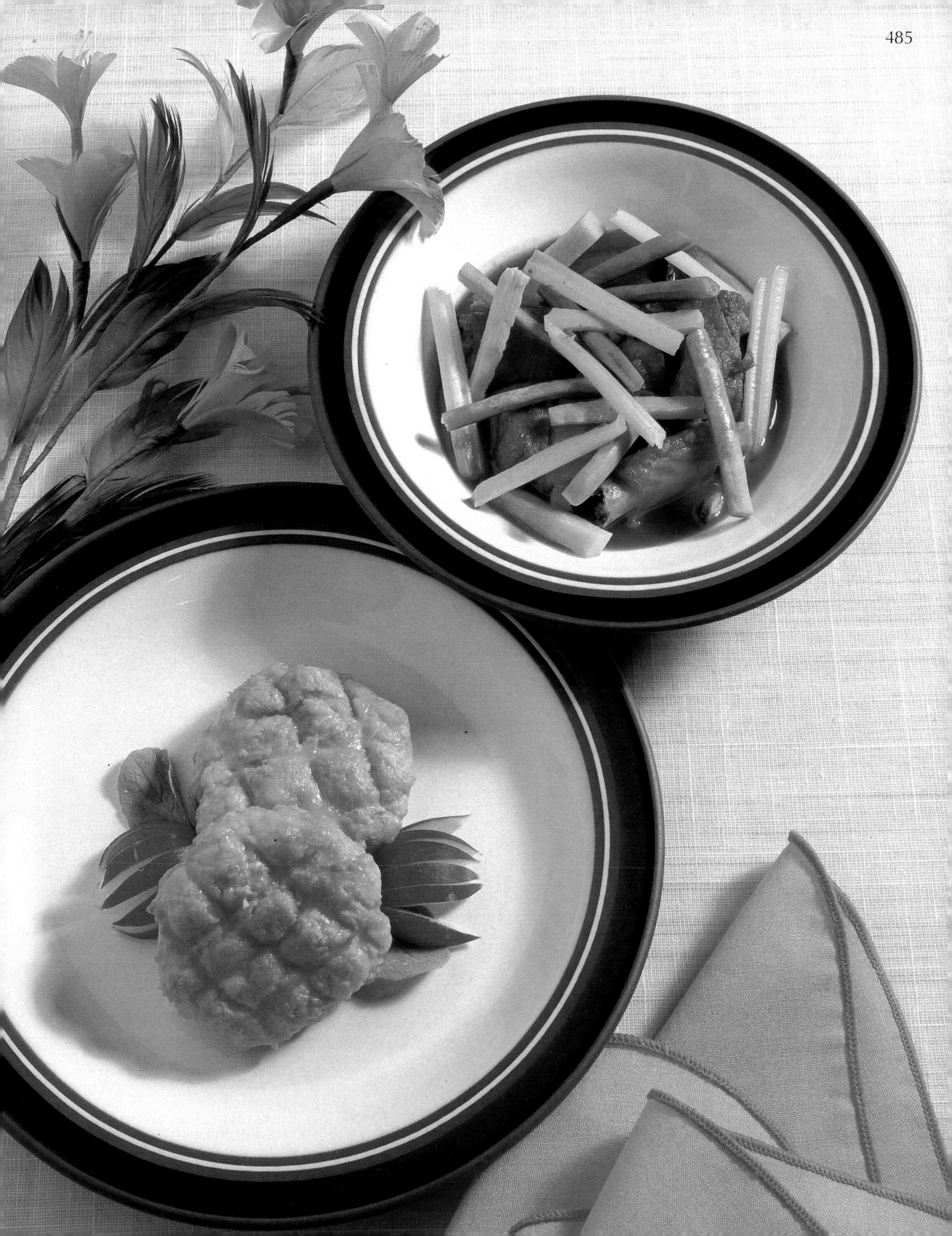

Deep Frying

Lemony Marinated Herring

PREPARATION TIME: 15 minutes	
COOKING TIME: 10-20 minutes	
SERVES: 4 people	

4 herrings, cleaned and heads removed
3 tbsps rice vinegar
2 tbsps soy sauce
2 tbsps sake
1 tbsp lemon juice
Cornstarch to dredge
Oil for frying

Score the fish diagonally 3 or 4 times on one side. Mix the vinegar, soy sauce, sake and lemon juice together and sprinkle over the fish. Leave in a cool place to marinate for 15 minutes. Heat oil to 350°F (180°C) in a deep-fat fryer or wok. Dredge the fish with cornstarch and fry in the hot oil, 2 fish at a time. Cook for 5-10 minutes. Drain on paper towels. Garnish with lemon and cucumber twigs, if desired.

Deep-Fried Pork

PREPARATION TIME: 15 minutes	
COOKING TIME: 5 minutes per batch	
SERVES: 4 people	

4 slices pork tenderloin, about ½ inch
  thick
Flour with salt and pepper
2 egg whites, lightly beaten
1 cup fresh breadcrumbs
Oil for frying
½ head Chinese cabbage
1 lime, sliced

Clip the edges of the pork slices to prevent curling and dip in the seasoned flour. Shake off excess flour and dip the pork into the egg white and then sprinkle with breadcrumbs.

This page: Taksuta-Age (Deep-Fried Chicken) (top) and Deep-Fried Pork (bottom). Facing page: Snowy Fried Shrimp (top) and Lemon Marinated Herring (bottom).

Heat the oil to 350°F (180°C) in a deep-fat fryer or wok. Fry 1 or 2 slices at a time for about 5 minutes. Remove the pork and drain on paper towels. Slice each piece diagonally into ½ inch thick strips. Serve assembled on a bed of shredded Chinese cabbage and garnish with lime slices.

Snowy Fried Shrimp

PREPARATION TIME: 20 minutes

COOKING TIME: 2 minutes per batch

SERVES: 4 people

1½ lbs cooked jumbo shrimp, peeled
2oz harusame or saifan (soy flour noodles)
½ cup flour with salt and pepper
2 egg whites
Oil for frying

De-vein the shrimp and score diagonally on the underside. Cut the noodles into ¼-½ inch pieces. Beat the egg whites until foamy. Dip the shrimp into the seasoned flour and shake off surplus. Dip into egg white and then sprinkle on the noodles until each shrimp is completely covered. Heat oil in a deep-fat fryer or wok to 325°F (160°C). Add the shrimp to the hot oil and fry a few at a time until the noodles look opaque, about 2 minutes. Drain well before serving. They should not be allowed to brown.

Vegetable Tempura

PREPARATION TIME: 30 minutes

COOKING TIME: 2 minutes per batch

SERVES: 4 people

Selection of the following ingredients prepared as directed:
Celery, cut into sticks
Artichoke hearts, halved
Lotus root, sliced in rounds about ¼ inch thick
Mushrooms, whole fresh or dried, soaked 30 minutes, with stems removed
Green peppers, cut in ¼ inch thick rings or strips
Onions, cut in ¼ inch rings
Parsnips, peeled and cut into sticks
Asparagus tips
Turnips, peeled and cubed
Pea pods, ends trimmed and strings removed if necessary
Green beans, ends trimmed
Eggplant, cut in half. Cut away flesh, leaving ⅛ inch clinging to the skin. Cut the skin into fan shapes about 1½ inches long
Zucchini, cut in half lengthwise and then into thin slices across
Okra, stems removed and pods left whole
Broccoli, cut into flowerets
Cauliflower, cut into flowerets
Parsley, snipped into small bunches
Sweet potato, peeled and sliced into ½ inch rounds
Carrots, peeled and cut into diagonal slices
Cucumber, cut in quarters lengthwise and then into 1 inch wedges
Oil for frying

DIPPING SAUCE
½ cup chicken stock
4 tbsps soy sauce
4 tbsps sherry or sake
Pinch sugar
Small piece daikon radish, grated
Small piece ginger, grated

BATTER
1 egg yolk
1¼ cups iced water
1 cup all-purpose flour

Prepare the vegetables as directed. Mix all the ingredients for the sauce except the radish and ginger. Pour the sauce into 4 small bowls. Place a small mound of grated radish and one of grated ginger on each of 4 plates. Heat oil in a deep-fat fryer to 350°F (180°C). A wok may also be used. Beat the egg yolk lightly and beat in the water. Sift in the flour and stir with a table knife. The batter should look lumpy and under-mixed. Dip each vegetable in the batter and shake off the excess. Lower ingredients carefully into the hot oil and cook for about 2 minutes, turning once or twice with a metal spoon. Fry only 3 or 4 pieces at a time and fry only 1 kind of vegetable at a time. Do not coat too many vegetables in advance. Drain fried vegetables on paper towels on a rack for a few seconds before serving. Serve while still hot and crisp. Each person may mix a desired amount of the grated radish and ginger into the dipping sauce to eat with the tempura.

Taksuta-Age (Deep-Fried Chicken)

PREPARATION TIME: 15 minutes, plus marinating time

COOKING TIME: 2-3 minutes per batch

SERVES: 4 people

4 chicken breasts
3 tbsps soy sauce
1 tbsp mirin or sweet sherry
1 tbsp rice vinegar
2 tbps sugar
1 clove garlic, minced
2oz flour, with a pinch of salt and pepper
Oil for frying

Cut the chicken into 1 inch cubes and combine with all remaining ingredients except flour in a deep bowl and leave to marinate, covered, for about 1 hour in a cool place. Stir occasionally to coat the chicken evenly. Remove the chicken from the marinade with a draining spoon. Toss in the seasoned flour to coat. Heat the oil in a deep-fat fryer or wok to 350°F (180°C) and fry the chicken, a few pieces at a time. Cook until golden brown and crisp, about 2-3 minutes per batch. Drain on paper towels a few seconds before serving. Serve with extra soy sauce for dipping, if desired.

Facing page: Vegetable Tempura.

Fish Tempura

PREPARATION TIME: 30 minutes

COOKING TIME: 2 minutes per batch

SERVES: 4 people

12 uncooked jumbo shrimp
2 whitefish fillets, skinned and cut into
    2 x ¾ inch strips
Small whole fish such as smelt or
    whitebait
Squid, cleaned and cut into 1 x 3 inch
    strips and dredged with flour
Oil for frying

DIPPING SAUCE
⅓ cup soy sauce
Juice and zest of 1 lemon or lime
¼ cup dashi

BATTER
1 egg yolk
1 cup iced water
1 cup all-purpose flour, sifted

Shell the shrimp, leaving only the tail shell on the end of each. De-vein if necessary. Wash the whole fish and pat dry. Prepare other fish as directed. Mix the dipping sauce ingredients and pour into small bowls. Heat oil in a deep-fat fryer to 350°F (180°C). A wok may also be used. To make the batter, beat the egg yolk lightly and gradually beat in the iced water. Sift in the flour and stir the batter with a table knife. Batter will be lumpy and look under-mixed. Dip each piece of fish in the batter and shake off the excess. Lower ingredients carefully into the hot oil and cook for about 2 minutes, turning once or twice with a metal spoon. Fry only 3 or 4 pieces of fish at a time, and only 1 kind of fish at a time. Do not coat too many pieces of fish in advance. Drain on a rack with

cubes. Heat the oil in a deep-fat fryer or wok to 350°F (180°C). Reduce heat slightly and add the tofu cubes to the hot oil. Deep-fry 1-2 minutes or until cubes float to the surface. Turn them over and fry a further 1 minute. Remove from the oil with a draining spoon and drain on a rack or paper towels. Cook tofu in several batches. Meanwhile, bring the stock to the boil in a saucepan. Add the beans and bonito flakes and simmer gently for 5 minutes until the beans are just tender. Transfer the beans to a serving dish with a draining spoon. Arrange them in a circle and keep warm. Rapidly boil the cooking liquid to reduce by half and pour over the beans. Pile the deep-fried tofu into the center of the beans to serve.

Chicken Croquettes

PREPARATION TIME: 20 minutes

COOKING TIME: 3-5 minutes per batch

SERVES: 4 people

8oz ground chicken
8oz cooked, mashed potatoes
½ small onion, finely chopped
1 clove garlic, minced
2 tbsps chopped parsley
Salt
Pepper
1 tbsp soy sauce
1 egg, beaten
1 cup breadcrumbs
Oil for frying

Combine the chicken, potatoes, onion, garlic, parsley, salt, pepper and soy sauce together in a mixing bowl. Add the egg and mix well. Form the mixture into small cylinder shapes about 2 x ½ inch. Roll in breadcrumbs and chill briefly. Heat oil to 350°F (180°C) in a deep-fat fryer or wok. Lower the croquettes carefully into the hot oil and fry for about 3-5 minutes, until golden brown and crisp. Cook in small batches. Drain on paper towels on a rack for a few seconds before serving. Serve with soy sauce for dipping if desired.

paper towels for a few seconds before serving. Serve with the sauce for dipping while still hot and crisp.

Facing page: Fish Tempura. This page: Deep-Fried Tofu with Green Beans (top) and Chicken Croquettes (bottom).

Deep-Fried Tofu with Green Beans

PREPARATION TIME: 20 minutes

COOKING TIME: 5 minutes for beans, 1-2 minutes per batch for tofu

SERVES: 4 people

1lb tofu
1 cup chicken stock
8oz green beans, trimmed
1 tbsp bonito flakes
Oil for frying

Drain and press tofu to remove excess moisture and cut into 1 inch

JAPANESE COOKING

Vinegared Foods and Salads

Spinach and Bean Sprouts with Wasabi

PREPARATION TIME: 15 minutes

COOKING TIME: 1 minutes

SERVES: 4 people

1lb fresh spinach, washed well and stalks removed
4oz bean sprouts

DRESSING
2 tbsps rice vinegar
2 tbsps sugar
1 tbsp soy sauce
½ tsp wasabi powder mixed to a paste with water

Cook the spinach 1 minute in a covered saucepan with only the water that clings to the leaves after washing. Refresh under cold water, press to remove excess moisture and leave to drain. Combine leaves with bean sprouts. Mix dressing ingredients very well and pour over salad. Toss lightly and serve in individual bowls.

Daikon and Carrot Salad

PREPARATION TIME: 25 minutes

SERVES: 4 people

4 small oranges
½ daikon radish, peeled and coarsely grated
1 large carrot, peeled and coarsely grated
1 small piece ginger, grated
Rice vinegar
2 tbsps sugar
Pinch salt

GARNISH
Radish flowers and leaves

Cut the oranges in half and squeeze for juice. Measure the juice and add an equal amount of vinegar. Add the sugar and salt and mix well. Cook over low heat to dissolve sugar and evaporate vinegar fumes. Set the dressing aside to cool. Cut a slice from the rounded end of the orange shells so that they stand level. Do not cut completely through the base. Scoop out the orange pulp and cut

This page: Daikon and Carrot Salad. Facing page: Bean Salad with Sesame Dressing (top) and Spinach and Bean Sprouts with Wasabi (bottom).

the edge in scallops or points if desired. Mix radish, carrot and ginger with the dressing. Leave to stand 30 minutes. Fill orange shells with the salad and serve chilled.

Gold Salad

PREPARATION TIME: 20 minutes

COOKING TIME: 6-8 minutes

SERVES: 4 people

20 *spears white asparagus, stalks trimmed*
Salt

SAUCE
2 egg yolks
2 tbsps rice vinegar
2 tsps dry mustard
1 tbsp sugar
2 tsps cornstarch
4 tbsps dashi
Chopped parsley

Cut the asparagus into 2 inch diagonal pieces, leaving the tips whole. Bring 2 cups water to the boil. Add a pinch of salt and the asparagus. Cook 2-3 minutes. Asparagus should still be crisp. Rinse in cold water and drain. Combine all ingredients for the sauce in a double boiler or in a small bowl in a bain marie. Stirring constantly, cook over boiling water to thicken. Remove and stir or wisk until the sauce cools. It should be the consistency of mayonnaise. Divide asparagus into 4 bowls, spoon over the sauce and sprinkle on chopped parsley.

GARNISH
3 green onions, very finely chopped

Pre-heat a broiler, or cook over charcoal. Dry mushrooms well. Cut stalks off and sprinkle caps with salt. Cut the tofu into ½ inch slices. Brush lightly with oil on both sides. Broil with the mushrooms, about 3 minutes per side, turning once. Cut mushrooms and tofu into thin slices. Arrange on dishes and mix the sauce ingredients. Pour over the mushrooms and tofu. Garnish with the onion. Serve hot.

Okra with Garlic and Seven Spice Pepper

PREPARATION TIME: 15 minutes

COOKING TIME: 5 minutes

SERVES: 4 people

40 okra pods
1 tbsp soy sauce
2 cloves garlic, grated finely
Seven spice pepper

Wash the okra well. Keep stem end on and put okra into boiling, salted water. Cook 5 minutes. Refresh under cold water and drain well. Cut off the stem ends. If the pods are small, leave whole. If large cut on the diagonal into ½ inch lengths. Sprinkle over soy sauce, garlic and pepper. Toss and serve in small bowls.

Lima Beans in Tofu Dressing

PREPARATION TIME: 25 minutes

COOKING TIME: 5 minutes

SERVES: 4 people

2lbs fresh lima beans (weight when shelled)
Salt

DRESSING
1 8oz cake tofu
2 tbsps sugar
Pinch salt
2 tsps sesame oil
½ tsp soy sauce

Facing page: Okra with Garlic and Seven Spice Pepper (top) and Lima Beans in Tofu Dressing (bottom). This page: Gold Salad (top) and Vinegared Mushroom Salad with Tofu (bottom).

Vinegared Mushroom Salad with Tofu

PREPARATION TIME: 30 minutes

COOKING TIME: 3 minutes

SERVES: 4 people

12 large shiitake mushrooms, soaked 30 minutes
1 8oz cake tofu, drained
Salt
Oil

SAUCE
3 tbsps lemon juice
3 tbsps rice vinegar
6 tbsps soy sauce
Dash mirin

3 tbsps hot water
Black sesame seeds

Cook the beans in lots of boiling, salted water for about 5 minutes. Reserve the water. Rinse beans in cold water and peel off their outer skins, using only the bright green inner beans. Lower the cake of tofu carefully into the boiling water left from the beans. Leave tofu in the water about 5 seconds and remove with a draining spoon. Drain well, wrap in cheesecloth and press gently to extract all moisture. Blend in a food processor or blender with remaining dressing ingredients except sesame seeds. Pour over beans and sprinkle on sesame seeds.

Vinegared Crab

| **PREPARATION TIME:** 25 minutes |
| **COOKING TIME:** 3 minutes |
| **SERVES:** 4 people |

1 small cucumber, grated
1 large cooked crab
1 small piece ginger, grated

SAUCE
2 tbsps rice vinegar
2 tbsps dashi
4 tbsps mirin
1 tbsps soy sauce

GARNISH
Chinese cabbage
Grated pickled ginger

Sprinkle cucumber with salt and leave to stand 30 minutes. Bring sauce ingredients to the boil and set aside to cool. Pour into small bowls. Rinse and drain the cucumber. Press to remove excess moisture. Crack legs and claws off the crab. Remove the meat from the claws and leave the thin legs whole. Separate the underbody from the shell and remove the stomach sac and gills and discard. Scrape all the brown meat from the shell and crack the body into 4 pieces. Use a skewer to pick out the meat. Combine all meat with the ginger and cucumber and toss carefully. Arrange Chinese cabbage on plates or trays and pile salad on,

This page: Vinegared Crab. Facing page: Sushi.

leaving some of the leaves showing on each plate. Garnish with whole crab legs and pickled ginger. Serve the sauce for dipping.

Bean Salad with Sesame Dressing

| **PREPARATION TIME:** 15 minutes |
| **COOKING TIME:** 2 minutes |
| **SERVES:** 4 people |

8oz green beans, trimmed and cut in 2 inch lengths
Salt

DRESSING
2 tbsps sesame paste
1 tbsp sugar
2 tsps soy sauce
2 tsps rice vinegar
Black sesame seeds

Bring water to the boil in a large pan with a pinch of salt. Add the beans and cook for 2 minutes after the water comes back to the boil. Drain and refresh under cold water. Leave to drain and dry. Mix all ingredients for the dressing except sesame seeds. Spoon over the beans and toss lightly. Sprinkle on seeds and serve in individual bowls.

JAPANESE COOKING

Rice, Noodles and Pickles

Sushi

PREPARATION TIME: 40 minutes

COOKING TIME: 18 minutes

SERVES: 6-8 people

RICE
2½ cups short grain rice
Small piece konbu seaweed
3½ cups water
1 tbsp sake

ROLLED SUSHI
4 sheets nori
½ cucumber
2 pieces pickled red ginger
Wasabi horseradish

LAYERED SUSHI
2 sheets nori
½ cucumber
4oz smoked salmon, thinly sliced

SWEET VINEGAR
8 tbsps rice vinegar
3 tbsps sugar
Pinch salt

Rinse raw rice until water is almost clear. Leave in a colander 1 hour to drain. Meanwhile toast sheets of nori over a gas flame for 1 minute to freshen. Mix wasabi with enough water to make a paste. Slice the cucumber in half lengthwise. Reserve one half and quarter the other half. Mix the sweet vinegar ingredients and heat slowly in a small saucepan until sugar is dissolved. Leave to cool completely. Bring the water to the boil in a large pan with the piece of konbu. Remove the seaweed as soon as the water reaches a rolling boil. Add the sake and rice. Bring back to the boil and cook for 30 seconds on high heat. Lower the heat and cook for a further 12 minutes, covered.

Turn up the heat again and cook for 5 minutes to evaporate excess moisture. Take the pan off the heat and leave to stand, covered, for 10-15 minutes. Transfer the hot rice to a clean bowl and toss with the sweet vinegar. Cover the bowl with a damp towel until ready to use. Place 1 sheet of nori on a clean towel or piece of wax paper. If you have Japanese

bamboo mats these are ideal to use. Divide rice mixture in half and reserve half, covered. Divide half the mixture in fourths and spread some on the sheet of nori across the end closest to you. Spread some of the wasabi carefully over the rice. Cut a quarter of the cucumber to fit the sheet of nori and place on top of the rice. Cover the cucumber with another layer of rice and press it around firmly. Fold the end of the nori over the rice and tuck in the sides. Roll up using the towel, paper or mat to help you. Roll tightly, tucking in the sides as you roll. Repeat with the remaining rice, the remaining quarter of cucumber and use the same method with the pickled ginger, leaving out the wasabi. Leave each roll to stand, seam side down, for at least 2 minutes before slicing into 4-6 pieces with a dampened knife.

To make the layered sushi, line 2 6 or 8 inch oblong pans with plastic wrap. Divide the remaining rice mixture in half. Press half of that into one of the pans. Place the nori on top of the rice and cover with another layer of rice. Slice the cucumber lengthwise into thin slices. Place on top of the rice. Cover with another sheet of plastic wrap and place another pan of the same size on top. Press down and weight lightly. Leave to stand 5-10 minutes before removing from the pan and slicing the sushi into 2 inch pieces. Use the same method with the remaining rice and top with smoked salmon. Arrange the rolled and layered sushi on a large serving plate and give each person a bowl of soy sauce for dipping if desired.

Chrysanthemum Rice

PREPARATION TIME: 30 minutes

COOKING TIME: 30 minutes

MAKES: 15 balls

1 cup short grain rice
1¼ cups water
3 tbsps soy sauce
½ sheet nori
1 tbsp toasted sesame seeds
1 piece ginger, grated
6 eggs
3 tbsps dashi
1 tbsp sugar
1 tbsp sherry or sake
Oil for frying
Red caviar to garnish

Cook rice as for Chicken Donbun. Sprinkle soy sauce over warm rice, toss and cover with a damp cloth. Pre-heat oven to 250°F (130°C), place a sheet of nori on a baking tray and let dry for 3-4 minutes. When dry, crumble the nori. Add to the rice with the toasted sesame seeds and ginger, and toss lightly. With dampened hands, divide rice into 15 balls. Place 1 ball in the center of a piece of cheesecloth, gather up the ends and twist cloth to form a firm ball of rice. Remove rice ball from the cloth and repeat with all the remaining rice. Dampen fingers and flatten the rice balls slightly. Cover with a damp cloth and set aside. Combine eggs, dashi, sugar and

This page: Sekihan (Red Rice) (top) and Chicken Donbun (bottom). Facing page: Chrysanthemum Rice (top) and Onigiri (bottom).

sherry or sake in a bowl and beat well. Lightly oil a 6 inch omelet pan or frying pan and heat. Add about 4 tbsps of the egg mixture to the pan and cook over medium heat for 1½ minutes, until edges are dry. Turn omelet over and continue cooking until set, about 30 seconds-1 minute. Transfer to a plate and repeat with remaining egg mixture. Let cool completely and then cut into thin

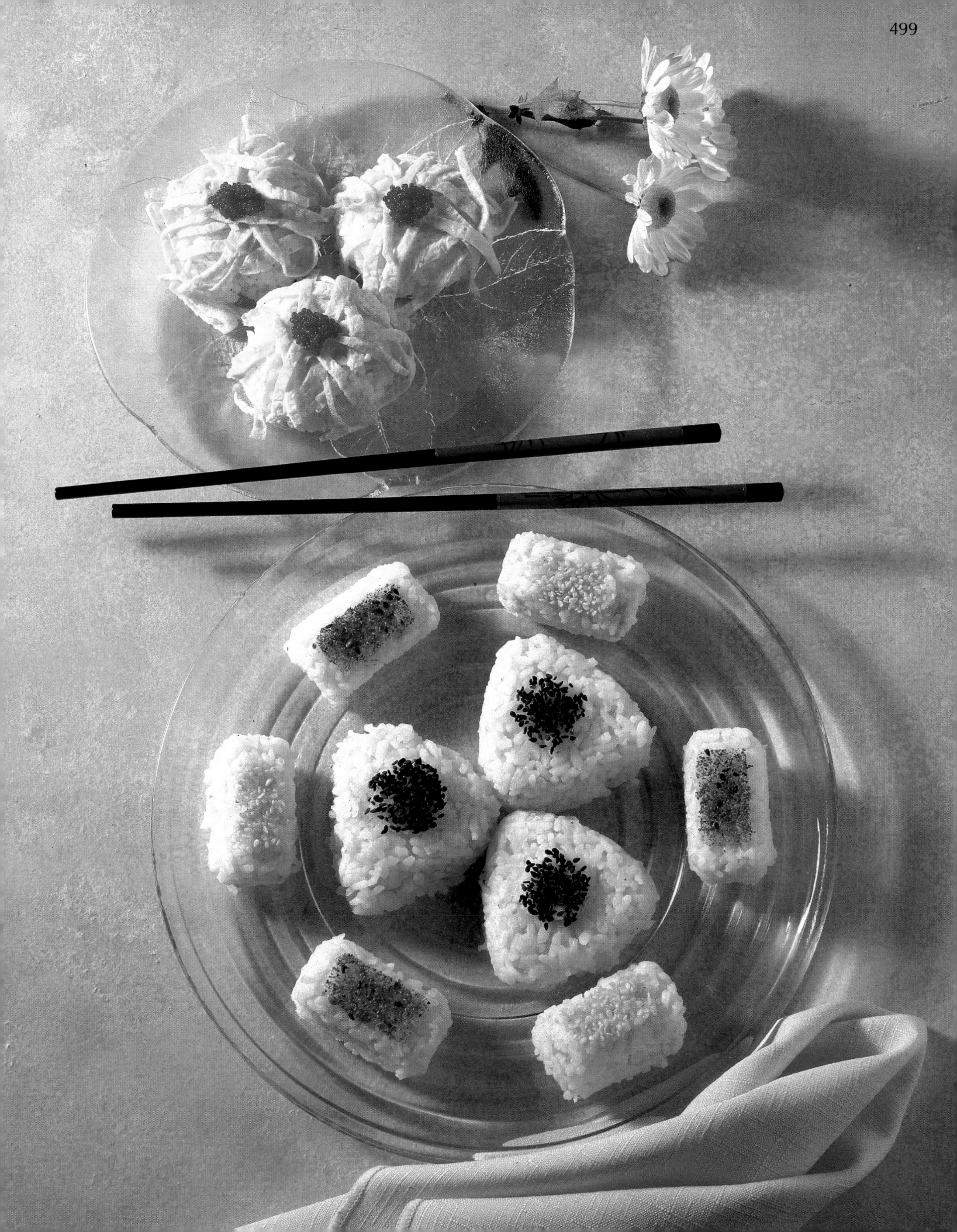

strips, about 3-4 inch long. Lay the omelet strips over each rice ball to form "chrysanthemum petals." Make a slight indentation in the middle of each one and fill with a little red caviar.

Chicken Donbun

| PREPARATION TIME: 15 minutes |
| COOKING TIME: 40 minutes |
| SERVES: 4 people |

8oz cooked chicken
1 cup short grain rice
1½ cups water
1 cup chicken stock
2 tbsps sweet sherry or mirin
2 tbsps soy sauce
8oz fresh mushrooms, sliced
4oz peas
3 eggs
1 tsp salt

Cut the chicken into bite-sized pieces and set aside. Rinse the rice under cold water until the water runs almost clear. Leave in a colander to drain. Put the rice and water into a heavy-based saucepan and bring to the boil. Reduce the heat and simmer, covered, for 15 minutes until the rice is tender and the water is just absorbed. Stir and leave to stand, covered for 10-15 minutes before using. Put the stock, sherry, soy sauce, mushrooms and peas into a saucepan and bring to the boil. Reduce heat and simmer for 1-2 minutes until vegetables are tender. Add the rice and chicken and stir gently. Beat the egg and salt together and add to the ingredients in the saucepan. Cook over low heat, stirring occasionally until egg is just set. Serve immediately.

Sekihan (Red Rice)

| PREPARATION TIME: 15 minutes plus soaking time |
| COOKING TIME: 55-57 minutes |
| SERVES: 4 people |

¼ cup a dzuki beans (small red beans), soaked overnight
1½ cups short grain rice
2 tbsps black sesame seeds

Rinse beans and place in a saucepan with 2 cups water. Bring to the boil and then simmer, uncovered, for 10-12 minutes or until beans begin to soften. Drain and reserve the cooking liquid. Wash the rice until the water runs almost clear. Soak the rice in half the bean liquid for about 2 hours. Reserve remaining bean liquid. Drain the rice and mix with beans. Spread both out on a plate in an even layer. Place the plate in the top part of a steamer or on a rack above boiling water. Cover tightly and steam 15 minutes. Uncover and spoon over about ⅓ of the remaining bean liquid. Re-cover and steam a further 10 minutes. Repeat the procedure twice more during cooking. Rice and beans should steam about 45 minutes. Toss the red rice to fluff it up and sprinkle over sesame seeds to serve.

Garnished Noodles

| PREPARATION TIME: 25 minutes |
| COOKING TIME: 20 minutes |
| SERVES: 4 people |

SAUCE
3 tbsps white wine vinegar
3 tbsps soy sauce
2 tsps sugar
½ cup chicken stock or dashi
1lb soba noodles
4 cups water

GARNISHES
Cucumber, diced
4oz small, cooked and peeled shrimp
Celery leaves
2 sheets nori, toasted and crumbled or shredded

Combine vinegar, soy sauce, stock/dashi in a saucepan and bring to the boil. Remove from the heat and keep warm. Bring water to the boil and add the noodles. Stir once and bring back to the boil. Simmer gently until tender, about 5 minutes. Drain in a colander and rinse with hot water. Divide the noodles among 4 serving dishes and arrange garnishes on top. Pour over the sauce and serve.

Five-Colored Noodles

| PREPARATION TIME: 25 minutes |
| COOKING TIME: 18-20 minutes |
| SERVES: 4 people |

8oz ubon or somen noodles
4 cups water
½ cup chicken stock
1 carrot cut into diagonal slices
1 small turnip, diced
4 dried shiitake mushrooms, soaked 30 minutes, drained and stalks removed, and sliced
4oz green beans, cut into 1½ inch strips
2 tsps cornstarch
3 tbsps soy sauce
4 tsps black sesame seeds

Cook noodles as for Garnished Noodles. Rinse under cold water and drain thoroughly. In a saucepan, bring the stock to the boil; add carrot, turnip, mushrooms and beans and cover the pan. Simmer 8-10 minutes until just tender. Blend cornstarch and soy sauce together and add to the stock. Continue cooking until slightly thickened. Divide the noodles among 4 serving bowls and pour over the vegetables. Sprinkle with black sesame seeds and serve.

Onigiri

| PREPARATION TIME: 30 minutes |
| COOKING TIME: 25 minutes |
| SERVES: 6 people |

1lb short grain rice
2½ cups water
4 tbsps black sesame seeds
Seven spice pepper
2 sheets nori

Facing page: Five-Colored Noodles (top) and Garnished Noodles (bottom).

Cook rice as for Chicken Donbun. Dampen hands with salt water and shape hot rice into cakes, triangles and oblongs. Rice molds are available in various shapes and may be used instead of the hand-shaping method. Place the molds on a flat surface and fill with rice. Use the pusher to press the rice firmly into shape and then remove the mold. Toast the nori sheets over a gas flame and cut into strips. Wrap a strip around each rice oblong. Decorate one of the other shapes with black sesame seeds and the other with the seven spice pepper. Serve warm. In Japan, these are often eaten as snacks.

Cauliflower and Broccoli Pickles

PREPARATION TIME: 20 minutes

COOKING TIME: 3 minutes

SERVES: 4 people

1 small head cauliflower, cut in flowerets
4oz broccoli, cut in flowerets

DRESSING
1 tbsp wasabi horseradish
6 tbsps soy sauce
2 tbsps mirin
Black sesame seeds

Bring lots of salted water to the boil in a large saucepan and add the prepared vegetables. Mix the remaining ingredients and set aside. Cook vegetables about 3 minutes. Drain and refresh under cold water. Leave to dry. Toss with the dressing and refrigerate 3 hours before serving.

Cucumber Pickles

PREPARATION TIME: 30 minutes

SERVES: 4 people

2 tsps sesame seeds, mixed with 1 tbsp oil
1 cucumber
2-4 tbsps soy sauce
Bonito flakes

Spread the sesame seeds over the bottom of a heavy frying pan and cook over gentle heat until lightly browned. Peel the cucumbers and cut into 1 inch irregular wedges. Combine all ingredients except the bonito flakes and leave to marinate 20 minutes in a cool place. Sprinkle bonito flakes on top before serving.

Lemon Turnips

PREPARATION TIME: 20 minutes plus chilling time

SERVES: 4 people

4 medium turnips
Juice and rind of ½ lemon

This page: Cauliflower and Broccoli Pickles. Facing page: Lemon Turnips (top) and Cucumber Pickles (bottom).

Salt
1 small piece nori, shredded

Peel turnips and cut into large dice. Combine all the ingredients except nori. Put into a large bowl. Press a smaller bowl on top and weight. Refrigerate overnight. When ready to serve, refresh nori over a gas flame and shred finely. Sprinkle over the top of the pickle.

Desserts

sugar until dissolved. Sprinkle on the agar-agar and whisk until dissolved. Dampen a 4 cup loaf pan and pour in the mixture. Leave in the refrigerator to set. Unmold onto a serving dish. Slice the kiwi fruit and arrange on top of the jelly.

Sweet Tempura

PREPARATION TIME: 20 minutes

COOKING TIME: 2-3 minutes per batch

SERVES: 4 people

Selection of the following prepared as directed:
Strawberries, hulled, washed and drained
Kiwi fruit, peeled and cut into ¼ inch slices
Apples, cored and cut into wedges, lightly sprinkled with lemon juice
Pears, peeled, cored and cut into wedges, lightly sprinkled with lemon juice
Pineapple, peeled, cored and cut in rings or pieces
Banana, peeled and sliced, lightly sprinkled with lemon juice
Plums, small ones left whole
Tangerine, peeled and segmented
Melon, peeled, seeded and cut into cubes or wedges

BATTER
1 egg
½ cup water
¾ cup all-purpose flour
¼ cup cornstarch

Clear honey

Orange and Kiwi Jelly

PREPARATION TIME: 20 minutes

SERVES: 4-6 people

1½ cups orange juice
½ cup water

½ cup sugar
2 tsps agar-agar
1 or 2 kiwi fruit, peeled

Put orange juice and water into a saucepan and heat until boiling. Remove from the heat and stir in the

This page: Sweet Tempura. Facing page: Orange and Kiwi Jelly.

Prepare fruit before preparing the batter. Pre-heat oil in a deep-fat fryer or wok to 350°F (180°C). Lightly beat egg and stir in the water. Sift in the flour and cornstarch and stir in with a table knife. Do not overmix; batter should be lumpy. Dip the fruit into the batter and lower carefully into the hot oil. Cook for 2-3 minutes until lightly golden and crisp. Cook in small batches and cook only one kind of fruit at a time. Drain a few seconds on paper towels. Arrange on serving plates and drizzle with honey. Serve immediately.

Nishiki-Tamago (Brocade Eggs)

PREPARATION TIME: 15 minutes
COOKING TIME: 20 minutes
OVEN TEMPERATURE: 325°F (150°C)

10 eggs
Scant 1 cup sugar
Pinch salt

Bring a large saucepan of water to the boil. Carefully lower in the eggs and bring back to the boil. Cook the eggs 10 minutes from the time the water begins to boil. Run cold water over the eggs until they are completely cooled. If prepared in advance, leave in shells in cold water. To prepare, peel eggs and push the whites and yolks through a metal strainer, keeping them separate. Egg whites can be finely chopped in a food processor. Mix the whites with a pinch of salt and about ⅓ cup of the sugar. Mix the egg yolks with remaining sugar. Place the whites in a square pan and press down lightly. Cover with the yolk mixture and press again. Bake for 10 minutes. Allow to cool completely and cut into 1-2 inch pieces.

Sweet Potato and Chestnut Pudding

PREPARATION TIME: 30 minutes
COOKING TIME: 30 minutes

SERVES: 6-8 people

10oz sweet potatoes, peeled and sliced
4oz can whole chestnuts in syrup
3 tbsps sugar
2 tbsps mirin or sherry
1 tbsp cornstarch
4 tbsps water

Soak sweet potatoes in cold water for 30 minutes. Place in fresh water in a large saucepan. Cover and bring to the boil. Cook about 20 minutes, or until very soft. Drain and dry over low heat, mashing with a fork or potato masher until smooth.

Meanwhile drain the chestnuts and reserve the syrup. Mix syrup with sugar and bring slowly to the boil in a heavy-based pan. Cook until the sugar dissolves and mixture thickens slightly. Mix half the syrup with the sweet potatoes. Cook the potatoes again over moderate heat, beating constantly with a wooden spoon until the potatoes thicken. Chop half the chestnuts roughly and add to the potatoes. Mound the pudding into a serving dish and decorate with whole chestnuts. Mix the remaining syrup with the mirin and the cornstarch dissolved in the water. Bring syrup to

the boil. Stir and cook until thickened. Allow to cool completely and pour over the pudding to serve.

Almond Sesame Cookies

PREPARATION TIME: 15 minutes

COOKING TIME: 10-20 minutes

OVEN TEMPERATURE: 325°F (150°C)

MAKES: 20

2 tbsps sesame oil
½ cup water
1 cup raisins
1 cup sesame seeds
1 egg, beaten
Few drops almond extract
½ cup sugar
1 cup all- purpose flour and 1 tsp baking powder
1 cup whole-wheat flour
20 whole almonds

Pre-heat oven. Place the sesame oil, water, raisins, sesame seeds, egg and almond extract in a bowl and mix well. Sift in sugar, the flours and

Facing page: Nishiki-Tamago (Brocade Eggs) (top) and Almond Sesame Cookies (bottom). This page: Sweet Potato and Chestnut Pudding.

baking powder, if using and mix to a stiff dough. Divide the mixture into 20 portions and roll each into a ball. Arrange the balls on a greased baking sheet and press an almond into the top of each, flattening them slightly. Bake 10 minutes depending on the number of cookies. The cookies should be crisp and golden when done.

MICROWAVE ENTERTAINING

Introduction

Giving a party is supposed to be fun. Frequently, however, the thought fills some people with terror. The remedy for this is advance planning and dependable equipment, and one appliance that can help enormously is the microwave oven. It comes to the rescue in so many ways, from speedy preparation of sauces to last minute reheating of vegetables. Use it in combination with your labor-saving appliances, such as food processors and blenders, and really make entertaining easy.

Advance preparation is one of the best ways of insuring against that last-minute panic, and the following points are worth considering:

● Be flexible with the menu. Plan ahead, but be prepared to make final decisions depending on what is available and looks best when you are in the shops.

● Buy ingredients that will keep a few days in advance. Buy fresh ingredients the day before the party.

● Make a timetable. Write down the order in which you need to prepare, cook, reheat and serve dishes.

● Prepare appetizers and desserts in advance and reheat in your microwave oven as necessary at the last minute. If one of the dishes can be served cold, so much the better.

● If the main course is to be accompanied by a sauce, choose one that can be made in advance, and then frozen and reheated successfully.

● Pre-cook main courses if they will not spoil with standing. In particular, poultry can be cooked and then reheated in a sauce, and meat can be browned in advance. One of the great advantages of the microwave is that it reheats without drying out the food.

● Pre-cook rice, potatoes and pasta. All of these reheat successfully in a microwave oven. Choose vegetables that can be parboiled and reheated, too.

● Reheat directly on serving dishes whenever possible, thus saving time and the chore of washing up. The microwave is perfect for this.

● If you forget to take cheese or butter out of the refrigerator, both can be softened by heating on a LOW or DEFROST setting for 15-20 seconds.

When planning your menu, keep color, texture and shape in mind when choosing the food for each course, so that you have an interesting and varied meal. Also keep in mind the style of each dish; for example, don't choose an informal appetizer to precede a very formal main course and dessert.

While you are unlikely to forget that white wine goes with fish and white meats and that red wine should be served with red meats, you may be surprised at how pleasant the combination of a light red wine and salmon can be. Even though chicken and veal are white meats, if they are served in a dark, rich sauce they need a red wine. Smoked fish or spicy food can present a problem, but a Hock or Alsace wine is a good choice when a white wine is necessary. If choosing a dessert wine confuses you, remember that Champagne is always delicious!

With a well-planned menu and a microwave oven in the kitchen, you will have more time to enjoy yourself with your guests. Entertaining will be more "entertaining".

All the recipes in this book were prepared in an oven with a 700 watt maximum output. For 500 watt ovens add 40 seconds for each minute stated in the recipe. For 600 watt ovens add 20 seconds for each minute stated in the recipe. If using a 650 watt oven only a slight increase in overall time is necessary.

Dinner Party Menus

MENU 1

Garlic Vegetables

PREPARATION TIME: 15 minutes

MICROWAVE COOKING TIME:
11-14 minutes plus standing time

SERVES: 6 people

1 small head cauliflower, broken into
    small flowerets
4oz broccoli
2oz pea pods
½ red pepper, seeded and finely sliced
½ yellow pepper, seeded and finely sliced
4 green onions, thinly sliced on the
    diagonal

DRESSING
½ cup prepared mayonnaise
2 cloves garlic, crushed
1 tbsp chopped parsley and chives, mixed
Pinch salt and pepper

GARNISH
1 hard-boiled egg, finely chopped

Place the cauliflower flowerets in a casserole with 4 tbsps salted water. Cover and cook on HIGH for 6-8 minutes, cut the broccoli spears into flowerets the same size as the cauliflower and keep the stalks for other use or discard. Place in a casserole with 2 tbsps salted water and cover loosely. Cook on HIGH for 4-5 minutes. Top and tail the pea pods and add to the broccoli 1-2 minutes before the end of cooking time. Drain all the vegetables and combine with the sliced red and yellow pepper and the green onions. Mix all the dressing ingredients together and stir carefully into the vegetables. Place the vegetables on serving plates and heat through for 1 minute on HIGH. Top with the chopped hard-boiled egg before serving. Surround with lettuce leaves or shredded lettuce if desired. Serve with French bread or melba toast.

Involtini alla Romana

PREPARATION TIME: 30 minutes

MICROWAVE COOKING TIME:
15-19 minutes

SERVES: 6 people

6 veal escalopes (about 4-6oz each)
6 slices Parma ham
8oz garlic cheese
1 tbsp chopped fresh oregano or basil or ½
    tbsp dried
Salt and pepper

SAUCE
14oz canned tomatoes
1 onion, roughly chopped
Salt and pepper
1 bay leaf
Pinch nutmeg
4 tbsps dry white wine
6 tomatoes, peeled, seeded and cut into
    thin strips
1 tbsp chopped parsley
Grated Parmesan cheese (optional)

Flatten the veal between 2 sheets of wax paper using a rolling pin or meat mallet. Place a slice of Parma ham on top of each veal escalope. Mix the cheese and the marjoram together and divide evenly among the veal escalopes. Place the cheese in the middle and roll the veal and ham around the cheese. Arrange in a circle in a dish and cook, uncovered, on HIGH for 8-10 minutes. Set aside while preparing the sauce. Combine all the ingredients except the chopped parsley, the tomato strips and cheese in a small, deep bowl. Cook on HIGH, uncovered, for 6-8 minutes or until the onion has softened and the sauce has reduced. Purée in a food processor or blender and sieve out the seeds. Arrange veal in a serving dish, pour over the sauce and sprinkle on the chopped parsley and the tomato strips. Reheat for 1 minute on HIGH before serving. Sprinkle with cheese, if desired. Serve with pasta or Italian rice.

Zabaglione

PREPARATION TIME: 25 minutes

MICROWAVE COOKING TIME:
3½ minutes

SERVES: 6 people

½ cup marsala or sweet sherry
6 egg yolks
3 tbsps sugar
2 tsps grated lemon rind

**Menu 1: Zabaglione (top left),
Involtini alla Romana (top right)
and Garlic Vegetables (bottom).**

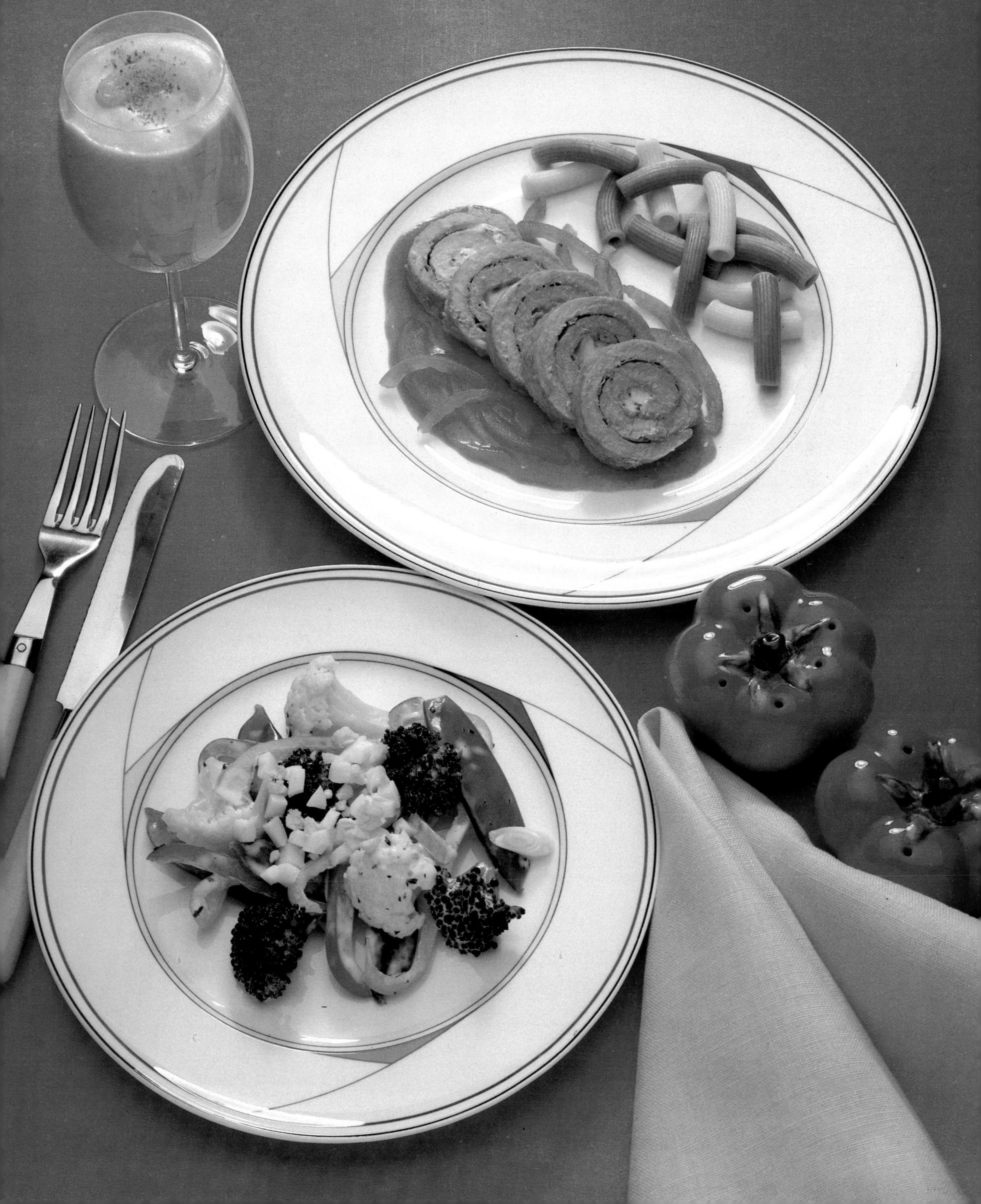

4-6 large peaches, nectarines or apricots,
   peeled
Lemon juice

Microwave meringues, crushed

Peel the peaches or nectarines according to the recipe for Peches Melba. Crush 3 or 4 meringues coarsely or use ratafia biscuits. Place the meringues or biscuits in the bottom of each of 6 dessert glasses. Cut the fruit in half and remove the stones. Slice thinly, toss in lemon juice and divide the fruit among the glasses. To prepare the zabaglione pour the marsala into a glass measure and microwave on HIGH for 30-45 seconds. Whisk the egg yolks, sugar and lemon rind together in a large bowl and then gradually whisk in the hot liqueur. Microwave the mixture on LOW or DEFROST for 1½ minutes, remove and whisk well and then continue to cook on the same setting for a further 1½ minutes, whisking halfway through the cooking time. Whisk again briefly and then spoon the mixture on top of the fruit and meringues or biscuits. Sprinkle with grated nutmeg if desired.

MENU 2

Salmon Quenelles

PREPARATION TIME: 10-15 minutes

MICROWAVE COOKING TIME: 20-21 minutes

SERVES: 4 people

1lb salmon
1 bay leaf
1 slice onion
1 blade mace
½ cup water
3 slices bread, crusts removed
3 tbsps heavy cream
2 egg whites
Salt and pepper

SAUCE
½ cup butter
2 egg yolks
1 tbsp white wine vinegar
1 tbsp lemon juice
1 tbsp green peppercorns, drained and
   rinsed if packed in brine
2 tbsps heavy cream
Salt and pepper

Skin the salmon and remove any bones. Place the skin with the bones, bay leaf, onion slice, blade mace and water in a bowl. Cook, uncovered, on HIGH 2-3 minutes or until boiling. Reduce the setting and cook for 10 minutes on LOW. Strain the liquid and make up to 6 tbsps with water if necessary. If the liquid exceeds 6 tbsps, continue cooking on HIGH until reduced. Cut up the fish and purée in a food processor with the bread, egg whites and fish cooking liquid. Blend in the cream by hand and season with salt and pepper. Pour 2 cups of hot water into a large, shallow dish. Cook on HIGH for 2-3 minutes or until very hot or boiling. Divide the fish mixture into equal portions and shape into ovals using 2 spoons. Place spaced well apart into the hot water and cover the dish. Cook on HIGH for 6 minutes, repositioning the fish quenelles halfway through cooking. Leave to stand while preparing the sauce. Melt the butter for 1½ minutes on HIGH and beat the egg yolks with the remaining ingredients. Whisk the egg yolks into the hot butter and cook on MEDIUM for 1 minute, stirring after 15 seconds. Do not allow the sauce to boil. If the sauce begins to curdle, place the bowl in another bowl of iced water to stop the cooking. Continue cooking the sauce for the remaining 15 seconds or until thickened. Stir in the peppercorns and cream. Serve with the salmon quenelles.

Lemon Duckling

PREPARATION TIME: 30 minutes plus marinating time

MICROWAVE COOKING TIME: 30 minutes

SERVES: 6 people

6 duck breast fillets, about 6oz each

MARINADE
2 tbsps vegetable oil
Juice of 2 lemons
1 clove garlic, crushed
½ tsp ground coriander
Salt and pepper
1 tbsp chopped parsley
1 bay leaf

SAUCE
Zest of 4 lemons
2 lemons segmented
2 tsps cornstarch
1½ tbsps water
½ cup chicken stock
1 tbsp soy sauce
2 tsps honey
Pinch salt and pepper

Wipe the duck breasts with paper towels and then score the skin to make a diamond pattern. Combine the marinade ingredients in a shallow dish or plastic bag, add the duck and turn to coat well. Cover and leave in the refrigerator for 4 hours, turning occasionally. Drain and reserve the marinade, discarding the bay leaf. Heat a browning dish according to the manufacturer's directions. Place the duck breasts skin side down three at a time on the dish and cook on HIGH for 3 minutes. Turn over and cook for a further 10 minutes, rearranging the duck once or twice

Menu 2: Fig and Apricot Charlottes (top), Lemon Duckling (center) and Salmon Quenelles (bottom).

during cooking. Leave to stand for 5 minutes while cooking the second batch. If desired, the duck may be browned under a preheated broiler for 1-2 minutes for crisper skin. Mix cornstarch and water in a small, deep bowl. Add the reserved marinade and stock and cook on HIGH for 2 minutes, stirring once or twice. Add the lemon segments, zest, soy sauce and honey. Pour the sauce over the duck to serve and garnish with lemon slices and fresh coriander if desired. Serve with rice.

Fig and Apricot Charlottes

PREPARATION TIME: 25 minutes

MICROWAVE COOKING TIME:
1-2 minutes plus standing time

SERVES: 6 people

8oz dried figs
8oz dried apricots
½ cup brandy
1lb cream or curd cheese
½ cup thick natural yogurt
3 tbsps honey
Halved toasted almonds
½ cup heavy cream
Nutmeg

Place the figs and the apricots in a deep bowl with the brandy and heat for 30 seconds-1 minute on HIGH. Leave to stand, covered, 2-3 minutes. Drain off the brandy and reserve. Place a circle of wax paper in the bottom of 6 individual custard cups. Cut the figs in half and press them flat. Press the apricots to flatten slightly. Use the fruit to line the sides of the dishes, seed side of the fig inside. Soften the cream or curd cheese for 30 seconds- 1 minute on MEDIUM. Stir in the yogurt, honey and the reserved brandy. Spoon the mixture into the molds, pressing down firmly against the base and the fruit lining the sides. Fold any fruit ends over the cheese filling and chill or freeze. To serve from frozen, leave overnight in a refrigerator and then at room temperature for 1 hour before serving. Turn the charlottes out onto a serving plate and carefully pour cream around the base of each. Remove the paper circles from the top and decorate with toasted almonds. Sprinkle nutmeg on the cream.

MENU 3

Lima Beans, Scallops and Bacon

PREPARATION TIME: 25 minutes

MICROWAVE COOKING TIME:
17-20 minutes

SERVES: 6 people

1½ lbs shelled fresh or frozen lima beans
6 rashers bacon, rind and bones removed
12 scallops, roes attached if possible

DRESSING
4 tbsps oil
1 shallot, finely chopped
1½ tbsps white wine vinegar
2 tsps Dijon mustard
Pinch sugar
Salt and pepper
1 tsp chopped thyme, parsley or chervil

Combine the lima beans with 6-8 tbsps hot water in a casserole. Cover and cook on HIGH for 5-6 minutes. Leave to stand, covered, while preparing the remaining ingredients. Place the bacon on a microwave rack or between 2-3 layers of paper towels on a plate. Cook on HIGH for 4-5 minutes, turning over halfway through. Leave to stand and, when cool, crumble or chop coarsely. Place the scallops in a circle in a shallow dish or casserole and cover the top loosely. Cook on MEDIUM for 7-8 minutes or until just firm. In a medium size bowl, combine the oil and the shallot and cook for 1 minute on HIGH, or until the shallot is just softened. Leave to cool and combine with the remaining dressing ingredients. If the lima beans are old, peel off the outer skins. If they are young, tender beans the outer skin may be left on. Add the beans and the bacon to the dressing and set aside. Cut the scallops in half through the middle or cut the white muscles into quarters and leave the roes whole. Add to the lima beans and the bacon in the dressing and cover the bowl. Heat through on HIGH for 1 minute and serve immediately on a bed of lettuce, radicchio, curly endive or lambs lettuce (mache).

Chicken Veronique

PREPARATION TIME: 35 minutes

MICROWAVE COOKING TIME:
40-50 minutes

SERVES: 6 people

6 boned chicken breasts, skinned
1 cup white wine
1 bay leaf
6 black peppercorns
1 slice onion
2 tbsps butter or margarine
1½ tbsps flour
2 tsps chopped fresh tarragon or 1 tsp dried tarragon
Salt and pepper
1 cup light cream
6oz green seedless grapes
Salt and white pepper

Menu 3: Fruit Shortcake (top), Chicken Veronique (center) and Lima Beans, Scallops and Bacon (bottom).

ALMOND RICE PILAF
2 tbsps butter or margarine
½ cup sliced almonds
1 medium onion, finely chopped
Pinch saffron
1 cup long-grain rice
1½ cups hot chicken stock or water

Place the chicken in a casserole with the wine, bay leaf, peppercorns and onion slice. Cover with pierced plastic wrap and cook on HIGH for 20-25 minutes or until the juices from the chicken run clear. Melt the butter for the sauce for 30 seconds on HIGH and stir in the flour. Strain on the chicken cooking liquid and stir in gradually. Add salt, pepper and tarragon and cook on HIGH for 3-5 minutes, or until thickened. Stir in the cream, add the grapes and leave the sauce to stand, covered, while preparing the pilaf. Melt the butter or margarine in a large bowl or casserole and add the almonds. Cook on HIGH for 1-2 minutes or until the almonds begin to brown. Add the onion and cook a further 2 minutes to soften the onion and to brown the almonds. Add the saffron, rice and hot stock or water. Stir well and cover the bowl. Cook on HIGH for 13-14 minutes, stirring occasionally. Leave to stand for 10 minutes before serving. To serve, place 1 chicken breast on each serving dish, loosely cover and reheat for 1-2 minutes on HIGH. Reheat the sauce for 1 minute on HIGH and coat some over each chicken breast. Serve the rest of the sauce separately and place a portion of almond rice pilaf on each serving plate. Garnish each serving with mint leaves and small bunches of grapes if desired.

Fruit Shortcake

PREPARATION TIME: 35 minutes

MICROWAVE COOKING TIME: 9½ minutes

SERVES: 6 people

PASTRY
2 cups all-purpose flour
1 tbsp ground cinnamon

4 tbsps powdered sugar
½ cup plus 2 tbsps butter or margarine, softened

TOPPING
1 cup redcurrant jelly
1lb strawberries, raspberries or blackberries
½ cup whipped cream
Shelled pistachio nuts or angelica, washed and cut into small diamonds

Sift the flour, cinnamon and sugar together, rub in the butter until the mixture is like fine breadcrumbs or work in a food processor. Place a circle of wax paper in the bottom of a 9 inch round dish. Press in the mixture and smooth down firmly. Cook on LOW or DEFROST for 8 minutes. If brown spots form, cover them with small pieces of foil and continue cooking. The shortcake is done when a skewer inserted into the center of the cake comes out clean. Cool for at least 1 hour in the baking dish. Remove the shortcake and place on a serving plate. Melt the redcurrant jelly in a small bowl on HIGH for 1 minute. Stir and then push through a strainer into a clean bowl. Brush a thin layer of jelly to within ½ inch of the edge of the pastry and allow to set slightly. Arrange the fruit on top of the jelly. If the strawberries are large, cut in half and place cut side down on the jelly. Reheat the jelly 30 seconds on HIGH and stir. Brush the fruit with a thin layer of jelly, making sure the holes between the fruit are filled with jelly. Allow to set and cool completely. Pipe rosettes of cream around the outside edge of the fruit and decorate with nuts or angelica.

Menu 4: Petits Vacherins (top), Veal with Wild Mushrooms (center) and Jerusalem Artichoke Soup (bottom).

MENU 4

Jerusalem Artichoke Soup

PREPARATION TIME: 25 minutes

MICROWAVE COOKING TIME:
8-9 minutes

SERVES: 6 people

8oz Jerusalem artichokes, peeled and
    sliced
2 potatoes, peeled and sliced
3½ cups chicken or vegetable stock
Salt and pepper
2 tbsps butter (optional)
½ cup whipping cream

GARNISH
1 small jar red caviar
6 tbsps thick yogurt
2 tbsps chopped fresh chives

Place the artichokes and potatoes in
a large, deep bowl. Cover the bowl
loosely with plastic wrap and cook
on HIGH for 6 minutes or until soft.
Add the stock, salt and pepper and
the butter if using. Cover and cook 8
minutes on HIGH or until the stock
just comes to the boil. Allow to cool
slightly and pour into a food
processor or blender and purée until
smooth. Add the cream and adjust
the seasoning. Reheat for 2-3 minutes
on HIGH before serving and garnish
each serving with a spoonful of
yogurt, ½ tsp red caviar and some
chives.

Veal with Wild Mushrooms

PREPARATION TIME: 25 minutes

MICROWAVE COOKING TIME:
14-15 minutes

SERVES: 6 people

2lbs veal, cut in large chunks
12 oyster or other wild mushrooms
4 tbsps butter or margarine
4 tbsps Dijon mustard
4 tbsps honey
4 tbsps Worcestershire sauce

VEGETABLE ACCOMPANIMENT
8oz salsify, peeled and cut into 3 inch
    pieces
3 carrots, peeled and cut to the same size
    as the salsify
½ a celeriac root, peeled and cut into
    strips
1 tbsp chopped parsley
1 tbsp fresh rosemary leaves
4 tbsps heavy cream

Mix together the mustard, honey,
Worcestershire sauce and veal. Heat
a browning dish according to the
manufacturer's directions and melt
the butter. When foaming, add the
veal in small batches, pressing down
firmly on one side, turning over and
pressing down again to seal both
sides. Cook in 2 batches. Cook on
HIGH for 5 minutes. Add the
mushrooms and cook 1 minute on
HIGH, cover and keep them warm.
Combine the meat juices with all of
the vegetables and toss well to coat.
Add the herbs and salt and pepper
and microwave, uncovered, on
HIGH for 2 minutes. Cover and
continue cooking on HIGH for 6
minutes or until the salsify is tender.
Stir in the cream. Reheat the veal for
1-2 minutes on HIGH and serve with
the vegetables.

Petits Vacherins

PREPARATION TIME: 20 minutes

MICROWAVE COOKING TIME:
6 minutes

SERVES: 6 people

MERINGUES
1 egg white
4 cups powdered sugar
¼ cup finely chopped walnuts

SAUCE
12oz raspberries
Lemon juice to taste
Powdered sugar to taste

TOPPING
¾ cup whipping cream
Walnut halves
Reserved raspberries

To make the meringues, put the egg
white into a bowl and whisk lightly
with a fork. Add enough of the
powdered sugar, sifted, to give a firm,
pliable dough. It may not be
necessary to add all the sugar. Keep
the mixture covered while shaping
the meringues. Put out a portion on a
surface dusted with more powdered
sugar and form a sausage about the
thickness of a little finger. Cut into
1 inch pieces and place well apart on
wax paper on a plate or microwave
baking sheet. Cook for about
1 minute or until dry and crisp.
Reserve 6-12 raspberries for
decoration and put the rest into a
food processor or blender with the
lemon juice. Purée until smooth and
add sugar to taste. Process again to
mix the sugar and sieve the sauce to
remove the seeds. Divide the sauce
equally among 6 dessert plates and
place a meringue on top of the sauce
on each plate. Crush 6 of the
meringues and set aside. Any
remaining meringues may be frozen
or stored in an airtight container.
Whip the cream and pipe on top of
each meringue. Sprinkle with the
reserved crushed meringue and
decorate with walnut halves and the
reserved raspberries.

MENU 5

Oeufs en Croustade

PREPARATION TIME: 30 minutes
MICROWAVE COOKING TIME: 22-24 minutes
SERVES: 6 people

12 slices whole-wheat bread, crusts removed
6 tbsps butter

FILLING
4oz mushrooms, finely chopped
1 shallot, finely chopped
2 tsps butter or margarine
2 tsps flour
1 tbsp sherry
4 tbsps light cream
12 quail eggs

SAUCE
1 tbsp butter or margarine
1 tbsp flour
½ cup milk
1 tsp chopped parsley
1 small cap pimento, finely chopped
Salt and pepper
Paprika

Roll the slices of bread to flatten. Cut into 3 inch rounds with a pastry cutter. Melt the butter for 30 seconds on HIGH and brush over both sides of the bread rounds. Mold into small custard cups and cook for 3 minutes on HIGH until crisp. Remove from the custard cups and place on a serving plate. Combine the mushrooms, shallot and butter for the filling in a small bowl and heat for 2-3 minutes on HIGH, or until the shallot is soft and the mushrooms are cooked. Stir in the flour and add the sherry and cream. Season lightly with salt and pepper and cook on HIGH for 2-3 minutes or until thickened. Allow to cool slightly. Melt the butter for the sauce for 30 seconds on HIGH and stir in the flour. Beat in the milk gradually until smooth and cook for 2-3 minutes on HIGH, or until thickened. Add the parsley and the pimento, season lightly with salt and pepper and set aside, with plastic wrap pressed directly over the sauce. Bring water in a shallow dish to the boil with 1 tsp vinegar and a pinch of salt. This should take about 8 minutes. Carefully break each quail egg onto a saucer and gently lower the egg into the water. Return to the oven and cook on HIGH for 30 seconds-1 minute or until nearly set. Leave to stand for 1-2 minutes to complete cooking. Eggs may be cooked in advance and kept in cold water. Place the mushroom mixture in the bottom of each tartlet shell. Drain the quail eggs and place 1 egg in each tartlet. Spoon over the sauce and dust lightly with paprika. Arrange the tartlets in a circle on a serving dish and heat through for 1-2 minutes on MEDIUM. Serve immediately.

Quail with Garlic and Green Olives

PREPARATION TIME: 30 minutes
MICROWAVE COOKING TIME: 23-34 minutes
SERVES: 6 people

6 quail
4 tbsps butter or margarine
6 cloves garlic
1 cup brown stock
½ cup dry white wine
1½ tbsps cornstarch
½ tsp thyme
1 tbsp chopped parsley
Salt and pepper
18 large green olives, pitted and quartered
1 tsp Dijon mustard
Salt and pepper

POMMES PAILLASSON
4 tbsps butter or margarine
1lb potatoes, peeled and coarsely grated
Salt and pepper

First prepare the potatoes. Melt the butter in a round, glass dish for 1½ minutes on HIGH. Layer in the grated potatoes, pressing down well and seasoning in between each layer. Loosely cover the dish with plastic wrap and cook on HIGH for 10-15 minutes. Set aside while preparing the quail. Heat a browning dish according to the manufacturer's directions. Melt the butter and when foaming brown the quail, 2 at a time, on HIGH for 2-3 minutes. Combine all the remaining ingredients except the olives in a casserole dish and add the quail and the juices from the browning dish. Cover and cook on HIGH for a further 6-8 minutes. Stir the sauce occasionally while the quail are cooking. To serve, turn out the potatoes onto a heatproof serving dish and brown the top under a preheated broiler. Remove the quail from the sauce and trim them if necessary. Arrange the quail on top of the potato cake, cover and keep warm. Purée the sauce in a food processor or blender until the garlic is completely broken down. Sieve if desired and add the olives. Season with salt and pepper and reheat the sauce on HIGH for 1-2 minutes. Spoon some of the sauce over the quail to serve and serve the rest of the sauce separately. Serve with a green vegetable or carrots in parsley butter.

Chocolate Orange Mousse

PREPARATION TIME: 20 minutes
MICROWAVE COOKING TIME: 4-5 minutes
SERVES: 6 people

6oz semi-sweet chocolate
1 cup heavy cream
1 egg
Grated rind of half an orange
2 tsps orange juice

DECORATION
Orange rind cut into thin strips
½ cup heavy cream, whipped

Chop the chocolate into small pieces and combine with the cream. Heat

Menu 5: Oeufs en Croustade
(below), Quail with Garlic and
Green Olives (bottom) and
Chocolate Orange Mousse (far
right).

on HIGH for 2-3 minutes, stirring frequently until the chocolate has melted and the mixture is smooth. Beat the egg with the orange rind and juice and gradually beat in the chocolate mixture. Pour into 6 individual dessert dishes and heat for

1 minute on HIGH to thicken. Chill until set. To serve, whip the remaining cream and pipe 1 rosette on top of each serving dish. Place the strips of orange rind in a small bowl with 4 tbsps water and heat for 1 minute on HIGH to soften. Drain

and rinse under cold water and pat dry. Sprinkle on top of the mousse to serve.

MENU 6

Avocado and Chicken Livers

PREPARATION TIME: 25 minutes

MICROWAVE COOKING TIME: 4½-5½ minutes

SERVES: 6 people

2 ripe avocados
8oz chicken livers
2 tbsps butter or margarine
1 shallot, finely chopped
1 tbsp sherry
4-6 tomatoes, peeled, seeded and thinly sliced

DRESSING
8 tbsps oil
Juice of 1 small lemon
2 tsps chopped fresh herbs
Pinch sugar
Salt and pepper
1 head curly endive

Heat a browning dish according to the manufacturer's instructions. Pick over the chicken livers and trim away any discolored parts. Melt the butter in the browning dish and add the chicken livers, tossing to coat well. Add the shallot and cook on HIGH for 4-5 minutes, or until the shallot is softened and the livers are just barely pink inside. Pour over the sherry and set aside. Cut the avocados in half and remove the stones. Peel and cut each avocado half into thin slices. Combine all the dressing ingredients and mix with the tomatoes. Arrange a bed of curly endive on each serving plate and place the avocados on top so that the slices form a fan. Spoon over the dressing. Slice the chicken

livers thinly and place a portion at the bottom of each avocado fan along with some tomato slices. Loosely cover the dishes and reheat for 30 seconds on HIGH before serving.

Monkfish Medallions Paprika

PREPARATION TIME: 25 minutes

MICROWAVE COOKING TIME: 16-19 minutes

SERVES: 6 people

1lb monkfish tails, skinned and cut into ½ inch slices
6 tbsps white wine
1 red pepper, seeded and sliced
½ cup heavy cream
1 tbsp paprika
1 tbsp cornstarch
Salt and pepper
8oz fresh pasta
2 cups boiling water
1 tbsp oil
Pinch salt

Place the sliced monkfish and the wine in a shallow dish and cover loosely with plastic wrap. Cook on HIGH for 4 minutes. Place the red pepper in a deep bowl, cover loosely and cook on HIGH for 1-2 minutes to soften. Add the heavy cream and paprika and cook on HIGH for 2-3 minutes. Mix the cornstarch with the cooking liquid from the fish and add the cream and pepper. Add a pinch of salt and pepper to taste and cook on HIGH for a further 2-3 minutes or until thickened. Cover and set

aside while preparing the pasta. Pour the boiling water into a deep bowl, add a pinch of salt and the pasta. Loosely cover and cook on HIGH for 6 minutes. Leave to stand for 3 minutes before draining. Place the pasta in a serving dish and arrange the monkfish slices on top. Pour over the sauce to serve. If necessary, reheat on HIGH for 1-2 minutes.

Oeufs à la Neige

PREPARATION TIME: 25 minutes

MICROWAVE COOKING TIME: 23-26 minutes

SERVES: 6 people

MERINGUE
2 egg whites
3 tbsps sugar
2 drops vanilla extract

ORANGE CUSTARD
1½ cups milk
Grated rind of ½ an orange
1 tbsp sugar
4 egg yolks
½ tsp cornstarch

CARAMEL TOPPING
6 tbsps sugar
6 tbsps water

Menu 6: Oeufs à la Neige (top), Monkfish Medallions Paprika (center) and Avocado and Chicken Livers (bottom).

To make the meringues, whisk the egg whites until stiff but not dry. Add the sugar gradually, whisking continuously until the meringue is stiff, smooth and shiny. Fill a large, shallow dish with hot water. Shape the meringue with 2 damp tablespoons into egg shapes and slide them carefully onto the hot water. Cook on LOW or DEFROST for 2-3 minutes. Turn the meringues over and cook again on LOW or DEFROST for a further 2-3 minutes.

Heat the milk and the orange rind for the custard on HIGH for 2 minutes. Beat the sugar, egg yolks and cornstarch until light, and gradually pour on the milk, beating constantly. Cook the custard on LOW or DEFROST for about 12 minutes, stirring every 30 seconds. Remove the custard when it coats the back of a spoon. Pour into a large serving dish or individual dishes and chill. Carefully float the meringues on top of the custard. To prepare the

caramel topping, combine the sugar and water in a small, deep bowl and cook on HIGH for 5-6 minutes until golden. Do not allow the syrup to become too dark as it will continue to cook after it is removed from the oven. Dip the caramel bowl into another bowl of cold water to stop the cooking and to thicken the caramel slightly. Using a fork, drizzle the caramel over the meringues on top of the custard and allow it to set before serving.

MENU 7

Watercress Soup

PREPARATION TIME: 20 minutes

MICROWAVE COOKING TIME: 14-17 minutes

SERVES: 6 people

4 medium-sized potatoes, peeled and
  thinly sliced
1 small onion, finely chopped
2 tbsps butter or margarine
3½ cups vegetable or chicken stock
1 bay leaf
Salt and pepper
2 bunches watercress, well washed and
  thick stems removed
½ cup heavy cream
Nutmeg

GARNISH
Reserved small watercress leaves

Place the potatoes, onion and butter into a large, deep bowl and loosely cover with plastic wrap. Cook on HIGH for 4-6 minutes or until the potatoes and onions are beginning to soften. Pour on the stock and add the bay leaf, salt and pepper. Re-cover the bowl and cook a further 8 minutes on HIGH or until the stock just comes to the boil. Allow to cool slightly and pour into a food processor or blender. Reserve 6 small sprigs of watercress for garnish and roughly chop the rest. Place the watercress in the blender or food processor with the soup and purée

until smooth. The soup should be lightly flecked with green. Add the cream to the soup and adjust the seasoning. Add a pinch of nutmeg and reheat on HIGH 2-3 minutes before serving. Garnish with the small watercress leaves.

Plié a l'Indienne

PREPARATION TIME: 25 minutes

MICROWAVE COOKING TIME: 9½ minutes

SERVES: 6 people

12 flounder fillets
1 bay leaf
1 slice onion
6 black peppercorns
1 cup water
2 tbsps butter or margarine
1½ tbsps flour
½-1 tbsp mild curry powder
1 tsp turmeric
Salt and pepper
4 tbsps light cream
1 small can pineapple pieces

GARNISH
Toasted almonds
Desiccated coconut

Place the fish in a shallow dish with the bay leaf, onion slice, peppercorns and water. Loosely cover with plastic

wrap and cook on HIGH for 4 minutes. Leave to stand while preparing the sauce. Melt the butter for 30 seconds on HIGH and stir in the flour. Strain on the fish cooking liquid and add the curry powder, turmeric and salt and pepper. Cook on HIGH for 5 minutes. Stir in the cream and drained pineapple, cover and set aside. Place the fish in a serving dish or on individual plates and coat with the sauce. Sprinkle with toasted almonds and desiccated coconut. Serve with rice.

Almond Float with Fresh Fruit

PREPARATION TIME: 25 minutes

MICROWAVE COOKING TIME: 13-15 minutes

SERVES: 6 people

1 tbsp gelatine
4 tbsps cold water
½ cup milk
1 tbsp sugar
½ tsp almond extract
Few drops red food coloring (optional)

Menu 7: Almond Float with Fresh Fruit (top), Plié a l'Indienne (center) and Watercress Soup (bottom).

Assortment of fruits such as lychees, peeled, kiwi fruit, peeled and sliced, star fruit, thinly sliced, kumquats, thinly sliced, papayas, peeled, seeded and thinly sliced or cut into cubes, melon, peeled, seeded and thinly sliced or cut into cubes

SYRUP
½ cup sugar
1 cup water
Almond extract or amaretto (almond liqueur)

Sprinkle the gelatine over the water in a small bowl or cup and leave to soften for 5 minutes. Melt on HIGH for 15-20 seconds or until clear. Mix the milk with an equal amount of water and add the sugar. Heat for 2-3 minutes on HIGH to dissolve the sugar. Allow to cool and stir in the gelatine and the almond extract and coloring if using, and pour into a shallow, rectangular dish. Chill in the refrigerator until set. Meanwhile, prepare the syrup. Combine the water and sugar in a deep bowl and stir well. Cook on HIGH for 8-10 minutes or until the sugar is completely dissolved and the syrup is boiling. Do not allow the syrup to brown. Check carefully, it may be necessary to remove the syrup from the oven before the end of cooking time. Leave to cool completely and add the almond extract or amaretto. Chill the syrup completely and, when the almond float is set and the syrup is cold, prepare the fruit as directed. Cut the almond float into diamond shapes about 3 inches in length. Place 2 diamond shapes on each of 6 serving plates and arrange an assortment of fruit around them. Spoon over the syrup to serve.

MENU 8

Green Beans, Pâté and Mushrooms

PREPARATION TIME: 20 minutes
MICROWAVE COOKING TIME: 9½-11 minutes
SERVES: 6 people

1lb young green beans
8oz mushrooms
4oz firm pâté

DRESSING
4 tbsps oil
1 clove garlic, crushed
2 tsps chopped chives
1 tsp chopped parsley
1½ tsps white wine vinegar
Salt and pepper

Cook the green beans in 2 tbsps salted water for 6 minutes on HIGH. Stir occasionally and leave to stand for 1-2 minutes. The beans should still be crisp. While the beans are standing, combine the mushrooms with half of the measured oil from the dressing in a small bowl and cook on HIGH for 1-2 minutes or until just softened. Slice the pâté into thin strips or cut into small cubes. Combine the remaining dressing ingredients with the mushrooms and toss with the green beans. Add the pâté and mix carefully. Heat through on HIGH for 30 seconds-1 minute before serving. Pile the mixture onto serving plates lined with lettuce leaves if desired.

Sole d'Epinard

PREPARATION TIME: 30 minutes
MICROWAVE COOKING TIME: 14-17 minutes
SERVES: 6 people

FILLING
8oz fresh spinach, stems removed and well washed
Salt and pepper
Nutmeg
3 slices white bread, crusts removed and made into crumbs
1 egg white
2 tbsps heavy cream

6 double fillets of sole
4 tbsps dry white wine

SAUCE
2 tbsps butter
2 tbsps flour
1 cup milk
Juice and rind of 1 lemon
Salt and pepper

TOPPING
Parmesan cheese, grated
Dry breadcrumbs

GARNISH
Lemon slices

Cook the spinach for 4 minutes on HIGH in a roasting bag or casserole, well covered. Drain and chop in a food processor with the salt and pepper, nutmeg and breadcrumbs. Add the egg white and process once or twice to mix. Stir in the cream by hand. Spread evenly over the fish fillets and fold or roll up. Place fish in a dish in a circle with the wine and cover with plastic wrap. Cook on HIGH for 4-5 minutes. Melt the butter for 30 seconds on HIGH and add the flour. Strain in the cooking liquid from the fish, add the milk and beat well. Cook on HIGH 3-5 minutes until thickened. Add the lemon rind and juice, salt and pepper. Arrange the sole in a serving dish and pour over the sauce. Mix the Parmesan cheese and the breadcrumbs together and sprinkle over the top. Brown under a preheated broiler or cook a further 2

Menu 8: Tartelettes aux Fruits (top), Sole d'Epinard (center) and Green Beans, Pâté and Mushrooms (bottom).

minutes on HIGH. Garnish with lemon slices. Serve with boiled potatoes or rice.

Tartelettes aux Fruits

PREPARATION TIME: 40 minutes

MICROWAVE COOKING TIME: 5½-8 minutes

SERVES: 6 people

PASTRY
1 cup all-purpose flour
2 tbsps toasted ground hazelnuts or almonds
5 tbsps butter or margarine
2 tsps sugar
1 egg yolk

FILLING
1 cup milk
2 egg yolks
4 tbsps sugar
2 tbsps cornstarch
¼ tsp almond extract

TOPPING
Selection of fresh fruit such as white or black grapes, strawberries, satsumas, apricots, cherries or kiwi fruit

GLAZE
Apricot jam
Redcurrant jelly

Rub the fat and flour for the pastry together until the mixture resembles fine breadcrumbs. Add the sugar and nuts and stir in the egg yolk. Knead lightly, wrap in plastic wrap and chill in the refrigerator for 30 minutes.

Alternatively, prepare the pastry in a food processor, taking care not to over-mix. Roll the pastry out thinly on a floured board and cut into 12 rounds about 2 inches in diameter. Use the pastry to line microwave muffin trays or small custard cups. Prick the bases with a fork and cook on HIGH for 3 minutes. Cook in two batches of 6. Allow the pastry to cool slightly in the baking dishes and then transfer to a wire rack to cool completely. To make the filling, heat the milk for 1-2 minutes on HIGH, or until boiling. Beat the egg yolks, sugar cornstarch and almond extract together until light. Gradually pour on the milk, beating well. Return to the microwave oven and cook on HIGH for 1-2 minutes, stirring every 15 seconds until thick and smooth. Place wax paper directly over the top of the filling to allow it to cool without forming a skin. When the filling is nearly cool, spoon in equal amounts into each pastry shell. Cut the grapes in half and remove the seeds. Place them cut side down on top of the filling or cut into quarters and arrange in attractive patterns. Arrange the other fruit as desired, making sure that all the pith is removed from the satsuma segments. Melt the apricot jam and the redcurrant jelly in two separate bowls for 30 seconds to 1 minute on HIGH. Sieve both and use the apricot jam for the light colored fruit and the redcurrant jelly for the red fruit. Brush the glazes on the fruit while the glaze is still warm. Allow the glaze to set before serving.

MENU 9

Pea Pods and Jumbo Shrimp

PREPARATION TIME: 25 minutes

MICROWAVE COOKING TIME: 3-4 minutes

SERVES: 6 people

8oz pea pods
6oz jumbo shrimp, cooked and shelled
2 green onions, shredded or thinly sliced

Menu 9: Marrons en Chemise (top left) Noisettes d'Agneau Maltaise (top right) and Pea Pods and Jumbo Shrimp (bottom).

4-6 water chestnuts, thinly sliced

DRESSING
4 tbsps oil
Dash sesame oil
1 tsp grated fresh ginger
½ clove garlic, crushed
Juice and grated rind of half a lemon
Salt and pepper

Top and tail the pea pods and place in a bowl or casserole with 2 tbsps salted water. Cover loosely and cook on HIGH for 1-2 minutes. Set aside while preparing the other ingredients. Slice the water chestnuts thinly and slice the jumbo shrimp in half through the middle. Heat the oil with the sesame oil, ginger and garlic on HIGH for 1 minute. Allow to cool and combine with the remaining dressing ingredients. Drain the pea pods and combine with the shrimp, water chestnuts and green onions. Mix with the dressing ingredients and place on serving dishes. Reheat through on HIGH for 1 minute before serving.

Noisettes d'Agneau Maltaise

PREPARATION TIME: 30 minutes

MICROWAVE COOKING TIME: 26-32 minutes

SERVES: 6 people

6 noisettes of lamb cut from the best end, about 1½ inch thick
Oil

SAUCE MALTAISE
2 egg yolks
½ cup butter
Salt and pepper
Grated rind of ½ a blood orange

POMMES DUCHESSE
1½ lbs potatoes, peeled and cut into even-sized pieces
Salt and pepper
2 tbsps butter
2-4 tbsps hot milk

1 large egg, beaten
Paprika

First prepare the potatoes. Place them in a large bowl with a pinch of salt and 4 tbsps water. Cover with pierced plastic wrap and cook on HIGH for 5-10 minutes. Leave to stand for 5 minutes. Mash until smooth and then beat in the butter and pepper. Beat in the hot milk until smooth. Allow to cool slightly and then beat in the egg, reserving about half. Mix very well and fill a pastry bag fitted with a rosette tube. Pipe swirls of potato onto a plate covered with wax paper. Chill thoroughly. Heat a browning dish according to the manufacturer's directions. Lightly oil the surface and cook the noisettes 2 or 3 at a time, pressing them down against the hot browning dish on both sides to seal. Cook the noisettes on HIGH for about 7 minutes. Cover and keep warm while preparing the sauce. Melt the butter for 2 minutes on HIGH in a large glass measure. Beat the egg yolks together with orange rind. Add a pinch of salt and white pepper and gradually beat into the hot butter. Cook on MEDIUM for 1 minute, whisking after 15 seconds and at 15 second intervals thereafter. If the sauce begins to curdle, dip the glass measure into a bowl of iced water to stop the cooking and whisk well. Continue cooking until the sauce thickens. Cover the sauce and set aside. To finish the potatoes, brush with additional beaten egg mixed with a pinch of salt and sprinkle lightly with paprika. Cook on HIGH for 3-4 minutes until piping hot. Brown under a preheated broiler if desired. Reheat the noisettes for 1-2 minutes on HIGH if necessary and place on a serving dish, removing the string around each.
Spoon over some of the sauce and garnish with the segmented orange if desired. Place a swirl of potato on each plate and serve immediately.

Marrons en Chemise

PREPARATION TIME: 30 minutes

MICROWAVE COOKING TIME: 5-7 minutes

SERVES: 6 people

WHITE CHOCOLATE MOUSSE
1 cup milk
4oz white chocolate, roughly chopped
2 egg yolks, 1 white reserved
2 tbsps sugar
3 tbsps water
1 tbsp gelatine
½ cup whipping cream

Approximately 1 cup crème de marron (sweetened chestnut spread)

DECORATION
2-3 squares semi-sweet chocolate

Heat the milk for 2-3 minutes on HIGH with the chopped white chocolate. Beat the egg yolks and the sugar together until light. Gradually pour on the milk, stirring constantly. Return to the oven and cook on HIGH for 2-3 minutes, stirring every 15 seconds until the mixture coats the back of a spoon. Allow to cool. Meanwhile, sprinkle the gelatine on top of the water in a small bowl. Allow to stand for 5-10 minutes to soften and then melt on HIGH for 20-30 seconds. Pour into the cooled custard and set the bowl in another bowl of iced water. Allow to cool completely and stir frequently to help the gelatine to set evenly. Meanwhile, whip the cream and the egg white and fold into the custard when the gelatine is nearly set. Spoon the crème de marron into the bottom of each of 6 small dessert dishes. Pour the white chocolate mousse on top to cover before the mousse sets completely. Chill in the refrigerator until firm. To decorate, melt the chocolate for 20-30 seconds on HIGH, stirring frequently. Put into a small pastry bag fitted with a writing tube. Pipe out a lacy design on top of the white chocolate mousse and let the chocolate set before serving. Mousse may be prepared and assembled the day before serving. Decorate with chocolate no more than 2 hours in advance.

MENU 10

Tomato Farcis

PREPARATION TIME: 25 minutes

MICROWAVE COOKING TIME:
9-12 minutes

SERVES: 6 people

6 large tomatoes, peeled

FILLING
6oz low fat soft cheese
3oz cooked ham, finely chopped
1 clove garlic, crushed
1 tbsp chopped parsley
2 tsps chopped fresh thyme or ½ tsp dried
    thyme

GARNISH
Whole chives

ACCOMPANIMENT
Hot butter toast or melba toast

To peel the tomatoes, place 4 cups water in a large bowl, cover with plastic wrap and microwave on HIGH for 8-11 minutes or until boiling. Place 2 of the tomatoes in the water and leave to stand for 1-1½ minutes. Remove the tomatoes to another bowl of cold water and bring the hot water back to the boil. Repeat with the remaining 4 tomatoes. The skin should peel off easily. On the rounded end of the tomato, cut a slice about ½ inch. Scoop out the pulp, sieve and set aside the juice. Combine the tomato juice with the filling ingredients and spoon into the tomatoes. Set the tops on at an angle and place the tomatoes in a circle on a plate. Heat on HIGH for 1 minute and place on individual serving plates. Garnish the plates with whole fresh chives and serve with the toast.

Scallops aux Herbes

PREPARATION TIME: 25 minutes

MICROWAVE COOKING TIME:
23-24 minutes plus standing time

SERVES: 6 people

18-24 scallops with roes attached
6 tbsps dry white wine
1 bay leaf

SAUCE
¾ cup heavy cream
3 tbsps chopped mixed herbs such as
    tarragon, chives, chervil or marjoram
Salt and pepper
Squeeze lemon juice

WILD RICE PILAF
½ cup long-grain rice
½ cup wild rice
½ cup chopped walnuts
Salt and pepper

Place the scallops in a shallow dish with the white wine and bay leaf. Cover and cook on MEDIUM for 3 minutes. Leave to stand while preparing the remaining ingredients. Boil the cream for 5 minutes on HIGH. Add 2 tbsps of the cooking liquid from the scallops and cook a further 2-3 minutes on HIGH. Stir in the herbs, salt, pepper and lemon juice. To cook the rice, place in a casserole with 2 cups boiling, salted water. Cook on HIGH for 12 minutes and leave to stand 5-10 minutes. Drain any water that is not absorbed and add the walnuts. Reheat on HIGH for 2 minutes. Add the scallops to the sauce and reheat on HIGH for 1 minute. Serve the scallops on a bed of rice.

Petites Galettes Normandes

PREPARATION TIME: 30 minutes

MICROWAVE COOKING TIME:
10-11 minutes plus standing time

SERVES: 6 people

PASTRY
1 cup all-purpose flour
1 tsp ground allspice

4 tbsps butter or margarine
2 tsps brown sugar
1 egg yolk

FILLING
1lb dessert apples, peeled, cored and sliced
½ tsp ground cinnamon
2 tbsps apricot jam
1 cup heavy cream, whipped

TO DECORATE
6 browned hazelnuts

To make the pastry, sift the flour with the sugar and the allspice and rub in the butter until the mixture resembles fine breadcrumbs. Add the egg yolk and mix to a soft dough. Knead lightly and wrap in plastic wrap and chill in the refrigerator for 30 minutes. Alternatively, make the pastry in a food processor. Roll the pastry out thinly and cut into 12 rounds, 6 at 3 inches and 6 at 2 inches diameter. Place the rounds on a plate or microwave baking sheet and cook on HIGH for 3 minutes. Cook the pastry in 2 batches. Allow to cool slightly on the dish or baking sheet and then transfer to a wire rack to cool. Combine the apples, cinnamon and apricot jam in a casserole, cover and cook on HIGH for 4-5 minutes. Leave to stand for 5 minutes, uncovered, and leave to cool. Place a large round of pastry on a serving plate and top with some of the apple filling. Whip the cream until soft peaks form and pipe or spoon on top of the apple. Place the smaller round of pastry on top of the cream and pipe a rosette on top. Decorate the rosette with a hazelnut and sprinkle lightly with powdered sugar if desired.

Overleaf: Menu 10 – Tomato Farcis (left), Scallops aux Herbes (center) and Petites Galettes Normandes (right).

MENU 11

Spinach Mousse with Tomato Tarragon Sauce

PREPARATION TIME: 25 minutes

MICROWAVE COOKING TIME:
18-22 minutes plus standing time

SERVES: 6 people

½ cup whipping cream
½ clove garlic, crushed
1lb fresh spinach, stems removed and
    leaves well washed
2 eggs
Salt and pepper
Grated nutmeg

SAUCE
14oz canned plum tomatoes
1 shallot, roughly chopped
3 sprigs fresh tarragon or 2 tsps dried
    tarragon leaves
Salt and pepper
Pinch sugar
2 tsps tomato paste
1 tbsp white wine or tarragon vinegar

GARNISH
3 tomatoes, peeled, seeded and cut into
    small dice

To prepare the spinach mousse, place the spinach in a roasting bag and tie loosely with string. Cook on HIGH for 4-5 minutes or until wilted. Leave to stand for 1-2 minutes and drain if necessary. Combine in a food processor with the garlic, eggs, salt, pepper and nutmeg. Blend until a smooth purée. Stir in the cream by hand. Grease 6 small custard cups lightly with butter and place a round of wax paper in the bottom. Divide the mixture between the custard cups and cook in a shallow dish of hot water to come halfway up the sides of the custard cups. Loosely cover the dish and cook on HIGH for 5-6 minutes. The mousses should feel firm when lightly pressed and should rise slightly in the dishes. Set aside while preparing the sauce. Combine all the sauce ingredients except the vinegar in a deep bowl and loosely cover. Cook on HIGH for 8-10 minutes, until boiling rapidly.

Allow to stand for 3-5 minutes and sieve or purée in a food processor. Push through a strainer to remove the seeds and stir in the vinegar. Place an equal portion of the sauce on each of 6 serving dishes and turn out the spinach mousses on top. Reheat 1 minute on HIGH. Place a spoonful of the tomato dice on top of each mousse and serve immediately.

Beef Stroganoff

PREPARATION TIME: 25 minutes

MICROWAVE COOKING TIME:
14½ minutes

SERVES: 6 people

4 tbsps butter or margarine
2lbs rump or sirloin steak, trimmed and
    cut into thin strips
8oz mushrooms, sliced if large
1 clove garlic, crushed
2 tbsps flour
4 tbsps brown stock
4 tbsps brandy or sherry
Salt and pepper
½ cup sour cream or whole milk yogurt
4 tbsps snipped chives

Heat a browning dish according to the manufacturer's directions. Melt the butter and, when foaming, brown the meat in three or four batches. Pour the contents of the browning dish into a casserole and sprinkle over the flour. Gradually stir in the stock and the brandy or sherry. Add salt and pepper to taste and cook on HIGH for 4 minutes. Add the mushrooms and cook for a further 4 minutes, covered. Add salt and pepper to taste and stir in the chives. Gently stir in the sour cream and cook for 30 seconds on HIGH. Serve with noodles.

Kissel

PREPARATION TIME: 20 minutes

MICROWAVE COOKING TIME:
9-11 minutes

SERVES: 6 people

4oz blackcurrants, canned or frozen
4oz redcurrants, canned or frozen
4oz canned or frozen black cherries, pitted
4 tbsps sugar
4 tbsps water
Grated rind and juice of 1 orange
1 cinnamon stick
4oz raspberries, fresh or frozen
4oz strawberries, fresh or frozen
1 tbsp arrowroot or cornstarch mixed with
    4 tbsps brandy

TOPPING
½ cup heavy cream, whipped
½ cup natural yogurt or sour cream
1 tbsp powdered sugar
Grated nutmeg

Place the blackcurrants, redcurrants and cherries in a deep bowl along with their juices. Add the sugar, water, grated rind and juice of the orange and cinnamon stick. Cover with pierced plastic wrap and cook on HIGH for 7-8 minutes or until boiling. Strain, reserving the syrup. Place the fruit in another bowl with the strawberries and raspberries. Mix the arrowroot or cornstarch with the brandy, add to the reserved syrup and cook, about 2-3 minutes on HIGH until thickened and clear. Remove the cinnamon stick and pour over the fruit. Stir well and leave to cool slightly. To serve, spoon the fruit mixture into glasses or dessert dishes. Whip the cream lightly and fold in the powdered sugar and sour cream or natural yogurt. Top each serving with some of the cream and sprinkle on nutmeg to serve.

Menu 11: Kissel (top), Beef Stroganoff (center) and Spinach Mousse with Tomato Tarragon Sauce (bottom).

MENU 12

Coquilles aux Poissons Fumé

PREPARATION TIME: 25 minutes
MICROWAVE COOKING TIME: 22-30 minutes
SERVES: 6 people

¾ lb smoked haddock fillets
¾ lb smoked cod fillets
½ cup dry white wine
1 bay leaf
3 parsley stalks

SAUCE
1 shallot, finely chopped
½ clove garlic, chopped
½ cup dry white wine
½ cup cooking liquid from the fish
2 tbsps butter or margarine
2 tbsps flour
Pinch turmeric
½ tsp dill seed
½ cup heavy cream
Squeeze lemon juice
Salt and pepper

GARNISH
Sprigs of fresh dill
2oz smoked salmon, cut into thin strips

Cut the fish into 1 inch pieces, place in a shallow casserole, pour over the wine and add the parsley and bay leaf. Loosely cover and cook on HIGH for 1-2 minutes. Leave to stand, covered, while preparing the remaining ingredients. For the sauce, put the shallots, garlic, wine, turmeric and dill seed into a small, deep bowl or glass measure. Cook on HIGH for 8-10 minutes, or until boiling. Allow to boil another 2-3 minutes to reduce slightly. Strain the liquid and reserve. Melt the butter in a small casserole for 30 seconds on HIGH and stir in the flour. Pour in the reduced wine mixture and strain on the required amount of fish cooking liquid. Stir well and cook on HIGH for 4-5 minutes, or until thickened. Pour the cream into a deep bowl or glass measure and cook on HIGH for 6-8 minutes to reduce. Pour into the

sauce and blend well. Season with salt and pepper. Divide the haddock and cod among 6 shells or shell-shaped dishes. Pour over the sauce, loosely cover the dishes and reheat on HIGH for 1-2 minutes. Garnish the dishes with strips of smoked salmon and sprigs of fresh dill.

Lamb Poivrade

PREPARATION TIME: 35 minutes
MICROWAVE COOKING TIME: 26-30 minutes
SERVES: 6 people

4 best end necks of lamb

SAUCE
2 tbsps butter or margarine
2 tbsps flour
1 onion, finely chopped
1 clove garlic, crushed
1 cup rich brown stock
4 tbsps dry white wine
1 tsp tomato paste
1 bay leaf
1 sprig thyme
Salt
1 tbsp green peppercorns, slightly crushed
    (drained and rinsed if packed in brine)

POMMES DAUPHINOISE
4 tbsps butter or margarine
1 clove garlic, peeled
1lb potatoes, peeled and thinly sliced
½ cup light cream
1 egg, beaten
Salt and pepper
Grated nutmeg
½ cup grated Gruyère cheese

First prepare the potatoes. Melt the butter in a round dish or casserole with the garlic for 1½ minutes on HIGH. Remove the garlic clove and arrange the potatoes in neat layers, seasoning with salt, pepper and nutmeg in between each layer. Cover the dish with plastic wrap and cook

on HIGH for 9 minutes. Remove the dish from the oven. Whisk the cream and the egg together and pour evenly over the potatoes, shaking the dish gently to allow it to seep down the sides to the bottom. Re-cover and cook on HIGH for 6 minutes more. Uncover the dish, sprinkle the cheese over the top and leave to stand while preparing the lamb. Trim away the bones and all the fat from each best end neck of lamb until only the eye of the meat remains. Slice into ½ inch thick slices. Heat a browning dish according to the manufacturer's directions and lightly grease with oil. Press the slices of lamb down firmly on one side and turn over and press again to seal both sides. Cook in several batches. Set aside, covered, while preparing the sauce. Put the remaining butter in the browning dish and add the onion and flour. Cook on HIGH for 3-4 minutes or until the onion and the flour are beginning to brown. Deglaze the browning dish with some of the stock and pour the contents into a casserole dish. Add the remaining stock, white wine, tomato paste, bay leaf and sprig of thyme. Season with salt and cook on HIGH 3-5 minutes or until thickened. If desired, a few drops of gravy browning may be added to make the sauce darker. Add the peppercorns and the lamb and stir well. Cover and cook on HIGH for 3 minutes to heat through and finish cooking the lamb. Reheat the potatoes for 1-2 minutes on HIGH. Brown under a preheated broiler and cut into even-sized portions. Serve with the Lamb Poivrade and lightly cooked pea pods.

**Menu 12: Pêches Melba (top left),
Pommes Dauphinoise (top right)
Lamb Poivrade (center) and
Coquilles aux Poissons Fumé
(bottom).**

Pêches Melba

PREPARATION TIME: 25 minutes

MICROWAVE COOKING TIME:
10-14 minutes

SERVES: 6 people

2 cups vanilla ice cream
6 ripe peaches
8oz raspberries, fresh or frozen
2 tsps lemon juice
Powdered sugar to taste
4 tbsps raspberry liqueur
Ground blanched almonds

Place the vanilla ice cream in a bowl
and soften for 20-30 seconds on
HIGH. Place in a pastry bag and
quickly pipe the ice cream in swirls
into 6 individual dishes, filling them
halfway. Freeze the dishes until the
ice cream is firm. Meanwhile, place
4 cups water in a large bowl. Cover
with plastic wrap and heat on HIGH
for 8-11 minutes or until boiling.
Place 3 of the peaches in the water
and allow to stand for 1-2 minutes.
Remove the fruit to a bowl of cold
water and then peel. Return the bowl
to the oven and reboil the water.
Repeat with the remaining 3 peaches.
To prepare the sauce, combine the
raspberries and lemon juice in a deep
bowl and cook on HIGH for 2-3
minutes. Place in a food processor or
liquidizer and purée until smooth.
Add powdered sugar to taste and
process once or twice to mix well.
Strain out the seeds and push as
much of the purée through the sieve
as possible. Stir in the raspberry
liqueur and set the sauce aside.
Soften the ice cream at room
temperature for 15 minutes. To serve,
place a peach on top of the ice cream
in each dish and spoon over some of
the raspberry sauce. Sprinkle the top
of the peaches with some of the
blanched ground almonds. Serve the
remaining sauce separately.

MENU 13

Consommé Valentine

PREPARATION TIME: 20 minutes

MICROWAVE COOKING TIME:
10-11 minutes

SERVES: 6 people

1 large carrot, thinly sliced
1-2 turnips, depending upon size, peeled
   and thinly sliced
1 tbsp chopped chervil or parsley
4 cups canned or freshly prepared chicken
   or beef consommé
4 tbsps sherry

Cut each slice of carrot and turnip
into a heart shape with a small
cookie cutter. Place the carrots and
turnips in separate bowls with 1 tbsp
water in each. Loosely cover the
bowls with plastic wrap and cook on
HIGH for 2-3 minutes. Leave to
stand while reheating the consommé.
Pour the consommé into a
microwave proof soup tureen or
individual bowls and add the sherry
and chervil or parsley. Cover loosely
and cook on HIGH for 8 minutes for
the soup tureen or 2-3 minutes for
individual bowls. Halfway through
the reheating time, add the drained
carrot and turnip hearts. Serve hot.

Poulet au Concombres

PREPARATION TIME: 30 minutes

MICROWAVE COOKING TIME:
20-28 minutes

SERVES: 6 people

6 chicken breasts, skinned and boned
1 cup chicken stock
1 small cucumber, seeded and cut into
   thin strips, but not peeled
2 tbsps butter or margarine
1½ tbsps flour
Salt and pepper
¾ cup light cream
2 tbsps chopped fresh dill or 1 tbsp dried
   dill weed

GARNISH
Whole sprigs of fresh dill

Place the chicken breasts in a dish in
a circle and pour over the chicken
stock. Cover with pierced plastic
wrap and cook on HIGH for 15-20
minutes or until the juices from the
chicken run clear. If desired, cut the
chicken breasts into thin strips.
Alternatively, leave whole if they
have retained their shape. Melt the
butter for 30 seconds on HIGH and
stir in the flour. Strain on the cooking
liquid from the chicken and add the
cream. Season with salt and pepper
and add the chopped dill. Cook on
HIGH for 3-5 minutes, stirring
occasionally until thickened. Place
the chicken in a serving dish with the
cucumber strips, loosely cover and
reheat on HIGH for 2-3 minutes.
Pour over the sauce to serve. Garnish
with fresh dill.

Pavlova

PREPARATION TIME: 30 minutes

MICROWAVE COOKING TIME:
3 minutes

SERVES: 6 people

6 egg whites
1½ cups sugar
¼ tsp vanilla extract
2 tsps cornstarch
1 tsp white distilled vinegar
½ cup toasted sliced almonds

**Menu 13: Pavlova (top), Consommé
Valentine (center) and Poulet au
Concombres (bottom).**

FILLING
*1 small pineapple, peeled, cored and cut
into pieces or 8oz canned pineapple
pieces, drained*
2 kiwi fruit, peeled and sliced
1 passion fruit
*4oz fresh strawberries (if available) or 2
oranges, peeled and segmented*
1 cup whipping cream
Powdered sugar

Beat the egg whites until stiff peaks

form. Add the sugar, a spoonful at a
time, beating well in between each
addition, until the meringue is stiff
and glossy. Fold in the vanilla,
vinegar and cornstarch. Spread the
meringue in a circle on the plate or
serving dish and make a deep well in
the center. Do not spread to the edge
of the plate. Sprinkle with the
toasted almonds and cook on HIGH
for 3 minutes. Allow to cool
completely. Mix half the fruit with

half the cream and fill the well in the
center of the pavlova. Reserve the
passion fruit for the top. Spoon or
pipe the remaining cream into the
center of the pavlova and decorate
the top with the remaining fruit,
scooping out the seeds and pulp
from the passion fruit to drizzle on
top as a sauce. Sprinkle lightly with
powdered sugar and chill before
serving.

MENU 14

Artichokes with Orange Mousseline Sauce

PREPARATION TIME: 30 minutes

MICROWAVE COOKING TIME:
17½-23 minutes

SERVES: 6 people

6 medium globe artichokes
½ cup salted water
2 tbsps lemon juice
1 bay leaf

SAUCE
½ cup butter
1 tbsp orange juice
1 tbsp lemon juice
2 egg yolks
1 tsp chopped tarragon
Salt and pepper
4 tbsps whipped cream

Wash the artichokes and trim off the
stems and the lower leaves. Trim the
pointed ends off all the leaves and
place the artichokes in a large
casserole or bowl with the salted
water, lemon juice and bay leaf. Cook
on HIGH for 15-20 minutes, turning
the dish or re-arranging the
artichokes twice during cooking. To
test if the artichokes are cooked, pull
one of the leaves from the bottom, it
should come away easily. Drain the
artichokes upside down on paper
towels and leave to cool. To prepare
the sauce, heat the butter in a glass
measure for 2 minutes on HIGH.
Beat the egg yolks and the orange

and lemon juice together with salt
and pepper and tarragon. Gradually
whisk the egg yolks into the butter.
Cook on MEDIUM for 1 minute,
whisking well after 15 seconds. Do
not allow the sauce to boil. If the
sauce looks curdled, dip the glass
measure into a bowl of iced water
and whisk well. Continue heating
until the sauce thickens. Allow to
cool slightly and fold in the whipped
cream. Carefully separate the center
leaves on the artichoke and, using a
teaspoon, remove the thistle-like
choke from the inside. Reshape the
artichoke and place 1 on each serving
plate. Reheat on HIGH for 30
seconds-1 minute and serve with the
mousseline sauce.

Stuffed Trout

PREPARATION TIME: 35 minutes

MICROWAVE COOKING TIME:
39-44 minutes

SERVES: 6 people

6 even-sized rainbow trout, boned

FILLING
6oz crab meat
1 tbsp snipped chives
1 package low fat soft cheese
*5 slices bread, crusts removed made into
crumbs*
Cayenne pepper
Salt
6 tbsps butter

Juice of half a lemon
2 tbsps chopped parsley

GARNISH
Lemon slices

NEW POTATOES
1lb new potatoes, scrubbed but not peeled
1 cup water
Salt
3 tbsps butter or margarine

Ask the fishmonger to bone the
trout. Mix the filling ingredients
together and stuff each trout. Cover
the heads and tails with foil and place
the trout, three at a time, in a shallow
dish. Cover with plastic wrap and
cook 12 minutes on HIGH. Set the
trout aside while cooking the
remaining fish. In a deep bowl,
microwave the butter for 2 minutes
on HIGH until lightly brown. Add
the lemon juice and parsley and set
aside. To cook the potatoes, place
them in a casserole dish with salt and
water. Cover and cook on HIGH for
10-14 minutes. Drain and reheat with
the butter 1-2 minutes. Leave to
stand, covered. Reheat the fish for
2 minutes on HIGH and pour over
the butter to serve. Garnish with
lemon slices.

**Menu 14: Artichokes with Orange
Mousseline Sauce (top left),
Flummery (top right) and Stuffed
Trout (bottom).**

Flummery

PREPARATION TIME: 30 minutes	
MICROWAVE COOKING TIME: 9-10 minutes	
SERVES: 6 people	

2 tbsps butter or margarine
1 cup porridge oats
1 pint milk
2 tbsps cornstarch
1 tbsp gelatine
3 tbsps water
2-3 tbsps honey
3 tbsps Scotch or malt whiskey
½ cup heavy cream
4oz berries such as blackberries, blackcurrants, blueberries or strawberries

Melt the butter for the topping on HIGH for 30 seconds and stir in the oats. Cook for a further 3 minutes on HIGH, stirring occasionally, until the oats are evenly browned. Set aside. Mix the milk and the cornstarch together in a deep bowl and cook on HIGH for 5-6 minutes, stirring every minute until the mixture thickens. Allow to cool, covered with wax paper to prevent a skin from forming. Sprinkle the gelatine over the water and allow to soak for 5 minutes. Cook on HIGH for 15-20 seconds to dissolve. Stir the gelatine, honey and whiskey into the thickened milk mixture. Whip the cream until soft peaks form and fold into the mixture. Taste the berries and sweeten with more honey if desired. Place some of the berries in the bottom of a glass dessert dish and sprinkle over some of the topping. Spoon in flummery mixture and continue alternating with the oats, fruit and mixture for the 6 dishes. Finish with a layer of oats and a few pieces of fruit. Serve cold.

MENU 15

Cream of Smoked Salmon Soup

PREPARATION TIME: 15 minutes	
MICROWAVE COOKING TIME: 11-14 minutes	
SERVES: 6 people	

¾ lb whitefish, skinned, boned and cut into 1 inch chunks
9oz smoked salmon, cut into 1 inch pieces, with 6 thin strips reserved for garnish
3 tbsps butter or margarine
3 tbsps flour
½ cup dry white wine
3½ cups milk
½ cup heavy cream
Freshly ground white pepper
1 tsp tomato paste (optional)

GARNISH
Sour cream
Chopped chives

Combine the whitefish and smoked salmon with the white wine in a large, deep bowl. Cover and cook on HIGH for 2-3 minutes. Leave to stand for 1-2 minutes before spooning into a food processor or blender. Add the milk and purée until smooth. Rinse out the bowl and melt the butter for 1 minute on HIGH. Stir in the flour and gradually pour in the milk and fish mixture. Heat for 3-5 minutes on HIGH, or until thickened. Add the pepper and the cream and reheat a further 5 minutes on HIGH. If the color of the soup is too pale, add 1 tsp tomato paste. Garnish with sour cream, chopped chives and the reserved strips of smoked salmon.

Fillet Steaks Rossini

PREPARATION TIME: 20 minutes	
MICROWAVE COOKING TIME: 14-18 minutes	
SERVES: 6 people	

MADEIRA SAUCE
2 tbsps butter
2 tbsps flour
1 small onion, finely chopped
1 cup rich brown stock
4 tbsps Madeira or sherry
½ tsp tomato paste
1 bay leaf
Salt and pepper
Gravy browning (optional)
6 filet mignons
2 tbsps butter or margarine

GARNISH
3oz firm pâté
6 mushroom caps, fluted if desired

Heat a browning dish according to the manufacturer's directions and add the butter for the Madeira sauce. Add the onion and the flour and cook on HIGH, stirring frequently, until the flour and the onions brown lightly – this should take about 5 minutes. Deglaze the browning dish with some of the brown stock and spoon the contents into a deep bowl. Add the remaining stock and the bay leaf. Cook on HIGH for 3-5 minutes or until thickened. Strain into a clean bowl and discard the onions and bay leaf. Add the Madeira, tomato paste, salt and pepper and gravy browning, if using. Cover the sauce and set it aside. Clean the browning dish and reheat. Add the butter for the steaks and, when foaming, place three steaks on the browning dish and press down firmly. Turn over and press again to seal both sides. Cook the steaks on HIGH for 4 minutes. Repeat with the remaining steaks. Place all the steaks on individual serving dishes. Top each with a round, thin slice of pâté, cover well and keep warm. Add the mushrooms to the browning dish and cook for 1-2 minutes on HIGH, stirring occasionally. Place 1 mushroom on top of each slice of pâté and re-cover the meat. Reheat the Madeira sauce on HIGH for 1-2 minutes and spoon some over each steak. Serve the remaining sauce separately. Serve with an accompaniment of green beans cooked with thinly sliced red peppers.

Raspberry Sorbet in Chocolate Cups

PREPARATION TIME: 35 minutes

MICROWAVE COOKING TIME: 6 minutes

SERVES: 6 people

RASPBERRY SORBET
8oz fresh or frozen raspberries
¾ cup sugar
2 tbsps lemon juice
1 egg white, stiffly beaten

CHOCOLATE CUPS
3 squares semi-sweet chocolate
1½ tsps vegetable shortening

TO SERVE
6 tbsps raspberry liqueur
12 whole raspberries
Mint leaves

If using frozen raspberries, thaw on DEFROST for about 1-2 minutes. Purée the fruit in a food processor or blender and sieve to remove the seeds. Combine the sugar with ½ cup water in a deep bowl or glass measure. Heat on HIGH for 4 minutes, stirring every minute. Allow the syrup to cool and add the lemon juice. Stir in the fruit purée and pour the mixture into a freezer container. Freeze until the mixture is slushy, return to the food processor and beat until smooth. Return to the freezer and freeze again until almost solid. Take out the mixture and process again in the food processor or blender, adding the stiffly beaten egg

Menu 15: Raspberry Sorbet in Chocolate Cups (top), Fillet Steaks Rossini (center) and Cream of Smoked Salmon Soup (bottom).

white. Return to the freezer until firm. To make the chocolate cups, combine the chocolate in a small bowl with the vegetable shortening and cook on HIGH for 2-2½ minutes until melted. Stir frequently while melting. Use a double layer of cup cake liners and fill 6 cases with an

equal amount of chocolate. Tilt case to coat the sides to within ¼ inch of the top. Continue to tilt to form a thick chocolate layer. Alternatively, brush on the chocolate with a pastry brush. Chill until set. Thirty minutes before serving, remove the sorbet from the freezer to allow it to soften. Alternatively, heat the container on HIGH for 20 seconds to soften. Carefully peel away the paper from the chocolate cups and place 1 on each serving plate. Fill with 1 scoop of sorbet and pour a spoonful of raspberry liqueur over the sorbet. Garnish with fresh raspberries and mint leaves.

Brunch

Apricot Cheesecake

PREPARATION TIME: 40 minutes

MICROWAVE COOKING TIME:
12-17 minutes

SERVES: 8 people

BASE
1 cup all-purpose flour, sifted
Pinch salt
2 tbsps butter or margarine
2 tsps fresh yeast
2 tsps sugar
1 egg, separated

FILLING AND TOPPING
8oz cream or curd cheese
2 tbsps sugar
Grated rind of 1 lemon
4 tbsps light cream
1 egg, separated
*1lb fresh or canned apricots, halved and
    stoned*
Demerara sugar

Sift the flour and salt and rub in the butter by hand or with a food processor. Mix the yeast with 1 tbsp warm water and the sugar. Beat the egg yolk and add to the flour with the yeast. Mix together to form a smooth dough by hand or with a food processor and then knead for about 10 minutes, by hand on a lightly-floured surface. Roll the dough out to line a 9 inch round dish. Trim the edges and cover the dish with plastic wrap. Heat on HIGH for 15 seconds and then leave to rise for about 30 minutes or until a finger mark stays when the dough is lightly pressed. Cook on HIGH for 3-4 minutes, turning the dish occasionally. Leave to cool in the dish. To prepare the filling, mix the cheese, sugar, lemon rind, cream and

the egg yolk together until smooth. Whisk both the egg whites until stiff but not dry and fold into the cheese mixture. Chop half of the apricots and arrange them over the dough base. Spoon the cheese mixture over the apricots and arrange the remaining apricot halves over the top of the cheese. Cook on HIGH for 4-5 minutes or until just beginning to set. Sprinkle with the demerara sugar and continue cooking for 5-8 minutes until the center is set. Turn the dish occasionally while the cheesecake is cooking. The top may be browned under a preheated broiler before serving if desired.

Red Fruit Compôte

PREPARATION TIME: 20 minutes

MICROWAVE COOKING TIME:
7-8 minutes

SERVES: 8 people

*2lbs of the following fruits: cranberries;
    redcurrants, topped and tailed; cherries,
    fresh or canned, pitted; plums, halved
    and stoned; strawberries; raspberries.*
½ cup sugar
2 tbsps cornstarch
½ cup orange juice

TOPPING
Natural yogurt
Ground cinnamon

Combine the cranberries, redcurrants and plums with sugar in a large, deep bowl. Cover and cook on HIGH for 3 minutes. If the cherries are fresh, add them with the cranberries, redcurrants and plums. If canned cherries are used, add them and

their juice to the cooked fruit. Combine the cornstarch and the orange juice in a small, deep bowl or a glass measure. Strain on ½ cup of the cooked fruit juice and stir well. Cook on HIGH 4-5 minutes, or until thickened. Fold carefully into the cooked fruit and allow the mixture to cool. When completely cooled add the strawberries and raspberries and chill before serving. Serve topped with natural yogurt sprinkled with cinnamon.

Red Flannel Hash

PREPARATION TIME: 20 minutes

MICROWAVE COOKING TIME:
19-22 minutes

SERVES: 8 people

6 potatoes, peeled and cut into small dice
2lbs corned beef
1 onion, finely chopped
4 cooked beets, peeled and diced
Salt and pepper
2 tbsps Worcestershire sauce
Dash tabasco
3 tbsps butter or margarine
Chopped parsley

Place the potatoes in a large bowl with 6 tbsps water. Cover with plastic wrap and cook on HIGH for 5 minutes. Cut the corned beef roughly and drain the potatoes. Mix with the onions, beets and seasonings. Place the mixture into a shallow dish or

**Facing page: Apricot Cheesecake
(top) and Red Fruit Compôte
(bottom).**

30 seconds on HIGH and add the onion. Cook for 1-2 minutes to soften slightly and stir in the flour. Gradually stir in the stock and sherry. Add the thyme and tomato paste, spoon in the kidneys and mushrooms, scraping the browning dish to remove the meat juices. Add a pinch of salt and pepper and cover the casserole. Cook on HIGH for 3 minutes. Stir well and cook a further 2 minutes on HIGH or until the kidneys are just tender. Stir in the cream and sprinkle with chopped parsley. Serve on, or surrounded by, triangles of hot, buttered toast, with the crusts removed.

Oeufs Florentine

PREPARATION TIME: 20 minutes

MICROWAVE COOKING TIME: 11½-13 minutes

SERVES: 4 people

1lb fresh spinach
4 eggs

SAUCE
4oz butter
Juice of ½ a lemon
Pinch cayenne pepper
Pinch dry mustard
2 egg yolks
Salt and pepper
Paprika

Wash the spinach well and remove any thick stalks. Place in a roasting bag and tie loosely with string. Cook on HIGH for 5-6 minutes, drain if necessary before using. To poach the eggs, pour 6 tbsps of hot water and a few drops of vinegar into each of 4 small dishes. Microwave on HIGH for about 1-2 minutes to bring to the boil. Break an egg into each dish and pierce the yolk with a skewer. Arrange the dishes in a circle and cook on HIGH for 2½-3 minutes.

individual dishes and dot the top with butter or margarine. Cook on HIGH for 9-12 minutes. Leave to stand for 5 minutes before serving sprinkled with chopped parsley. Poached eggs may be served on top.

Sherried Kidneys and Mushrooms

PREPARATION TIME: 15 minutes

MICROWAVE COOKING TIME: 18 minutes

SERVES: 8 people

4-6 veal kidneys, cored and cut into small pieces

8oz even-sized mushrooms, left whole
1 onion, finely chopped
3 tbsps butter or margarine
3 tbsps flour
1 clove garlic, crushed
1 cup brown stock
½ cup dry sherry
¼ tsp thyme
1 tbsp tomato paste
3 tbsps heavy cream
Chopped parsley
Toast

Heat a browning dish according to the manufacturer's directions. Melt 1 tbsp of the butter and, when foaming, place in the kidneys and mushrooms. Cook for 3 minutes on HIGH, in two batches. Melt the remaining butter in a casserole for

This page: Oeufs Florentine. Facing page: Red Flannel Hash (top) and Sherried Kidneys and Mushrooms (bottom).

Alternatively, cook on MEDIUM for 3-3¼ minutes. Allow the eggs to stand in the water for 30 seconds-1 minute before removing. If preparing the eggs in advance, place cooked eggs in a dish of cold water and keep until needed. To prepare the sauce, place the butter in a large, glass measure and heat on HIGH for 1½-2 minutes. Mix the lemon juice with the cayenne pepper, mustard and egg yolks and beat into the hot butter. Beat well and then add salt and pepper to taste. Cook on MEDIUM for 1 minute. Whisk the sauce thoroughly after 15 seconds and then continue cooking for another 15 seconds. Do not allow the sauce to boil. If the sauce begins to curdle, dip the glass measure into a bowl of cold water to stop the cooking. Whisk well and continue cooking until the sauce thickens. Season the spinach with salt and pepper and some grated nutmeg, if desired. Divide the spinach between 4 serving dishes. Spread it out evenly, leaving a slight well in the center. Drain the poached eggs and place 1 egg in each dish. Cover the dishes and reheat on HIGH for 30 seconds. Pour over the sauce and serve immediately. To double the recipe, increase cooking time by half as much again.

Kedgeree

PREPARATION TIME: 25 minutes

MICROWAVE COOKING TIME:
27-32 minutes plus standing time

SERVES: 8 people

1lb smoked haddock or cod
1 cup long-grain rice
2 tsps oil
6oz cooked, peeled shrimp
2 hard-boiled eggs
1-2 tsps mild curry powder
¾ cup light cream
Chopped parsley
Nutmeg

Place the fish in a covered casserole and cook on HIGH for 10-12 minutes. Flake the fish and discard the skin and bones. Place the rice in a

large, deep bowl with 2 cups boiling water, a pinch of salt and the oil. Cover with plastic wrap and cook on HIGH for 12 minutes, stirring halfway through to separate the grains. Leave to stand for 7 minutes. Drain if all the water has not been absorbed. Stir in the flaked fish and shrimp and leave covered. Place the curry powder and the cream in a glass measure or a small, deep bowl. Cook on HIGH for 3-5 minutes or until almost boiling. Chop 1 of the hard-boiled eggs and add it to the rice and fish with the cream. Stir

This page: Kedgeree. Facing page: Scones (top) and Shortbread (bottom).

gently and spoon into a serving dish. Garnish the top with the remaining hard-boiled egg sliced, chopped or cut into eighths. Sprinkle over chopped parsley and paprika before serving. If necessary, reheat the kedgeree for 2-3 minutes on HIGH before garnishing with the hard-boiled egg.

MICROWAVE ENTERTAINING

Treats for Tea

Shortbread

PREPARATION TIME: 15 minutes

MICROWAVE COOKING TIME:
4½-6 minutes

MAKES: 10

½ cup butter or margarine
4 tbsps sugar
1 cup all-purpose flour
4 tbsps rice flour
Pinch salt
4oz semi-sweet chocolate

Put the flour into a bowl with the rice flour and a pinch of salt. Rub in the butter or margarine until the mixture resembles fine breadcrumbs. Stir in half the sugar and knead the ingredients together lightly to form a dough. Line an 7 inch flan dish with wax paper. Alternatively, line the whole dish with plastic wrap. Press in the prepared shortbread mixture and smooth the top. Mark into 10 wedges and prick well with a fork. Cook on HIGH for 3-4 minutes. Sprinkle with the remaining sugar and allow to cool slightly. Cut through the markings in the wedges, remove from the dish and allow to cool on a wire rack. Melt the chocolate for 1½-2 minutes on MEDIUM, stirring until smooth. Holding the pointed end of each wedge of shortbread, place in the chocolate to coat about 2 inches or drizzle over the chocolate. Allow the chocolate to set and cool completely before serving.

Scones

PREPARATION TIME: 15 minutes

MICROWAVE COOKING TIME:
2-3½ minutes

MAKES: 9

1 cup whole-wheat flour
1½ tsps baking powder
Pinch salt
2 tbsps butter or margarine
½ cup golden raisins

6 tbsps milk

Sift the flour, baking powder and a pinch of salt into a mixing bowl. Return the bran to the bowl. Cut in the butter or margarine until the mixture resembles fine breadcrumbs. This may be done in a food processor or by hand. Stir in the golden raisins by hand and add the milk, gradually, until the dough comes together. It may not be necessary to add all the milk. Knead the dough lightly and turn it out onto a floured surface. Roll out to a thickness of ½-1 inch. Using a 2 inch round pastry cutter, cut the dough into approximately 9 rounds. The dough may also be cut into squares. Sprinkle each scone lightly with a mixture of sugar and cinnamon and place close together around the edge of a 9 inch round dish or microwave baking tray. Cook on HIGH for 2-3½ minutes or until the scones spring back lightly when touched. If necessary, rearrange the scones several times during cooking. Serve warm with jam and cream or butter.

Dundee Cake

PREPARATION TIME: 20 minutes

MICROWAVE COOKING TIME:
41-47 minutes plus standing time

MAKES: 1 cake

¾ cup butter or margarine
¾ cup dark brown sugar
3 eggs, lightly beaten
2 tbsps molasses
2 tbsps whiskey
2 cups all-purpose flour
1½ tbsps baking powder
1 tbsp allspice
½ cup chopped almonds
½ cup candied cherries, chopped
4½ cups mixed dried fruit (raisins, golden raisins, currants, candied peel)

DECORATION
Apricot jam
Blanched halved almonds
Candied cherries, halved

Soften the butter or margarine in a large bowl for 10-20 seconds on HIGH. Gradually beat in the sugar until light and fluffy. Beat in the eggs, one at a time, and add the molasses and whiskey. Beat until smooth and then sift in the flour, baking powder and spice. Carefully fold into the cream mixture and add the fruit, nuts

and cherries. Use a 7 inch straight-sided deep baking dish, lightly greased and lined with wax paper. Spoon the prepared cake mixture into the dish and cook on LOW or DEFROST for 40-45 minutes. Leave to stand for 5 minutes before removing from the dish to cool on a wire rack. Melt the apricot jam for 1-2 minutes on HIGH, stir and sieve. Brush a thin layer of jam over the top of the cake while it is still warm and decorate with the almond and candied cherries before the jam sets completely. Leave to cool completely before serving.

Orange Cake

PREPARATION TIME: 25 minutes

MICROWAVE COOKING TIME:
7½ minutes plus standing time

MAKES: 1 cake

¾ cup butter or margarine
¾ cup sugar
3 eggs
Grated rind of 2 oranges
1½ cups all-purpose flour
2 tsps baking powder
Orange juice or milk

ORANGE FROSTING
2 cups sifted powdered sugar
Juice of 1 orange made up to 4-5 tbsps with water
Rind of 1 orange cut into thin strips

Lightly grease the base and sides of a 7 inch diameter deep cake dish. Line the base with a circle of wax paper. Soften the butter or margarine for 30 seconds on HIGH in a large bowl. Mix in the sugar and, when light and fluffy, gradually beat in the eggs. Add the grated rind while beating in the eggs. Sift the flour and the baking powder together and fold into the mixture. Add enough orange juice or milk to bring the mixture to a thick dropping consistency. Spoon the mixture into the prepared dish and smooth down the top. Cook on HIGH for 6 minutes. Leave the cake

to stand in its dish on a flat surface for 5 minutes and then loosen the sides. Turn the cake out onto a wire rack set over a tray. For the frosting, place the orange juice and water, if using, in a deep bowl with the strips of orange rind. Cook on HIGH for 1 minute to soften the orange rind and to heat the liquid. Sift in about ¾ of the powdered sugar and stir to mix. The frosting should coat the back of a spoon and slowly run off if it is thick enough. Add remaining sugar if necessary or thin down with more hot water. When the cake is completely cool, pour the frosting onto the top and ease down the sides with a spatula. Allow to set completely before serving.

Apricot Nut Loaf

PREPARATION TIME: 20 minutes

MICROWAVE COOKING TIME:
4-5 minutes

MAKES: 1 loaf

4oz dried apricots, chopped
½ cup water
5 tbsps margarine
5 tbsps light brown sugar
1 cup all-purpose flour
1½ tsps baking powder
¼ tsp mixed spice or ground allspice
¼ tsp cinnamon
1 egg, slightly beaten
2 tsps golden syrup
3 tbsps milk
½ cup chopped almonds or walnuts

Combine the apricots and water in a small bowl and cover loosely. Heat on HIGH for 2 minutes and leave to stand for 30 minutes. Combine the remaining ingredients except the nuts and mix well. Drain the apricots and reserve the juice. Stir the nuts and apricots into the loaf mixture, adding enough of the reserved apricot juice to bring to a soft dropping

Facing page: Dundee Cake.

consistency. Line a loaf dish with wax paper and spoon in the loaf mixture. Microwave on HIGH for 4 minutes. Reduce the setting to LOW and continue cooking for 8-9 minutes. Stand for 5 minutes before removing from the dish. When cool, sprinkle the top with powdered sugar.

Chocolate Walnut Layer Cake

PREPARATION TIME: 25 minutes

MICROWAVE COOKING TIME:
11½-14 minutes plus standing time

MAKES: 1 cake

CHOCOLATE CAKE
1 cup butter or margarine
1⅛ cups brown sugar
½ cup vegetable oil
4 eggs
1½ cups all-purpose flour
2 tsps baking powder
4 tbsps cocoa

FILLING
3 tbsps butter or margarine
½ cup walnuts, finely chopped
2 tbsps light cream or evaporated milk
2 cups powdered sugar
½ tsp rum extract

TOPPING
4oz semi-sweet chocolate
Walnut halves
Powdered sugar

Line a 7 inch microwave cake dish with plastic wrap or place a wax paper circle in the bottom of a greased dish. Place the butter or margarine in a deep bowl and microwave on HIGH for 10-20 seconds to soften. Using an electric mixer, add the sugar and the oil gradually, making sure the sugar is well blended and the mixture is light and fluffy. When the sugar is no longer grainy, gradually beat in the eggs. If the mixture begins to curdle, add a little flour and whisk again. Put the remaining flour with the baking powder and cocoa and fold into the

cream mixture. Pour the mixture into the baking dish and cook on HIGH for 7 minutes. Leave to cool on a flat surface in the dish for 5-10 minutes and then remove to a cooling rack. While the cake cools, prepare the filling. Microwave the butter or margarine in a small mixing bowl on HIGH for about 1 minute or until melted. Stir in the walnuts and heat a further 2-4 minutes on HIGH until the butter and the nuts are light brown. Stir every 2 minutes. Sift in the powdered sugar and beat well. Gradually add the cream until the filling is of spreading consistency. Add the rum extract and set aside. Cut the cake horizontally into 3 layers and sandwich with the walnut filling. Break up the chocolate for the topping and put it into a small bowl.

This page: Apricot Nut Loaf (top) and Orange Cake (bottom). Facing page: Chocolate Walnut Layer Cake.

Microwave on MEDIUM for 1½-2 minutes, stirring often until the chocolate is spreadable. Using a spatula, spread the chocolate onto the top of the cake. Toss the walnuts into the powdered sugar to coat lightly. Shake off the excess sugar and, when the chocolate topping is nearly set, arrange the walnuts around the outside edge of the cake. Allow the chocolate to set completely before cutting to serve.

Cocktail Savories

Shrimp on Horseback

PREPARATION TIME: 30 minutes

MICROWAVE COOKING TIME: 7-8 minutes

MAKES: 16

8 slices bacon, rinds and bones removed
16 large uncooked shrimp, peeled but tail ends left on
1 large green pepper, seeded and cut into 16 even-sized pieces
16 anchovy fillets, soaked in 4 tbsps milk
4 tbsps lemon juice
Dash tabasco
16 whole chives (optional)

Precook the bacon on a microwave roasting rack or on a plate with paper towels. Place two layers of paper towels on a plate and arrange 4 slices of bacon on the towel; cover with another sheet of paper towel. Arrange another 4 slices on top and cover with another towel. If using a microwave roasting rack place the strips of bacon in an even layer. Cook on HIGH for 4 minutes, or until the bacon is slightly brown but not completely cooked. Meanwhile, drain the anchovies, rinse in cold water and pat dry. Place a shrimp on top of each slice of pepper and wrap an anchovy around the middle. Sprinkle with lemon juice and a dash of tabasco. Cut the bacon strips in half and wrap one half around each shrimp. If using chives, soften for 15 seconds on HIGH in a small dish of water. Drain and tie up each shrimp roll. Alternatively, secure with wooden picks. Place the shrimp on a plate or in a microwave baking dish. Cook on HIGH for 3-4 minutes or until the shrimp are cooked.

Sweet and Sour Sausages

PREPARATION TIME: 25 minutes

MICROWAVE COOKING TIME: 6-10 minutes plus standing time

SERVES: 6-8 people

1lb pork sausages
2 tbsps oil
8oz canned pineapple pieces, drained and juice reserved
1 large or 2 small green peppers, seeded and cut into 1 inch pieces
8oz cherry tomatoes (if unavailable, substitute 1 large or 2 small sweet red peppers, seeded and cut into 1 inch pieces)

SAUCE
1 tbsp cornstarch
2 tbsps brown sugar
¼ tsp ground ginger
1 clove garlic, crushed
1 tbsp tomato ketchup
1 tbsp soy sauce
Reserved pineapple juice

Heat a browning dish according to the manufacturer's directions. Prick the sausage skins all over with a fork. When the browning dish is hot, add the oil and the sausages and cook for 3 minutes on HIGH, turning frequently to brown evenly. Drain the sausages on paper towels and cut them into 1 inch pieces. Combine all the sauce ingredients, stirring in the reserved pineapple juice gradually. Combine the sauce with all the other ingredients, except tomatoes, in a casserole dish and cook on HIGH for 3-7 minutes or until the sauce is thickened, stirring carefully two or three times. Add tomatoes and leave to stand 1-2 minutes. Provide wooden picks for serving.

Chicken Satays with Peppers

PREPARATION TIME: 25 minutes plus marinating time

MICROWAVE COOKING TIME: 11-15 minutes

SERVES: 6-8 people

4 chicken breasts, skinned and boned
3 small peppers, red, green and yellow

MARINADE
4 tbsps oil
Grated rind and juice of 1 lime
1 tsp dry mustard powder
1 tbsp light soy sauce
1 clove garlic, crushed

BASTING SAUCE
1 shallot, finely chopped
1 clove garlic, crushed
1 tbsp tomato paste
½ chili pepper, finely chopped
4 tbsps chicken stock
1 tbsp soy sauce
2 tbsps smooth peanut butter

GARNISH
Lime wedges

Facing page: Sweet and Sour Sausages.

Cut the chicken breasts into 1 inch pieces. Seed the pepper and cut them into pieces the same size as the chicken. Thread three pieces of chicken and three pieces of pepper, alternating the colors, onto small wooden skewers. Place them in a shallow microwave ovenproof dish. Mix together the marinade ingredients and pour over the satays. Cover with plastic wrap and leave to stand for 2 hours or overnight in the refrigerator. Turn the satays often to coat them evenly. Place all the sauce ingredients in a blender or food processor and purée until smooth. Pour into a small bowl and cook on HIGH for 5-6 minutes, until boiling, stirring frequently. Heat a browning

This page: Shrimp on Horseback. Facing page: Chicken Satays with Peppers (top) and Lamb and Mint Meatballs (bottom).

dish according to the manufacturer's directions and when hot place the satays on the dish, turning to lightly brown all sides. Cook in the browning dish or on a microwave oven rack for 5-7 minutes, turning frequently and basting with the sauce. Combine any remaining sauce with the remaining marinade and reheat on HIGH for 1-2 minutes. Before serving, brush the satays lightly with sauce and serve the remaining sauce separately.

Lamb and Mint Meatballs

PREPARATION TIME: 20 minutes

MICROWAVE COOKING TIME: 8 minutes

SERVES: 6-8 people

1lb ground lamb
1 medium onion, roughly chopped
¼ tsp ground allspice
Salt and pepper
2 tsps chopped fresh mint
2 tsps chopped fresh parsley
4 slices bread, crusts removed
Water
Fresh mint leaves, as large as possible

GARNISH
Lemon twists

Chop the onion in a food processor until fine. Add the lamb, allspice, salt, pepper, chopped mint, chopped parsley and the bread slices, torn into small pieces. Process again to mix, but do not overwork the meat. Add about 4 tbsps water and process again briefly. The mixture should be very moist but still hold together. Use more water if necessary. Pat the mixture into 1 inch balls. Wrap each meatball in a mint leaf. Place the meatballs on a microwave baking sheet or in a shallow dish. Place the ends of the mint leaves on the bottom. Cook on HIGH for 5 minutes. Turn over and reposition the meatballs and cook a further 3 minutes on HIGH or until fully cooked. Garnish serving dish with lemon twists.

Hot Salmon and Horseradish Pinwheels

PREPARATION TIME: 25 minutes

MICROWAVE COOKING TIME: 1-2 minutes 20 seconds

SERVES: 6-8 people

8oz smoked salmon, thinly sliced
8oz cream, curd or low fat soft cheese
1 tbsp prepared horseradish sauce
2 tsps chopped fresh or dried dill
1 medium-sized cucumber, cut into

½ inch thick rounds

Place slices of smoked salmon on separate sheets of plastic wrap. Soften the cheese for 20 seconds on HIGH and mix with the horseradish and dill. Divide the cheese mixture among all the slices of smoked salmon and spread evenly. Roll-up the salmon jelly roll fashion and wrap tightly in the plastic wrap. Place in

the freezer until well chilled and firm, but not frozen. Score the skin of the cucumber, lengthwise, with the prongs of a fork, if desired. Slice the cucumber and sprinkle lightly with salt. Leave to drain on paper towels for 30 minutes. Rinse well and pat dry. Slice the salmon rolls crosswise into ¼ inch slices. Place one slice on each slice of cucumber and arrange in a circle on a plate or microwave

This page: Hot Salmon and Horseradish Pinwheels. Facing page: Pâté en Gelée.

baking sheet. Heat for 1-2 minutes on HIGH before serving.

MICROWAVE ENTERTAINING

Buffet

Pâte en Gelée

PREPARATION TIME: 25 minutes
plus chilling time

MICROWAVE COOKING TIME:
27-30 minutes

SERVES: 8-10 people

8oz rindless streaky bacon
1lb coarsely ground pork
8oz ground veal
8oz pork liver, skinned
1 clove garlic, crushed
¼ tsp ground allspice
2 tbsps aspic powder
¼ tsp ground nutmeg
¼ tsp ground ginger
2 cups water and white wine mixed half
*   and half*
½ tsp thyme
1 tsp chopped parsley
Salt and pepper
½ cup heavy cream
2 tbsps brandy
5oz thick-cut gammon or ham
2 bay leaves

DECORATION
Fresh herbs
Capers
Green peppercorns

Stretch the bacon with the back of a knife and use it to line a 6 cup glass loaf dish. Combine the ground meats, liver, garlic, spices, herbs, salt and pepper in a food processor and work to chop roughly. Add the cream and the brandy and process once or twice to mix. Cut the ham or gammon into strips and set aside. Place ⅓ of the meat mixture into the lined terrine and spread smoothly. Place a layer of ham or gammon on top and then cover with a layer of meat. Repeat with the remaining gammon and meat mixture, smooth down the top and fold any overlapping strips of bacon. Place 2 bay leaves on the top and cover the dish with plastic wrap. Cook on MEDIUM for 12 minutes. Allow the pâté to rest for 5 minutes. Cook on MEDIUM for a further 20 minutes. Cover the top of the pâté with foil and weight down. Chill for at least 2-4 hours or overnight. To serve, prepare aspic as for the Salmon in Aspic. Slice the pâté in ¼ inch slices and place them on a cooling rack. Decorate the slices with small sprigs of fresh herbs, capers, green peppercorns or pimento. Pour a small amount of nearly set aspic over the top of the decoration to set it. When the aspic is completely set, coat the whole slice of pâté with a thin layer of nearly set aspic. Allow to set and then arrange on a serving plate slightly overlapping. Put any remaining aspic in a tray, turn out when set and cut into cubes or chop roughly. Pile the aspic in the middle of the pâté slices to serve.

Salmon in Aspic

PREPARATION TIME: 35 minutes

MICROWAVE COOKING TIME: 32-39 minutes

SERVES: 8-10 people

3¼ lbs whole salmon or salmon trout
Whole dill or fennel
Oil for brushing
2 tbsps aspic powder
2 cups water and white wine mixed half and half
Fresh herbs for decoration
Pimento
Lemon or lime slices
Fresh bay leaves

Rinse the salmon and dry well. Trim off the fins and brush the skin lightly with oil. Place dill or fennel inside the fish for extra flavor. Cover the head and tail with foil and cover the foil with a double thickness of plastic wrap. Make a steam hole with a sharp knife on either side of the dorsal fin. Curve the fish to fit the turntable and then loosely tie the head to the tail with a slip knot. Cook on LOW or DEFROST for 26-29 minutes. Remove the string, plastic wrap and foil halfway through cooking time. To test if the salmon is cooked, insert a sharp knife into one of the steam holes at the dorsal fin. The blade should pass easily through the fish if it is fully cooked. Allow the fish to cool slightly and then peel away the skin using a filleting knife or a table knife. Cover the fish loosely with plastic wrap and allow to cool completely. Remove the herbs from inside the fish and discard them. Place the fish on a serving dish while preparing the aspic and decorations. Bring the water and wine to the boil in a deep bowl or glass measure. This should take about 4-6 minutes. Stir in the aspic powder and heat 1-2

minutes on HIGH to dissolve it completely. Place the bowl or glass measure into a bowl of iced water and allow the aspic to cool completely, until almost set. Brush a thin layer of the aspic over the salmon and allow it to set. To re-use the aspic, melt 1-2 minutes on HIGH and stir gently. Allow to thicken slightly again in iced water and spoon a thin layer over the salmon. When almost set, decorate with small sprigs of fresh herbs, lemon slices, bay leaves and pimento. Reheat the aspic once more and thicken it again over ice. Carefully spoon the thickened aspic over the decorations and leave to set completely. Pour the remaining aspic into a shallow pan and set in the refrigerator. Remove the set aspic and turn out onto a dampened cutting board. Cut into small cubes or chop roughly. Use to decorate serving dish for the salmon along with small bunches of fresh herbs and lemon slices.

Salad Singapore

PREPARATION TIME: 25 minutes plus marinating time

MICROWAVE COOKING TIME: 10-15 minutes

SERVES: 6-8 people

1 3¼ lb chicken
1 tsp freshly ground black pepper
1 tsp ground mustard
1 tsp ground ginger
1 clove garlic, crushed
½ tsp ground turmeric
1 tsp mild curry powder
2 tbsps vegetable oil
4 tbsps raw peanuts
8oz zucchini, sliced diagonally
1 red pepper, seeded and shredded
8oz pea pods
1 medium-sized cucumber
2 tbsps desiccated coconut

Skin and bone the chicken and cut the meat into shreds. Mix all the spices together and toss with the chicken. Allow to stand in the

refrigerator for at least 2 hours. Heat a browning dish according to the manufacturer's directions and add the oil. Add the peanuts and cook on HIGH for 2-3 minutes, stirring frequently until lightly browned. Remove the peanuts with a draining spoon and add the zucchini, red pepper and pea pods to the browning dish. Return to the microwave oven and cook on HIGH for 2 minutes. Place in a serving dish and keep warm. If necessary, add another 1 tbsp oil to the browning dish and reheat. Add the chicken and cook in small batches for 5-7 minutes on HIGH. Cut the cucumber into thin strips and add to the vegetables in the serving dish. Add the chicken and the peanuts and toss thoroughly. Sprinkle over the desiccated coconut and reheat for 1-2 minutes on HIGH if desired before serving. May also be served cold.

Potato, Cucumber and Dill Salad

PREPARATION TIME: 20 minutes

MICROWAVE COOKING TIME: 16-22 minutes

SERVES: 6-8 people

1lb even-sized small new potatoes, scrubbed
3 sprigs dill
Salt
1 cucumber, cut into 1 inch chunks

DRESSING
1 whole egg and 1 egg yolk
½ pint oil
2 tbsps chopped fresh dill or 1 tbsp dried dill
1 tbsp mild mustard
1 tbsp white wine vinegar
1 green onion, finely chopped

GARNISH
Sprigs of fresh dill

Facing page: Salmon in Aspic.

Put the potatoes into a large bowl with the dill and salt. Pour over enough boiling water to cover. Cover the bowl with pierced plastic wrap and cook on HIGH for 15-20 minutes or until the potatoes are tender. Do not allow the potatoes to boil too rapidly. Reduce the setting to MEDIUM if necessary. Drain and leave the potatoes to cool. Prepare the dressing in a food processor. Combine the eggs with all the remaining ingredients except the oil. With the machine running, gradually pour the oil through the feed tube in a thin, steady stream. Add salt and

This page: Boeuf Niçoise. Facing page: Cheesecake (top) and Chocolate Truffle Cake (bottom).

pepper to taste. Place the chunks of cucumber in a casserole with 4 tbsps water. Cook on HIGH for 1-2 minutes to blanch. Rinse immediately under cold water and leave to dry. Combine the potatoes and the cucumbers in a bowl with the dressing. Transfer to a serving dish and garnish with sprigs of fresh dill.

Chocolate Truffle Cake

PREPARATION TIME: 20 minutes

MICROWAVE COOKING TIME: 7 minutes

SERVES: 8-10 people

12oz semi-sweet chocolate
½ cup butter
4 tbsps brandy or rum
2 eggs
2 cups graham crackers, crushed
½ cup chopped blanched almonds
1 cup whipped cream
Chocolate curls

Melt the chocolate and butter together on MEDIUM for 5 minutes. Beat in the eggs and heat a further 2 minutes on MEDIUM, stirring twice to thicken the eggs. Stir in the brandy, biscuits and chopped almonds. Spread into a 7 inch springform or removable base pan. Chill overnight until firm. Transfer to a serving dish and pile the cream on top. Decorate the top with chocolate curls. To prepare chocolate curls, take a thick block of semi-sweet chocolate and microwave on MEDIUM LOW for 30-60 seconds or until the chocolate is just barely warm. Turn the chocolate once or twice while heating. To form the curls, draw a swivel vegetable peeler towards you across the edge of the chocolate in a continuous, even motion. Chocolate curls may be kept in an airtight container.

Cheesecake

PREPARATION TIME: 30 minutes

MICROWAVE COOKING TIME: 14-25½ minutes

SERVES: 6-8 people

FILLING
1lb cream cheese
⅔ cup sugar
Pinch salt
⅓ cup light cream
Rind and juice of ½ lemon
Pinch ground coriander
4 eggs

CRUST
4 tbsps butter or margarine
¾ cup graham crackers, crushed
2 tbsps sugar

TOPPING
1 kiwi fruit, peeled and thinly sliced
2-3 satsumas, pith carefully removed
4oz fresh strawberries, washed and halved or raspberries (if strawberries or raspberries are unavailable, use purple grapes, halved and seeded)
Green seedless grapes, halved
Apricot jam

Place the cream cheese in a bowl and microwave on MEDIUM for 1 minute or until softened. Beat in the sugar, salt, cream and lemon rind. Gradually blend in the lemon juice and eggs. Cook on HIGH for 4-7 minutes, stirring very well every 2 minutes. Line the bottom of a 9 inch round baking dish with a circle of wax paper. Pour in the cream cheese mixture and cook on MEDIUM for 7-15 minutes or until almost set. Meanwhile prepare the crust. Mix the crushed graham crackers in a food processor or blender with the sugar. Work until fine. Melt the butter for 1½-2 minutes on HIGH. With the machine running, pour in the butter to mix with the crumbs. When the cheese filling is nearly set, carefully spoon over the crumb crust. Press down lightly and cook on HIGH for 1½ minutes. Allow the cheesecake to cool in the dish and then refrigerate overnight. To decorate, loosen the cheesecake from the sides of the dish and turn out onto a serving plate. Carefully peel away the disc of paper from the top. Arrange the various prepared fruits in circles on top of the cheesecake. Melt the apricot jam for 1 minute on HIGH and strain. Brush the fruit with a light layer of warm glaze, making sure that all the fruit is covered completely. Allow the glaze to set before serving.

Boeuf Niçoise

PREPARATION TIME: 30 minutes plus chilling time

MICROWAVE COOKING TIME: 23-31 minutes

SERVES: 8-10 people

1lb beef tenderloin

SALAD
1 head cauliflower, trimmed into flowerets
8oz broccoli, trimmed into flowerets
8oz green beans, trimmed
8 tomatoes, peeled and quartered
½ cup black olives, stoned

DRESSING
4oz olive oil
2 tbsps white wine vinegar
2 tsps Dijon mustard
2 tsps chopped fresh basil
1 tsp chopped fresh parsley
Salt and pepper

Place the meat on a microwave roasting rack with the thinner portion of the meat tucked under for an even shape. Tie with string to keep the shape. Wrap the ends of the beef with foil, shiny side down, and cook on HIGH for 3 minutes. Remove the foil from the beef and reduce the power to MEDIUM. Cook a further 5-8 minutes longer, turning the beef over once. Allow to stand until cool. The meat should be rare. If desired, brush the beef lightly with gravy browning before beginning to cook. Bring 4 cups water to the boil in a large glass bowl for 8-11 minutes on HIGH. Drop in 4 tomatoes and leave for 5 seconds. Remove to a bowl of iced water and reboil the water. Repeat with a further 4 tomatoes. Skin the tomatoes, quarter them and set them aside. Place the cauliflower flowerets in a casserole dish with 4 tbsps water and a pinch of salt. Cover the dish

This page: Salad Singapore (top) and Potato, Cucumber and Dill Salad (bottom). Facing page: Raspberry Ripple Cake.

and cook on HIGH for 4-5 minutes. Place the broccoli flowerets in the water after 2 minutes of cooking time. Drain the vegetables and rinse under cold water to stop the cooking. Cook the beans in a casserole dish with 6 tbsps water. Cover the dish

and cook on HIGH for 3-4 minutes. Rinse the beans under cold water to stop the cooking and leave them to drain with the cauliflower and the broccoli. Mix the dressing ingredients together in a large bowl and when the vegetables are dry add them to the dressing along with the tomatoes and the olives. Toss the vegetables to coat, then leave in the refrigerator for 1 hour to marinate. To assemble the salad, slice the beef thinly and arrange on a serving plate in a semi-circle with the slices overlapping. Using a draining spoon, pile the vegetable salad onto the plate. Pour some of the remaining dressing over the meat before serving.

A Children's Party

Raspberry Ripple Cake

PREPARATION TIME: 2 minutes

MICROWAVE COOKING TIME: 11-13 minutes

MAKES: 1 cake

¾ cup butter or margarine
¾ cup sugar
3 eggs, lightly beaten
1½ cups all-purpose flour
Salt
2 tsps baking powder
3 tbsps seedless raspberry jam
2 tbsps hot water (optional)
Few drops red food coloring

FROSTING
3 tbsps seedless raspberry jam
4 cups powdered sugar
Hot water

Heat butter or margarine for 1 minute on HIGH to soften. Beat until creamy, and gradually beat in the sugar until light and fluffy. Gradually beat in the eggs until the mixture is mousse-like and all the eggs have been incorporated. Sift in the flour with a pinch of salt and the baking powder. Fold the dry ingredients into the butter, sugar and eggs. Divide the mixture into two bowls and add the raspberry jam and red food coloring to half the mixture. Stir thoroughly. Add hot water to the plain half as necessary to bring the mixture to soft dropping consistency. Line a round or decorative microwave cake dish with plastic wrap. Fill with spoonfuls of the two mixtures, alternating the colors. Draw a knife or spatula through the mixtures to marble the two colors. Cook for 6-8 minutes on HIGH, turning the dish occasionally if it is not a round shape. If the corners of the cake appear to be overcooking, cover with foil if your oven manufacturer allows its use. Leave in the dish for 5 minutes before turning out to cool. Soften the jam for the frosting for 20 seconds on HIGH and beat until smooth. Fill a pastry bag fitted with a small writing tube with the jam. Heat about 1 cup water on HIGH for 4-5 minutes. Sift in the powdered sugar gradually, beating until the frosting coats the back of a spoon but runs off slowly. It may not be necessary to add all the sugar. Pour over the cake, using a spatula to help spread the frosting. Pipe thin lines of jam over the cake before the frosting sets completely. Quickly swirl the jam through the frosting with a skewer and allow to set completely before cutting to serve.

Chocolate Marshmallow Turtles

PREPARATION TIME: 15 minutes

MICROWAVE COOKING TIME:
2 minutes 15 seconds-4½ minutes

MAKES: 12

48 shelled pecans
12 marshmallows
½ cup chocolate chips
1 tbsp vegetable shortening

Put the pecans in groups of 4 on a microwave baking sheet lined with nonstick paper. Place a marshmallow on top of the pecans. Microwave on HIGH for 15-30 seconds or until the marshmallows just start to puff. Place the chocolate chips and the vegetable shortening in a small bowl. Microwave on MEDIUM for 2-4 minutes, stirring frequently until the chocolate melts. Spoon over the top of each turtle to cover the marshmallow. Leave to set completely before serving.

Chocolate Squares

PREPARATION TIME: 30 minutes

MICROWAVE COOKING TIME:
5 minutes

MAKES: 16

4 tbsps butter or margarine
6oz semi-sweet chocolate
2 tbsps golden syrup or honey
2 cups graham crackers, crushed
Colored candied cherries

Place the butter or margarine, chocolate and syrup or honey in a small, deep bowl and heat on MEDIUM for 5 minutes, stirring occasionally until the chocolate melts. Stir in the biscuit crumbs and mix thoroughly. Grease a shallow 7 inch square pan and spoon in the chocolate mixture. Smooth the top and mark into squares with a sharp knife. Cut the candied cherries in half and put a half on top of each square, alternating the colors. Leave to set completely and then cut into squares to serve.

Granola Bars

PREPARATION TIME: 15 minutes

MICROWAVE COOKING TIME:
7-8 minutes

MAKES: 12

6 cups toasted fruit and nut granola
½ cup butter or margarine
½ cup dark brown sugar
Pinch salt
2 eggs, beaten
Few drops vanilla extract

Place the butter or margarine in a glass measure and microwave for 45 seconds-1 minute on HIGH. Combine the brown sugar, salt, eggs and flavoring in a large bowl and gradually beat in the melted butter. Add the granola and stir to coat well. Lightly grease a 12 x 8 inch baking dish and press in the mixture. Cook on HIGH for 6-8 minutes or until just firm to the touch. If the corners of the mixture seem to be cooking before the center, place foil across all 4 corners and continue cooking. Press the mixture with a spatula every few minutes to smooth down. Before allowing to cool, cut the mixture into 12 bars. Allow to cool

completely before removing from the dish.

Animal Crackers

PREPARATION TIME: 20 minutes

MICROWAVE COOKING TIME:
2-4 minutes

MAKES: 24

1 cup all-purpose flour
½ cup whole-wheat flour
2 tbsps sugar
½ tsp bicarbonate of soda
¼ tsp salt
¼ tsp ground cinnamon
4 tbsps vegetable shortening
1 tbsp butter or margarine
2 tbsps water
1 tbsp honey

1 tbsp molasses
Few drops vanilla extract

Sift the flours with the sugar, bicarbonate of soda, salt and cinnamon into a deep bowl. Return the bran to the bowl. Cut in the vegetable shortening and butter or margarine until the particles are the size of small peas. This may also be done in a food processor. Combine the water, honey, molasses and vanilla in a small bowl. Mix with the dry ingredients, tossing and mashing with a fork until the particles cling together. Form into a ball, cover with plastic wrap and refrigerate at least 1 hour. Divide the dough in half and roll out to ¼ inch thickness on a well-floured surface. Flour the rolling pin frequently while rolling out. Cut the dough with animal shaped cookie cutters. Prick lightly with a fork and

Facing page: Animal Crackers (top) and Chocolate Marshmallow Turtles (bottom). This page: Granola Bars (top) and Chocolate Squares (bottom).

transfer to a plate or microwave baking sheet lined with wax paper. Cook 12 cookies at a time arranged in a circle around the edge of the plate or baking sheet. Cook on HIGH for 1-2 minutes or until the surface of the dough is dry and firm to touch. Cool on a wire rack. Sprinkle lightly with powdered sugar or decorate with melted chocolate or colored frostings.

INDEX

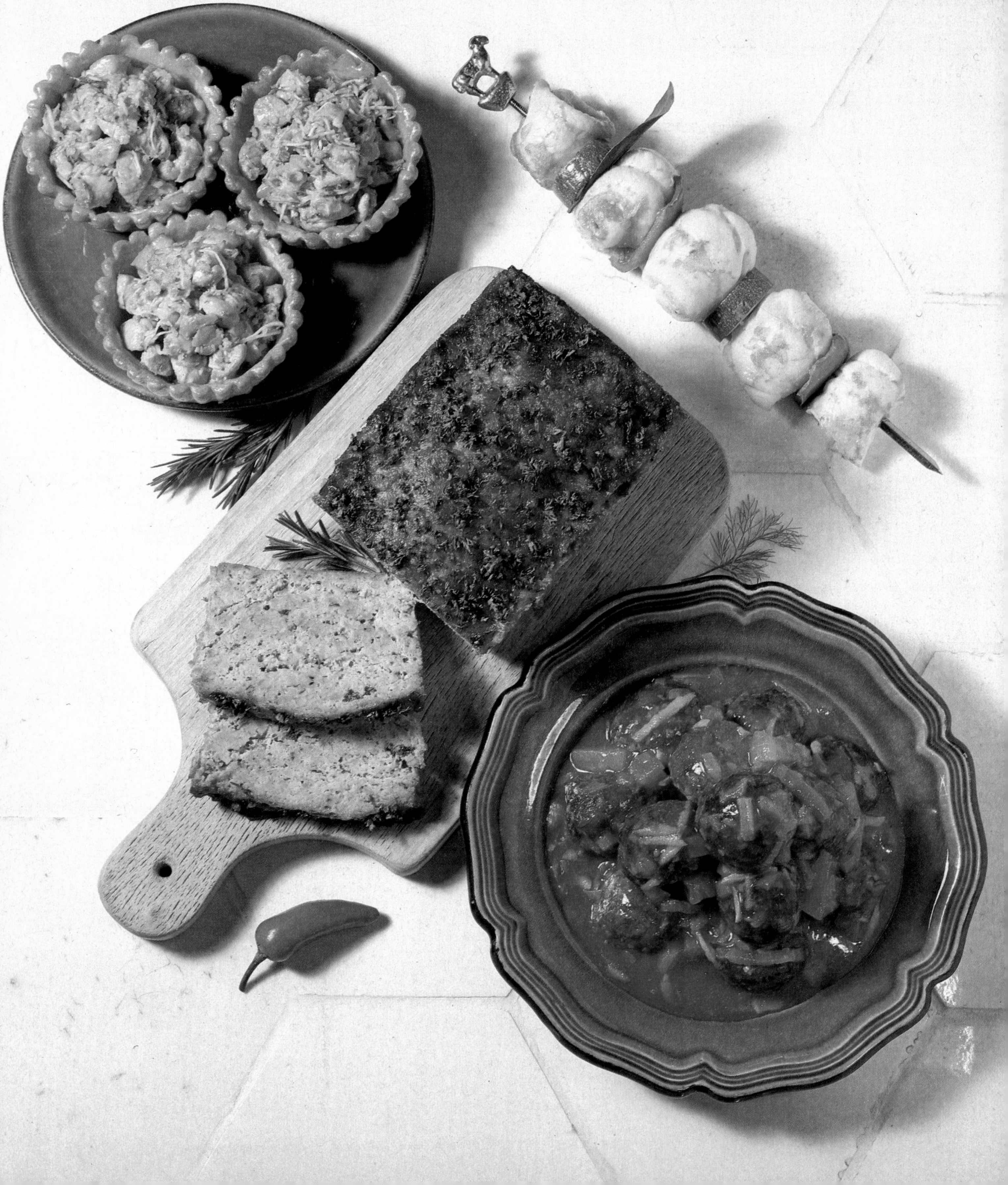